JAVA™ STUDIO CREATOR FIELD GUIDE

SECOND EDITION

GAIL ANDERSON • PAUL ANDERSON

Sun Microsystems Press
A Prentice Hall Title

PH PTR

Prentice Hall PTR, Upper Saddle River, NJ 07458
www.phptr.com

PH PTR

© 2006 Gail Anderson and Paul Anderson
Published by Prentice Hall PTR
Prentice-Hall, Inc.
Upper Saddle River, NJ 07458

Sun Microsystems Press
A Prentice Hall Title

Contents

CHAPTER 8 INTRODUCING DATA PROVIDERS 336

Foreword

The developers who set out to build Java Studio Creator had a very difficult task: to make the creation of sophisticated enterprise applications easy.

The set of technologies that comprise Java2 Enterprise Edition (J2EE) is huge. The good side is that J2EE is battle hardened and field proven to be an excellent base for large scale mission critical applications. There are many excellent books that cover all of the aspects of J2EE in great detail. But all of this leads to the bad side of J2EE: it can be difficult and time-consuming to learn and use. Tremendous effort goes into making J2EE as simple as possible, but it remains daunting.

Java Studio Creator is a huge leap in the simplification of the process of developing J2EE based web applications. Developers don't need to deal with all of the gory details: Creator just handles them. Instead, developers can focus on what their application does and looks like in a very simple and straightforward way. They weave together data sources through a simple drag-and-drop interface. Very little knowledge of Java or J2EE is required to develop applications in Creator. Creator not only simplifies the process: it also accelerates it.

This book contains all that you need to know to generate enterprise applications using Creator. It doesn't require that you know anything about J2EE or even Java: there are gentle introductory chapters that lead you through what you need to know. This is a great entry point for developers from other platforms (like Visual Basic!) to enter the world of large-scale, mission-critical applications. It's fun. Take the plunge.

James Gosling
Sun Microsystems, Inc.

Preface

You're about to embark on a journey that we hope will prove both enjoyable and fruitful. Certainly the aim of any application development tool is to help developers become efficient and allow them to spend time on creative tasks while the tool silently generates the drudgery for them. To that end, we hope this book will teach you the ins and outs of Creator so that you can quickly begin to build web applications.

How This Book Is Organized

Creator2 has significant enhancements over the first version of Creator and we've completely revamped (and grown!) this text to reflect the "new" Creator. In a nutshell, you'll see an improved design time experience, with an advanced page design editor and component style editor. Creator2 includes a complete set of new (and more numerous) UI components sporting an improved theme-based look and intuitive property names. Data providers give you a consistent interface with the persistence tier and NetBeans provides the underpinnings of the IDE. Building portlet-based projects, consuming EJBs, and using AJAX-enabled components round out the list of improvements. Enjoy!

Chapter 1 introduces the world of Java and its supporting technologies. Creator depends on these well-established Java technologies to do its job. With the Java programming language and XML, JavaServer Faces component system, and NetBeans tool building technology, Creator has tapped the available standards. Here we provide a gentle introduction to these topics, so you'll get the "big picture" of how Creator fits into the Java world. We also spend time on the Java programming language since you will use Java often with Creator. If you come from another programming environment, we want you to feel comfortable right away with Java-based web applications.

Chapter 2 introduces Creator, with the aim of getting you up to speed with its various windows, the design canvas, and its editors. Knowing how to move around in the IDE will quickly make you productive. You'll also build your first project from scratch.

Chapter 3 is your "Components Catalog." This reference chapter lets you choose the best component for your application from Creator's store of components, validators, and data converters. We'll also point you to places in the book where these components are used in complete projects.

Chapter 4 is all about working with the Java source editor, managing your code with the Concurrent Versioning System (CVS), and performing project-level tasks, such as refactoring. Creator is built on the NetBeans IDE, which provides the backbone for these software management tasks.

Chapter 5 introduces Page Navigation in Creator. You'll learn how to specify page flow in a web application and understand which components are suitable for page navigation. We'll also discuss Creator's navigation model and illustrate page navigation with several projects.

Chapter 6 discusses the anatomy of Creator projects. JavaBeans components (beans) provide one of the key supporting technologies that Creator uses. Developers who understand the advantages of JavaBeans components can build robust applications with reusable components. The chapter also delves into the JSF/Creator page request life cycle so that you can best leverage Creator's life cycle callback methods.

Chapter 7 covers features that help you with web page design and layout. Page fragments give your application a consistent look and several layout components help you design your page layout. Creator's Cascading Style Sheet (CSS) editor lets you build page and component style rules.

Chapter 8 introduces data providers, a standard layer connecting your web application's components to a persistence tier, such as database, web service, JavaBeans component, or Enterprise JavaBeans (EJB) component. We explore the data provider interface and show you common ways to work with data providers in your projects.

Chapter 9 shows you how to use a database with Creator. You'll build projects with essential database operations, such as read, update, insert, and delete. Creator's data-aware components make linking to a database (via data providers) easy and straightforward.

Chapter 10 shows you how to access a web service from a Creator-built application. Creator bundles a selection of web services; you can also add additional web services to the IDE. In this chapter, you'll build an application that uses the Google Search Web Service.

Enterprise JavaBeans (EJBs) provide a powerful model for distributed systems. Creator lets you build applications that consume EJBs, automatically generating the code to invoke methods on deployed objects. Chapter 11 shows you how to invoke EJB methods and manipulate returned data through standard data providers.

With Creator, you can create a JSF portlet application that conforms to the Java Specification Request (JSR) 168 Portlet specification. Chapter 12 covers portlet application development, including examples on using web services, database access, and portlet Edit and Help modes.

Chapter 13 shows you how to customize a web application with Creator. You'll learn how to localize/internationalize an application. We also show you how to write and install custom validation methods. Anxious to use AJAX technology? We include several examples that use an auto-complete AJAX-enabled text field.

Chapter 14 shows you how to use Creator's debugger in your projects. You'll learn how to set breakpoints, look at the server log file, respond to exceptions, and use the NetBeans HTTP monitor.

About the Examples

Java Studio Creator Field Guide, Second Edition is an example-driven book. All example projects that we describe in these chapters are provided prebuilt in the example download bundle. The database chapter includes a sample Music database, which we also provide in the download bundle. The example code is available on the Sun Microsystem Creator2 web site.

```
http://developers.sun.com/prodtech/javatools/
   jscreator/index.jsp
```

You can also download the example code from the authors' web site at

```
http://www.asgteach.com
```

We recommend you visit both web sites to keep current with the latest Creator updates!

Notational Conventions

We've applied a rather "light hand" with font conventions in an attempt to keep the page uncluttered. Here are the conventions we follow.

Element	*Font and Example*
property name	`text` property, `cellpadding` property
code comments	`// User event code here . . .`
component name	text field `loanAmount`
Creator components	output text, text field, drop down list
filename	**color1.properties**, **Page1.jsp**
Java class	String, Object, Integer
Java code	`username.setValue("rave4u")`
JavaBeans components	LoginBean, ColorBean, Page1
JSF EL expressions	`#{Page1.colorBean.redValue}`
JSP code, HTML code	`<f:loadBundle>`, `<img>`
key combinations	press **<Alt+Shift+I>**; press **<Enter>**
menu selections	View Page1 Java Class, Music > Tables
project name	Login1, Echo
user input	Type the text **Music1**, specify **loginBean**

About the Front Cover

I.M. Pei's Glass Pyramid is an apt symbol for a book on Java Studio Creator. The pyramid serves as the entrance to the Louvre Museum in Paris. Truly international, it was designed by a Chinese-American, who is both an engineer and an artist. We were drawn to its elegant simplicity of glass and light, its multiple facets, and the blending of a structure that is modern yet simultaneously representative of Ancient Egypt.

Java Studio Creator is built on the same concept of layered architecture. Based on JavaServer Faces technology, Creator leverages the existing Java 2 Platform Enterprise Edition (J2EE) architecture and of course, the solid foundations of Java and its runtime environment. Likewise, the Glass Pyramid is an extraordinary example of layered architecture whose backdrop is a traditional Renaissance palace. The Louvre itself houses artistic treasures dating from antiquity, perhaps none more famous than Leonardo da Vinci's Mona Lisa.

Gail and Paul Anderson
Anderson Software Group, Inc.

Acknowledgments

Without the help of others, not only would this text be lacking in timeliness and accuracy, but its very existence is questionable.

Jim Inscore of Sun Microsystems blazed the path for this project, taking care of both administration and coordinating technical help. Without his desire to see this project a reality, the Second Edition would have remained unrealized.

Many people from the Sun Microsystems Creator Team helped us directly and indirectly by answering technical questions, giving us insights into design and architectural issues, providing updated "bits" so that we could always work with a current system, and providing valuable feedback to early drafts. We'd like to especially acknowledge Winston Prakash. He gave us crucial technical support and answered many questions. He was our go-to guy and we cannot praise his dedication to this project enough!

Octavian Tanase and Sandip Chitale were also on the frontline for us, helping with various technical questions throughout the entire writing process. Octavian also was central dispatch for our questions, feeding them to the right Creator Team member. Thus, we'd also like to thank those who answered when asked for help: David Botterill, David Folk, Chau Nguyen, Tor Norbye, Matt Bohm, Craig McClanahan, Chris Kutler, Edwin Goei, Dongmei Cao, Vaughn Spurlin, and Dusan Pavlica. Valerie Lipman was in on the early proposed content talks. Valuable feedback also came from one of our readers, Les Hawkins.

The Second Edition builds on the initial work of the First Edition. Greg Doench, our editor at Prentice Hall, made that possible. Vicky Hilpert of Vietsbronn, Germany helped with the German translations and Blanca Lazaro helped with the Spanish. Thanks also to our family (especially Sara and Kellen) and friends for love and support.

Lastly, we'd like to thank James Gosling for giving us all Java.

JAVA™ STUDIO CREATOR

FIELD GUIDE

JAVA TECHNOLOGY OVERVIEW

Topics in This Chapter

- The Java Programming Language
- JavaBeans Components
- NetBeans Software
- The XML Language
- The J2EE Architecture
- JavaServer Faces Technology
- JDBC and Databases
- Ant Build Tool
- Web Services
- EJBs and Portlets

Chapter 1

Welcome to Creator! Creator is an IDE (Integrated Development Environment) that helps you build web applications. While many IDEs out in the world do that, Creator is unique in that it is built on a layered technology anchored in Java. At the core of this technology is the Java programming language. Java includes a compiler that produces portable bytecode and a Java Virtual Machine (JVM) that runs this byte code on any processor. Java is an important part of Creator because it makes your web applications portable.

But Java is more than just a programming language. It is also a *technology platform*. Many large systems have been developed that use Java as their core. These systems are highly scalable and provide services and structure that address some of the high-volume, distributed computing environments of today.

1.1 Introduction

Creator depends on multiple technologies, so it's worthwhile touching on them in this chapter. If you're new to Java, many of its parts and acronyms can be daunting. Java technologies are divided into related packages containing classes and interfaces. To build an application, you might need parts of one system and parts of another. This chapter provides you with a road map of Java technologies and documentation sources to help you design your web applications with Creator.

We'll begin with an overview of the Java programming language. This will help you get comfortable writing Java code to customize your Creator applications. But before we do that, we show you how to find the documentation for Java classes and methods. This will help you use them with confidence in your programs.

Most of the documentation for a Java Application Program Interface (API) can be accessed through Creator's Help System, located under Help in the main menu. Sometimes all you need is the name of the package or the system to find out what API a class, interface, or method belongs to. Java consists of the basic language (all packages under `java`) and Java extensions (all packages under `javax`). Once you locate a package, you can explore the interfaces and classes and learn about the methods they implement.

You can also access the Java documentation online. Here's a good starting point for the Java API documentation.

```
http://java.sun.com/docs/
```

This page contains links to the Java 2 Platform Standard Edition, which contains the core APIs. It also has a link to all of the other Java APIs and technologies, found at

```
http://java.sun.com/reference/docs/index.html
```

Creator is also built on the technology of JavaServer Faces (JSF). You can find the current JSF API documentation at

```
http://java.sun.com/j2ee/javaserverfaces/1.0/docs/api/
index.html
```

JSF is described as part of the J2EE Tutorial, which can be found at

```
http://java.sun.com/j2ee/1.4/docs/tutorial/doc/index.html
```

These are all important references for you. We've included them at the beginning of this book so it's easy to find them later (when you're deep in the challenges of web application development). For now, let's begin with Java as a programming language. Then we'll look at some of the other supporting technologies on which Creator is built.

1.2 The Java Programming Language

This cursory overview of the Java programming language is for readers who come from a non-Java programming environment. It's not meant to be an in-depth reference, but a starting point. Much of Creator involves manipulating components through the design canvas and the components' property sheets. However, there are times when you must add code to a Java page bean (the supporting Java code for your web application's page) or use a JavaBeans component in your application. You'll want a basic understanding of Java to more easily use Creator.

Object-Oriented Programming

Languages like C and Basic are procedure-oriented languages, which means data and functions are separated. To write programs, you either pass data as arguments to functions or make your data global to functions. This arrangement can be problematic when you need to hide data like passwords, customer identification codes, and network addresses. Procedure-oriented designs work fine when you write simple programs but are often not suitable to more complex tasks like distributed programming and web applications. Function libraries help, but error handling can be difficult and global variables may introduce side effects during program maintenance.

Object-oriented programming, on the other hand, combines data and functions into units called *objects*. Languages like Java hide private data (*fields*) from user programs and expose only functions (*methods*) as a public interface. This concept of *encapsulation* allows you to control how callers access your objects. It allows you to break up applications into groups of objects that behave in a similar way, a concept called *abstraction*. In Java, you implement an object with a Java class and your object's public interface becomes its *outside view.* Java has inheritance to create new data types as extensions of existing types. Java also has interfaces, which allow objects to implement required behaviors of certain classes of objects. All of these concepts help separate an object's implementation (inside view) from its interface (outside view).

All objects created from the same class have the same data type. Java is a strongly typed language, and all objects are implicitly derived from type `Object` (except the built-in primitive types of `int`, `boolean`, `char`, `double`, `long`, etc.). You can convert an object from one type to another with a converter. Casting to a different type is only allowed if the conversion is known by the compiler. Creator's Java editor helps you create well-formed statements with dynamic syntax analysis and code completion choices. You'll see how this works in Chapter 2.

Error handling has always been a tough problem to solve, but with web applications error handling is even more difficult. Processing errors can occur on the server but need to propagate in a well-behaved way back to the user. Java implements exception handling to handle errors as objects and recover gracefully. The Java compiler forces programmers to use the built-in exception handling mechanism.

And, Java forbids global variables, a restriction that helps program maintenance.

Creating Objects

Operator `new` creates objects in Java. You don't have to worry about destroying them, because Java uses a garbage collection mechanism to automatically destroy objects which are no longer used by your program.

```
Point p = new Point();         // create a Point at (0, 0)
Point q = new Point(10, 20); // create a Point at (10, 20)
```

Operator `new` creates an object at run time and returns its address in memory to the caller. In Java, you use *references* (`p` and `q`) to store the addresses of objects so that you can refer to them later. Every reference has a type (`Point`), and objects can be built with arguments to initialize their data. In this example, we create two `Point` objects with `x` and `y` coordinates, one with a default of (0, 0) and the other one with (10, 20).

Once you create an object, you can call its methods with a reference.

```
p.move(30, 30);          // move object p to (30, 30)
q.up();                  // move object q up in y direction
p.right();               // move object p right in x direction

int xp = p.getX();       // get x coordinate of object p
int yp = p.getY();       // get y coordinate of object p
q.setX(5);               // change x coordinate in object q
p.setY(25);              // change y coordinate in object p
```

As you can see, you can do a lot of things with `Point` objects. It's possible to move a `Point` object to a new location, or make it go up or to the right, all of which affect one or more of a `Point` object's coordinates. We also have getter methods to return the x and y coordinates separately and setter methods to change them.

Why is this all this worthwhile? Because a `Point` object's data (`x` and `y` coordinates) are *hidden*. The only way you can manipulate a `Point` object is through its public methods. This makes it easier to maintain the integrity of `Point` objects.

Classes

Java already has a Point class in its API, but for the purposes of this discussion, let's roll our own. Here's our Java Point class, which describes the functionality we've shown you.

Listing 1.1 Point class

```
// Point.java - Point class
class Point {
// Fields
  private double x, y;          // x and y coordinates

// Constructors
  public Point(double x, double y) { move(x, y); }
  public Point() { move(0, 0); }

// Instance Methods
  public void move(double x, double y) {
    this.x = x;   this.y = y;
  }
  public void up() { y++; }
  public void down() { y--; }
  public void right() { x++; }
  public void left() { x--; }

  // getters
  public double getX() { return x; }
  public double getY() { return y; }

  // setters
  public void setX(double x) { this.x = x; }
  public void setY(double y) { this.y = y; }
}
```

The Point class is divided into three sections: Fields, Constructors, and Instance Methods. Fields hold internal data, constructors initialize the fields, and instance methods are called by you with references. Note that the fields for x and y are *private*. This enforces data encapsulation in object-oriented programming, since users may not access these values directly. Everything else, however, is declared public, making it accessible to all clients.

The Point class has two *constructors* to build Point objects. The first constructor accepts two double arguments, and the second one is a default constructor with no arguments. Note that both constructors call the move() method to initialize the x and y fields. Method move() uses the Java this keyword to distinguish local variable names in the method from class field names in the object. The `setX()` and `setY()` methods use the same technique.[1]

Most of the `Point` methods use void for their return type, which means the method does not return anything. The ++ and -- operators increment or decrement their values by one, respectively. Each method has a *signature*, which is another name for a function's argument list. Note that a signature may be empty.

Packages

The `Point` class definition lives in a file called **Point.java**. In Java, you must name a file with the same name as your class name. This makes it convenient for the Java run-time interpreter to find class definitions when it's time to instantiate (create) objects. When all classes live in the same directory, it's easy to compile and run Java programs.

In the real world, however, classes have to live in different places, so Java has *packages* that allow you to group related classes. A package in Java is both a directory and a library. This means a one-to-one correspondence exists between a package hierarchy name and a file's pathname in a directory structure. Unique package names are typically formed by reversing Internet domain names (`com.mycompany`). Java also provides access to packages from class paths and JAR (Java Archive) files.

Suppose you want to store the `Point` class in a package called `MyPackage.examples`. Here's how you do it.

```
package MyPackage.examples;
class Point {
   . . .
}
```

Package names with dot (.) delimiters map directly to path names, so **Point.java** lives in the **examples** directory under the **MyPackage** directory. A Java *import* statement makes it easy to use class names without fully qualifying their package names. Import statements are also applicable to class names from any Java API.

```
// Another Java program
import java.util.Date;
import javax.faces.context.*;
import MyPackage.examples.Point;
```

---

1. The `this` reference is not necessary if you use different names for the arguments.

The first import statement provides the `Date` class name to our Java program from the `java.util` package. The second import uses a wildcard (*) to make *all* class definitions available from `javax.faces.context`. The last import brings our `Point` class into scope from package `MyPackage.examples`.

Exceptions

We mentioned earlier that one of the downfalls of procedure-oriented languages is that subroutine libraries don't handle errors well. This is because libraries can only detect problems, not fix them. Even with libraries that support elaborate error mechanisms, you cannot force someone to check a function's return value or peek at a global error flag. For these and other reasons, it has been difficult to write distributed software that gracefully recovers from errors.

Object-oriented languages like Java have a built-in exception handling mechanism that lets you handle error conditions as objects. When an error occurs inside a try block of critical code, an exception object can be thrown from a library method back to a catch handler. Inside user code, these catch handlers may call methods in the exception object to do a range of different things, like display error messages, retry, or take other actions.

The exception handling mechanism is built around three Java keywords: `throw`, `catch`, and `try`. Here's a simple example to show you how it works.

```
class SomeClass {
   . . .
   public void doSomething(String input) {
      int number;
      try {
         number = Integer.parseInt(input);
      }
      catch (NumberFormatException e) {
         String msg = e.getMessage();
         // do something with msg
      }
      . . .
   }
}
```

Suppose a method called `doSomething()` needs to convert a string of characters (input) to an integer value in memory (number). In Java, the call to `Integer.parseInt()` performs the necessary conversion for you, but what about malformed string arguments? Fortunately, the `parseInt()` method throws a `NumberFormatException` if the input string has illegal characters. All we do is place this call in a try block and use a catch handler to generate an error message when the exception is caught.

All that's left is to show you how the exception gets thrown. This is often called a *throw point*.

```
class Integer {
  public static int parseInt(String input)
                         throws NumberFormatException {
    . . .
    // input string has bad chars
    throw new NumberFormatException("illegal chars");
  }
  . . .
}
```

The static `parseInt()` method[2] illustrates two important points about exceptions. First, the throws clause in the method signature announces that `parseInt()` throws an exception object of type `NumberFormatException`. The throws clause allows the Java compiler to enforce error handling. To call the `parseInt()` method, you must put the call inside a try block or in a method that also has the same throws clause. Second, operator `new` calls the `NumberFormatException` constructor to build an exception object. This exception object is built with an error string argument and thrown to a catch handler whose signature *matches* the type of the exception object (`NumberFormat` Exception).[3] As you have seen, a catch handler calls `getMessage()` with the exception object to access the error message.

Why are Java exceptions important? As you develop web applications with Creator, you'll have to deal with thrown exceptions. Fortunately, Creator has a built-in debugger that helps you monitor exceptions. In the Chapter 14, we show you how to set breakpoints to track exceptions in your web application (see "Detecting Exceptions" on page 669).

Inheritance

The concept of code reuse is a major goal of object-oriented programming. When designing a new class, you may derive it from an existing one. Inheritance, therefore, implements an "is a" relationship between classes. Inheritance also makes it easy to hook into existing frameworks so that you can take on

---

2. Inside class `Integer`, the `static` keyword means you don't have to instantiate an `Integer` object to call `parseInt()`. Instead, you call the static method with a class name rather than a reference.
3. The match doesn't have to be exact. The exception thrown can match the catch handler's object exactly or any exception object derived from it by inheritance. To catch any possible exception, you can use the superclass `Exception`. We discuss inheritance in the next section.

new functionalities. With inheritance, you can retain the existing structure and behavior of an existing class and specialize certain aspects of it to suit your needs.

In Java, inheritance is implemented by *extending* classes. When you extend one class from another, the public methods of the "parent" class become part of the public interface of the "child class." The parent class is called a *superclass* and the child class is called a *subclass*. Here are some examples.

```
class Pixel extends Point {
   . . .
}

class NumberFormatException extends IllegalArgumentException {
   . . .
}
```

In the first example, `Point` is a superclass and `Pixel` is a subclass. A `Pixel` "is a" `Point` with, say, color. Inside the `Pixel` class, a color field with setter and getter methods can assist in manipulating colors. `Pixel` objects, however, are `Point` objects, so you can move them up, down, left or right, and you can get or set their `x` and `y` coordinates. (You can also invoke any of `Point`'s public methods with a reference to a `Pixel` object.) Note that you don't have to write any code in the `Pixel` class to do these things because they have been inherited from the `Point` class. Likewise, in `NumberFormatException`, you may introduce new methods but inherit the functionality of `IllegalArgumentException`.

Another point about inheritance. You can write your own version of a method in a subclass that has the same name and signature as the method in the superclass. Suppose, for instance, we add a `clear()` method in our `Point` class to reset `Point` objects back to (0, 0). In the `Pixel` class that extends from `Point`, we may *override* the `clear()` method.[4] This new version could move a `Pixel` object to (0, 0) *and* reset its color. Note that `clear()` in class `Point` is called for `Point` objects, but `clear()` in class `Pixel` will be called for `Pixel` objects. With a `Point` reference set to either type of object, different behaviors happen when you call this method.

It's important to understand that these kinds of method calls in Java are resolved at run time. This is called *dynamic binding*. In the object-oriented paradigm, dynamic binding means that the resolution of method calls with objects

---

4. Creator uses this same feature by providing methods that are called at different points in the JSF page request life cycle. You can override any of these methods and thus provide your own code, "hooking" into the page request life cycle. We show you how to do this in Chapter 6 (see "The Creator-JSF Life Cycle" on page 260).

is delayed until you run a program. In web applications and other types of distributed software, dynamic binding plays a key role in how objects call methods from different machines across a network or from different processes in a multitasking system.

Interfaces

In Java, a method with a signature and no code body is called an *abstract* method. Abstract methods must be overridden in subclasses and help define *interfaces*. A Java interface is like a class but has no fields and only abstract public methods. Interfaces are important because they specify a *contract*. Any new class that implements an interface must provide code for the interface's methods.

Here's an example of an interface.

```
interface Encryptable {
   void encode(String key);
   String decode();
}

class Password implements Encryptable {
   . . .
   void encode(String key) { . . . }
   String decode() { . . . }
}
```

The `Encryptable` interface contains only the abstract public methods `encode()` and `decode()`. Class `Password` implements the `Encryptable` interface and must provide implementations for these methods. Remember, interfaces are types, just like classes. This means you can implement the same interface with other classes and treat them all as `Encryptable` types.

Java prohibits a class from inheriting from more than one superclass, but it does allow classes to implement multiple interfaces. Interfaces, therefore, allow arbitrary classes to "take on" the characteristics of any given interface.

One of the most common interfaces implemented by classes in Java is the `Serializable` interface. When an object implements `Serializable`, you can use it in a networked environment or make it *persistent* (this means the state of an object can be saved and restored by different clients). There are methods to serialize the object (before sending it over the network or storing it) and to deserialize it (after retrieving it from the network or reading it from storage).

1.3 JavaBeans Components

A JavaBeans component is a Java class with certain structure requirements. Javabeans components define and manipulate properties, which are objects of a certain type. A JavaBeans component must have a default constructor so that it can be instantiated when needed. Beans also have getter and setter methods that manipulate a bean property and conform to a specific naming convention. These structural requirements make it possible for development tools and other programs to create JavaBeans components and manipulate their properties.

Here's a simple example of a JavaBeans component.

```
public class Book {
  private String title;
  private String author;
  public Book() { setTitle(""); setAuthor(""); }
  public void setTitle(String t) { title = t; }
  public String getTitle() { return title; }
  public void setAuthor(String a) { author = a; }
  public String getAuthor() { return author; }
}
```

Why are JavaBeans components important? First and most important, they are accessible to Creator. When you write a JavaBeans component that conforms to the specified design convention, you may use it with Creator and bind JSF components to bean properties. Second, JavaBeans components can encapsulate business logic. This helps separate your User Interface (UI) components or presentation from the business data model.

In subsequent chapters, we show you several examples of JavaBeans components. We'll use a `LoginBean` to handle users that login with names and passwords and show you a `LoanBean` that calculates mortgage payments for loans. The `Point` class in Listing 1.1 on page 7 is another example of a JavaBeans component.

1.4 NetBeans Software

NetBeans software is an open source IDE written in the Java programming language. It also includes an API that supports building any type of application. The IDE has support for Java, but its architecture is flexible and extensible, making support for other languages possible.

NetBeans is an Open Source project. You can view more information on its history, structure, and relationship with Sun Microsystems at its web site

```
http://www.netbeans.org/
```

NetBeans and Creator are related because Creator is based on the NetBeans platform. In building Creator, Sun is offering an IDE aimed specifically at creating web-based applications. Thus, the IDE integrates page design with generated JSP source and page bean components. NetBeans provides features such as source code completion, workspace manipulation of windows, expandable tree views of files and components, and debugging facilities. Because NetBeans is extensible, the Creator architects included Java language features such as inheritance to adapt components from NetBeans into Creator applications with the necessary IDE functions.

1.5 The XML Language

XML is a metalanguage that dictates how to define custom languages and describe data. The name is an acronym for Extensible Markup Language. XML is not a programming language, however. In fact, it's based on simple character text in which the data are surrounded by text markup that documents data. This means you can use XML to describe almost anything. Since XML is self-describing, it's easy to read with tools and other programs to decide what actions to take. You can transport XML documents easily between systems or across the Internet, and virtually any type of data can be expressed and validated in an XML document. Furthermore, XML is portable because it's language and system independent.

Creator uses XML to define several configuration files as well as the source for the JSP web pages. Here's an example XML file (**managed-beans.xml**) that Creator generates for managing a JavaBeans component in a web application.

```
<faces-config>
  <managed-bean>
    <managed-bean-name>LoanBean</managed-bean-name>
    <managed-bean-class>asg.bean_examples.LoanBean
        </managed-bean-class>
    <managed-bean-scope>session</managed-bean-scope>
  </managed-bean>
</faces-config>
```

Every XML file has opening tags (`<tag>`) and closing tags (`</tag>`) that define self-describing information. Here, we specify a `managed-bean` element to tell Creator what it needs to know about the LoanBean component. This includes its name (LoanBean), class name and package (`asg.bean_examples.LoanBean`), and the scope of the bean (session). When you add your own JavaBeans components to Creator as managed beans, Creator generates this configuration information for you.

Creator maintains and updates its XML files for you, but it's a good idea to be familiar with XML syntax. This will allow you to customize the Creator XML files if necessary.

1.6 The J2EE Architecture

The J2EE platform gives you a multitiered application model to develop distributed components. Although any number of tiers is possible, we'll use a three-tier architecture for the applications in this book. Figure 1–1 shows the approach.

The client machine supports web browsers, applets, and stand-alone applications. A client application may be as simple as a command-line program running as an administrator client or a graphical user interface created from Java Swing or Abstract Window Toolkit (AWT) components. Regardless, the J2EE specification encourages *thin clients* in the presentation tier. A thin client is a lightweight interface that does not perform database queries, implement business logic, or connect to legacy code. These types of "heavyweight" operations preferably belong to other tiers.

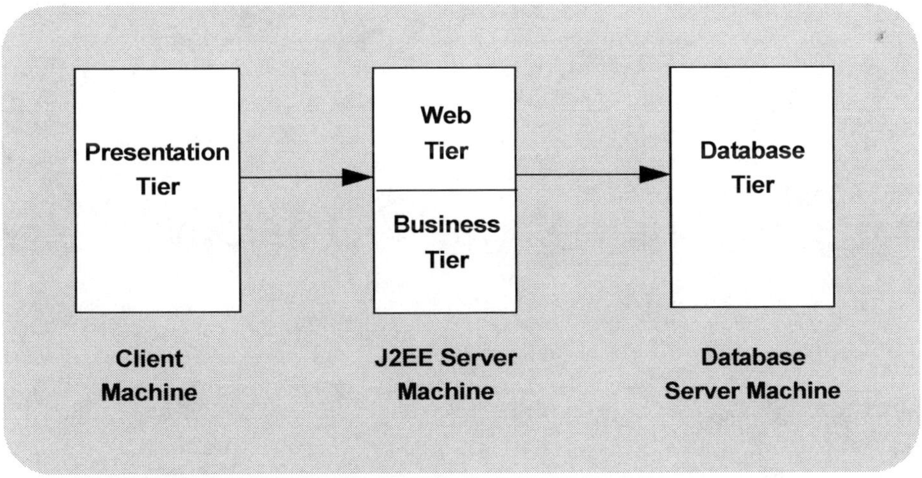

Figure 1–1 **Three-tier J2EE architecture**

The J2EE server machine is the center of the architecture. This middle tier contains web components and business objects managed by the application server. The web components dynamically process user requests and construct responses to client applications. The business objects implement the logic of a business domain. Both components are managed by a J2EE application server that provides these components with important system services, such as security, transaction management, naming and directory lookups, and remote connectivity. By placing these services under control of the J2EE application server, client components focus on either presentation logic or business logic. And, business objects are easier for developers to write. Furthermore, the architecture *encourages* the separation of business logic from presentation logic (or model from view).

The database server machine handles the database back end. This includes mainframe transactions, databases, Enterprise Resource Planning (ERP) systems, and legacy code. Another advantage of the three-tier architecture is that older systems can take on a whole new "look" by using the J2EE platform. This is the approach many businesses are taking as they integrate legacy systems into a modern distributed computing environment and expose application services and data to the web.

1.7 Java Servlet Technology

The Java Servlet component technology presents a request-response programming model in the middle tier. Servlets let you define HTTP-specific servlet classes that accept data from clients and pass them on to business objects for processing. Servlets run under the control of the J2EE application server and often extend applications hosted by web servers. Servlet code is written in Java and compiled. It is particularly suited to server-side processing for web applications since each Servlet session is handled in its own thread.

1.8 JavaServer Pages Technology

A JavaServer Pages (JSP) page is a text-based document interspersed with Java code. A JSP engine translates JSP text into Java Servlet code. It is then dynamically compiled and executed. This component technology lets you create dynamic web pages in the middle tier. JSP pages contain static template data (HTML, WML, and XML) and JSP elements that determine how a page constructs dynamic content. The JSP API provides an efficient, thread-based mechanism to create dynamic page content.

Creator uses JavaServer Faces (JSF), which is built on both the servlet and JSP technologies. However, by using Creator, you are shielded from much of the details of not only JSP and servlet programming, but JSF details as well.

1.9 JDBC API and Database Access

Java Data Base Connectivity (JDBC) is an API that lets you invoke SQL commands from Java methods in the middle tier. Typically, you use the JDBC API to access a database from servlets or JSP pages. The JDBC API has an application-level interface for database access and a service provider interface to attach JDBC drivers to the J2EE platform. In support of JDBC, J2EE application servers manage a pool of database connections. This pool provides business objects efficient access to database servers.

The JDBC `CachedRowSet` API is a newer technology that makes database access more flexible. Creator accesses configured data sources using a `CachedRowSet` object, a JavaBeans component that is scrollable, updatable, and serializable. These components are disconnected from the database, caching its rows into memory. When web applications modify data in the cached rowset object, the result propagates back to the data source through a subsequent connection. By default, Creator instantiates a cached rowset object in session scope.

The concept of *data providers* is also important because it produces a level of abstraction for data flow within Creator's application environment. Creator's data providers allow you to change the source of data (say, from a database table to a web services call or an EJB method) by hooking the data provider to a different data source.

We introduce data providers in Chapter 8 and show how to use them with databases in Chapter 9.

1.10 JavaServer Faces Technology

The JavaServer Faces (JSF) technology helps you develop web applications using a server-side user interface (UI) component framework. The JSF API gives you a rich set of UI components and lets you handle events, validate and convert user input, define page navigation, and support internationalization. JSF has custom tag libraries for connecting components to server-side objects. We show you these components and tag libraries in Chapter 3.

JSF incorporates many of the lower level tasks that JSP developers are used to doing. Unlike JSP applications, however, applications developed with JSF can map HTTP requests to component-specific event handlers and manage UI elements as stateful objects on the server. This means JSF offers a better separation of model and presentation. The JSF API is also layered directly on top of the Servlet API.

1.11 Ant Build Tool

Ant is a tool from the Apache Software Foundation (`www.apache.org`) that helps you manage the "build" of a software application. The name is an acronym for "Another Neat Tool" and is similar in concept to older build tools like `make` under Unix and `gmake` under Linux. However, Ant is XML-based, it's easier to use, and it's platform independent.

Ant is written in Java and accepts instructions from XML documents. Ant is well suited for performing complicated and repetitive tasks. Creator uses Ant to compile and deploy your web applications. Ant gets its instructions for building a system from the configuration file, **build.xml**. You won't have to know too much about Ant to use Creator, but you should be aware that it's behind the scenes doing a lot of work for you.

1.12 Web Services

Web services are software APIs that are accessible over a network in a heterogeneous environment. Network accessibility is achieved by means of a set of XML-based open standards such as the Web Services Description Language (WSDL), the Simple Object Access Protocol (SOAP), and Universal Description, Discovery, and Integration (UDDI). Web service providers and clients use these standards to define, publish, and access web services.

Creator's application server (J2EE 1.4) provides support for web services. In Creator, you can access methods of a web service by dragging its node onto the design canvas. We show you web services with Creator in Chapter 10.

1.13 Enterprise JavaBeans (EJB)

EJB is a component technology that helps developers create business objects in the middle tier. These business objects (enterprise beans) consist of fields and methods that implement business logic. EJBs are server-side components written in Java that serve as building blocks for enterprise systems. They perform specific tasks by themselves, or forward operations to other enterprise beans. EJBs are under control of the J2EE application server. We show you how to access EJBs from Creator applications in Chapter 11.

1.14 Portlets

A portlet is an application that runs on a web site managed by a server called a *portal*. A portal server manages multiple portlet applications, displaying them on the web page together. Each portlet consumes a fragment of the page and manages its own information and user interaction. Portlet application developers will typically target portlets to run under portals provided by various portal vendors.

You can use Creator to develop portlets. Creator builds JSF portlets. This means your design-time experience in building portlet web application using the visual, drag-and-drop features of Creator will be familiar. Most of the interaction with the IDE is exactly the same as it is for non-portlet JSF projects. We show you how to create portlets in Chapter 12.

1.15 Key Point Summary

- Creator is an IDE built on layered Java technologies that helps you build web applications.
- Procedure-oriented languages separate data and functions, whereas object-oriented languages combine them.
- Encapsulation enforces data hiding and allows you to control access to your objects.
- Java is a strongly typed object-oriented language with a large set of APIs that help you develop portable web applications.
- In Java, operator `new` returns a reference to a newly created object so that you can call methods with the reference.
- Java classes have fields, constructors, and instance methods. The `private` keyword is used for encapsulation, and the `public` keyword grants access to clients.
- Java packages allow you to store class files and retrieve them with `import` statements in Java programs.
- Java uses `try`, `catch`, and `throw` to handle error conditions with a built-in exception handling mechanism.
- Inheritance is a code reuse mechanism that implements an "is a" relationship between classes.
- Dynamically bound method calls are resolved at run time in Java. Dynamic binding is essential with distributed web applications.
- An interface has no fields and only abstract public methods. A class that implements an interface must provide code for the interface's methods.
- The J2EE architecture is a multitiered application model to develop distributed components.

- Java Servlets let you define HTTP-specific servlet classes that accept data from clients and pass them on to business objects for processing.
- A JSP page is a text-based document interspersed with Java code that allows you to create dynamic web pages.
- JDBC is an API for database access from servlets, JSP pages, or JSF. Creator uses data providers to introduce a level of abstraction between Creator UI components and sources of data.
- JavaServer Faces (JSF) helps you develop web applications using a server-side user interface component framework. Creator generates and manages all of the configuration files required by JSF.
- A JavaBeans component is a Java class with a default constructor and setter and getter methods to manipulate its properties.
- NetBeans is a standards-based IDE and platform written in the Java programming language. Java Studio Creator is based on the NetBeans platform.
- XML is a self-describing, text-based language that documents data and makes it easy to transport between systems.
- Ant is a Java build tool that helps you compile and deploy web applications.
- Web services are software APIs that are accessible over a network in a heterogeneous environment.
- EJBs are server-side components written in Java that implement business logic and serve as building blocks for enterprise systems.
- Portlets are applications that consume a portion of a web page. They run on web sites managed by a portal server and execute along with other portlets on the page.
- Portlets help divide web pages into smaller, more manageable fragments.

CREATOR BASICS

Topics in This Chapter

- Creator Window Layout
- Visual Design Editor
- Components and Clips Palette
- Source Editors/Code Completion
- Page Navigation Editor
- Outline Window
- Projects Window
- Servers and Resources
- Creator Help System
- Basic Project Building

Chapter 2

Sun Java Studio Creator makes it easy to work with web applications from multiple points of view. This chapter explores some of Creator's basic capabilities, the different windows (views) and the way in which you use them to build your application. We show you how to manipulate your application through the drag-and-drop mechanism for placing components, configuring components in the Properties window, controlling page flow with the Page Navigation editor, and selecting services from the Servers window.

2.1 Examples Installation

We assume that you've successfully installed Creator. The best source of information for installing Creator is Sun's product information page at the following URL.

```
http://developers.sun.com/prodtech/javatools/jscreator/
```

Creator runs on a variety of platforms and can be configured with different application servers and JDBC database drivers. However, to run all our examples we've used the bundled application server (Sun Java System Application Server 8.2) and the bundled database server (Derby). Once you've configured

Creator for your system, the examples you build here should run the same on your system.

Download Examples

You can download the examples for this book at the Sun Creator web site. The examples are packed in a zip file. When you unzip the file, you'll see the **FieldGuide2/Examples** directory and subdirectories for the various chapters and projects. As each chapter references the examples, you will be instructed on how to access the files.

You're now ready to start the tour of Creator.

2.2 Creator Views

Figure 2–1 shows Creator's initial window layout in its default configuration. When you first bring it up, no projects are open and Creator displays its Welcome window.

There are other windows besides those shown in the initial window layout. As you'll see, you can hide and display windows, as well as move them around. As we begin this tour of Creator, you'll probably want to run Creator while reading the text.

Welcome Window

The Welcome window lets you create new projects or work on existing ones. Figure 2–2 shows the Welcome window in more detail. It lists the projects you've worked on recently and offers selection buttons for opening existing projects or creating new projects. If you hover with the mouse over a recently opened project name, Creator displays the full pathname of the project in a tooltip.

To demonstrate Creator, let's open a project that we've already built. The project is included in the book's download bundle, in directory **FieldGuide2/Examples/Navigation/Projects/Login1**.

Creator Tip

We show you how to build this project from scratch in Chapter 5 (see "Dynamic Navigation" on page 206). For our tour of the IDE, however, we'll use the pre-built project from the examples download.

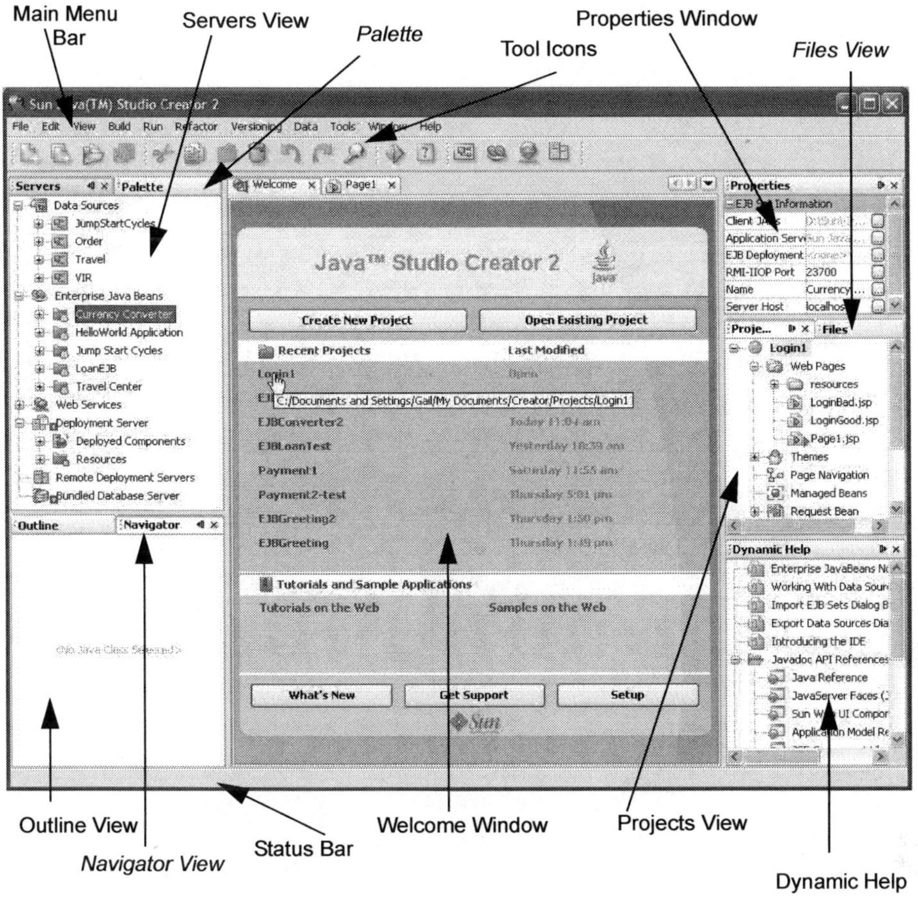

Figure 2–1 **Creator's initial window layout**

1. Select the Open Existing Project button and browse to the **FieldGuide2/Examples/Navigation/Projects** directory.
2. Select **Login1** (look for the projects icon) and click Open Project Folder. This opens the **Login1** project in the Creator IDE.
3. Page1 should display in the visual editor, as shown in Figure 2–3. If Page1 does not open in the design editor, find the Projects view (its default position is on the right, under the Properties view).
4. In the Projects view, expand node Login1, then Web Pages. Double-click **Page1.jsp**. Page1 should now appear in the design editor.

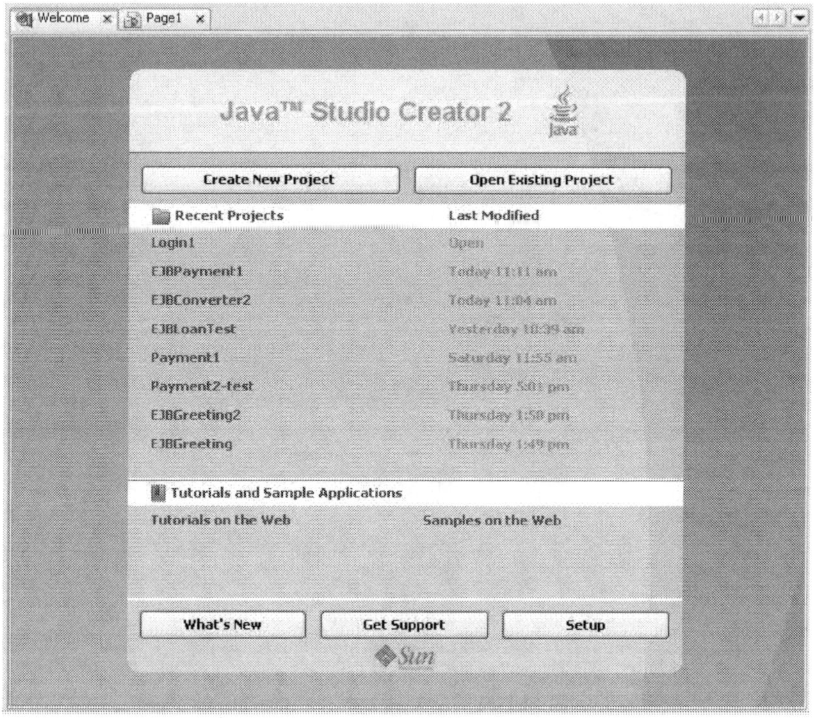

Figure 2–2 **Creator's Welcome window**

Design Editor

Figure 2–3 shows a close-up of the design canvas (the visual design editor) of Page1. You see the design grid and the components we've placed on the canvas. The design editor lets you visually populate the page with components.

Page1 contains a "virtual form." Virtual forms are accessible on a page by selecting the Show Virtual Forms icon on the editing toolbar, as shown in Figure 2–3. Virtual forms let you assign different components to different actions on the page. We show you how to use virtual forms in "Configure Virtual Forms" on page 216 (for project Login1 in Chapter 5) and in "Virtual Forms" on page 417 (for project MusicAdd in Chapter 9).

Select the text field component. The design canvas marks the component with selection and resizing handles. Now move the text field component around on the grid. You'll note that it snaps to the gird marks automatically when you release the mouse. You can temporarily disable the snap to grid feature by moving the component and pressing the Shift key at the same time. You can also select more than one component at a time (use **<Shift+Click>**) and Cre-

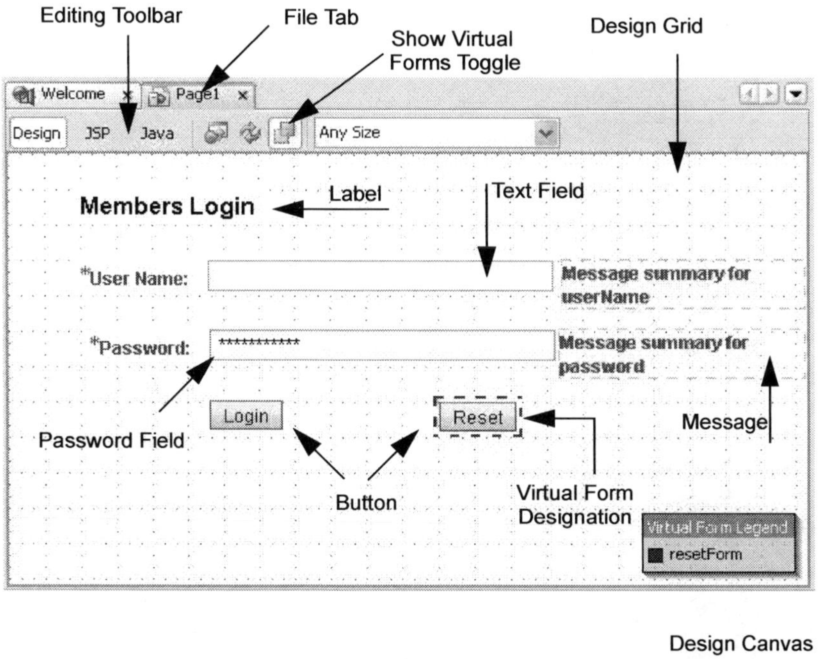

Figure 2–3 **Creator's design canvas showing project Login1**

ator provides options to align components. We cover the mechanics of page design in Chapter 7 (see "Using the Visual Design Editor" on page 273).

Note that when you make modifications to a page, Creator indicates that changes have been made to the project by appending an asterisk to the file name tab. Once you save your project by clicking the Save All icon in the toolbar (or selecting File > Save All from the main menu), the Save All icon is disabled and the asterisk is cleared from the file name tab.

Typically applications consist of more than one page. You can have more than one of your project's pages open at a time (currently, there's just one page open). When you open other files, a file tab appears at the top of the editor pane. The file tab lets you select other files to display in the editor pane.

Creator lets you configure your display's workspace to suit the tasks you're working on. All the windows can be hidden when not needed (click the small x in a window's title bar to close it) and moved (grab the window's title bar and move it to a new location). To view a hidden window, select View from the menu bar and then the window name. Figure 2–4 shows the View menu with the various windows you can open, along with a key stroke shortcut for opening each window.

You can also dock Creator windows by selecting the pushpin in the window title bar. This action minimizes the window along the left or right side of the

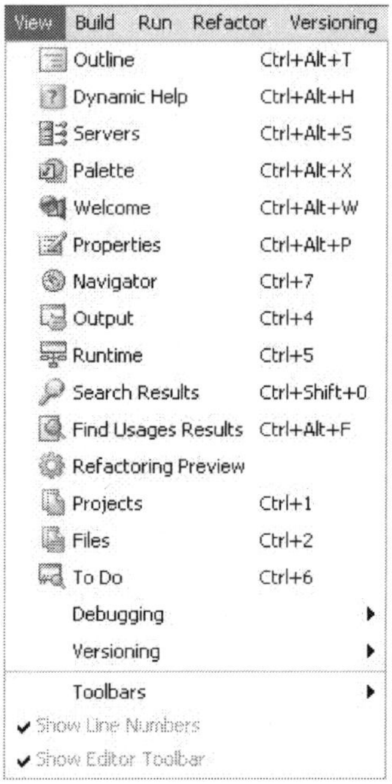

Figure 2–4 **Creator's View Menu allows you to select specific views of your project**

workspace. Make it visible again by moving the cursor over its docked position. Toggling the pushpin icon undocks the window. Figure 2–5 shows the Properties view with both the Projects and Files windows docked.

Properties

As you select individual components, their properties appear in the Properties window. Select the text field component on the design canvas. This brings up its Properties window, as shown in Figure 2–5.

Creator lets you configure the components you use by manipulating their properties. When you change a component's properties, Creator automatically updates the underlying JSP source for you. Let's look at several properties of the text field component. If you hold the cursor over any property value, Creator displays its setting in a tooltip.

Components have many properties in common; other properties are unique to the specific component type. The `id` property uniquely identifies the component on the page. Creator generates the name for you, but you can change it (as we have in this example) to more easily work with generated code. The `label` property enables you to specify a textual label associated with the text field. The red asterisk next to the label in the design view indicates that input is

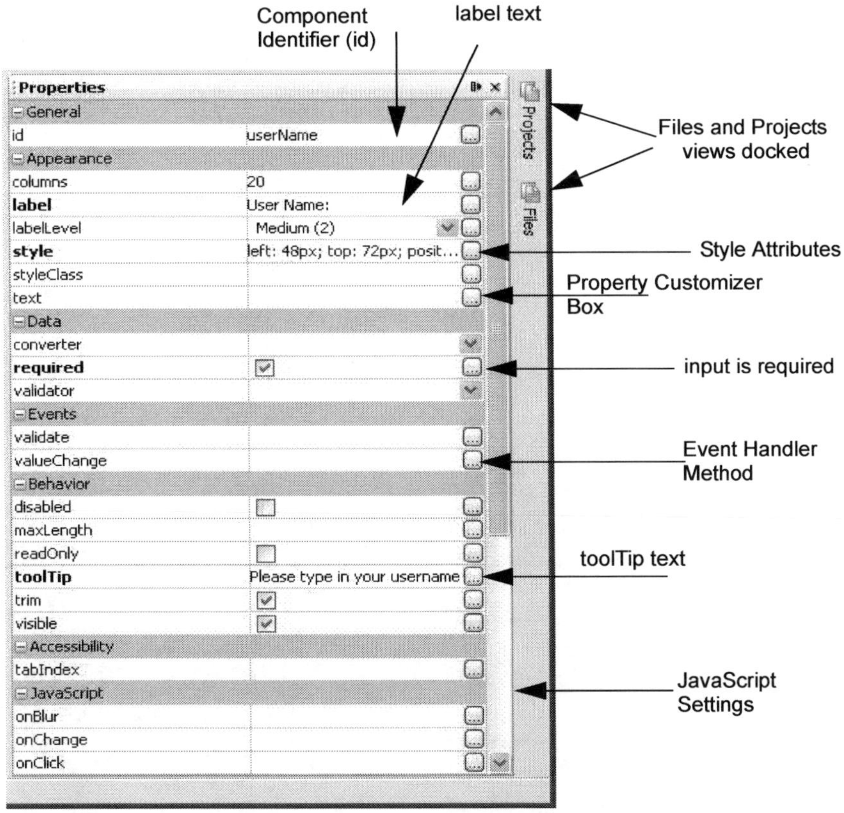

Figure 2–5 **Properties window for text field component "userName"**

required for this component. Property `text` holds the text that the user submits. You can use the `style` property to change a component's appearance. The `style` property's `position` tag reflects the component's position on the page. When you move the component in the design view, Creator updates this for you.

Property `styleClass` takes previously defined CSS style classes (you can apply more than one). File **stylesheet.css** (under Web Pages > resources in the Projects window) is the default style sheet for your projects. We cover `style`, `styleClass` and using Creator's preconfigured Themes in Chapter 7.

Text field components can take a converter (specified in property `converter`) and a validator (property `validator`). The `validate` and `valueChange` properties (under Events) expect method names and are used to provide custom validation or to process input when the component's text value changes.

Click on the text field component (again) in the design canvas until Creator displays a gray outline around the component. Now type in some text and finish editing with **<Enter>**. The text you type appears opposite property `text` in the Properties window. To reset the property, click the customizer box opposite property `text`. Creator pops up a Property Customizer dialog, as shown in Figure 2–6. Select Unset Property. This is a handy way to return a property value to its unset state.

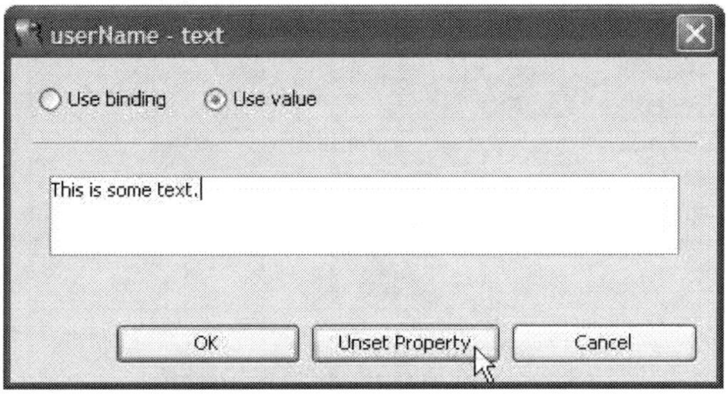

Figure 2–6 **Property customizer dialog for property text**

Each property's customizer is tailored to the specific property. For example, select the Login button on the design canvas. In the Properties window, click the property customizer box opposite property `style`. Creator pops up an elaborate style editor. Experiment with some of the settings (change the font style or color, for example) and see how the button changes in the design view. You can also preview the look. Right-click inside the design view and select Preview in Browser. Figure 2–7 shows a preview of Login1 with a different appearance for the Login button.

Palette

Creator provides a rich set of basic components, as well as special-function components such as Calendar, File Upload, Tab Set, and Tree. The palette is divided into sections that can be expanded or collapsed. Figure 2–8 shows the Basic Components palette, which includes all of the components on Page1 of project Login1. In Figure 2–8 you also see the Layout and Composite Components palette.

The palette lets you drag and drop components on the page of your application. Once a component is on a page, you can reposition it with the mouse or configure it with the Properties window.

Figure 2–9 shows the Validators and Converters palette. Creator's converters and validators let you specify how to convert and validate input. Because con-

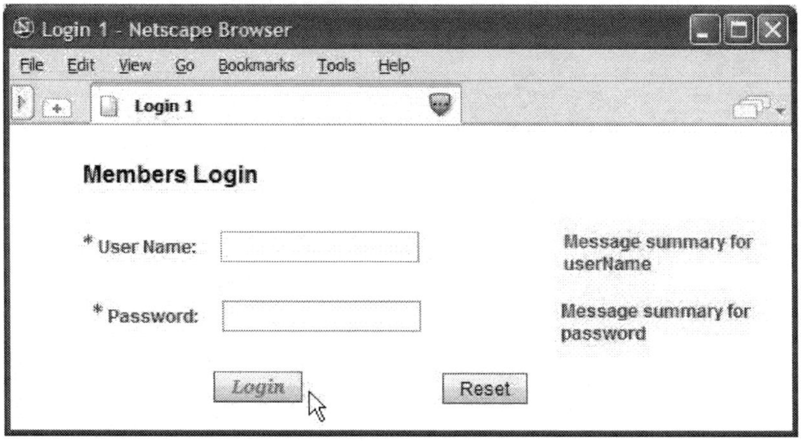

Figure 2–7 **Preview in Browser for Login1**

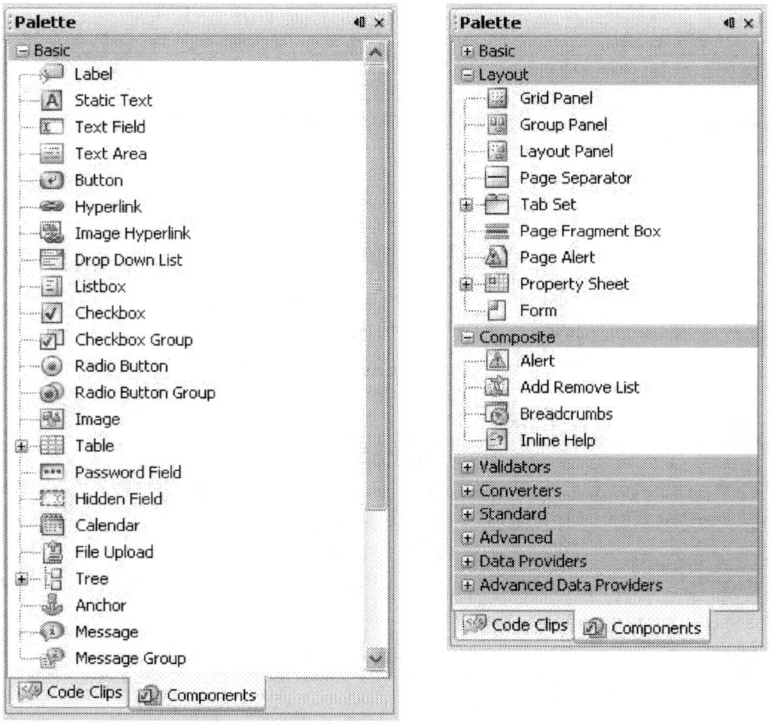

Figure 2–8 **Basic, Layout and Composite Components palette**

version and validation are built into the JSF application model, developers can concentrate on providing event handling code for valid input.

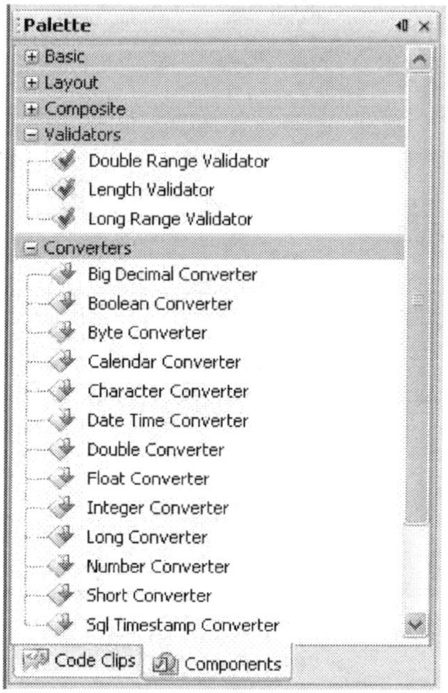

Figure 2–9 **Creator Validators and Converters Components palette**

You select converters and validators just like the UI components. When you drag one to the canvas and drop it on top of a component, the validator or converter binds to that component. To test this, select the Length Validator and drop it on top of the `userName` text field component. You'll see a length validator `lengthValidator1` defined for the text field's `validator` property in the Properties window.

Note that components, validators, and converters all have associated icons in the palette. Creator uses these icons consistently so you can easily spot what kind of component you're working with. For example, select the Login button component on the design canvas and examine the Outline view. You'll see that the icon next to the button components (Login and Reset) matches component Button in the Basic Components palette.

Outline

Figure 2–10 is the Page1 Outline view for project **Login1**. (Its default placement is in the lower-left portion of the display.) The Outline window is handy for showing both visual and nonvisual components for the page that's currently displayed in the design canvas. You can select the preconfigured managed beans, RequestBean1, SessionBean1 and ApplicationBean1. These JavaBeans components hold your project's data that belong in either request (page), session or application scope, respectively. (We discuss scope issues for web application objects in "Scope of Web Applications" on page 224.)

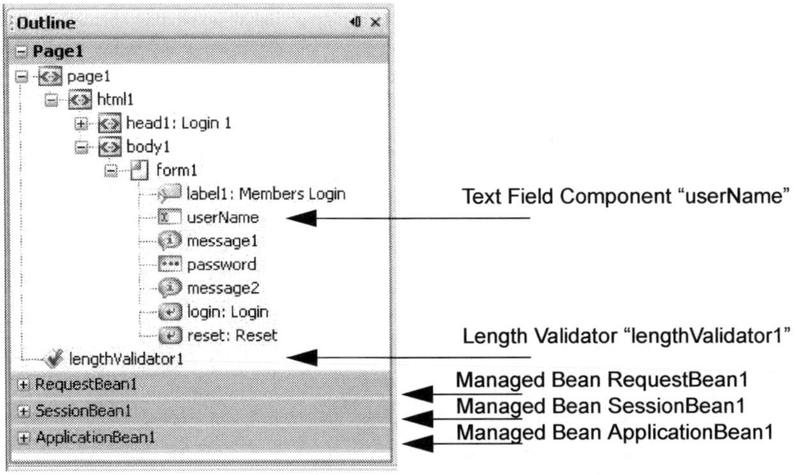

Figure 2–10 **Creator's Outline window for project Login1**

Some components are composite components (they contain nested elements). The Outline window shows composite components as nodes that you can expand and compress with '+' and '-' as needed. Suppose, for example, you select grid panel for layout. When you add components to this grid panel, they appear nested underneath the panel component in the Outline view.

The length validator component on the `userName` text field appears as component `lengthValidator1` in the Outline view. Select the length validator and examine it in the Properties view. Specify values for properties `maximum` (use **10**) and `minimum` (use **3**). This limits input for the `userName` text field component to a string that is between 3 and 10 characters long.

Now let's look at the Projects window.

Projects

Figure 2–11 shows the Projects window for project **Login1**. Its default location is in the lower-right corner. Whereas the Outline view displays components for individual pages and managed beans, the Projects window displays your entire project, organized in a logical hierarchy. (Since Creator lets you open more than one project at a time, the Projects window displays all currently opened projects.) Project **Login1** contains three JSP pages under the Web Pages node: **Page1.jsp**, **LoginGood.jsp**, and **LoginBad.jsp**. Double-click any one of them to bring it up in the design canvas. When the page opens, Creator displays a file name tab so you can easily switch among different open files in the design canvas.

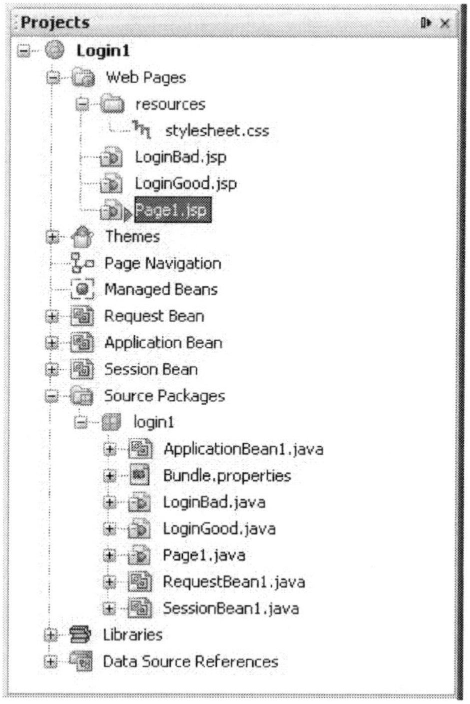

Figure 2–11 **Creator's Project Navigator window for project Login1**

When you create your own projects, each page has its own Java component "page bean." These are Java classes that conform to the JavaBeans structure we mention in Chapter 1 (see "JavaBeans Components" on page 13). To see the Java files in this project, expand the Source Packages node (click on the '+'), then the **login1** folder. When you double-click on any of the Java files, Creator brings it up in the Java source editor. (We'll examine the Java source editor shortly.) Without going to the editor, you can also see Java classes, fields, constructors, and methods by expanding the '+' next to each level of the Java file.

The Projects view displays Creator's "scoped beans." These are pre-configured JavaBeans components that store data for your project in different scopes. You can use request scope (Request Bean), application scope (Application Bean), or session scope (Session Bean). Many of the projects in this text add properties to these beans. We discuss JSF scoping issues in Chapter 6 (see "Predefined Creator Java Objects" on page 226).

The Projects view also lists the resources node, which lives under the Web Pages node. The resources node typically holds file **stylesheet.css** and any image files. Creator uses the libraries listed in the Libraries node to display, build, and deploy your application. These class files (compiled Java classes) are stored in special archive files called JAR (Java Archive) files. You can see the name, as well as the contents (down to the field and method names) of any JAR file by expanding the nodes under Libraries. We show you how to add a JAR file to your project in Chapter 13 (see "Add the asg.jar Jar File" on page 595).

Files

The Projects window shows you a logical view of your project. Sometimes you may need to access a configuration file that is not included in the Projects view. In such a case, use the Files view, as shown in Figure 2–12.

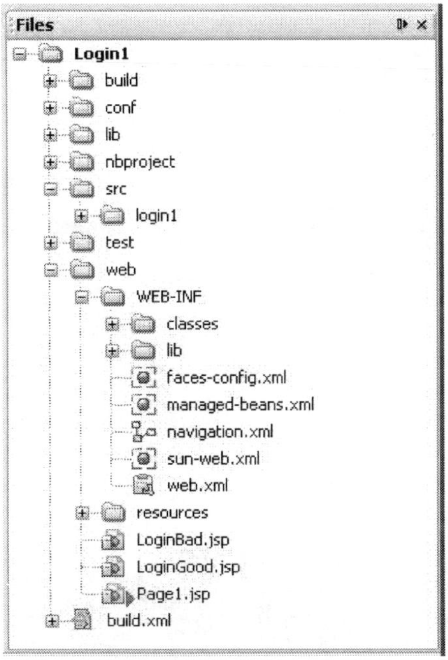

Figure 2–12 **Files view for project Login1**

The Files view shows all of the files in your project. For example, expand node **web > WEB-INF** and double-click file **web.xml**. Creator brings up file **web.xml** in a specialized Creator-configuration XML editor, as shown in Figure 2–13.

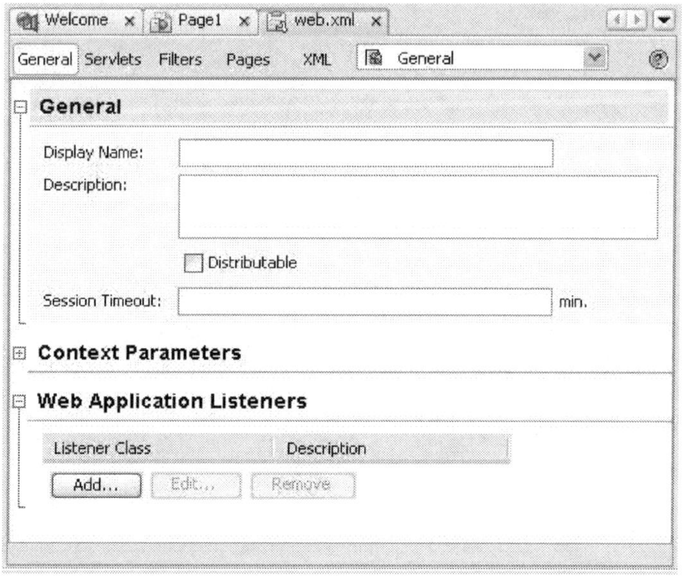

Figure 2–13 **Editing file web.xml**

File **web.xml** lets you set various project-level configuration parameters, such as Session Timeout, Filters, or special error pages. Close this file by clicking the small x in the **web.xml** file tab.

JSP Editor

As you drop components on the page and configure them with the Properties window, Creator generates JSP source code for your application. You can view the JSP representation of a page by clicking the JSP button in the editing toolbar, as shown in Figure 2–14.

Normally, you will not need to edit this page directly, but studying it is a good way to understand how Creator UI components work and how to manage their properties. You'll see a close correspondence between the JSP tags and the components' properties as shown in the Properties window. If you do edit the JSP source directly, you can easily return to the design view. Creator always keeps the design view synchronized with the JSP source.

Tags in the JSP source use a JSF Expression Language (EL) to refer to methods and properties in the Java page bean. For example, the login button's `action` property is set to `#{Page1.login_action}`, which references method `login_action()` in class **Page1.java**.

Creator also generates and maintains code for the "page bean," the Java backing code generated for each page. Let's look at the Java source for **Page1.java** now.

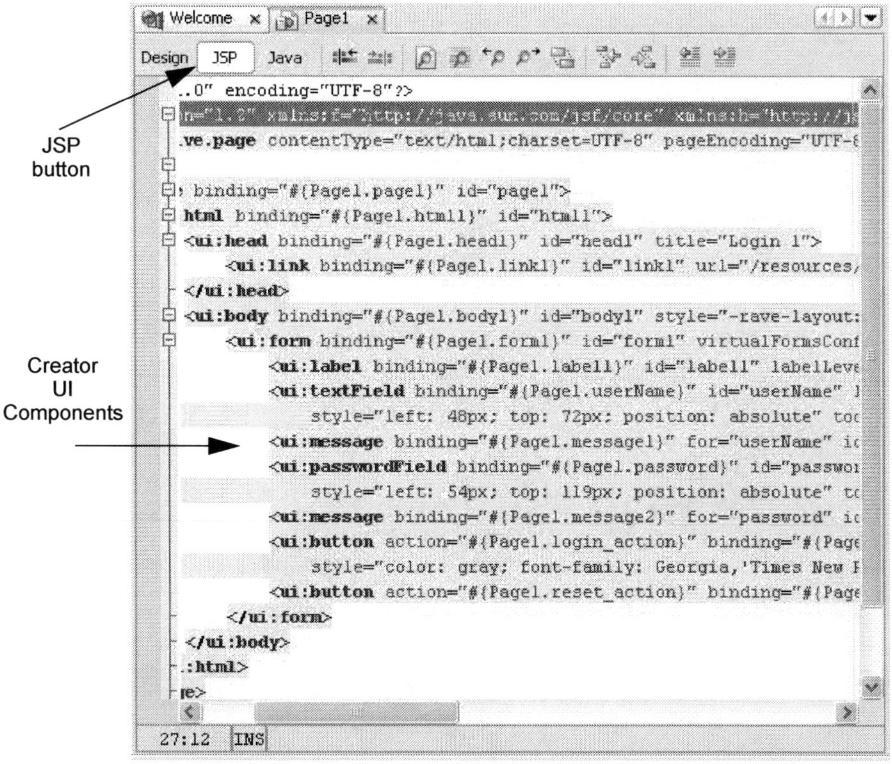

Figure 2–14 **Page1.jsp XML Editor**

Java Source Editor

Click the Design button and return to the Page1 design view. As you build your application, not only does Creator generate JSP source that defines and configures your component, but it also maintains the page bean. For example, Creator makes it easy for you to code event handlers (methods that perform customized tasks when the user selects an option from a drop down list or clicks a button). Double-click button Login in the design view. Creator generates a default event handler for this button and puts the cursor at the method in the Java source editor. If this method was previously generated (as it was here), Creator brings up the editor and puts the cursor at the method, as shown in Figure 2–15. Here you see method `login_action()` in file **Page1.java**.

You can always bring up a page's Java code by selecting the Java button in the editing toolbar. This Java file is a bean (conforming to a JavaBeans structure) and its properties consist of the components you place on the page. Each

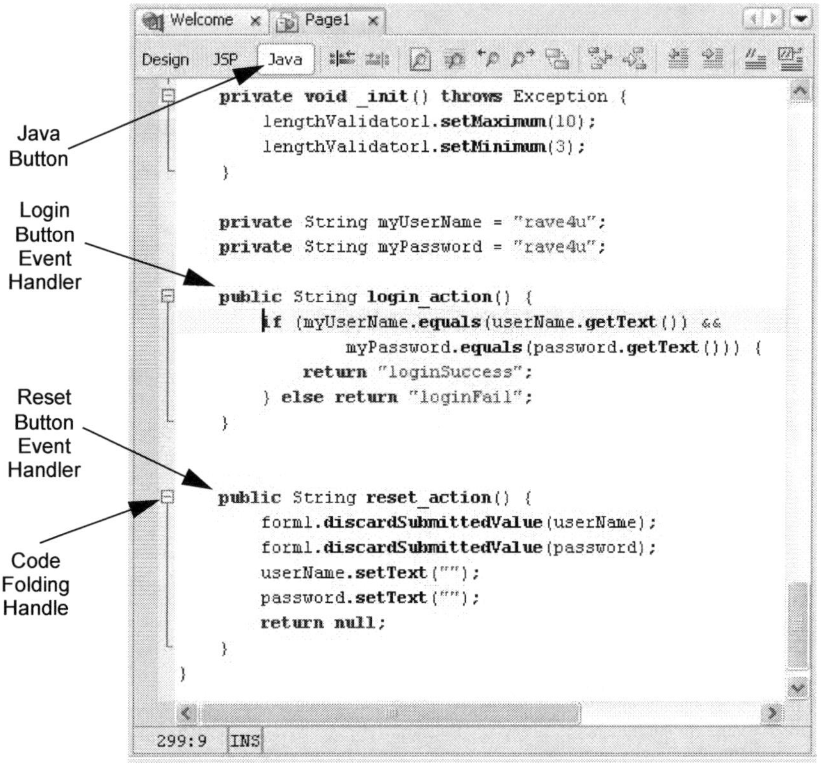

Figure 2–15 **Page1.java in Java source editor**

component corresponds to a private variable and has a getter and setter. This allows the JSF EL expression to access properties of the page bean.

All of Creator's editors are based on NetBeans. The Editor Module is a full-featured source editor and provides code completion (we show an example shortly), a set of abbreviations, and fast import with **<Alt+Shift+I>**. The editor also has several useful commands: Reformat Code (handy when pasting code from an external source), Fix Imports (adds needed import statements as well as removes unused ones), and Show Javadoc (displays documentation for classes and methods). There are more selections in the context menu (right-click inside the editor to see the menu). Sections of the Creator-generated code are folded by default to help keep the editing pane uncluttered. You can unfold (select '+') or fold (select '-') sections as you work with the source code. You can also view line numbers: place the mouse in the blue left-margin, right-click, and select Show Line Numbers.

To see the set of abbreviations for the Java editor, select Tools > Options from the main menu bar. The Options dialog pops up. Under Options, select Editing

> Editor Settings > Java Editor. On the right side of the display, click the small editing box next to Abbreviations. Creator pops up the window shown in Figure 2–16.

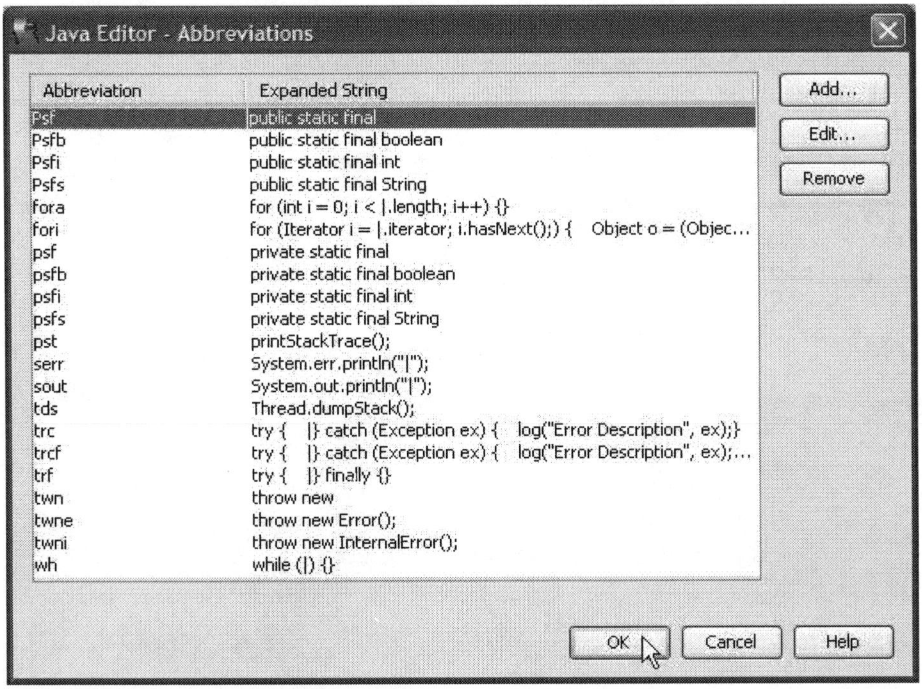

Figure 2–16 **Java source editor list of abbreviations**

The window lists the abbreviations in effect for your Java editor. (You can edit, add, or remove any item.) For example, to place a `for` loop in your Java source file, type the sequence **fora** (*for array*) followed by **<Space>**. The editor generates

```
for (int i = 0; i < .length; i++) {
}
```

and places the cursor in front of `.length` so that you can add an array name. (`.length` refers to the length of the array object. This code snippet lets you easily loop through the elements of the array.)

The Java source editor also helps you with Java syntax and code completion. All Java keywords are bold, and variables and literal Strings have unique colors.

When you add statements to your Java source code, the editor dynamically marks syntax errors (in red, of course). The editor also pops up windows to help with code completion and package location for classes you need to reference (press **<Ctrl+Space>** to activate the code completion window). If available, code completion includes Javadoc help. For example, Figure 2–17 shows the code completion mechanism as you highlight method `equals()` and press **<Ctrl+Space>**.

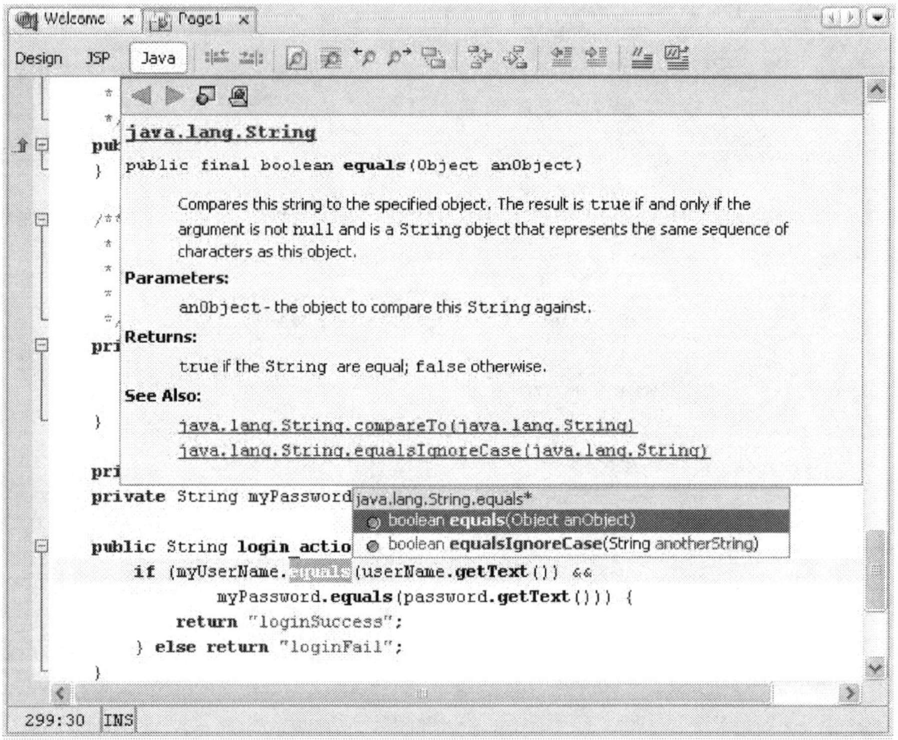

Figure 2–17 **Java source editor code completion**

When you use the down-arrow to select the second method, `equalsIgnore-Case()`, the help mechanism displays its Javadoc documentation. (To retrieve Javadoc documentation on any class in your source file, select it and press **<Ctrl+Shift+Space>**.) The Java Source editor is discussed in more detail in Chapter 4 (see "Using the Java Source Editor" on page 136).

When the Java source editor is active, Creator also activates the Navigator window, as shown in Figure 2–18. The Navigator window lets you go to a method or field within the Java source editor by clicking its name in the window. In Figure 2–18, the cursor hovers over method `destroy()`, displaying help in a tooltip.

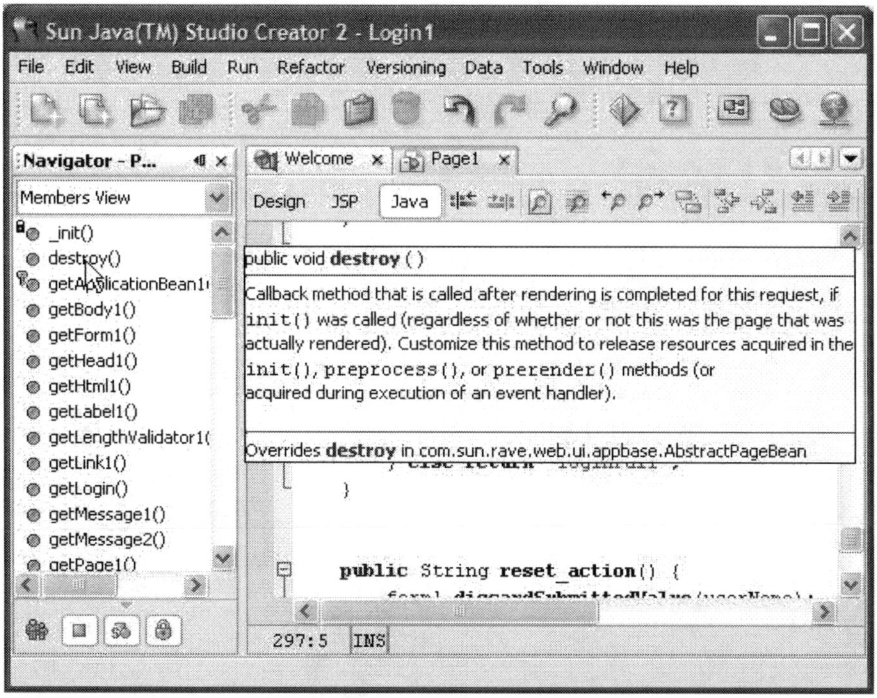

Figure 2–18 **Navigator view and help for method destroy() displayed**

Code Clips Palette

When the Java Source editor is displayed, Creator replaces the Components palette with the Code Clips palette, as shown in Figure 2–19. Here we show several sections, including the code clips for Application Data. Highlight clip Store Value in Session in this section. If you hold the cursor over the clip name, Creator displays a snippet window. You can drag and drop the clip directly into your Java source file.

To view or edit a clip, select it, right-click, and choose Edit Code Clip. Figure 2–20 shows the Store Value in Session code clip.

The Code Clips palette is divided into categories to show sample code for different programming tasks. For example, if you click Application Data, you'll see a listing of clips that let you access application data from different scopes in your web application.

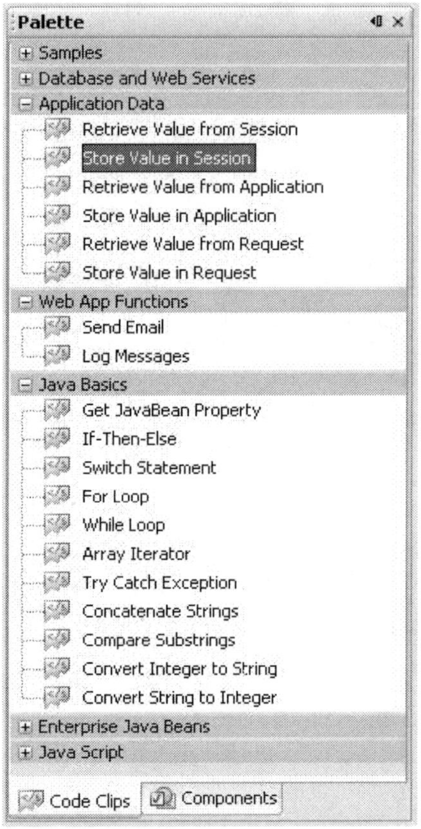

Figure 2–19 **Java Clips Palette**

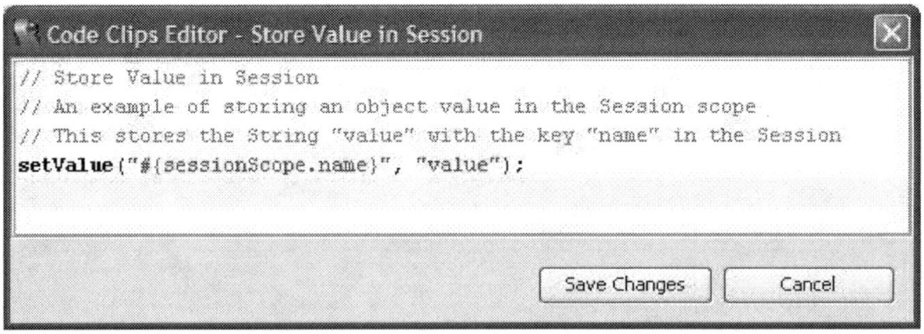

Figure 2–20 **Code Clips Editor**

Page Navigation Editor

Return to the Java Source window and examine method `login_action()`. You'll see that `login_action()` returns one of two Strings (either `"loginFail"` or `"loginSuccess"`) to the action event handler. The action event handler then passes the String on to the navigation handler to determine page flow. Let's look at the Page Navigation editor now.

1. From the top of the Java source window, select the Design button. This returns you to the design canvas for this page.
2. Now right-click in the design canvas and select Page Navigation from the context menu. Creator brings up the Page Navigation editor for project **Login1**, as shown in Figure 2–21.

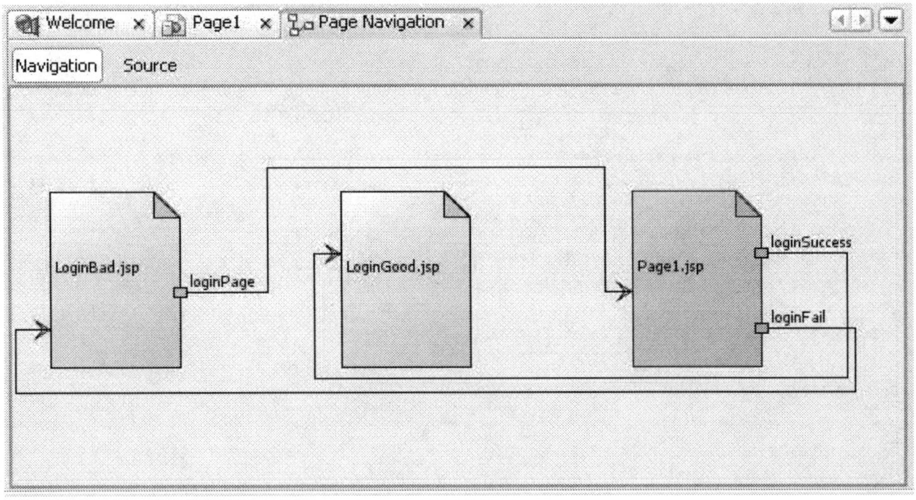

Figure 2–21 **Page navigation editor for project Login1**

There are three pages in this project. The Page Navigation editor displays each page and indicates page flow logic with labeled arrows. The two labels originating from page **Page1.jsp** correspond to the return Strings in action method `login_action()`.

Chapter 5 shows you how to specify navigation in your applications (see "Page Navigation" on page 188). The Page Navigation editor is also a handy way to bring up any of the project's pages: just double-click inside the page. Once you've visited the Page Navigation editor, Creator displays a file tab called **Page Navigation** so you can easily return to it.

Before we explore our project any further, let's have you deploy and run the application. From the menu bar, select Run > Run Main Project. (Or, click the green Run arrow on the icon toolbar, which also builds and runs your project.)

Output Window

Figure 2–22 shows the output window after building and deploying project Login1. Creator uses the Ant build tool to control project builds. This Ant build process requires compiling Java source files and assembling resources used by the project into an archive file called a WAR (Web Archive) file. Ant reads its instructions from a Creator-generated XML configuration file, called **build.xml**, in the project's directory structure.

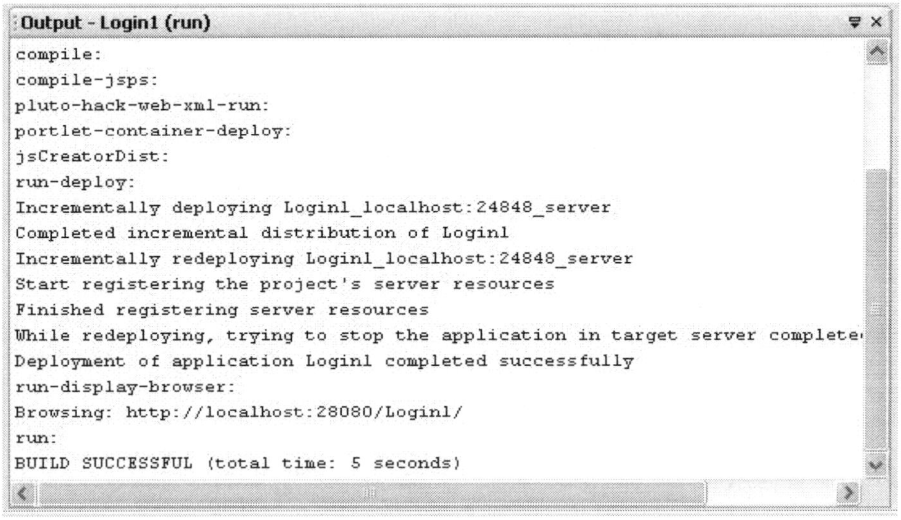

Figure 2–22 **Output window after building and deploying project Login1**

If problems occur during the build process, Creator displays messages in the Output window. A compilation error with the Java source is the type of error that causes the build to fail. When a build succeeds (the window shows `BUILD SUCCESSFUL`, as you see Figure 2–22), Creator tells the application server to deploy the application. If the application server is not running, Creator starts it for you. If errors occur in this step, messages appear in the Outline window from the application server.

Finally, it's possible that the deployment is successful but a runtime error occurs. In this situation, the system throws an exception and displays a stack trace on the browser's web page. Likely sources for these errors are problems with JSF tags on the JSP page, resources that are not available for the runtime class loader, or objects that have not been properly initialized.

When the build/deployment process is complete, Creator brings up your browser with the correct URL. (Here the status window displays "Browsing: `http://localhost:28080/Login1/`.") To run project **Login1** with the Sun bundled Application Server, Creator generates this web address.

```
http://localhost:28080/Login1/
```

You use `localhost` if you're running the application server on your own machine; otherwise, use the Internet address or host name where the server is running. The port number `28080` is unique to Sun's bundled J2EE application server. Other servers will use a different port number here.

Note that the Context Root is **/Login1** for this application. The application server builds a directory structure for each deployed application; the context root is the "base address" for all the resources that your application uses.

Figure 2–23 shows the **Login1** project deployed and running in a browser. The Password field's tooltip is displayed. Both the User Name and Password input fields have asterisks, indicating required input. Type in some values for User Name and Password. If you leave the User Name field empty or type less than 3 characters or more than 10, you'll get a validation error. (The minimum and maximum number of characters only apply if you added a length validator earlier.) The correct User Name and Password is "rave4u" for both fields.

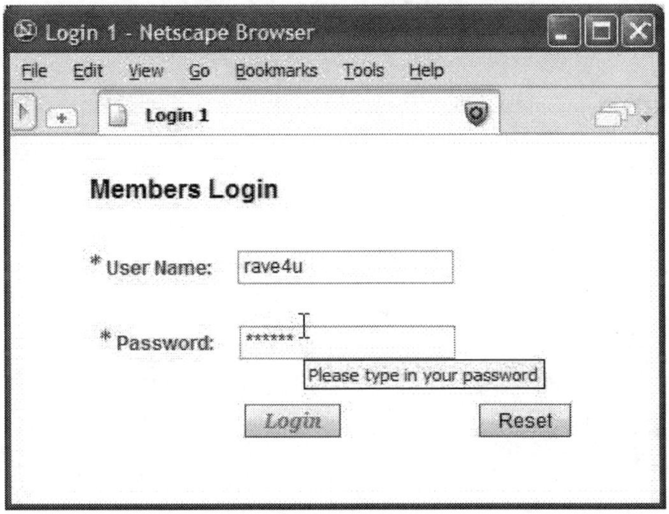

Figure 2–23 **Project Login1 running in a browser**

If you supply the correct values and click the Login button, the program displays page **LoginGood.jsp**. Incorrect values display **LoginBad.jsp**.

It's time now to explore the Servers window, located in the upper-left portion of your Creator display. Click the tab labeled Servers to see this window.

Servers

Figure 2–24 shows the Servers window after you've deployed project **Login1**. Various categories of servers are listed here, including Data Sources, Enterprise JavaBeans, Web Services, Deployment Server, Remote Deployment Servers, and Bundled Database Server.

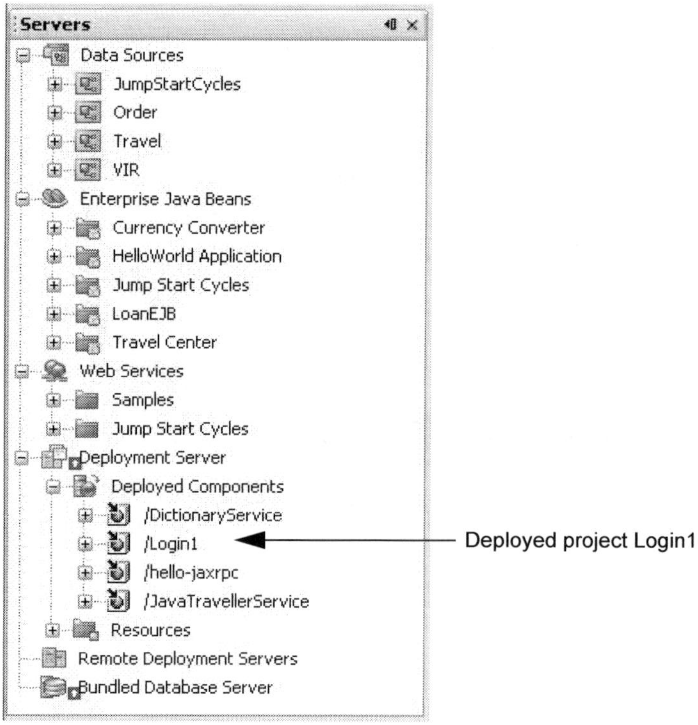

Figure 2–24 **Servers window**

The Data Sources node is a JDBC database connection. Creator bundles a database server and the Data Sources node connects to the bundled database by default. You can configure a different database. Creator comes configured with several sample databases, which are visible if you expand the Data Sources node.

Creator Tip

The Database Server must be running to inspect the sample database tables. If the Bundled Database Server is not running, right-click node Bundled Database Server and select Start Bundled Database.

Let's expand the Travel > Tables node and view the database tables. As you select different tables, Creator displays their properties in the Properties window. Expand a table further to examine its database table field names, as shown in Figure 2–25. Here, we expand table PERSON, displaying field names PERSONID, NAME, JOBTITLE, and FREQUENTFLYER.

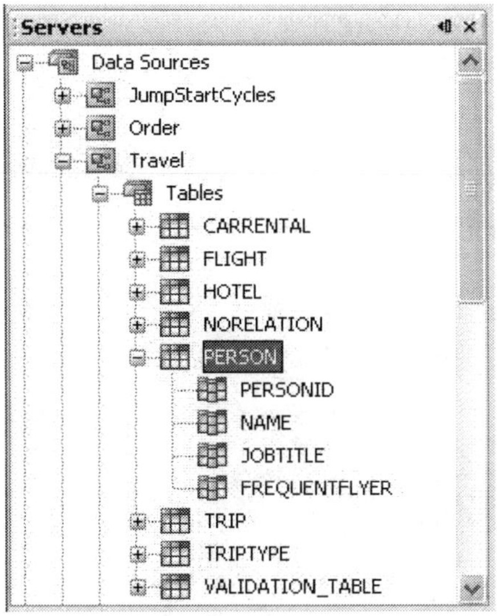

Figure 2–25 **Inspecting the Travel Database tables (Person)**

When you double-click a table name, Creator displays the data in the editor pane with a default query, as shown in Figure 2–26. You can close the table view by clicking the small x on the Query 1 tab. We discuss creating web applications that access databases in Chapter 9 (see "Accessing Databases" on page 372).

The second resource in the Servers window is the Enterprise JavaBeans node. Creator has a few sample EJBs deployed on the bundled Application Server, which you can access within your projects. Expand node Enterprise JavaBeans > Travel Center > TravelEJB, as shown in Figure 2–27. The TravelEJB provides some of the same data as the Travel database. With Creator, you can bind data to components exactly the same with EJBs as you can with data source tables. We show you how to use EJBs in Chapter 11.

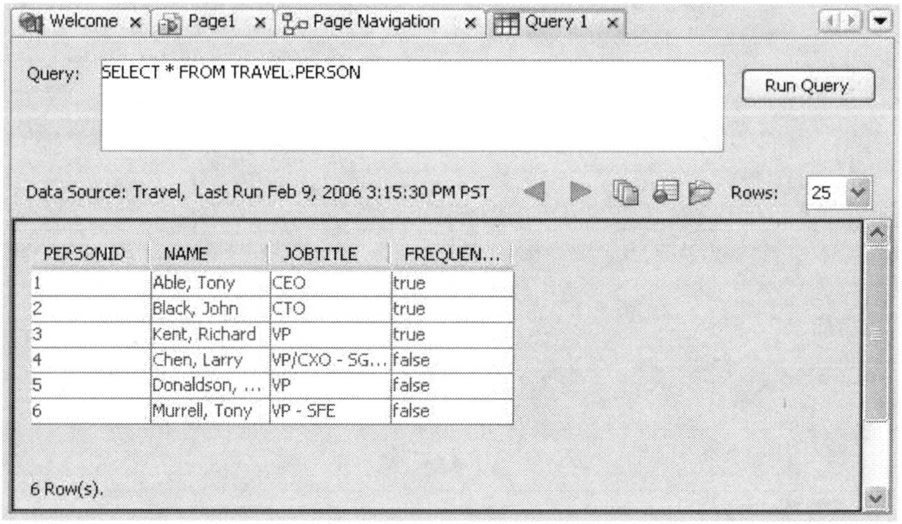

Figure 2–26 **Display data from the Person table**

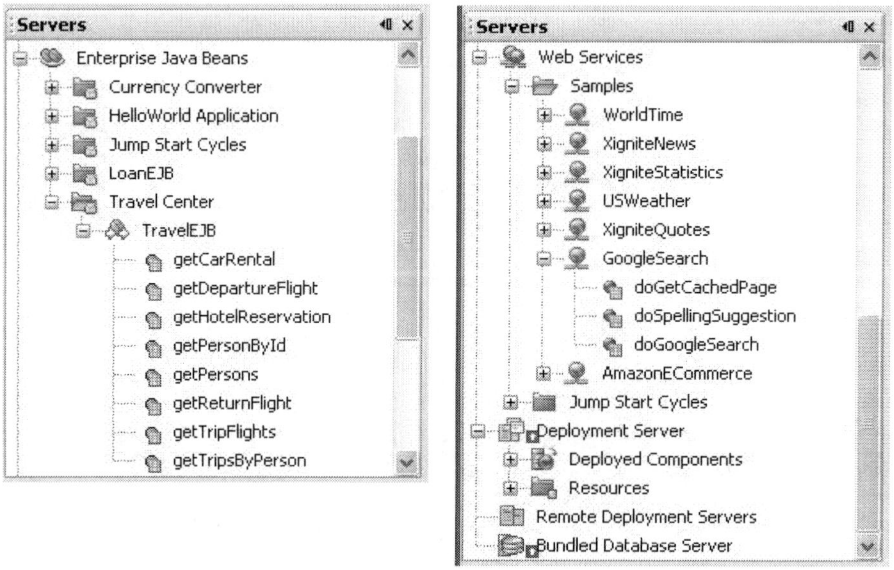

Figure 2–27 **EJB and Web Services resources shown in the Servers window**

Another server resource is Web Services, which provides access to remote APIs from Creator applications. This requires the cooperation of several Java technologies, which we discussed in Chapter 1. The Creator installation includes a client to access the Google Web Services. In Chapter 10 we show you how to create an application with the Google web service API. The Google Search web service methods are shown in Figure 2–27.

The bundled Deployment Server allows you to deploy and run Creator applications on your machine. The Deployed Components node shows you the currently deployed components (including the Login1 application you just deployed). From the Deployment Server node, you can start and stop the server, access the Administrative Console, or view the server's log (right-click Deployment Server to view the context menu with these options).

Creator Tip

The application server must be running for access to the administration console. Use user name **admin** *and password* **adminadmin**.

Debugging Windows

Creator has a debugger that lets you perform typical debugging tasks, such as setting breakpoints, tracing the call stack, tracking local variables, and setting watches. Use the View > Debugging menu to choose which debugging windows to enable, as shown in Figure 2–28.

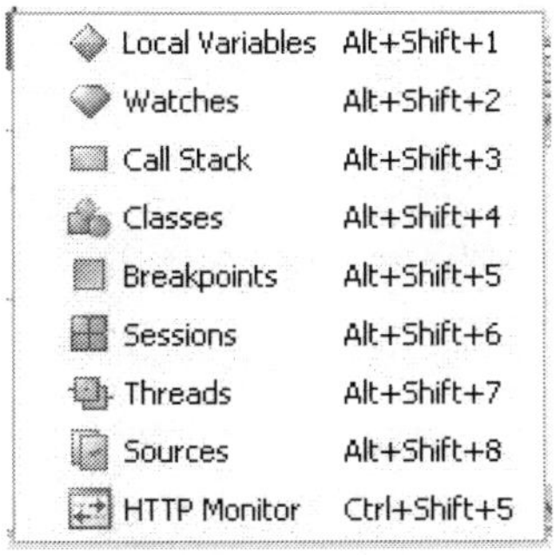

Figure 2–28 **View > Debugging Menu Choices**

To run your application in "debug mode," click on Run > Debug Main Project from the menu bar. The application server has to stop and restart if it's not already in debug mode. In Chapter 14 we walk you through the debugger options, setting breakpoints, stepping through code, and other debugging activities.

Creator Help System

The Creator Help System is probably the most useful window for readers new to Creator. This help system includes a Dynamic Help display, search capability, contents, and an index. The easiest way to access the help system is to select Help > Dynamic Help from the main menu. The selections displayed are context sensitive.

As an example, in the Page1 design view, select one of the Message components and choose Help > Dynamic Help. Creator displays a help window with topics relating to the message component as shown in Figure 2–29.

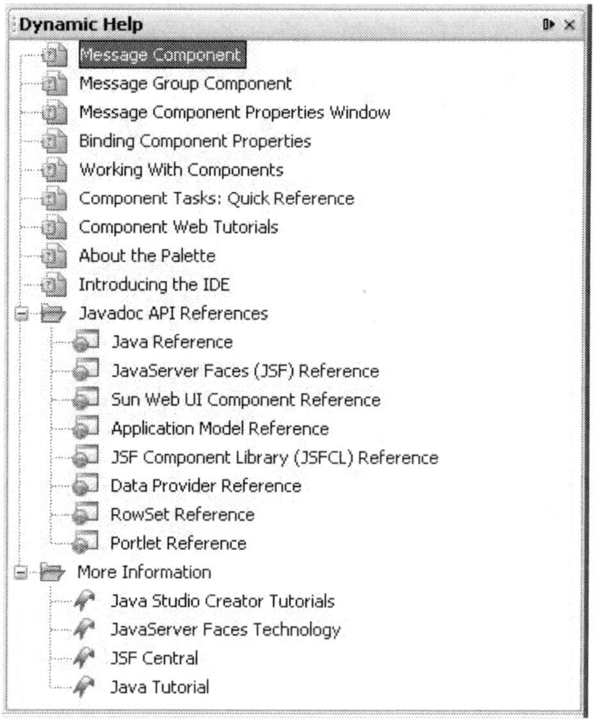

Figure 2–29 **Dynamic Help window**

When you double-click a selection, Creator displays the help information (see Figure 2–30).

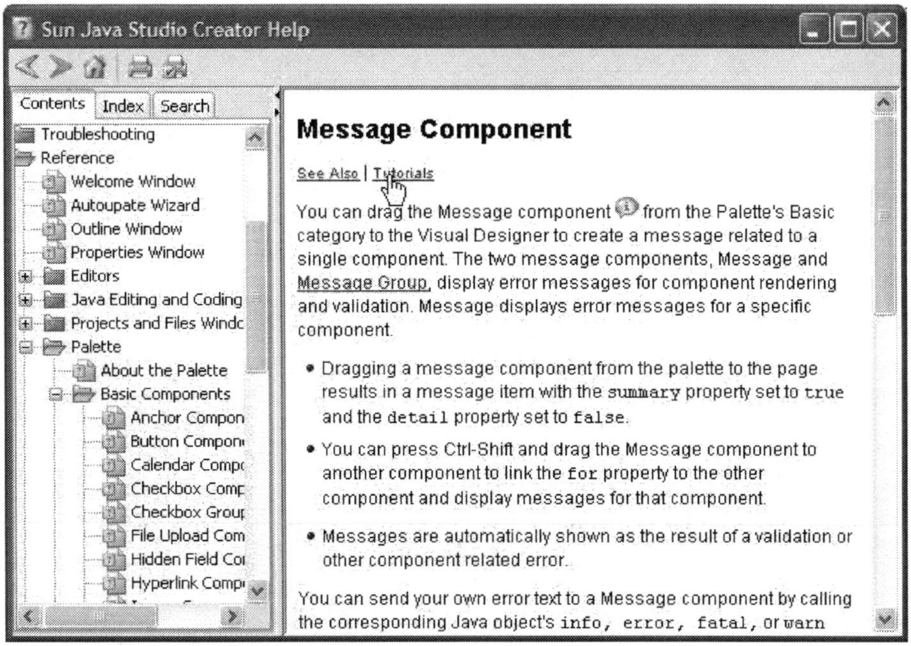

Figure 2–30 **Creator Help system**

2.3 Sample Application

Now that you're comfortable with Creator, let's create a simple web application. Even though this application is simplistic, it shows some of the power in Creator. Figure 2–31 provides a preview of this web application.

Create a Project

Close project **Login1** if it's open.

1. From the Projects window, right-click the project node **Login1** and select Close Project from the context menu.
2. From Creator's Welcome Page, select Create New Project. From the New Project dialog, under Categories select **Web** and under Projects select **JSF Web Application.** Click Next.

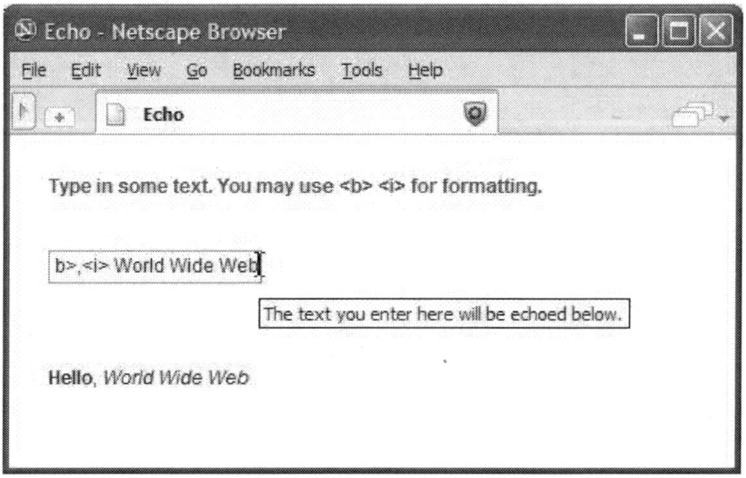

Figure 2–31 **Web application Echo running in a browser**

3. In the New Web Application dialog, specify **Echo** for Project Name and click Finish.

   After creating the project, Creator comes up in the design view of the editor pane. You can now set the title.

4. Select `Title` in the Properties window and type in the text **Echo**. Finish by pressing **<Enter>**.

Add Components to the Page

Creator makes the Components palette visible after you create a project. Using the design editor, you'll add three components to the page: a label, a text field, and a static text component. Figure 2–32 shows the design view with all the components added to the page.

1. From the Basic Components palette, select Label and drag it over to the design canvas. Drop it on the page, near the top on the left side.
2. The label remains selected after you drop it on the page. Supply the text **Type in some text. You may use <b> <i> for formatting.** Finish by pressing **<Enter>**. Creator sets the `text` property to this text (verify this in the Properties view) and displays the text on the page. The default font setting (property `labelLevel`) for a label's text is Medium(2), which can be changed in the Properties window.

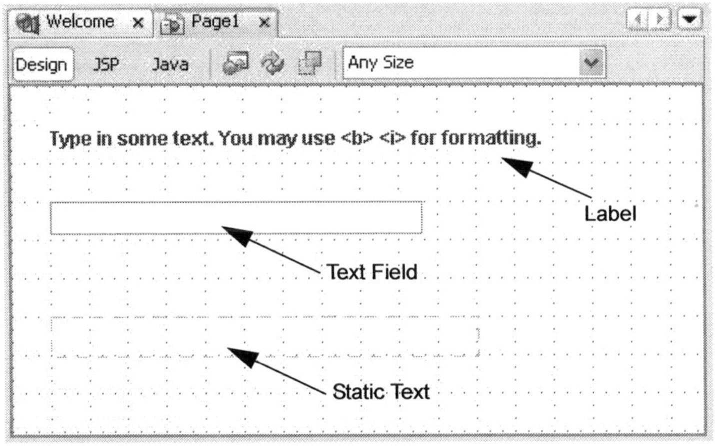

Figure 2–32 **Project Echo in the design view**

3. From the Basic Components palette, select component Text Field and place it on the design canvas underneath the label you just added.
4. Make sure the text field is selected. In the Properties window under Behavior, change its `toolTip` property to **The text you enter here will be echoed below**. Finish with **<Enter>**. This will appear as a tooltip when the user hovers the mouse over the text field in the browser.
5. From the Basic Components palette, select Static Text component and place it under the text field. Resize it so that it is approximately 11 grids wide, as shown in Figure 2–32.
6. Select the static text component. In the Properties window under Data, *uncheck* property `escape`. This allows HTML formatting tags to pass through unaltered to the browser.

You've finished adding the components. Now you will use property binding to bind the text field component `text` property to the static text component `text` property. Here's how.

1. Select the static text component (`staticText1`), right-click, and choose Property Bindings from the context menu. Creator brings up the Property Bindings dialog as shown in Figure 2–33.
2. Under Select bindable property, choose **text** ***Object***.
3. Under Select binding target, expand **Page1 > page1 > html1 > body1 > form1** by clicking the '+' at each level.
4. Select component **textField1** (the text field component you added). Expand the component by clicking '+' on `textField1` and select **text** ***Object***. (The properties are listed in alphabetical order, so `text` is near the end.)

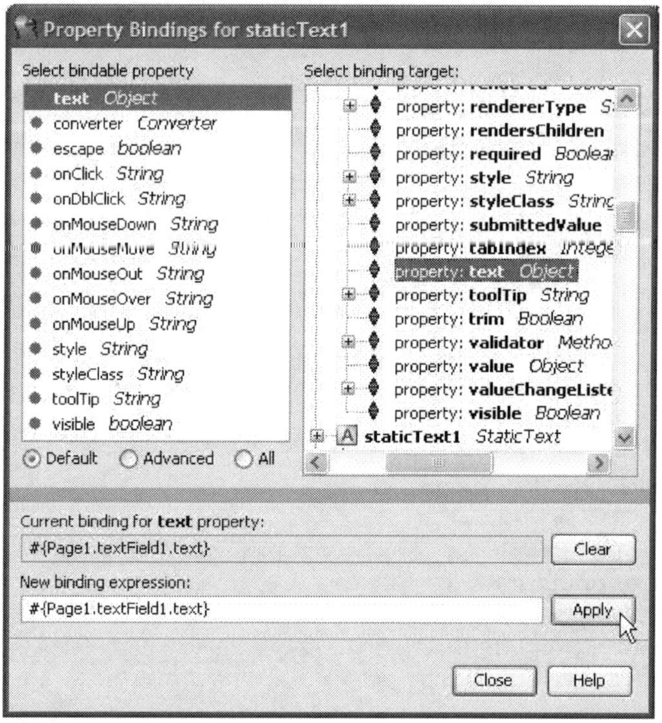

Figure 2–33 **Property Bindings dialog**

5. Click the Apply button. (If you don't click the Apply button, Creator doesn't set the property binding.) Under Current binding for **text** property, you should see the following JSF EL expression

```
#{Page1.textField1.text}
```

6. Click Close to finish

So, what did all this accomplish? You've just configured *property binding* on the static text component (id `staticText1`). This means JSF gets the `text` property (the text that is displayed on the page) for `staticText1` *from* the text field's `text` property (component `textField1`). This, in turn, means that whatever you type in for input will be echoed in the static text's display when you press **<Enter>**. Note that Creator and JSF made all this possible without you writing any Java code!

Is a button necessary to submit the page? As it turns out, when you hit **<Enter>** after entering text in the text field, the default action is to submit the page. This puts the JSF life cycle events in motion and the page is rendered with the new text displayed in the static text component. We discuss the JSF life cycle events in detail in Chapter 6 (see "The Creator-JSF Life Cycle" on page 260). Because you unchecked the `escape` property, any formatting tags are unaltered by the component and passed directly through to the browser.

Deploy and Run

You've finished creating the application. Now it's time to build, deploy, and run it. From the menu bar, select Run > Run Main Project (or select the Run Main Project green arrow icon on the toolbar). Creator builds the application, deploys it, and brings up a browser with the **Echo** web application running.

Figure 2–31 on page 52 shows what the browser window displays after you type **<b>Hello</b>, <i>World Wide Web** inside the text field followed by **<Enter>**. Note that bold tags mark the word Hello and italic marks the phrase World Wide Web. The text field tooltip appears as the user hovers the mouse over the text field component.

This completes our tour of Creator. The next chapter provides a detailed description of the Creator UI components, validators, and converters.

2.4 Key Point Summary

- Creator has multiple windows to give you different views of the project that you're working on. The windows can be sized, docked and undocked, or hidden.
- From the main menu, select View and the desired window name to enable viewing.
- Use the Welcome Window to select a Project to open or to create a new project.
- The design canvas allows you to manipulate components on a page and control their size and placement. Grid lines provide an easy way to align components.
- Use the Components palette to drag and drop a component on the design canvas.
- Use the Converters and Validators sections in the palette to select data converters and input validators for your project.
- The Properties window allows you to inspect and edit a component's properties. Each component type displays a different list of properties.
- A component's `text` attribute typically contains text that is rendered on the page (such as labels on buttons, input text fields, and static text fields). Use the `toolTip` property to create a tooltip for the component and the `style`

property to change font characteristics. Property `styleClass` lets you apply previously defined style definitions.
- You can apply Property Binding and "connect" the value of one component to another or to a data object in request, session, or application scope.
- The Outline window shows all of the elements on a page, including nonvisual components such as converters, validators, or EJB or Web Services clients.
- The Projects view gives you a logical view of your project, including Web Pages, Source Packages, Libraries, the pre-configured beans, and Page Navigation.
- The Files view lets you see all the files in your project.
- The JSP Source editor displays a page's source. Most of the page includes JSF tags for components and their properties. As you make changes to your pages in the design canvas, Creator synchronizes the JSP and Java source.
- Creator's editors are based on NetBeans and reflect a rich functionality for editing Java source, JSP source, and XML files.
- The Java Source editor displays the Java source for each "page bean," a JavaBeans component that manipulates each page's elements. You typically place event handler code or custom initialization code in the Java page bean.
- The Java Source editor includes a code completion mechanism that provides pop-up windows with possible method names (use **<Ctrl+Space>** to invoke) and Javadoc documentation for classes and objects in your program (use **<Ctrl+Shift+Space>** to invoke). The Java editor also includes a dynamic syntax analyzer to warn you about compilation errors before you compile.
- The Code Clips palette provides sample Java code to accomplish common programming tasks. The Clips are organized into categories based on function. You can select a clip and drop the code into your Java source.
- The Page Navigation editor lets you specify page flow. This editor generates a navigation configuration file, **navigation.xml**.
- When you build your project, the Output window provides diagnostic feedback and completion status.
- The Servers window displays Data Sources, Enterprise JavaBeans, Web Services, Deployment Server, and Database Server nodes.
- The Deployment Server node lets you start and stop the application server and undeploy running web applications.
- You can view database table data by expanding the Data Sources node and selecting individual tables. Creator displays the data in the editor pane when you right-click a table name and select View Data.
- The Debugger Window displays several views that are helpful when you are debugging your project. You can set breakpoints and monitor the call stack, local variables, and watches with the debugger.
- The Creator Help system provides a table of contents, index, and search mechanism to help you use Creator effectively. The help system is dynamic

and displays help information based on how you're currently interacting with Creator.

CREATOR COMPONENTS

Topics in This Chapter

- JSF Overview
- Component Categories
- Basic Components
- Layout Components
- Composite Components
- Converters and Validators
- Component Library Manager
- Importing a Component Library

Chapter 3

Sun Java Studio Creator's design palette presents a wide variety of components to choose from. These components include buttons, text fields, checkboxes, listboxes, radio buttons, hyperlinks, images, tables, tree nodes, grid panels, and so on—in short, anything you need to design a web page. You can select a component, drag it to the design canvas, and drop it at the location of your choice. In addition, you can choose validator components to verify user input and converter components for data conversions. Creator maintains a design canvas with your web page layout and generates Java code for you, along with JSP and XML statements to configure and deploy your application.

In this chapter we present a catalog of Creator User Interface (UI) components, validators, and converters. We also provide references to examples in this book where they are used. The examples will help you understand how to use the Creator UI components in your projects.

3.1 JSF Overview

The Creator UI components work within a JSF web application environment. With the JSF framework, these components let you handle events, validate and convert user input, define page navigation, and support internationalization. JSF also connects components to server side objects. Let's start with the architecture of JSF to give you the "big picture" of what's going on.

JSF Architecture

Figure 3–1 shows the architecture used with JSF.

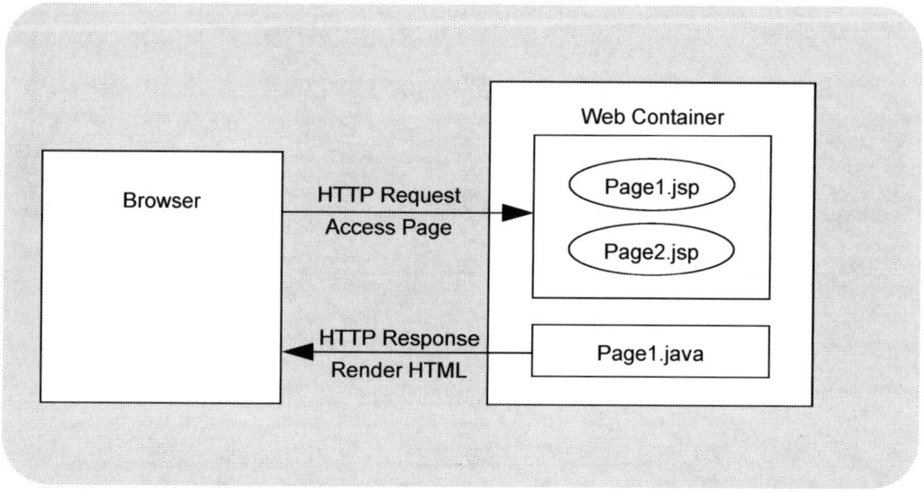

Figure 3–1 **JSF architecture**

Your browser interacts with the web container through one or more JSP pages (**Page1.jsp** and **Page2.jsp**). These are JSP pages containing JSF tags. The supporting page bean (**Page1.java**) manages the objects referenced by the JSP pages. Note that the JSP pages handle HTTP requests when a page is accessed, whereas the Java files render HTML for the HTTP response.

The JSP Page

Suppose a web page has a static text component (`staticText1`) that displays "In what year were you born?", a button to click (`button1`), and a text field (`textField1`) for the year (restricted to the range 1900 to 1999). When these components are moved from the palette to the design canvas, Creator generates the component tags in the JSP file. Each Creator UI component also becomes a property in the generated Java page bean. To understand how this all works, let's start with how the static text component is defined in **Page1.jsp**.

```
<ui:staticText id="staticText1"
    binding="#{Page1.staticText1}"
    style="font-size: 18pt; left: 96px; top: 96px;
       position: absolute"
    text="In what year were you born?"/>
```

The JSP file is expressed in XML. Creator generates this file for you and keeps it synchronized with your page design. As you modify components with the Properties window, Creator updates the JSP code as well as the Java code as necessary. Creator generates the required tags for your components in the JSP page. You can always access the JSP page by selecting the JSP label in the editing toolbar above the design canvas.

In this example, the static text component displays "In what year were you born" on the page. Its `id` property (unique page identification) is `staticText1` and its `binding` property (the corresponding property in the Page1 page bean) is also `staticText1`. The `style` property specifies its location on the page with the left and top settings in pixels. This property also makes the text appear in 18-point font size.

JSF Expression Language (EL)

JSF uses a specialized syntax to access JavaBeans components with its tags. For example, the notation

```
#{Page1.staticText1}
```

references the `staticText1` property in JavaBeans component Page1. In the JSP file (**Page1.jsp**), the generated component tags reference properties in the supporting page bean, as follows.

```
binding="#{Page1.staticText1}"
```

Now let's look at the generated tags for a button component in **Page1.jsp**.

```
<ui:button id="button1"
    binding="#{Page1.button1}"
    action="#{Page1.button1_action}"
    style="left: 72px; top: 168px; position: absolute"
    text="Click for your age"/>
```

Elements `binding` and `action` are UI component tag library properties whose values are set with JSF EL. Element `binding` is the button component's page bean reference, and `action` references a special action event method `button1_action()`, also in Page1. Here, method `button1_action()` is called when the users clicks the button controlled by component `button1`.

Converters and Validators

What about the text field component? Recall that this component must read a year (in the range 1900 to 1999) from the user. Here's how the input text field component is configured in **Page1.jsp**.

```
<ui:textfield id="textField1"
    binding="#{Page1.textField1}"
    converter="#{Page1.integerConverter1}"
    style="left: 192px; top: 168px; position: absolute"
    validator="#{Page1.longRangeValidator1.validate}"/>
```

Text field components display and accept text, but `textField1` must work with integer numbers in this example. Consequently, a JSF conversion component (`integerConverter1`) is necessary to convert String input to integer values. Input is restricted to a specific range of numbers (1900 to 1999), so we'll need a JSF validator (`longRangeValidator1`) for the input, too.

```
converter="#{Page1.integerConverter1}"
validator="#{Page1.longRangeValidator1.validate}"
```

In both cases, JSF EL references the components that perform the conversion and validation.

Event Handling

JSF uses a delegation event model to handle events generated by user actions (clicking a button, changing a selection in a drop down list, pressing **<Enter>** after editing a text field, for example). It's helpful to have an understanding of the pieces that work together to make responding to events a well-behaved system.

The Event Source is a component that is capable of generating an event. Different components generate different event types. Button components and hyperlink components (for example) generate action events. Drop down list components generate value change events.

Event Objects are generated by components (the Event Source). An Event Object is basically a message that is passed from the Event Source to an Event Listener. The Event Object contains information about the Event.

Event Listeners are specialized objects created by JSF that know what to do when an event is generated. Different types of listeners can respond to different types of events. For example, ActionEventListeners respond to action events and ValueChangeListeners respond to value change events.

Using the "Publish-Subscribe" design pattern, Event Listener Registration keeps track of which objects "care about" an event occurring. Objects that "care" are those that register themselves through the Event Listener Registration. After registering with the Event Source, Event Listeners are notified when an action occurs. Notification means their special event method is called with the event object as a parameter. Fortunately, Creator generates all the method stubs, event listeners, and event registration for you. Here is an example of the default value change method that JSF calls when a value change event is generated from a drop down list component.

```
public void dropDown1_processValueChange(
        ValueChangeEvent event) {
   // TODO: Replace with your code
   . . .
}
```

Web application developers provide the specialized event-processing code (whatever actions your web application must perform in responding to the value change event).

Action events are common with most applications and Creator generates the action event handlers for you. Action events can be used to write processing code in response to a button click. In addition, action events return String values to a navigation handler, which allow you to invoke a different web page. Here is the default event handler Creator generates for a button (with property `id` set to `button1`).

```
public String button1_action() {
   // TODO: Process the button click action.
   // Return value is a navigation
   // case name where null will return to the same page.
   . . .
   return null;
}
```

Note that action events implement navigation by returning String values. A null string means you stay on the same page. A different String (`"Button-Click"`, for example) instructs the navigation handler to go to a different page.

Java Page Bean

Now let's show you the Java page bean file, **Page1.java**. Creator generates Java code in the Java page bean for the components you select from the design palette. Each component becomes a property of the supporting page bean, and the component instance is bound to that property.

Here's the **Page1.java** file for our simple web application with two text fields and a button. Again, Creator generates this file for you.

```
public class Page1 extends AbstractPageBean {

   private Button button1 = new Button();
   private TextField textField1 = new TextField();
   private TextField textField2 = new TextField();

   private LongRangeValidator longRangeValidator1 =
        new LongRangeValidator();
   private IntegerConverter integerConverter1 =
        new IntegerConverter();

   // getters and setters for components
   . . .

   public Page1() {
   }

   // Creator-generated life cycle code omitted . . .

   public String button1_action() {
     // TODO: Process the button click action.
     // Return value is a navigation
     // case name where null will return to the same page.
     return null;
   }
}
```

Note that Page1 extends AbstractPageBean. The private fields are generated for each UI component you place on the page and the getter and setter methods make them accessible as properties. Here are the getters and setters for the static text component.

```
public TextField getTextField1() {
   return textField1;
}

public void setTextField1(TextField tf) {
   this.textField1 = tf;
}
```

In our example a public `init()` method calls a private `_init()` method in the Java page bean to set the minimum and maximum ranges for the JSF validator component (`longRangeValidator1`). When you set these values for the validator by using Creator's Properties window, Creator generates the statements in the private `_init()` method to configure the validator for you. This is done before the managed components are initialized.

```
private void _init() throws Exception {
     longRangeValidator1.setMaximum(1999L);
     longRangeValidator1.setMinimum(1900L);
}

public void init() {
     super.init();
     try {
        _init();
     }

     catch (Exception e) {
        log("Page1 Initialization Failure", e);
        throw e instanceof FacesException ?
           (FacesException)e : new FacesException(e);
     }
     // Perform application initialization that must complete
     // *after* managed components are initialized
     // TODO - add your own initialization code here
}
```

3.2 Components

Creator allows you to select UI components from a design palette for your application. These components are implemented with a JSP custom tag library for rendering components in HTML.

When you select a component and drag it to the design canvas, Creator generates code in the page's JSP source as well as support code in the associated Java page bean. Furthermore, Creator displays each component in the Outline view, including any support components that may not be visible. Once you place a component on the design canvas, you can modify its properties and behavior through the Properties window, through the JSP code, or through modifications to the Java page bean. In general, it's preferable to edit properties of a component with Creator's Properties window. However, writing code to handle action and value change events must be done in the Java page bean file.

Components Palette

The Components Palette is divided into three groups: Basic, Layout, and Composite. Each component includes the component name and an icon that you can drag and drop on the design canvas. Figure 3–2 shows you the component groups and all of their components.

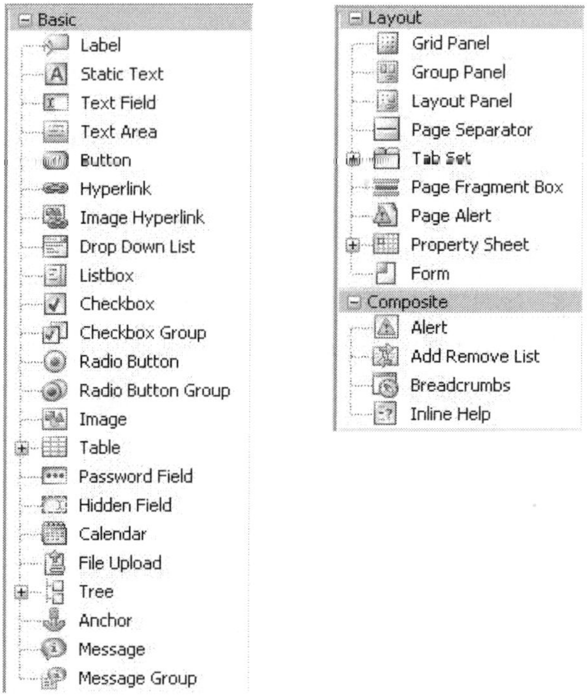

Figure 3–2 **Component palette**

Creator Tip

The Components palette also includes the Standard Components, the JSF Reference Implementation components bundled with the first version of Creator. These are included for backward compatibility with imported Creator1 projects only. For newly created projects, use the components in the Basic, Layout, and Composite sections.

Component Properties

This chapter presents a catalog of Creator components so that you can easily look up their behavior and use them in your applications. Many components share common properties and code generation features, however. Let's start with the definitions of these properties so that you can see how they're used.

text

The `text` property stores a component's main textual characteristics. Its meaning depends on the component. For example, `text` stores the text of a button label, the display text of a static text component, or the input for a text field. The `text` property can also store the text for a password field and hidden field components.

The `text` property is a Java `Object` type. Creator allows you to bind a component's `text` property to a JavaBeans property, a data source, or even a localized message in a properties file.

label

The `label` property is a text string that provides text labeling for a component on a web page. Examples of components that have label properties are text fields, checkboxes, radio buttons, and drop down lists.

The `label` property is a Java `Object` type. Creator allows you to bind a component's `label` property to a JavaBeans property, a data source, or a localized message in a properties file.

toolTip

The `toolTip` property is a text string for a component's tooltip.

style

The `style` property holds Cascading Style Sheet (CSS) strings for properties such as font family, font size, and position parameters. These determine the type of font used, its point size, and placement on the design canvas. Creator provides a sophisticated CSS style editor that helps you configure a component's `style` property. (For a detailed discussion of the style editor, see "Using the Style Editor" on page 282.)

styleClass

The `styleClass` property allows you to specify predefined CSS style classes. You can place CSS style class definitions in the default style sheet, **stylesheet.css** (found in the Projects window under Web Pages > resources). We show you examples of property `styleClass` in Chapter 7 (see "Using Property styleClass" on page 284).

id

The `id` property is a page-unique string that identifies a component on the web page. Creator generates the component's `id` for you, but you can use the Properties window to change it.

Creator Tip

We recommend renaming the default id when you have components on the page with event handling methods (action or value change methods). Providing meaningful names for the id property makes Creator generate methods with meaningful names. This makes your Java code easier to read.

rendered

The `rendered` boolean property controls whether a component will be rendered during the Render Response Phase of the JSF life cycle.

visible

The `visible` boolean property controls whether a rendered component will be visible on the page.

action

The `action` property is important for Action and Link components, such as buttons and hyperlinks. This property references a method in the page bean that returns a String for JSF's navigation handler. Chapter 5 discusses page navigation in detail. The application writer may provide application-specific statements in the action method, process information to determine page flow, or both. To generate an action event handler, double-click the component in the design canvas. Creator brings up the Java source editor and puts the cursor at the first line of the action event handler.

binding

Creator sets the `binding` property for all components you place on the page. A `binding` property binds the component instance to a property in the page bean. Since Creator maintains this property for you, there is no reason for you to change it. For example, if you add a button component to a web application's initial page (**Page1.jsp**), the default `binding` property for the button component is

```
binding="#{Page1.button1}"
```

This JSF EL expression references the `button1` property of managed bean Page1 and binds the component instance to the bean property. Now you can write code in the **Page1.java** page bean to access the button component and dynamically control its properties.

JavaScript

JavaScript allows client side processing activated with mouse events (for example, clicking a component, giving focus to a component, or moving the mouse over a component). The browser executes the JavaScript on the client machine without any server involvement. You can attach a mouse event to a component by specifying a JavaScript element in the component's Properties window for that event. Not all Creator UI components detect the same mouse events.

For example, suppose you want to obtain a confirmation from the user before activating a button's Delete operation. In the design view, select the button. In the Properties view under JavaScript, specify the following JavaScript for property `onClick`.

```
return confirm('Are You Sure You Want To Delete?');
```

When the user clicks the button, a confirmation window appears, as shown in Figure 3–3. If the user selects OK, the button's action event handler method is invoked. Otherwise, the button click is ignored.

Figure 3–3 **JavaScript confirmation dialog defined for property onClick**

Input Components

Components that collect input (text field, password field, text area, drop down list, listbox, for example) share common properties to control and validate input. Let's look at some of these properties now.

validator

The `validator` property references a method that performs validation on its value. JSF provides three standard validators: a length validator for strings, a long range validator for integral types, and a double range validator for floating types. You can also write your own custom validation method. See "Add a Validation Method" on page 617 (Chapter 13).

converter

The `converter` property references a converter component that builds the correct type of object. Once the conversion has taken place, you can retrieve the object by casting it to the desired type.

maxlength

The `maxlength` property limits input to a specified number of characters. (This is *not* the same as length validation.) Setting `maxlength` causes a component to stop accepting input after the user has typed in the maximum characters allowed. No error messages are produced.

required

The boolean `required` property specifies whether or not input is necessary for the component. If the user leaves an input component's field empty and `required` is set, an error message is produced during the validation phase.

valueChange

A value change event occurs when an input component's selection changes or its text changes. If you want to perform processing based on input change, double-click the component in the design view. Creator generates a `process-ValueChange()` event method for you in the Java page bean. You can add your own processing code to this method.

Auto-Submit on Change

The Auto-Submit on Change feature submits the page for processing when an input component generates a value change event. To enable Auto-Submit on Change, select the component in the design canvas, right-click, and choose Auto-Submit on Change. This sets the `onChange` property to the following Java-Script element, shown here for a Text Area component.

```
common_timeoutSubmitForm(this.form, 'textArea1');
```

The input component has `id` property `textArea1`. When the input value of the text area changes, the page is submitted, allowing immediate processing (instead of waiting for a button click or hyperlink selection).

Virtual Forms

Virtual Forms allow the application developer to build web pages that provide more than one function (or use case). For example, a single web page might allow a user to either login or create a new username. The login use case requires a username and password before clicking the "Login" button. The create new username use case requires additional fields (perhaps a new password that must be entered twice, as well as a username). By grouping input components into separate virtual forms, you avoid interference when a validator requires input for a component that is not needed to fulfill another use case. Here are several examples of virtual forms use shown in the text.

Book Examples

- "Configure Virtual Forms" on page 216 (Chapter 5). Uses virtual forms allow a Reset button to clear input fields.
- "Virtual Forms" on page 417 and "Configure Virtual Forms" on page 420 (Chapter 9). Uses virtual forms to provide add, update, and cancel use cases on the same page.

Data-Aware Components

Creator offers a selection of data-aware components that can bind a data provider to a database table, a web services method, an EJB method, or a JavaBeans component. The table component is particularly suited for displaying data, but you can also choose from among the drop down list, checkbox, listbox, or radio button components.

Creator automatically supplies a converter for non-String data fields when you bind to a data provider with known data types. If there are any conversion errors, you will only see error messages if you have placed message components on the page.

Creator Tip

We recommend placing a message group component on the page when you're using the data-aware components (see "Message Group" on page 90).

Data Providers

A data provider is an abstraction for a data source. Creator has data providers for database tables, web services, EJBs, maps, arrays, and lists. Data providers are useful because they offer a common interface for accessing different sources of data.

When you drop a database table on a data-aware component, Creator configures the appropriate data provider for you. Similarly, if you drop a web services method or EJB method on a component, Creator configures a data provider. You can also explicitly select data providers for arbitrary objects, such as arrays or lists. Chapter 8 introduces data providers and Chapter 9 uses data providers with database accesses. Chapter 10 shows you data providers with web services and Chapter 11 shows you data providers with EJB methods.

3.3 Basic Components

The following catalog of basic components describes each component and gives you common usage scenarios. To show you how a basic component can be useful in a Creator project, we also point you to relevant examples in other chapters of this book. The basic components are listed alphabetically for easy lookup.

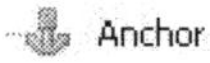

Anchor

The anchor component helps position link targets within a page. Anchor components are non-visual and often used with hyperlinks to scroll pages. By default, an anchor is rendered in HTML as `<a name=targetname></a>`.

Figure 3–4 shows an anchor component dropped on the design canvas.

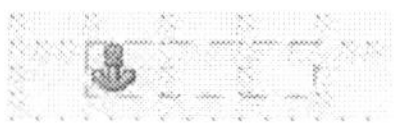

Figure 3–4 **Anchor component**

Suppose, for example, you place a hyperlink at the bottom of a page and drop an anchor component called `anchorTop` at the top of the page. To jump to the top of the page, set the `url` property of the hyperlink to the following.

```
/faces/Page1.jsp#anchorTop
```

It's also possible to link to anchor components in other pages.

Book Examples

- "Add Components to the Page" on page 298 (Chapter 7). Uses anchor components with hyperlinks to control page scrolling.

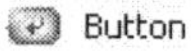

Button

The button component is an example of a "command component." Buttons perform an action when they are activated (clicked). This can happen during server-side processing (a method that processes an action event) or with a navigational action that determines page flow. The button component is one of the most-often-used components in web design. By default, buttons are rendered as HTML `<input type=button>` tags.

Figure 3–5 shows a button component and tooltip in a web page with a browser. The message shown was set in the button's `toolTip` property.

Figure 3–5 **Button component**

Buttons can be used for "simple" or dynamic navigation between web pages. With simple navigation, a button's `action` method returns a String that matches a case label in the navigation rules generated for the application. We show you how to create this type of navigation in "Add Page Navigation" on page 195. Dynamic navigation is useful when you need to figure out the next page based on some sort of processing. In this case, the `action` method returns a String based on the processing. See "Create New Web Pages" on page 212 for an example of dynamic navigation.

In Creator, you connect the a button click (an action event) to an event processing method by double-clicking the button component in the Creator design canvas. This brings up the matching `button_action()` method (where `button` is the component's `id` property) in the Java page bean so that you can add your processing code.

The button's `text` property is its label. You can bind this value to a property or to a value in a properties file.

Book Examples

- "Add Button Components" on page 193 (Chapter 5). Uses a button to initiate navigation.
- "Place Button, Label and Static Text Components" on page 257 (Chapter 6). Uses a button to submit a page for processing.

- "Add a Button Component" on page 452 (Chapter 10). Uses a button to invoke an action event method.
- "Modify the Components for Localized Text" on page 599 (Chapter 13). Configures a button for internationalization.

Calendar

The calendar component lets users enter dates on a page, either by typing in a specific date or by selecting a date from a pop-up calendar. Figure 3–6 is an example of a calendar component in the visual editor with a Enter Date label.

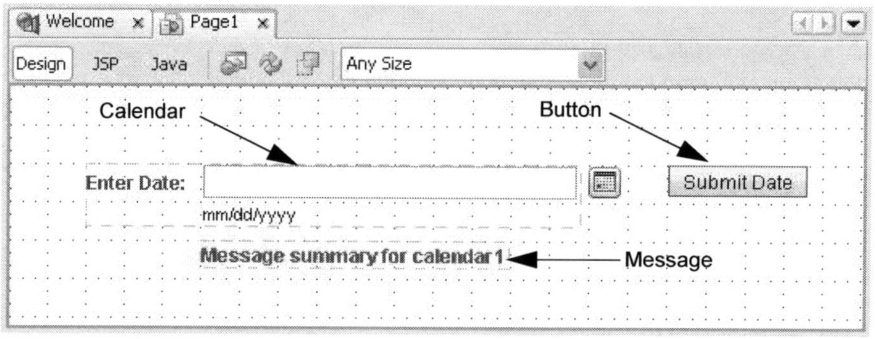

Figure 3–6 **Calendar component**

When you click the calendar icon, a pop-up window lets you select a date from a drop down list of months and years. Otherwise, just type a specific date into the component's text field.

The calendar component automatically validates the input date. You control the range by setting properties `minDate` and `maxDate`. The minimum date defaults to the current date and the maximum defaults to today's date four years from now. Most applications will need to customize these values. Here is an example that sets the minimum date to January 1, 1975 and the maximum to December 31, 2020. You typically add this initialization code to the page bean's `init()` method.

```
// Set minimum date to January 1, 1975
// Method getTime() returns java.util.Date
calendar1.setMinDate(
     new GregorianCalendar(1975, 0, 1).getTime());
// Set maximum date to December 31, 2020
calendar1.setMaxDate(
     new GregorianCalendar(2020, 11, 31).getTime());
```

Creator Tip

You cannot supply String values for these properties in the Properties window, but you can provide property binding expressions (to objects of type Date) or you can set the minimum and maximum values as shown in the page bean. Use a message group or message component to display validation error messages on the page.

The date format defaults to the default format for the locale, but you can use the `dateFormatPattern` property to select different date format patterns.

Property `selectDate` holds the user-supplied date, which you can bind to an object or a data provider. You can also right-click the calendar component and select Edit Event Handler from the pop-up menu. The `validate` option lets you insert Java code that validates user input, and the `processValueChange` option lets you insert Java code that executes when a component's value has changed.

Book Examples

- "Configure the Calendar Component" on page 355 (Chapter 8). Uses a calendar component and shows you how to configure its settings.

Checkbox

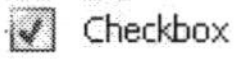

The checkbox component uses a boolean on/off setting as a choice for a user. Checkboxes are often used as standalone components (that is, not part of a checkbox group) on a page. Figure 3–7 shows part of a page with a checkbox component. Here we set the `label` property to the text string shown and the `selected` property to `true`, which displays a check mark.

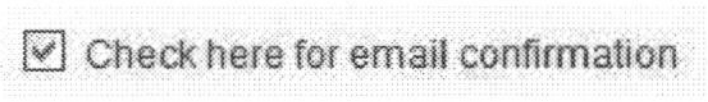

Figure 3–7 **Checkbox component**

There are two important properties with checkboxes. The `selected` property indicates whether or not a checkbox is selected and checked on the page. The `selectedValue` property allows you to store and retrieve an arbitrary data value associated with the checkbox. A check box is considered to be selected when the value of the `selected` property is equal to the value of the `selectedValue` property. You can bind the `selected` property of a checkbox to an object, such as a JavaBeans property or a data source object.

Use method `isChecked()` to determine if the component is selected.

Book Examples

- "Configure Checkbox Components" on page 430 (Chapter 9). Uses checkboxes in columns with table components.
- "Specify Property Bindings" on page 582 (Chapter 12). Uses standalone checkbox components and binds them to SessionBean properties.

Checkbox Group

Checkbox Group

The checkbox group component groups a set of checkboxes. You can specify their items with a dialog accessed from the Properties window or dynamically fill them from a database or JavaBeans component. When you use a checkbox group, users may select any number of checkbox options (including none unless the `required` property is checked). Checkboxes are rendered as an HTML `<table>` element with rows and columns. Figure 3–8 shows a checkbox group component when you drop it on the design canvas.

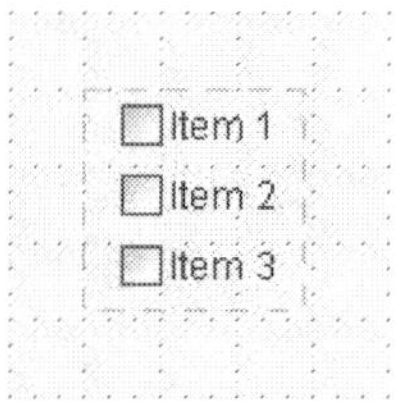

Figure 3–8 **Checkbox group component**

A checkbox group component is appropriate when you want to give the user a list of choices with the phrasing "please check all that apply."[1] The selection items may be hardcoded with the Properties window or generated dynamically at run time. Creator automatically supplies a converter for non-String data fields when you fill the list from a database source. The checkbox group component also accepts data binding. The `selected` property of the checkbox group returns an array of `Objects` consisting of the checked selections.

Adding a checkbox group component to your web page creates three elements: the checkbox group component, an embedded selection list, and a "default items" list used for initializing the selection choices. To specify the choices, select `checkboxGroup1DefaultOptions` in the Outline view. In the Properties window, click the editing box opposite property `options`. Creator pops-up a dialog so that you can add, edit, or remove items. (This is the same

---

1. If you'd like to limit the choice to only one from a list, use the radio button group component (see "Radio Button Group" on page 93).

dialog used to specify Display/Value pairs for the Listbox component. See Figure 3–20 on page 87.)

Example

Figure 3–9 shows a checkbox group component on a web page. The default layout for a checkbox group is a single vertical column, so we set the `columns` property to the number of checkboxes (4) to get a horizontal layout. Note that a user may select more than one choice (including none or all).

Figure 3–9 **Checkbox group component**

Here is the Java code to display choices selected from the checkbox group (whose `id` property is `checkboxGroup1`) in a static text component. Note that we assign the selected values to a `sides` String array. Casting is necessary since the `getSelected()` method returns an `Object` array. The `for` loop concatenates selected values with space delimiters. This code is placed in the button event handler method.

```
public String button1_action() {
   String choices = "";
   String[] sides = (String[])checkboxGroup1.getSelected();
   for (int i = 0; i < sides.length; i++) {
      choices = choices + " " + sides[i];
   }
   staticText1.setValue(choices);
   return null;
}
```

Drop Down List

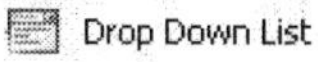

The drop down list component is an extremely versatile component, rendered as an HTML `<select>` element (a drop down list). A drop down list allows a user to select one item from a set of items, as shown in Figure 3–10.

The selection items may be hardcoded with a dialog accessed from the Properties window or generated dynamically at run time. Creator automatically supplies a converter for non-String data fields when you fill the list from a

Figure 3–10 **Checkbox group component**

database source. This component also accepts data binding. The `selected` property determines the value of the currently selected item.

When a drop down list component is used with a data provider that wrappers a database data source, you typically bind the database table's primary key field with the Value field. You select an appropriate field from the data table for the dropdown component's Display field. Figure 3–11 shows the Bind to Data dialog that lets you configure the drop down list and the data provider. Here the Value field is the RECORDINGID field (the primary key) and the Display field is RECORDINGTITLE. Thus, the dropdown component's `getSelected()` method will return the primary key. This is useful for setting SQL query parameters from a drop down list component's selection value (see Chapter 9, "Connect Dropdown List to Query" on page 408).

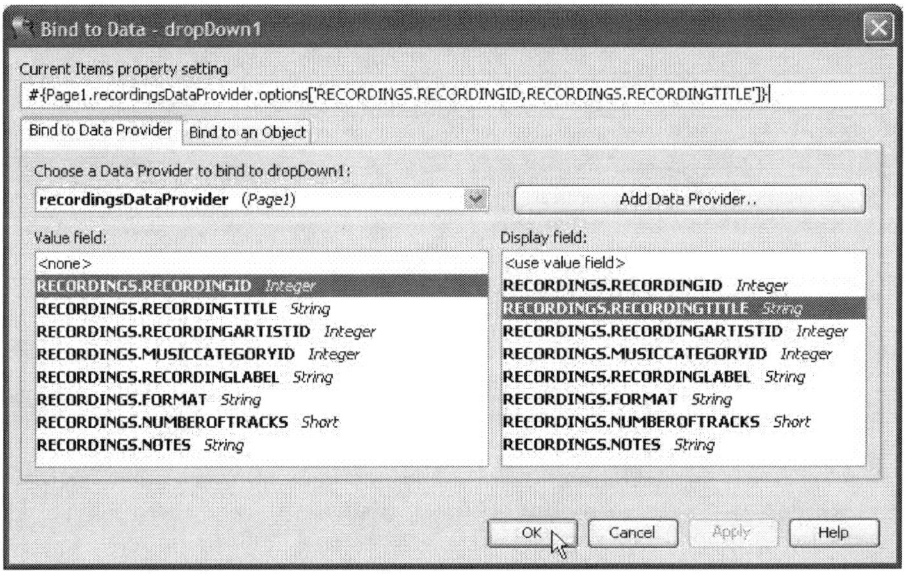

Figure 3–11 **Bind to Data dialog with a drop down list**

The nonvisual component `dropDown1DefaultOptions` supplies text for the selections. To input text items, select the `dropDown1DefaultOptions` element in the Outline view and click the `options` property in the Properties window. A dialog pops up that lets you type in Display/Value pairs for each selection item (see Figure 3–20 on page 87). To supply options for a drop down list using data stored in application scope (for example), see "Add ApplicationBean1 Data" on page 577.

When the user selects a different item from a drop down list component, the system generates a value change event. To submit the page for immediate processing on a value change event, set the Auto-Submit on Change feature. To provide event handling code for a value change event, double-click the drop down list component on the design canvas. Creator generates a default `processValueChange()` method and brings up the Java source editor for you.

Book Examples

- "Add a Drop Down List" on page 202 (Chapter 5). Uses a drop down list with navigation.
- "Add a Data Source" on page 401 (Chapter 9). Fills the selection list from a database data source.
- "Add ApplicationBean1 Data" on page 577 (Chapter 12). Shows how to instantiate data in an `Options[]` array appropriate for a selection component, such as drop down list or listbox.
- "Specify Property Bindings" on page 582 (Chapter 12). Uses a drop down list to bind a SessionBean property.
- "Add Components to Page1" on page 607 (Chapter 13). Uses a drop down list to specify locale.

File Upload

File Upload

The file upload component lets users locate a file on their system and upload it to a server. You can upload text files, images, and other types of data files (`.zip` or `.jar` files, even executables). This component is similar to an HTML `<input type="file">` element. Figure 3–12 shows a file upload component on the design canvas.

Figure 3–12 **File upload component**

For security reasons, file upload components are not supported in portlet projects. You can upload files up to one megabyte in size by default. To upload larger files, modify the `maxsize` parameter for the `UploadFilter` entry in the web application's **web.xml** file.

The read-only `uploadedFile` property provides a `UploadedFile` interface with methods that let you read the file and write it to disk. There are also methods to access the file's name, size in bytes, and type (`text/plain` or `image/jpeg`).

Creator Tip

Be careful with file names that have spaces, they are not supported. It is also not possible to nest a file upload component within a tab set component.

Example

Figure 3–13 shows you a web page with a file upload component. Note that the file upload component has a built-in Browse button to let users locate a file on their system. When the "Get File Now" button is clicked, the file contents are written to the server and displayed in the scrollable text area on the page. A message group component displays status.

Here is the Java code for the button handler that uploads the file, displays the file in the text area, and writes the data to the server.

```
public String filer_action() {
   // read file from client
   UploadedFile uploadedFile =
          (UploadedFile)fileUpload1.getUploadedFile();
   String uploadedFileName = uploadedFile.getOriginalName();
   String FileName = uploadedFileName.substring
        (uploadedFileName.lastIndexOf(File.separatorChar) + 1);
   info("Uploaded file from " + uploadedFileName +
         ", size is " + uploadedFile.getSize() + " bytes");

   // write data to text area component
   textArea1.setText(uploadedFile.getAsString());

   // save file contents to server on C:
   try {
     File file = new File("C:" + File.separatorChar + "Saved" +
                 File.separatorChar + FileName);
     info("Saved file to " + file) ;
     uploadedFile.write(file);

   } catch (Exception ex) {
       error("Cannot upload file: " + FileName);
   }
   return null;
}
```

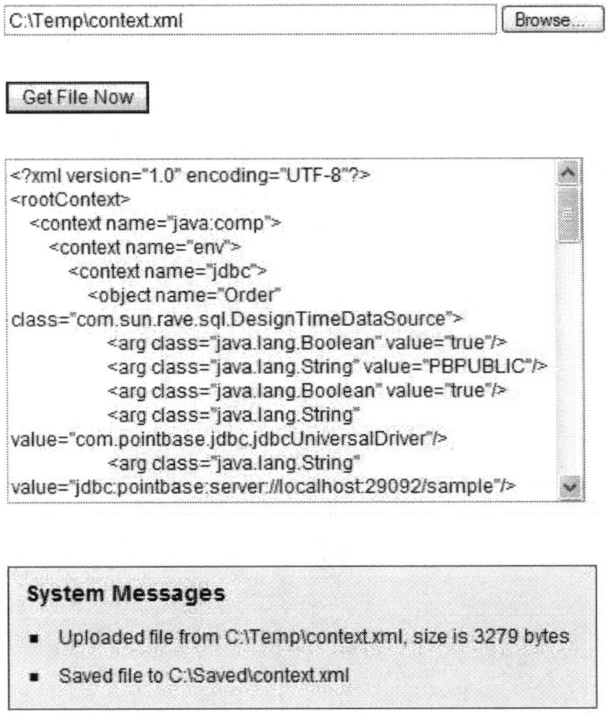

Figure 3–13 **File upload component**

Hidden Field

The hidden field component is a non-visual form field that is not displayed on the design canvas or in a browser window. The hidden field component is generated as an HTML `<input type="hidden">` element. Hidden field components do not appear in the design view, but you can access their properties from the Outline window.

Web developers typically use hidden field components to store data used by Javascript on the page. Hidden field components are also handy for storing page data, as an alternative to saving and restoring in session scope. The `text` property of a hidden field component holds the data that is sent to the server.

Note that anyone can examine an HTML document's source to locate a "hidden" field. Hidden fields, like password fields, are extended from the same component classes as text field and therefore have the same configurable properties.

Hyperlink

Hyperlink

Hyperlink components are action components that provide navigation to other pages as well as to a location on a page (with the anchor component). A hyperlink component is also useful when a page's URL information is data driven and no processing is necessary (you set property `url`). Figure 3–14 shows a hyperlink for a home page in a browser window.

Figure 3–14 **Hyperlink component**

To add event handling code, select the hyperlink component in the design canvas and double-click. This brings up the `hyperlink1_action()` method (where `hyperlink1` is the component's `id` property) in the Java source editor.

Creator Tip

If you want the hyperlink to show an image rather than text, use the image hyperlink component (see "Image Hyperlink" on page 84).

Book Examples

- "Add Components to Page LoginBad" on page 213 (Chapter 5). Uses a hyperlink component with navigation.
- "Using Hyperlink with a Nested Static Text" on page 458 (Chapter 10). Uses a hyperlink and a nested static text component (for formatting) to provide a link to URLs returned from a Google web services search.

- "Modify the Components for Localized Text" on page 599 (Chapter 13). Configures a hyperlink component for localization.

Image

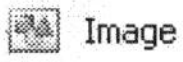

Image components display graphics from a file or a URL. The image component is rendered as an HTML <img> element. Figure 3–15 shows an image component after dropping it on the design canvas.

Figure 3–15 **Image component**

Once you place an image component on the design canvas, there are several ways to set its image. The image may be a file (JPEG, GIF, PNG), a URL web location, or a built-in theme. To set the image, right-click on the image component and choose Set Image. The Image Customizer dialog appears with radio buttons Choose File, Enter URL, and Set Theme Icon. Figure 3–16 shows the Image Customizer dialog with the Set Theme Icon selected and `ALARM_CRITICAL_MEDIUM` set for the image.

Selecting Choose File in this dialog lets you navigate to an image file in your file system and copy it to the **resources** node in your project. When you choose this option, the image component's `url` property is set to **resources/*image_filename*,** where ***image_filename*** is the image file.

Creator Tip

You can also add an image by dragging its file node from the file explorer dialog to your page.

The dialog also lets you enter a URL to a web location for the file. As before, the `url` property of the image component will be set to the URL you enter. Alternatively, you can select the `url` property in the Properties window and select the Use Binding radio button. This allows you to bind the property to a data object.

Book Examples

- "Add the Google Logo" on page 451 (Chapter 10). Puts an image on the page.

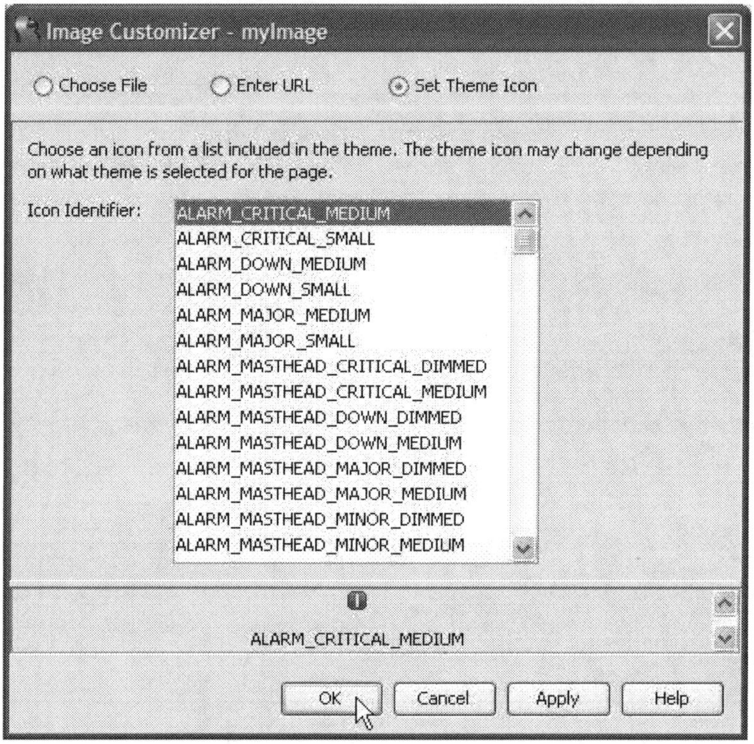

Figure 3–16 **Image customizer dialog**

Image Hyperlink

Image Hyperlink

The image hyperlink component is similar to a hyperlink, except that it supports images in addition to text. When you right-click an image hyperlink component, the Image Customizer dialog lets you set the image to a file (JPEG, GIF, PNG), a URL web location, or a built-in theme (see Figure 3–16).

The `imageURL` property specifies an image file or a URL on the web. The `icon` property holds the theme. Figure 3–17 shows an image hyperlink in a browser window.

As with hyperlinks, you can specify an action event handler. To add event handling code, select the image hyperlink component in the design canvas and double-click. Creator generates a default action event method and brings up the page bean in the Java source editor. The cursor is set to the `imageHyperlink1_action()` method (where `imageHyperlink1` is the component's `id` property).

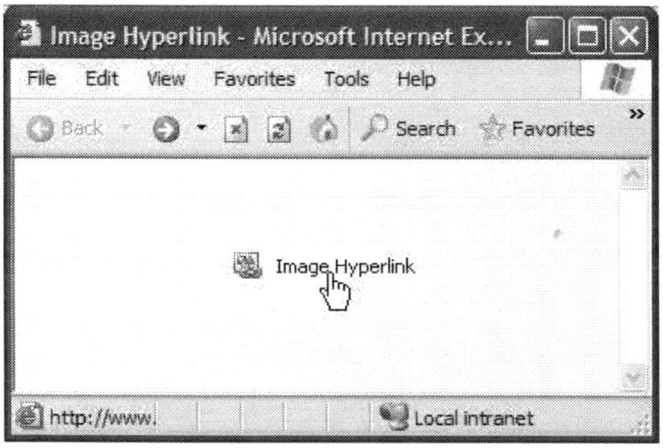

Figure 3–17 **Image hyperlink component**

Book Examples

- "Banner Page Fragment" on page 309 (Chapter 7). Uses an image hyperlink with a page fragment.
- "Add an Image Hyperlink Component" on page 481 (Chapter 10). Uses image hyperlinks to page through Google search results.
- "Add Components to the Page" on page 562 (Chapter 12). Uses image hyperlinks to page through Google search results.

Label

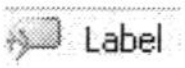

The label component is typically used to associate text with input components, such as text fields and checkboxes. Labels are rendered as HTML `<label>` elements when they are associated with components and as `<span>` elements when they are not. Figure 3–18 shows a label on the design canvas.

Figure 3–18 **Label component**

A label's `for` property associates the label with another component. When you bind the `for` property of a label to a text field, for instance, the label component displays an asterisk if the text field's `required` property is set to true. Furthermore, if invalid input is supplied to the server, the page will highlight the label component's text in red. These behaviors make labels highly useful in pages where input components are heavily used.

Label components also have data binding. You can bind a label's `text` property to a data source, a JavaBeans property, or text from a resource bundle.

Creator Tip

Input components have a dedicated `label` *property that you can alternatively use for label text, but these labels cannot be easily resized or aligned. Instead, use the label component for more flexibility with component placement and style control.*

Book Examples

- "Add a Label Component" on page 207 (Chapter 5). Uses a label to place a heading on a page.
- "Modify the Components for Localized Text" on page 599 (Chapter 13). Sets the label's text from a localized **.properties** file.
- "Add Components for Input" on page 620 (Chapter 13). Sets the label's `for` property to a text field component and sets the label's `text` property from a localized **.properties** file.

Listbox

Listbox

The listbox component allows users to select items from a list of items. The selection items may be hardcoded with a dialog accessed from the Properties window or generated dynamically at run time. Figure 3–19 shows a listbox component on the design canvas after configuring the options list.

Creator automatically supplies a converter for non-String data fields when you fill the list from a data provider source. The `multiple` property determines whether the user may select one item or multiple items in the listbox. (With `multiple` set, press **<Ctrl+Click>** to select more than one item.) The `rows` property controls the number of items to display.

When a listbox component's data provider wraps a database data source, you typically bind the database table's primary key field with the Value field. You select an appropriate field from the data table for the listbox component's Display field. Figure 3–11 on page 78 shows the (equivalent) Bind to Data dialog for a drop down list that lets you configure the data provider.

The nonvisual component `listbox1DefaultOptions` supplies text for the selections. To specify selection items, select the `listbox1DefaultOptions` element in the Outline view and click the `options` property in the Properties win-

Figure 3–19 **Listbox component**

dow. A dialog pops up that lets you type in Display/Value pairs for each selection item, as shown in Figure 3–20. Text in the Display column appears on the page. The `selected` property (or method `getSelected()`) returns the corresponding text of the selected item from the Value column.

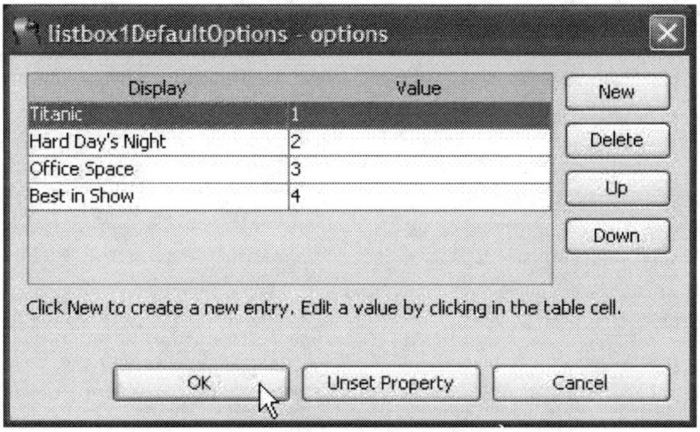

Figure 3–20 **Dialog to select text items for listbox component**

When the user selects a different item from a listbox component, the system generates a value change event. To submit the page for immediate processing on a value change event, set the Auto-Submit on Change feature. To provide event handling code for a value change event, double-click the listbox component on the design canvas. Creator generates a default `processValueChange()` method and brings up the Java source editor for you.

Book Examples

- "Add a Listbox Component" on page 400 (Chapter 9). Fills the selection list from a database data source. Uses listbox for a master-detail database read.
- "Add Components to the Page" on page 516 (Chapter 11). Fills the selection list from an EJB data source.
- "Add ApplicationBean1 Data" on page 577 (Chapter 12). Shows how to instantiate data in an `Options[]` array appropriate for a selection component, such as drop down list or listbox.

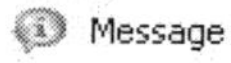

Message

The message component displays error messages generated by other components. Typically, these messages are data conversion or input validation errors. When the validator or converter detects errors, it sends a message to the JSF context on behalf of the component. Message components can retrieve and display these messages. Message components are particularly useful on a web page that contains multiple input components. When you associate a unique message component with each input component, validation or conversion error messages clearly indicate the source of the input error. By default, a message component has its `ShowSummary` property set to `true` and its `ShowDetail` property set to `false`. Figure 3–21 shows a message component initially dropped on the design canvas.

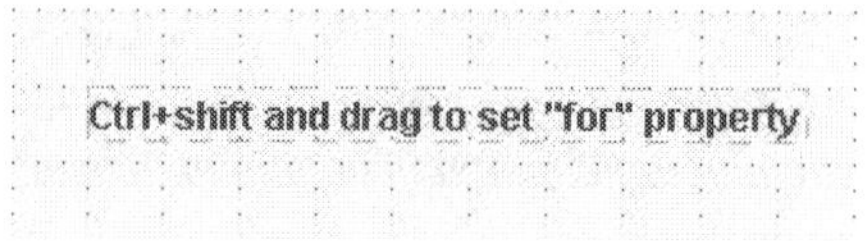

Figure 3–21 **Message component**

To associate a message component to an input component, select the message component, press **<Ctrl+Shift>**, and drag the arrow generated by Creator to the target component. This sets the `for` property to the `id` property of the input component. Figure 3–22 is an example page with a submit button and two message components associated with input text fields. Note that the names of the text fields (`textfield1` and `textfield2`) appear in the message text, indicating that the `for` property has been set for each message component.

You can use the message component's `style` property to format the appearance of your error messages.

You can also send your own message to a message component with the `info()`, `error()`, `fatal()`, or `warn()` methods. These methods are all rendered using distinct styles. You must include the message component's target compo-

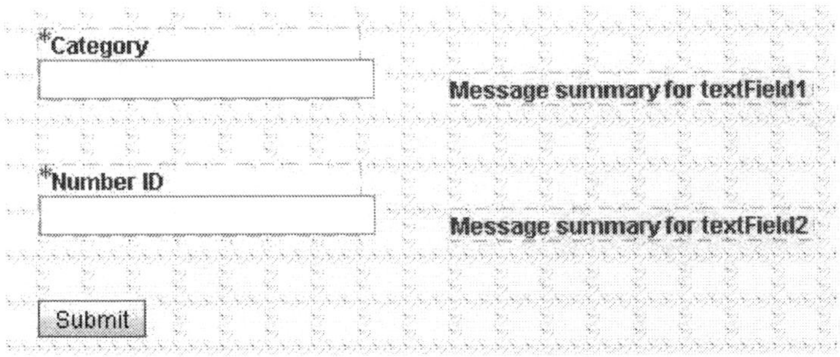

Figure 3–22 **Message components with `for` property set**

nent `id` with the call, however. The following code shows the approach. Here, inside the listbox's value change event handler, we send a warning that the listbox component's value has changed. Note that component id `listbox1` is the first parameter for method `warn()`.

```
public void listbox1_processValueChange(
        ValueChangeEvent event) {
  warn(listbox1, "Value changed!");
}
```

Creator Tip

The message component displays a single message only. If you need to display multiple messages, or you don't want to specify a particular component, use component Message Group instead.

Book Examples

- "Use Validators and Converters" on page 252 (Chapter 6). Uses a message component to report data conversion errors for a text field component.
- "Add a Message Component" on page 474 (Chapter 10). Uses a message component to report validation errors for a text field component.
- "Add Components to the Page" on page 562 (Chapter 12). Uses a message component to report validation errors.
- "Add Components for Input" on page 620 (Chapter 13). Uses a message component to report validation errors from a custom validator method.

Message Group

Message Group

Message group components display run-time errors for page-level messages originating from multiple components or for system (global) messages. With message group components, you can limit the message group to display global errors only (that is, exclude component errors), or display errors for all components on the page, including errors with the page itself.

Figure 3–23 is a page with a submit button, input text fields with associated message components, and a message group component to report global errors. The message group component's `showGlobalOnly` property is set to true.

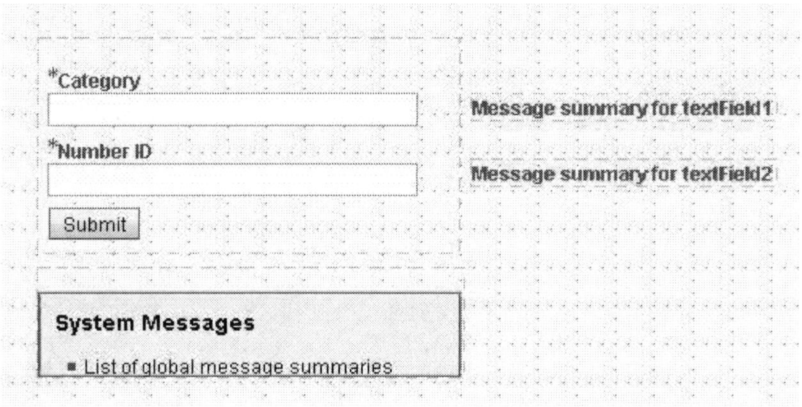

Figure 3–23 **Message group components**

Set property `showGlobalOnly` when one or more message components appear on the page with a message group component. This prevents a component's validation or conversion error message from appearing twice.

You can also use the message group `style` property to format the appearance of your error messages in the System Messages box.

Creator Tip

It's a good idea to routinely place a message group component on your pages, especially when accessing a database, web service, or EJB. Recall that JSF writes FacesException messages to the JSF context. You will only see these messages if a message group or message component is on the page.

Book Examples

- "Add a Message Group Component" on page 386 (Chapter 9). Uses a message group component to report database access errors.
- "Message and Message Group Components" on page 474 (Chapter 10). Uses a message group component to report system (global) errors.
- "Add Components to the Page" on page 502 (Chapter 11). Uses a message group component to show all error messages when there is only one input component.
- "Add the Google Web Service Client" on page 566 (Chapter 12). Uses a message group component to report system (global) errors.

Password Field

Password Field

The password field component allows users to input a single line of text. Echoed text is replaced by a single character, such as a black dot or an asterisk. Password field components are useful for handling sensitive data input, like passwords and PIN numbers. The password field component is rendered as an HTML `<input type=password>` element. When a password field is rendered, its previous value is always cleared. Figure 3–24 shows a password field dropped on the design canvas.

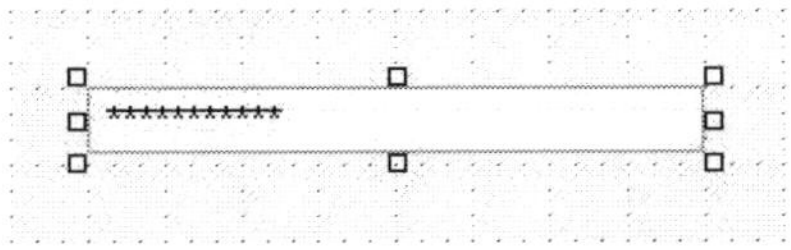

Figure 3–24 **Password field component**

In all other respects, a password field component behaves just like a text field. The input string is stored in the component's `password` property. When you change the text, a value change event is generated. The password field's `getPassword()` method reads the text and `setPassword()` sets it. You can also bind the `password` property to an object or data provider.

Password field components can have validators. Length validators, required validators, and range validators are all possible to check input text. Note that value change events occur only if no validation errors are detected.

When a password field component generates a value change event, the JSF implementation invokes the value change event handler for that component. You can use the password field's `label` property to set the label text on a page. It's a good idea have message components associated with password fields to report validation or conversion errors. To create a tooltip, set the password field's `toolTip` property.

Book Examples

- "Create the Form's Input Components" on page 208 (Chapter 5). Uses a password field to gather input for a password field.
- "Bind Input Components" on page 237 (Chapter 6). Shows property binding with the password field component.
- "Modify the Components for Localized Text" on page 599 (Chapter 13). Shows how to localize an application that contains a password field (the password component's `toolTip` is bound to the properties file).

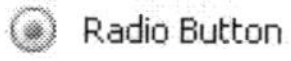

Radio Button

The radio button component uses a boolean on/off setting as a choice for a user. Radio buttons can appear as standalone components on a page (not part of a radio button group). Figure 3–25 shows part of a page with two radio button components. Here we set the `label` property to the text strings shown. You can treat two or more radio buttons as a group by setting each radio button's `name` property to the same value. When radio buttons are part of the same group, only one radio button can be selected (set to true).

Figure 3–25 **Radio button component**

There are two important properties with radio buttons. The `selected` property indicates that a radio button is selected and clicked on the page. The `selectedValue` property allows you to pass data values for the radio button. It's also possible to bind the `selected` property of a radio button to an object, such as a JavaBeans or a data source. A radio button is considered to be selected when the value of the `selected` property is equal to the value of the `selectedValue` property.

Use the `isChecked()` method to determine if the component is selected. To use radio buttons in table component columns, set the `name` property to the same value to group all the radio buttons in the column.

Creator Tip

Radio buttons by themselves (not in a group) are used sparingly in web pages because users cannot deselect a single radio button once it is selected. If you want users to select and deselect their choices, use checkboxes (see "Checkbox" on page 75).

Radio Button Group

Radio Button Group

The radio button group component lets you group radio buttons on a page. When a user selects a choice from a radio button group, each choice deselects the previous one. This means only one button within the group is "on" at a time.[2] Radio button groups are rendered as an HTML `<table>` element with rows and columns. Figure 3–26 shows a radio button group component after you drop it on to the design canvas.

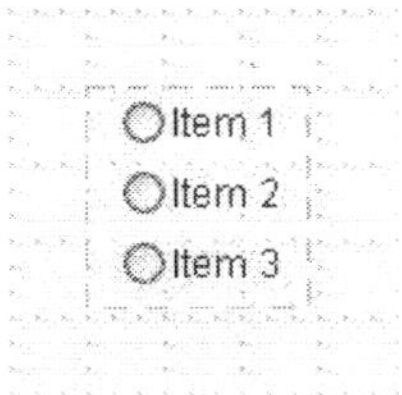

Figure 3–26 **Radio button group component**

The selection items can be hardcoded with the Properties window or dynamically generated at run time. Creator automatically supplies a converter for non-String data fields when you fill the list from a database source. This component also accepts data binding. The `selected` property of the radio button group returns the selected item.

To specify the choices, select `radioButtonGroup1DefaultItems` in the Outline view. In the Properties window, click the editing box opposite property `options`. Creator pops up a dialog so that you can add, edit, or remove items. (This is the same dialog box used to specify Display/Value fields for the Listbox component. See Figure 3–20 on page 87.)

Example

Figure 3–27 shows a radio button group component on a web page. The default layout for a radio button group is a single vertical column, so we set the `col-`

2. If you need to select more than one item at a time, use the checkbox group component (see "Checkbox Group" on page 76.)

`umns` property to the number of radio buttons (3) to get a horizontal layout. Note that a user may select only one choice.

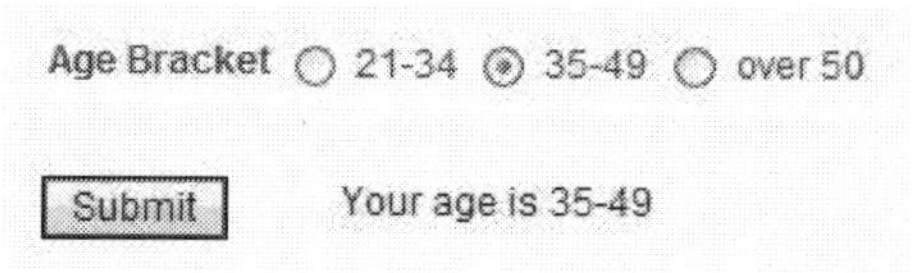

Figure 3–27 **Radio button group component**

Here is the code in the button's event handler that displays the user's selection in a static text component. The code that accesses the radio button group component is bold.

```
public String button1_action() {
   String choice = (String)ageBracket.getSelected();
   staticText1.setText("Your age is  " + choice);
   return null;
}
```

Static Text

Static Text

Of all the components, static text is probably used the most often in web pages. A static text component lets you display any kind of textual information, like instructions, titles, and headings. Static text components typically display String data, but you can bind them to objects, JavaBeans properties, and data providers. Figure 3–28 shows a static text component after dropping it on the design canvas.

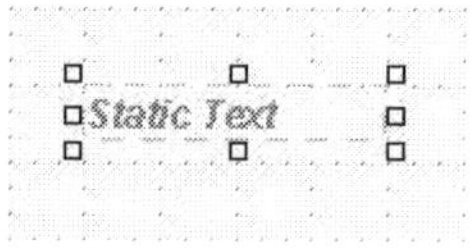

Figure 3–28 **Static text component**

With data converters and formatters, static text components can display almost any type of data. An embedded static text component is the default for a table component. Static text components may be embedded in hyperlink components to allow embedded HTML in the hyperlink's text display.

The `text` property of a static text component stores the text that is displayed. From a user's point of view, static text components are read-only. The `setText()` method sets its text and `getText()` reads it. You can resize static text components on the design page, but Creator expands them if you leave them unsized.

Static text components are rendered as plain text, which may include HTML formatting tags. This means you can build entire HTML pages by concatenating a string of HTML tags with text and assigning it to the component's `text` property.

Creator Tip

To enable correct rendering of HTML tags, make sure you set the `escape` *property to* `false` *in the Properties window. Also, avoid using static text as labels for other components. Use either a separate label component or the label property of the component.*

Book Examples

- "Place Button, Label and Static Text Components" on page 257 (Chapter 6). Binds an output component to a JavaBeans property and applies a number converter.
- "Add Components to the Page" on page 298 (Chapter 7). Uses an embedded static text component in a grid panel. Builds the static text component's `text` by concatenating HTML tags and unchecking the `escape` property.
- "Using Hyperlink with a Nested Static Text" on page 458 (Chapter 10). Uses an embedded static text component in a hyperlink to store HTML text.
- "Configure the Table" on page 477 (Chapter 10). Uses an embedded static text component to improve HTML formatting.
- "Add Static Text Component to the Page" on page 586 (Chapter 12). Uses a static text component for formatting text using HTML tags in a portlet.

Table

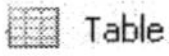

The table component is a composite component with rows and columns. Tables typically have nested columns, which in turn contain other display components (such as static text components, buttons, or text fields). Table components render as HTML `<table>` elements.

A table node in the design palette has nested column and row group components (see Figure 3–29). Dragging these components to a table in the design canvas adds columns and row groups to the table. Figure 3–29 also shows a table component initially dropped on the design canvas with the default of five rows by three columns.

Figure 3–30 shows the Outline view for the default table component. Note that each column in a table has a static text field to display data, but you can replace it with other components (checkboxes, hyperlinks, for instance). Every

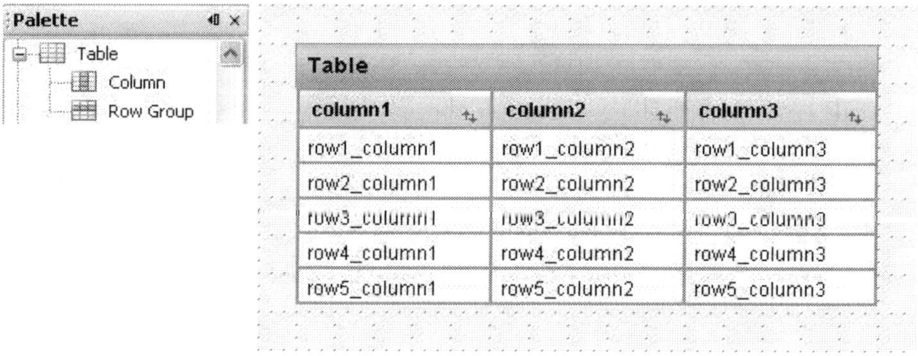

Figure 3–29 **Table component**

table component also has a default data provider (`defaultTableDataProvider`, a non-visual component).

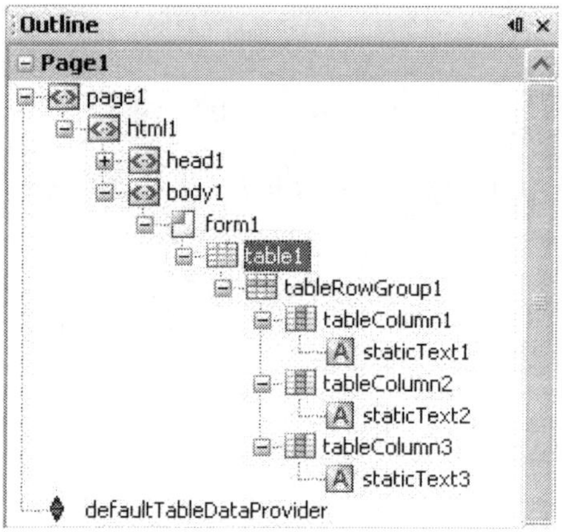

Figure 3–30 **Table component Outline view**

Creator Tip

Creator provides an enhanced selection mechanism for composite components, such as the table component. In the design canvas, click on any row in a table column and look in the Outline view and Properties window to see which component is selected. Now click again and you'll see the outer nested component's properties. Successive clicks let you cycle through each nesting level of a component.

Table components are typically filled dynamically with data from a data provider attached to a data source (database table), web services method, EJB method, or JavaBeans property. When you fill a table component with data from a data provider, Creator lets you control the layout, including the columns to display, the number of headers and footers, and the component you use in each column. You can also apply data converters to any field (column).

When you bind a data provider to a table component in the design canvas, Creator automatically fills the table with the data and generates the needed columns. Creator also generates headers from the field names and applies the necessary converters.

Example

Figure 3–31 shows Creator's design canvas with a table component bound to the TRACKS table from the Music Database in Chapter 9. This table has three columns (with headings from the database metadata). Creator shows the column's data type as "123" for numeric data and "abc" for String data. For data that is not text, Creator applies a converter for you.[3] In this table, an embedded static text component is used for the display.

TRACKNUMBER	TRACKTITLE	TRACKLENGTH
123	abc	abc
123	abc	abc
123	abc	abc

Figure 3–31 **Binding table component with an external database table**

3. For example, if a primary key field is integer data, Creator applies an Integer converter to the component. Creator performs this action for all the data-aware components.

Creator automatically sizes the columns and dynamically generates the correct number of rows. When you bind a table component to a database table, Creator generates a default query for you. You can modify this query by selecting the associated rowset from the nonvisual display. We show you how to work with database queries in Chapter 9 (see "Modify the SQL Query" on page 405.)

Figure 3–32 shows Creator's dialog for manipulating a table component's layout. Select the table component in the Design or Outline view, right-click, and choose Table Layout. Here, the dialog shows the columns from the TRACKS database table. You can choose which columns to display, the header and footer text, and the underlying component that holds the data.

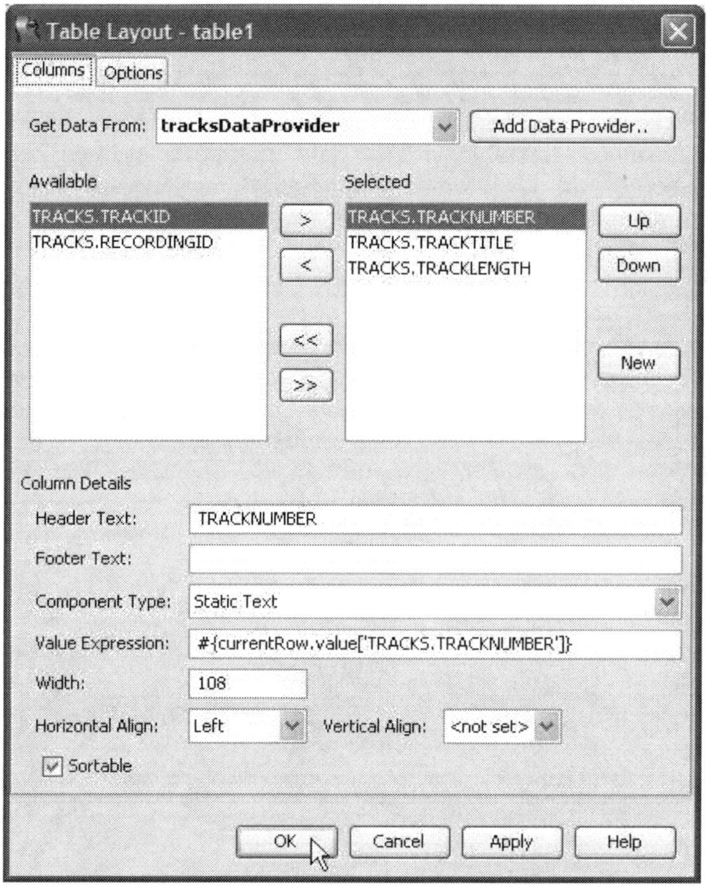

Figure 3–32 **Table Layout dialog: specifying columns**

Figure 3–33 shows Creator's dialog for specifying options for the table. Here you can set the table's title, description (summary), footer, and a message to display if the table is submitted without data. The checkboxes let you enable various options for the table component, including buttons to select all rows, clear sorting, open or close the table's sort panel, and enable pagination and a page size number. After making your selections, click Apply, then OK.

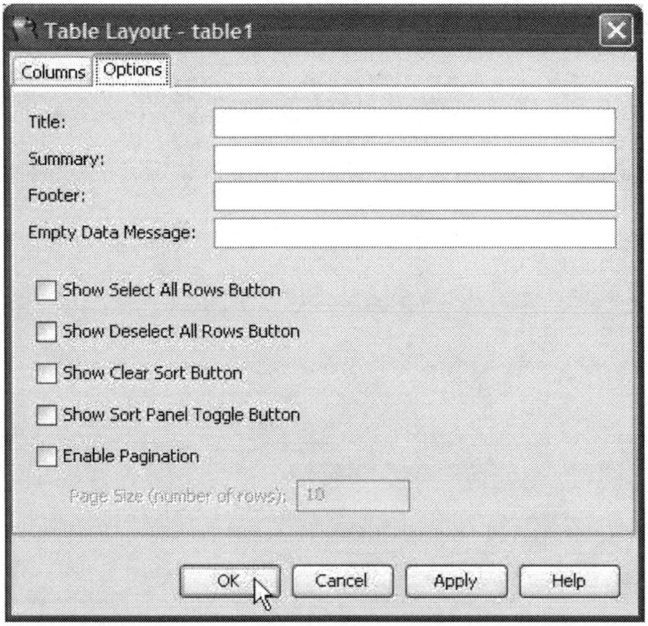

Figure 3–33 **Table Layout dialog: specifying options**

Book Examples

- "Configure the Table" on page 360 (Chapter 8). Uses a table component with an object list data provider. Enables table pagination.
- "Configure Table Component" on page 397 (Chapter 9). Uses a table component with an SQL query parameter.
- "Add a Table Component" on page 402 (Chapter 9). Builds a master-detail relationship using data binding with a table component.
- "Modify the Table Layout" on page 412 (Chapter 9). Uses a table component with text field components for updating data.
- "Add Components" on page 429 (Chapter 9). Uses a table component with checkboxes.

- "Add a Table Component" on page 477 (Chapter 10). Uses a table component with an object array data provider and web services.
- "Configure Table Component" on page 556 (Chapter 12). Uses a table component with portlets and database access.

Text Area

Text Area

Text area components gather textual information for multiple lines. This component is similar to a text field, but you build it with rows and columns (see Figure 3–34). Its standard look displays several lines, and a vertical scrollbar appears if the number of lines exceeds the number of rows. Text area components let you specify their size, provide text for a tooltip, and bind their `text` property to objects or data providers. Text area components are rendered as an HTML `<textarea>` element.

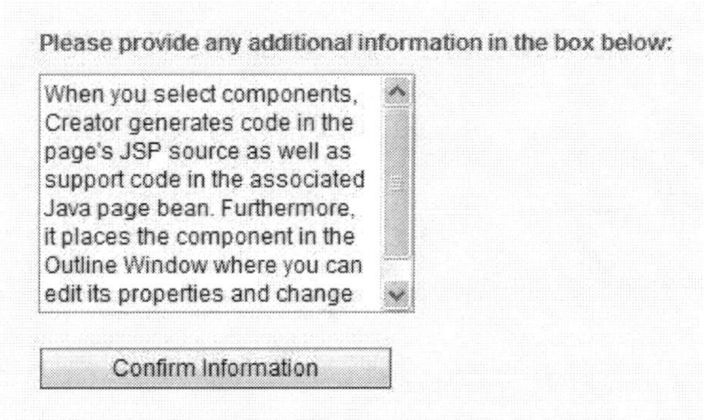

Figure 3–34 **Text area component on a web page**

Text area components are common with web applications that solicit free-form text. Examples are composing letters, listing comments, sending email, posting to guest books, filing bug reports, or reviewing products.

The `getText()` method retrieves the text and `setText()` sets it. The text is sent to the server when the page is submitted. Like the listbox component, text areas work with value change events and the `processValueChange()` event handler. To configure this method, double-click the text area component in the design view. Creator generates the event handler method in the Java page bean for you.

Example

You can bind the `text` property to a session bean property to automatically save submitted text in session scope. For example, here is the generated JSP code for a text area component that binds its `text` property to session bean property `userInfo` (shown in bold).

```
<ui:textArea binding="#{Page1.textArea1}" id="textArea1"
   style="height: 120px; left: 48px; top: 72px;
   position: absolute"
   text="#{SessionBean1.userInfo}"/>
```

Text Field

Text Field

The text field component enables users to input a single line of text. The input string is stored in the component's `text` property, and a value change event is generated when you change the text. The component's `getText()` method reads the text and `setText()` sets it. The text is sent to the server when the page is submitted. Text field components are rendered as an HTML `<input type="text">` element.

Figure 3–35 shows a text field in a browser window that prompts for a person's first name. The text field's `label` and `toolTip` properties are set to the strings shown. The boolean `required` property makes a red asterisk appear with the label and alerts the user that input is mandatory.

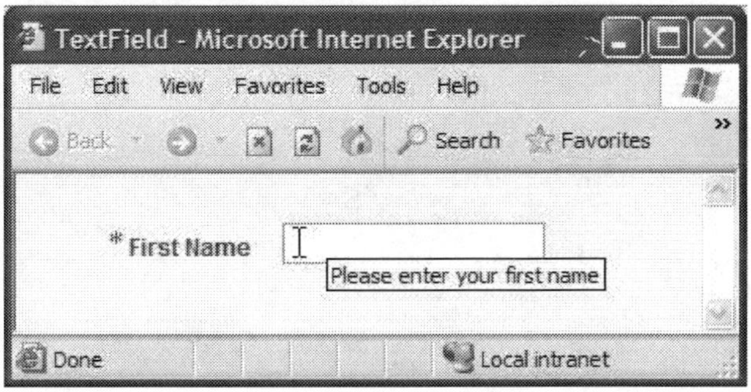

Figure 3–35 **Text field component on a web page**

With text fields, you can attach a length validator, a required validator, or range validators (with converted numerical values). Value change events occur only if no validation errors are detected. When a text field component generates a value change event, the JSF implementation invokes the value change event handler for that component. Message components are handy for reporting validation or conversion errors with text fields. (See "Message" on page 88.)

You can also attach a data converter to a text field. To do this, select the convertor you want from the `converter` property in the Properties window under

Data. When you apply a data converter, the type of the `text` property changes from String (the default) to the converted type. If you don't want all input components on the page to be validated, use virtual forms (see "Configure Virtual Forms" on page 216).

Text fields may be embedded in table components and you can bind them to data or other objects. Figure 3–36 shows the Property Bindings dialog box for binding a text field component to a JavaBeans property. Here, we bind text field `username` with the `username` property in the JavaBeans component loginBean.

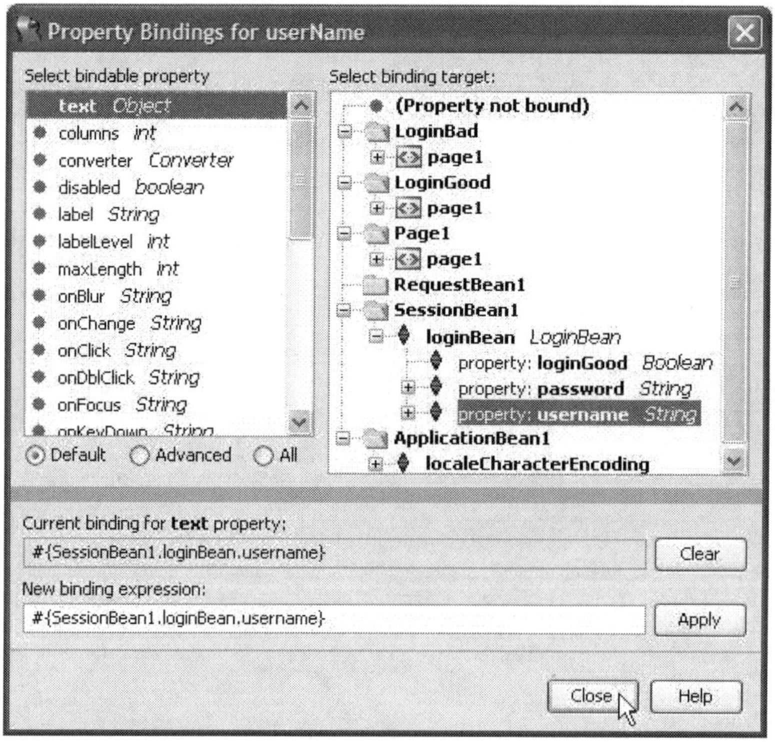

Figure 3–36 **Property Bindings dialog with text field component**

Book Examples

- "Configure Virtual Forms" on page 216 (Chapter 5). Excludes validation of text field components with virtual forms.
- "Bind Input Components" on page 237 (Chapter 6). Shows binding properties with a text field.

- "Create the Form's Input Components" on page 250 (Chapter 6). Shows text fields with converters and validators.
- "Add Components to the Page" on page 298 (Chapter 7). Uses a text field in a nested grid panel.
- "Modify the Table Layout" on page 412 (Chapter 9). Uses text fields with a table component.
- "Add Components" on page 417 (Chapter 9). Uses text fields to gather input for database row insert operations. Uses virtual forms.
- "Add a Text Field Component" on page 451 (Chapter 10). Shows validators.
- "Add Components for Input" on page 620 (Chapter 13). Uses text fields with a custom validator method.

Tree

Tree

The tree component lets you render data in an expandable list with a hierarchical tree structure. In web applications, trees are useful for navigating through nested data, like file systems and categories. A tree component contains tree nodes, which act like hyperlinks. In the design palette, a nested tree node component appears when you expand a tree node, as shown in Figure 3–37.

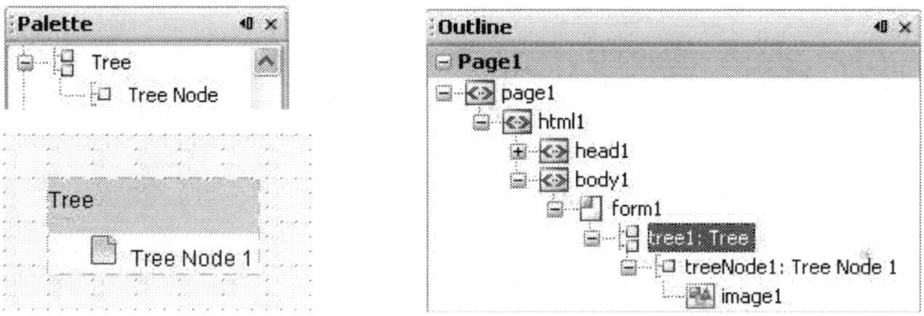

Figure 3–37 **Tree component**

Figure 3–37 also shows you the design canvas for a tree component and its Outline view. Note that a tree node has an embedded image component. Once you expand a tree component and drop it on the design page, you can drop tree node components to build nested structures.

Initially, when you drop a tree component on a page, the root node is labeled Tree and the subnode is labeled Tree Node 1. The `text` property lets you set the strings to be rendered for these nodes, and the `toolTip` property gives users more information about the node.

Creator Tip

When you drop tree node components on tree components, pay attention to what Creator outlines in blue. If the entire tree component is blue, the tree node will render as a sibling of the tree component. Otherwise, the tree node will render as a nested node underneath the node outlined in blue.

There are several important properties with tree components. The `url` property lets you navigate to another page or display data like a PDF or JPEG file. Binding the `action` property to an action event handler makes the tree node automatically submit the current page. The `clientSide` boolean property controls whether a request to the server is made each time a user expands or collapses a node.

Example

Figure 3–38 shows a tree component called Download Site with tree nodes Home Page and Music. Underneath the Music node are the nested tree nodes Jazz, Rock, and Country.

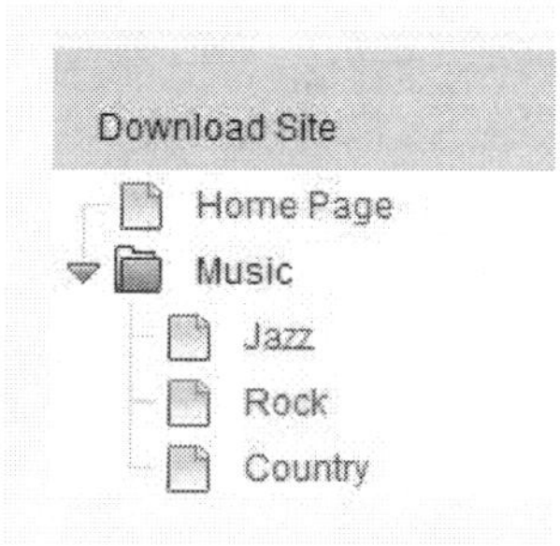

Figure 3–38 **Example tree component**

Note that the image for a tree node is a page icon if it is not nested. Otherwise, a folder icon appears with an arrow if the node has children (nested nodes). On a web page, users may expand or collapse the folder to see the nested nodes by clicking the arrow icon.

Suppose a web application displays PDF files for the Jazz, Rock, and Country music categories. When you select a tree node on the design page and click the `url` property customizer box, a dialog appears to set the property. Clicking the Add File button lets you browse for the location of the PDF file you want to display. Figure 3–39 shows this dialog for the Jazz tree node.

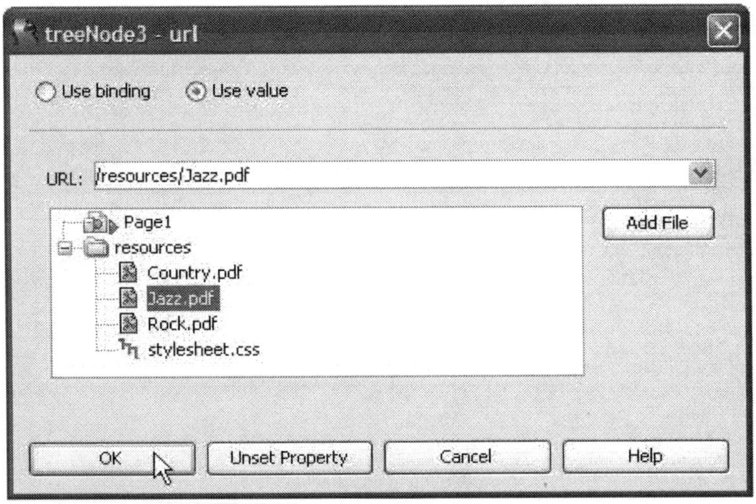

Figure 3–39 **Url dialog for tree node component**

Creator Tip

At the time of this writing, tree node selection events do not work in portlet projects.

3.4 Layout Components

The following catalog of layout components describes each component and gives you common usage scenarios. To show you how layout components can be useful in a Creator project, we also point you to relevant examples in other chapters of this book. The layout components are listed alphabetically for easy lookup.

Form

Form

The IDE makes sure that every new page that you create already has one form component. If you want to add more forms, drag the form component from the design palette and drop it on the page. This is usually not necessary in most applications, but you may want to manage certain components in their own forms. If you add a new form component to a page, it appears in the Outline view along with `form1`, the default form (see Figure 3–40). New form components render as selected boxes in the design canvas.

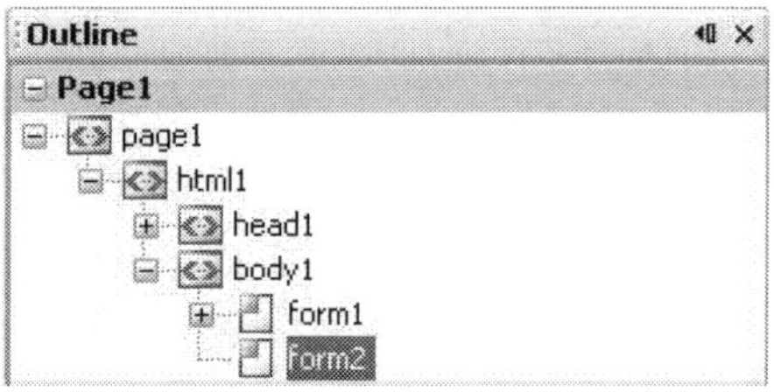

Figure 3–40 **Form component Outline view**

Creator Tip

If you need nested forms, use a virtual form (see "Virtual Forms" on page 70). Although you can always delete form components that you add to a page, it is not possible to delete the default form component, since every page must have one.

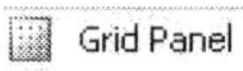

Grid Panel

A grid panel component is a general-purpose container that groups other components and controls their layout. When you drop a grid panel on the design canvas, you can place other components inside of the grid panel. Creator fills the grid panel with your components in a grid (rows and columns) layout. The components appear on the grid panel in the order that you drop them. (You can rearrange components later by "re-dropping" them on the grid panel.) Grid panels render as HTML `<table>` elements.

By default, grid panels have one column but you can modify the `columns` property to add more columns. The grid panel displays its components left to right to fit the number of columns you specify. It also resizes the number of rows based on how many components you have in the grid panel. Figure 3–41 shows a grid panel (box of dashed lines) in the design canvas containing a button, checkbox, and radio button. The grid panel on the left is a vertical layout (one column, the default). Next to it is a grid panel with `columns` set to 3.

The grid panel is particularly useful when you don't know how much space a component will take up on the page. For example, if a static text component is built dynamically and you want to place another component after it on the

Figure 3–41 **Grid panel components**

page, you can nest both components in a grid panel. The layout mechanism adjusts the relative position of each component appropriately.

The grid panel component has other properties that control its appearance. These properties include `bgcolor` for background color, `cellspacing` and `cellpadding` for cell width spacing, and `border` for the width of the grid panel's border lines.

Creator Tip

Use the Outline view rather than the design canvas to work with nested components. It's much easier to place components on top of a desired target with the Outline view. Rendering in the design view often obscures the specific target component that you're trying to drop onto.

Book Examples

- "Add a Grid Panel Component" on page 193 (Chapter 5). Uses a grid panel to hold button components.
- "Add Components to the Page" on page 298 (Chapter 7). Uses nested grid panels to help with component layout.
- "Layout and Grouping with Grid Panel" on page 457 (Chapter 10). Uses a grid panel to group different components and control their rendering.
- "Add Components to the Page" on page 502 (Chapter 11). Uses a grid panel and nested grid panel to help with layout. Uses static text components as placeholders in grid panels.
- "Add Components to the Page" on page 521 (Chapter 11). Uses a grid panel with table components to help with layout.
- "Using Grid Panel to Improve Page Layout" on page 597 (Chapter 13). Uses a grid panel to handle layout for components rendered with text read from properties files.
- "Adding Components to the Page" on page 619 (Chapter 13). Uses a grid panel to help with layout.

Group Panel

Group Panel

A group panel is a general-purpose container that groups components and controls their layout. Whereas grid panels place components in a grid configuration (you specify the number of columns), a group panel component uses a flow layout. Depending on the width of the panel, group panels arrange components one after the other in a flow. When there's not enough room in the first row, Creator continues with placement in a second row. Like grid panels, the order in which you drop components on a group panel is the same order that they appear on the page.

A group panel component renders as an HTML `<span>` element and the page bean implements a group panel as a `PanelGroup` object. (If you set property `block` to true, a group panel renders as an HTML `<div>` element.) Figure 3–42 shows a group panel (box of dashed lines) in the design canvas containing a button, checkbox, and radio button.

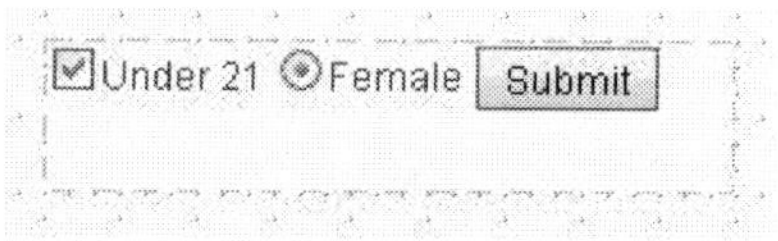

Figure 3–42 **Group panel component**

Creator Tip

Group panels are handy for grouping nested components. It's possible, for example, to place a group panel inside cells of a grid panel. This technique lets you create interesting web pages by placing groups of components in each cell of a grid panel. From the grid panel's perspective, these nested components are treated as a single cell.

Layout Panel

Layout Panel

The layout panel component is a container that groups components and lets you choose a layout mode. When you drag a layout panel component from the component palette and drop it on the design canvas, the IDE gives you a Flow Layout by default. As you drop components in the layout panel, the IDE aligns them from left to right on the top line, moving them to the next line if there is not enough room. This makes layout panels behave like group panels as you add components.

If, on the other hand, you'd like to use the design canvas to position components at arbitrary (absolute) places in the panel, change the `panelLayout` property to Grid Layout (use the drop down list in the Properties window). Now each component will be positioned relative to the nearest grid lines. This makes layout panels behave like Creator's design canvas (the default grid layout).

Figure 3–43 shows a layout panel (box of dashed lines) in flow layout mode containing a drop down list, a listbox, and a button.

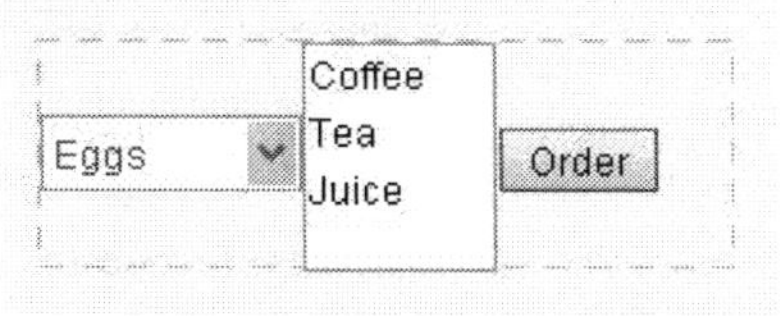

Figure 3–43 **Layout panel component**

Layout panel components are also the default for tab set components (see "Tab Set" on page 114).

Book Examples

- "Add Components to the Page" on page 289 (Chapter 7). Uses a layout panel in Grid Layout mode to position components.
- See TabSet3 project in the Creator download file (**FieldGuide2/Examples/WebPageDesign/Projects/TabSet3**). Uses a tab set component with embedded layout panels for each tab selection.

Page Alert

The page alert component displays messages on a separate page. If you don't want to use a separate page, use an alert component from the Composite palette (see "Alert" on page 118). Page alerts are useful because they have recognizable icons and configurable messages. Figure 3–44 shows the page alert component after you drop it on the design canvas.

Figure 3–44 **Page alert component**

The `type` property in the Properties view contains a drop down list of icons and alert types. There are four types of alerts: error, warning, information, or question. The `summary` property displays a brief text message for the alert, and the `detail` property lets you display a longer, more detailed message. You can also right-click a page alert component and bind its properties to a Javabeans property or another object.

Figure 3–45 shows two page alerts in a browser window. The left alert displays a brief information message. The right alert shows an error alert with a brief reason for the alert followed by a detailed suggestion.

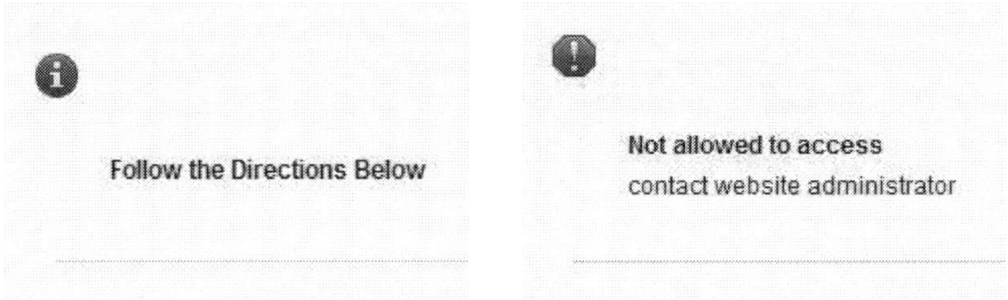

Figure 3–45 **Page alert components**

Page Fragment Box

Page Fragment Box

Page fragments are separate, reusable components that you include in multiple web pages. The Page Fragment Box component generates a JSP directive that includes a JSP file fragment in your page. Page fragments let you build web pages that have consistent form. You may, for instance, use page fragments to include the same graphic header in all pages of an application.

When you select a page fragment component and drop it on the design canvas, Creator pops up a dialog that lets you create a new page fragment or select an existing one. Figure 3–46 shows the Select Page Fragment dialog.

Page fragment files show up in the Projects view Web Pages > resources node as a **.jspf** file. In the Outline view, a page fragment box appears as a node underneath an HTML `<div>` element. The name of this node has the format **directive.include:*fragment_file*.jspf**, where ***fragment_file*** is the name of your page fragment file. Figure 3–47 shows the Outline view for the **Fragment1.jspf** page fragment.

Once you have a page fragment box, you can add visual elements to it as needed. A typical example is a page fragment consisting of a banner with a company's logo (an image component). As you create pages in your web application, drag a page fragment box component to the page, position it, and specify the page fragment name.

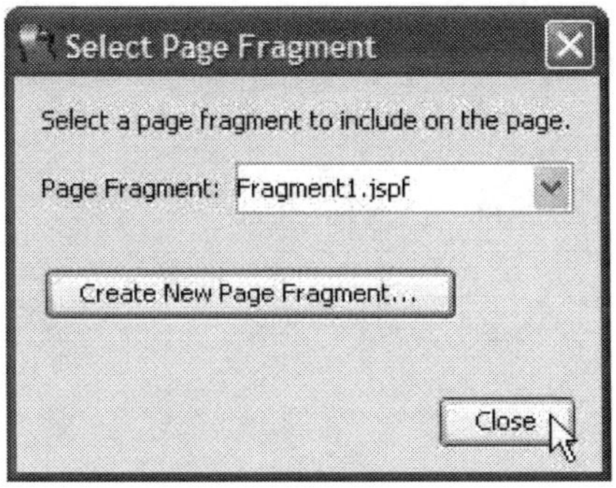

Figure 3–46 **Select Page Fragment dialog**

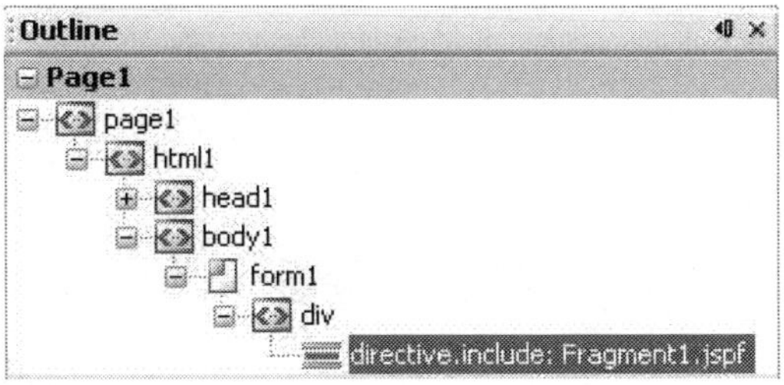

Figure 3–47 **Page fragment Outline view**

Creator Tip

When adding components to page fragments, make sure the id of any new component does not conflict with any component id names on the including page. Also, virtual forms are not allowed within page fragments.

Book Examples

- "Banner Page Fragment" on page 309 (Chapter 7). Uses page fragment box components to create uniform looking pages.
- "Using Tab Sets and Page Fragments" on page 327 (Chapter 7). Uses a page fragment box with tab set components.

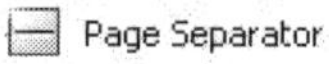

Page Separator

The page separator component creates a horizontal line on your page. This lets you separate other components for a better visual layout. Page separator components are rendered as HTML <hr> elements. You can change a page separator's width and appearance in the Properties view. In the page bean, a page separator component is a `PageSeparator` object.

Figure 3–48 shows a page separator with a drop-down list, text field, and submit button.

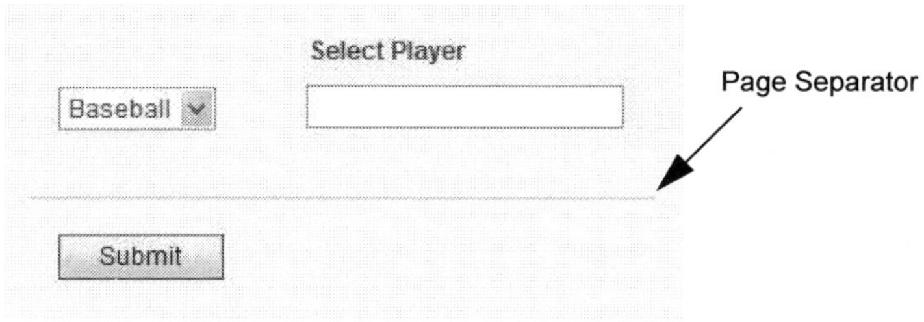

Figure 3–48 **Page separator component**

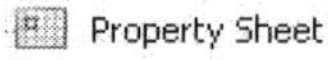

Property Sheet

The property sheet component is a layout composite component. In the design palette, property sheets contain nodes for nested property sheet section components and property components (see Figure 3–49).

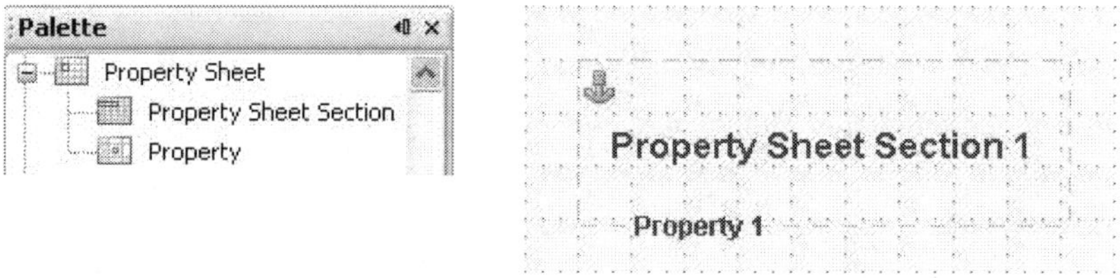

Figure 3–49 **Property sheet component**

When you drag a property sheet component to the design canvas, the initial layout is one sheet section containing one property, as shown in Figure 3–49. It's possible to have multiple sheet sections on a page with header strings initialized with the sheet section's `label` property. You can also have multiple property components within each sheet section.

Property components are containers with labels, optional help text, and default formatting. By default, the property component displays read-only data, but you can attach input components, such as calendars, drop-down lists, or text fields. To add new properties, drop a property component on a property sheet section, or right-click the property sheet section component and select Add Property. After creating property components, the Outline view is helpful for dropping input components on a selected property. Figure 3–50 shows a layout with one sheet section (`section1`) and four properties. Each property has its own input component.

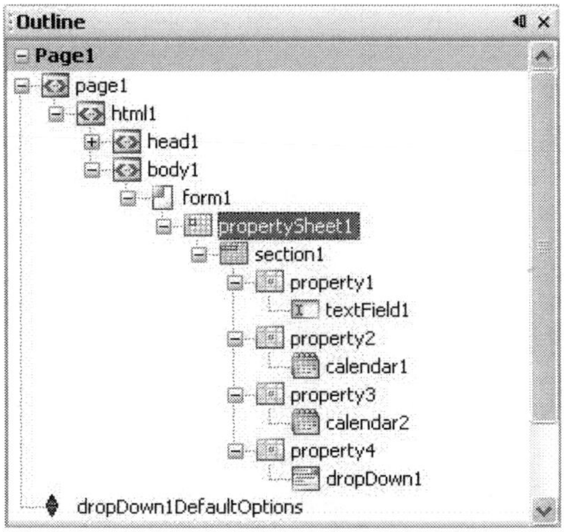

Figure 3–50 **Property sheet Outline view**

There are several important properties for property sheet components. The `requiredFields` property displays a required fields message (and red asterisk) when set to `true`. A property sheet component also contains an anchor component by default (see "Anchor" on page 72). If you set the `jumpLinks` property, the property sheet displays links to its sections at the top of the property sheet. If a property has an input component, you can set the optional `required` property for that component to force data entry on the page.

Example

Property sheets are handy for creating data entry forms. Figure 3–51 shows an entry form for a rental car reservation in a browser window.

Here, we have one property sheet set up with properties and input components. Note that this property sheet has required fields for most of the input

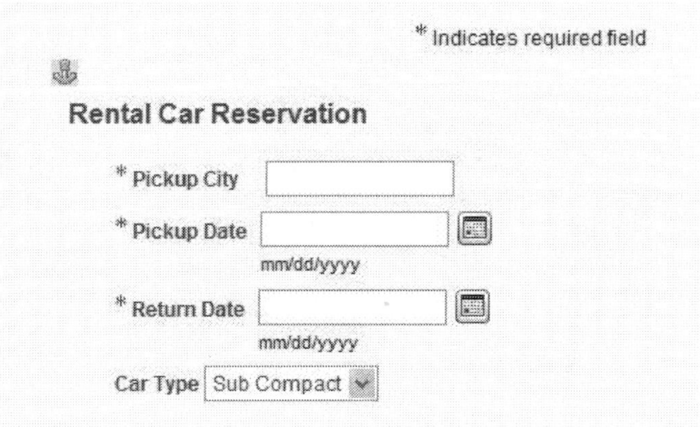

Figure 3–51 **Property sheet example**

components. The drop-down selection is not required for input and defaults to the initial string `Sub Compact`. The `requiredFields` property is set here to display the required fields message.

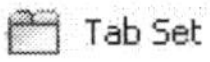

Tab Set

The tab set is a layout composite component. In the design palette, tab sets contain a nested tab component node (see Figure 3–52). Tab set components let you click tabs to view alternate sets of components or navigate to different pages. Each tab in a tab set is a tab component with configurable properties. To add a new tab, right-click the tab set component and choose Add Tab or drop a new tab component on a tab set (or another tab component for nested tabs).

In the Outline view, tab components provide a default layout panel (see Figure 3–52) to hold components that become visible when a user clicks a tab. Each layout panel's `panelLayout` property is set to Grid Layout by default, but you can change it to Flow Layout in the Properties view. If you use tab sets to navigate between pages, be sure to delete each tab component's layout panel. The `selected` property of a tab set component determines which tab is initially selected. Tab selections also change color when you select them.

You can create an event handler by double clicking any tab component of a tab set in the design view. It's also possible to bind a tab component's text property to an object or data provider.

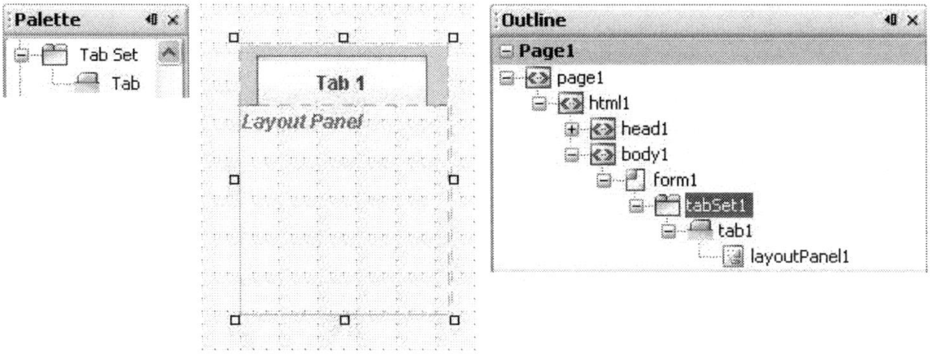

Figure 3–52 **Tab set component**

Creator Tip

When you drop a tab component to the left or right of an existing tab in a tab set, the tab component appears in the same row of tabs. Otherwise, the tab component will be a child of the tab component that you drop it on. You can have at most three levels of tabs in any tab set.

Figure 3–53 shows the design canvas for a tab set with three tab components. In the Outline view, each tab component has its own layout panel.

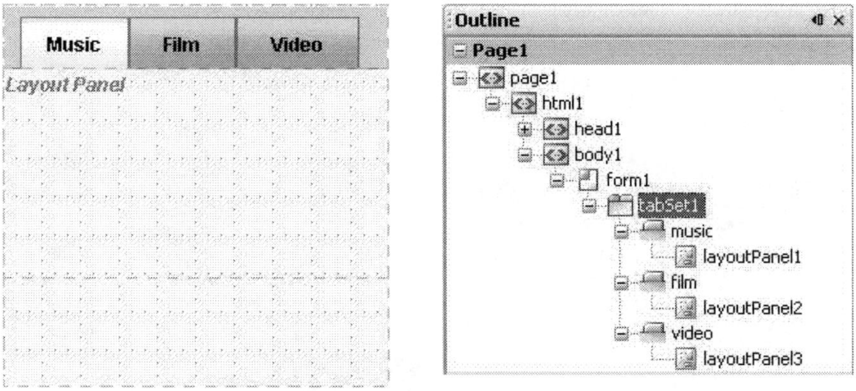

Figure 3–53 **Design canvas and Outline view of tab set**

Book Examples

- "Using Separate Tab Sets" on page 324 (Chapter 7). Uses separate tab set components to navigate among pages.
- "Add Tab Set and Tabs to CactusBanner" on page 329 (Chapter 7). Uses a tab set component with a page fragment for navigation.
- See TabSet3 project in the Creator download file (**FieldGuide2/Examples/WebPageDesign/Projects/TabSet3**). Uses a tab set component on one page to display different sets of components.

3.5 Composite Components

The following catalog of composite components describes each component and gives you common usage scenarios. The composite components are listed alphabetically for easy lookup.

Add Remove List

Add Remove List

The add remove list component lets users select items from one list and add or remove them from another list. The component displays two listboxes and two buttons. One listbox displays available options and the other displays selected options. The buttons let you add or remove options from the two listboxes.

Figure 3–54 shows the layout after you drop the add remove list component on the design canvas and fill in the selection items in the available listbox.

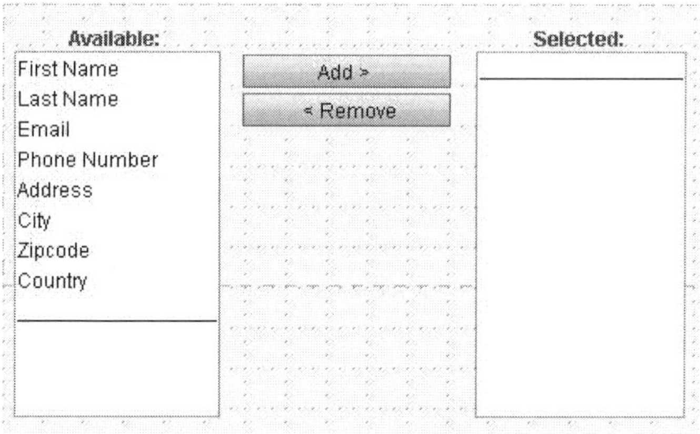

Figure 3–54 **Add remove list component**

The selection items can be set through the Properties window or dynamically generated at run time. Creator automatically supplies a converter for non-String data fields when you fill the list from a data provider. The `selected` property of the add remove list returns the selected items. The `items` property associates the component with a data provider.

To specify the choices, select the non-visual `addRemoveList1DefaultItems` component in the Outline view. In the Properties window, click the editing box opposite property `options`. Creator pops up a dialog so that you can add, edit, or remove items. (This is the same dialog box used to specify Display/Value fields with the Listbox component. See Figure 3–20 on page 87.)

You can also right-click the add remove list component and select Edit Event Handler from the pop-up menu. The `validate` option lets you insert Java code that validates user input, and the `processValueChange` option lets you insert Java code that executes when a component's value has changed.

Example

Let's add a submit button and a static text field to the sample page shown in Figure 3–54. In a browser window, the submit button determines which selections were made and the static text field displays them. Figure 3–55 shows the results of clicking the Submit button after adding an email, city, and country to the selected listbox. The static text field displays the selected string items.

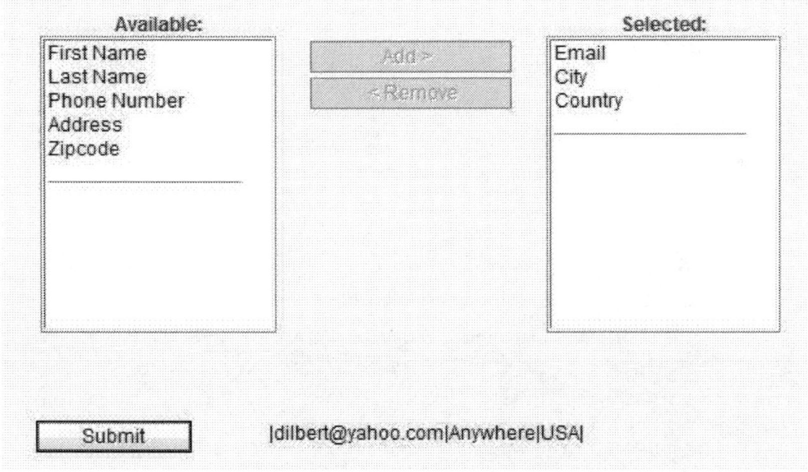

Figure 3–55 **Add remove list component with selections**

Here is the Java code for the Submit button event handler method that reads the selections from the add remove list component and displays the strings in the static text component.

```
public String submit_action() {
    String selections = addRemoveList1.getSelectedValues();
    staticText1.setText(selections);
    return null;
}
```

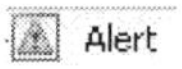

Alert

The alert component lets you display messages on a page. Alerts have recognizable icons and configurable messages. When you drag an alert component from the palette and drop it on to the design canvas, the default is an error alert, as shown in Figure 3–56.

Figure 3–56 **Alert component**

The `type` property in the Property view contains a drop down list of icons and alert types. The are four types of alerts: success, error, warning, and information. The `summary` property displays a brief text message for the alert, and the `detail` property lets you display a longer, more detailed message. If the `summary` property is empty, the component won't display on the page. You can also right-click a page alert component and bind its properties to a Javabeans property or another object.

Component alert includes an embedded hyperlink component, which you access by setting property `linkText`. To specify an action event handler for the hyperlink component, right-click the alert component and select Edit action Event handler.

Example 1

Figure 3–57 shows a page with a success alert directing users to a second page. To show the check mark icon, we set the alert component's `type` property to `success`. The `summary` and `detail` properties are set to "Item in Stock" and "To Process Your Order", respectively. Users are directed to another page via the `linkText` property, set to the string "Click Here".

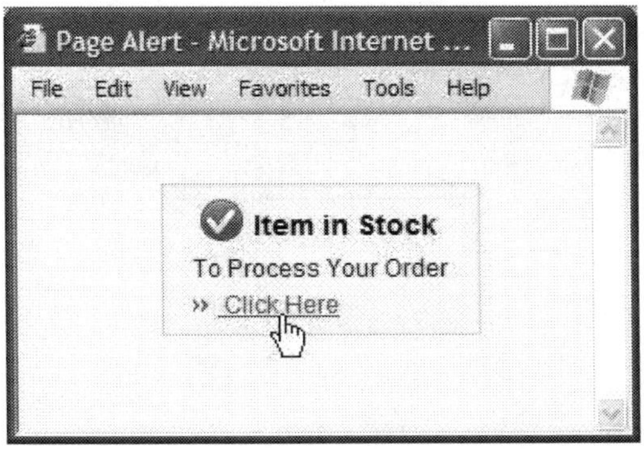

Figure 3–57 **Success alert with page navigation**

To implement page navigation, we use Creator's page navigation editor to specify navigation. Figure 3–58 shows the page navigation editor connecting the two JSP pages with string "`alertOutcome`".

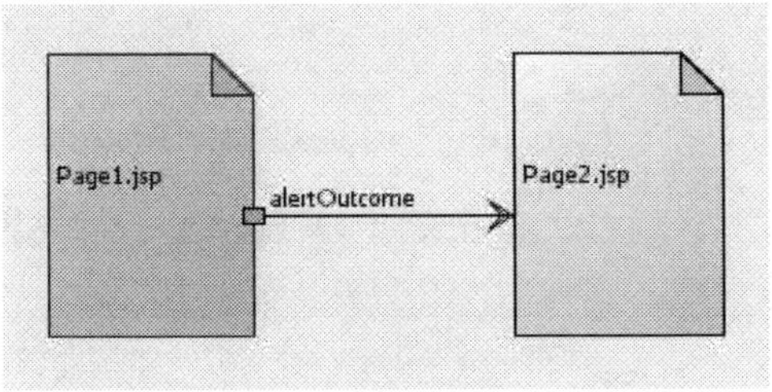

Figure 3–58 **Page navigation editor**

The IDE generates an event handler when you double-click the alert component. Here is the Java code for the alert event handler method, which simply returns the same string used by the page navigator.

```
public String alert1_action() {
    return "alertOutcome";
}
```

Example 2

You can use alert components in place of message or message group components. Figure 3–59 shows project Color1 (see "Custom Validation Method" on page 611) running in a browser. We replaced the three message components with alert components (with property id of `redAlert`, `greenAlert`, and `blueAlert`).

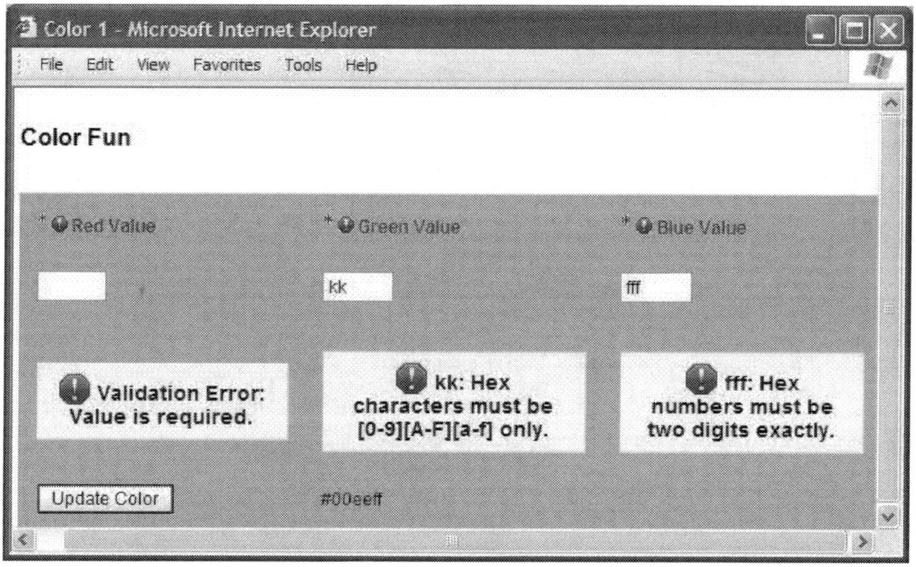

Figure 3–59 **Using alert instead of message to display validation errors**

In the page bean method `prerender()`, we invoke helper method `setAlertMessage()` to set the alert's `summary` property with a component-specific message from the FacesContext.

```
public void prerender() {
  setAlertMessage(alertRed,  redInput);
  setAlertMessage(alertGreen, greenInput);
  setAlertMessage(alertBlue, blueInput);
}
```

Method `setAlertMessage()` obtains the FacesContext and any messages associated with `inComp`, its argument's component. FacesContext method `getMessages()` returns an Iterator of FacesMessages for the component's `clientId` passed as an argument. Conveniently, the alert component does not display if its `summary` property is empty.

```
private void setAlertMessage(Alert ac, UIComponent inComp) {
  FacesContext context = FacesContext.getCurrentInstance();
  Iterator mi = context.getMessages(
        inComp.getClientId(context));
```

```
    String newMessage = "";
    while (mi.hasNext()) {
      newMessage += ((FacesMessage)mi.next()).getSummary()+" ";
    }
    ac.setSummary(newMessage);
  }
```

Breadcrumbs

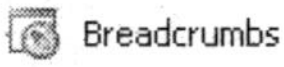

The breadcrumbs component is a default layout for hyperlinks. The name comes from an old hiker's trick where you drop breadcrumbs on a trail to find your way back and not get lost. With applications having many different web pages, breadcrumbs typically show a user's location by displaying the path through the page hierarchy to the current page.

When you drag a breadcrumbs component from the palette and drop it on the design canvas, the IDE includes a nested hyperlink component for every page in the application. Figure 3–60 shows the Design view and Outline view for a breadcrumbs component with two pages.

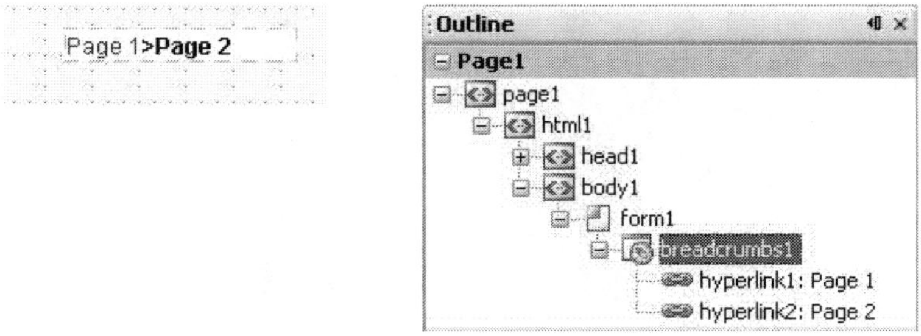

Figure 3–60 **Breadcrumbs component**

In the Design view, the breadcrumbs component separates hyperlinks by right angle brackets (>). By default, the initial component has a single hyperlink that points to the current page.

The `url` and `action` properties of each hyperlink are set the same way for breadcrumb components (see “Hyperlink” on page 82). You populate a list of hyperlinks by setting the `pages` property of a breadcrumb component to point to any array or list of `HyperLink` objects. You can also bind the `pages` property to a JavaBeans component or data provider.

Creator Tip

With portlets, the IDE does not provide a default hyperlink for breadcrumb components. You must add the hyperlinks yourself.

Example

Suppose an application has separate web pages to help users edit, compile, debug, and test a program. On the test page, it may be important to refer to the previous pages for information that relate to testing. Figure 3–61 shows a breadcrumbs component in a browser with links to the previous pages visited by the user.

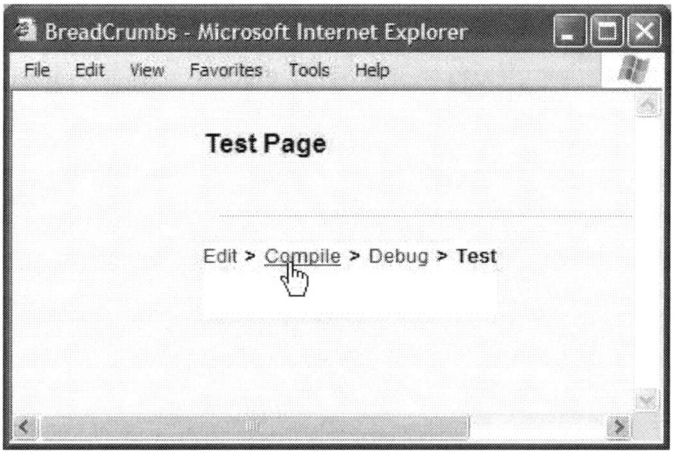

Figure 3–61 **Breadcrumbs Example**

Property `url` of each hyperlink in the breadcrumbs component is set to the page that was previously visited.

Inline Help

Inline Help

The inline help component is similar to a label. However, inline help components are restricted to displaying short help information for users on web pages. Once you drop an inline help component on the design canvas, you can type text directly in the component box. You may resize the box and the text wraps automatically. Figure 3–62 shows an inline help component on the design canvas.

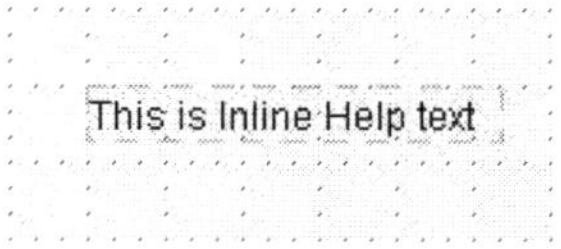

Figure 3–62 **Inline help component**

The inline help component has a `type` property which may be set to `page` (the default) or `field` in the Properties view. Page view is a larger font that applies to a page, whereas field view is a smaller font to help describe individual components. You can set the `style` property of an inline component using the Style Editor and the `styleClass` property using the styleClass Property editor. The `text` property can also be bound to an object or data provider.

Example

Figure 3–63 shows a page in a web browser with an inline help component at the top with `type` property set to **page**. Below the Confirm Selection button, a second inline help component appears with its `type` property set to **field**.

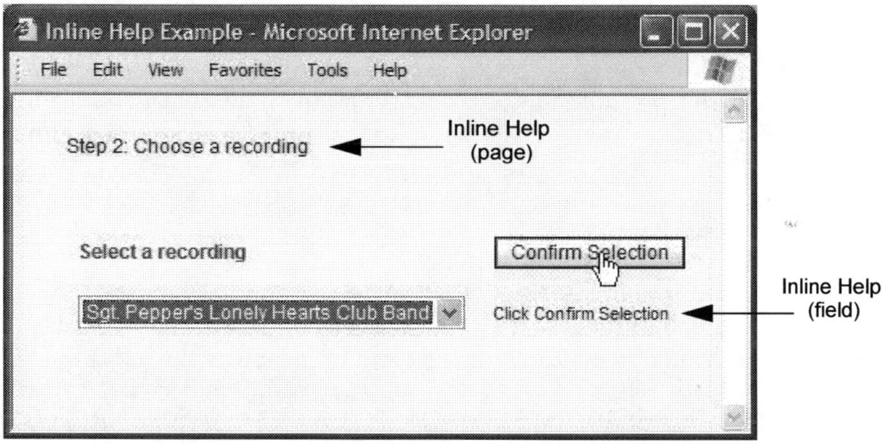

Figure 3–63 **Inline help example**

3.6 Validators

Creator provides a set of standard objects that validate user input gathered through UI components. The JSF architecture builds validation into the page request life cycle process, making validation an easy task for the developer to specify. Figure 3–64 shows the available validators in the Creator Components palette.

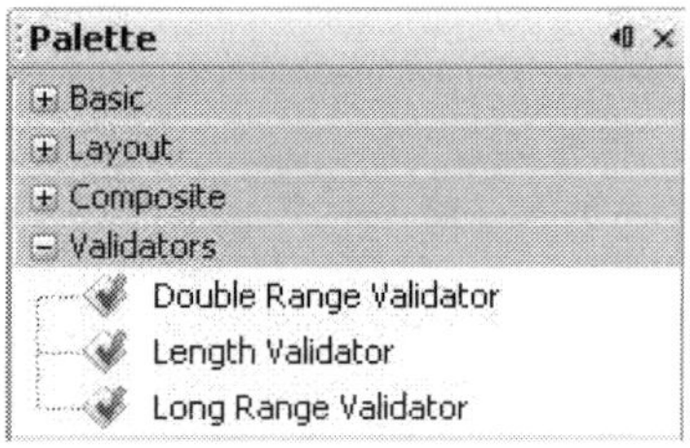

Figure 3–64 **Validators**

Validation Model

In Creator, you attach a validator object to a component by selecting a validator from the design palette and dropping it onto the component in the design canvas. You can also select a validator from the drop down list opposite property `validator` in an input component's Properties view. Validators have properties that you can manipulate to specify range limits (for example).

The JSF life cycle (see Figure 6–16 on page 262) includes a Process Validations phase. For components that have registered validators, JSF will validate the component's data. When validation errors occur, the affected component is marked "invalid" and an error message is sent to the JSF context.

Validation errors affect the life cycle process. Validation errors cause the page to proceed directly to the Render Response phase, skipping the Update Model Values phase and Invoke Application phase. This means events such as button clicks are not processed. When a page has multiple components with registered validators, all input is validated. This is helpful to the user since feedback (error messages) for the entire page can be displayed. Table 3.1 describes the validators in more detail.

There are three standard validators: a Double Range Validator for floating types, a Length Validator for strings, and a Long Range Validator for integral values. You can also write your own custom validation method. Note that each standard validator has properties for minimum and maximum values. The Length validator works with String data, and the Double Range and Long

Table 3.1 JSF Validators

Name	*Description*	*Example*
Double Range Validator	Specify minimum and maximum values.	"Use Validators and Converters" on page 252 (Chapter 6). Uses a Double Range Validator with a text field to check the range of a double.
Length Validator	Specify minimum and maximum values. Does not detect empty input fields (you use required property of component).	"Add a Validator" on page 472 (Chapter 10). Uses a Length Validator with a text field.
Long Range Validator	Specify minimum and maximum values.	"Place Interest Rate and Term Components" on page 254 (Chapter 6). Uses a Long Range Validator with a text field to check the range of an Integer value.
Custom Validate Method	`validate-HexString()` method checks for a 2-digit hex string	"Add a Validation Method" on page 617 (Chapter 13). Shows how to implement your own validation method.

Range validators are typically used with converters to convert a component's data to the correct type.

Table 3.1 also points you to examples in the book that show you how to use the validators. This includes an example of a custom Validate Method called `validateHexString()` that checks for a 2-digit hexadecimal string in a web application.

3.7 Converters

JSF strives to separate presentation data (the data that users read and possibly modify) from internal data or model data. To accomplish this, you should use JavaBeans components, EJB components, JDBC cached rowsets, and other application-specific structures to represent model data and behaviors. JSF also makes sure that any data conversions between the two views are consistent and well-defined.

Figure 3–65 shows the available converters in the Creator design palette.

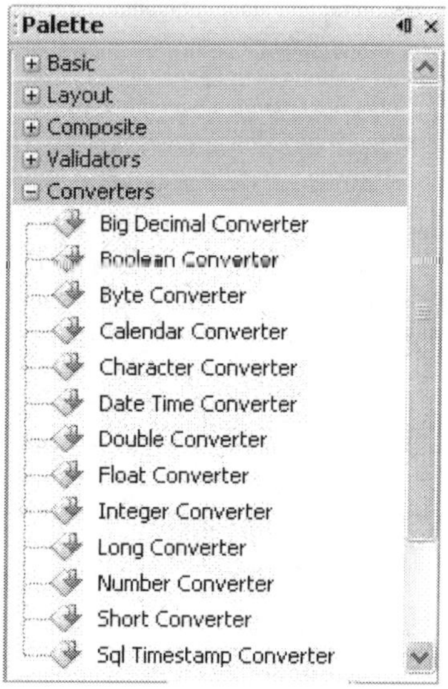

Figure 3–65 **Converters**

Conversion Model

A UI component (components for input such as text fields or components for output such as labels and static text components) can take a data converter to convert its data to a specific type. Typically (but not always), the component may be bound to a JavaBeans property of that type. For example, in project **Payment1** (see "LoanBean" on page 242), we bind a text field component (`loanAmount`) to the `amount` property of LoanBean. Property `amount` is a Double, so we apply a Double converter to the text field component.

Like the validation process, JSF sets aside specific times to perform conversions. For an input component, conversion applies to the submitted input before validation. When errors occur, the affected component is marked "invalid" and conversion error messages are sent to the JSF context. JSF proceeds to the Render Response phase in this case.

Creator applies converters automatically to data-aware components when the source data type is not a String. Table 3.2 describes the converters available on Creator's palette.

Most of the converters are straightforward and provide a conversion that's obvious from their name. Note that all converters use wrapper classes (subclassed from `Object`) instead of the primitive types. This allows the `text` property (type `Object`) to accept all of these types.

Table 3.2 JSF Converters

Name	*Description/Example*
Big Decimal Converter	Converts between String and java.math.BigDecimal.
Boolean Converter	Converts between String and Boolean.
Byte Converter	Converts between String and Byte.
Calendar Converter	Converts between String and java.util.Calendar.
Character Converter	Converts between String and Character.
Date Time Converter	"Configure the Table" on page 360 (Chapter 8). Converts between String and java.util.Date.
Double Converter	"Use Validators and Converters" on page 252 (Chapter 6). Shows a double converter with an interest rate value and a loan amount value.
Float Converter	Converts between String and Float.
Integer Converter	"Place Interest Rate and Term Components" on page 254 (Chapter 6). Shows an integer converter with a loan term value.
Long Converter	Converts between String and Long.
Number Converter	"Place Button, Label and Static Text Components" on page 257 (Chapter 6). Shows a number converter with a currency value.
Short Converter	Converts between String and Short.
Sql Timestamp Converter	Converts between String and java.sql.Timestamp.

The Date time converter, Number converter, and Sql Timestamp converter require a bit more explanation, however, so let's do that now.

Date Time Converter

The Date Time Converter converts a component's data to a `java.util.Date`. When you apply a Date Time Converter to a text field, the textual input is converted. The field on the page is updated with a standard format during the Render Response phase. You can always configure a Date Time Converter's format if you need to. If you don't specify a locale, the Date Time Converter uses the default locale (see "A Word About Locales" on page 593).

The Date Time Converter uses the format rules and patterns of the `DateFormat` class. See the tutorial at `http://java.sun.com/docs/books/tutorial/i18n/format/dateFormat.html` for more information on formatting; see also the Javadoc for the DateFormat class at `http://java.sun.com/j2se/1.4.2/docs/api/java/text/DateFormat.html`.

The Date Time Converter uses a default pattern if you don't configure it differently. The data are assumed to be a date (as opposed to time) using the pattern MMM d, yyyy. Although full names for the month are accepted, the Date Time Converter shortens it to three letters and rejects numerical values. On input, you must supply a comma. See "Configure the Table" on page 360 for an example of applying the Date Time Converter to a table column.

Of course, your choices for other formats are more flexible. Table 3.3 shows the results of applying the Date Time Converter to a specific date (April 5, 1985) in String format. The table shows several formatting patterns and the effect of setting the `dateStyle` property to `medium`, `long`, and `full`.

Table 3.3 Date Time Converter

Property/Pattern	***Result***
`medium`	Apr 5, 1985
`long`	April 5, 1985
`full`	Friday April 5, 1985
`MM-dd-yy`	04-05-85
`EEE, MMM d, "yy`	Fri, Apr 5, '85

Number Converter

A Number Converter lets you manipulate numerical data using either a pattern, or specifying minimum and maximum digits and fraction digits. Since numbers are sensitive to language and locale, a Number Converter can use locale.

The Number Converter uses a pattern with separate properties for manipulating a format (such as currency symbol, integer digits, fraction digits, and locale). We use a Number Converter to convert a double to a dollar (String) value here (see "Place Button, Label and Static Text Components" on page 257). Also see Figure 11–8 on page 505, which shows the Number Format dialog. We use it in Figure 11–8 to convert a BigDecimal value to String for output, using pattern "USD #,###.00" for a currency amount in U.S. dollars.

Sql Timestamp Converter

The Sql timestamp converter converts data between String values and `java.sql.Timestamp` data types. It is also useful for binding a component to a database column of type TIMESTAMP. You can use to convert input data to type TIMESTAMP or display TIMESTAMP values on the web page.

3.8 AJAX Components

Asynchronous JavaScript Technology and XML (AJAX) is a web development technique for building interactive web applications. Its main purpose is to allow asynchronous updates on a web page without refreshing the whole page and without performing a submit and postback. Creator provides a component library that includes experimental-technology AJAX components. To use these components, install the Update Center's most recent AJAX component library and add it to the Components palette. Figure 3–66 shows the BluePrints AJAX Components and Support Beans installed in the Components palette.

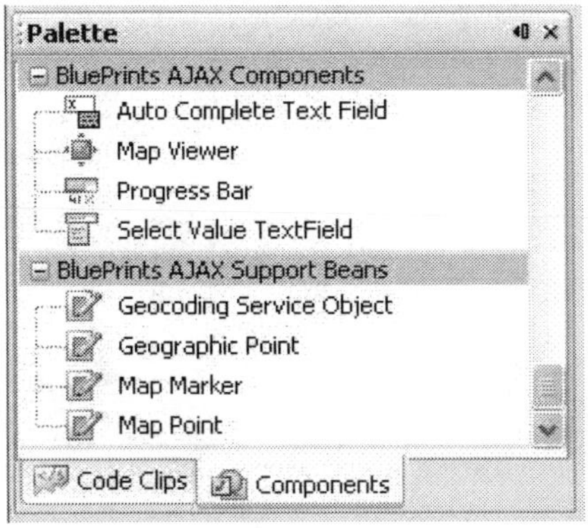

Figure 3–66 **BluePrints AJAX Components and Support Beans**

In this section, we'll show you how to use the Component Library Manager to add the AJAX component library to the palette. We show you how to use the AJAX-enabled Auto Complete Text Field component in Chapter 13 (see "Using AJAX-Enabled Components" on page 628 and "Using AJAX-Enabled Components with Web Services" on page 638).

Creator Tip

Since the AJAX-enabled components are under development, you should make sure you have installed the most recent component library from the Update Center.

Importing a Component Library

The first step in using one of the AJAX-enabled components is to import the target component library into Creator.

1. From the Creator main menu, select **Tools > Component Library Manager.** Creator brings up the Component Library Manager dialog, as shown in Figure 3–67. (Alternatively, right-click on one of the Component sections in the Components palette and select **Manage Component Libraries.**)

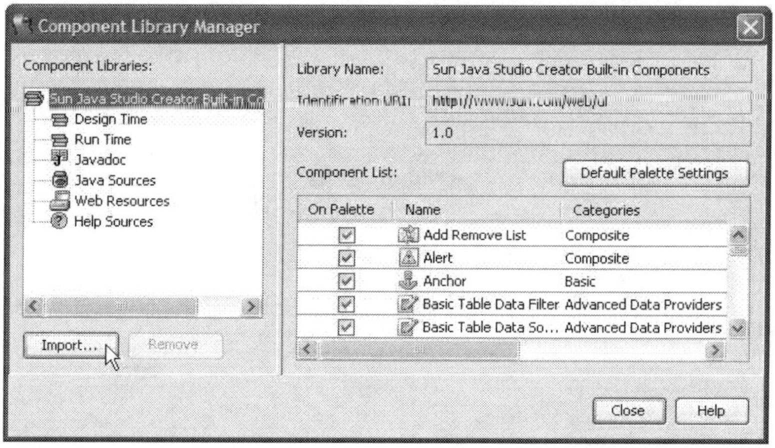

Figure 3–67 **Component Library Manager Dialog**

2. Click Import. Creator brings up the Import Component Library dialog.
3. Click Browse and navigate to the directory **samples/complib**.
4. Select **ui.complib** and click Open.
5. You'll see BluePrints AJAX Components and Support Beans in the text field under radio button Import into Palette Categories defined by Library, as shown in Figure 3–68. Click OK.
6. The Component Library Manager dialog now shows the BluePrints AJAX Components listed under the Component Libraries. The Component List includes the Auto Complete Text Field, Map Viewer, Progress Bar, and Select Value TextField (and support beans) as shown in Figure 3–69. Click Close to close the Component Library Manager dialog.
7. From the Components palette, open the BluePrints AJAX Components section to see these components added to the palette (as shown in Figure 3–66).

Creator Tip

More components will be included in the BluePrints AJAX Components Library as they are developed.

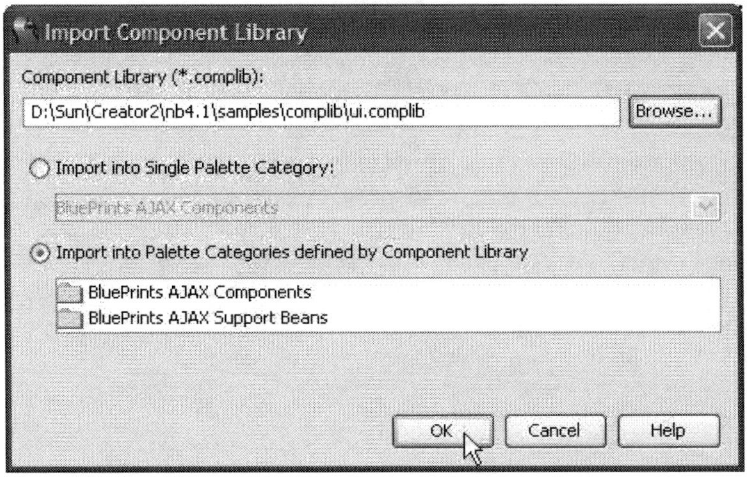

Figure 3–68 **Import Component Library Dialog**

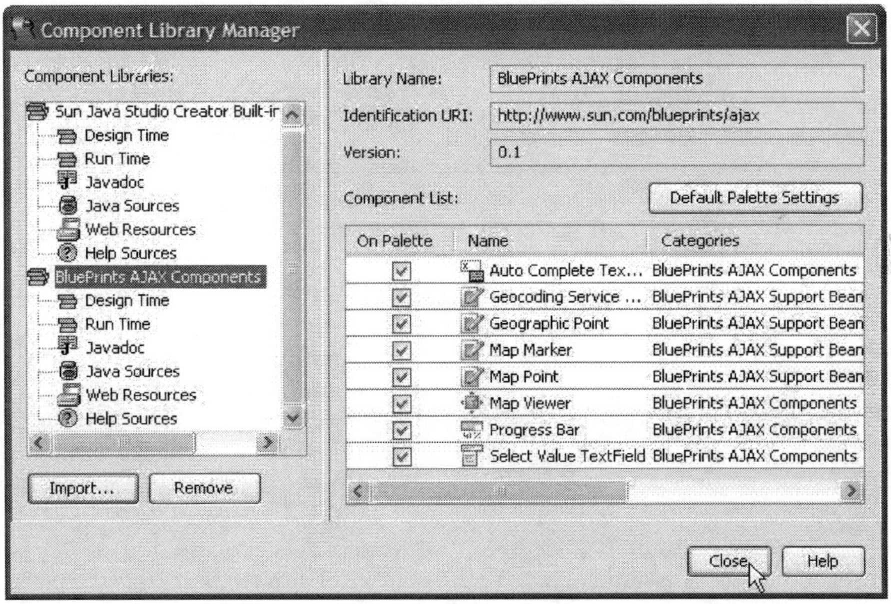

Figure 3–69 **After importing the BluePrints AJAX component library**

3.9 Key Point Summary

- Creator's design palette contains components, validators, converters, and data providers.
- Creator's components are rendered in HTML.
- Creator components share many properties in common, such as `text`, `toolTip`, `style`, `id`, and `binding`.
- Creator components that manipulate data can accept converters to convert data to an from String form. You can also use converters to format data on output.
- Input components share common properties, such as `validator`, `maxlength`, `required`, `valueChangeListener`, and `onChange`.
- A value change event occurs when an input component's selection changes or its text changes.
- Creator generates a `processValueChange()` method when you double-click an input component.
- The Auto-Submit on Change feature submits a page when an input component fires a value change event. Creator generates a JavaScript element and configures the component's `onChange` property to implement this feature.
- Table components (table and grid panel) have properties to control appearance, such as `bgcolor`, `border`, `cellspacing`, `cellpadding`, and `columns`.
- Creator provides component binding with data providers that wrap data sources, JavaBeans components, web services return objects, and EJB return objects. You can also apply property binding to arbitrary application data. This simplifies transferring data between the presentation view and the model view.
- A table component is data aware and offers sophisticated layout choices. By specifying headers, footers, and embedded component types for its columns, the page designer can build a custom page for displaying data.
- You can enable paging controls with table components. This is useful for database queries or other data that produce more than a single page of data.
- JSF has data converters that encourage the separation of model and presentation data. The Creator converters seamlessly convert presentation data to and from model data.
- The Creator validators validate user input before events are processed. Validation and conversion errors short-circuit the normal life cycle request mechanism and re-render the page with error messages.
- Use a message or message group component to display validation or conversion errors on a web page.
- Use message group components to display system or global errors.

- You can write your own custom validation method and hook it into the JSF validation cycle.
- Use the Component Library Manager to import component libraries to Creator's Components palette, as well as to configure the palette.
- Creator includes a bundled BluePrints AJAX Components library, an experimental technology set of components that use AJAX.

SOFTWARE DEVELOPMENT

Topics in This Chapter

- Editing Java Code
- Refactoring
- Source Code Control with CVS
- Creating Non-Web Projects

Chapter 4

Sun Java Studio Creator has an integrated development environment (IDE) that greatly simplifies the "edit-compile-deploy" cycle of complex web applications. Based on NetBeans, the IDE has code generation and navigation features that make it easy and pleasurable to edit and compile programs. In addition to keyboard shortcuts and code completion, the IDE also provides code refactoring and CVS source code control. All of these features make up a development environment that helps you create, manage, and maintain your web applications.

This chapter shows you how to use the Source Editor to write Java code effectively. You will learn how to customize the IDE to your tastes and create a comfortable environment to develop applications. We'll also show you how to refactor your code when it becomes necessary to make large changes, like changing the name of a method or a heavily-used class. Because source code maintainability is so vital today with complex web projects, we'll show you how to put your code under CVS source code control. Along the way, there will be plenty of examples to help you understand how to use these features[1] in Creator projects.

---

1. This chapter focuses only on editing, refactoring, and versioning in the IDE. To learn more about Creator's software development features beyond these topics, consult the NetBeans documentation.

4.1 Using the Java Source Editor

The Java source editor is where you'll spend a lot of your time in Creator. This section shows you useful features that make it easier to develop your applications.

Finding What You Need

Creator allows you to customize the Java editor to suit your individual tastes. If you select Tools > Options from the Creator toolbar and select Java Editor under the Editing > Editor Settings node, you will see General and Expert settings for the editor, as shown in Figure 4–1.

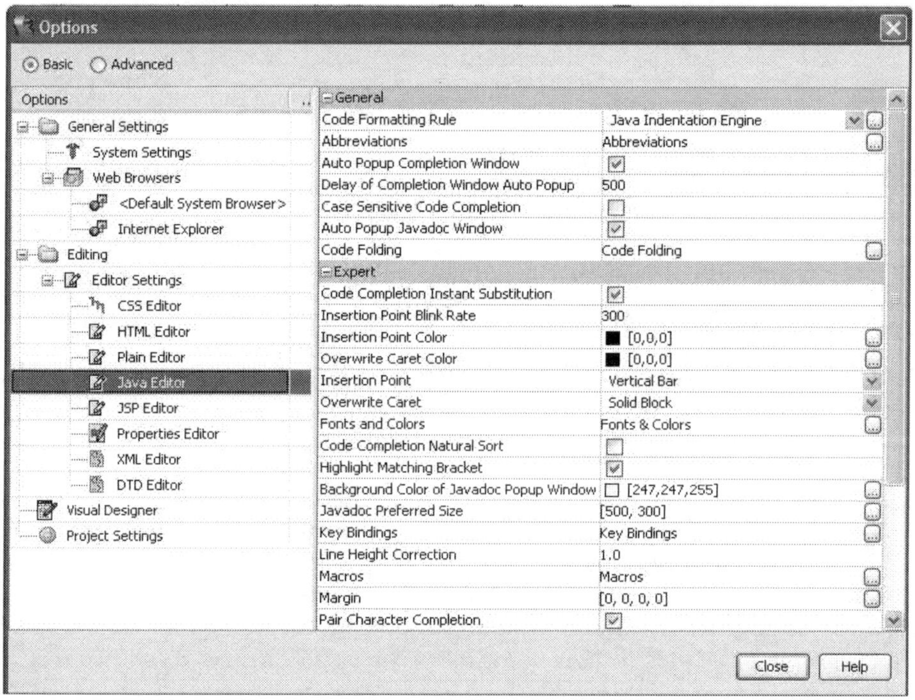

Figure 4–1 **Java Editor Basic Options**

Note that you can do basic things like change code formatting rules, add new editor abbreviations, or modify code folding for imports and methods. If you are feeling like an expert, you can change fonts and colors, key bindings, and even the insertion blink rate (to save on your eyes). Take a few moments to click on the customizer boxes with several of the features here, and you will learn a lot about what you can do to customize the editor.

If you click the Advanced radio button in the Options dialog, you will see the Java Code Formatting Rule settings under the Editing > Code Formatting Rules node. Figure 4–2 shows the list of configurable rules that affect code formatting.

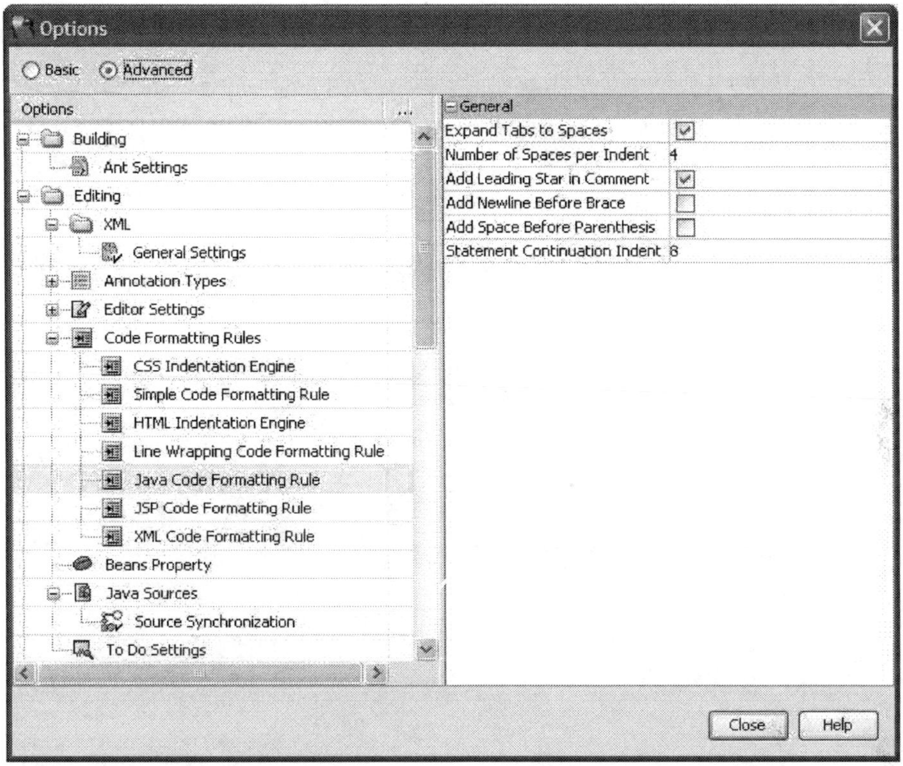

Figure 4–2 **Java Editor Advanced Options**

Formatting Code

Java code is automatically formatted in Creator according to default rules. Members of classes, for example, are indented four spaces, continued statements are indented eight spaces, and any tabs that you enter are converted to spaces. No spaces are placed before an opening parenthesis, and an opening curly brace is put on the same line as a class or method declaration.

To reformat all the code in any file in Creator, type **<Ctrl+Shift+F>**. (Alternatively, right-click inside the editor and select Reformat Code from the context menu.) This is very handy right after you paste a code fragment from another file into your source code. To indent blocks of code manually, type **<Tab>** or **<Ctrl+T>**. Typing **<Shift+Tab>** or **<Ctrl+D>** reverses indents.

You can change any of Creator's default settings for code formatting by accessing the Java Indentation Engine. This can be done directly with the Java Code Formatting Rule in the Advanced Options dialog (see Figure 4–2), or by clicking on the customizer box for Code Formatting Rule in the Basic Options dialog (see Figure 4–1).

Fonts and Colors

The Basic Options dialog (Figure 4–1) lets you configure font size and style, as well as the foreground and background colors of the editor. Under Expert, click the customizer box for Fonts and Colors. Figure 4–3 shows the settings for Java Method calls.

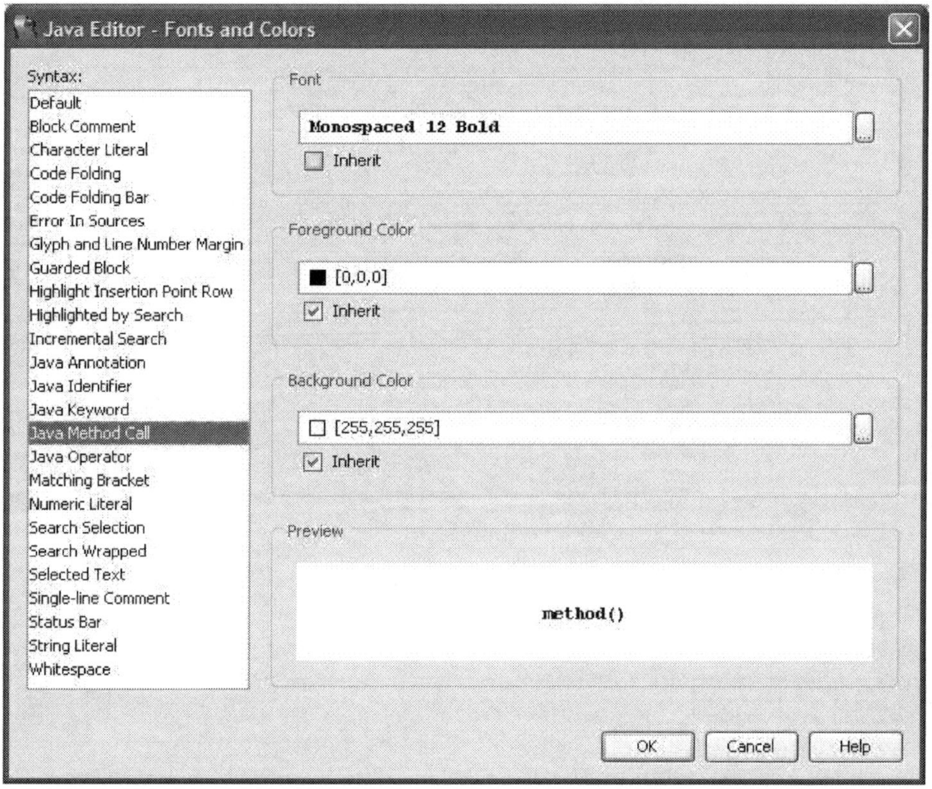

Figure 4–3 **Fonts and Colors Dialog**

Clicking the customizer box for a Foreground or Background Color brings up a color palette to choose a different RGB value. Likewise, clicking the customizer box for a Font allows you to change its style and point size. The Inherit checkbox indicates whether or not a font or color should be inherited from the Default syntax category.

Code Completion

One of the handier features of the IDE is code completion, which lets you type part of a Java identifier and let the IDE finish the expression for you. To use this feature, activate a code completion box with one of the following:

- Type a few characters in an expression, then press **<Ctrl+Space>** or **<Ctrl+\>**.
- Pause after you type a period (.) in an expression (this gives you a choice of method names).
- Type the `import` keyword followed by a space.

A code completion box contains a list of choices to select from. After you choose what you want, just press **<Enter>** to finish. To close the code completion box without choosing anything, press the **<Esc>** key.

Figure 4–4 shows a code completion box and associated Javadoc popup window. Here we typed `new List` followed by **<Ctrl+\>** and selected `ListDataProvider` in the code completion box. Note that the Javadoc window provides the documentation for this class. After you press **<Enter>**, the IDE completes the class name and adds the import statement for the class to your code.

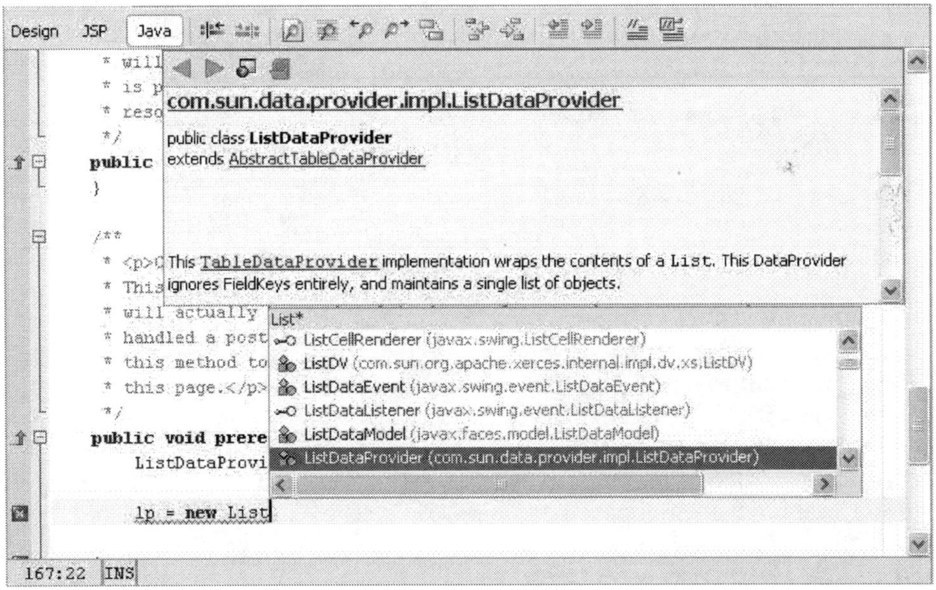

Figure 4–4 **Code Completion and Javadoc popup**

Disabling Code Completion

You can disable the code completion box and Javadoc popups if you don't want them active. To do this, choose Tools > Options from the Creator menu, expand the Editing > Editor Settings node, and select Java Editor. Under General, select from any of the following.

- To disable the code completion box - uncheck the checkbox for Auto Popup Completion Window.
- To disable Javadoc popups - uncheck the checkbox for Auto Popup Javadoc Window.
- To change the code completion box display delay time - modify the default of 500 milliseconds for the Delay of Completion Window Auto Popup.

Note that changing these options disables only the automatic appearance of what the IDE does. Once disabled, you can still manually activate code completion with **<Ctrl+Space>** (or **<Ctrl+\>**). Likewise, typing **<Ctrl+Shift+Space>** manually activates Javadoc popups.

Show Line Numbers

You can toggle whether or not the Java source editor shows line numbers. Place the cursor in the blue left-margin area and right-click. Select Show Line Numbers from the context menu to enable line numbers. This is especially convenient for identifying the source of an exception or debugging activities.

Code Folding

The Editor lets you collapse (or fold) certain sections of code to make room for other lines. You may fold methods, inner classes, import blocks, and Javadoc comments. Clicking a box icon in the left margin allows you to fold/unfold code that is bracketed by a vertical line extending down from the icon.

It's also possible to configure the IDE to fold code for you automatically. To do this, click Tools > Options from the toolbar and select Editing > Editor Settings > Java Editor. In the property window for Code Folding, click the customizer box (see Figure 4–1) and select the checkbox for any code element that you would like folded by default.

To access the code folding commands, right-click in the editor window and select Code Folds from the context menu. Or, select Window > Code Folds from the toolbar. Figure 4–5 shows the context menu for Code Folding and its shortcuts.

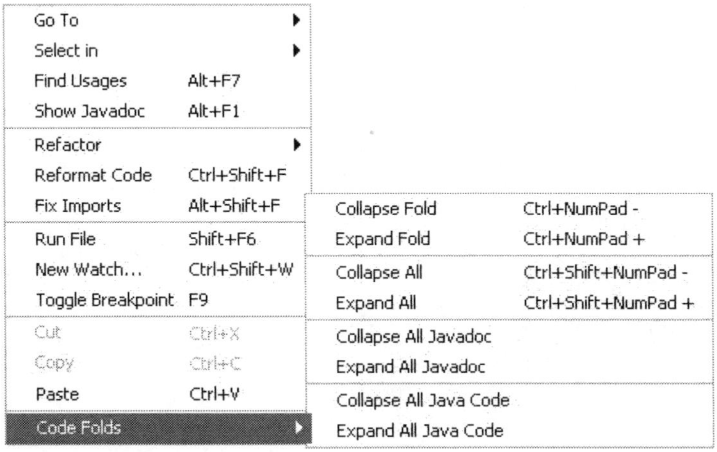

Figure 4–5 **Code Folds**

Handling Imports

There are several ways to manage import statements in Creator. Here are the choices:

- Fast Import (**<Alt+Shift+I>**) - lets you add an import statement to your code for the currently selected identifier. Figure 4–6, for example, shows an Import Class dialog for the selected identifier, `ListDataProvider`. Although only one import shows up here, this technique lets you choose the import statement you want from a list in the dialog.
- Fix Imports (**<Alt+Shift+F>**) - lets you insert any missing import statements for the entire file. Figure 4–7 shows the context menu when you right-click in the editor window and move the cursor to the Fix Imports selection.
- Code Completion - you can also generate import statements with code completion. Just type part of the class name with an open code completion box and an import statement will be added to your code automatically.

Using Javadoc

A Javadoc popup window appears for any selected class when you type **<Ctrl+Shift+Space>**. Press **<Esc>** to remove it. Additionally, you may open a web browser for a selected class within the IDE. Just right-click the class and choose Show Javadoc (or **<Alt+F1>**) from the context menu. You may close the internal browser window by clicking the **x** in the Javadoc tab.

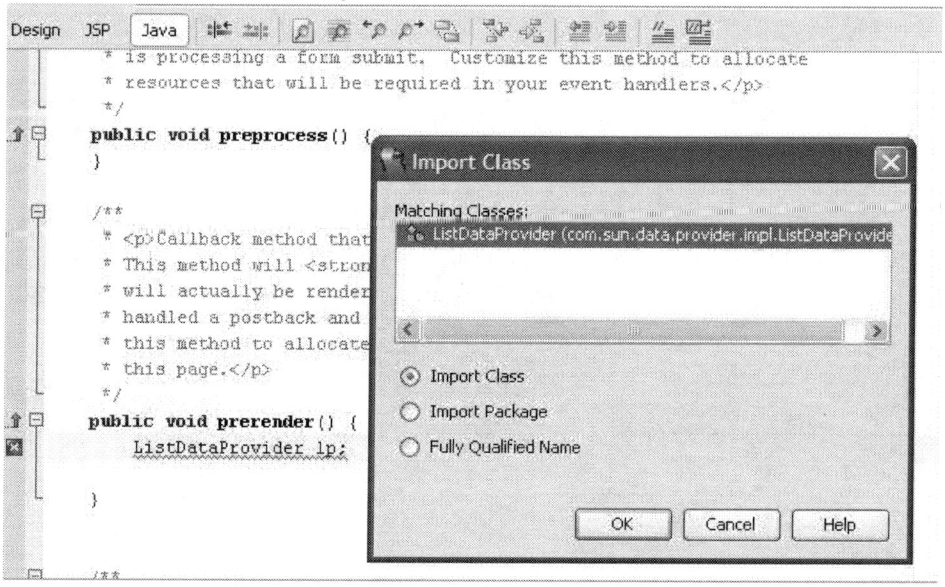

Figure 4–6 **Fast Import using <Alt+Shift+I>**

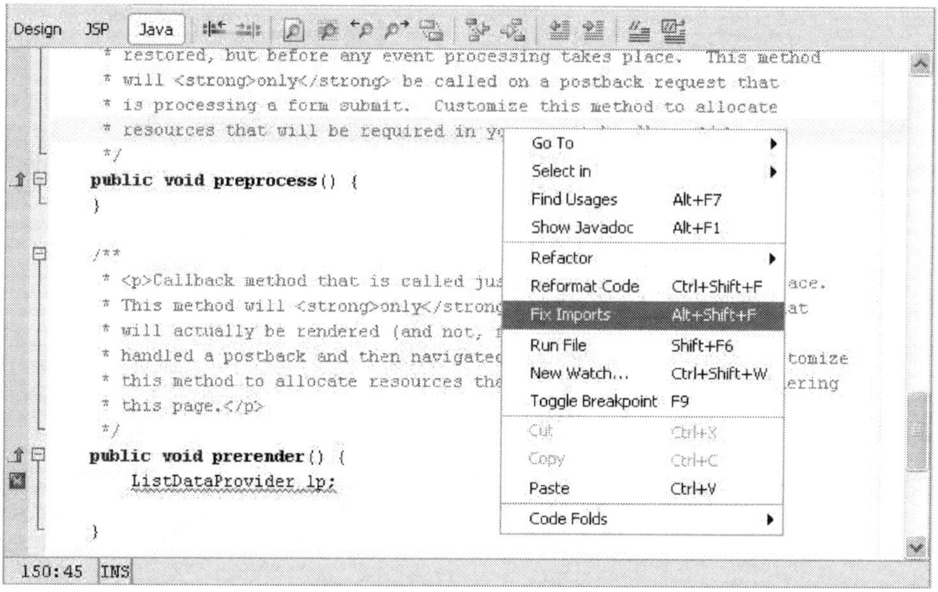

Figure 4–7 **Fix Imports using <Alt+Shift+F>**

Abbreviations

The editor has an internal list of abbreviations that generate commonly used keywords, identifiers, and code idioms. Just click on the Abbreviations customizer box in the Basic Options dialog under General (see Figure 4–1). Figure 4–8 shows the default list of abbreviations. Type the abbreviation, press the **<Space>**, and the editor fills in the expanded keywords or expressions for you. If an abbreviation is the same as the text you want to type, press **<Shift+Space>** to keep it from expanding.

The `fora` and `fori` abbreviations are very handy for generating `for` loops and the `trc`, `trcf`, and `trf` abbreviations for `try`/`catch`/`finally` can save a lot of typing time. Note that the Abbreviations dialog allows you to edit or remove an abbreviation or add your own.

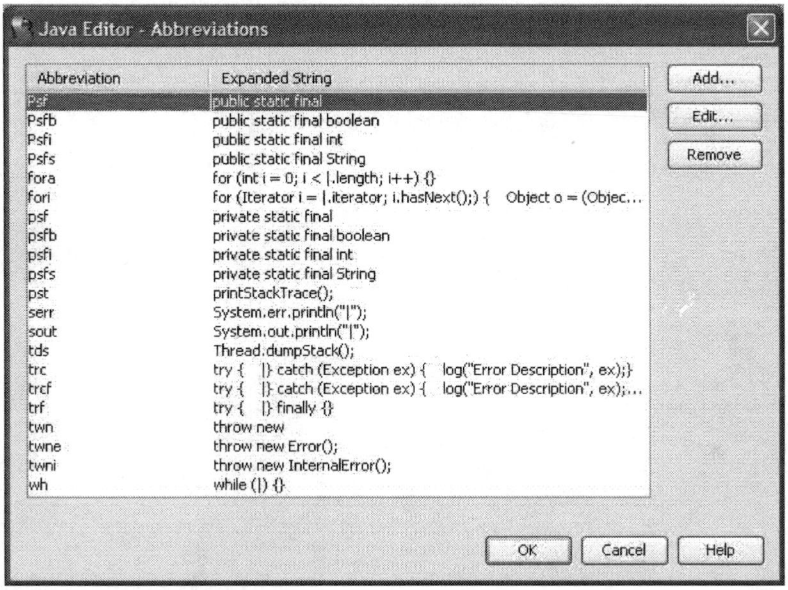

Figure 4–8 **Abbreviations Dialog**

Generating Methods

The IDE helps you generate code when extending a class or implementing an interface. Let's show you how to do this now.

Overriding Methods

When you extend a class, overriding multiple methods and getting everything right can be a tedious process. Creator's IDE has an Override and Implement

Methods dialog to help you generate the code from a list of allowable methods for an extended class. Here are the steps.

1. Define your class and type `extends` *`ClassName`*.
2. Select Tools > Override Methods from the toolbar (or press **<Ctrl+I>**).
3. Select the method(s) you want the IDE to override for your extended class.

Figure 4–9 shows the Override and Implements Methods dialog for a class extended from `ListProvider`. Here we override the `appendRow()` and `canInsertRow()` methods. The Generate Super Calls checkbox makes the IDE include calls to the super implementation of the method. Uncheck this box if you don't want this behavior.

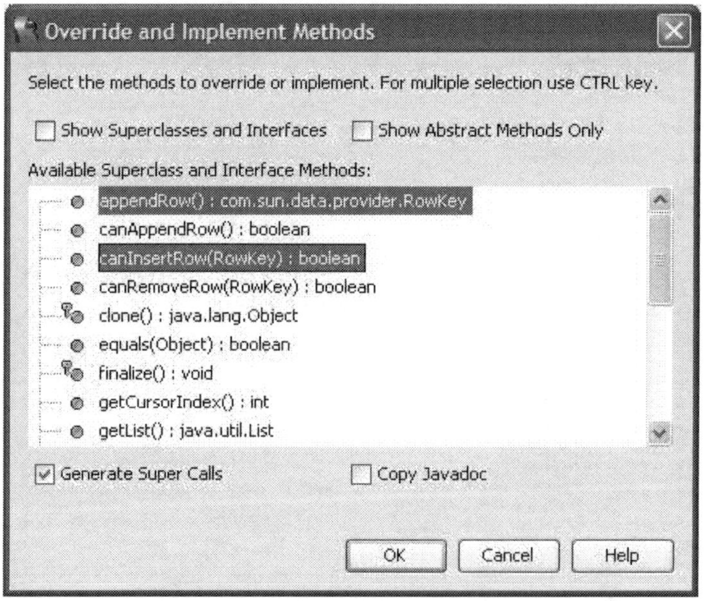

Figure 4–9 **Override and Implement Methods Dialog**

Implementing Interfaces

When you create a class that implements an interface, there can be many methods to implement. The IDE's Synchronize feature helps you generate the necessary methods. Here are the steps.

1. Define your class and type `implements` *`InterfaceName`*.
2. Select Tools > Synchronize from the toolbar.
3. Select the method(s) you want the IDE to implement.

You can also have the IDE automatically prompt you to generate methods when you create a class that implements an interface. Here are the steps.

1. Select Tools > Options from the toolbar and click the Advanced radio button.
2. Expand the Editing > Java Sources node and select Source Synchronization. Under General in the properties window, select the Synchronization Enabled checkbox.

Figure 4–10 shows a Confirm Changes dialog when creating a class that implements the `DataProvider` interface.

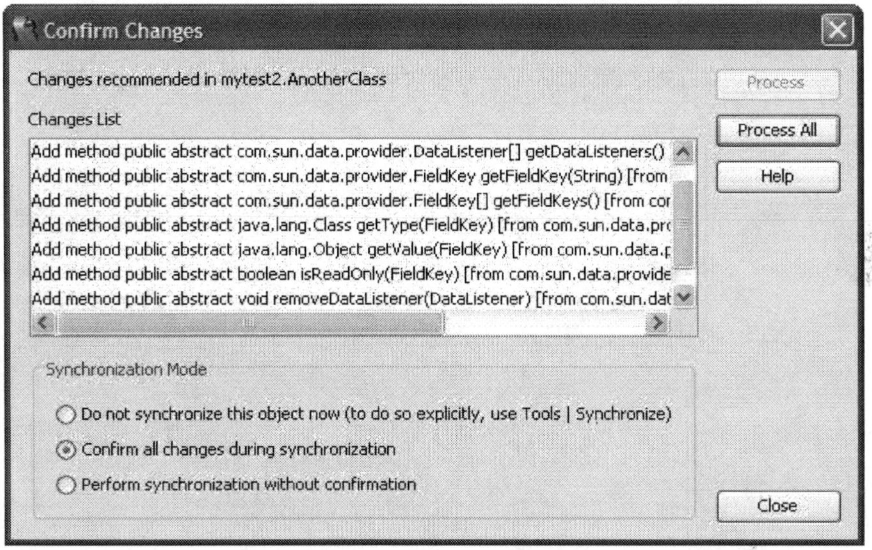

Figure 4–10 **Confirm Changes Dialog for Implementing Interfaces**

Generating Properties

With the IDE, it's easy to generate properties that conform to the JavaBeans component model. Here are the steps.

1. In the Projects window, expand your project node.
2. Right-click on a bean pattern node (Session Bean, Application Bean, etc.)
3. Choose Add > Property.
4. In the New Property Pattern dialog, type in the name of your property and select its type (String is the default). Under Mode, select Read/Write (default), Read Only, or Write Only.
5. Choose the options you want for code generation of the property.
6. When you click OK, the IDE will generate a field for the property and the getter and setter methods for the field.

Figure 4–11 shows a New Property Pattern dialog for the `status` property.

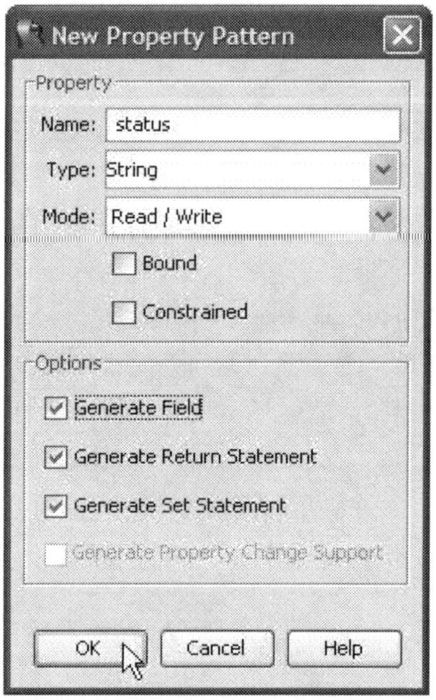

Figure 4–11 **New Property Pattern Dialog**

Searching and Replacing

The IDE has several find commands that help you search and replace in your code. These commands work with the current open file or with other project files. Let's show you how to use these different find commands.

Find Command

Selecting Edit > Find from the toolbar (or typing **<Ctrl+F>**) lets you find specific character combinations in your current open file. You can match case, look for whole words, search backwards, and use regular expressions in your search. After you close a Find dialog, you can move to the next occurrence with **<F3>** or move to the previous occurrence with **<Shift+F3>**.

To search and replace, select Edit > Replace from the toolbar (or type **<Ctrl+H>**) and fill in the fields for Find What and Replace With. Figure 4–12 shows a Find command that searches for `isRowAvailable` in the current open file.

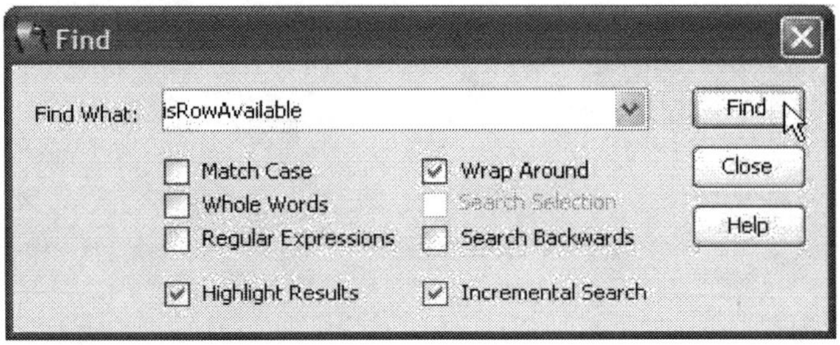

Figure 4–12 **Find command**

Find Usages Command

The Find Usages command displays lines in your project according to what you specify. Just select Edit > Find Usages from the toolbar (or type **<Alt+F7>**). You may also bring up this command by right-clicking on a class, method, or field name and selecting Find Usages from the context menu. The Find Usages command is case-insensitive and doesn't match parts of words, but you can have it look for a variety of different things, such as:

- Class, interface, method, or field declarations
- Method declarations or variables of classes and interfaces
- Specific occurrences, like new instances, imports, extending classes, implementing interfaces, casts, and throwing exceptions
- Methods or fields of a specific type
- Getters and setters of a field
- Method invocation
- Overriding methods
- Comments that refer to an identifier

The results of the Find Usages command appear in a separate Usages window at the bottom of your screen (like the Output window). Figure 4–13 shows an example of a Usages window. Here we show the results of a Find Usages command for the variable `retValue`. Double-clicking on any of the `retValue` occurrences takes you to the spot in the file where it's used.

Find in Projects Command

The Find in Projects command lets you search project files for characters in a file, filename characters, file type, file modification dates, and version control status. Just select Edit > Find in Projects (or type **<Ctrl+Shift+F>**) from the toolbar, or right-click a folder in the Files window and select Find from the context menu. Figure 4–14 shows the Find in Projects dialog for the text `SessionBean`.

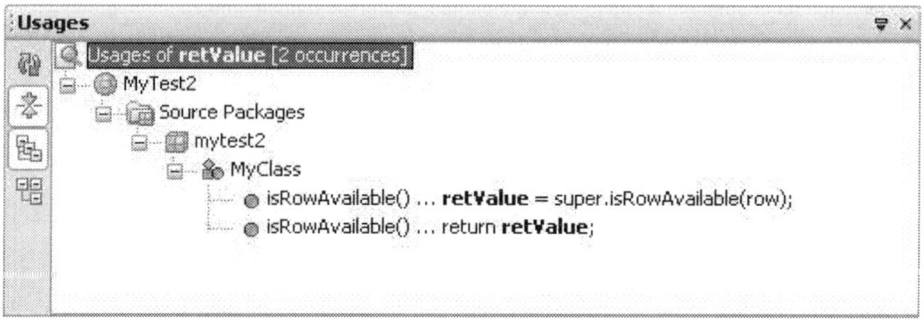

Figure 4–13 **Find Usages command**

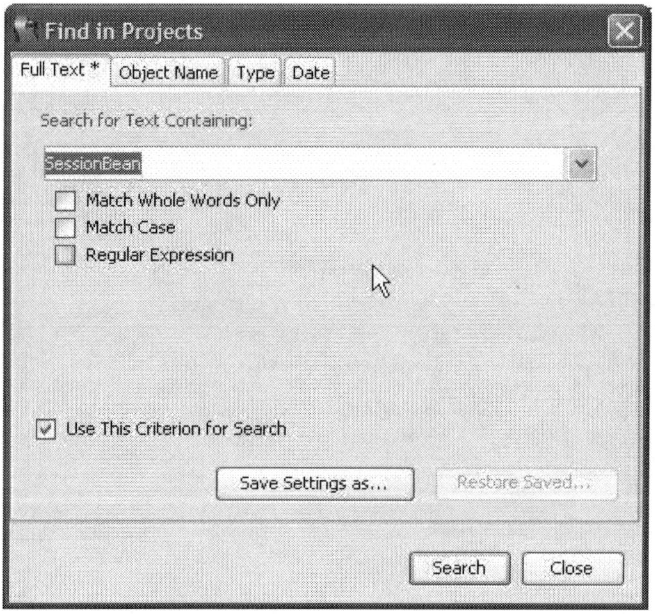

Figure 4–14 **Find in Projects command**

The results of a Find in Projects command appear in a Search Results window at the bottom of your screen. With full-text searches, you can expand nodes to see which files contain your patterns. Double-clicking on any of the occurrences takes you to the spot in the file where it is used. Figure 4–15 shows the Search Results window for the text `SessionBean`.

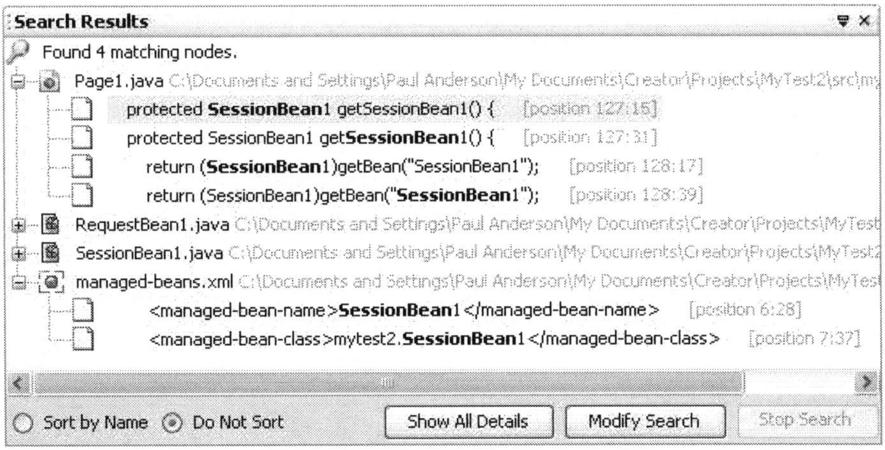

Figure 4–15 **Search Results window**

Navigating Files

When you right-click in the editor window and select Go To, a context menu lists ways to navigate from your current file to other places. You may navigate to the super implementation of a class, a specific line number, a declaration, or to the source code for a class, method, or field. Figure 4–16 shows the context menu for Go To and its shortcuts.

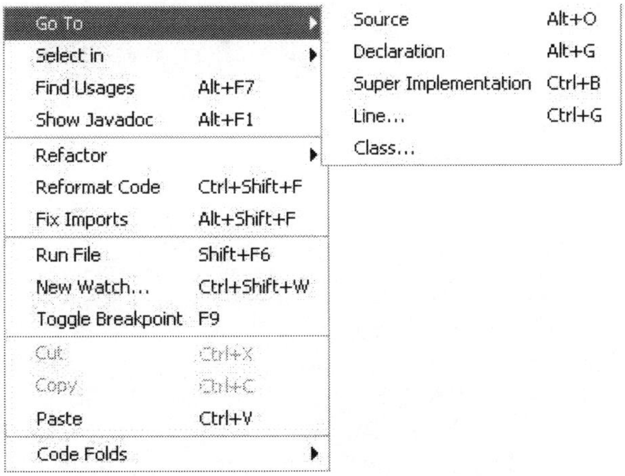

Figure 4–16 **Navigation with Go To**

If you right-click in the editor window and choose Select in, you can navigate to other project files or to other files in the same package. These options are also available from the toolbar by clicking Window > Select Document in. Figure 4–17 shows the context menu for Select In and its shortcuts.

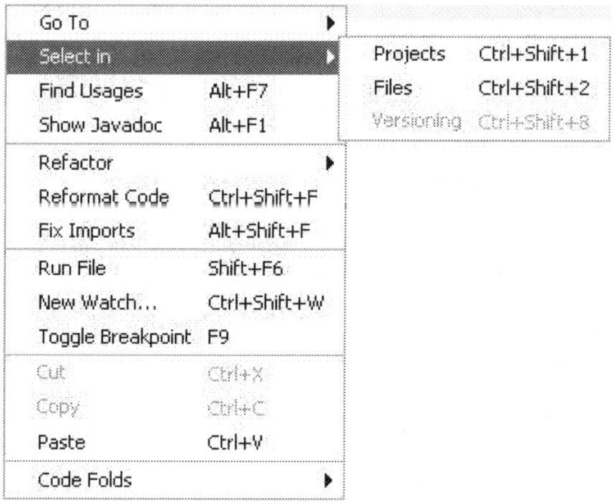

Figure 4–17 **Navigation with Select in**

Task Lists

During a hectic software development project, who wants to write notes on post-its to remind themselves to do something important? To help with this, the IDE supports *task lists.* Task lists provide a way to document and clean up any loose ends in your code.

Task lists manage special "tag" words that you mark in your code. These tag words typically appear in comments, such as

```
// TODO: add your event handler here..
// PENDING: Gail will write this code
```

To see what tag words are available for your task list, click Tools > Options from the toolbar, click the Advanced radio button, and select the Editing > To Do Settings node. Click the Task tags customizer box to see the list of tags and their priorities. Figure 4–18 shows the Task Tags dialog.
Note that it's possible to change or delete the default list of tags, and you can add you own tag to the task list. You can also change a tag's priority. The available priorities are High, Medium-High, Medium, Medium-Low, and Low. By default, all tags have Medium priority, except the <<<<<< tag, which has High priority.

To view the task list, select View > To Do (or type **<Ctrl+6>**) from the toolbar. This brings up the To Do window, which appears at the bottom of your screen (like the Output window). Inside the To Do window, you can view tasks for the

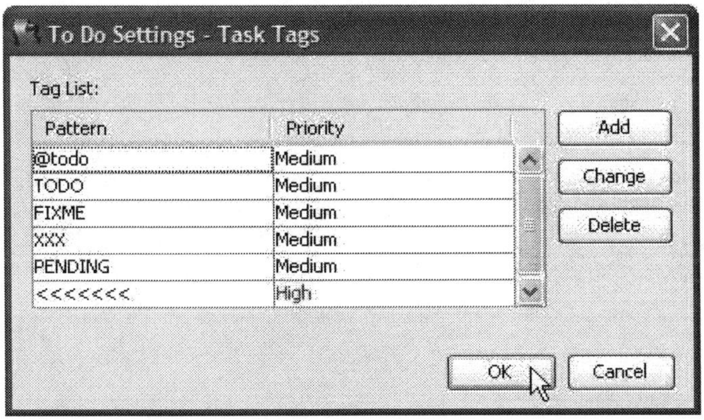

Figure 4–18 **Task Tags dialog**

current file, all open files, or for a specific folder. If you right-click in the window and select List Options, you can sort the task list by task, location, or priority. If you double-click any tag line in the task list, the editor highlights the source code line in the file where the tag appears. Figure 4–19 shows an example of a task list in the To Do window for opened files.

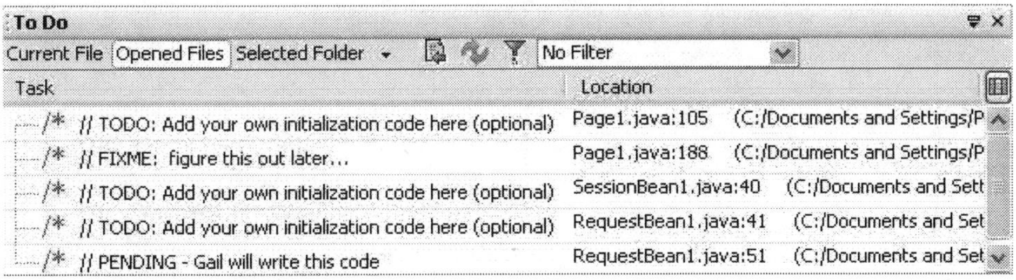

Figure 4–19 **To Do window**

The To Do window also supports a handy feature called *filters*, which allow you to limit what you see in this window. If you click on the filter icon (to the left of the combo box on the toolbar), the IDE brings up an Edit Filters dialog. To create a new filter, click on the New button and type a filter name in the Name field. Below this, you may specify more than one criteria and match any or all of the criteria. When you're done, your newly defined filter will appear in the combo box on the toolbar of the To Do window.

Figure 4–20 shows you how to create a filter for the PENDING tag. This makes the To Do window display only the PENDING tag lines when you select PENDING in the Combo box.

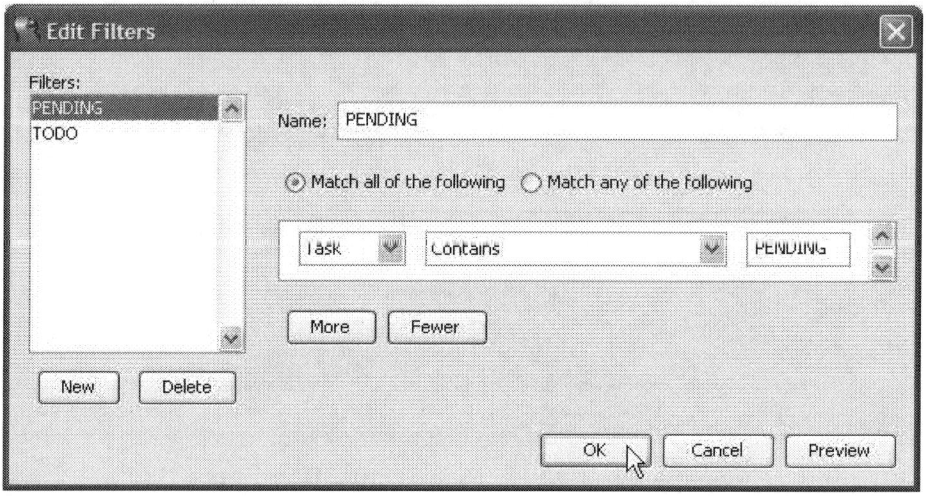

Figure 4–20 **Task Edit Filters dialog**

4.2 Refactoring

Sometimes you need to make "global" changes to your project, like renaming a heavily-used class, field, or method. You might also have to add a new parameter to a method or move a class to a different package. You could do these things manually, but it would be tedious, error-prone, and well, a lot of work. A better approach is to have the IDE help you. Making these kinds of modifications is called *refactoring*. In this section we'll show you how to use the refactoring features of the IDE. This knowledge can save you a lot of time, especially in large projects with many files.

What is Refactoring?

Refactoring is transforming and restructuring source code so that the refactored code behaves the same as the original source. In an object-oriented development environment like Java, refactoring must apply to classes, fields, and methods. Some examples of refactoring are relatively simple, like renaming a class, field, or a method. Other types of refactoring are more complicated, like changing the signature of a method or moving a class to a different package.

Here are several reasons why you would refactor your source code.

- You want to add a new feature to your code.

- You need to remove unnecessary repetitions.
- You want to reduce complexity for better understanding.
- You want to make your code more maintainable for others.

Let's explore how Creator's IDE helps you refactor. We'll show you how to use the refactoring features in the IDE and explain how to use them with existing projects. As you will see, the IDE not only lets you preview the changes before you make them, but the IDE also gives you a chance to undo your refactoring changes if you make a mistake.

Here are the refactoring features in the IDE.

- ***Find Usages*** - determine where classes, fields, and methods are used in your source code.
- ***Renaming*** - change the name of a class, field, or method. Automatically updates all the references to these elements in your source code.
- ***Encapsulating Fields*** - generates getter and setter methods for fields. Optionally updates all references to a field using the getters and setters.
- ***Change Method Signatures*** - add parameters to methods and change the method's visibility.
- ***Move Classes*** - move a class to another package or inside another class. Automatically updates your source code to reference the class from its new location.

Refactoring Window

All the refactoring commands make use of a refactoring window, which appears at the bottom of your screen in the IDE (in the same place as the output window). This window is created when you execute a refactoring command. The window provides a preview of files and class elements that are affected by each refactoring command.

Here's what you can do in the Refactoring window.

- Allow or disallow a refactoring change.
- Open the file in the editor for the line(s) to be refactored.
- Refresh the refactoring preview.
- Exit without making any changes.
- Apply the refactoring changes.

We'll show you how to use the refactoring window in the forthcoming examples.

Payment Project

Let's begin with an existing Creator project called **Payment1**, a monthly payment calculator. (Project Payment1 is in the download for this book under **FieldGuide2/Examples/JavaBeans/Projects**.) Open Project Payment1 and deploy it by selecting Run Main Project on the Creator toolbar (or click the Run icon). When the web page comes up in your browser, you will see the payment for a default loan amount, interest rate, and loan term. Try different values for each parameter and click the Calculate button to see the recalculated loan payment.

We'll actually have you build this project from scratch in a later chapter, but let's use it now to demonstrate refactoring.

Copy Project

This step is optional. If you don't want to copy the project, simply skip this section and make modifications to the **Payment1** project.

1. Bring up project **Payment1** in Creator, if it's not already opened.
2. From the Projects window, right-click node Payment1 and select Save Project As. Provide the new name **PaymentRF**.
3. Close project Payment1. Right-click PaymentRF and select Set Main Project. You'll make changes to the PaymentRF project.
4. Expand PaymentRF > Web Pages and open **Page1.jsp** in the design view.
5. Click anywhere in the background of the design canvas of the PaymentRF project. In the Properties window, change the page's `Title` property to **Payment Calculator - Refactor**.

Find Usages

When it's time to refactor, the first thing you'll want to do is issue a Find Usages command. You already know how to determine where classes, fields, and methods are used in your source code (see "Find Usages Command" on page 147), but let's look at this technique again as it relates to refactoring.

The Payment Calculator project uses a LoanBean class to calculate payments from the input parameters supplied on the web page. Let's use the Find Usages command to determine where this LoanBean class is used in our source code.

1. Bring up the Projects view, if it is not already opened.
2. Expand the Source Packages > asg.bean_examples node.
3. Right-click **LoanBean.java** and select Find Usages in the context menu.
4. In the Find Usages dialog, click the Search in Comments checkbox, then click the Next button.

5. The IDE displays a Usages window. Click the Show Physical View icon in the bottom left margin of the window. The Usages window shows you all the occurrences of the LoanBean class in the project (see Figure 4–21).
6. Double-click any of the LoanBean references in the window. This takes you to the appropriate line in **LoanBean.java** or **SessionBean1.java** where these statements appear.

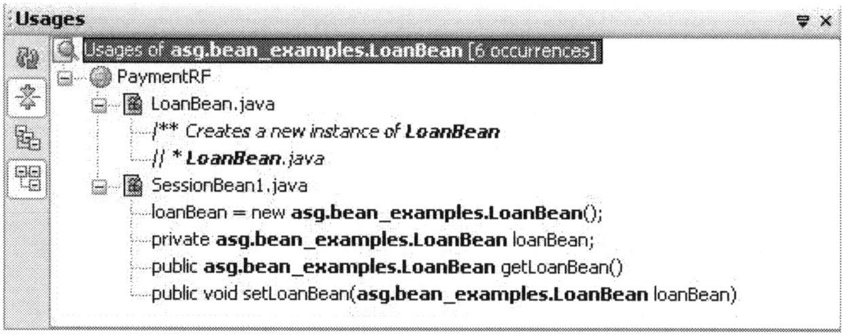

Figure 4–21 **Find Usages for LoanBean**

Renaming Classes

Let's change the name of the LoanBean class in this project. The Find Usages command shows the LoanBean object is instantiated in **SessionBean1.java**. It also lists the other places in this file where the LoanBean class is referenced.

Here are the refactoring steps to change the name of the LoanBean class and all its references in the project.

1. Double-click **LoanBean.java** in the Projects view. This brings up this file in the editor window.
2. Find the LoanBean class declaration in **LoanBean.java** and right-click the LoanBean name. Select Refactor > Rename from the context menu.
3. In the Rename dialog, type **MyLoanBean** in the New Name field and click the Apply Rename on Comments checkbox.
4. Make sure the Preview All Changes checkbox is checked in the Rename dialog.
5. Click the Next button.
6. The IDE displays a Refactoring window. Click the Show Physical View icon in the bottom left margin of the window. Figure 4–22 shows seven occurrences (including comments) of the LoanBean class in the project.

The Refactoring window lists all the occurrences of LoanBean in two files, **LoanBean.java** and **SessionBean1.java**. The checkboxes next to each refactoring line let you allow (checked) or disallow (unchecked) the refactoring. There are buttons in the left margin of the window to refresh the refactoring data, col-

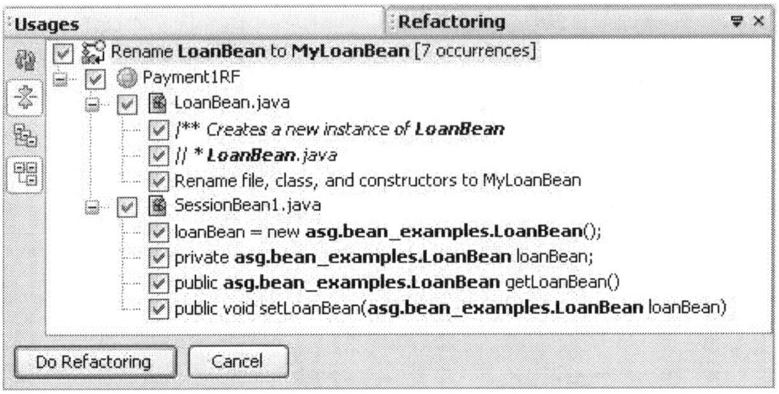

Figure 4–22 **Refactoring window**

lapse the nodes in the tree, and show the logical and physical views of the refactoring lines.

Let's finish the class name refactoring now.

1. Leave all the checkboxes checked in the Refactoring window.
2. Click the Do Refactoring button.
3. Click the **x** in the top right corner of the Usages window to remove this window from the display.
4. Verify that the file name **MyLoanBean.java** now appears in the Projects view.
5. Right-click the MyLoanBean class name in **MyLoanBean.java** and select Find Usages in the context menu. In the Find Usages dialog, make sure the Search in Comments checkbox is still checked.
6. Click the Next button. In the Usages window, click the Show Physical View icon in the bottom left margin of the window. You should see the newly applied changes from the refactoring, including MyLoanBean as the new class name (Figure 4–23).
7. Right-click the PaymentRF project in the Projects window and select Clean and Build Project (this may take a few moments). Verify that your project compiles without errors.

Undo and Redo

Everything should have worked fine here, but let's show you the Undo and Redo commands anyway. Select Refactor > Undo [Rename] from the Creator toolbar (you can also right-click in the editor and select this from the context menu). You'll see all your refactoring changes restored back to their original values. This can be very valuable when you realize that a refactoring did not do exactly what you wanted.

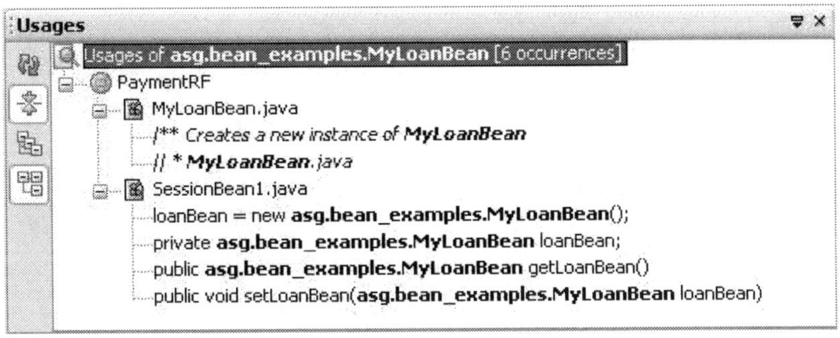

Figure 4–23 **Find Usages for MyLoanBean**

After an undo command, it's possible to redo refactoring changes by selecting Refactor > Redo [Rename] from the toolbar or from the context menu. Let's leave our changes undone for now and show you another way to refactor classes.

Refactoring for Renamed Files

Refactoring is also done when you rename class files in the Projects or Files window. This brings up the Refactor Code for Renamed File(s) dialog. Let's show you how to rename your LoanBean class with this technique.

1. Switch from the Projects view to the Files view.
2. Under PaymentRF, open the src > asg > bean_examples node.
3. Right-click **LoanBean.java** and select Rename.
4. In the Rename dialog, type **MyLoanBean** in the New Name field. Click OK.
5. The Refactor Code for Renamed File(s) dialog appears (see Figure 4–24). Click Next.
6. The IDE displays a Refactoring window. Click the Show Physical View icon in the bottom left margin of the window. The refactoring changes should be the same as what you did before (see Figure 4–22 on page 156).
7. Click Do Refactoring.
8. Verify that the file name **MyLoanBean.java** now appears in the Files view.
9. Right-click the PaymentRF project in the Projects window and select Clean and Build Project (this may take a few moments). Verify that your project compiles without errors.

Creator Tip

Make sure you use the IDE to rename class files. If you rename your files with Windows explorer or other file system utilities, Creator won't be able to track your changes.

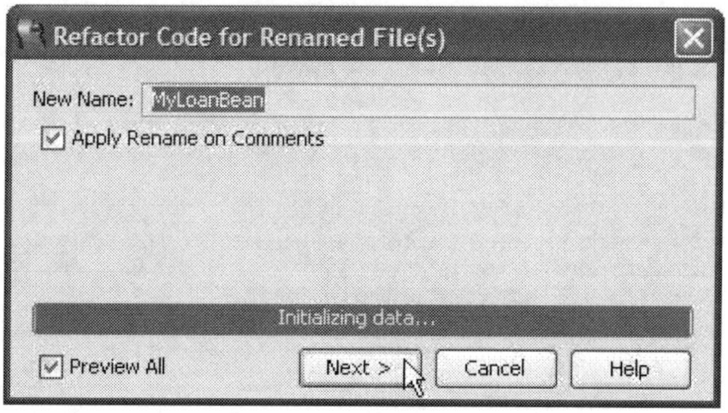

Figure 4–24 **Refactor code for renamed file**

Renaming Fields and Methods

Renaming a class field or method is done the same way as renaming a class. Here are the steps.

1. Find the field or method you want to rename in the editor. In the Projects view, expand the source file nodes until you find the field or method you want.
2. Right-click the field or method and select Refactor > Rename from the context menu.
3. In the Rename dialog, type the New Name for the field or method.
4. Click the Next button.
5. In the Refactoring window, review the lines of code that will be refactored. Clear any checkboxes for code that you do not want changed.
6. Click the Do Refactoring button to make the changes.
7. Right-click on your project name in the Projects view and select Clean and Build Project. Verify that your project compiles without errors.

Creator Tip

Be careful with refactoring fields and methods of JavaBeans components. With JavaBeans, the setters and getters use naming conventions which could be disrupted by an improper refactoring. Refactoring JavaBeans could also adversely affect bindings and other assumptions made by the IDE.

Encapsulating Fields

Refactoring lets you encapsulate fields, which insures that class fields can only be accessed by getter and setter methods. This type of encapsulation enforces data hiding and improves maintainability. Typically, a class field's visibility is restricted to private, whereas the getter and setters for the field are marked as public. Other visibility choices are possible (protected with inheritance access, for instance).

The IDE supports the following refactoring features for Encapsulating Fields.

- Generate getter and setter methods for fields.
- Modify the visibility modifier for the fields and the getters and setters.
- Replace references to field names with calls to the getters or setters.

Let's modify our Payment Calculator project and show you how to encapsulate a field and generate setters and getters for the field. Here are the steps.

1. Open **MyLoanBean.java** in the editor if it is not already open.
2. Add the following field declaration to your code, right below the MyLoanBean constructor.

```
private String version = "Version 1.0";
```

3. Select the `version` field. Choose Refactor > Encapsulate Fields from the toolbar (or right-click the `version` field and select this option from the context menu).
4. In the Encapsulate Fields dialog, make sure the `version` field's checkbox is checked. Select `protected` in the combo boxes for both the Fields' Visibility and the Accessors' Visibility (see Figure 4–25). Click Next.
5. The IDE displays a Refactoring window. Click the Show Physical View icon in the bottom left margin of the window. The Refactoring window shows the changes that will be made to encapsulate the `version` field (Figure 4–26).

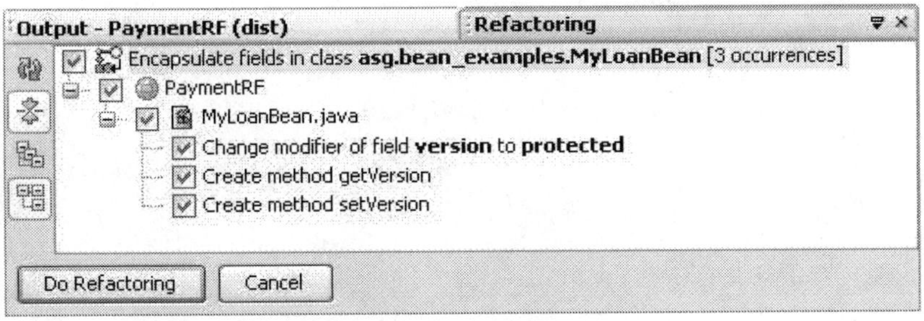

Figure 4–26 **Refactoring window for Encapsulate Fields**

6. Click Do Refactoring. Verify that the code for setter method `setVersion()` and getter method `getVersion()` now appear in **MyLoanBean.java** with protected visibility. The `version` field should be protected as well.

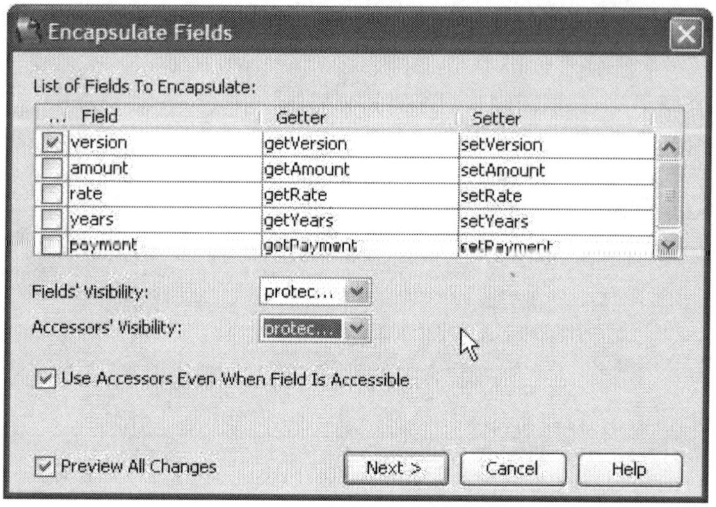

Figure 4–25 **Encapsulate Fields dialog**

7. Right-click your project name in the Projects view and select Clean and Build Project (this may take a few moments). Verify that your project compiles without errors.

Changing Method Signatures

The design of class methods is crucial to the behaviors of object-oriented designs and reusable classes. During the early stages of development, it's easy to develop methods with several parameters and change them when you need to. But near the end of a large development cycle, changing the signature of a heavily used class method can be a time-sink, because the change often propagates to a large number of invocations in source code. Refactoring can be a big help here, because the IDE can update all the method calls for you.

The IDE supports the following refactoring features for Changing Method Signatures.

- Add parameters to a method's signature.
- Reorder the parameters in a method's signature.
- Change the visibility for a method.

Creator Tip

Refactoring does not allow you to remove a parameter from a method's signature. You can't refactor a method's return type, either. If you need to do these things in your project, you'll have to do it manually.

Generate New Method

Before we show you how to refactor a method's signature, let's add a new method to the MyLoanBean class and call it from the Payment Calculator. Here are the steps.

1. Open **MyLoanBean.java** in the editor if it is not already open.
2. Add the following method to your code, right below the `setVersion()` and `getVersion()` methods.

```
public String getInfo() { return version; }
```

3. Return to **Page1.java** in the editor and click the Design button to bring up the design view.
4. Double-click the Calculate button. This generates a `calculate_action()` method in **Page1.java**. Add the following code before the return statement (new code is in **bold**).

```
public String calculate_action() {
   // TODO: Process the button click action...
   log(getSessionBean1().getLoanBean().getInfo());
   return null;
}
```

5. Click the Run icon on the toolbar to deploy the Payment Calculator application. Type input values on the page and click the Calculate button.
6. In the Servers window, right-click Deployment Server and select View Server Log.
7. In the Output window, you should see the string "Version 1.0" appear in the server log.

Add Method Parameter

Now let's add a new parameter to our `getInfo()` method and refactor it in our project. Here are the steps.

1. Select the `getInfo()` method in the editor. Select Refactor > Change Method Parameters from the toolbar (or right-click the `getInfo()` method and select this option from the context menu).
2. In the Change Method Parameters dialog, type **who** for Name, **String** for Type, and "paul" for Default Value. To edit these, you'll need to double-click each cell.
3. Leave the Access Modifier public and make sure the Preview All Changes checkbox is checked (see Figure 4–27). Click Next.

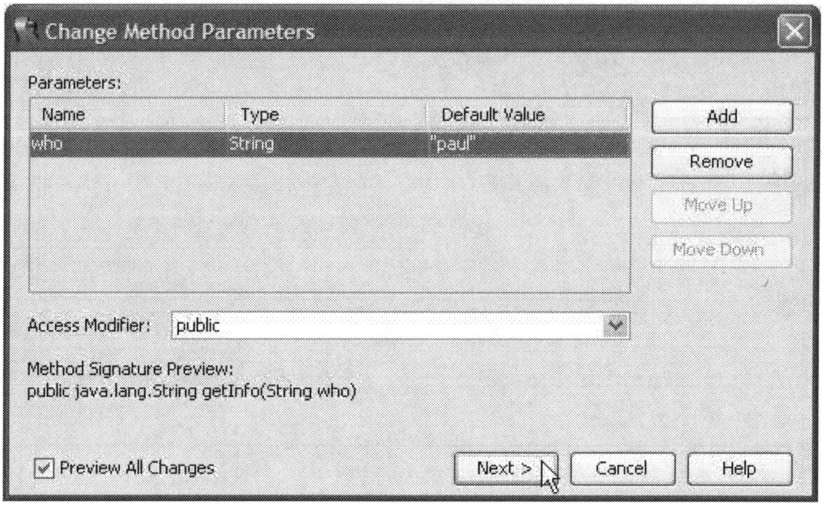

Figure 4–27 **Change Method Parameters dialog**

4. The IDE displays a Refactoring window. Click the Show Physical View icon in the bottom left margin of the window.The Refactoring window shows the changes that will be made to refactor the `getInfo()` method (see Figure 4–28).

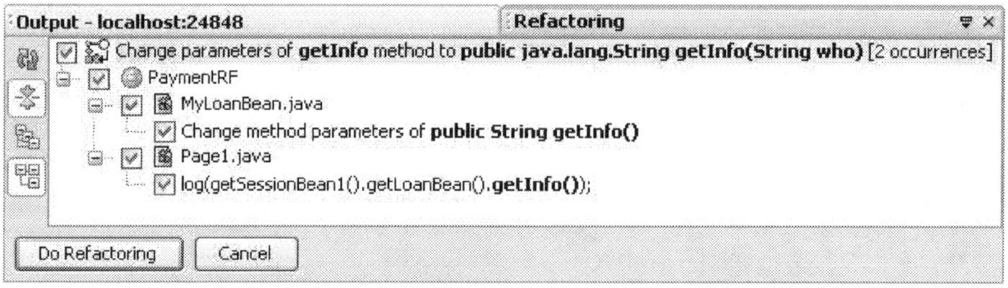

Figure 4–28 **Refactoring window for Changing a Method's signature**

5. Click Do Refactoring. Verify that a new parameter was added to the `get-Info()` method in **MyLoanBean.java**. Modify this code as follows (new code is **bold**).

```
public String getInfo(String who) {
  return version + "-" + who;
}
```

6. Verify that the call to `getInfo()` in **Page1.java** was modified, too. Here's what it should look like (new code is **bold**).

```
public String calculate_action() {
   // TODO: Process the button click action...
   log(getSessionBean1().getLoanBean().getInfo("paul"));
   return null;
}
```

Now deploy, run, and test the project.

1. Right-click your project name in the Projects view and select Clean and Build Project (this may take a few moments). Verify that your project compiles without errors.
2. Click the Run icon on the toolbar to deploy the Payment Calculator application. Type input values on the page and click the Calculate button.
3. In the Servers window, right-click Deployment Server and select View Server Log.
4. In the Output window, you should see the string "Version 1.0-paul" appear in the server log.

Reordering Parameters

Reordering parameters in a method's signature is done the same way as adding a parameter. Here are the steps.

1. Select the method you want in the editor. Select Refactor > Change Method Parameters from the toolbar (or right-click the method and select this option from the context menu).
2. Select the parameter you want to move and click Move Up or Move Down. This changes its position in the list. Click Next.
3. In the Refactoring window, review the lines of code that will be refactored. Clear any checkboxes for code that you do not want changed.
4. Click Do Refactoring to make the changes.
5. Right-click your project name in the Projects view and select Clean and Build Project. Verify that your project compiles without errors.

Changing a Method's Visibility

The refactoring commands for a method's visibility are very similar to the others. Here are the steps.

1. Select the method you want in the editor. Select Refactor > Change Method Parameters from the toolbar (or right-click the method and select this option from the context menu).

2. Select an Access Modifier for the method's visibility from the combo box (options are public, protected, private, or default). Click Next.
3. In the Refactoring window, review the lines of code that will be refactored. Clear any checkboxes for code that you do not want changed.
4. Click the Do Refactoring button to make the changes.
5. Right-click your project name in the Projects view and select Clean and Build Project. Verify that your project compiles without errors.

Creator Tip

Note that the code for the `getInfo()` *method refers to the* `version` *field directly. By refactoring, you can make this method use the getter method for the field instead. To do this, select the* `version` *field and choose Refactor > Encapsulate Fields. Make sure the checkbox is checked for Use Accessors Even When Field is Accessible. Click Do Refactoring. You will see code in* `getInfo()` *that now calls* `getVersion()` *to get the* `version` *field's value.*

Moving Classes to Different Packages

Another important refactoring feature is moving a class from one package to a another. This kind of code change can certainly be a hassle to do manually, so refactoring is a big help here.

There are two approaches for moving a class between packages, so let's show you how to do both. Here are the steps for the first approach.

Moving Classes

1. Bring up the Projects view, if it is not already opened.
2. Under PaymentRF, expand the Source Packages > asg.bean_examples node. Note that **MyLoanBean.java** is contained in this package (Figure 4–29).
3. Right-click **MyLoanBean.java** and select Refactor > Move Class from the context menu.
4. In the Move Class dialog, select **payment1** from the combo box for To Package (see Figure 4–30).
5. Make sure the Preview All Changes checkbox is checked. Click Next.
6. The IDE displays a Refactoring window. Click the Show Physical View icon in the bottom left margin of the window.The Refactoring window shows the refactoring statements that move the MyLoanBean class to the **payment1** package (Figure 4–31).
7. Click Do Refactoring to make the changes. Verify that **MyLoanBean.java** has been moved to the **payment1** package in the Projects View (see Figure 4–32).

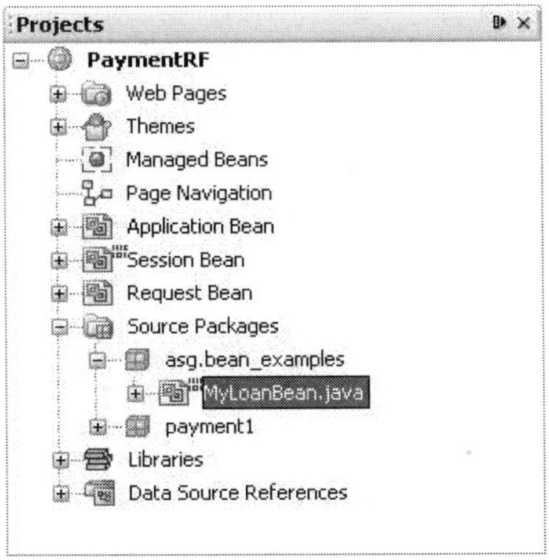

Figure 4–29 **Projects window before refactoring**

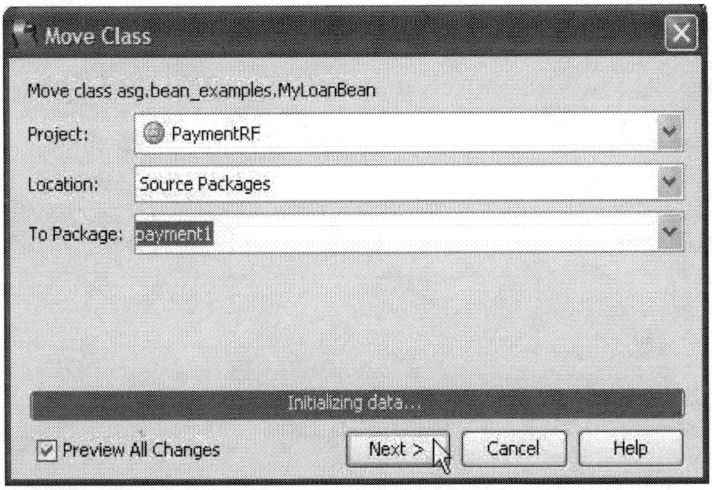

Figure 4–30 **Move Class dialog**

8. Right-click your project name in the Projects view and select Clean and Build Project (this may take a few moments). Verify that your project compiles without errors.
9. Click the Run icon on the toolbar to deploy the Payment Calculator application. Verify that everything works.

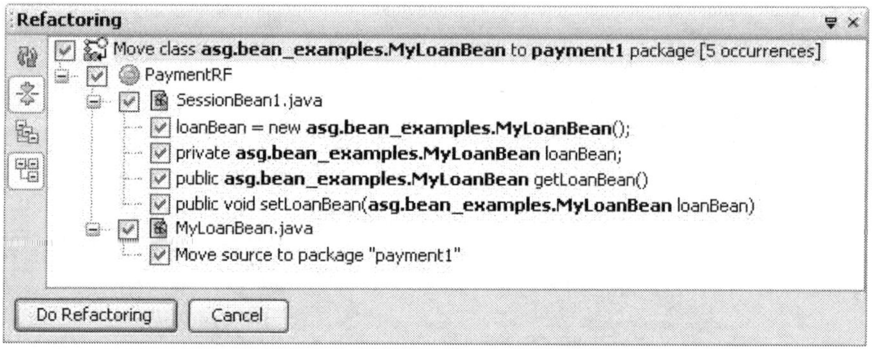

Figure 4–31 **Refactoring window for Move Class**

Figure 4–32 **Projects window after refactoring**

Refactoring for Moved Files

The IDE has other ways to move class files between packages. The Refactor Code for Moved Class dialog opens whenever you perform the following actions:

- Cut and paste files in the Projects or Files window.
- Drag and drop files in the Projects or Files window.

- Type a new package name in the Projects window for a package node.
- Type a new folder name in the Files window for a folder node.

Let's show you how to use this technique. Here are the steps.

1. Select Refactor > Undo [Move class] to put the MyLoanBean class back in the original package.
2. In the Projects view under PaymentRF, open the Source Packages > asg.bean_examples node.
3. Right-click **LoanBean.java** and select Cut.
4. Right-click package **payment1** and select Paste.
5. The Refactor Code for Moved Class dialog appears (Figure 4–33). Click

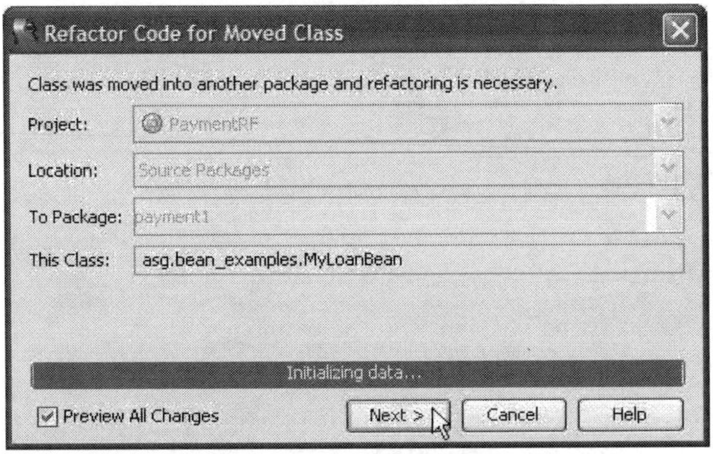

Figure 4–33 **Refactor Code for Moved Class dialog**

Next.

6. The IDE displays a Refactoring window. Click the Show Physical View icon in the bottom left margin of the window. The refactoring changes should be the same as what you did before (see Figure 4–31 on page 166).
7. Click Do Refactoring.
8. Verify that **MyLoanBean.java** has been moved to the **payment1** package in the Projects View (see Figure 4–32 on page 166).
9. Right-click the PaymentRF project in the Projects window and select Clean and Build Project (this may take a few moments). Verify that your project compiles without errors.

4.3 Source Code Control with CVS

Version control allows developers to track the changes they make to their source code. With version control, you can determine when a change was made and by whom. You can also use version control to track bugs and generate specific builds that might customize certain parts of your system. All this works for a single developer working on a project as well as a group working on the same project code.

Creator supports several Version Control Systems (VCS), but we'll show you CVS (Concurrent Versioning System) which is very popular with developers. You'll learn how to create CVS working directories and repositories, import source code into CVS, and check out modules. You'll also see how to commit editing changes to CVS, compare revisions, and examine log histories of code changes. As before, we'll use our Payment Calculator project to show you how to use CVS with Creator.

Copy Project

This step is optional. If you don't want to copy the project, simply skip this section and make modifications to the **Payment1** project.

1. Bring up project **Payment1** in Creator, if it's not already opened.
2. From the Projects window, right-click node Payment1 and select Save Project As. Provide the new name **PaymentCVS**.
3. Close project Payment1. Right-click PaymentCVS and select Set Main Project. You'll make changes to the PaymentCVS project.
4. Expand PaymentCVS > Web Pages and open **Page1.jsp** in the design view.
5. Click anywhere in the background of the design canvas of the PaymentCVS project. In the Properties window, change the page's `Title` property to **Payment Calculator - CVS**.

Setting up CVS

The IDE provides two ways to work with CVS in Creator. You can use the built-in CVS client in Creator (written in Java) that helps you connect to CVS repositories on remote machines. Or, you can install CVS locally and have the IDE work with CVS directly on your machine. This is the approach we'll show you here.

Installing CVS

If you don't have CVS installed on your system already, it's fairly easy to find an open source version on the web for CVS. Download the appropriate version for your machine and install it. Make sure you can run the **cvs** command from a command prompt window.

Create CVS Profile

In CVS, you will need to setup two directories: a *repository* directory, which stores a project's full revision history, and a *working* directory to store the files in your project. Here are the steps.

1. Outside the IDE, create a directory or folder for your CVS repository. Make sure this is a safe place where accidental deletions are unlikely (a **temp** directory, for instance, would be a poor choice).
2. Outside the IDE, create a directory or folder for your CVS working directory. (You can skip this step if you already have a directory with source files and you're willing to use this directory for version control.)
3. From the Creator toolbar, select Versioning > Versioning Manager. In the dialog box, click the Add button.
4. In the Add Versioned Directory dialog, select CVS for the System Profile.
5. Fill in the location of the CVS working directory you created in Step 2.
6. Set the Repository Path to the name of the CVS repository you created in Step 1.
7. Click the Use Command-Line CVS Client radio button and make sure **cvs** is set for your CVS executable.
8. Uncheck the Perform Checkout checkbox and Click Finish (see Figure 4–34).
9. When you return to the Add Versioned Directory dialog, you should see your working directory appear. Click Close to exit this dialog.

Initialize CVS Repository

Now that the CVS repository directory has been created, you need to initialize it. Here are the steps.

1. From the Creator toolbar, select Versioning > CVS > Init Local Repository. This brings up the CVS Init dialog.
2. Select your Repository Path in this dialog, click the Set As Default button to remember these values, then click OK (see Figure 4–35).

Importing Files

Now that you've setup and initialized your CVS directories, the next step is to import source files into the CVS repository. This is very straightforward, the only thing you have to watch are your own binary file types, like images and jar files.

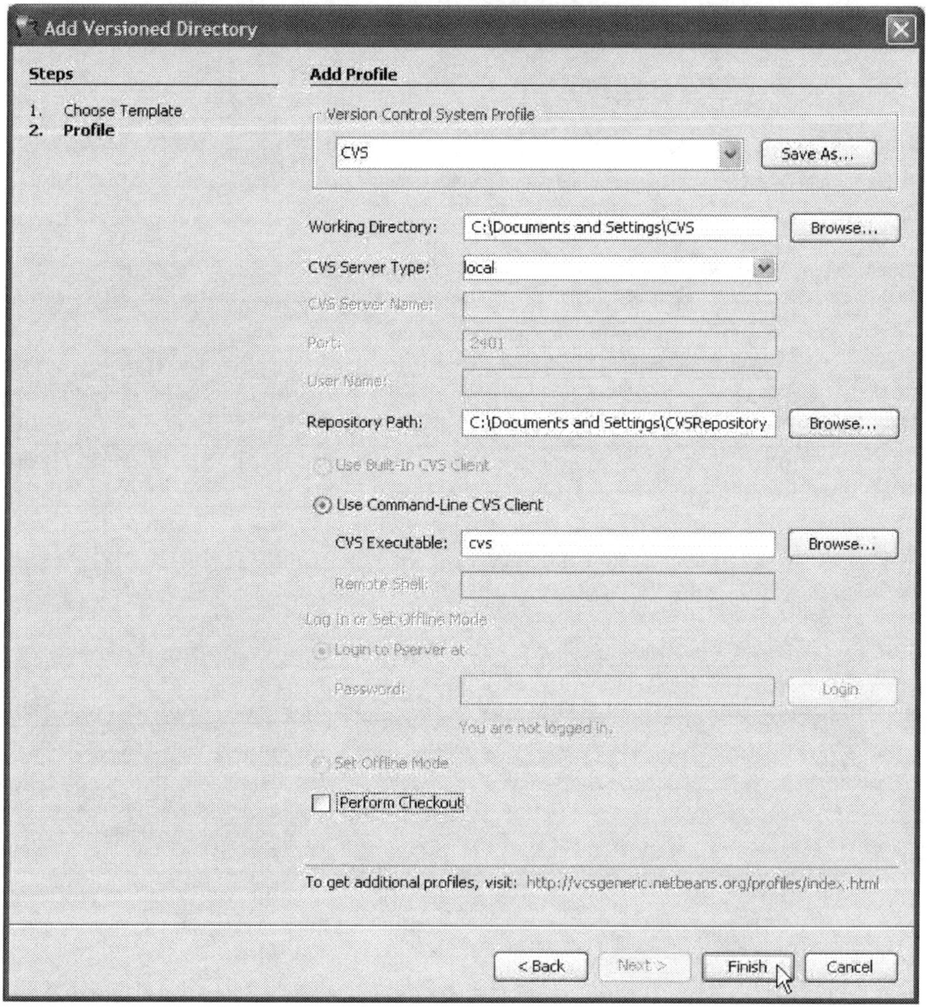

Figure 4–34 **CVS Profile Dialog**

Creator Tip

Version control works by storing your changes as textual diff statements. You don't want to import your own binary files (images, jar files, etc.) into the repository, because textual diffs won't work. The easiest thing to do is to remove binary files from your project directory before you import. After you checkout the files into your working directory, you can use the CVS > Add command to put the binary files back in your project. (See "Creator Tip" on page 180.)

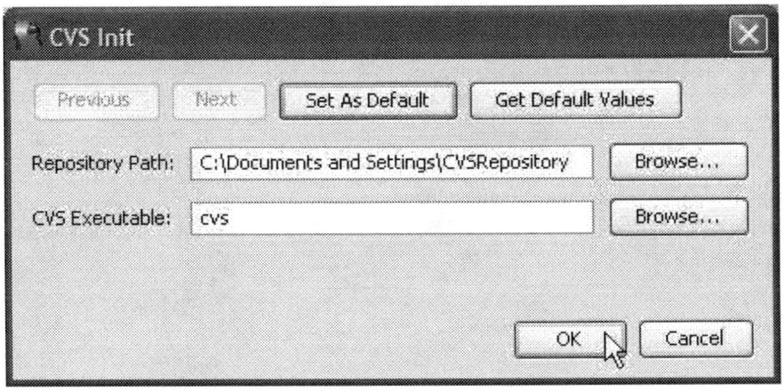

Figure 4–35 **Initialize CVS Repository**

Here are the steps to import the Payment source files into the CVS repository.

1. From the Creator toolbar, select Versioning > CVS > Import. This brings up the CVS Import dialog.
2. In this dialog, set Directory to Import to the location of your source files to import.
3. Choose **local** for the CVS Server Type.
4. Set the Repository Path to your CVS repository directory.
5. Type **PaymentCVS** for your Repository directory.
6. Click the Use Command-Line CVS Client radio button and make sure **cvs** is set for your CVS executable.
7. Fill in Logging Message, Vendor Tag, and Release Tag as shown, and uncheck the Perform Checkout After Import checkbox.
8. Click the Set As Default button to store these values.
9. Click OK (see Figure 4–36). In the VCS Output window under Standard Output, you should see a list of imported files in your repository.

Checking Out Files

Now that the files are residing in the CVS repository, you must check them out into your CVS working directory. This directory is where you will make your changes under version control. Here are the steps.

1. From the Creator toolbar, select Versioning > CVS > Check Out. This brings up the CVS Checkout dialog.
2. In this dialog, set the Working Directory to the name of your CVS working directory.
3. Choose **local** for the CVS Server Type.
4. Set the Repository Path to your CVS repository directory.

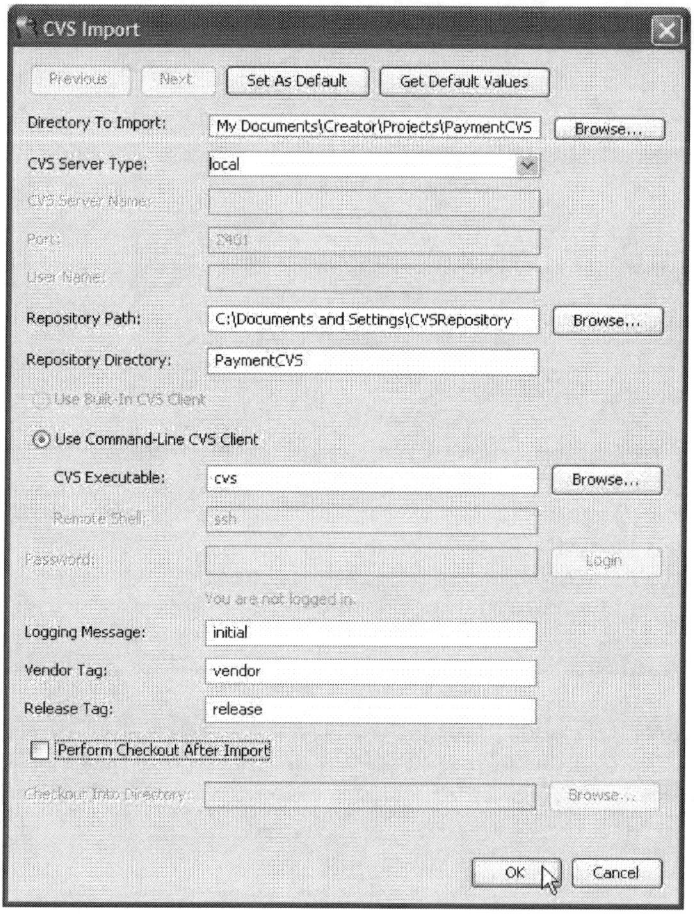

Figure 4–36 **CVS Import Dialog**

5. Click the Use Command-Line CVS Client radio button and make sure **cvs** is set for your CVS executable.
6. Click the Module(s) radio button and type in **PaymentCVS**.
7. Click OK (see Figure 4–37). In the VCS Output window under Standard Output, you should see a list of checked-out files in your working directory.

Updating Source Files

In this section we'll show you how to access files in your working directory, edit their contents, then update them under CVS version control.

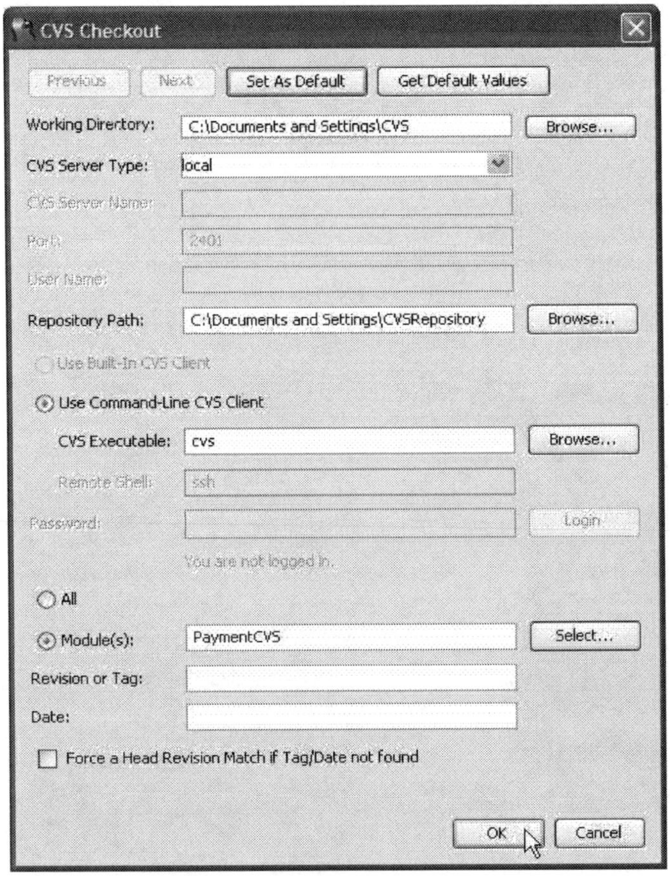

Figure 4–37 **CVS Checkout Dialog**

Versioning Window

Before you make a change to your code, let's open the Versioning window and see what the PaymentCVS project looks like. Here are the steps.

1. From the Creator toolbar, Select View > Versioning > Versioning (or type **<Ctrl+8>**).
2. The Versioning window appears in the top left portion of the screen. Expand the source nodes for src > asg > bean_examples > LoanBean.java, src > payment1 > Page1.java, and web > Page1.jsp (see Figure 4–38).

Note that all **.java** and **.jsp** files are listed as Up-to-date with 1.1.1.1 being the Initial revision.

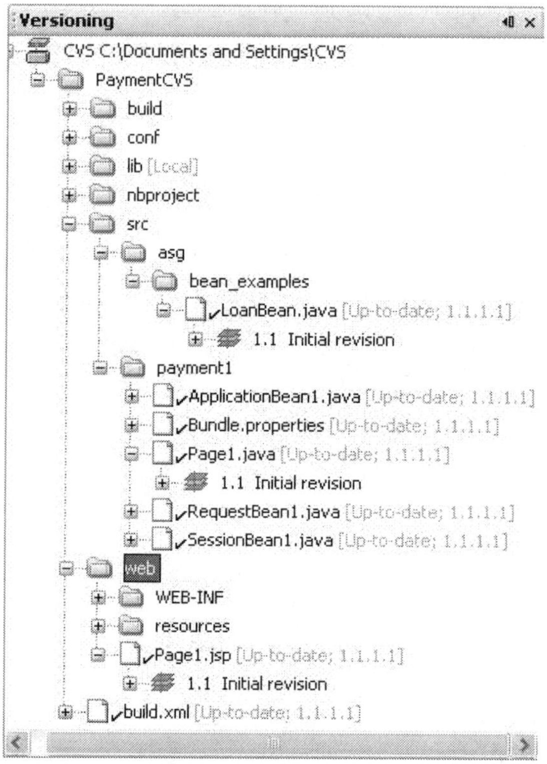

Figure 4–38 **CVS Versioning Window**

Editing Source Files

Let's modify our project code and test it. Here are the steps.

1. Bring up **Page1.jsp** in the Design view. On the page for the Payment Calculator, double click the Calculate button. This generates a `calculate_action()` button handler code in **Page1.java**.
2. Let's write to the log file for a button push. Add the following code before the return statement (new code is in **bold**).

```
public String calculate_action() {
   // TODO: Process the button click action...
   log("Version 1.1");
   return null;
}
```

3. Save your changes. Note that **Page1.java** and **Page1.jsp** are marked as Locally Modified in the Versioning window.
4. Click the Run icon on the toolbar to deploy the Payment Calculator application. Type input values on the page and click the Calculate button.
5. In the Servers window, right-click Deployment Server and select View Server Log.
6. In the Output window, you should see the string "Version 1.1" appear in the server log.

Committing Source Files

Now that you've tested the code to make sure it works, let's store your changes under version control. Here are the steps.

1. In the Versioning window, right-click **Page1.java** and select CVS > Update. This ensures that your local copies of the files are up-to-date. You should see a successful update appear in the VCS Output window under the Standard Output tab.
2. Right-click **Page1.java** again and choose CVS > Commit. This brings up a CVS Commit dialog for **Page1.java**.
3. In the window for Enter Reason, type **log button push**.
4. Follow these same steps for **Page1.jsp**. Provide the same input **log button push** for Enter Reason when you commit.
5. The Versioning window should now mark the **Page1.java** and **Page1.jsp** files Up-to-date as revision 1.2 (see Figure 4–39).

Comparing File Revisions

During a hectic software development cycle, it's often necessary to compare file revisions and track down what happens as code evolves. This helps everyone understand what changes were made, by whom, and when.

At this point, you have revision 1.1 (initial) and revision 1.2 (log button push) for both the **Page1.java** and **Page1.jsp** files. Let's look at **Page1.java** and show you how to see the changes you just made to the project for that file. Here are the steps.

1. In the Versioning window, right-click on the 1.1 Initial revision under **Page1.java** and select Diff Graphical.
2. A **Page1.java [VCS Diff]** graphical visualizer window appears, showing you the changes between revision 1.1 on the left and your working file (revision 1.2) on the right (see Figure 4–40).

The Graphical Visualizer gives you a side-by-side view of the changes in the main window. You'll see changed lines highlighted in blue, lines added since an earlier revision highlighted in green, and lines removed highlighted in red.

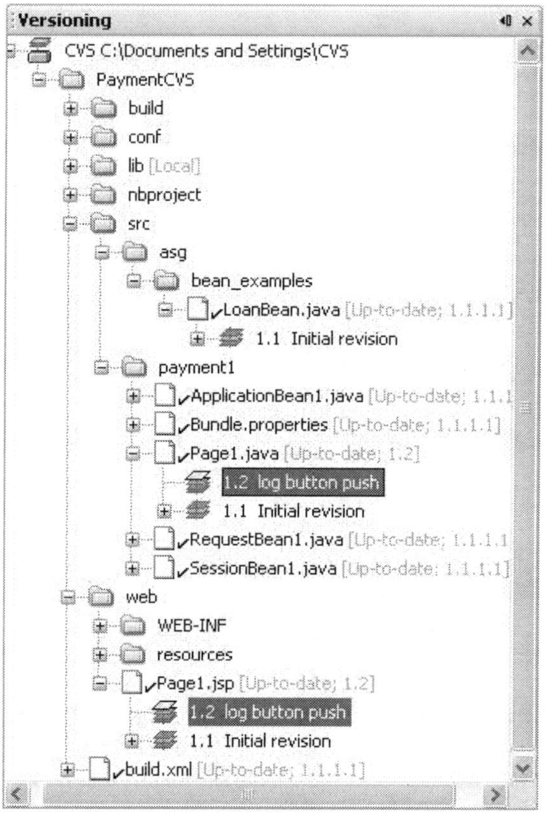

Figure 4–39 **Commit CVS files**

Try the Graphical Visualizer with **Page1.jsp** to see the differences between its two revisions. You can also **<Shift+Click>** revision nodes in the Versioning window and right-click either of the nodes to select Diff Graphical.

Creator Tip

The Visualizer also lets you see the differences between revisions as text differences. To see your changes in this format, click the Visualizer combo box and select Textual Diff Viewer.

Viewing History

During software development, it's important to track the changes that have made to a module and by whom. This sections shows you how to use the CVS History command to get this information.

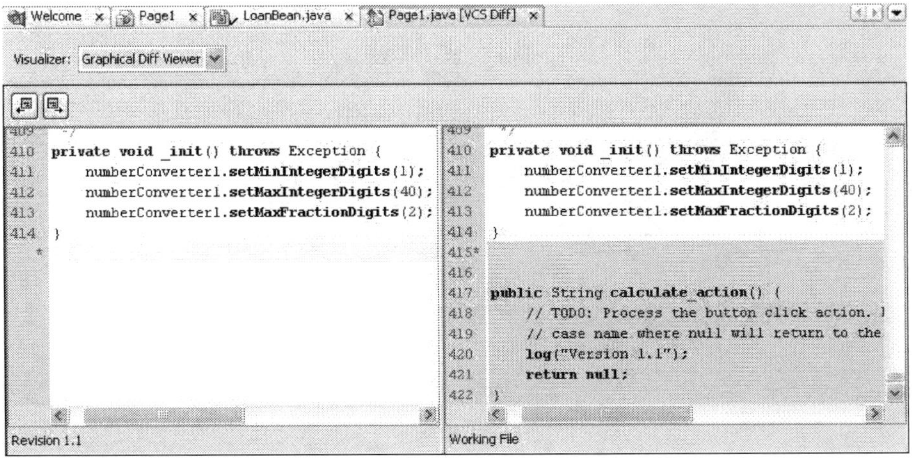

Figure 4–40 **CVS Graphical Visualizer**

History Log

The CVS History Log command gives you a full list of a file's revisions, tags, and commit history. Let's show you what this looks like for the changes we made to **Page1.java**. Here are the steps.

1. Right-click **Page1.java** in the Versioning window.
2. Select CVS > History > Log.
3. A history log should appear in the IDE main window displaying the complete revision history of **Page1.java** (see Figure 4–41).

History Annotation

Another useful CVS history command is annotation. The CVS History Annotation command displays information about each line in source file, including when a line was changed and by whom. Let's try this out with our **Page1.java** file. Here are the steps.

1. Right-click **Page1.java** in the Versioning window.
2. Select CVS > History > Annotate.
3. A history annotation should appear in the IDE main window displaying the revision history of **Page1.java** line-by-line. In Figure 4–42, we show you which lines in the file were introduced for revision 1.2 and by whom.

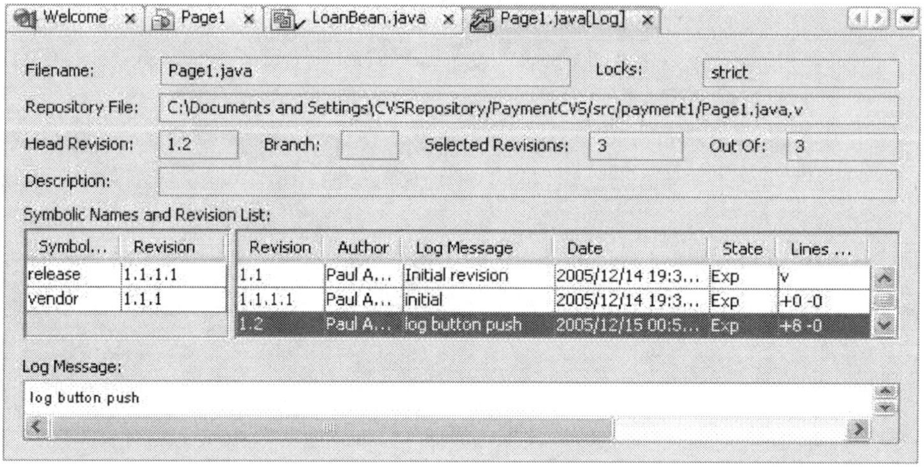

Figure 4–41 **CVS History Log**

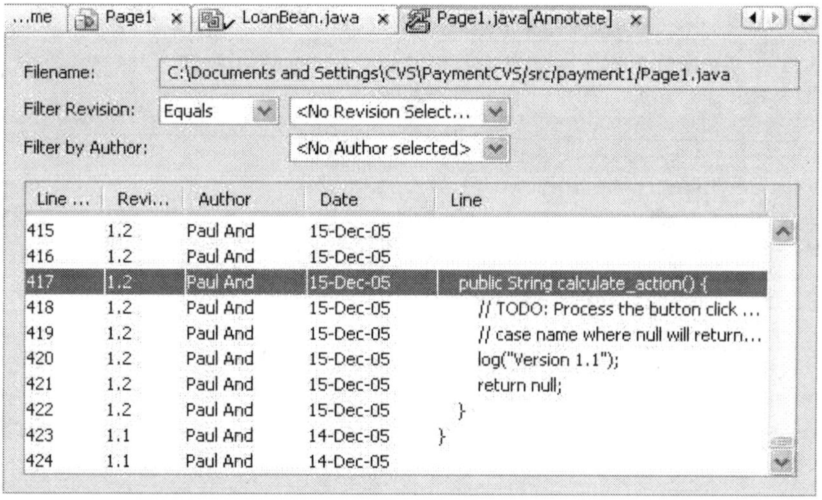

Figure 4–42 **CVS History Annotation**

Adding and Removing Files

After you import your source files and check them out, CVS allows you to add and remove source files from your CVS working directory. This section shows you how to use these commands.

Add Command

The CVS Add command lets you schedule a new file to be added to your working directory. The CVS status of a file must be set to Local, or the CVS Add command is not available for that file.

Let's create a new java file in our working directory and add it to the repository. We'll also commit this file and put it under version control. Here are the steps.

1. In the Files window, right-click src > asg > bean_examples and select New > Java Class.
2. Type **DemoBean** for the New Class Name in the New Java Class dialog. Click the Finish button.
3. In the Versioning window, the **DemoBean.java** file should appear under the bean_examples node, marked as Local.
4. Right-click **DemoBean.java** and select CVS > Add. This brings up the CVS Add dialog.
5. Type **Demo Bean** for the File Description and click the Textual radio button.
6. Check the Proceed with Commit If Add Succeeds checkbox. Click OK (see Figure 4–43).

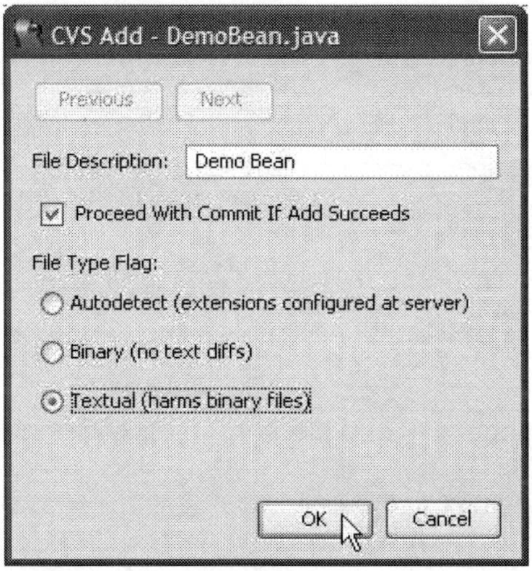

Figure 4–43 **CVS Add Dialog**

7. In the VCS Output window, an Update tab will open and display status. Since you clicked the commit radio button in the CVS Add dialog, CVS will commit the file after the Add succeeds. In the CVS Commit dialog, type **Initial revision** in the window for Enter Reason.

8. The Versioning window should now reflect the CVS status change of **DemoBean.java** to Up-to-date with revision 1.1 (see Figure 4–44).

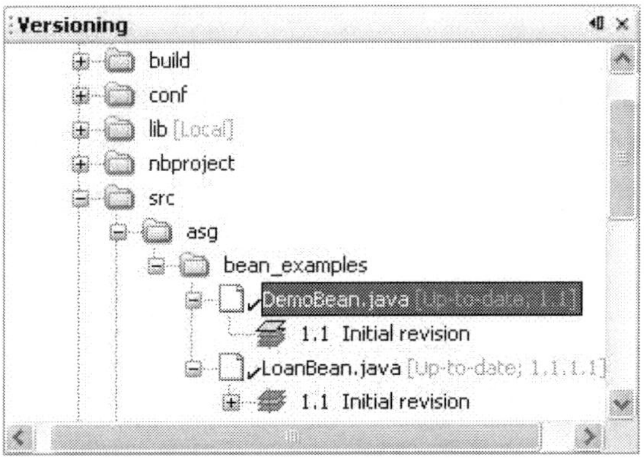

Figure 4–44 **CVS Add New File**

Creator Tip

Check the Textual radio button for text files and the Binary radio button for binary files. Use the CVS > Add command to restore binary files (images and jar files) that you removed during a CVS import. (See "Creator Tip" on page 170.) If you do not check the commit checkbox in the Add dialog, your file will not be added to CVS until you run the CVS > Commit command.

Remove Command

The CVS Remove command deletes your local copy and schedules the file for removal from the CVS repository. To show you how this works, let's delete the **DemoBean.java** file you just added. Here are the steps.

1. In the Versioning window, right-click **DemoBean.java** and select CVS > Remove.
2. Click Yes in the Question dialog. The CVS Remove dialog will appear.
3. Check the Proceed with Commit If Remove Succeeds checkbox. Click OK (see Figure 4–45).
4. In the VCS Output window, an Update tab will open and display status. Since you clicked the commit radio button in the CVS Remove dialog, CVS will commit the file after the Remove succeeds. In the CVS Commit dialog, type **Not necessary** in the window for Enter Reason.
5. In the Versioning and Projects windows, the **DemoBean.java** will not appear.

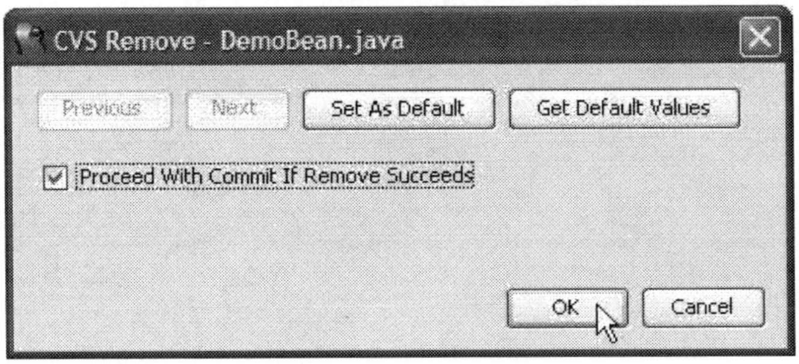

Figure 4–45 **CVS Remove File**

Configuring CVS Settings

The IDE lets you configure CVS with settings that apply to a single local working directory or globally for all projects under version control. Let's show you how to access these settings for CVS management.

Local Settings

The IDE lets you view or change settings for your working directory. Here are the steps for the PaymentCVS project.

1. From the Creator toolbar, select Versioning > Versioning Manager. In the Versioning Manager dialog, select the working directory and click Edit. (Or, right-click the working directory in the Versioning window and select Customize.)
2. The Customizer dialog has four tabs: Profile, Advanced, Environment, and Properties. Figure 4–46 shows the settings under the Properties tab. Note that changes made in the Customizer apply only to the working directory you select.

Global Settings

It's also possible to view or modify global settings that apply to all CVS working directories and repositories. Here are the steps.

1. From the Creator toolbar, select Tools > Options.
2. Click the Advanced radio button.
3. Expand the Source Creation and Management node and Version Control Settings node.
4. Click CVS. Figure 4–47 shows the General Properties window. Clicking any customizer box here grants you access to a wide variety of different configuration parameters that you can view or modify.

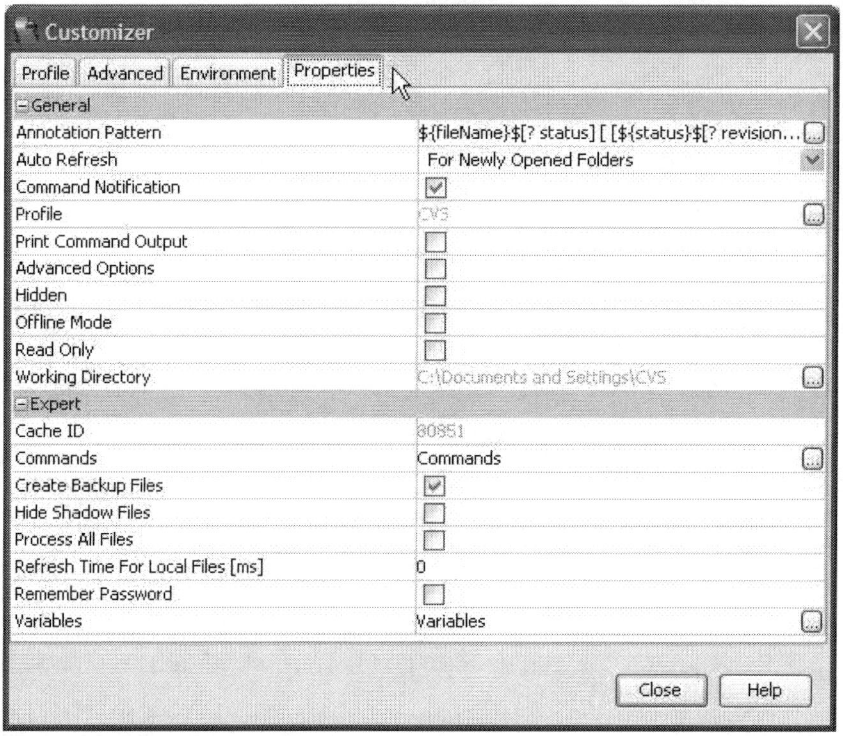

Figure 4–46 **CVS Customizer for Working Directory**

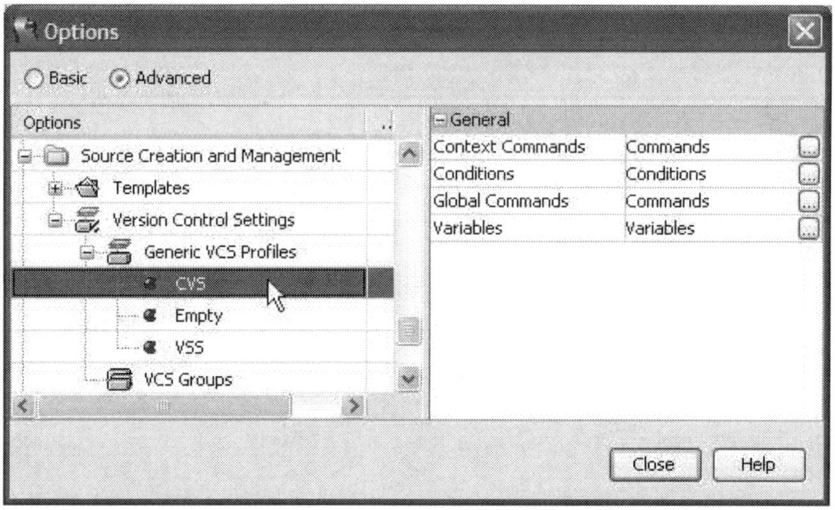

Figure 4–47 **CVS Global Options**

Advanced CVS Features

The IDE also implements more advanced features of CVS, such as branches and merging. A *branch* allows you to maintain different versions of a code base. This can be handy when a customer requires a different version of your code or you need to build a demo program. After creating a branch, any committed changes that you make apply only to that branch.

CVS also supports code *merging*. This can be useful when it's time to incorporate branch code back into a code "trunk" or to merge file revisions. Merging in CVS can be a bit tricky because *merge conflicts* are possible. This can happen when more than one developer changes the same line of source code. The IDE helps you graphically resolve merge conflicts before committing the code to version control.

Branches and merging are beyond the scope of this book, but you should know enough about CVS now to apply these advanced features if you need them.

4.4 Creating Non-Web Projects

While Creator is a great IDE for creating and managing web applications, you might also want to create non-web projects, such as stand-alone Java programs. With general projects, the IDE generates an Ant script to build, run, and debug your project. You can also add testing. In this section, you'll step through building a general project with a very useful goal: the project creates a sample database that you'll use later on in this book to explore Creator's database access facilities.

The MusicBuild project consists of a single Java class, a library that you'll add through the Libraries node, and the default JDK that comes installed with Creator. When you run the project, it generates sample database tables, table constraints, and records for a Music Library.

This project is included in the book's download. If you don't want to step through the building process, you can bring up the project in the IDE. The project is located at **FieldGuide2/Examples/Projects/MusicBuild**.

Create a General Project

Here are the steps to create the MusicBuild project.

1. Close any projects that are open. From the Creator Welcome page, click the Create New Project button.
2. In the New Project dialog, select **General** under Categories and **Java Class Library** under Projects. Click Next.

3. In the New Java Class Library dialog, specify project name as **MusicBuild**.
4. Click Finish.

After creating the project, Creator builds the structure for your project, which you can inspect through the Projects window.

Add a Java Package

Here are the steps to add a Java package under the Source Packages node.

1. In the Projects window, expand the Source Packages node. You'll see that Creator generates a default package node for you.
2. Right-click the Source Packages node and select New > Java Package. Creator displays the New Java Package dialog.
3. For Package Name, specify **asg.databuild**. Click Finish. Creator replaces the default package node with package **asg.databuild**.

Add a Java Class File

Here are the steps to add the main Java file to this project.

1. In the Projects window, select package **asg.databuild**. Right-click and select **New > Java Class**.
2. In the New Java Class dialog, specify class name **DerbyMusicDB**. Creator generates class file **DerbyMusicDB.java**.
3. Copy and paste the contents of **DerbyMusicDB.java** found in your Creator book download at **FieldGuide2/Examples/Database/utils**.
4. Go ahead and build the project (don't run it yet, though). From the main menu, select **Build > Build Main Project**.There should be no build errors in the Output window.

Add a JAR/Folder

The **DerbyMusicDB** class uses Java's JDBC package to connect to the bundled database. In order for this program to work, you must make the database driver class available at runtime (found in jar file **derbyclient.jar**). You must also make sure that the bundled database server is running (before running the project).

Here are the steps to add the **derbyclient** JAR file to the project.

1. From the Projects window, select Libraries, right-click, and select **Add JAR/Folder** from the context menu. Creator displays the Add JAR/Folder dialog.

2. Browse to the Creator installation directory and locate the derbyclient JAR file, **<Creator-Installation-Directory>/rave2.0/core/derbyclient.jar**. Click Open, as shown in Figure 4–48.

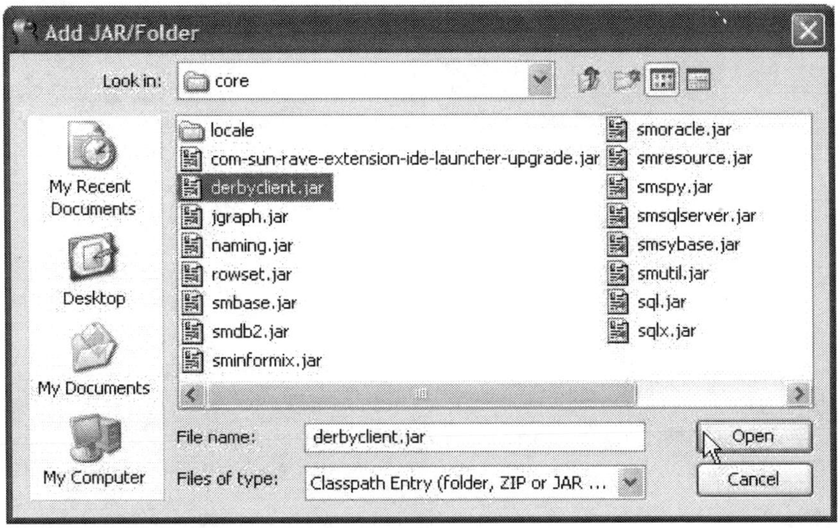

Figure 4–48 **Add JAR/Folder dialog**

After adding the **derbyclient** JAR file to your project, the Projects window should display its name under Libraries, as shown in Figure 4–49.

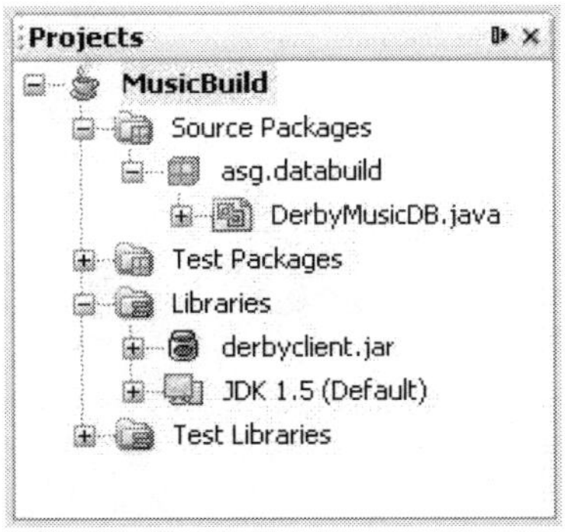

Figure 4–49 **Projects view for project MusicBuild**

Build and Run Project

Now you are ready to build and run project **MusicBuild**. Click the green Run Main Project icon from the icon toolbar or select Run > Run Main Project from the main menu.

After running the program, the Output window should tell you the Music database was created. Once you add the Music schema as a data source to Creator's IDE, you can build web applications with design-time support for data-aware components. We show you how to do this in Chapter 9. See "Configuring the Bundled Database" on page 376.

4.5 Key Point Summary

- The IDE greatly simplifies the "edit-compile-deploy" cycle of complex web applications.
- Keyboard shortcuts and code completion help make coding easier.
- The IDE lets you format your code, change fonts and colors, collapse (fold) sections of code, generate import statements, and use abbreviations for heavily used Java keywords and expressions.
- Javadoc popup windows make it easy to locate documentation for Java classes.
- The IDE helps you generate code when extending a Java class or implementing a Java interface.
- The IDE generates properties that conform to the JavaBeans component model.
- Task lists provide a way to document and clean up loose ends in your code.
- Refactoring is transforming and restructuring source code so that the refactored code behaves the same as the original source.
- With refactoring, you may rename a class, field, or method, generate getter and setter methods for fields, change method signatures, and move classes to another package.
- The IDE supports Undo/Redo for refactoring commands.
- Creator supports CVS (Concurrent Version System), one of several Version Control Systems (VCS).
- With CVS, you may place source code under version control, generate revisions, compare revisions, and examine log histories of code changes.
- A CVS repository is a directory that stores a project's full revision history.
- A CVS working directory stores the source code of your project.
- The IDE lets you setup CVS profiles and configure the CVS environment when you work with project code under version control.
- Importing files in CVS is placing project source code under version control.
- Committing source files is storing your edited changes in CVS.

- The IDE has a Graphical Visualizer to help you compare different revisions in CVS.
- History logs in CVS help you document what source code lines were changed in each revision and by whom.
- After importing source code files into the repository and checking them out to your working directory, you may add new files to your project or remove them.
- The IDE also lets you create non-web projects, such as stand-alone Java programs.

PAGE NAVIGATION

Topics in This Chapter

- JSF Navigation Model
- Page Navigation Editor
- Navigation Rules
- Command Components and Navigation
- Static Navigation
- Simple Navigation
- Noncommand Components
- Dynamic Navigation
- Action Event Handlers
- Virtual Forms

Chapter 5

Most web applications consist of multiple pages. A significant design task in building web applications is deciding page flow: that is, how you get from one page to another. Many commercial web sites consist of a "main" (or home) web page with links to other pages. These are frequently static links that simply bring up the requested page without any processing or decision making. Other web sites require more flexibility in their page navigation. Even if the next page is known, the web application may perform bookkeeping tasks or other processing before launching the next page. Finally, clicking a button may involve dynamic processing whose outcome determines the next page. For example, a login sequence results in either a successful login (and you go to the Welcome page) or a failed login (where you are rebuffed or are invited to try again).

Fortunately, Creator excels at page navigation. It uses the JavaServer Faces navigation model in concert with an easy-to-use Page Navigation editor that lets you draw page flow arrows to define navigation rules. Creator generates the underlying configuration files for you. You retain the needed flexibility through coding the action methods that return outcome Strings to the navigation handler. Let's see how this works.

5.1 Navigation Model

JSF navigation is a rule-based system. Each application contains a navigation configuration file, **navigation.xml**, that has rules for choosing the next page to display after a user clicks a button or a hyperlink component. Like the other configuration files, **navigation.xml** consists of XML elements. Here is a sample rule for changing pages from Page1 to MusicBrowser.

```
<navigation-rule>
      <from-view-id>/Page1.jsp</from-view-id>
      <navigation-case>
        <from-outcome>musicBrowse</from-outcome>
        <to-view-id>/MusicBrowser.jsp</to-view-id>
      </navigation-case>
</navigation-rule>
```

Element `from-view-id` identifies the origination page and `to-view-id` identifies the target page. Element `from-outcome` specifies the String value that is returned from an action method or action label associated with a command component. Clicking that component generates the String which is passed to the navigation handler. With these rules, the navigational handler can then identify the target page.

In Creator, you specify the navigation rules by connecting your web pages with labeled page flow arrows in the Page Navigation editor. For each rule you construct, Creator generates an origin page, a destination page, and the outcome label that identifies it. Creator assumes that your origin page contains either a hyperlink component or a button component that generates an action event when the user clicks it. The action event implements the navigation. That is, it returns the string that matches the label associated with that navigation rule.

Figure 5–1 is a UML activity diagram summarizing the steps in the navigation system.

Creator implements both static and dynamic navigation. With static navigation, a command component specifies an action *label* that matches the `from-outcome` property value from the navigation rules. Often, however, you need to process information before you can determine which page to invoke (for example, a login scenario can succeed or fail). To do this, the component's action property specifies an action *method*. The action method returns a navigation label that depends on the results of its processing.

By the way, the navigation model understands a default rule. If the action method returns null or a string that isn't defined in the navigation rules, the navigation model renders the same page. You'll see this behavior if you add a button to your page but do not define an action method. Or, if you don't

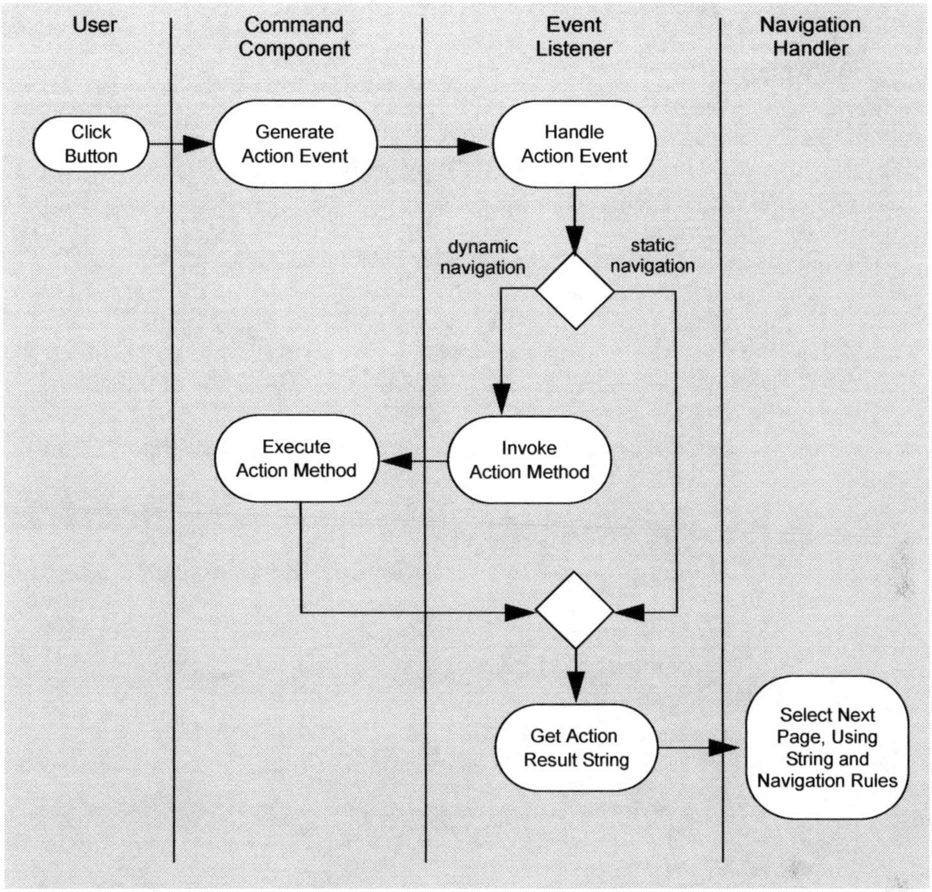

Figure 5–1 **JSF Navigation Model: Page Navigation UML activity diagram**

change the default return value of null. When you click the button, it appears as if nothing happens. However, JSF invokes the page request process and the current page is redisplayed.

5.2 Simple Navigation

The first example we work through illustrates simple navigation. That is, each button component (or you could just as easily use a hyperlink component) takes the user to one page. No processing is involved after the user clicks the button. For simple navigation you can either use action labels or action event handlers. We'll show you both here.

Create a New Project

1. In the Welcome Page, select button Create New Project.
2. In the New Project dialog, select **Web** under Categories and **JSF Web Application** under Project. Click Next.
3. In the New JSF Web Application dialog, specify project name as **Navigate1**. Click Finish.

After creating the project, Creator comes up in the design view of the editor pane. You can now set the title.

4. Select property `Title` in the Properties window and type the text **Navigate 1**. Finish by pressing **<Enter>**. (Alternatively, if you click in the small square opposite the property name, a pop-up dialog lets you edit the title. Click OK to complete editing.) Figure 5–2 shows the components you'll add to the project's initial page.

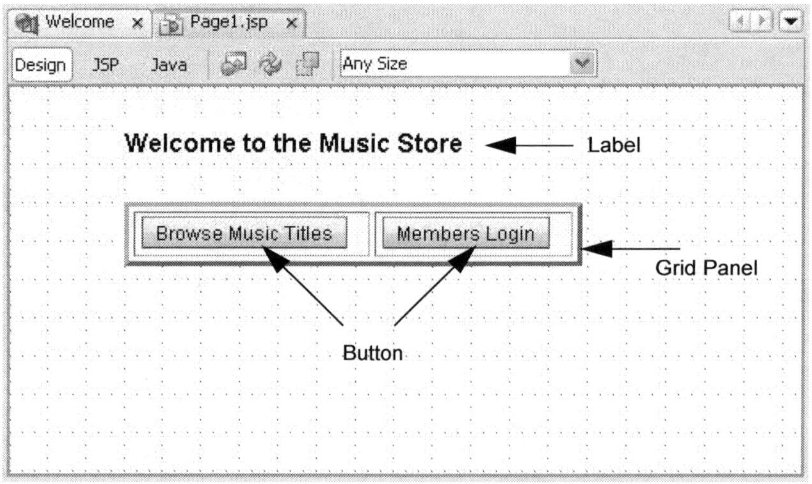

Figure 5–2 **Design view for project Navigate1**

Add a Label Component

First, use a label component to place a heading on the page.

1. From the Basic Components palette, select Label. Drag it over to the design canvas and place it near the top of the page. Don't resize it.

2. Make sure that it's selected and type in **Welcome to the Music Store**, ending with **<Enter>**. This changes the `text` property. The component should now display these words.
3. In the Properties window under Appearance, edit the `labelLevel` property. Select `Strong (1)` from the drop down menu.The output text should now appear with its new style characteristics (bold and larger).

Add a Grid Panel Component

A grid panel component is a container that holds nested components, organized as a grid. You'll use it to hold two button components in a single row. (Adding a grid panel component for this project is optional.)

1. Expand the Layout section of the components palette, if it's not already. Select Grid Panel from the Layout Components palette and drag it to the design canvas. Place it underneath the label component. Creator builds a grid panel component with `id` property set to `gridPanel1`.
2. Make sure the grid panel is selected. In the Properties window under General, specify **lightyellow** for property `bgcolor`.
3. Still in the Properties window, change `border` to **3**, `cellpadding` to **3**, `cellspacing` to **3**, and `columns` to **2**.

Creator Tip

Grid panel is a container component that uses a grid layout. It places the components in the container in the order that you drop them on the panel. A grid panel dynamically creates rows to hold the components according to how many columns you've specified. (If you don't specify the number of columns, it defaults to 1.) After you add the button components, you'll see them nested beneath the grid panel node in the page's Outline view.

Add Button Components

Now add two button components to the grid panel.

1. From the Basic Components palette, select Button and drag the component to the design canvas. Drop it directly on top of the grid panel you added previously. Change its `id` property to **browseMusic** and its `text` property to **Browse Music Titles**. Note that the grid panel automatically resizes itself as you add components to it.

Creator Tip

Changing the `id` *property is important here because you want more meaningful names than those generated by Creator. When you have multiple components that generate action events, it is much easier to work with meaningful method and property names in the Java page bean.*

2. Select a second Button and drop it onto the grid panel. Creator will place the second button to the right of the first.
3. Change the button's `id` property to **loginButton** and its `text` property to **Members Login.**

Besides buttons, you can also use hyperlink components. These components have action methods and can be used with the JSF navigation model, too.

Deploy and Test Run

Your web application is only partially done, but this is a good point to deploy and run it. Click the green arrow on the Creator toolbar. Note that the page is redisplayed when you click the buttons; that's because there are no navigation rules yet. Figure 5–3 shows what the initial page looks like.

Figure 5–3 **Simple navigation web application**

Add Page Navigation

Creator makes it particularly easy to add page navigation to your web application. In this section, we show you how to do this with the Page Navigation editor. Let's enhance your application to have a total of three web pages. The first page, **Page1**, contains all of the components you just added, which include two buttons that take the user to separate pages in the application. Here are the steps to create the new pages and add page flow definitions with Creator's Page Navigation editor.

1. From the design canvas view, place the mouse in the canvas (anywhere in the background), right-click, and select Page Navigation. This brings up the Page Navigation editor. You see the initial web page, **Page1.jsp**, in the Page Navigation editor pane.
2. Place the mouse anywhere in the editor pane (in the background area) and right-click. From the context menu select New Page. Provide the name **MusicBrowser** instead of the default (Page2). This creates a new page called **MusicBrowser.jsp**.
3. Repeat this process to create another page called **LoginStart**.

The Page Navigation editor now displays the three pages of your application in the editor pane: **Page1.jsp**, **MusicBrowser.jsp**, and **LoginStart.jsp**. (You can see the pages in the Projects view as well, under the Web Pages node.)

There is also a tab at the top of the editor pane labeled **Page Navigation**. This refers to the XML-based configuration file (**navigation.xml**) that contains your application's navigation rules. As you define page flow cases, Creator generates the navigation rules for you.

New Rules!

In this next step, you'll connect the pages and provide navigation case labels that the navigation handler uses to control page flow.

1. Click the mouse inside page **Page1.jsp**. The page changes color, enlarges, and displays its buttons.
2. Inside page **Page1.jsp**, select button **browseMusic**, click, and drag the arrow to page **MusicBrowser.jsp**. When you unclick, you'll see an arrow with a label. Change the label from case1 to **musicBrowse** (finish by pressing **<Enter>**). *Be sure to select the button. When you enlarge the page, you'll see the navigation arrow originates directly from the button.*
3. For the second case, start once again inside **Page1.jsp**, select button **loginButton**, click, and drag the arrow to page **LoginStart.jsp**. This time change the label name to **userLogin**.

Figure 5–4 shows the Page Navigation editor pane with the web pages and navigation labels you just created. Note that the page flow arrows originate from the buttons in **Page1.jsp** and point to the target pages.

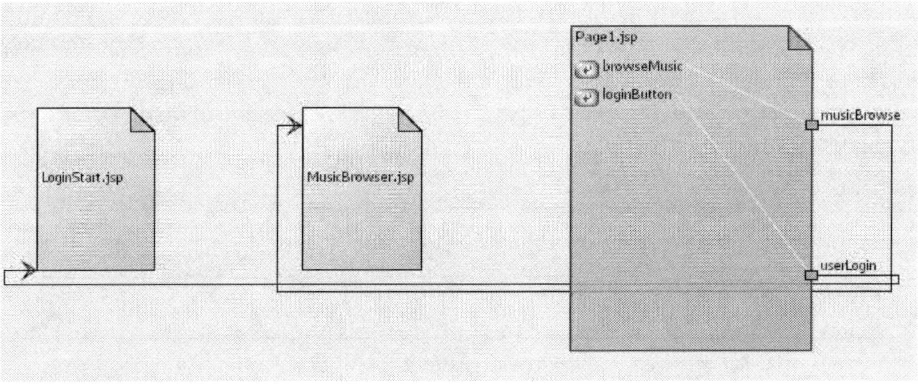

Figure 5–4 **Navigating from page Page1.jsp**

Creator Tip

As you create your navigation rules, Creator displays the property values in the Properties window for that rule. For example, if you select the musicBrowse arrow, you'll see the properties for that rule displayed (see Figure 5–5). You can always use the Properties window to change a selected page flow arrow or rename a label.

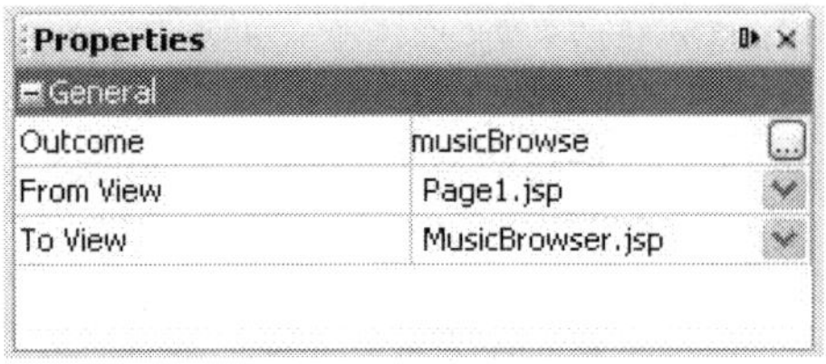

Figure 5–5 **Properties window for a navigation rule**

To view the navigation configuration file that Creator generates, select the Source button at the top of the Page Navigation editor pane. Here is the file for this application.

```
<faces-config>
    <navigation-rule>
        <from-view-id>/Page1.jsp</from-view-id>
        <navigation-case>
            <from-outcome>musicBrowse</from-outcome>
            <to-view-id>/MusicBrowser.jsp</to-view-id>
        </navigation-case>

      <navigation-case>
            <from-outcome>userLogin</from-outcome>
            <to-view-id>/LoginStart.jsp</to-view-id>
        </navigation-case>
    </navigation-rule>
</faces-config>
```

This XML code defines one navigation rule with two separate navigation cases. Creator can collapse both cases into a single rule since they share the same origination page (**Page1.jsp**, the value of property `from-view-id`). The `from-outcome` property corresponds to the labels you supplied to the Page Navigation editor. These are the labels that Creator uses to configure the button components' action properties. Let's look at that now.

1. Click the tab labeled **Page1** at the top of the editor to return to the design view for this page.
2. Now click the JSP button in the editing toolbar. Creator displays the JSP source for this page.
3. Scroll down to the JSP specification for the buttons as shown here.

```
<ui:button action="musicBrowse" binding="#{Page1.browseMusic}"
   id="browseMusic" text="Browse Music Titles"/>

<ui:button action="userLogin" binding="#{Page1.loginButton}"
   id="loginButton" text="Members Login"/>
```

When you configure the navigation rules, Creator updates the JSP source for these components to specify an action label (static navigation). In the browser, JSF sends the string to JSF's Navigation Handler that corresponds to the button's action label. Action labels provide a simple, straightforward way to specify navigation rules. However, they preclude using an action event handler to provide additional processing. After you finish building the application, you'll add action event handlers. This provides another way to use command components with navigation.

Add Label Components

Before testing the application, you'll now add label components to both target pages (**MusicBrowser.jsp** and **LoginStart.jsp**). You can access the design canvas of each page by double-clicking the page in the Page Navigation editor, by selecting the page name in the tab at the top of the editor pane (if it has been opened previously), or by double-clicking the page name in the Projects window.

1. For each page, select it and bring it up in the page design editor.
2. From the Basic Components palette, select Label and drag it to the design canvas.
3. Modify its `text` attribute so that it displays a title that indicates which page you navigated to.
4. Optionally, modify the `labelLevel` property to manipulate the text font and size.

Deploy and Run

Go ahead and deploy the application. When you click a button, the system displays the appropriate page. You can use the browser's back arrow to return to the main page. If you'd prefer to have a button or hyperlink component to navigate back, you can easily add these components to each of the target pages. Of course, you'll need to define the additional navigational rules in the Page Navigation editor. Figure 5–3 on page 194 shows the initial page in this web application.

Creator Tip

When you navigate to one of the target pages, the page loads slowly the first time. This is because the application server must generate Java source from the JSP, compile, and execute the code. It is faster after the first time because the code has already been generated and compiled.

Add Event Handler Code

Now let's add event handler code for the two buttons you just added.

1. Bring up **Page1** in the page design editor. Select the Browse Music Titles button (make sure the you select the button and not the grid panel). Double-click the button. Creator generates the event handler method for you and places the cursor inside the method in **Page1.java**.
2. Return to the design view and double-click the second button. Creator generates the action method in **Page1.java** for the **loginButton** component.

The action methods for both buttons follow. Note that the return values (in bold) match the case labels you used in the Page Navigation editor. Creator uses the action labels and automatically supplies these as the return String value in the action event handler.

```
public String browseMusic_action() {
   // TODO: Replace with your code
   return "musicBrowse";
}

public String loginButton_action() {
   // TODO: Replace with your code
   return "userLogin";
}
```

Action methods have a consistent format: they are always public methods that return a String and take no parameters. A null return value is ignored by the navigation handler (and therefore redisplays the same page).

Why use an action method instead of a simple action label? The action event handler gives you the added flexibility to add processing code before you navigate to a new page. It also allows you to set the value of the return string based on the outcome of some processing—we'll see this later in the chapter (see "Dynamic Navigation" on page 206).

When you define action methods, Creator generates the necessary JSP source for the button components. Click the JSP button in the editing toolbar. Here are the tags. Note that now the `action` property references the event method in the Java page bean.

```
<ui:button action="#{Page1.browseMusic_action}"
   binding="#{Page1.browseMusic}" id="browseMusic"
   text="Browse Music Titles"/>

<ui:button action="#{Page1.loginButton_action}"
   binding="#{Page1.loginButton}" id="loginButton"
   text="Members Login"/>
```

Return to the Page Navigation editor and select **Page1.jsp**, as shown in Figure 5–6. Note that now each button includes an event handler icon to show that the component has an associated action method instead of an action label.

Deploy and Run

Deploy the application. The navigation will work the same as before.

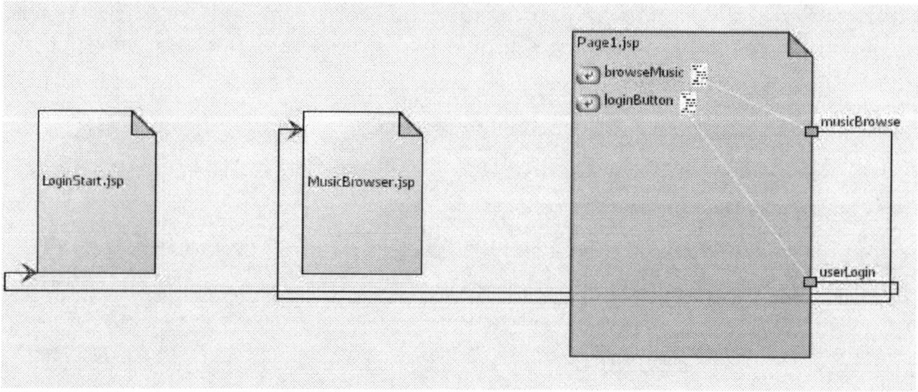

Figure 5–6 **Navigation using action event handlers**

Draggable Mode

Before moving on to the next project, let's take a closer look at the Navigation Editor and some of its user interface options.

1. With Project Navigate1 open in the IDE, return to the Navigation Editor (right-click in the background of any page and select Navigation Editor from the context menu). Creator brings up the three pages and shows the navigation cases linking the pages.
2. Right-click anywhere in the background and select Draggable from the context menu. This puts the editor in draggable mode, as shown in Figure 5–7.

In draggable mode you can move the pages around. Move a page by holding down the Shift key while you select the page and move it. When a project contains a large number of pages, it's useful to move the pages to control how the links are laid out.

You can also change the link style. Figure 5–7 shows the links in the standard style (links are drawn with direct lines). To change the link style, right-click in the background and select Wired Link. Now the links are drawn with line segments, as shown in Figure 5–8.

Creator Tip

You can only change the link style when the Navigation Editor is in Draggable Mode.

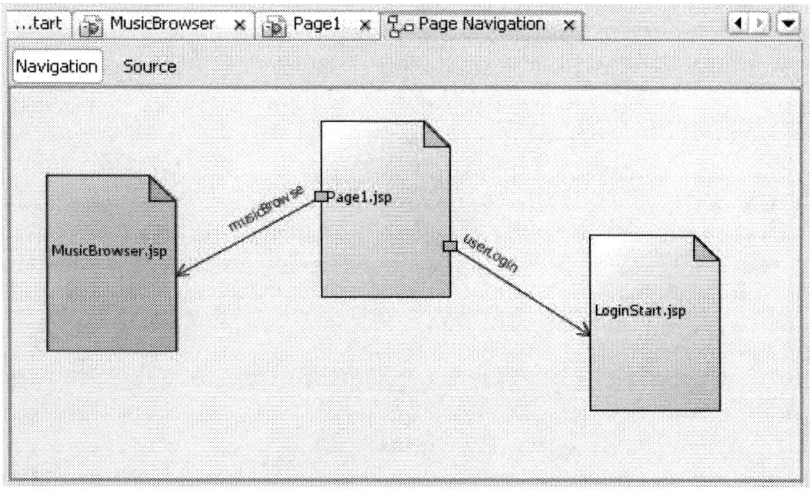

Figure 5–7 **Draggable mode in the Navigation Editor**

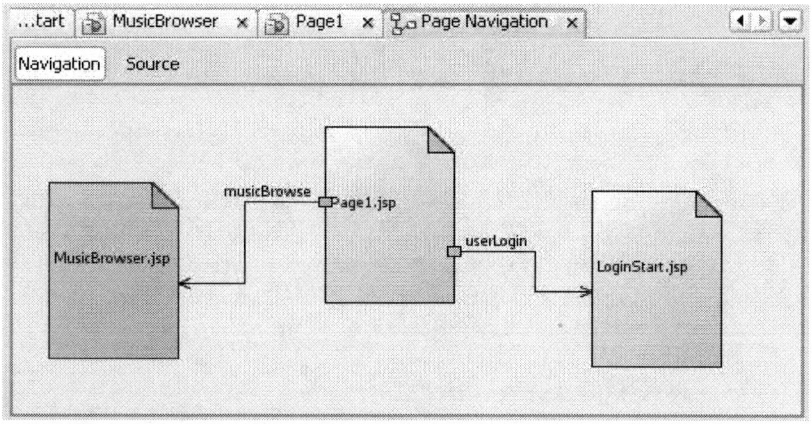

Figure 5–8 **Changing the link style to Wired Link**

5.3 Noncommand Components

The JSF navigation model is set up to work with command components (those components that generate action events). Action event handlers return a String that the navigation handler uses to determine which page to launch next.

However, you can use other components to initiate navigation, although it's not quite as seamless. Basically, you need to provide a String directly to the navigation handler that matches the navigation rules you defined. Let's modify the **Navigate1** project to use a drop down list component instead of buttons to hold the navigation choices.

Copy the Project

To avoid starting from scratch, copy the **Navigate1** project to a new project. This step is optional. If you don't want to copy the project, simply skip this section and continue making modifications to the **Navigate1** project.

1. Bring up project Navigate1 in Creator, if it's not already opened.
2. From the Projects window, right-click node Navigate1 and select Save Project As. Provide the new name **Navigate2**.
3. Close project Navigate1. Right-click Navigate2 and select **Set Main Project**. You'll make changes to the Navigate2 project.
4. Expand Navigate2 > Web Pages and open **Page1.jsp** in the design view.
5. Click anywhere in the background of the Navigate2 project. In the Properties window, change the page's `Title` property to **Navigate 2**.

Delete the Buttons

1. From the design canvas of the first page **Page1.jsp**, select and delete the two button components. (Make sure you select the buttons and not the grid panel. Use the page's Outline view to select and delete them if you want.)
2. In the editing toolbar, select the Java button to bring up the Java page bean.
3. In the Java source (**Page1.java**), remove the action methods associated with the button components you just deleted. These are `browseMusic_action()` and `loginButton_action()`.

Add a Drop Down List

1. Return to the design canvas by selecting the Design button at the top of the editor pane. From the Basic Components palette, select Drop Down List and drop it on top of the grid panel component. (If you elected not to use the grid panel component, just place the Drop Down List onto the page.)
2. In the Page1 Outline view, select the `dropDown1DefaultOptions` element (at the very bottom of the view).
3. In its Properties window, click the small editing square opposite property `options`. An options editing dialog box appears. Replace the default items by double-clicking inside each table cell to edit. For the first entry, use **Home** for Display and Value **home**. The second entry is Display **Browse Music Titles** and Value **musicBrowse**. The third entry is Display **Members Login** and

Value **userLogin**. Figure 5–9 shows the drop down component options editing dialog. When you're done, click OK.

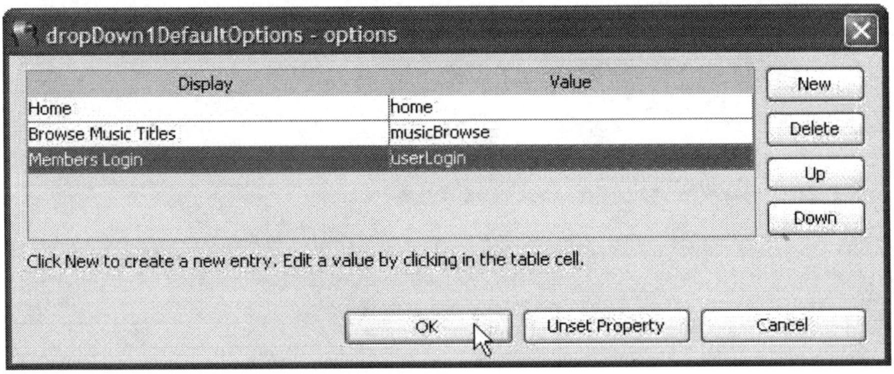

Figure 5–9 **Drop down options editing dialog**

4. In the design canvas, select the drop down list component. Right-click and check `Auto-submit on change` (it's currently *unchecked*). This sets the JavaScript property `onChange` to `common_timeoutSubmitForm(this.form, 'gridPanel1:dropDown1');` which submits the page when the user changes the drop down list component's selection.

Value Change Event vs. Action Event

Before we go any further, an explanation is warranted for adding three navigation choices to the drop down menu component. Why is this necessary? Remember, the event type is called value *change*. If we present the user with a drop down menu item that contains navigation choices and one of the choices is preselected, this preselection prohibits the user from selecting it with an accompanying value *change* event. Simply, there is no change in value since it is already selected. Therefore, we create an initial (preselected) choice, **Home**, representing the current page.

A page designer has another choice. You can always place a button next to the drop down menu. After the user makes a selection (whether it be a value change or not), he or she clicks the button and the button's action event handler can return the drop down menu selection's String value.

Creator Tip

When you key off a value change event, the event handler will only be called if the selection component has actually changed. The event handler will not be called when you select the displayed choice.

Match the Navigation Labels

The drop down list component's default options includes both a *label* (which is displayed in the drop down's menu) and a *value,* which is returned by method `getSelected()`). Therefore, the navigation labels you specified using the Page Navigation editor work just fine with the matching values you supplied to the drop down component's options (**musicBrowse** and **userLogin**).

Add Event Handler Code

When the user changes the selection in a drop down list component, a value change event is generated. A value change event is not hooked into the navigation system the way that an action event is. But in the event handler, we can grab the new value and pass it directly to the navigation handler. You'll be adding code to do this.

Creator Tip

The code you are about to add will cause the Java source editor to complain because it doesn't have all of the necessary import statements. After you add the code, we'll show you a shortcut for fixing the imports.

1. Make sure that Page1 is active in the page design editor.
2. Double-click on the drop down list. Creator brings up the Java page bean and puts the cursor in the newly generated event handling method for the drop down list component, `dropDown1_processValueChange()`.
3. Add the code from the book's download examples (copy and paste file **FieldGuide2/Examples/Navigation/snippets/Navigate2_valueChange.txt**). This code "gets at" the context and application objects associated with this web application to access the navigation handler. The last statement sends the navigation String (the selected value in the drop down list component) to the navigation handler. The added code is bold.

```
public void dropDown1_processValueChange(
        ValueChangeEvent vce){
   // TODO: Replace with your code
   FacesContext context = FacesContext.getCurrentInstance();

   Application application = context.getApplication();
   NavigationHandler navigator =
        application.getNavigationHandler();
   navigator.handleNavigation(context, null,
        (String)dropDown1.getSelected());
}
```

Your code will be underlined in red because the Java file is lacking import statements. Here's how to add the needed import statements.

4. Click anywhere inside the word `FacesContext` and type **<Alt+Shift+F>**. Creator pops up the Fix Imports dialog and adds the following import statements to the source at the top of **Page1.java**:

```
import javax.faces.application.Application;
import javax.faces.application.NavigationHandler;
import javax.faces.context.FacesContext;
```

This procedure eliminates the red underlines in your code and any "unresolved symbol" errors in the event handler code. (You can add the import statements individually using **<Alt+Shift+I>** but fixing them all at once is easier.)

Add Button Components

You'll now add button components to return to the Welcome (home) page of the application.

1. In the Projects window, expand the Web Pages node and double-click **LoginStart.jsp**. Creator brings up the page in the design view.
2. From the Basic Components palette, select Button and drop it onto the page.
3. The button label text will be selected. Type in **Home** followed by **<Enter>**.
4. Repeat these steps to add a button to page **MusicBrowser.jsp**. Make its label **Home** as well.

You'll now add navigation rules for the button components you just added.

1. Right-click in the background of the **MusicBrowser** page and select Page Navigation. Creator brings up the Navigation editor.
2. Click inside **MusicBrowser.jsp**. Creator enlarges the page. Click the button component inside **MusicBrowser.jsp**, drag the cursor to **Page1.jsp**, and release the mouse. Creator draws a navigation arrow.
3. Change the case label to **home**.
4. Now click inside **LoginStart.jsp**. When the page enlarges, click the button component inside **LoginStart.jsp**, drag the cursor to **Page1.jsp**, and release the mouse.
5. Change the case label to **home**.

Deploy and Run

Deploy and run the application. Figure 5–10 shows the drop down list component with the page navigation choices. You can see that command components (button and hyperlink) are easier to use for navigation, but with a bit of extra coding you can make other components work too.

Figure 5–10 **Using a drop down list component for navigation**

Creator Tip

If you use the browser's back arrow to return to the home page, the drop down component displays the page you came from. If you return using the Home button, however, the drop down displays Home.

5.4 Dynamic Navigation

You've seen an example of simple navigation, in which each component's action event returns a label that corresponds to a navigation rule. Now you're going to work through an example that shows dynamic navigation. Here, an action method can return a different label depending on some processing it performs. You'll see that dynamic navigation is also straightforward with Creator.

This example sets up a login sequence whereby the user is required to give a username and password to gain access to the next page. We've simplified the processing criteria to concentrate on the navigation issues, but in the next chapter we expand this example for an improved architectural configuration (using JavaBeans component architecture).

Create a New Project

Creator Tip

In this section, you will use the same name (Login1) as the project we showed you in Chapter 2 ("Creator Basics"). However, this time you'll build the project from scratch. If project Login1 is already included in your default Creator Projects directory, you may want to delete it or move it before continuing.

1. In the Welcome Page, select button Create New Project.
2. In the New Project dialog, select **Web** under Categories and **JSF Web Application** under Project. Click Next.
3. In the New Web Application dialog, specify project name as **Login1**. Click Finish.

After creating the project, Creator comes up in the design view of the editor pane for Page1.jsp. You can now set the title.

4. Select `Title` in the Properties window and type in the text **Login 1**. Finish by pressing **<Enter>**.

Add a Label Component

You'll use a label component to place a heading on the page.

1. From the Basic Components palette, select Label. Drag it over to the design canvas and place it near the top of the page.
2. Make sure that it's selected. Start typing **Members Login** and press **<Enter>**. The `text` attribute in the Properties window will show these words and the label component will display them.
3. In the Properties window under Appearance, edit the `labelLevel` attribute. Using the drop down menu, select option `Strong (1)` to alter the font style and size of the text. The label's text should now appear with its new style characteristics.

Create the Form's Input Components

The application uses the next set of components to gather input for the member's username and password. For the username, you'll add a a text field and a message component. Figure 5–11 shows the design canvas with all the components added to the page. Note that this project uses virtual forms, which you'll configure later.

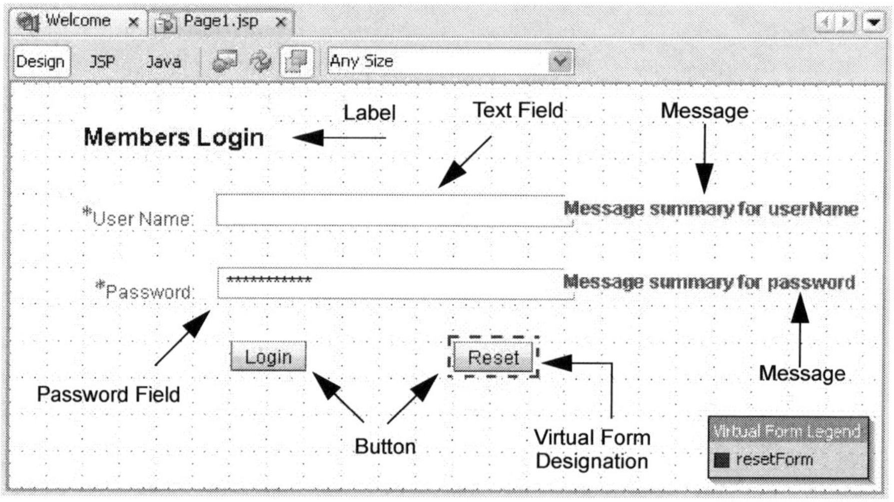

Figure 5–11 **Design canvas showing components for project Login1**

1. From the Basic palette, select Text Field and add it to the design canvas. Change its `id` property to **userName**.
2. In the text field's Properties window under Appearance, change the `label` property to **User Name:**.
3. In the Properties window under Data, check the `required` property. This automatically adds a red asterisk in front of its label, letting the user know that input is required. Now when you process the input in the event handler, you don't have to worry about checking for null values or empty strings.
4. In the Properties window under Behavior, change the `toolTip` property to **Please type in your username**. When the application is running and the user holds the mouse over the text field, this tooltip will appear.
5. From the Basic Components palette, select Message and add it to the design canvas to the right of the **userName** text field.
6. Press and hold **<Ctrl+Shift>** while dragging the mouse (you'll see an arrow), releasing the mouse when it is over the text field component. This step asso-

ciates the message component with the text field, making any conversion or validation error messages associated with the **userName** text field appear in this message component. This step sets the message component's `for` property (in the Properties window under Behavior) to the `id` of the text field component (**userName**).

For the password field, you'll need a password field component and a message component for error messages. The password field component performs several functions that make it particularly suitable for gathering sensitive data. First, it replaces the text that you enter with a constant character (the default is a black dot or an asterisk). Second, when the page is refreshed or you return to the page, the field is cleared. Thus, if you leave your workstation and someone else uses your computer, the new user can't "borrow" your password entry by simply selecting the browser's back button until the login page is reached.

Place the password components directly underneath the username components added above. You will follow the same procedure.

1. From the Basic Components palette, select Password Field and add it to the design canvas. Change its `id` property to **password**.
2. In the password field's Properties window under Appearance, change the `label` property to **Password:**.
3. In the Properties window under Data, check the `required` property.
4. Still in the Properties window under Behavior, change the `toolTip` property to **Please type in your password**.
5. From the Basic Components palette, select Message and add it to the design canvas to the right of the password field.
6. Press and hold **<Ctrl+Shift>** while dragging the mouse, releasing the mouse when it is over the password field component. This sets the message component's `for` property to the `id` of the password field component (**password**).

Creator Tip

*To align the password field on the right with the userName text field, use **<Shift+Click>** to select both components. With the mouse positioned over the userName text field, right-click and select **Align > Right**.*

To check the placement of the components on the page, right-click in the design canvas and choose Preview in Browser. Creator renders the components in a page in your browser.

Add Button Components

This application uses two button components: one to submit the form data to be processed for logging in. The second button clears the two input fields so that the user can start over. After adding the components, you'll add code for the button event handlers.

1. From the Basic Components palette, select the Button component and drag it to the design canvas. Position it under the two input components.
2. Make sure it's selected and type the text **Login** followed by **<Enter>**. This sets the button's `text` property, which is displayed as its label.
3. In the Properties window under General, change its component name (`id` property) to **login**.
4. Repeat these steps and add a second button to the design canvas.
5. Make sure it's selected and change its `text` property to **Reset**.
6. In the Properties window under General, change its `id` property to **reset**.

tabIndex Property

Components that can be selected, such as input components like text fields or command components such as buttons, have an inherent "tab order" on the page. The default tab order is the order that you place them on the page. For example, if you followed these instructions exactly, the tab order of this page is the text field, the password field, the login button, and lastly, the reset button. While the application is running, if you place the cursor in the text field and hit the **<Tab>** key, you will select the components in the tab order.

To change the tab order, supply a value for property `tabIndex` (in the Properties window under Accessibility) beginning with 1 for the first component that should be selected. You can skip numbers if you think you'll add components in the middle later.

Deploy and Test Run

Although you haven't yet added any functionality to the button components, it's a good idea to deploy and run the application now. Go ahead and click the green chevron in the toolbar. When the login page comes up, type in usernames and passwords. Of course, clicking the buttons won't do anything, but you should see an error message if you leave an input field empty. Figure 5–12 shows the initial page of the **Login1** web application. The user is holding the cursor over the password field to display the tooltip.

Add Event Handler Code

Now let's add event handler code to both of the buttons on Page1.

1. Make sure that Page1 is in the design canvas. The button components should be visible.

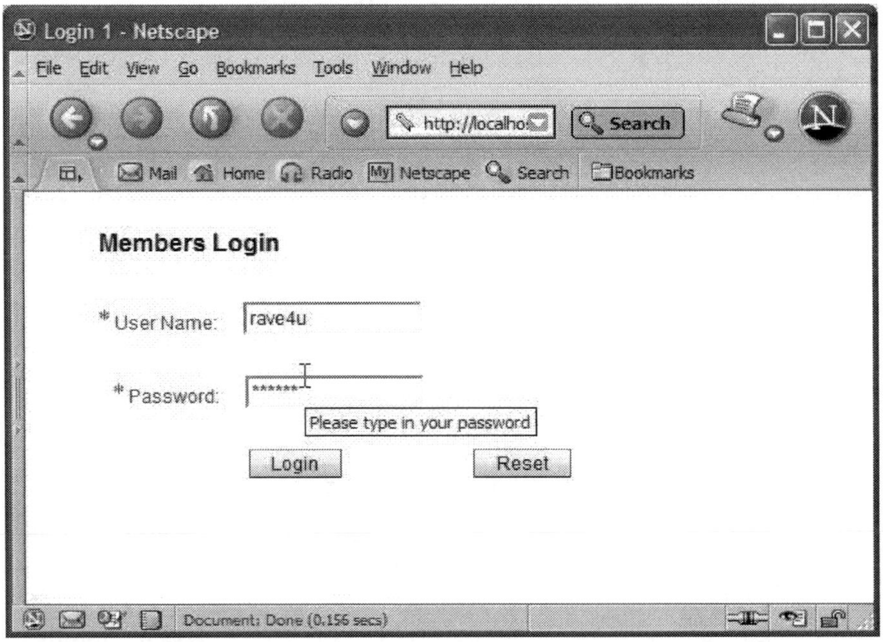

Figure 5–12 **Login page web application**

2. From the design view, double-click the Reset button. This takes you to the Java page bean, **Page1.java**. Creator generates the event handler method for you and places the cursor inside the method.
3. Add following code to the Reset button event handler, `reset_action()`, which clears the input components. Copy and paste from the file **FieldGuide2/Examples/Navigation/snippets/Login1_resetAction.txt**. (The added code is bold.)

```
public String reset_action() {
  // TODO: Replace with your code
  userName.setText("");
  password.setText("");
  return null;
}
```

4. Return to the design view by clicking the Design button in the editing toolbar. Double-click the Login button component. Creator now generates the event handler for the Login button.This takes you to the Java page bean, **Page1.java**.

5. Add the following code to the Login button event handler, `login_action()`. Copy and paste from file **FieldGuide2/Examples/Navigation/snippets/Login1_loginAction.txt**. The added code is bold. (Be sure to delete the `return null` statement.)

```
public String login_action() {
   // TODO: Replace with your code
   if (myUserName.equals(userName.getValue()) &&
     myPassword.equals(password.getValue())) {
   return "loginSuccess";
   } else return "loginFail";
}
```

(Ignore the errors flagged in red for now.) The `"loginSuccess"` and `"loginFail"` String values correspond to the page's navigation rules for going to page **LoginGood.jsp** and **LoginBad.jsp**, respectively. This is called "dynamic" navigation because the event handler dynamically figures out the outcome according to the result of the `if` statement.

6. Add the following two lines of code (place them above method `login_action()`). These statements define values for private variables `myUserName` and `myPassword`. These are the "correct" values the user must supply for a successful login. Choose whatever values you'd like for testing the application (and they don't have to be the same). Here's the code. Copy and paste from file **FieldGuide2/Examples/Navigation/snippets/Login1_declareVars.txt**. (After you add this code, the errors flagged in red will disappear.)

```
private String myUserName = "rave4u";
private String myPassword = "rave4u";
```

Create New Web Pages

This application has a total of three web pages. The first page, **Page1**, contains all of the components you have just added, including a Login button that will take the user to either a **LoginGood** page (if the login process succeeds) or **LoginBad** page (if the login process fails). First you'll create these new pages, add components to them, and then specify the page navigation rules.

1. In the Projects view for project Login1, expand node Web Pages. Right-click Web Pages and select **New > Page**. Creator pops up the New Page dialog.
2. Specify **LoginGood** for File Name and click Finish. Creator brings up page **LoginGood.jsp** in the design view and adds **LoginGood.jsp** to the Projects view under Web Pages.

3. Repeat these steps and add page **LoginBad.jsp**. Creator now displays page **LoginBad.jsp** in the design view and adds **LoginBad.jsp** to the Projects view.

Add Components to Page LoginBad

When the login process fails because the values typed into the input fields do not match the Strings stored in the Java page bean, the system loads page **LoginBad.jsp**. Here you display a failure message to the user and include a hyperlink component to return to the login page, **Page1.jsp**.

1. Make sure that **LoginBad.jsp** is active in the design view.
2. In the Properties window, supply the text **Failed Login** followed by **<Enter>** for the page's `Title` property.
3. From the Basic Components palette, select component Static Text and drag it onto the design canvas. Position it at the top.
4. Make sure the component is selected and type **Invalid username or password. To try again, click**. Finish by pressing **<Enter>**. This changes the `text` property.
5. Now select the Hyperlink component from the Basic Components palette and drag it onto the design canvas. Position it to the right of the static text component.
6. Make sure that the hyperlink component is selected and type in the text **HERE** followed by **<Enter>**. This changes its `text` property.
7. In the Properties view, change the hyperlink's id property to **loginpage**.

Add a Component to Page LoginGood

Now you'll add a component to **LoginGood.jsp**.

1. Make sure that page **LoginGood.jsp** active in the design view by selecting its tab from the top of the editor pane.
2. In the Properties window, supply the text **Login Good** followed by **<Enter>** for the page's `Title` property.
3. From the Basic Components palette, select component Label and drag it onto the design canvas. Position it at the top.
4. Make sure the component is selected and type in **Welcome to our Members-Only Page.** Finish by pressing **<Enter>**.
5. In the Property window under Appearance, modify the `labelLevel` property to `Strong (1)` using the drop down selection.
6. Click the Save All icon to save all the project's pages (or select File > Save All from the main menu).

Specify Page Navigation

In the next steps, you'll connect the pages and provide navigation case labels that you use to control the page flow.

1. Page **LoginGood.jsp** should be active in the design view. Right-click anywhere in the background of the page and select Page Navigation from the context menu. Creator brings up the Page Navigation editor and displays the project's three pages.
2. Place the mouse inside page **Page1.jsp** and click. The page enlarges and the navigation editor displays its two command components. Make sure that you don't select the buttons (click anywhere in the blank page area) and drag the arrow to page **LoginGood.jsp**. When you unclick, you'll see an arrow with a label. Change the label from case1 to **loginSuccess**.
3. Once again, select **Page1.jsp** (again, don't select any components) and drag the arrow to page **LoginBad.jsp**. This time change the label name to **loginFail**.
4. Finally, you'll add a third rule. Select page **LoginBad.jsp**. The navigation editor enlarges the page and displays the hyperlink component (`loginpage`) you added previously. Select the hyperlink component and hold and drag the mouse to page **Page1.jsp**. Change its label to **loginPage**. This sets the static navigation label for the hyperlink component.

Figure 5–13 shows the Page Navigation editor pane with the web pages and navigation labels you just created.

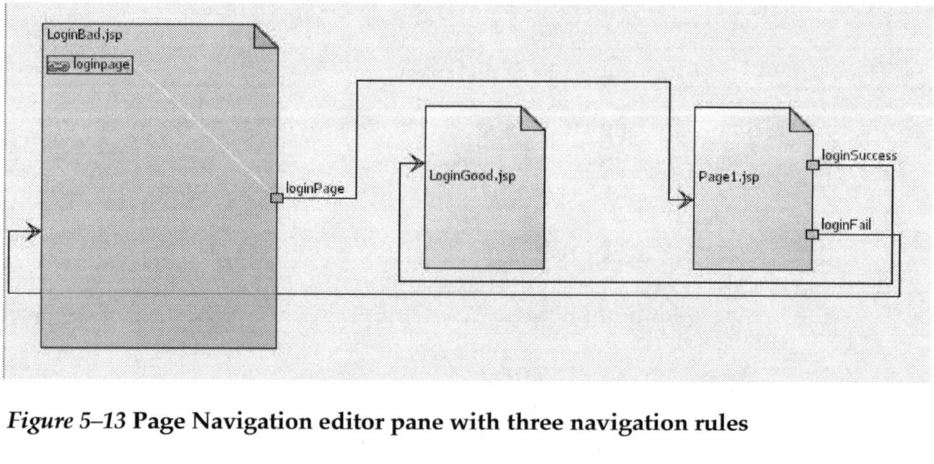

Figure 5–13 **Page Navigation editor pane with three navigation rules**

Behind the scenes Creator is generating code for its Navigation Rules in file **navigation.xml**. To see what it generates, select the Source tab at the top of the Page Navigation editor pane. Here is the file.

```
<faces-config>
    <navigation-rule>
        <from-view-id>/Page1.jsp</from-view-id>
        <navigation-case>
            <from-outcome>loginSuccess</from-outcome>
            <to-view-id>/LoginGood.jsp</to-view-id>
        </navigation-case>

       <navigation-case>
            <from-outcome>loginFail</from-outcome>
            <to-view-id>/LoginBad.jsp</to-view-id>
        </navigation-case>
    </navigation-rule>

  <navigation-rule>
        <from-view-id>/LoginBad.jsp</from-view-id>
        <navigation-case>
            <from-outcome>loginPage</from-outcome>
            <to-view-id>/Page1.jsp</to-view-id>
        </navigation-case>
    </navigation-rule>
</faces-config>
```

This XML file has two rules originating from **Page1.jsp** and one rule from page **LoginBad.jsp**. The `from-outcome` attribute corresponds to the labels you supplied to the Page Navigation editor. Note that these labels match the strings returned in the Login button's action event handler on **Page1.jsp**. What about the hyperlink component?

1. Select the tab labeled **LoginBad** on top of the editor pane. Creator displays the design view for this page.
2. Now select the JSP button in the editing toolbar to see the JSP source.
3. Scroll down to view the hyperlink component's JSP, as follows.

```
<ui:hyperlink action="loginPage"
  binding="#{LoginBad.loginpage}" id="loginpage"
  style="left: 336px; top: 48px; position: absolute"
  text="HERE"/>
```

The `action="loginPage"` supplies the required navigation case label when the user selects the hyperlink component making a specific action event handler unnecessary.

Deploy and Test

Deploy and test the application by clicking the green chevron on the toolbar. Go ahead and type in test usernames and passwords. Check both the failure and success cases (type **rave4u** for both the username and password), as well as leaving one or more of the input fields blank. You'll note that in order for the Reset button to clear the fields, *both* fields must contain some text. Let's remove this constraint.

Configure Virtual Forms

This project is an excellent example illustrating virtual forms. Why do you need virtual forms here? The page has two buttons, and each button performs a distinct (and opposing) function. The login button submits the username and password values to an event handler that determines whether or not the user has supplied correct values. Before this processing takes place, component validation makes sure there is input in each component. If validation fails, the JSF life cycle process skips to the Render Response phase and displays the error message. If validation succeeds, normal event processing occurs and the login button's event handler is invoked. (We delve into the JSF life cycle later. See "JSF Life Cycle" on page 261.)

If the user selects the Reset button, its event handler clears the input for both the text field and password field components. However, if one or more of these components is already blank, component validation kicks in and once again processing skips to the Render Response phase. The user becomes quickly annoyed because he or she has to supply input before the Reset button's event handler can be invoked to clear the form!

The solution is to use virtual forms. Configure the Reset button in its own virtual form (which excludes the input components). When the user selects the Reset button, the input components are not included with the page submission and validation is not performed. Here are the steps to do this.

1. Make sure that Page1 appears in the Design view. Select the Reset button component, right-click, and select Configure Virtual Forms . . .. Creator pops up the Configure Virtual Forms dialog for component `reset`.
2. Click the New button. Creator makes a new virtual form with color code blue. Edit the virtual form's Name to **resetForm** (double-click the field name and it becomes editable) and change the Submit field to **Yes** using the drop down selection. Figure 5–14 shows what the dialog looks like at this point.
3. Click Apply then OK. The Design view now shows the Reset button with a blue-dotted line, indicating that it is the submit component for the blue virtual form.

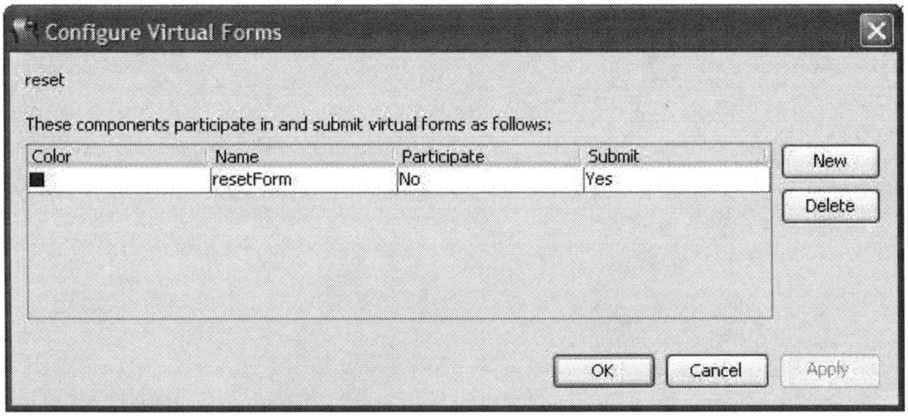

Figure 5–14 **Configure Virtual Forms dialog**

If the Design view does not show the virtual form, toggle the Virtual Form icon on the editing toolbar, as shown in Figure 5–15. The Virtual Form icon is next to the Refresh icon above the editing pane.

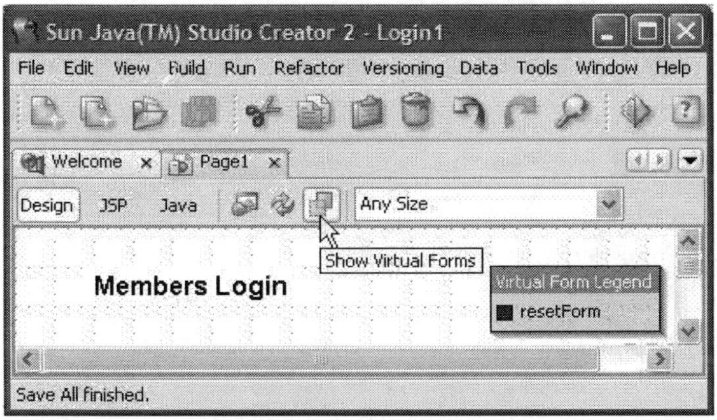

Figure 5–15 **Show Virtual Forms icon**

Placing the Reset button in its own virtual form *almost* fixes the problem. When the user clicks the Reset button, the input components are not included in the page submission. Even though the `required` property for the input components is checked, validation does not take place when user clicks the Reset button. Since all of the input components go with the Login button, these do not need to go into a separate virtual form. Therefore, a second virtual form for the Login button, the text field, and the password field components is not necessary.

However, if you deploy and run the project as is, you'll see that now the Reset button *does not clear* the submitted input from the two text field components. (Submitted values are the unconverted and unvalidated data in the input fields.) When you use virtual forms, all submitted values of non-participating components are retained by default. This prevents the loss of any non-participating input, saving the user from having to re-submit unprocessed data. In this situation, however, we must override the default behavior and discard the submitted values for the two input field components.

1. From the Page1 design view, double-click the Reset button. Creator brings up **Page1.java** and places the cursor at the first line of the `reset_action()` event handler.
2. Add following code to the Reset button event handler, `reset_action()`. Copy and paste from the file **FieldGuide2/Examples/Navigation/snippets/Login1_discard.txt**. (The added code is bold.)

```
public String reset_action() {
   // TODO: Replace with your code
   form1.discardSubmittedValue(userName);
   form1.discardSubmittedValue(password);
   userName.setText("");
   password.setText("");
   return null;
}
```

The `form1` Form component includes method `discardSubmittedValue()` to discard submitted values of non-participating input fields. Its argument is the component id of the input component (which must be non-participating). A second form of the method (`discardSubmittedValues()`) accepts a virtual form name and discards the submitted values of all participating components in the named virtual form. The virtual form specified cannot be the form submitted during the current request.

Deploy and Run

Deploy and run the application. Test using the Reset button with the input components empty and not empty. You can see that using virtual forms has made handling this web page much cleaner. Also, note that when you return to the login page, the password input field is cleared. Figure 5–12 on page 211 shows the login page.

Design Tip

The `login_action()` *event handler performs a simple String comparison between the input field values and the private variables in the Java page bean. We elected to show you this code because it is simple and we really wanted to emphasize page navigation. However, it is better to remove the computation for determining the "success" of a login from the action method and encapsulate it in a JavaBeans object. The changes are small, but the architectural advantages are striking. In Chapter 6 ("Anatomy of a Creator Project"), we show you how to encapsulate this computation.*

5.5 Key Point Summary

- JSF navigation is a rule-based system. When you create page flow links, Creator generates the rules for you and stores them in the XML configuration file, **navigation.xml**.
- Creator supports static, simple, and dynamic navigation.
- In static navigation, the command component's `action` property supplies a string to the navigation handler.
- In simple navigation, the command component's action event handler returns a String that matches a navigation case label. You can optionally specify processing code within the action method.
- In dynamic navigation, the command component's action event handler performs some processing that affects the String value that it returns.
- The action event listener passes the String associated with clicking a button or hyperlink component to the navigation handler.
- You can use other components with navigation, but you have to manually code their event handlers to pass an appropriate String to the navigation handler.
- Dynamic navigation provides more flexibility than static navigation. With dynamic navigation you can add processing in the event handler (to determine the next page or just to perform some housekeeping updates).
- With Creator's Page Navigation editor, you can create new web pages and connect the pages in your application with page flow case labels. Creator generates the navigation rules that the navigation handler uses to manage your application's page flow.
- Use Virtual Forms to control which input components are included in a page submission. Virtual Forms make it easier to control when conversion and validation take place for each component that supplies input.

ANATOMY OF A CREATOR PROJECT

Topics in This Chapter

- JavaBeans Components and Properties
- Managed Beans
- Object Scope
- Value Binding
- Conversion and Validation
- Life Cycle Events

Chapter 6

Before you wonder if we're trying to slip in a science class topic, let's explain what we mean by the *anatomy* of a Creator project. A Creator project has a certain structure that is dictated by the JSF model, as well as the structure imposed by the HTTP request-response protocol. Creator does a great job managing this structure for you, and you can build quite a range of applications without having to delve into the various configuration files that support the application. However, to best leverage both JSF and the artifacts included with the Creator product, an understanding of what we call the *application model*, that is, the structure of the application as well as its behavior, will be helpful as you design and build your web application.

To that end, in this chapter we'll introduce the concept of a JavaBeans object and the JSF and Creator life cycle. JSF's architecture includes the concept of *managed beans*. A managed bean is a JavaBeans object whose life cycle and scope is controlled by JSF. By carefully defining its public methods, you can make your managed bean and all of its properties available to the pages of a web application.

The JSF life cycle encompasses the steps that JSF performs to handle user requests and program events. Creator projects let you hook into this life cycle by providing methods that will be invoked at specific points in your application. While you can access the full JSF life cycle phases if you want, Creator presents a simplified model. We'll show you why this is useful.

JSF components support conversion, validation, and property binding. We'll give you project examples that use conversion, validation, and property binding and show how these fit into the life cycle phases.

The first step is to learn what a JavaBeans object is.

6.1 What Is a Bean?

A JavaBeans object or component (bean) is a Java class with certain structure requirements. When a Java class conforms to this structure, other programs (like Creator) can access the bean and inspect it intelligently. Furthermore, programs can inspect instances (objects) of the bean.

Because they follow certain design standards, beans can be reused in various applications. The JSF architecture is set up to allow the JSF user interface (UI) components to access JavaBeans objects.

Properties

One the most important characteristic of a bean is its ability to define and manipulate *properties*. A JavaBeans property is a value of a certain type. With a bean, you provide public methods to access a bean's properties. A property is frequently implemented by an instance variable, but not always. Sometimes properties are derived from the values of other instance variables in the Java class (especially with read-only properties). Properties can also be tied to events and have listeners that detect a change to a property's value.

Properties usually contain a single value. These are called *simple properties*. They can also be represented by an array of values. These are called *indexed properties*.

Setters and Getters

The public setters and getters define a bean's properties. A setter provides write access to a property and a getter provides read access. The names of these access methods are set by standards and determine the name of the property.

A getter is a public method that returns a reference to an object of the property's type (or if the type is a built-in type, it returns a value). It combines the word "get" with the property name, capitalizing its first letter. For example, if a JavaBeans object implements a property called `customer` (a String), its getter is

```
public String getCustomer() {
   return customer;
}
```

Similarly, a setter is a public method that takes an object of the property's type and returns `void`. Using the same convention, setters combine the word "set" with a property name whose initial letter is capitalized. A setter for the above `customer` property is

```
public void setCustomer(String c) {
  customer = c;
}
```

A boolean property's getter may have one of two forms. Suppose a JavaBeans object has a property called `onMailingList` (a boolean). Its getter can be implemented as

```
public boolean isOnMailingList() { ... }
```

or the traditional

```
public boolean getOnMailingList() { . . . }
```

Creator Tip

When you create a boolean property through the IDE, Creator uses the `is`*`PropertyName`*`()` *form for the getter.*

Note that what determines a bean's properties is the accessor methods you provide. When you create a JavaBeans object through Creator's IDE, Creator supports these conventions.

Default Constructor

There is one important rule to remember with JavaBeans components. A bean *must* define a public default constructor, that is, a constructor with no arguments.[1] Typically, JavaBeans objects are instantiated by a mechanism that precludes passing arguments to the constructor. The constructor's job is to provide any necessary initialization steps for the bean, including default values for the bean's properties.

Property Binding

When you write a JavaBeans object that conforms to these design standards, you can use them with Creator and bind JSF components to JavaBeans proper-

1. A public class with *no constructor* is also considered to have a public default constructor.

ties. This provides a powerful link between a UI component and the application's "model," that is, the business data that the application manipulates.

The binding is specified by the JSF EL (Expression Language). Typically, you bind the text property of a Creator component to a JavaBeans property. Creator provides a Property Bindings dialog that allows you to select a component's bindable property (many properties are bindable) and a binding target (see Figure 6–3, "Property Bindings dialog for component userName" on page 237). After you've applied the binding, Creator generates the necessary code in the page's JSP source. Here is an example of a static text component called `cost` bound to the `payment` property of LoanBean, which we show you later in this chapter. The binding with the LoanBean component is in bold.

```
<ui:staticText binding="#{Page1.cost}"
   converter="#{Page1.numberConverter1}" id="cost"
   style="left: 264px; top: 288px; position: absolute"
   text="#{SessionBean1.loanBean.payment}"/>
```

This binding means that the static text's `text` property is updated with the LoanBean's `payment` property during the page's request cycle. When you use binding in your application, JSF uses *Property Resolvers* to access the property. This instantiates the referenced object as needed and invokes the property's getters and setters. In this example, the LoanBean object is a property of SessionBean1 and has session scope. We explain later how this all works in more detail. But first, let's discuss object scope in web applications.

Scope of Web Applications

When a web application runs on the server, it consists of various programming objects whose life cycles depend on their *scope*. For example, a page generally lives in request scope and exists during the life cycle of a single request. Certain data, however, are available throughout the entire session. When a user puts items in a shopping cart, for example, the cart and all of its contents are generally in session scope. Each user running the application has his or her own session objects.

Sometimes data need to be shared among all users of a web application. For example, suppose a counter keeps track of how many users have accessed a web application. Such a counter needs to be accessible throughout all sessions and therefore must have application scope. Since it's important to understand object scope in your Creator projects, we define the different kinds for you.

Session scope means the object is available for one user throughout the entire session. Each user of the web application is given his or her own instance of any object with session scope. Objects in session scope exist until the session terminates—either until the session times out or until the application calls `invalidate()` on the `HttpSession` object. Session tracking is supported by the underlying Servlet technology in conjunction with the web application server.

Application scope means the object is available for all sessions within an application. A component with application scope usually contains application-wide data or processing, since all sessions share the same object.

Request scope means the object exists only for the duration of an HTTP request. When the application transitions from one page to the next, items in request scope are available until the response is sent back to the client making them available for the next page. This makes request scope objects convenient for passing temporary information from one page instance to the next. Data that keeps track of state, however, needs to survive past a single request and should be placed in session scope.

An object with scope *none* is instantiated each time it is referenced. This means that the object is not saved in any scope. You would use scope none when an object is closely tied to and dependent on another object. For example, an AddressBean with scope none is instantiated when a CustomerBean references it.

If one object references a second one, the allowable scope of the second object depends on the scope of the first object. Table 6.1 lists the allowable bindings in a JSF application.

Table 6.1 Well-behaved bindings between objects

Object1's Scope	*May Refer to Object2 in This Scope*
none	none
application	none, application
session	none, application, session
request	none, application, session, request

In general, (except for scope none) an object with a longer-living scope should not refer to an object with a shorter life span. For example, an object with session scope should not reference an object with request scope. On the other hand, an object of request scope may refer to an object stored in session scope because session scope has a longer life span. Objects with scope none may only reference other objects of the same scope (none).

Why is all this important? First of all, you need to understand scoping rules to create your JavaBeans objects properly in a Creator project. Then you must understand scoping rules to correctly instantiate and access your JavaBeans objects in the correctly scoped managed bean. Later in this chapter, we show you how to do this with the LoginBean in session scope (see "Modify Event Handler" on page 238).

Predefined Creator Java Objects

If you open any Creator project (or create a new one) from Creator's Projects window, you'll see three predefined beans: Session Bean, Request Bean, and Application Bean. These are all JavaBeans objects installed as *managed beans* with application scope, request scope, and session scope, respectively. These objects will be instantiated by the web server *as needed by your application*. That is, these objects (beans) will only be created if there is some reference to them. If you expand the Source Packages and the main project package nodes (in the Projects window), you'll see the Java sources for these beans, as well as the page beans for your web application's pages.

Each page has its own page bean. By default, **Page1.java** is the page bean for the first page of your application. The page bean is a JavaBeans object consisting of a property for each component you add to your page. Creator generates the Java source for this file (including the components' properties), and you can add code to it (such as event handler methods or user-defined initialization statements). Page1, therefore, is a JSF managed bean with request scope.

A project's managed beans (the predefined beans, the page beans, and any managed beans you add to your project) are described in file managed-beans.xml. To see this, double-click node Managed Beans in the Projects view. Creator displays the managed-beans.xml file.

RequestBean1.java provides a place for you to store request scope data for your application. This is where you store data that is available across different pages in the same HTTP request. The RequestBean1 component is a better alternative to SessionBean1 for passing transient user input from one page request to the next. Object RequestBean1 scales well since it goes away at the end of the request. See "Master Detail Application - Two Page" on page 390 for an example of a project that uses RequestBean1 to pass data to a second page. Here is its source. [2]

```
package project_name;

import com.sun.rave.web.ui.appbase.AbstractRequestBean;
import javax.faces.FacesException;
```

---

2. Creator hides (or "folds") some of the Creator-managed code by default to keep your editor pane uncluttered. To see this code, click the '+' in the editor pane's margin.

```
public class RequestBean1 extends AbstractRequestBean {
  . . . Creator-managed Component Definition . . .

  public RequestBean1() {
    . . . Creator-managed Component Initialization . . .
    // TODO: Add your own initialization code here (optional)
  }

  protected ApplicationBean1 getApplicationBean1() {
    return (ApplicationBean1)getBean("ApplicationBean1");
  }
  protected SessionBean1 getSessionBean1() {
    return (SessionBean1)getBean("SessionBean1");
  }
}
```

SessionBean1.java is where you place objects that you want to have session scope. You place data here that keep track of the state of a user's session. Examples include the contents of a shopping cart, login information about the user, or the value of the current row's primary key in a data table. Here is its source.

```
package project_name;

import com.sun.rave.web.ui.appbase.AbstractSessionBean;
import javax.faces.FacesException;

public class SessionBean1 extends AbstractSessionBean {

 . . . Creator-managed Component Definition . . .

  public SessionBean1() {
        . . . Creator-managed Component Initialization . . .
    // TODO: Add your own initialization code here (optional)
  }

  protected ApplicationBean1 getApplicationBean1() {
    return (ApplicationBean1)getBean("ApplicationBean1");
  }

  public void init() {
  }
  public void passivate() {
  }
  public void activate() {
  }
  public void destroy() {
  }
}
```

If you use SessionBean1 to store data as a property, you can configure it using the Add Property context menu from the Projects window (we show you how to do all this in our first example). Creator generates the appropriate getter and setter methods for you. Since SessionBean1 has session scope, all of its instance variables (including objects that are properties) will have session scope as well.

You'll notice that SessionBean1 includes methods for manipulating its state. An application that has many sessions active at one time may need to be moved to secondary storage or to a different container if container resources become scarce. Method `passivate()` is invoked by the application server when a session object is about to be transferred. Method `passivate()` should release any resources that cannot be serialized. Method `activate()` is invoked after the session object is restored to the container. You can place one-time initialization or resource acquisition code in method `init()`, which is invoked once when the object is initially created. Code to release resources or perform any cleanup goes in method `destroy()`, which is invoked just before the session object goes away.

ApplicationBean1.java will have only one instance within an application (and only if it is actually referenced) and the instance is shared among all sessions (users). It has similar structure to component SessionBean1 but does not require methods `activate()` and `passivate()`. You use ApplicationBean1 as a container for objects with application scope. Here is its source.

```
package project_name;

import com.sun.rave.web.ui.appbase.AbstractApplicationBean;
import javax.faces.FacesException;

public class ApplicationBean1 extends
            AbstractApplicationBean {

   . . . Creator-managed Component Definition . . .

   public ApplicationBean1() {
         . . .Creator-managed Component Initialization . . .
   // TODO: Add your own initialization code here (optional)
   }

   public void init() {
   }

   public void destroy() {
   }
```

```
    public String getLocaleCharacterEncoding() {
        return super.getLocaleCharacterEncoding();
    }
}
```

There's a lot more to tell you about leveraging managed beans, program scope, and JavaBeans objects, so let's get started. Once we've explored this chapter's two example projects, we'll return to examine the details of the life cycle phases and how these interact with property binding, page initialization and cleanup tasks, validation, and conversion issues.

6.2 LoginBean

In our first example using managed beans with Creator, you'll start with the web application you built in Chapter 5 (project **Login1**). You will add a reusable "component" (JavaBeans object) called LoginBean. LoginBean is a bean with the structure described in the previous section. LoginBean's purpose is twofold: it holds user login information and it processes a login request. By encapsulating both the login data and the processing procedure, the client (which is the JSF web application you are building) is shielded from the implementation details. Furthermore, by making LoginBean a JavaBeans object with session scope, any page you define in your project can access it throughout a session.

LoginBean Outside View

Let's begin by examining the LoginBean from its outside view, that is, the view from your application. Then we'll look at its source and show you how to install it in your project.

A bean that represents a user logging in should store the user's name and password. Therefore, the LoginBean will have two properties, one for `username` (a String) and another for `password` (also a String). To access these properties from JSF tags, use a JSF EL expression, as follows.

```
#{SessionBean1.loginBean.username}
```

Note that `username` is a property of `loginBean`, which in turn is a property of SessionBean1 (the default managed bean with session scope). Likewise, the expression

```
#{SessionBean1.loginBean.password}
```

references `loginBean's` `password` property in SessionBean1. In Java code, these map to the property's accessor methods: `getUsername()`, `setUsername()`, `getPassword()`, and `setPassword()`.

Once a user of your web application types a username and password and these values are stored in the LoginBean, the bean can tell you if that user's login information is valid. The LoginBean has a boolean property for that, called `loginGood`. Since this is a read-only property, you'll need to provide getter `isLoginGood()`.

Note that a client does not need to know how LoginBean determines whether a login is valid, making it easier for bean providers to change how this is done. For example, our initial implementation of LoginBean compares the web application user's login data with constants stored in the Java source. Another implementation could access a database and look up the user's name and password. To the client, however, the calling method is unchanged. You still invoke method `isLoginGood()`.

Advantages of JavaBeans Objects

In an earlier chapter (see "Design Tip" on page 219), we said that using a JavaBeans object offers striking advantages over placing code in a Java page bean. We were referring to the ability to change a JavaBeans object's implementation without affecting its clients, as well as the ability to encapsulate business logic and data. For example, in project **Login1** you placed the code for a valid login sequence inside the action event handler of the Java page bean, **Page1.jsp**. In general, it's not a good idea to put business logic in the Java page bean. Instead, you should encapsulate all business logic inside business components implemented as beans. This approach separates the presentation code (UI components and event handlers in the Java page bean) from the model code (business logic).

Reusability is another big advantage of JavaBeans objects that implement business logic. Because you don't put any UI-specific code (output formatting, for example) in LoginBean, there's no reason why another web application cannot easily use it.

Property Binding with Creator Components

When objects are implemented as JavaBeans, it's easy to use binding with the JSF components you define on your page. This means you don't need to write explicit Java code to set the LoginBean properties using the component's `getText()` method. By binding the component's `text` property to a property in LoginBean, you're essentially performing the Java code implicitly. Suppose, for example, the following code appears in an event handler that reads a text field component called `username`.

```
loginBean.setUsername(userName.getText());
```

Or, in the `prerender()` method, you might use the following code to display the value that's stored in the LoginBean instance.

```
userName.setText(loginBean.getUsername());
```

With object binding, however, all of this is accomplished behind the scenes (we show you how to specify binding shortly). Creator generates the JSF tags for you. For example, to bind the `userName` text field component's `text` property to the `username` property of LoginBean, Creator generates the following JSF tag (the relevant expression is bold).

```
<ui:textField binding="#{Page1.userName}" id="userName"
   label="User Name: " required="true"
   style="left: 48px; top: 72px; position: absolute"
   text="#{SessionBean1.loginBean.username}"
   toolTip="Please type in your username"/>
```

Binding this JSF component to LoginBean means that JSF displays the text that is in the `username` property of LoginBean in the JSF's component's input field. And conversely, JSF puts the text that is in the `text` property of the text field component in the `username` property of LoginBean.

Let's use LoginBean to improve the **Login1** project. Here's a step-by-step approach.

Copy the Project

To avoid starting from scratch, copy the Login1 project to a new project called Login2. This step is optional. If you don't want to copy the project, simply skip this section and continue making modifications to the Login1 project.

1. Bring up project Login1 in Creator, if it's not already opened.
2. From the Projects window, right-click node Login1 and select Save Project As. Provide the new name **Login2**.
3. Close project Login1. Right-click Login2 and select Set Main Project. You'll make changes to the Login2 project.
4. Expand Login2 > Web Pages and open **Page1.jsp** in the design view.

5. Click anywhere in the background of the design canvas of the Login2 project. In the Properties window, change the page's `Title` property to **Login 2**.

Add LoginBean to Your Project

LoginBean is a reusable JavaBeans object that you will configure with *session scope*. Session scope means that the object is available for the duration of one user's session. Each user of the web application is given his or her own instance of the LoginBean object. To do this, you'll create the Java source file within the Login2 project. Then you'll add the code that provides the LoginBean behavior we describe earlier. Finally, you'll add the newly created LoginBean component to your project as a Session Bean property.

1. In the Projects window, expand node Source Packages.
2. Right-click Source Packages and select **New > Java Package**. Creator pops up a New Java Package dialog.
3. Supply the name **asg.bean_examples** and click Finish.
4. Select package name **asg.bean_examples** and select **New > Java Class**. Creator pops up a New Java Class dialog as shown in Figure 6–1.

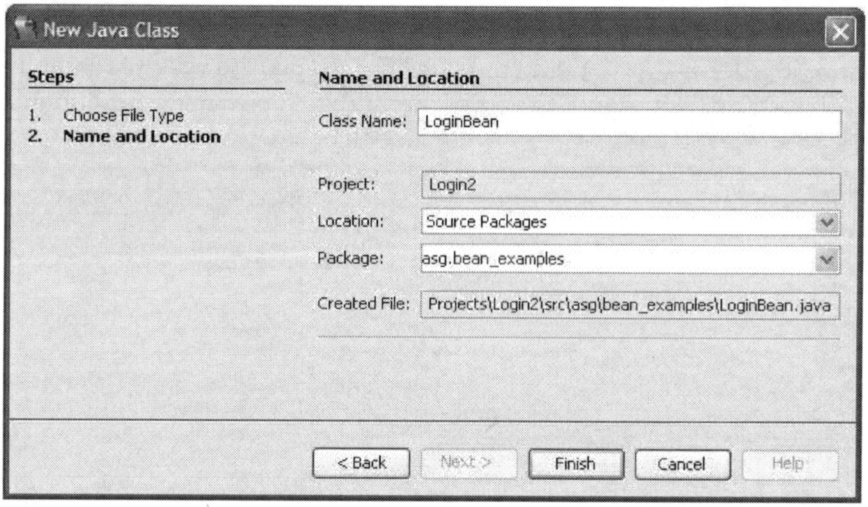

Figure 6–1 **New Java Class dialog**

5. For Class Name, specify **LoginBean** and click Finish. Creator generates Java source file **LoginBean.java** and puts it under the package name **asg.bean_examples**. Creator writes the file to your project's source code directory **Login2/src** (which is visible in the Files view by expanding **Login2 > src > asg > bean_examples**).

After Creator generates the Java source file, it appears in the Java source editor so that you can modify it.

Configure LoginBean.java

First let's add the data fields that maintain the state of the LoginBean component, then you'll add the initialization code to the constructor, and finally, you'll add the code that provides access to the component's properties.

1. Make sure that **LoginBean.java** is active in the Java source editor.
2. Put the cursor in the file after the LoginBean class declaration (above the constructor).
3. Copy and paste the following statements that generate data fields. Use file **FieldGuide2/Examples/JavaBeans/snippets/Login2_loginBean_fields.txt** from your Creator book download.

```
private String username;
private String password;

private String correctName;
private String correctPassword;
```

4. Find the `LoginBean()` constructor and place the cursor after the initial brace.
5. Copy and paste the following initialization code. Use file **FieldGuide2/Examples/JavaBeans/snippets/Login2_loginBean_init.txt**. Reformat the code using **<Ctrl+Shift+F>** if necessary.

```
username = "xxx";
password = "xxx";
correctName = "rave4u";
correctPassword = "rave4u";
```

6. Place the cursor after the constructor. The following code provides the setters and getters for properties `username` and `password` and the getter for property `loginGood`. Copy and paste from file **FieldGuide2/Examples/JavaBeans/snippets/Login2_loginBean_properties.txt.**

```
public boolean isLoginGood() {
  return (username.equals(correctName) &&
    password.equals(correctPassword));
}
```

```
public void setUsername(String name) {
  username = name;
}

public void setPassword(String word) {
  password = word;
}

public String getUsername() {
  return username;
}

public String getPassword() {
  return password;
}
```

7. You're finished editing file **LoginBean.java**. Click the Save All icon on the toolbar to save these changes.

LoginBean has three properties, `username`, `password`, and `loginGood`. It also has two additional fields (`correctName` and `correctPassword`), but these fields are not properties. LoginBean's default constructor sets the four fields with initial values. (Property `loginGood` is read-only and does not correspond to an instance variable.)

Boolean method `isLoginGood()` returns true if the login information in `username` and `password` is valid. Our implementation checks the property values against the internal fields `correctName` and `correctPassword`. Other implementations of valid login information are possible.

The remaining methods implement the setters (`setUsername()` and `setPassword()`) and getters (`getUsername()` and `getPassword()`) for the bean's other properties.

Add a LoginBean Property to SessionBean1

You've added the LoginBean source, but now you need to make the component accessible within your project. Since LoginBean should have session scope, let's add it to managed bean SessionBean1 as a property. This will enable JSF to automatically instantiate LoginBean when it instantiates SessionBean1. This will also make LoginBean available to the UI components as a SessionBean1 property.

1. In the Projects window, select component **Session Bean**, right-click, and select **Add > Property**. This pops up the New Property Pattern dialog.

Figure 6–2 **New Property Pattern dialog**

2. Fill in the dialog as shown in Figure 6–2. Under Name specify **loginBean**, under Type specify **asg.bean_examples.LoginBean**, and under Mode, select **Read/Write**.

Creator Tip

Since Name and Type are case sensitive, make sure you copy the capitalizations exactly. Also, note that we're using the fully qualified pathname for Type. This means you won't have to provide an import statement in the Session Bean source.

3. Make sure that options Generate Field, Generate Return Statement, and Generate Set Statement are all checked. Click OK to add property `loginBean` to SessionBean1.
4. Still in the Projects window, double-click the node **Session Bean**. This brings up the file **SessionBean1.java** in the Java source editor. Here are the getter / setter methods Creator generated.

```
/**
 * Holds value of property loginBean.
 */
private asg.bean_examples.LoginBean loginBean;

/**
 * Getter for property loginBean.
 * @return Value of property loginBean.
 */
public asg.bean_examples.LoginBean getLoginBean() {
  return this.loginBean;
}

/**
 * Setter for property loginBean.
 * @param loginBean New value of property loginBean.
 */
public void setLoginBean(
      asg.bean_examples.LoginBean loginBean) {
  this.loginBean = loginBean;
}
```

Now you'll add Java code that instantiates (with operator `new`) the LoginBean object.

5. In the Java source editor (you're still editing file **SessionBean1.java**), add instantiation with operator `new` for property `loginBean` inside the SessionBean1 `init()` method, as shown.

```
public void init() {
  loginBean = new asg.bean_examples.LoginBean();
}
```

Creator2 has simplified the event processing life cycle. All of the page beans, SessionBean1, and ApplicationBean1 include method `init()`. Customize `init()` with code to initialize any required data.

The code that you added to **SessionBean1.java** makes the `loginBean` object a property of SessionBean1. Thus, to access the `username` property of `loginBean` (for example), use the following JSF EL expression.

```
#{SessionBean1.loginBean.username}
```

Creator Tip

Although you've added property loginBean to SessionBean1, it is not yet visible within the IDE. To make it accessible, you'll build the project, close it, and then re-open it. From the main menu, select Build > Build Main Project. Now close the project. When you re-open the project in the IDE, you should see property loginBean in the SessionBean1 Outline view.

Bind Input Components

To implement binding for both the text field and the password field components, return to the design canvas (select the **Page1** tab at the top of the editor pane). Click button Design to make the design view active.

1. From the design canvas, select text field `userName`.
2. Right-click and choose Property Bindings from the menu. Creator displays the Property Bindings dialog as shown in Figure 6–3.

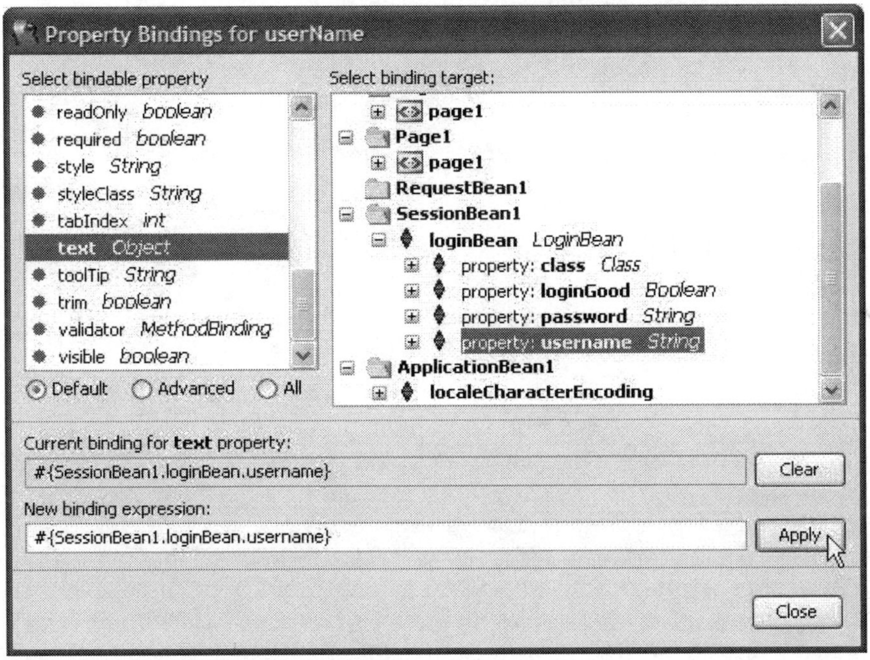

Figure 6–3 **Property Bindings dialog for component userName**

3. In the Select bindable property window, choose **text *Object***.
4. In the Select binding target window, expand the **SessionBean1** and **loginBean** nodes.

5. Select the **username** property under **loginBean**. Click Apply. The following expression is displayed under Current binding for **text** property.

```
#{SessionBean1.loginBean.username}
```

6. Click Close.
7. Repeat steps 1 through 6 to bind the `password` property of component `password` to `#{SessionBean1.loginBean.password}`.

Modify Event Handler

You also need to update the **Page1.java** event handler to invoke the LoginBean's `isLoginGood()` method. To do that, you have to access the LoginBean component.

1. From the Page design view, select the Login button and double-click. Creator brings up the page bean **Page1.java** in the Java source editor and puts the cursor at the first statement of the `login_action()` method.
2. Remove the following private variables `myUserName` and `myPassword` from the code. (This code is left over from project Login1; you'll find it just above method `login_action()`.)

```
private String myUserName = "rave4u";
private String myPassword = "rave4u";
```

3. Move the cursor to the opening brace in method `login_action()` and press **<Enter>** to add a new line.
4. Add the following statement to obtain a reference to the LoginBean object from SessionBean1.

```
LoginBean login = getSessionBean1().getLoginBean();
```

   Method `getSessionBean1()` returns a reference to the SessionBean1 object, giving you access to SessionBean1's `loginBean` property.

5. We've once again introduced syntax errors because of LoginBean. Use the Fix Imports shortcut **<Alt+Shift+F>** to have Creator add the import class statement for LoginBean to your source file.

```
import asg.bean_examples.LoginBean;
```

6. Modify the `if` statement to call LoginBean's getter, `isLoginGood()`.

```
if (login.isLoginGood()) {
...
```

At this point, no red underlines should appear in your source code. If you still see them, check the syntax again before moving on.

Listing 6.1 shows the complete method.

Listing 6.1 Action event handler `login_action()`

```
public String login_action() {
  LoginBean login = getSessionBean1().getLoginBean();

  if (login.isLoginGood()) {
    return "loginSuccess";
  }
  else return "loginFail";
}
```

After calling getter `isLoginGood()`, the event handler returns either `"loginSuccess"` or `"loginFail"`. These are the labels you used when you specified navigation page flow for the project in Chapter 5.

Modify Page LoginGood.jsp

Because the LoginBean has session scope, it's available throughout the session. The successful login page, **LoginGood.jsp**, will access LoginBean to personalize the welcome greeting for the user. You can do this simply enough by binding the label component to the LoginBean's `username` property. Here's how.

1. In the Projects window, select **LoginGood.jsp** under the Web Pages node.
2. Double-click page **LoginGood.jsp**. This brings up the design canvas for this page.
3. Select the label component `label1`.
4. Right-click and select Property Bindings. The Property Bindings dialog pops up. Under Select bindable property choose **text *Object***. Under Select binding target choose **SessionBean1 > loginBean > username**. Click Apply.
5. Now under New binding expression, edit the JSF EL expression to add the text **Welcome,** in front of the binding expression, as shown in Figure 6–4.

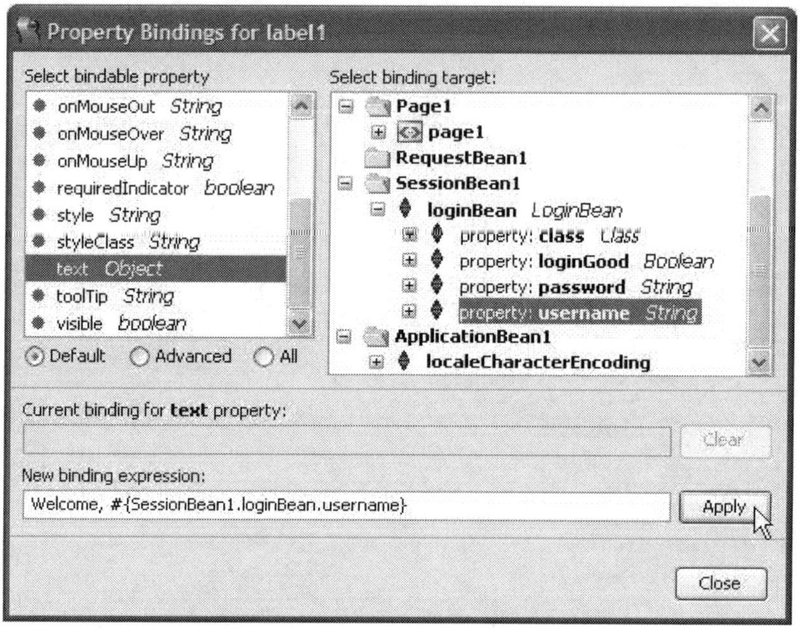

Figure 6–4 **Property Bindings dialog for component label1**

The new binding expression should be set to:

```
Welcome, #{SessionBean1.loginBean.username}
```

6. Click Apply then Close.

Note that you've concatenated a plain string with a property binding expression. You can also concatenate one or more property binding expressions together. The string and binding expression now appear inside the label component in the design view.

7. Click the JSP button in the editing toolbar. Here is the updated JSP tag for the label component you placed on the **LoginGood.jsp** page. The property binding is in bold.

```
<ui:label binding="#{LoginGood.label1}" id="label1"
  labelLevel="1"
  style="left: 72px; top: 24px; position: absolute"
  text="Welcome,#{SessionBean1.loginBean.username}"/>
```

Deploy and Run

Deploy and run the application by clicking the green arrow in the toolbar. Figure 6–5 shows the login page when the web application first comes up.

Figure 6–5 **Login web application that uses LoginBean**

Note that the User Name text field component displays "xxx." This is because the LoginBean constructor initializes the `username` field with "xxx." When you specify binding, JSF automatically instantiates LoginBean and updates the text field component's `text` property with the initialized value in LoginBean's `username` property.

The same initialization occurs with the password component and LoginBean's `password` property. However, because the rendering mechanism of the password field component replaces the text with constant characters to hide the password, you don't see LoginBean's default initialization here (you see stars or dots).

Go ahead and type in various usernames and passwords. Again, check both the failure and success cases, and leave one or more of the input fields blank. Also, note that when you return to the login page, the password field is cleared.

Figure 6–6 shows page **LoginGood.jsp** after a successful login scenario. (Type **rave4u** for both the username and password.) The page displays the

Username, thanks to the binding of the label component with the LoginBean's `username` property.

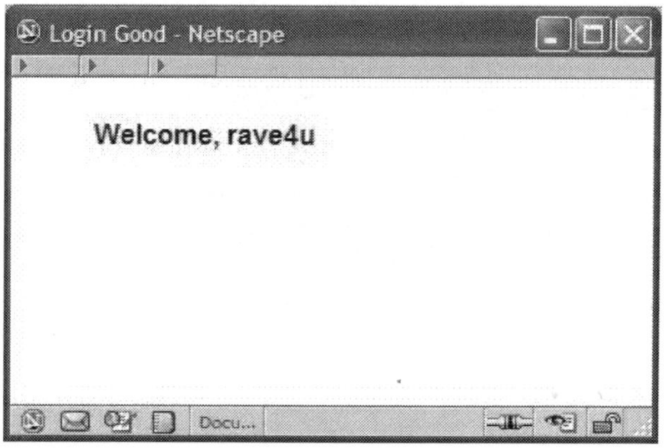

Figure 6–6 **A successful login session**

6.3 LoanBean

The project that you'll build in this section uses a JavaBeans business object called LoanBean. The LoanBean JavaBeans object is interesting because we accomplish the web application's functionality completely through binding properties with converters and validators to manage input and output. Once you install LoanBean as a session bean property, there is no code to write! All the hard work is accomplished by the architecture of the JSF components, the functionality of the converters and validators, and the ability to plug in an application-specific bean. Furthermore, the LoanBean code is compact and straightforward. This is a poster-child example for using layered technologies in an IDE environment.

LoanBean Outside View

The LoanBean JavaBeans object computes a monthly payment for a long-term, fixed-rate loan based on a loan amount, annual interest rate, and term (the length of the loan in years). The monthly payment is returned from getter `getPayment()`, making `payment` a property of LoanBean. Although `payment` is a property of LoanBean, it is a *derived* property. This means its value is computed from the values of the bean's other properties. Since `payment` is a derived property, LoanBean does not require a setter method for it.

LoanBean's other three properties are amount (the loan amount), rate (the annual interest rate), and years (the loan's term). Following the conventions of building a conforming JavaBeans object, LoanBean contains setters and getters for each of these three properties.

To build this application, you'll be placing text field components on the design canvas to allow the user to specify amounts for the LoanBean's properties. You'll use converters to convert String input into the necessary data types and validators to control the range of these values. You'll also bind Creator components' text properties to the LoanBean properties.

After supplying input parameters for the loan, the user clicks a Calculate button to see the monthly payment. The application displays the payment information in a static text component that is bound to the LoanBean's payment property. With the help of converters and formatters, JSF updates the page automatically. Figure 6–7 shows what this web application looks like.

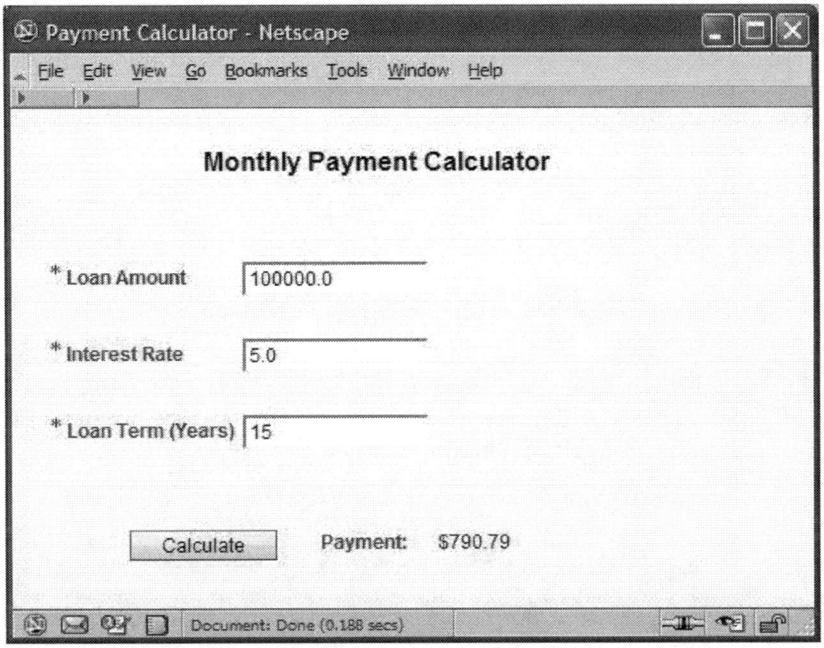

Figure 6–7 **Project Payment1 running in a browser**

Create a New Project

To build this application, you create the project, place a title on the page, and add the LoanBean managed bean to the project. After configuring the LoanBean component, you add the other components to gather input and report a monthly payment amount. This involves adding labels, specifying tooltips, applying converters and validators, and specifying binding between the user interface components (the "presentation" components) and the JavaBeans objects (the "model"). Let's begin.

1. From Creator's Welcome Page, select button Create New Project. Creator displays New Project dialog. Under Categories, select Web. Under Projects, select JSF Web Application. Click Next.
2. In the New Web Application dialog under Project Name, specify **Payment1**. Click Finish.

   After initializing the project, Creator comes up in the design view of the editor pane. You can now set the title.

3. Click anywhere in the middle of the design canvas and select `Title` in the Properties window. Change the title to **Payment Calculator**. Finish by pressing **<Enter>**.
4. Change the page's background color. In the Properties window, select the small editing square next to attribute `Background`. Creator pops up a color selection dialog. Choose the yellow swatch in the top row. This corresponds to RGB value 255, 255, 204 (a variation of yellow).

Add a Label Component

You'll add a label component to put a heading on the page.

1. From the Basic Component palette, select component Label and drag it to the top of the page.
2. When you drop it onto the design canvas, it remains selected and you can begin typing. Type in **Monthly Payment Calculator**. Finish with **<Enter>**. (Don't resize the component; Creator will stretch it to fit the text.)
3. In the Properties window, change property `id` to **titleLabel**.
4. In the Properties window, select **Strong(1)** for the `labelLevel` property.
5. Save the changes by selecting **File > Save All** from the main menu bar.

Add LoanBean to Your Project

These steps create the LoanBean Java source file and add it to your project.

1. Select the Projects window.
2. Under Payment1, expand the Source Packages node.
3. Select the Source Packages node, right-click, and select **New > Java Package** from the menu. Creator displays the New Java Package dialog.

4. Specify name **asg.bean_examples** and click Finish. This adds package **asg.bean_examples** under node Java Sources.
5. Select package **asg.bean_examples**, right-click, and select **New > Java Class** from the menu. Creator displays the Java Class dialog, as shown in Figure 6–8.

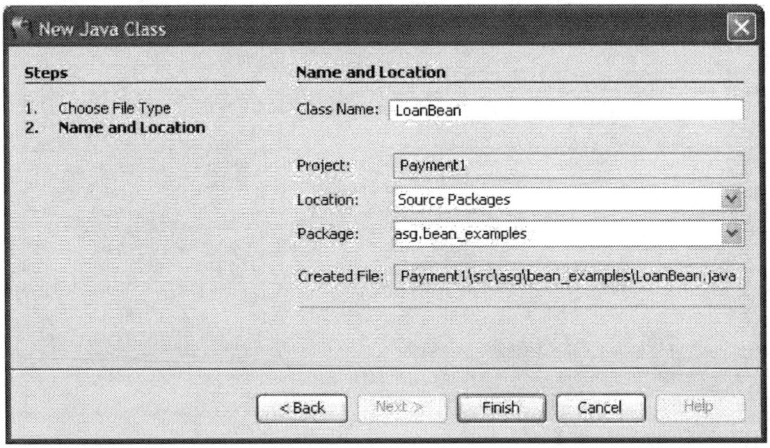

Figure 6–8 **New Java Class dialog**

6. Specify name **LoanBean** and click Finish. You've just added a stub for class **LoanBean.java**, which Creator brings up for you in the Java source editor. Note that Creator generates standard Javadoc comments for you.

You now define LoanBean's properties and specify custom code for its constructor and one of its getters.

1. The first property you will add is property `amount`. In the Projects Window, right-click node **LoanBean.java** and select **Add > Property**. Creator displays the New Property Pattern dialog as shown in Figure 6–9.
2. Fill in the dialog. For Name, specify **amount**[3], for Type select **Double**[4], and for Mode select **Read/Write**. Verify that the default Options (Generate Field, Generate Return Statement, and Generate Set Statement) are all checked.
3. Click OK. You see that Creator has added the code to **LoanBean.java** for property `amount`.

You will add three more properties to LoanBean. Table 6.2 displays the property name, type, mode (read/write or read-only), and options for each

3. All property names should have an initial lowercase letter.
4. Note that you specify type *Double* (the wrapper class), not *double* (the primitive type).

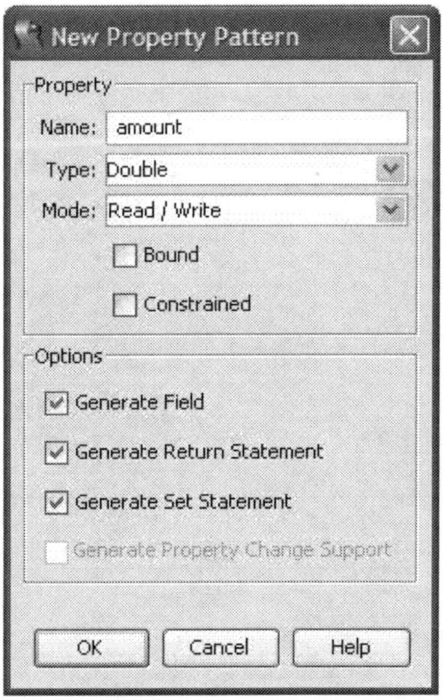

Figure 6–9 **New Property Pattern dialog**

property in **LoanBean.java**. Use the table as a guide to add the three remaining properties using the New Property Pattern dialog. Note that property `years` is type Integer and property `payment` is read only. Add these properties now.

Table 6.2 Properties for LoanBean component

Name	*Type*	*Mode*	*Options*
`amount`	`Double`	Read/Write	Generate Field Generate Return Statement Generate Set Statement
`rate`	`Double`	Read/Write	Generate Field Generate Return Statement Generate Set Statement
`years`	`Integer`	Read/Write	Generate Field Generate Return Statement Generate Set Statement
`payment`	`Double`	Read Only	Generate Field Generate Return Statement

You'll now supply initialization code for the constructor and payment calculation code for method `getPayment()`.

1. The Java source editor should still be active with file **LoanBean.java**.
2. In the code Navigator window (its default position is in the lower-left corner of the IDE), find the LoanBean constructor and double-click (look for the diamond icon that identifies the constructor). Creator highlights the constructor in the source code editor.
3. Add the constructor initialization code shown. Copy and paste from your Creator book's file **FieldGuide2/Examples/JavaBeans/snippets/Payment1_constructor.txt**. The added code is bold.

```
/** Creates a new instance of LoanBean */
public LoanBean() {
   amount = new Double(100000);
   rate = new Double(5.0);
   years = new Integer(15);
}
```

4. Add the `getPayment()` calculation code. In the code Navigator window, double-click method `getPayment()`. Creator puts the cursor at method `getPayment()` in the editor pane.
5. Copy and paste from your Creator book's file **FieldGuide2/Examples/JavaBeans/snippets/Payment1_getPayment.txt.** The added code is bold. Reformat the code (right-click and select Reformat Code) if the indentations are off.

```
public Double getPayment() {
   double monthly_interest = rate.doubleValue() / 1200;
   int months = years.intValue() * 12;
   payment = new Double(amount.doubleValue() *
      (monthly_interest/(1-Math.pow(1+monthly_interest,
            -1*months))));
   return payment;
}
```

6. Compile the Java code to make sure that there are no errors. Select **Build > Build Main Project** from the main menu bar and verify that the build is successful in the Output window. If not, fix the error(s) and rebuild.

This completes the source for LoanBean.

Add a LoanBean Property to SessionBean1

The LoanBean JavaBeans object provides a way to calculate a monthly payment amount based on input provided by the user. Even though this data is transient, you'll add it to session scope. (In this single-page example, adding LoanBean to either request or session scope makes no practical difference. However, in a later example, we add a second page and want to maintain the state of the loan bean property across page requests. Therefore, you'll add LoanBean as a property to the managed bean SessionBean1.) By making LoanBean a property of a managed bean, you make it available at design time, enabling you to easily bind its properties to UI components on the page.

1. In the Projects window, select node Session Bean, right-click, and select **Add > Property.**
2. Creator pops up the New Property Pattern dialog.
3. For Name, specify **loanBean**, for Type specify **asg.bean_examples.LoanBean**, and for Mode use the default **Read/Write**.
4. Click OK to add property `loanBean` to SessionBean1.
5. In the Projects window, double-click node Session Bean. This brings up the file **SessionBean1.java** in the Java source editor.
6. Scroll down to the end of the file where you'll see the getter and setter methods Creator generated. Here are the getter / setter methods for property `loanBean`.

```
/**
 * Holds value of property loanBean.
 */
private asg.bean_examples.LoanBean loanBean;

/**
 * Getter for property loanBean.
 * @return Value of property loanBean.
 */
public asg.bean_examples.LoanBean getLoanBean() {
  return this.loanBean;
}

/**
 * Setter for property loanBean.
 * @param loanBean New value of property loanBean.
 */
public void setLoanBean(asg.bean_examples.LoanBean loanBean) {
  this.loanBean = loanBean;
}
```

Now you'll add Java code that instantiates the LoanBean object.

1. In the Java source editor, add instantiation code with operator `new` for property `loanBean` in the SessionBean1 `init()` method, as follows.

```
public void init() {
   loanBean = new asg.bean_examples.LoanBean();
}
```

2. Save these changes by selecting the Save All icon from the toolbar.

Creator Tip

Although you've added property loanBean to SessionBean1, it is not yet visible within the IDE. To make it accessible, you'll build the project, close it, and then re-open it. From the main menu, select Build > Build Main Project. Now close the project. When you re-open the project in the IDE, you should see property loanBean in the SessionBean1 Outline view.

LoanBean.java Code

Listing 6.2 contains the source for **LoanBean.java**. You've already seen the source in the Java source editor, but we show it here for completeness. We omit the Creator-generated Javadoc comments.

Listing 6.2 LoanBean.java

```
package asg.bean_examples;

public class LoanBean {
   /** Creates a new instance of LoanBean */
   public LoanBean() {
      amount = new Double(100000);
      rate = new Double(5.0);
      years = new Integer(15);
   }

   private Double amount;

   public Double getAmount() {
      return this.amount;
   }

   public void setAmount(Double amount) {
      this.amount = amount;
   }
```

Listing 6.2 LoanBean.java *(continued)*

```
    private Double rate;

    public Double getRate() {
      return this.rate;
    }

    public void setRate(Double rate) {
      this.rate = rate;
    }

    private Integer years;

    public Integer getYears() {
      return this.years;
    }

    public void setYears(Integer years) {
      this.years = years;
    }

    private Double payment;

    public Double getPayment() {
      double monthly_interest = rate.doubleValue() / 1200;
      int months = years.intValue() * 12;
      payment = new Double(amount.doubleValue() *
                (monthly_interest/(1-Math.pow(1+
                  monthly_interest,1*months))));
      return payment;
    }
}
```

Create the Form's Input Components

The Monthly Payment Calculator web page requires a set of components to gather input for the parameters of the loan. There are three parameters: the loan amount, the interest rate, and the term. Each parameter has a label, a text field to gather input, and a message component to report validation and conversion errors. Figure 6–10 shows what the design canvas looks like with all of the components added to the page (we've labeled most of them for you).

Here are the steps to create the components for the loan amount parameter:

1. Switch back to the design canvas by selecting the tab labeled **Page1** at the top of the editor pane. Click button Design to make the design view active.

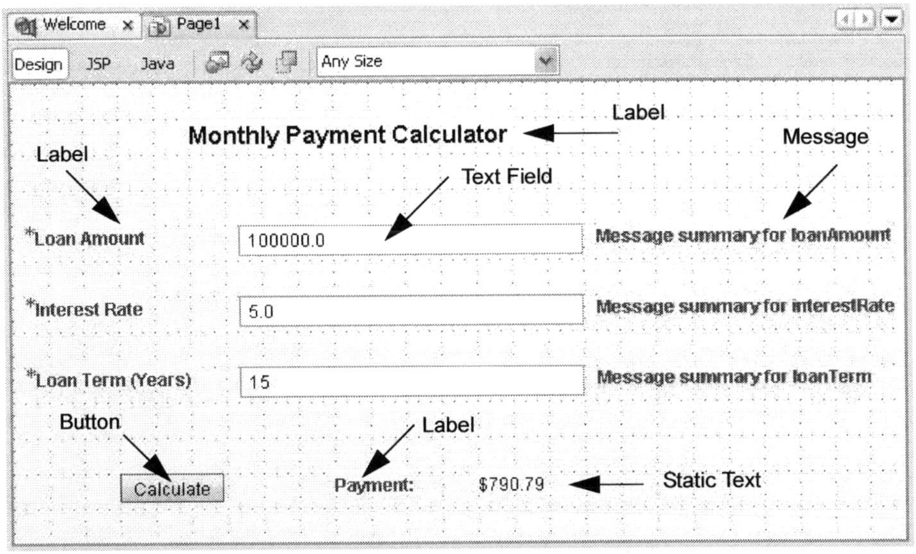

Figure 6–10 **Design canvas showing placement of components for project Payment1**

2. From the Basic Components palette, select Label and drag it onto the design canvas.
3. Make sure that the component remains selected and type in the text **Loan Amount**. Finish with **<Enter>**.
4. From the Basic Components palette, select Text Field and drop it onto the design canvas. Position it to the right of the label component you just added.
5. In the Properties window, change its `id` attribute to **loanAmount**.
6. In the Properties window under Data, make sure the `required` attribute is selected (checked). This ensures that the user supplies input for this field.
7. In the Properties window under Behavior, set the `toolTip` property to **Please supply the loan amount in dollars**. Finish with **<Enter>**.
8. In the Design view, select the label. Press and hold **<Ctrl+Shift>**, left-click the mouse, and drag the cursor to the `loanAmount` text field component to set the label's `for` property.

   Setting the label's `for` property to the text field defines an association between the label and the `loanAmount` text field. When the application is running, selecting the label as well as the text field places the cursor in the text field. Furthermore, Creator automatically prepends an asterisk (*) to the label's text indicating that its text field input is required. Validation and conversion errors will also affect the label's appearance

Creator Tip

Here, you can use either a Label component (and have more control over the placement of the label and its style characteristics) or you can supply label text through the text field's `label` *property. Both approaches allow the label text to reflect required input (with an asterisk) and modify the label's style when conversion or validation errors occur.*

Use Validators and Converters

The `loanAmount` text field collects a numerical string that represents the amount of the loan. The string data is used with UI components for the "presentation" part of the application. Internally, however, you'll store this information as a Double. Therefore, you need to convert the String to a Double and make sure its value is within a reasonable range with validation. To do this, you'll use a JSF Double Range Validator for validation and a JSF Double Converter for conversion. You can add these components to your project from the Validators and Converters palettes. Here's how.

1. In the Palette window, expand the Converters node. Select Double Converter, drag it to the design canvas, and drop it *on top of* the text field component `loanAmount`. In the Properties window, Creator sets the `converter` property under Data for `loanAmount` to `doubleConverter1`.
2. Repeat this step for the validator. In the Palette window, expand the Validators node. Select Double Range Validator, drag it to the design canvas, and drop it on top of the `loanAmount` text field component. Creator sets the `validator` property under Data for `loanAmount` to `doubleRangeValidator1` in the Properties window. Component `doubleRangeValidator1` also appears in the Page1 Outline view.

You've just applied a range validator for the loan amount. Now you specify its range (maximum and minimum).

1. In the Outline view, select the validator you just added for the `loanAmount` component, `doubleRangeValidator1`.
2. From the Properties window, set the minimum and maximum values to **1.0** and 1 million (**1000000.0**), respectively (or other values you deem reasonable).

Creator Tip

Creator displays properties in alphabetical order within each category, making property maximum appear before property minimum. Make sure that you supply the minimum and maximum values to the correct property name. If you reverse them, validation will always fail!

You also need a message component to display error messages resulting from conversion and validation errors.

1. From the Basic Components palette, select component Message. Drag it to the design canvas and position it to the right of the text field component `loanAmount`.
2. Press and hold **<Ctrl+Shift>**, left-click the mouse, and drag the cursor to the `loanAmount` text field component to set the `for` property as shown in Figure 6–11. This ties the message component to the `loanAmount` text field component. Any error messages generated by the component's validator or converter will be displayed on the page by this message component. In the design view, the message component now displays the text **Message summary for loanAmount.**

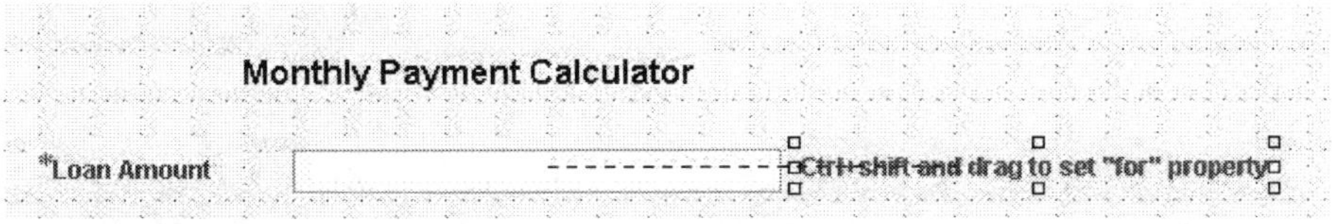

Figure 6–11 **Setting a Message component's** `for` **property**

Specify Property Binding

Now let's specify binding for the `loanAmount` text field's `text` property.

1. Make sure that the `loanAmount` component is selected.
2. Right-click and select Property Bindings from the menu. A dialog entitled Property Bindings for `loanAmount` pops up.
3. In the Select bindable property window, choose **text** *Object*.
4. In the Select binding target window, expand node **SessionBean1 > loanBean**, select property **amount**, and click Apply. Figure 6–12 shows the Property Bindings dialog.
5. In the Current binding for **text** property, Creator displays the expression

```
#{SessionBean1.loanBean.amount}
```

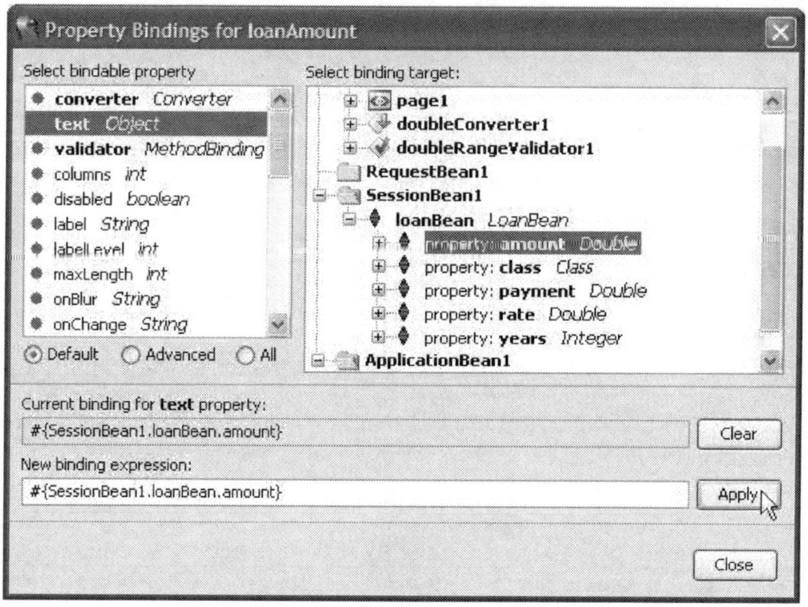

Figure 6–12 **Property Bindings for loanAmount**

6. Click Close. This binds the `text` property of the text field component `loan-Amount` to the `amount` property of LoanBean.
7. The text field component now displays the LoanBean's default value for the amount property (`100,000`). In the Properties view, property `text` displays the binding icon. If you hold the cursor over this attribute, a tooltip displays the above binding expression.

Place Interest Rate and Term Components

Ok, you've finished placing the components associated with gathering the loan amount parameter. You'll need to repeat these steps for the interest rate (which uses a Double converter and a Double range validator) and the loan term (which uses an Integer converter and Long range validator). Follow the same steps we showed you for the loan amount input.

1. First grab a label, then the text field, converter, and validator, and finally, the message component.
2. To make this easier, we've created tables that help you create the components and set their values. You may find it helpful to follow the instructions and descriptions we gave you for the loan amount parameter.Table 6.3 lists the components and their properties for the interest rate input.

Table 6.3 Components for interest rate input

Component	*Property*	*Setting*
Label (`label2`)	`for`	`interestRate` (set this property after you place text field `interestRate` on canvas)
	`text`	Interest Rate
Text Field	`id`	`interestRate`
	`toolTip`	Please specify the interest rate (APR)
	`converter`	`doubleConverter1` (the same converter you used for `loanAmount`; select the drop down opposite the `converter` property and choose `doubleConverter1`)
	`required`	true (checked)
	`validator`	`doubleRangeValidator2` (select Double Range Validator from the Validators palette)
	`text`	`#{SessionBean1.loanBean.rate}`
Double Range Validator (`doubleRangeValidator2`)	`maximum`	15.5
	`minimum`	0.001
Message (`message2`)	`for`	`interestRate` (press and hold **<Ctrl+Shift>**, left-click the mouse, and drag the cursor to the `interestRate` component)

3. Be sure to specify binding for `interestRate`'s `value` attribute with the LoanBean's `rate` property. Use the Property Binding dialog and select **SessionBean1 > loanBean > rate**.

Creator Tip

You can use the same Double converter for text field `interestRate` *that you used with text field* `loanAmount`. *After placing the text field on the design canvas, select the drop down opposite the* `converter` *property in the Properties window and choose* `doubleConverter1`.

Table 6.4 lists the components and their Properties settings for the loan term parameter.

Table 6.4 Components for loan term input

Component	*Property*	*Setting*
Label (`label3`)	`for`	`loanTerm` (set this attribute after you place text field `loanTerm` on canvas)
	`text`	Loan Term (Years)
Text Field	`id`	`loanTerm`
	`toolTip`	Please specify term of loan in years
	`converter`	`integerConverter1` (select Integer Converter from the Converters palette; will be set after you drop the converter onto the component)
	`required`	true (checked)
	`validator`	`longRangeValidator1` (will be set after you drop the validator onto the component)
	`text`	`#{SessionBean1.loanBean.years}`
Integer Converter (`integerConverter1`)		
Long Range Validator (`longRangeValidator1`)	`maximum`	99
	`minimum`	1
Message (`message3`)	`for`	`loanTerm` (press and hold **<Ctrl+Shift>**, left-click the mouse, and drag the cursor to the `loanTerm` component)

The text field component `loanTerm` requires an Integer converter and a Long range validator to control the allowable range. Specify binding with **SessionBean1 > loanBean > years**.

Place Button, Label and Static Text Components

On the last line of the web application page, you'll place a button, a label component, and a static text component that binds to the `payment` property of the LoanBean. Table 6.5 shows the components you need and their properties that control the payment display. Specify **SessionBean1 > loanBean > payment** to bind the static text's `text` property with the LoanBean's `payment` property.

Table 6.5 Components for monthly payment output

Component	*Property*	*Setting*
Button	`id`	`calculate`
	`text`	Calculate
Label (`label4`)	`text`	Payment:
Static Text	`id`	`cost`
	`converter`	`numberConverter1` (this will be set after you drop the Number Converter onto the component)
	`text`	`#{SessionBean1.loanBean.payment}`
Number Converter (`numberConverter1`)	`pattern`	$#,###.00

Here's how to apply and configure the Number converter.

1. From the Converters Components palette, select Number Converter and drop it on the static text component. Creator pops up the Number Format dialog so that you can configure the converter.
2. Select the Pattern radio button and provide pattern **$#,###.00**, as shown in Figure 6–13. This pattern supplies a dollar sign, a comma separator for thousands and millions (etc.), and supplies two digits to the right of the decimal point. (You can test the pattern by providing a sample number in the Example field and click Test. The resulting conversion appears in the Results window.) Click Apply, then OK to close the dialog.

Let's see how the button and static text components work with the LoanBean and the Number converter.

The button component does not have an action event handler defined in the Java page bean. The default action submits the page. This begins the life cycle process and updates the fields, including the static text component `cost`.

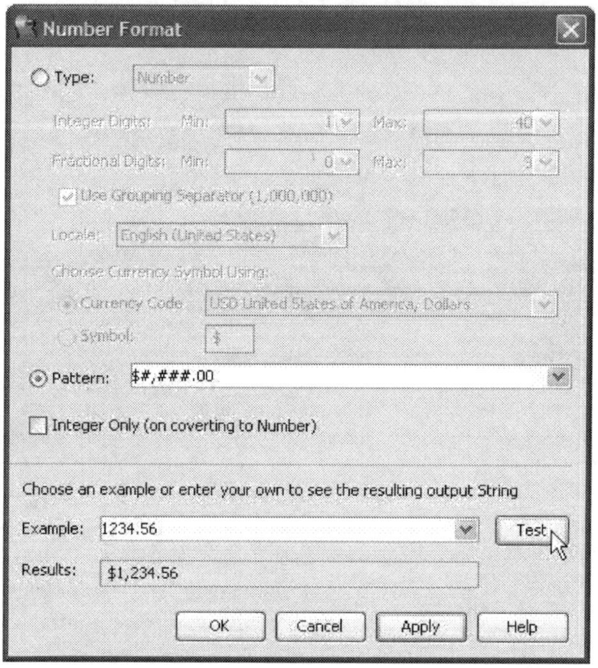

Figure 6–13 **Number Format dialog for number converter**

Static text component `cost` is bound to the `payment` property of the LoanBean. Recall that method `getPayment()` returns a Double. When you define a number converter for the static text component, the Double generated by the LoanBean component is converted to a String. We want the payment displayed in dollars and cents, however. Fortunately, the number converter has a `pattern` property that manipulates the Double as a comma-separated number with two digits to the right of the decimal point and a dollar sign in front. The pattern that accomplishes this is

```
$#,###.00
```

The number converter has additional properties to help you control the format of the output String, but this pattern fully specifies the format we need.

Deploy and Run

Figure 6–14 shows the Outline view of the JSF components, converters, and validators for project **Payment1**. Before deploying, you may find it helpful to compare your Outline view with the components shown here.

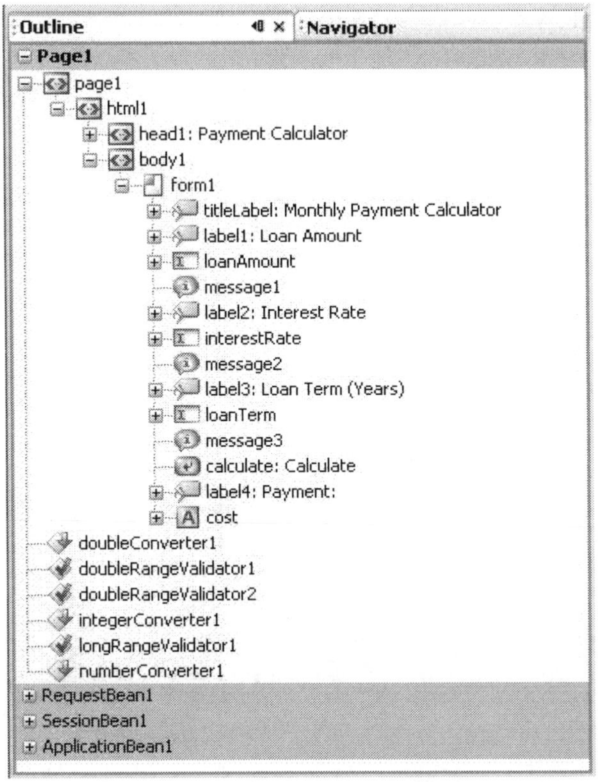

Figure 6–14 **Outline view for project Payment1**

Deploy and run the application by clicking the green arrow on the toolbar. Figure 6–15 shows the web application with new values for the loan amount, interest rate, and loan term. Note how the tooltip provides context help as the user holds the cursor over the interest rate text field component.

The payment amount is computed from the new values. When you change any of the loan parameters and click the Calculate button, a new payment appears. All this takes place because of the bindings between the text field components and the LoanBean properties (including the LoanBean `payment` property for output). Of course, the converters and validators play important roles as well.

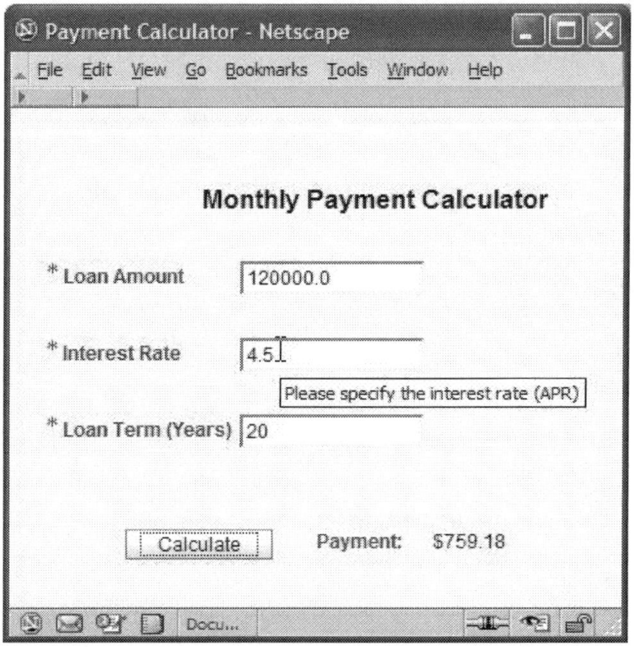

Figure 6–15 **Monthly payment calculator that uses LoanBean**

6.4 The Creator-JSF Life Cycle

Now that you've built two projects in this chapter (Login2 and Payment1) that involve page navigation, validation, conversion, JavaBeans objects, and saving state across page requests, you're ready to delve into the JSF life cycle and apply it to the Creator application model. We're going to present the JSF life cycle phases and explore what sorts of processing occurs in each phase. When viewed as a step-by-step sequence of events, the life cycle phases make sense and explain how the framework invokes your application's code.

What is not so straightforward, however, is how to consistently invoke initialization and cleanup code and have all scenarios handled. To that end, Creator provides a set of callback methods that allow you to control initialization code, cleanup code, and code that helps render your page. First, let's take a look at the JSF life cycle.

JSF Life Cycle

The JavaServer Faces framework provides a life cycle for a JSP request. The six steps in this life cycle process are shown in Figure 6–16[5]. While the steps always occur in the same order, it is important to note that not all six steps will necessarily be processed for every page request. For example, validation rules are applied to the request during Step 3 (Process Validations). If a component fails a validation, the page is returned with an error message and the process skips directly to Step 6 (Render Response). Furthermore, JSF (and indeed all HTTP-based frameworks) make a distinction between an *initial request* (invoking the first page of a web application, navigating to a new page with a redirect, or navigating to a page with an explicit URL (a bookmark)) and a *postback* (handling and processing a request due to user input). During an initial request, JSF executes only the first (Restore View) and last (Render Response) phases. When JSF handles a postback it potentially executes all six phases. Let's describe these phases.

Phase 1 - Restore View

This is a system-level phase, meaning that application code is not involved. JSF builds the view of the page and saves it in the FacesContext instance. (You accessed the FacesContext when you hooked into the navigation handler using a noncommand component in project Navigate2. See "Noncommand Components" on page 201.) The view consists of a tree of the UI components for the page. If this is an initial request, the view is empty and the system skips to the Render Response phase. There is no processing, since there is not yet any input supplied by the user. If this is a postback, the view already exists and the system continues to the Apply Request Values phase.

Phase 2 - Apply Request Values

During the Apply Request Values phase, any new input values are extracted and stored by the appropriate component. If the component's local value is not a String, it must be converted to the correct type. If the conversion fails, several steps occur.

1. An error message is generated and associated with the component.
2. The error message is queued on the FacesContext (it will be displayed later in the Render Response phase).

---

5. This diagram is adapted from "JavaServer Faces Standard Request-Response Life Cycle," in the J2EE 1.4 Tutorial. See `http://java.sun.com/j2ee/1.4/docs/tutorial/doc/index.html` for more information.

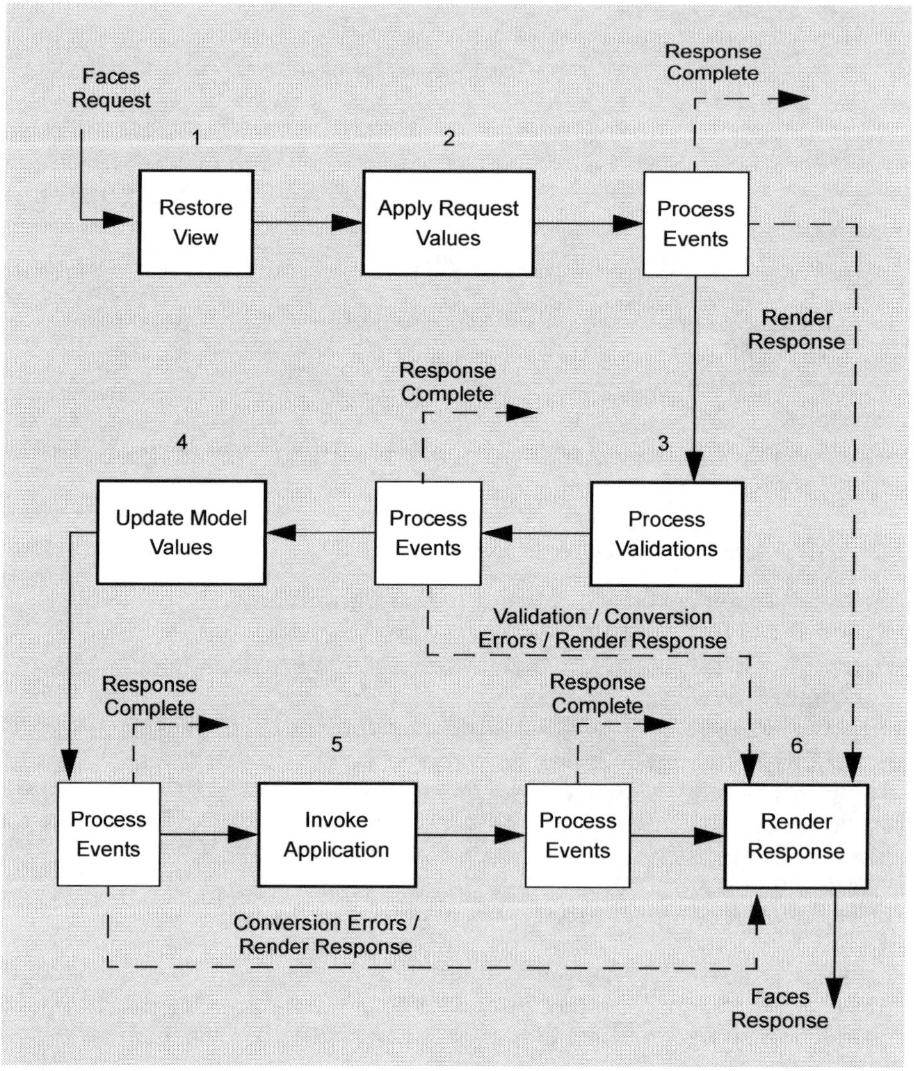

Figure 6–16 **JSF Request-Response Life Cycle Process**

3. The life cycle skips to the Render Response phase when this phase has completed (all of the components will process their input values).

   Skipping to the Render Response phase has several consequences.

- The same page will be rendered. This allows the user to see the input errors for all of the fields that have errors.

- Since the Process Validations phase is skipped, the system won't try to validate badly formed input.
- None of the business data will be updated (this happens in the Update Model Values phase).
- None of the event handlers will be invoked (this happens in the Invoke Applications phase).

Creator Tip

If any component on the page has its `immediate` *property set to true, then the validation, conversion, and events associated with this component take place during the Apply Request Values phase. For many cases, however, using virtual forms precludes the necessity of using the* `immediate` *property.*

As an example, in project Payment1 when the user types in new values for the loan amount, interest rate, and loan term, these values are converted from the character strings to Double and Integer values in this phase. If the user supplies non-numeric input, the conversion fails. A standard conversion error message is displayed during the Render Response phase in the relevant message component. None of the LoanBean properties are updated with the new values when the conversion error occurs, since processing skips to the Render Response phase.

Phase 3 - Process Validations

After component input has been converted (successfully) it is validated during the Process Validations phase. Validation is typically customized to the application. All input that has validation is validated. If any input fails validation, the same steps described above for failed conversion occur here. Thus, an error message is queued, processing skips to the Render Response phase, and the same page is rendered. The user thus receives feedback for all input that fails validation.

In the Payment1 project, if the user supplies input that can be converted but is outside the minimum and maximum limits you specify for the validator, the component is marked invalid.

Phase 4 - Update Model Values

During the Update Model Values phase, all input has been properly converted and validated. This is the phase which processes property bindings: the model data is updated with the values from the components. Thus, the model data has new values. For example, when the user submits a username and password in project Login2, these values are stored in the LoginBean component during this phase. Similarly, in project Payment1, the values supplied for the loan amount, interest rate, and term are stored in the LoanBean component. Because JSF executes this phase only after successfully completing the Process Validations phase, you are guaranteed that the updated model values will be valid. (Of course, the data may violate some business logic, but business logic validation usually occurs in the Invoke Application phase when event handler code is executed.)

Phase 5 - Invoke Application

During the Invoke Application phase, JSF processes any application-level events. Typical events include action events (for command components such as buttons and hyperlinks) or process value change events (for input components such as text fields or drop down lists). Action events return a String that is provided to the navigation handler which determines the next page to be displayed.

In project Login2, when you click the Login button, method `login_action()` processes the username and password you supply (this is the business logic). Depending on the outcome, the method returns either "loginSuccess" or "loginFail." The navigation handler then determines that either the LoginGood or LoginBad page should be displayed next.

In project Payment1, there are no specified event handlers. The property bindings mean that the model data (the LoanBean component) is updated with the user submitted values during Phase 4. Then property bindings come into play again when the components are rendered with the updated model data during Phase 6.

Phase 6 - Render Response

During this final phase, the page is rendered. If this is an initial request for this page, the components are added to the view at this time. If this is a postback, the components have already been added to the view.

If there are messages queued (from conversion or validation errors) and the page contains a message or message group component, these will be displayed. Conversely, if the page does *not* contain a message or message group component, no message will appear.

If there were no errors and if there are property bindings associated with any of the components, the component values are updated from model properties. For example, in project Payment1, the static text component that displays the monthly payment value is updated with the `payment` property of the LoanBean component at this time. Similarly, in project Login2, the label component on page LoginGood is updated with the `username` property of the LoginBean component.

If there were errors, the component values are not updated from the model data. To see this behavior, deploy and run project Login2. You'll note that the userName text field is initialized from the LoginBean username property (it is 'xxx'). Change the 'xxx' to something else (such as 'newusername'). Now clear the field for the password input and click Login. The password field fails validation, which means that the Process Validations phase skips to the Render Response phase. Since JSF skips the Update Model Values phase, the username and password properties in the LoginBean component are not updated. When the page is re-rendered, the password field is still empty and a validation error message appears. The username field contains the new input ('newusername') which was left unaltered in the component.

Creator Life Cycle Callback Methods

The JSF life cycle is relatively straightforward. What is a bit tricky is understanding the sequence of events when page navigation occurs. Recall that in the Creator model, each page bean has request scope. Therefore, for each request the page is created anew. When you navigate from one page to the next, the second page is created for the Render Response phase. The first page is not destroyed until after the Render Response phase.

Creator provides hooks into this life cycle process for the application developer. The initial release of Creator exposed methods that are invoked before and after each of the JSF life cycle events. For example, method beforeRenderResponse() is invoked before the Render Response phase and afterRenderResponse() is invoked after this phase. The process is muddied, however, by the following complications:

- Not all of the phases are always executed. If input fails to properly convert or fails validation, the life cycle process skips from the Process Validations phase to the Render Response phase.
- Because you may navigate to a new page, the beforeRenderResponse() method may not belong to the page that actually gets rendered.
- If this is the initial page (a Welcome page, for example) of the application, JSF has not yet constructed the view (the components that comprise the state of the application) when the page's constructor is invoked. Therefore, there wasn't a consistent place to put page initialization and cleanup code.

The current release of Creator addresses these issues by supplying callback methods that are available in any page bean, that is, the Java backing code that Creator generates for you whenever you create a web page through the IDE. Table 6.6 lists these methods (and you'll note that Creator generates stubs for them so that you can easily provide your own code).

The best way to see how these methods work is to step through a few use cases. Let's use project Login2, since this is a multi-page project.

Table 6.6 Creator Page Life Cycle Callback Methods

Method	*Description*
`init()`	Called after JSF either creates the Faces view or restores the Faces view, depending on whether this is a postback or an initial page. When navigation is involved, `init()` is called on the To Page after the processing is complete but before `prerender()` is invoked. Place any page or component initialization code here.
`preprocess()`	Called before Apply Request Values phase for the page bean that is processing this form submit. Since `preprocess()` is invoked before conversion and validation, you are guaranteed that this method will be called even if conversion or validation errors occur. (Method preprocess() is not invoked with an initial request.)
`prerender()`	Called before Render Response for the page bean that is about to be rendered. When you navigate to a new page, `prerender()` is always called on the To Page, not the From Page.
`destroy()`	Called after Render Response for all page beans for which `init()` was also called. When you navigate to a new page, `destroy()` will be called for both the From Page and the To Page. The From Page's `destroy()` method will be invoked first. Put any page cleanup code or state saving code here.

Use Case 1: Initial Request

When you navigate to the web application from a page outside application, this is an initial request.[6] That is, you supply the following URL to the browser:

```
http://hostname:port_number/Login2/
```

Here are the steps.

- JSF executes the Restore View phase for Page1.
  `Page1()` constructor is invoked.
  `Page1.init()` is invoked.
- JSF executes the Render Response phase for Page1. The text field components are initialized from the values in the LoginBean's properties.
  `Page1.prerender()` is invoked.
  `Page1.destroy()` is invoked.

---

6. Technically, an initial request also includes navigating to a new page with a redirect (not a forward) and navigating to a page with an explicit URL (bookmark).

Use Case 2: User Clicks Reset

Page1 of the Login2 project is rendered on the page and the user clicks the Reset button. Because you use virtual forms with this project, the application does not validate the input associated with the text fields. The text fields are cleared when the page is re-rendered (no navigation occurs). Here are the steps.

- JSF executes the Restore View phase for Page1.
  `Page1()` constructor is invoked.
  `Page1.init()` is invoked.
  `Page1.preprocess()` is invoked.

- JSF executes the Apply Request Values, Process Validations, Update Model Values, and Invoke Application phase.

  During the Invoke Application phase, method `Page1.reset_action()` is executed, clearing the text field values.

- JSF executes the Render Response phase for Page1. The text field components are not updated with the LoginBean's property values.
  `Page1.prerender()` is invoked.
  `Page1.destroy()` is invoked.

Use Case 3: User Fails to Login

In this case, the user supplies new values for username and password. These values don't flag validation errors, but the login sequence fails. Thus, the application navigates to the LoginBad page.

- JSF executes the Restore View phase for Page1.
  `Page1()` constructor is invoked.
  `Page1.init()` is invoked.
  `Page1.preprocess()` is invoked.

- JSF executes the Apply Request Values, Process Validations, Update Model Values, and Invoke Application phase.

  During the Apply Request Values phase the user input is stored in its associated component. No conversion is necessary and no errors occur. During the Process Validations phase, the input for username and password is validated and no validation errors occur. During Update Model Values, the input for username and password is copied into the LoginBean's corresponding properties. During the Invoke Application phase, method `Page1.login_action()` is executed. The submitted values stored in Login-

Bean are compared to LoginBean's `correctName` and `correctPassword` fields. The comparison fails and the String "loginFail" is passed to the navigation handler. JSF navigates to page LoginBad.

- JSF executes the Render Response phase for LoginBad.
  `LoginBad()` constructor is invoked.
  `LoginBad.init()` is invoked.
  `LoginBad.prerender()` is invoked.
  `Page1.destroy()` is invoked (From Page).
  `LoginBad.destroy()` is invoked (To Page).

Use Case 4: User Login is Successful

From Page1 the user supplies new values for username and password. These values don't flag validation errors and the login sequence is successful. Thus, the application navigates to the LoginGood page.

- JSF executes the Restore View phase for Page1.
  `Page1()` constructor is invoked.
  `Page1.init()` is invoked.
  `Page1.preprocess()` is invoked.

- JSF executes the Apply Request Values, Process Validations, Update Model Values, and Invoke Application phase.

  During the Apply Request Values phase the user input is stored in its associated component. No conversion is necessary and no errors occur. During the Process Validations phase, the input for username and password is validated and no validation error occur. During Update Model Values, the input for username and password is copied into the LoginBean's corresponding properties. During the Invoke Application phase, Page1's `login_action()` is executed. The submitted values stored in LoginBean are compared to LoginBean's `correctName` and `correctPassword` fields. The comparison succeeds and the String "loginSuccess" is passed to the navigation handler. JSF navigates to page LoginGood

- JSF executes the Render Response phase for LoginGood. The label component's `text` property is set with the value of the LoginBean `username` property which was updated with the submitted values during the Update Model Values phase above.
  `LoginGood()` constructor is invoked.
  `LoginGood.init()` is invoked.
  `LoginGood.prerender()` is invoked.
  `Page1.destroy()` is invoked (From Page).

`LoginGood.destroy()` is invoked (To Page).

6.5 Key Point Summary

The **Login2** and **Payment1** web applications illustrate the power of property bindings with JavaBeans objects that are business components. Used in conjunction with the appropriate converters (for non-String property values in the business objects) and validators, you can see how easy it is to isolate business logic from presentation code in your web applications.

Creator provides a set of life cycle call back methods that simplify the JSF life cycle phases. Use these methods for initialization, cleanup, and page rendering code.

- A JavaBeans object is a Java class that conforms to certain design standards.
- JavaBeans objects implement read-access properties with public getter methods.
- JavaBeans objects implement write-access properties with public setter methods.
- A JavaBeans object must have a public default constructor with no arguments.
- A JavaBeans object is a reusable component and helps separate business logic from presentation code.
- A JavaBeans object hides its implementation code by carefully defining its public methods (outside view).
- You can install a JavaBeans object as a property in one of Creator's default managed beans. A JavaBeans object configured as a property of the **Request1.java** page bean has request scope. Configuring it in **SessionBean1.java** gives it session scope and configuring it in **ApplicationBean1.java** gives it application scope.
- You can also install a JavaBeans object in a Creator project as a managed bean and specify its scope explicitly.
- The bean configuration file **managed-beans.xml** contains your JavaBeans object's name, class, and scope. It may also specify other properties of your bean.
- A managed bean with session scope is available for the duration of the session for one user.
- A managed bean with request scope is available for the duration of the request. When the application transitions from one page to the next, items in request scope are available for the next page.

- To specify a managed bean property within a JSF component tag, use the JSF EL expression

```
#{ManagedBeanName.propertyName}
```

  For example, here `loanBean` is a property of `SessionBean1`.

```
#{SessionBean1.loanBean}
```

- To specify a JavaBeans object's property that is itself a property of a managed bean, use the JSF EL expression

```
#{ManagedBeanName.javaBeanObjectName.propertyName}
```

  For example, here `amount` is a property of `loanBean`.

```
#{SessionBean1.loanBean.amount}
```

- To bind a JSF component's property to a property in a JavaBeans object, select the JSF component, right-click, and select Property Bindings. Creator displays the Property Bindings dialog which lets you specify the JSF component's bindable property and the binding target. The binding target can be a property of another JSF component.
- Creator provides four page bean life cycle methods: `init()`, `preprocess()`, `prerender()`, and `destroy()`.
- Place any page or component initialization code in method `init()`.
- Place any code that should be called before any of the JSF processing phases in `preprocess()`. Since `preprocess()` is invoked before conversion and validation, you are guaranteed that this method will be called even if conversion or validation errors occur.
- Place code that should be called before the page is rendered in `prerender()`. Only the `prerender()` method of the page that will actually be rendered is invoked.
- Method `destroy()` is invoked after the page is rendered. Place any page cleanup code or code that saves state here. When JSF navigates to a different page, the `destroy()` method of the From Page is invoked before the `destroy()` method of the To Page.
- Conversion, validation, event handling code and page navigation can all affect which methods are invoked throughout an application's life cycle.

WEB PAGE DESIGN

Topics in This Chapter

- Component Style
- Themes
- CSS Style Editor
- Page Layout
- Page Fragments
- Project Templates
- Navigation with Page Fragments
- Tab Sets

Chapter 7

Sun Java Studio Creator provides layout components, visual design editors, and style sheet editors to help you design visually pleasing pages for a coherent, unified-looking web application. In this chapter we explore some of the Creator tools and components available to you for page design.

Once you've designed your pages, you'd like to reuse the components, style settings, and logos and images on subsequent pages or in other projects. Cascading style sheets, page fragments, and project templates help designers build artifacts that can be reused. Although you will see some event handling code, page initialization code, and property patterns in the upcoming examples, this chapter concentrates on Creator's visual page design.

7.1 Using the Visual Design Editor

Creator's visual design editor runs in the main editor pane by default when you create a new project. Its main purpose is to help you select components and position them on the page using a page grid. You can also turn off the grid, temporarily disable it, or change the grid size.

Create a Project

Let's explore the main features of the design editor. To do this, you'll build a simple project with three static text components. Figure 7–1 shows the project in the design view with these components.

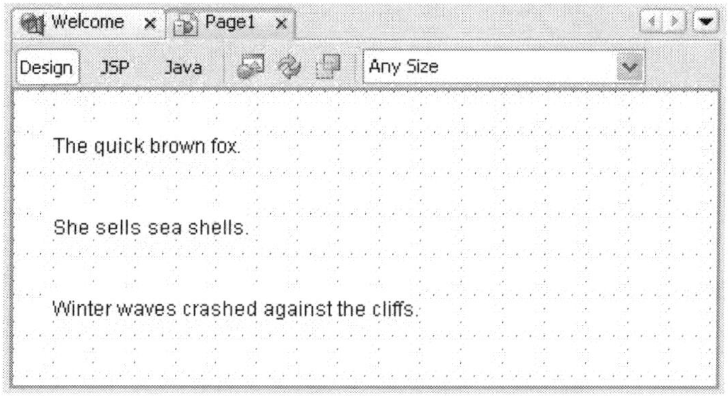

Figure 7–1 **Visual design editor in the editor pane**

1. From Creator's Welcome Page, select button Create New Project. Creator displays the New Project dialog. Under Categories, select Web. Under Projects, select JSF Web Application. Click Next.
2. In the New Web Application dialog under Project Name, specify **Design1**. Click Finish.

   After initializing the project, Creator comes up in the design view of the editor pane. You can now set the title.

3. In the Properties window, select property `Title` and specify title **Design1**. Finish by pressing **<Enter>**.

Add Components to the Page

Now let's add the static text components and specify the text for each one.

1. From the Basic Component palette, select component Static Text and drop it on the page. Don't worry about positioning yet.
2. The component is selected so that you can type in some text. Type in the text **The quick brown fox** followed by **<Enter>**.
3. Select component Static Text again and add it to the page under the first component.
4. Specify its text **She sells sea shells**.

5. Add a third static text component and specify its text **Winter waves crashed against the cliffs**.

Working with Components on the Page

By default, a project's layout is in grid mode. This allows you to position components on the page at an absolute location. The grid helps you with component alignment.

1. Select the first static text component. Creator marks the component selected and displays component resizing handles for you. With the component selected, you can move it to a different location. You'll note that it automatically snaps to the grid.
2. Select the same component a second time. The text area is selected (Creator displays a blue background) and the component is enabled for text editing. In this mode you can now issue typical editing short cuts, such **<Ctrl+C>** for copy or **<Ctrl+V>** for paste. You can also select a word, use the left and right arrow keys, or type replacement text.
3. Sometimes you'll want to move the component so that it doesn't snap to the grid lines. To temporarily turn off grid alignment, select the component, hold the Shift key, and use the mouse to adjust the component on the page.

You can configure Creator to change the grid size or disable it using the Tools menu.

1. In the main menu, select **Tools > Options**. In the Options dialog, select **Visual Designer**. Creator displays the options for the Visual Design Editor, as shown in Figure 7–2.
2. After making changes, click Close.

The Show Grid option controls whether or not the grid is visible in the editor. This is true by default. When the Snap to Grid option is set to true, the components align with the grid lines in the designer. The Grid Height and Grid Width values control the grid size and the Target Browser Window controls the size of the application's window in the browser.

Component Alignment

Each component has a context-sensitive menu that becomes visible when you select a component and right-click the mouse. The Align menu option provides component alignment criteria. While frequently you can align components by simply using the default behavior of snapping to the grid lines, occasionally you'll want to align components using other criteria. For example, here's how to center the three static text components.

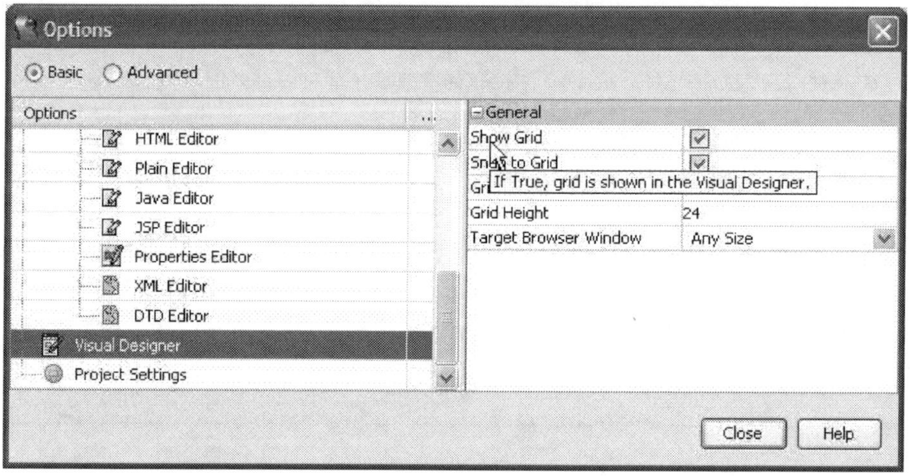

Figure 7–2 **Visual Designer Options dialog**

1. Choose one static component and position it on the grid at the desired location. Use the Shift key if you'd like to disable the snap to grid lines option.
2. You can select multiple components by selecting one, then selecting others while holding the Shift key. Alternatively, you can draw a box around the components you'd like to select, as shown in Figure 7–3. Click the mouse at a spot above and to the left of all the components. Drag the mouse towards the lower-right until all the components are enclosed in the selection box. When you release the mouse, all three components are selected.

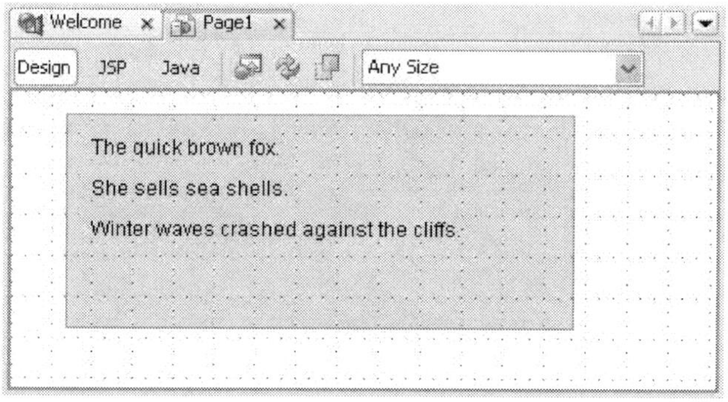

Figure 7–3 **Selecting multiple components**

3. Place the mouse over the component that you want to use as the alignment reference, right-click, and select **Align>Center**. The three components will be horizontally centered using the selected component as the alignment reference.

For horizontal alignment options, select Left, Center, or Right. For vertical alignment options, select Top, Middle, or Bottom.

Deploy and Run

After aligning the components, deploy and run the application. Figure 7–4 shows project Design1 running in the browser. The components were centered horizontally using the third component as the reference for the alignment.

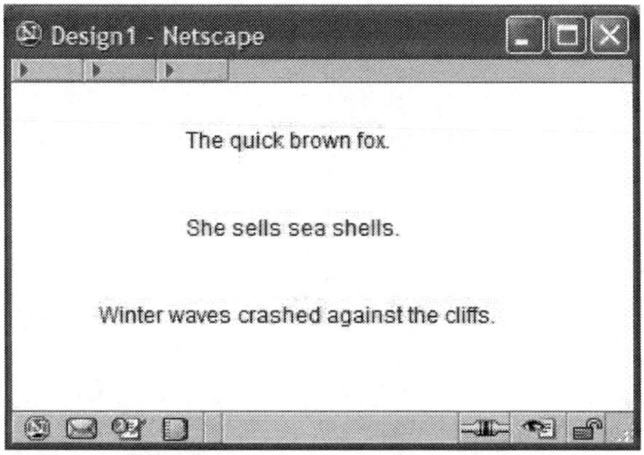

Figure 7–4 **Project Design1 running in a browser**

7.2 Themes

Creator gives web page designers a number of choices for specifying the look of a web page. The components from the Basic, Layout, and Composite sections of the palette are rendered using *themes*. A theme is a bundled set of cascading style sheets, JavaScript files, and images that apply to the components and the web page. Creator currently ships with four configured themes. The available themes for a project are listed in the Projects window under node Themes, as shown in Figure 7–5. The currently selected theme is marked with a triangle badge. To change the current theme, right-click a new theme selection and select **Set As Current Theme**.

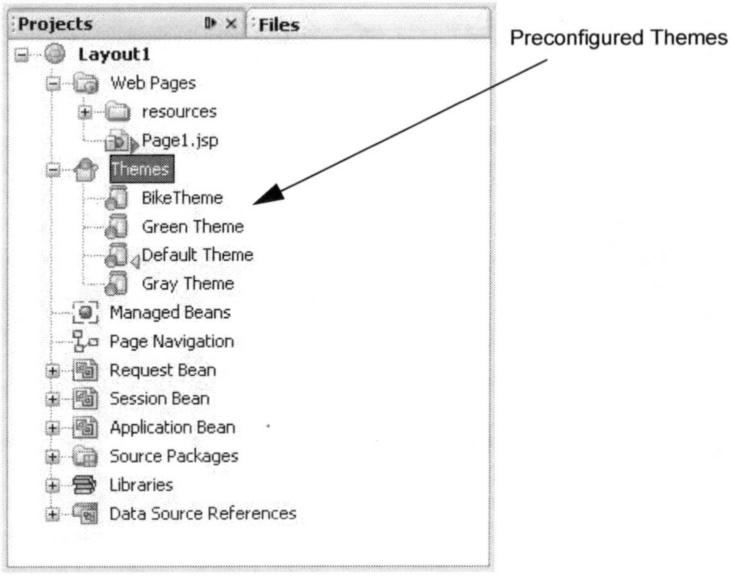

Figure 7–5 **Creator Themes available for projects**

Creator Tip

To make a new theme take effect for deployment, first stop the application server, then clean and rebuild the project.

The Default Theme provides a gradient blue color, giving the components a unified look. The Gray and Green Themes provide color variations with the same gradient appearance. The Gray Theme is useful when you want to give the components a neutral look (for example, if your color scheme does not mesh well with either blue or green). The Bike Theme is used with **Jump Start Cycles**, one of Sun's sample applications. Access sample applications at the following url:

```
http://developers.sun.com/prodtech/javatools/jscreator/reference/code/sampleapps/index.html
```

Changing the Look with Themes

Let's create a simple application, deploy it, and change its current theme. This application won't do much, but you'll see how several components are affected by theme selection. Figure 7–6 shows the project running in a browser. The page contains a hyperlink component, text field, label, static text component, and table. The application is built with the Default (blue) Theme.

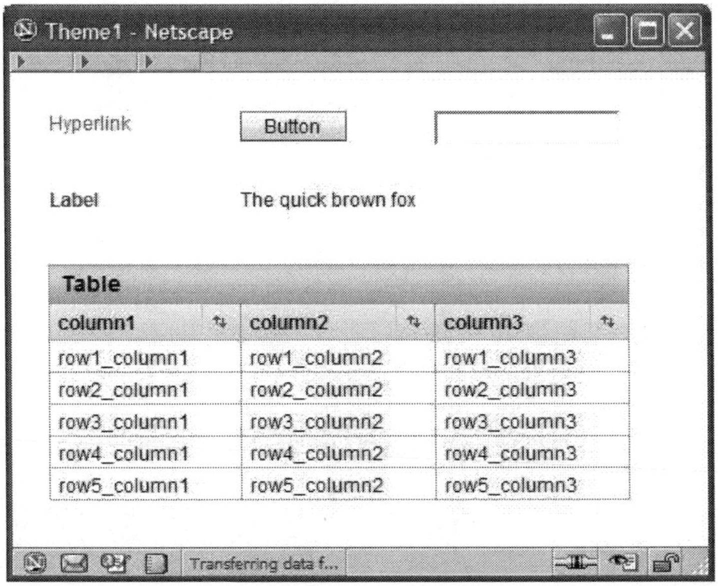

Figure 7–6 **Project Theme1 running in a browser**

1. From Creator's Welcome Page, select button Create New Project. Creator displays the New Project dialog. Under Categories, select Web. Under Projects, select JSF Web Application. Click Next.
2. In the New Web Application dialog under Project Name, specify **Theme1**. Click Finish.

   After initializing the project, Creator comes up in the design view of the editor pane. You can now set the title.

3. In the Properties window, select property `Title` and specify title **Theme1**. Finish by pressing **<Enter>**.
4. In the Projects window, expand the Themes node and make sure that the Default Theme is selected as the current theme (it should display a triangle badge).

Add Components to the Page

Using Figure 7–6 as a guide, add components to the page. Except for the static text component, all will retain their default settings.

1. From the Basic Component palette, select component Hyperlink and drag it to the top-left portion of the page.
2. Select component Button and place it to the right of the hyperlink component.
3. Select component Text Field and place it next to the button.
4. Select component Label and place it under the hyperlink component.
5. Select component Static Text and place it to the right of the label component. When you drop it on the design canvas, it remains selected and you can begin typing. Type in some text (**The quick brown fox**) and finish with **<Enter>**.
6. Finally, select component Table and place it on the page below the label component. Creator generates a table with default rows, columns, and data. The table component reflects the colors used by the different themes particularly well.
7. Deploy and run the application by clicking the Run arrow on the toolbar.

Change the Current Theme

Now let's change the current theme for this project and redeploy the application.

1. In the Projects window, expand the Themes node. Right-click Green Theme and select **Set As Current Theme**. Creator reminds you that you must stop the application server, then clean and rebuild the project before redeploying.
2. In the Projects window, expand the Libraries node and scroll down until you find the JAR file associated with the Green Theme library.
3. Expand the Green Theme library. You'll see the **defaulttheme-green.css** file as well as the images, properties, and JavaScript files associated with this theme. (You'll look at a cascading style sheet (**.css**) file shortly.)
4. In the Servers window, right-click Deployment Server and select **Start / Stop Server**. Click the Stop Server button.
5. Return to the Projects window, right-click the Theme1 project name, and select **Clean and Build Project**. (This step is necessary to make the application server use the correct JAR file for the selected theme.)
6. Deploy and run the application by clicking the Run arrow on the toolbar. The application should now display green-colored components.
7. Repeat Steps 1-6 above to change the current theme to the Bike Theme.

Creator Tip

Instead of deploying the application each time, you can right-click inside the visual design editor and select Preview in Browser for a quick look at a newly selected theme.

Modifying the Default Theme

The Default, Gray, and Green Themes are variations of the same theme. Is it possible to modify themes for different colors or use a different theme altogether? The style sheets and images that apply to components can theoretically be modified. The theme JAR files are installed in the Creator2 directory (currently at **rave2.0/modules/ext**). You can unpack the JAR file, edit the CSS file and images, and repackage them. Until Creator includes a theme-based editor, however, this remains a non-trivial task. Still, there's much you can do to control the appearance of your application. Let's continue to explore web page design options beginning with style.

7.3 About Style

You've probably noticed by now that each component has a `style` property that allows you to change the appearance of various features such as font (size, color, family, style), position, height, width, etc. Some components also contain "pass-through" HTML attributes, such as border and cellpadding that apply to table-type components. You specify style attributes by modifying the component's property sheet directly. This gives you control over the look of a specific component. It is also a handy way to experiment with different styles until you decide on an overall style for your application.

Property `style` accepts style declarations in the form

```
property1: value1; property2: value2; . . . propertyN: valueN
```

Let's look at an example.

Copy the Project

You'll make a copy of project Theme1 (call it Theme2) for this section. This step is optional. If you don't want to copy the project, simply skip this section and continue making modifications to the Theme1 project.

1. Bring up project Theme1 in Creator, if it's not already opened.
2. From the Projects window, right-click node Theme1 and select **Save Project As**. Provide the new name **Theme2**.
3. Close project Theme1. Right-click Theme2 and select **Set Main Project**. You'll make changes to the Theme2 project.
4. Expand **Theme2 > Web Pages** and open **Page1.jsp** in the design view.

5. Click anywhere in the background of the design canvas of the Theme2 project. In the Properties window, change the pages's `Title` property to **Theme2**.
6. Select the table component, right-click, and select **Delete** from the context menu to remove the component from the page (to simplify the page).

Using the Style Editor

Let's use the style editor to manipulate a component's look.

1. For project Theme2, restore the current theme to the Default Theme (blue-toned). Remember to stop the application server and clean and rebuild the project before proceeding.
2. In the Design View, select component `staticText1`.
3. In the Properties view, click the small editing box opposite property `style`. Creator pops up the Style Editor, as shown in Figure 7–7.

Creator provides a sophisticated Style Editor that lets you specify a component's style attributes. The Property Selection window lets you choose a property to edit. Depending on this selection, the editor displays windows that let you select values from a list or specify a custom value. When you change an attribute, the Results Display Window applies the style to the component.

Use the Style Editor to modify the static text component's `style` property.

1. Select **Font** in the Property Selection window.
2. In the Font-Family selection window, select the list of font-family values beginning with **Verdana**.
3. In the Size window, select font size **18**.
4. In the Style selection window, choose **italic** from the drop down menu. Note that the text in the Results Display windows reflects your selections.
5. Now select **Background** in the Property Selection window. The editor displays a different set of selection windows.
6. Select color **yellow** in the Background Color drop down menu.
7. Choose **Border** in the Property Selection window.
8. In the All selection window for Style select **solid**, for Width select **1px**, and for Color select **gray**.

Here is the new CSS Style setting for this component.

```
border: 1px solid gray; background-color: yellow;
  font-family: Verdana,Arial,Helvetica,sans-serif;
  font-size: 18px; font-style: italic; left: 120px; top: 72px;
  position: absolute
```

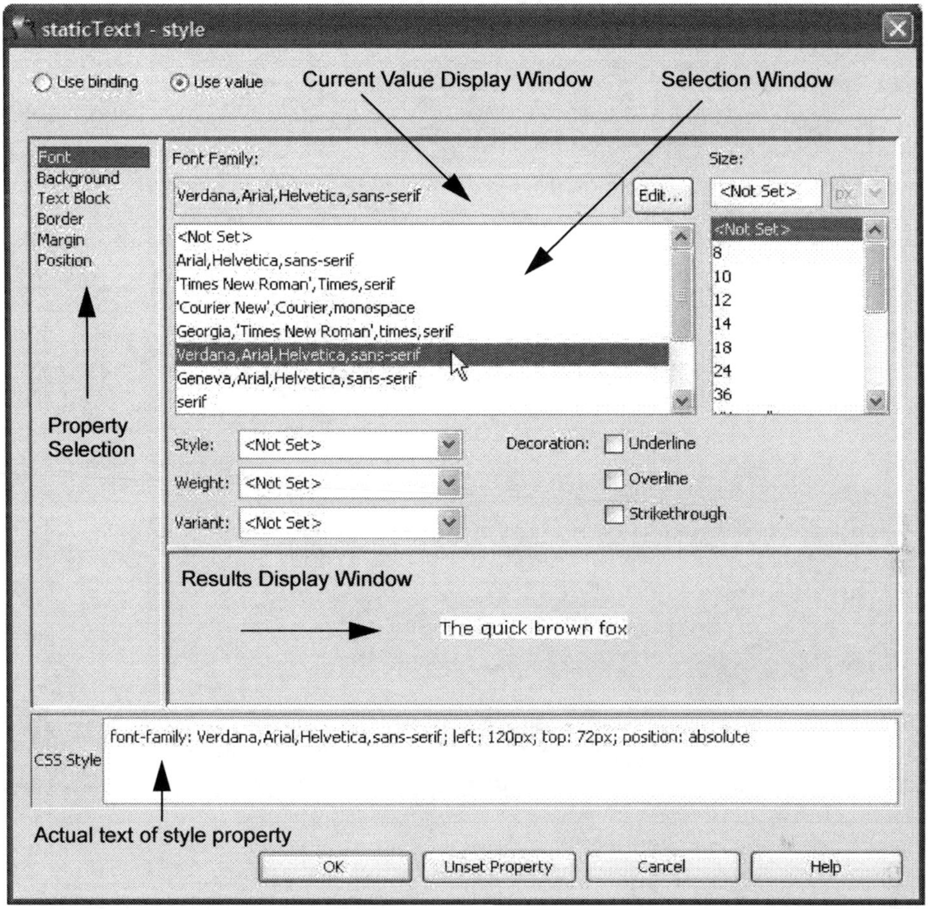

Figure 7–7 **Using the Style Editor**

9. Click OK. The page in the design view reflects the new style characteristics.

Deploy and Run

Right-click in the visual design editor and choose Preview in Browser, or deploy and run the application to check its appearance.

7.4 Cascading Style Sheets

Using a component's `style` property to control its look can be tedious. You must specify attributes for each component manually by editing its property sheet. Furthermore, it's difficult to employ a uniform look for a web page using only `style` property settings.

Creator uses Cascading Style Sheets (CSS) to control the look of its components and pages. CSS is a standard that allows a web designer to specify style characteristics. The style characteristics apply to a document in a *cascading* fashion: that is, a style applies to a given level and subsequent styles can in turn apply on top of these "inherited" styles. If you don't specify a property for an element, it generally inherits the property from its "parent." For example, you can specify that all text in a document is (color) navy. You can then specify that text in a footer is a smaller text size. The footer text will be *both* navy and the smaller size since the footer-specific style inherits all properties specified for the global style.

You can read more about Cascading Style Sheets at the Cascading Styles Home Page: `http://www.w3.org/Style/CSS/`. The web site also includes tutorials about how to use style sheets.

Using Property styleClass

All Creator components include property `styleClass`, which is a comma separated list of style classes. You define and store a style class in a text file called a *style sheet*. As stated earlier, using property `styleClass` helps web designers create a uniform look to all pages in a project. Creator provides a default style sheet, **stylesheet.css**, that is included in each project you create. When you add style classes to the style sheet, you can then reference them in the component's `styleClass` attribute. (Note that the bundled themes include a set of style rules that also apply to the components.)

A style sheet is a collection of style *rules*. Each rule consists of a *selector* and a *declarator*. The selector identifies an HTML element(s) or style class name(s) to which the rule applies. The curly braces encompass the declarator, which is the semi-colon separated list of property-value pairs. While the component's `style` attribute lists the property-value pairs for a given component, a rule is a collection of property-value pairs that is named.

Let's examine the default style sheet, **stylesheet.css**, in the Style Sheet Editor. In the Projects window for project Theme2, select **Web Pages > resources** and double-click file **stylesheet.css**. Creator brings up the style sheet in the Style Sheet Editor and highlights the first rule, `.list-header`.

```
.list-header {
  background-color: #eeeeee;
  font-size: larger;
  font-weight: bold;
}
```

There are three property-value pairs here: property `background-color` has value `#eeeeee`, property `font-size` has value `larger`, and property `font-weight` has value `bold`. Rules that contain an initial dot are *style classes*. Once you define them in the style sheet for your project, you can specify the class names in a component's `styleClass` attribute.

You can also define rules that apply to HTML elements such as `<body>`, `<th>` (table heading), `<td>` (table data). The `body` style rule is a good place to list global settings for your web application, such as basic font characteristics, text color, and background color. Let's do this now.

1. Scroll to the top and add the following comment.

```
/* Custom style rules */
```

2. Now add a rule for body followed by opening and closing braces.

```
/* Custom style rules */

body {
}
```

3. Put the cursor after the open brace and hit **<Enter>**. You see that Creator pops up a property selection dialog. Select **background-color** followed by **<Enter>**.
4. Creator now pops up a value selection dialog, as shown in Figure 7–8. Scroll down to the bottom and choose **more...** and hit **<Enter>**.
5. Creator pops up a Choose Color dialog. Select tab RGB and specify values **230, 230, 200**, as shown in Figure 7–9. Click OK. Creator fills in value `#e6e6c8` for property `background-color`.
6. Continue editing style class `body`. You can also use the style selection windows below the editing pane. Here is the style to use for `body`.

```
body {
   background-color: #e6e6c8;
   font-family: Verdana,Arial,Helvetica,sans-serif
}
```

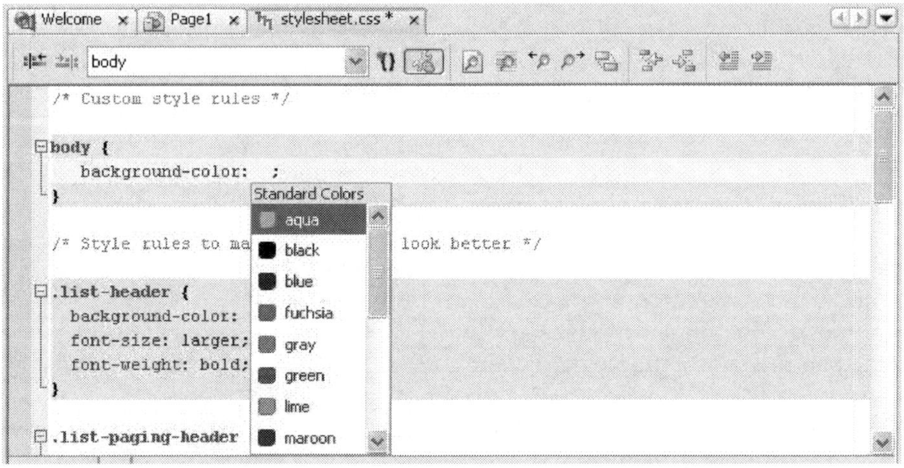

Figure 7–8 **Using the Style Sheet (CSS) Editor**

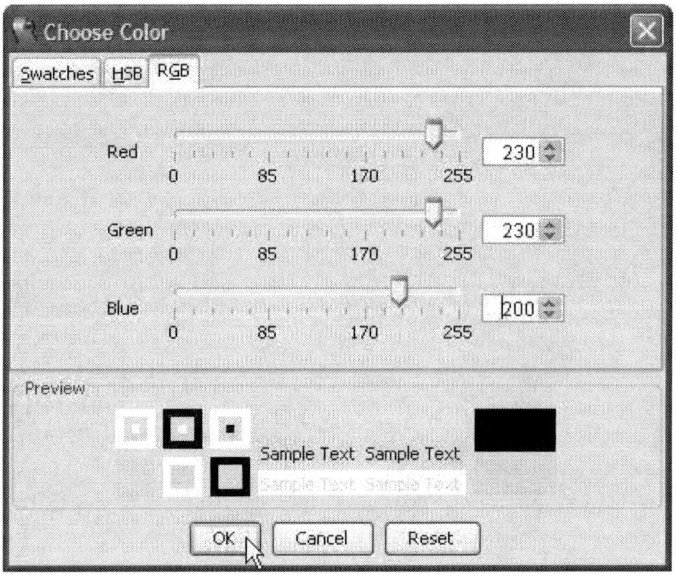

Figure 7–9 **Choose Color dialog**

7. Add a style class called `.headingStyle`, as follows. Use the style selection windows to specify `font-size` and `font-weight` (or just type them in).

```
.headingStyle {
    font-size: XX-large;
    font-weight: bold
}
```

8. Select the Save All icon on the toolbar to save the changes and close the Style Sheet Editor (click the small x in the **stylesheet.css** tab).

The `body` rule applies to all HTML `<body>` elements, as well as any elements declared inside of `<body>`. Thus, nested ("children") elements inherit the property-value settings from their enclosing ("parent") elements.

Return to the Page1 design view. You'll see that the background color and the font-family setting reflect the body style rule you defined. Now you'll apply the `.headingStyle` style class to the static text component.

1. In the design view, select the static text component (its text is "The quick brown fox").
2. Select the editing box opposite the `style` property. When the style editor pops up, select **Unset Property**. Creator clears its `style` setting (including its position value). The component is now in the upper-left corner.
3. Select it and move to its previous location (restoring its position values).
4. Make sure the component is still selected and type in the text **headingStyle** for property `styleClass` (do not use the initial dot from the style sheet file) followed by **<Enter>**. The static text component now has the extra large font size and is bold.

Deploy and Run

Deploy and run the project. Figure 7–10 shows the application running in a browser.

7.5 Page Layout

Creator provides several components that help you manipulate the layout of your web page. In this section, we'll examine components layout panel, grid panel, and anchor (paired with hyperlink). We'll keep the projects simple in order to concentrate on page layout issues.

Figure 7–10 **Project Theme2 running in a browser**

Layout Panel

Creator's palette includes several component containers that group or nest embedded components. With containers, you can uniformly control the "children" components' appearance, including position, style, and rendering. The layout panel component positions its components with either a flow layout, placing each component directly after the previous one, or a grid layout, letting you position components using the design editor. For this project, we'll also show you how to inspect the CSS style rules and HTML rendering that Creator generates for you. Finally, we'll show you how to center components on the page, even when the user resizes the browser window.

Create a Project

In the following project, you'll control components by grouping them together, allowing the components to share common style, position, and rendering attributes. You'll see how the layout panel lets you position components using the standard grid.

1. From Creator's Welcome Page, select button Create New Project. Creator displays the New Project dialog. Under Categories, select Web. Under Projects, select JSF Web Application. Click Next.
2. In the New Web Application dialog under Project Name, specify **Layout1**. Click Finish.

   After initializing the project, Creator comes up in the design view of the editor pane. You can now set the title.

3. In the Properties window, select property `Title` and specify title **Layout and Style**. Finish by pressing **<Enter>**.

Add Components to the Page

Figure 7–11 shows the design view of project Layout1. Use this as a guide as you add components to the page.

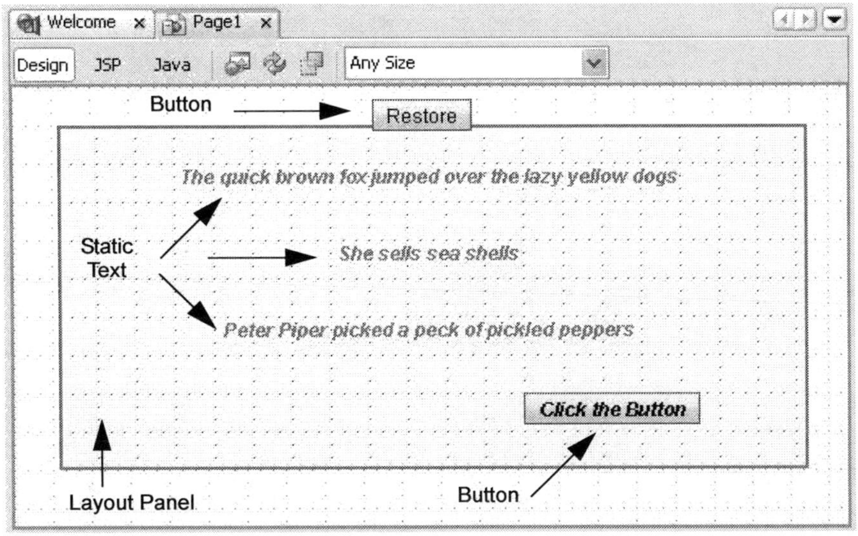

Figure 7–11 **Design view for project Layout1**

1. From the Layout section of the Component palette, select Layout Panel and drop it on the page. Enlarge it so that it is approximately 20 grids wide and 10 grids high.
2. Make sure the layout panel component is selected. In the Properties window opposite property `panelLayout`, select **Grid Layout** from the drop down list. This lets you use the design view's grid to position components that you'll add to the panel.
3. Still in the Properties window for the layout panel, click the small editing box opposite property `style`. Creator pops up the Style Editor.

As you've seen, there are several ways to modify a components' `style` property. We'll step you through using the editor, but you can also type in the style attributes manually. Refer to Figure 7–7 on page 283 for the window labels used here.

4. In the Property Selection window, select **Font**. In the center Font Family Selection Window, choose **Georgia,'Times New Roman',times,serif**. In the Size Selection Window, choose **12**. In the Style window, select **italic** from the drop down list. In the Weight window, select **bold** from the drop down list. In the Color window, select **gray** from the drop down list.
5. Now select **Background** in the Property Selection window. In the Background Color window, type the value **rgb(255,255,204)** followed by **<Enter>**. The small color indicator on the right will change to a muted yellow.
6. Select property **Border**. In the top row labeled All, for Style select **solid** and for Width select **2px**. Select OK to close the Style Editor. The layout panel now has a border and a new background color.

By changing the layout panel's `style` settings, you'll see how the children components are affected by the layout panel's `style`. Some style attributes are inherited (such as font characteristics); others are not (such as border). And some settings are overridden by more specific settings. We'll examine this in more detail after you add components to the layout panel.

1. From the Basic Components palette, select Static Text and drop it on the layout panel component. The static text component appears in the Page1 Outline view nested under the layout panel.
2. Type in the text **The quick brown fox jumped over the lazy yellow dogs** followed by **<Enter>**.
3. Change the static text `id` property to **line1**.
4. Add two more static text components with text **She sells sea shells** and **Peter Piper picked a peck of pickled peppers.** Change the id properties to `line2` and `line3`. All three static text components will be nested under the layout panel in the Page1 Outline view, as shown in Figure 7–12. (The screen shot also shows two button components, which you'll add later.)

Let's position the three static text components so that they're centered on the layout panel.

1. First, use the grid lines to evenly space the static text components vertically. Leave some room at the bottom of the panel for a button component.
2. Select the first static text component. Use **<Shift+Click>** to select all three static text components, as well as the layout panel.
3. Position the cursor inside the layout panel (anywhere in the background) and right-click. Select **Align > Center** from the context menu. Creator centers all three text components horizontally, using the layout panel as the reference component. The components should now be centered, as shown in Figure 7–11 on page 289.

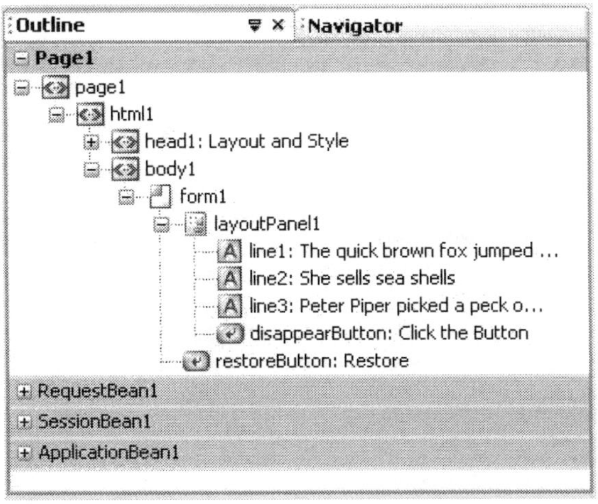

Figure 7–12 **Page1 Outline view for project Layout1**

Creator Tip

Note that the components are positioned relative to the layout panel component. If you re-position the layout panel on the page, the nested components retain their relative position inside the panel.

Now let's add two button components: one inside the layout panel and one outside.

1. From the Basic Component palette, select component Button and place it inside the layout panel. Position it under the three text components off-center to the right.
2. Change its text label to **Click the Button** (note that the button's font inherits the font style from the panel).
3. Change the button's `id` property to **disappearButton**.
4. From the Basic Component palette, select component Button again and place it on the page, centered above the layout panel (outside of the panel). The button component is not nested inside the panel component in the Page1 Outline view. Its font characteristics are therefore independent of the layout panel's settings.
5. Change its text label to **Restore**.
6. Change the button's `id` property **restoreButton**.

The event handling code for the buttons will make the layout panel disappear from the page (`disappearButton`) and then will restore it on the page (`restoreButton`).

1. In the design view, double-click the first button (`disappearButton`). Creator generates a default action event handler and brings up the Java source editor so that you can add event handling code.
2. Add the following code to the `disappearButton_action()` event handler (the added code is shown in bold).

```
public String disappearButton_action() {
   layoutPanel1.setRendered(false);
   restoreButton.setRendered(true);
   return null;
}
```

The event handler sets the `rendered` property of the layout panel to false, causing it (and all of its nested components) to disappear from the page. It makes the Restore button appear on the page.

1. Click label Design in the editing pane to return to the design view.
2. Double-click the Restore button, which brings up the action event handler in the Java source editor.
3. Add the following code to the `restoreButton_action()` event handler. The added code is bold. When the user clicks the button, the layout panel and all of its nested components will be rendered on the page. At the same time, the Restore button will disappear.

```
public String restoreButton_action() {
   layoutPanel1.setRendered(true);
   restoreButton.setRendered(false);
   return null;
}
```

4. Click label Design in the editing pane to return to the design view.
5. Select the Restore button. In the Properties view under Advanced (scroll down to see it), *uncheck* property `rendered`. The button disappears from the design view.

Creator Tip

Even though the component no longer appears on the design view, you can still select it in the Page1 Outline view. If you want to adjust it visually, turn the rendered property back on, make adjustments, and then turn it off again.

Deploy and Run

Deploy and run the application by selecting the green arrow in the icon toolbar. Figure 7–13 shows project Layout1 running in a browser. When you click the inside button, the layout panel disappears and the Restore button is rendered. Clicking the Restore button makes the layout panel reappear.

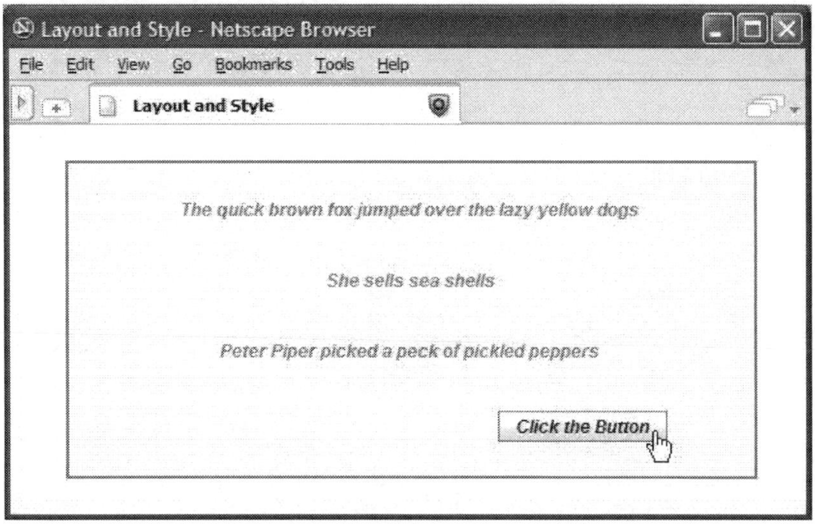

Figure 7–13 **Project Layout1 running in a browser**

More CSS Style Issues

Although this project is very simple, there are subtle style issues illustrated here. The style that a component finally acquires is an amalgamation from various sources, some of which may not be obvious. For example, the Creator components acquire a basic style from the pre-configured Theme style sheets. (This is why the button component has a gradient blue background image.) When you nest components inside container components, the nested ones can inherit styles from the enclosing component. (Thus, the button and the text components have a bold, italic font.) To help you figure out where style definitions originate, Creator has a hidden Document Object Model (DOM) inspector (*hidden* because it is not a formal part of the product). Let's examine several components in this project with the DOM inspector.

You access the DOM inspector by selecting a component with **<Ctrl+Alt+Click>**. Creator displays a Layout Inspector window that contains a tree of the page's components. HTML components are shown in angle <> brackets and the Creator component `id` appears (if there is one). The Properties window displays property values that can help you with various style attributes.

For example, select the third static component and type **<Ctrl+Alt+Click>**. Depending on where you actually place the cursor, a word is highlighted in red on the design view. Figure 7–14 shows the Layout Inspector (on the left) and the corresponding Properties window (on the right).

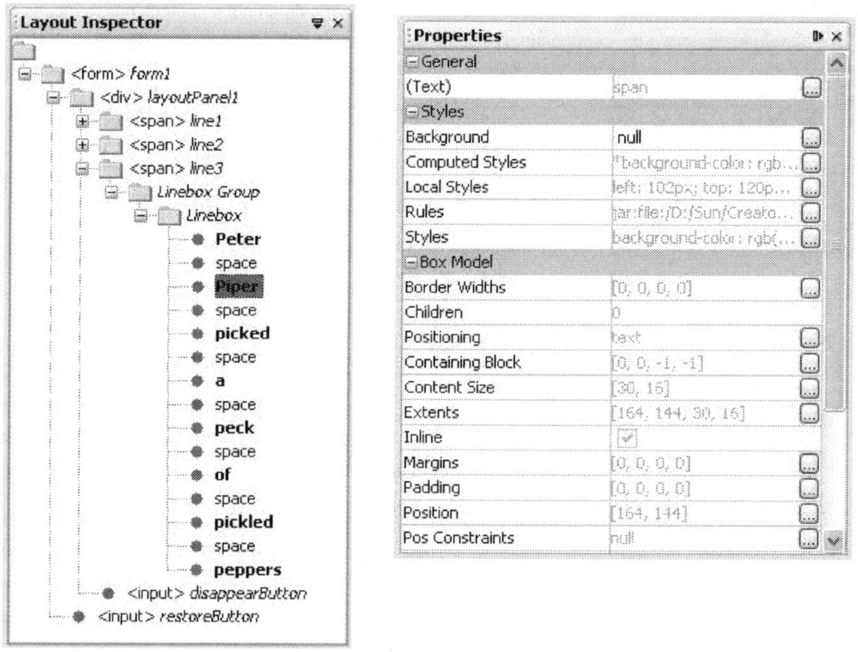

Figure 7–14 **Creator DOM Inspector**

Let's say you want to determine exactly where the text is set to italic. In the Properties window under Styles, there are several helpful windows. Computed Styles tells you where a style setting originates. Local Styles are the style rules set for this element (values not inherited), Rules are the CSS rules that apply to this element, and Styles is the grand total of all the styles that apply to this element.

In the Properties window, click the small box opposite property **Local Styles**. In the property customizer, you'll see that this element contains only positioning styles. Click Close. Now select property **Rules**. These are the style rules that apply to this element (found in file **css_master.css**). Click Close. Now select property **Computed Styles**. Creator pops up the customizer shown in Figure 7–15. Scroll up until you find the property setting for `font-style` (shown highlighted in the figure). You see that it's set to italic and it references Line 12 in **Page1.jsp**. Click Close and select JSP in the editing pane to open Page1 in the

JSP editor. Line 12 contains the component definition for <ui:panelLayout>, the layout panel that contains the text components. Thus, the text component *inherited* its `font-style` property value from the layout panel.

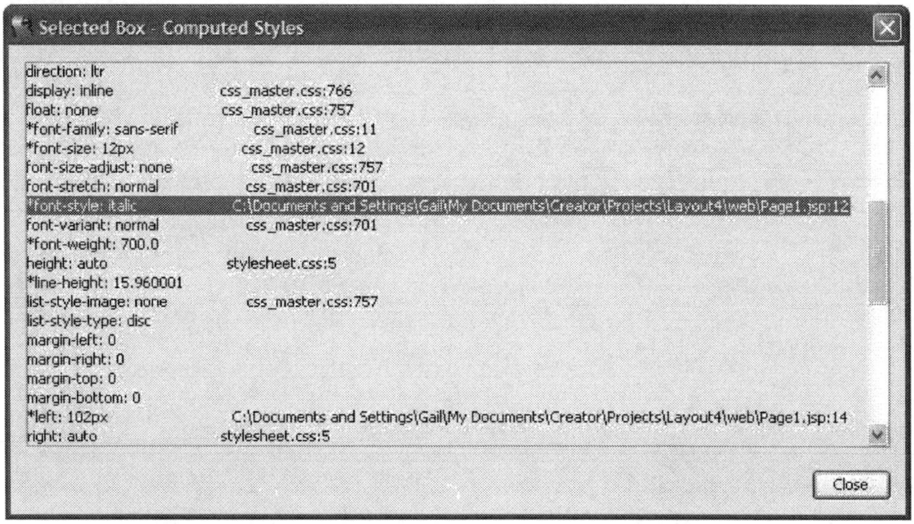

Figure 7–15 **Computed Styles property**

Finally, return to the design view (click Design in the editing toolbar) and re-select the text component with **<Shift+Alt+Click>**. Now select **Styles** (under Styles) in the Properties window. You'll see all of the styles that apply to the static text component.

Centering Components on a Page

Let's continue our exploration of manipulating style attributes to center the components in your browser window. You can apply centering horizontally, vertically, or both. To center a component horizontally, you must know the *width* of the target component. Likewise, to center a component vertically, you must know its *height*. The convenience of using containers is that you can center the container on the page, and then all of its children components retain their relative positions in the centered container.

We're going to center the components on the page both horizontally and vertically. You center the layout panel and separately center the Restore button (you might want to enable rendering for the Restore button until you're done modifying its style).

1. From the Page1 design view, select the layout panel. In the Properties window, select property `style` and bring up the style editor.

2. At the bottom on the window, you'll see the style settings for the component. Note the property settings for `width` and `height`. It will be something similar to the following (depending on how you sized the layout panel).

```
height: 212px; width: 460px;
```

To center horizontally, use `left: 50%`. To center vertically, use `top: 50%`. Unfortunately, these values will center the top-left corner of the layout panel. To compensate for this calculation, you adjust using negative values for `margin-left` and `margin-top`. The value should be *half the size* of the component's width (for `margin-left`) and *half the size* of its height (for `margin-top`).

Therefore, the new positioning values are as follows.

```
margin-left: -230px; margin-top: -106px; left: 50%; top: 50%;
```

3. Provide the above values for the layout panel's positioning and click OK. Creator will center the layout panel in the design view.
4. In the Page1 Outline view select the Restore button. In the Properties window under Advanced, enable rendering (check property `rendered`). The button will appear on the design canvas.
5. In the Properties window, select property `style` and bring up the style editor.

Creator Tip

Note that there are no set values for a button's height and width, because the component automatically sizes itself according to the text label. To find out its approximate size, you can resize it slightly and Creator will then make its size static. Use these values for the centering calculations and then return the component to automatic sizing by removing the static values for width and height.

6. The position values for the Restore button are as follows. Provide the values for the button in the Style editor and click OK.

```
margin-left: -33px; margin-top: -12px; left: 50%; top: 50%;
```

7. In the Restore button's Properties window under Advanced, *uncheck* property `rendered`.

Creator Tip

Note that if you adjust the position of the layout component or the Restore button in the design view, Creator replaces the percentage values you supplied for left and top with absolute position values. You'll have to re-edit the style property and supply the percentage settings.

Deploy and Run

Deploy and run project Layout1. Resize the browser window and check that the layout panel component remains centered. After you click the button, the Restore button appears. It should also be centered on the page. Figure 7–16 shows the component centered in the browser window.

Figure 7–16 **Project Layout1 with centered components**

Grid Panel

Creator provides another container component called a grid panel. The grid panel (as its name implies) provides a grid layout, whereby you specify the number of columns if you require more than the default of one. Creator places each component in the grid, positioning the component in the next available cell. With a single column, a component goes into a cell in the next row.

The grid panel gives the page designer additional options for controlling the page layout. For example, you can nest grid panels to achieve some advanced layout designs. In this section, we'll use the grid panel to control the page layout. We'll show you how to control component placement when you want to position a component after a variable-sized component (such as a table that contains an indeterminate number of rows).

Create a Project

In the following project, you'll control page layout by nesting components inside grid panels. Project LayoutMadness displays a table of numbers and their squares. The user specifies how many numbers should be displayed. To keep everything simple, the event handling code will generate HTML tags on the fly to build the table. This is a handy technique when you want to generate your own HTML tags.

1. From Creator's Welcome Page, select button Create New Project. Creator displays the New Project dialog. Under Categories, select Web. Under Projects, select JSF Web Application. Click Next.
2. In the New Web Application dialog under Project Name, specify **Layout-Madness.** Click Finish.

   After initializing the project, Creator comes up in the design view of the editor pane. You can now set the title.

3. In the Properties window, select property `Title` and specify title **Layout Madness.** Finish by pressing **<Enter>**.

Add Components to the Page

You'll add a grid panel to help with page layout. Inside, you'll add a nested grid panel that will hold a text field and button to gather and process the input. A static text component will display (using generated HTML elements) the table of squares and two hypertext/anchor component pairs will help with page scrolling. Figure 7–17 shows the design view.

Creator Tip

Note that we assigned contrasting background colors to the grid panels. This is helpful when you want to see how the grid panel is rendered and how it lays out its nested components. When you're satisfied with the layout, you can restore the grid panels' default background colors.

Figure 7–18 shows the Page1 Outline view for this project. You might want to consult it from time to time as you add the components to make sure that the nesting levels for the components are correct.

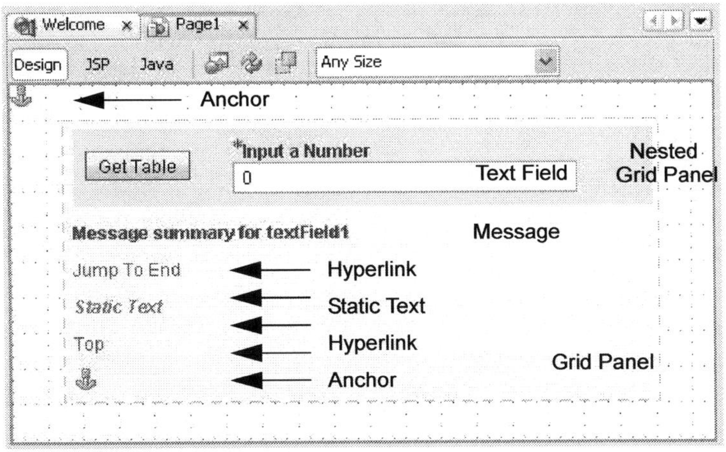

Figure 7–17 **Design view for project LayoutMadness**

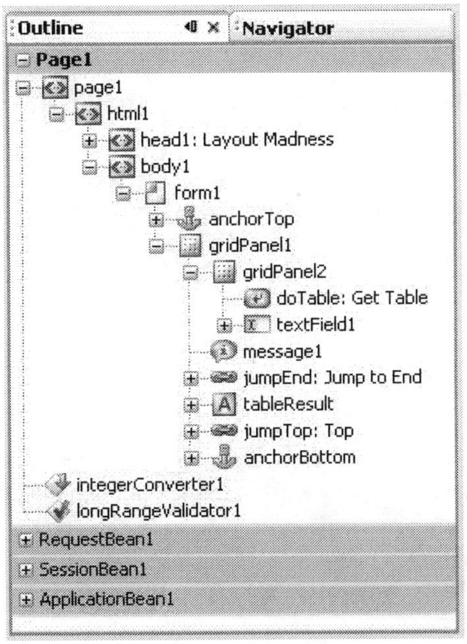

Figure 7–18 **Page1 Outline view for project LayoutMadness**

Creator Tip

Creator lists the components nested in the grid panel in the order that you place them on the page. If you need to rearrange the order, you can select a component, drag it up to its parent container, and re-drop it. This moves the component to the end of the list for that container.

1. From the Basic Components palette, select Anchor and place it on the page in the upper-left corner.
2. In the Properties window, change its id to **anchorTop**.
3. From the Layout Components palette, select Grid Panel and place it on the page.
4. In the Properties window for the grid panel, select property `style` and bring up the Style Editor.
5. In the Style Editor, select property Background. In the window for Background Color, provide the following RGB values.

```
rgb(255, 255, 215)
```

6. Select property Text Block. For Horizontal Alignment, select **center** from the drop down list.
7. Select property Position. Under Size, set Width to **400px**. Click OK to close the Style Editor. The grid panel will have a muted yellow background in the design view.
8. In the Properties window, set property `cellpadding` to **3** and property `cellspacing` to **3**. This will create space around the nested components.

   Now you'll add a second grid panel and nest it inside the first one.

1. In the Layout Components palette, select a Grid Panel component and drop it on top of the previous grid panel.
2. In its Properties window, set property `columns` to **2**, property `cellpadding` to **6**, and property `cellspacing` to **2**.
3. Click the editing box opposite property `style` and bring up the Style Editor for the nested grid panel.
4. In the Style Editor, select property Background. In the window for Background Color, provide the following RGB values.

```
rgb(232, 245, 202)
```

5. Select property Text Block. For Horizontal Alignment, select **center** from the drop down list. Click OK to close the Style Editor.

You'll place a button and a text field component inside the nested grid panel (component `gridPanel2`).

1. From the Basic Components palette, select Button and drop it on the nested grid panel. Make sure that the smaller, light-green panel is outlined in blue before you release the mouse.
2. The button's label is selected. Change its label to **Get Table**.
3. In the Properties window, change its `id` property to **doTable**.
4. From the Basic Components palette, select Text Field and drop it on top of the nested grid panel. Again, make sure that the panel is outlined in blue before you release the cursor.
5. In the Properties window for the text field, *check* property `required`.
6. In the Properties window for the text field, set property `label` to **Input a Number**. Because the field is required, Creator prepends an asterisk to the label.

The button and text fields components should be nested inside the second grid panel. Since the nested grid panel has two columns, these components are rendered side-by-side (each in its own cell in the same row). Let's configure the text field component now: you'll add an integer converter and a long range validator.

1. From the Converters Components palette, select Integer Converter and drop it on top of the text field component. The `converter` property for the text field is now set to `integerConvert1`.
2. From the Validators Components palette, select Long Range Validator and drop it on top of the text field component.
3. In the Page1 Outline view, select `longRangeValidator1`. In its Properties window, set maximum to **200** and minimum to **1**.

Now you'll add the rest of the components to the outer grid panel (component `gridPanel1`).

1. Since you've attached a validator and converter to the text field, you'll need a message component to display error messages. From the Basic Components palette, select Message and drop it on top of the outer grid panel. (Check component selection if you use the design view. Alternatively, you can drop the component on `gridPanel1` in the Page1 Outline view.)
2. In the design view, place the cursor inside the message component. Type **<Ctrl+Shift>**, hold, and left-click the mouse, releasing the cursor when it's over the text field component. The message component now displays "Message summary for textField1" on the design view.
3. From the Basic Components palette, select Hyperlink and drop the component on the outer grid panel.

4. Its text is selected. Change its `text` property to **Jump to End** followed by **<Enter>**. Change its `id` property to **jumpEnd**. You'll set its `url` property later.
5. From the Basic Components palette, select Static Text and drop it on the outer grid panel. In the Properties window, change its `id` property to **tableResult**. Under Data, *uncheck* property `escape`. This allows HTML tags to be interpreted.
6. From the Basic Components palette, select a second Hyperlink component. Drop it on the outer grid panel.
7. Change its text to **Top** followed by **<Enter>**. Change its `id` property to **jump-Top**.
8. From the Basic Components palette, select an Anchor component and drop it on the outer grid panel. Change its `id` property to **anchorBottom**.

The Page1 Outline view should now match the one shown in Figure 7–18 on page 299. Let's configure the two hyperlinks and connect them to the anchor components.

1. In the design view, select hyperlink component `jumpEnd`. In the Properties window, click the editing box opposite property `url`. Creator pops up the `url` property customizer, as shown in Figure 7–19.

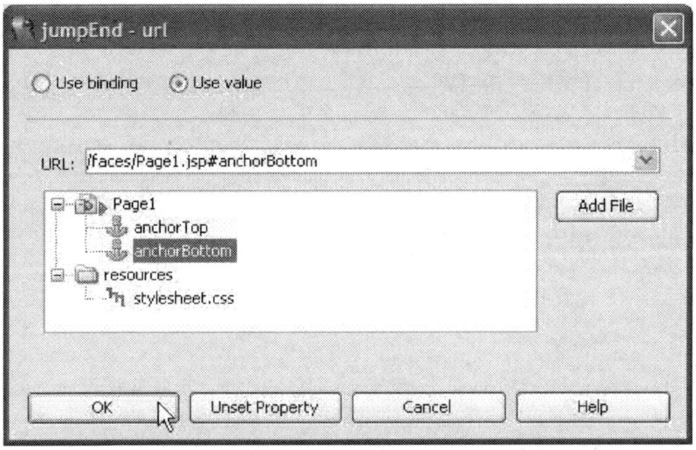

Figure 7–19 **Customizer for property url**

2. Select **anchorBottom** and click OK. This sets property `url` to

```
/faces/Page1.jsp#anchorBottom
```

3. Repeat steps 1 and 2 for the `jumpTop` hyperlink component and set its `url` property to **anchorTop**.

Let's finally add the event handling code for the button component.

1. In the design view, double-click button Get Table. Creator generates the default event handler and brings up **Page1.java** in the Java source editor.
2. Supply the following code. Copy and paste from the Creator download file **FieldGuide2/Examples/WebPageDesign/snippets/layout_doTable_action.txt**. The added code is bold.

```
public String doTable_action() {
   String str = "<table border=\"2\"" +
        " cellpadding=\"2\" width=\"400px\">";
   int nrows = ((Integer)textField1.getValue()).intValue();

   str = str + "<tr><th>Number</th><th>Square</th></tr>";
   for (int i = 1; i < nrows+1; i++) {
      str = str + "<tr><td>" + (i) +
            "</td><td>" + (i*i) + "</td></tr>";
   }

   str = str + "</table><p>";
   if (nrows > 0)
      tableResult.setValue(str);
   else tableResult.setValue(null);
   return null;
}
```

Method `doTable_action()` reads the value from the text field component (`textField1`) and uses it to compute a table of squares for that many numbers. The method generates the HTML code to dynamically build the table.

There's a few layout and design decisions we made that affect this project.

- First, we used grid panel to hold the components because we can't tell ahead of time how much space the static text (that holds the table of squares) will consume. By using a grid panel, Creator places all the components after each other in the next cell. If you tried to use absolute positioning you would not be able for format cleanly any component that came after the static text component.
- Second, we used anchor components since there is a possibility that the table won't fit on the page. This way, the user can easily jump to the end to view the bottom of the table. For the same reason, we added an anchor component so that the user can jump back to the top of the page.
- We configured the nested grid panel to have two columns, which holds both the button and the text field component in a single row. Then, the message component (which can display rather long messages) is in the outer grid panel in its own row.

- You can optionally center the outer grid panel using the component centering technique presented in the previous section. However, because the height of the grid panel is unknown, you cannot center it vertically. To center it horizontally, supply the following style positioning values for `gridPanel1`.

```
width: 400px; left: 50%; margin-left: -200px
```

Deploy and Run

Deploy and run project LayoutMadness. Figure 7–20 shows the project running in a browser (centered). The cursor is about to click the hyperlink component to jump to the end of the page.

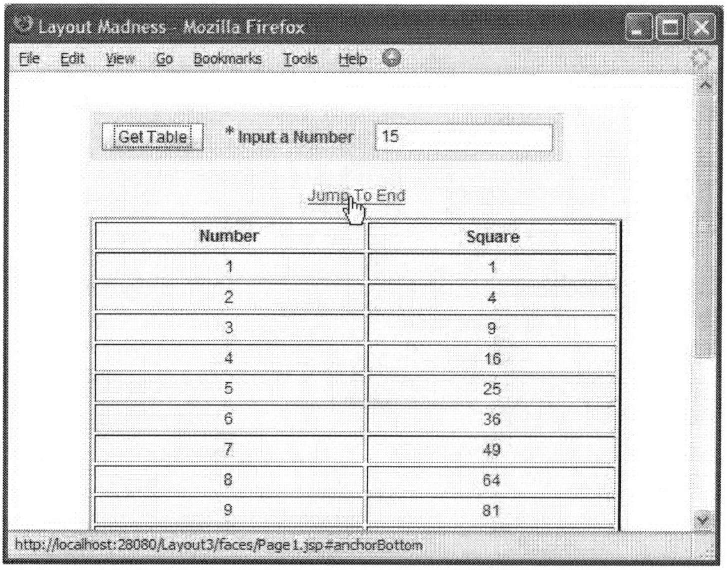

Figure 7–20 **Project LayoutMadness running in a browser**

7.6 Page Fragments

Page fragment components can be valuable to web page designers because they define building blocks for web pages. You can place components inside page fragments and then use the fragments within subsequent pages. Typically, page fragments hold parts of a web page that are standardized for a uniform look, such as images used as page headers, standard menus or navigation links, or even footers that contain copyright notices.

A page fragment is a helpful mechanism for reuse, but it does have some caveats. For one, page fragments are inserted inline into their containing document on the server. This means that a page fragment can only contain elements that are valid at the point of inclusion. As you work through the example in this section, note that page fragments are embedded in a `<div>` element (generated by Creator) and do not contain elements such as `<head>` or `<body>`, which already exist in the containing page.

To use page fragments in Creator, you first create a page fragment and then place it on the page. As an example, let's build a project for the hypothetical company called Cactus Consortium. This project has three pages: a Home (login) page, a Courses page, and a Books page. Figure 7–21 shows the layout of the Home page. The header is a page fragment that contains an image hyperlink component, the footer is a page fragment that contains a static text component, and the left menu is a page fragment that consists of a grid panel component holding navigation links (hyperlink components).

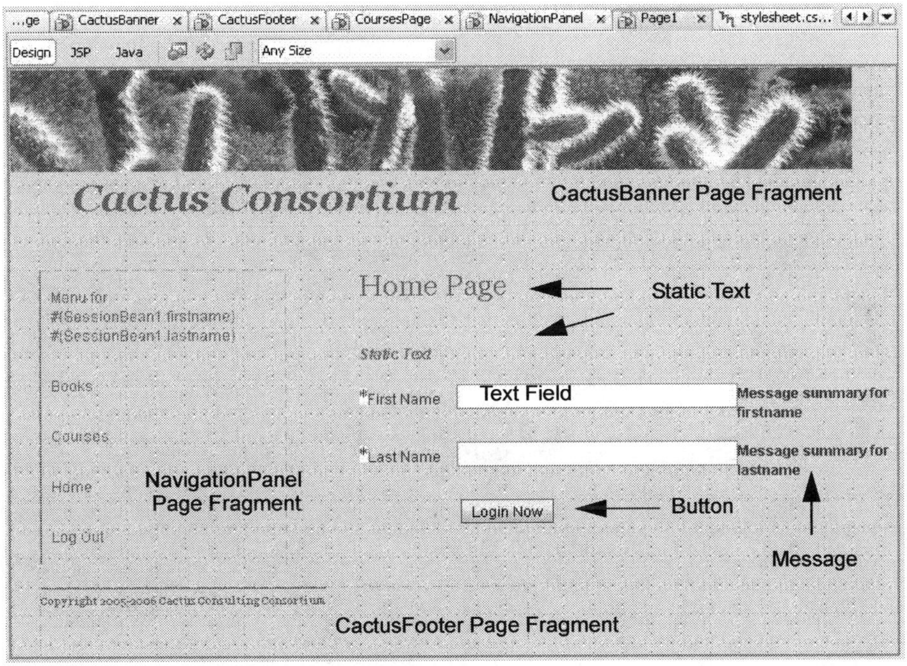

Figure 7–21 **Page layout using page fragments**

This web application requires users to login with their first and last names. The names are stored in session scope and adorn the navigation menu on the left. The user must login before navigating to subsequent pages.

The Books and Courses pages are prototype pages containing titles (and the page fragments for the uniform look).

Create a New Project

1. From Creator's Welcome Page, select button Create New Project. Creator displays the New Project dialog. Under Categories, select Web. Under Projects, select JSF Web Application. Click Next.
2. In the New Web Application dialog under Project Name, specify **Cactus1**. Click Finish.

After initializing the project, Creator comes up in the design view of the editor pane. You can now set the title.

3. In the Properties window, select property `Title` and specify title **Cactus Consulting**. Finish by pressing **<Enter>**.

Modify Default Style Sheet

Now you'll add some style rules to the default style sheet.

1. In the Project Navigator window, expand the resources node. You'll see the default style sheet, **stylesheet.css**.
2. Double click the **stylesheet.css** file name. Creator brings up this file in the editor pane.
3. Copy and paste the contents of file **FieldGuide2/Examples/WebPageDesign/snippets/stylerules.txt**, adding the new style rules to the beginning of the file. The new style rules are shown Listing 7.1.

Listing 7.1 New CSS Style Rules

```
/* Custom Style Rules for Cactus Consortium */

body {
   background-color: rgb(230,230,200);
   color: olive;
}
```

Listing 7.1 New CSS Style Rules *(continued)*

```
.headerStyle {
   font-family: Georgia,'Times New Roman',times,serif;
   font-size: 200%
}

.footerStyle {
   font-family: Georgia,'Times New Roman',times,serif;
   border-top-color: olive;
   border-top-style: solid;
   border-top-width: 1px;
   font-size: 75%
}

.bannerStyle {
   font-family: Georgia,'Times New Roman',times,serif;
   font-size: 24pt;
   font-style: italic;
   font-weight: bold
}

td, th {
    padding-left: .5em;
    padding-top: 1em;
    padding-bottom: 1em;
    padding-right: 1em;
}

.tableStyle {
   font-family: Georgia,'Times New Roman',times,serif;
   width: 200px;
   border-left-color: olive;
   border-left-style: solid;
   border-left-width: 1px;
}
```

You'll apply the style classes as you build the project. The `body` style rule applies to the entire project, setting the background color and the font color.

4. Save the modified CSS file by selecting the Save All icon on the toolbar and close file **stylesheet.css** (click the small x on the **stylesheet.css** tab). Note that Page1 now has a new background color.

Use the Gray Theme

The image and background colors for this application look better with the more neutral gray theme components.

1. In the Projects view, expand the Themes node, right-click Gray Theme and select **Set as Current Theme**.
2. After you restart the application server, Clean and Build the project to have the new theme take effect.

Add SessionBean1 Properties

This application displays the user's first and last names in different places (both in the navigation panel and the home page display). It also keeps track of whether the user is logged in or not. Since the application must save these values for each user session, you store all three variables in session scope. Program data scope is covered in detail in Chapter 6 (see "Scope of Web Applications" on page 224). Here's how to add these three properties (first name, last name, and login status) to SessionBean1, which puts the data in session scope.

1. In the Projects window, right-click Session Bean and select **Add > Property**. Creator pops up the New Property Pattern dialog.
2. For Name specify **firstname**, for Type specify **String**, and for Mode, specify the default **Read/Write**, as shown in Figure 7–22.
3. Click OK.
4. Repeat steps 1 through 3 and add property `lastname` to SessionBean1.
5. Add property `loggedIn` to SessionBean1. For this property, specify Name **loggedIn**, Type is **Boolean** (with an uppercase 'B'), and Mode is **Read/Write**. Click OK.

   When you add properties to SessionBean1, Creator generates code for the data field, as well as the getters and setters you need to access the data. Now you'll supply initialization code that you'll add to the `SessionBean1()` constructor.

1. In the Projects window, double-click Session Bean to bring **SessionBean1.java** up in the Java source editor.
2. Find the `SessionBean1()` constructor and add the following code after the comment, as shown. Copy and paste from the Creator download file

Figure 7–22 **New Property Pattern dialog**

FieldGuide2/Examples/WebPageDesign/snippets/cactus1_session_init.txt. The added code is bold.

```
public SessionBean1() {
// Creator-managed Component Initialization (folded)
// TODO: Add your own initialization code here (optional)
  firstname = "";
  lastname = "";
  loggedIn = new Boolean(false);
}
```

Banner Page Fragment

Figure 7–21 on page 305 shows the general layout of the home page, **Page1.jsp**. The first step is to create the banner page fragment, **CactusBanner.jspf**, placed across the top portion of the page.

1. Bring up Page1 in the design editor.
2. From the Layout Components palette, select Page Fragment Box and drag it over to the top-left corner of the page. Creator pops up the Select Page Fragment dialog.
3. Click Create New Page Fragment. Creator displays the Create Page Fragment dialog.

4. Specify Name **CactusBanner** and click OK. When you return to the Select Page Fragment dialog, **CactusBanner.jspf** appears in the selection window, as shown in Figure 7–23.

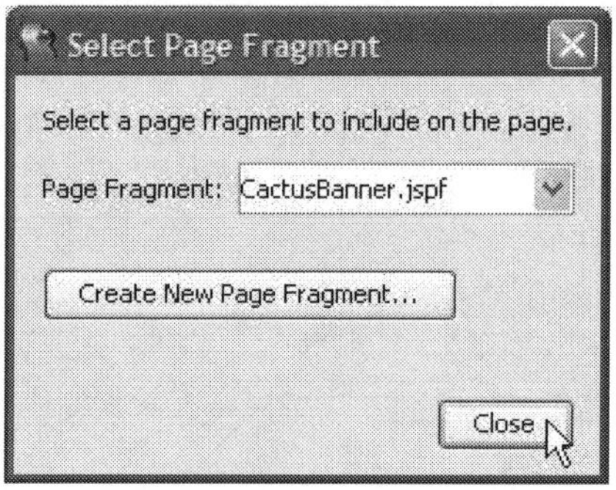

Figure 7–23 **Select Page Fragment dialog**

5. Click Close. Creator displays the (empty) CactusBanner page fragment in the design view and adds a <div> component and include directive to the Page1 Outline view.

Now you'll add components to the CactusBanner page fragment, as shown in Figure 7–24.

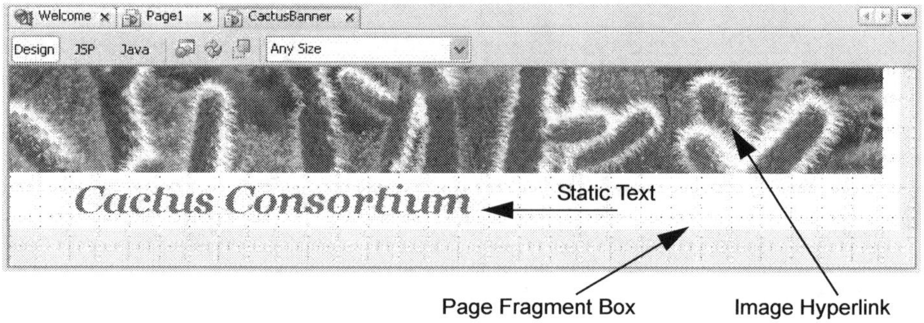

Figure 7–24 **CactusBanner Page Fragment**

1. In the Page1 design view, double-click the CactusBanner page fragment to bring up the design view for editing the page fragment.
2. Creator sets a page fragment's default size to 400px (width) by 200px (height). The white area in the design view indicates the page fragment's boundary.
3. In the Properties view, change the Height to **130px** and the Width to **700px**.

Place an image hyperlink on the page fragment.

1. From the Basic Components palette, select Image Hyperlink and place it in the top-left of the design view. Its top and left position parameters should both be zero. (Hold the mouse cursor over the `style` property in the Properties view to check its value.)
2. In the Properties window, click the editing box opposite property `imageURL`. Creator pops up a custom property editor.
3. Click Add File, navigate to your Creator download directory, and select file **FieldGuide2/Examples/WebPageDesign/images/cactus_banner.JPG**.
4. Select Add File. Creator copies the file to your project's resources directory. Make sure **cactus_banner.JPG** is selected and click OK. The image appears in the design view.
5. In the Properties window, click the editing box opposite property `text`. Click **Unset Property** in the property editor dialog. This removes the image hyperlink's default text from the design view.
6. In the Properties window under Behavior, set the `toolTip` to **Return to Home Page**. (When the user clicks on the image, you'll navigate back to the home page.)

Place a static text component on the page fragment.

1. From the Basic Components palette, select Static Text and place it inside the page fragment under the image on the design canvas.
2. It will be selected. Type in the text **Cactus Consortium** followed by **<Enter>**.
3. In the Properties window opposite property `styleClass`, specify **bannerStyle**. (This is one of the styles rules you added earlier to the project's style sheet.) The text now appears in a larger italic font and its color is olive.
4. Select the Save All icon on the toolbar to save these changes to your project.

Navigation Page Fragment

This project uses a grid panel to hold hyperlink components for navigation. You'll put this in a separate page fragment, **NavigationPanel.jspf**.

1. Return to the Page1 design view by selecting the Page1 tab above the editing pane.
2. From the Layout Components palette, select Page Fragment Box and drag it over to the left side of the page under the CactusBanner page fragment. Creator pops up the Select Page Fragment dialog.
3. Click Create New Page Fragment. Creator displays the Create Page Fragment dialog.

4. Specify Name **NavigationPanel** and click OK. When you return to the Select Page Fragment dialog, **NavigationPanel.jspf** appears in the selection window.
5. Click Close. Creator displays the (empty) NavigationPanel page fragment in the design view.

Now you'll add components to the NavigationPanel page fragment, as shown in Figure 7–25.

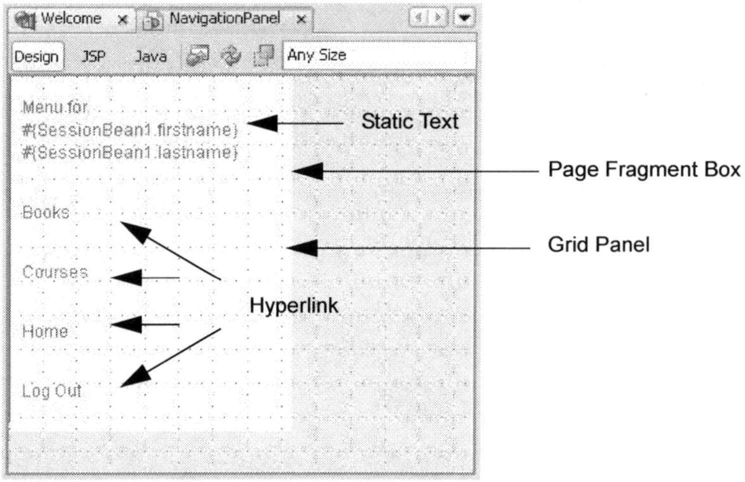

Figure 7–25 **NavigationPanel Page Fragment**

1. In the Page1 design view, double-click the NavigationPanel page fragment to bring it up in the design view.
2. In the Properties view, change the Height to **250px** and the Width to **200px**.

Place a grid panel to hold the navigation links.

1. From the Layout Components palette, select Grid Panel and place it on the page fragment in the top-left corner.
2. In the Properties view for property `styleClass`, specify **tableStyle**.

Add components to the grid panel.

1. From the Basic Components palette, select Static Text and drop it on the grid panel component. Make sure that the grid panel component is outlined in blue before you release the mouse.
2. The static text component is selected. Specify **Menu for #{SessionBean1.firstname} #{SessionBean1.lastname}** for the component's `text` property. This con-

catenates Session Bean property `firstname` and `lastname` with some text for the menu's heading.

As you add components to the grid panel, you'll see the effects of the style class you applied to the grid panel. For example, Creator wraps the text onto multiple lines instead of stretching the grid panel component because its width is fixed at 200 pixels. Also, the grid panel's cells have a generous margin because of the style rules applied to HTML elements `<th>` and `<td>` (Creator's grid panel is rendered with an HTML `<table>` element). Finally, the grid panel has a solid, 1px olive border on its left margin, which lengthens as you add components.

1. In the Properties window for the static text component, change the `id` property to **leftHeader**.
2. From the Basic Component palette, select Hyperlink and drop it on the grid panel component. (Again, make sure the grid panel is outlined in blue.)
3. Specify **Books** for its `text` property.
4. In the Properties window, change its `id` property to **booksPage**.
5. Repeat steps 4 through 6 to add a hyperlink component with `text` **Courses** and `id` **coursesPage**.
6. Repeat steps 4 through 6 to add a hyperlink component with `text` **Home** and `id` **homePage**.
7. Finally, add a hyperlink component with `text` **Log Out** and `id` **logout**.
8. Select the Save All icon on the toolbar to save these changes.

You'll specify the navigation for this project after you've added the Books and Courses pages.

CactusFooter Page Fragment

Each page in this project has a footer with a copyright designation. This information goes in its own page fragment, **CactusFooter.jspf**.

1. Return to the Page1 design view.
2. From the Layout Components palette, select Page Fragment Box and drag it over to the bottom-left of the design view under the NavigationPanel page fragment. Creator pops up the Select Page Fragment dialog.
3. Click Create New Page Fragment. Creator displays the Create Page Fragment dialog.
4. Specify Name **CactusFooter** and click OK. When you return to the Select Page Fragment dialog, **CactusFooter.jspf** appears in the selection window.
5. Click Close. Creator displays the (empty) CactusFooter page fragment in the design view.

Now you'll configure the CactusFooter page fragment, as shown in Figure 7–26.

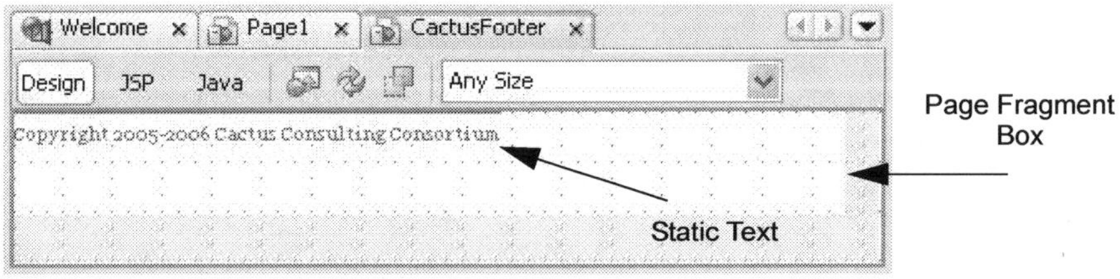

Figure 7–26 **CactusFooter Page Fragment**

1. In the Page1 design view, double-click the CactusFooter page fragment to bring it up in the design view.
2. In the Properties view, change the Height to **50px** and leave the Width at the default 400px.
3. From the Basic Components palette, select Static Text and drop it on the page fragment. Place it in the top-left corner.
4. The static text component is selected. Specify **Copyright 2005-2006 Cactus Consulting Consortium** for the component's `text` property.
5. In the Properties window, specify **footerStyle** for property `styleClass`. You'll see the font size shrink and a top border appear above the text.
6. Select the Save All icon on the toolbar to save the changes to your project and select the Page1 tab to return to the Page1 design view.

Add Pages

You've finished creating the page fragments. Now you'll create two more pages and add the page fragments to these pages as well.

1. Close the page fragments to keep the editor pane uncluttered. For each page fragment, click the small 'x' on the tab.
2. In the Projects window, right-click the Web Pages node and select **New > Page**. Creator displays the New Page dialog.
3. For File Name specify **BooksPage** and click Finish. Creator creates the new page and brings it up in the design view. Note that it has the new default background color you configured for this project.
4. Click anywhere in the background of the design view. In the Properties window for property `Title`, specify **Cactus Consulting - Books**.
5. Repeat Steps 1 through 3 and add another page with file name **CoursesPage** and page property `Title` **Cactus Consulting - Courses**.
6. Select the Save All icon on the toolbar to save the changes to your project and select the Page1 tab to return to the Page1 design view.

You have several ways to add the page fragments to CoursesPage and BooksPage. The brute-force approach is to simply add the three page fragments one at a time, positioning each one on the page at the same location. An easier approach is to copy and paste the three page fragments as a group onto the new pages. This second approach is more efficient and the one we'll use now.

1. Bring up Page1 in the design view. In the Page1 Outline view, use **<Shift+Click>** to select all three `div` elements and their nested page fragments, as shown in Figure 7–27. All three page fragments will also be selected in the design view.

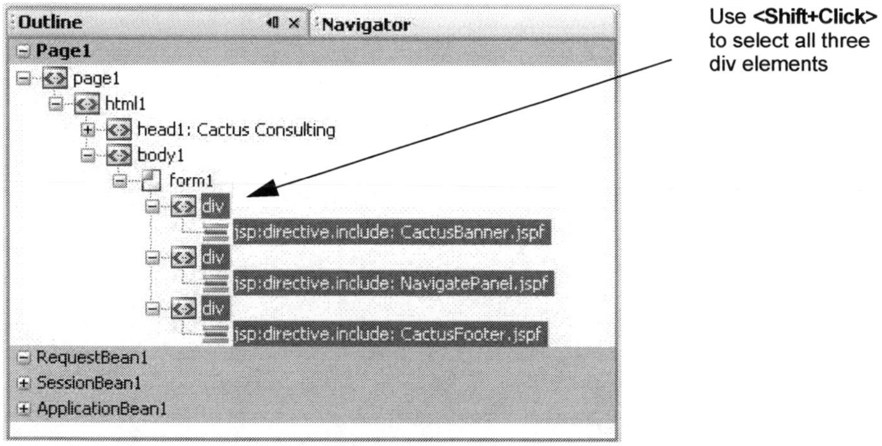

Figure 7–27 **Selecting all three div elements and the nested page fragments**

2. From the main menu, select **Edit > Copy** to copy the page fragments.
3. Now select the BooksPage tab on top of the editing pane to bring up BooksPage in the design view. In the BooksPage Outline view, expand nodes `page1 > html1 > body1` and select node `form1`. Right-click and select **Paste** from the context menu. Creator copies all three page fragments to the BooksPage, placing them in the equivalent positions on the page.
4. Select the CoursesPage tab and repeat the **Paste** operation on the `form1` component in the CoursesPage Outline view.

Page-Specific Content for Page1

You've created three pages that all share the same content. Now you'll add the page-specific components to each page. Let's start with Page1.

1. Select the Page1 tab above the editing panel to bring it up in the design view. Figure 7–21 on page 305 shows the design view with the page fragment

boxes and the page-specific components. Note that the page has a heading text component, a second static text component, text field components to provide login information, message components, and a button.

2. From the Basic Components palette, select Static Text and drop it on the page to the right of the navigation panel.
3. Specify the text **Home Page**.
4. In the Properties window, set the `id` property to **pageHeader**.
5. In the Properties window, set the `styleClass` property to **headerStyle**. The font-size and font-family now reflect the `headerStyle` style rule.
6. From the Basic Components palette, select Static Text and drop it on the page under static text component `pageHeader`.
7. In the Properties window, set its `id` property to **instructText**.

You'll now add two text field components and message components to go with them.

1. From the Basic Components palette, select Text Field and drop it on the page under the static text components you added.
2. In the Properties window, set the component's properties as follows. Set property `id` to **firstname**, property `label` to **First Name**, property `labelLevel` to **Weak (3)**, and property `required` to **true** (it should be checked). When you set the `required` property to true and provide label text, Creator prepends an asterisk to the label text so that the user knows the field is required.
3. In the design view, select the text field component, right-click, and select Property Bindings. Creator pops up the Property Bindings dialog. Under Select bindable property, click **text *Object***. Under Select binding target, expand SessionBean1 and select **firstname**. Click Apply and Close. This binds the text field to the SessionBean1 `firstname` property, `#{SessionBean1.firstname}`.
4. From the Basic Components palette, select Text Field and drop it on the page under the text field component you just added.
5. In the Properties window, set the component's properties as follows. Set property `id` to **lastname**, property `label` to **Last Name**, property `labelLevel` to **Weak (3)**, and property `required` to **true** (it should be checked).
6. In the design view, select the text field component, right-click, and select Property Bindings. Creator pops up the Property Bindings dialog. Under Select bindable property, click **text *Object***. Under Select binding target, expand SessionBean1 and select **lastname**. Click Apply and Close. This binds the text field to the SessionBean1 `lastname` property, `#{SessionBean1.lastname}`.

You need a message component to display error messages if the user does not provide input for the text components.

1. From the Basic Components palette, select Message and place it on the page to the right of the `firstname` text field component.
2. Press and hold **<Ctrl+Shift>** and left-click the mouse inside the message component. Drag the mouse and release it over the text field component. This sets the message component's `for` property to `firstname`, the `id` of the text field component. This means that the message component will display messages from the Faces context that are designated for the text field component. The message component's display text now reads "Message summary for firstname."
3. Repeat Steps 1 and 2 and set the `for` property to the `lastname` text field component.

You'll use a button component to submit the login information.

1. From the Basic Components palette, select Button and drop it on the page below the text field components.
2. Change the button's `text` property to **Login Now**.
3. Change the button's `id` property to **login**.
4. In the design view, double-click the Login Now button. Creator generates a default action handler and brings up **Page1.java** in the Java source editor.
5. Add the following event handler code (add the code in bold).

```
public String login_action() {
   getSessionBean1().setLoggedIn(new Boolean(true));
   return null;
}
```

This appears to be a rather terse event handler. The code sets the session bean property `loggedIn` to true. No special code is needed to check whether or not the user provided login information (validation does that for you) or specifically set the `firstname` and `lastname` session bean properties (the text field components property bindings do that for you). The only task left, then, is to set the `loggedIn` property.

When the page is rendered, it should display the logged in values stored in properties `firstname` and `lastname`. And, if the user has not logged in, it should display an instruction line requesting the user to log in. You'll put this logic in the predefined `prerender()` method.

1. **Page1.java** should still be active in the Java source editor. Locate method `prerender()`.

2. Add the following code. Copy and paste from **FieldGuide2/Examples/WebPageDesign/snippets/cactus1_prerender.txt**. The added code is bold.

```
public void prerender() {
   // see if user is logged in
   if (getSessionBean1().getLoggedIn().booleanValue()) {
     instructText.setValue(
          "Welcome, " + getSessionBean1().getFirstname() + " "
          + getSessionBean1().getLastname());

   } else
     instructText.setValue(
          "Please login using the form below.");
}
```

Page-Specific Content

Now let's add the header text for the BooksPage and CoursesPage.

1. Select the BooksPage tab from the top of the editor pane to bring up BooksPage in the design view.
2. From the Basic Components palette, select Static Text and place it on the page at the same location as the Home Page static text component on Page1.
3. Set its `text` property to **Books Page**, its `id` property to **pageHeader**, and its `styleClass` property to **headerStyle**.
4. Repeat Steps 1 through 3 to add a static text component to CoursesPage. Use the `text` **Courses Page**, `id` property **pageHeader**, and `styleClass` **headerStyle**.
5. Make sure that the `pageHeader` static text component is in the same location for all three pages. You can check visually or hold the cursor over the `style` property in the Properties window for the static text component and verify that the position attributes for all three components are the same.

Page Fragments and Navigation

You'll now provide the navigation rules for this application. The page fragment, **NavigationPanel.jspf**, contains the hyperlink components for navigation. Since this page fragment is on *each page*, you must specify navigation rules for each page. You can certainly do this in the Navigation Editor. You'll need six cases: two navigation arrows originate from each page to specify the other two pages. However, just a slight increase in the number of pages results in a messy graph using the Page Navigation visual editor. Therefore, you're going to cheat! Basically, you want three navigation cases (both the hyperlink components for Home and Log Out should navigate to Page1; the image hyperlink component also navigates to Page1), as follows.

1. Navigation label **Books** specifies page **BooksPage.jsp**.
2. Navigation label **Courses** specifies page **CoursesPage.jsp**.
3. Navigation label **Home** specifies page **Page1.jsp**.

As it turns out, JSF provides a sophisticated navigation handler that allows *wildcard* expressions. You'll define some basic rules and then modify the navigation configuration in the source editor to provide the wildcard expression.

1. Bring up the Page Navigation. Right-click anywhere in the background of any of the pages in the design editor and select **Page Navigation** from the context menu. You'll see the three pages in the Page Navigation editor.
2. Select **Page1.jsp** and when it enlarges, select the `booksPage` hyperlink and drag a navigation arrow to **BooksPage.jsp**.
3. Creator displays a navigation arrow. Change the case label to **Books**.
4. Select **Page1.jsp** and draw a navigation arrow from the `coursesPage` hyperlink to **CoursesPage.jsp**.
5. Change the case label to **Courses**.
6. Now select **CoursesPage.jsp** and when it enlarges, select the image hyperlink component and drag a navigation arrow to **Page1.jsp**. Change the case label to **Home**.
7. Starting with **CoursesPages.jsp** again, repeat this two more times, selecting the hyperlink components `logout` and `homePage`. For both of these navigation cases, change the case label to **Home**.

Using the navigation editor, you've configured all of the components so that their `action` property contains the correct navigation case label. Now you just have to generalize the cases so that the navigation handler goes to the correct page from any starting page. You have one rule and three cases.

1. Click the Source button in the navigation editor's toolbar to bring up **navigation.xml** in the source editor.
2. Modify the configuration file so that you have only one navigation rule with three navigation cases. Change the `<from-view-id>` element to **`/*`** (which matches *any* page).

3. Here is the modified file. (You can copy and paste from file **FieldGuide2/Examples/WebPageDesign/snippets/cactus1_navigation.txt** or provide the modifications by hand.)

```
<faces-config>
  <navigation-rule>
    <from-view-id>/*</from-view-id>
    <navigation-case>
      <from-outcome>Books</from-outcome>
      <to-view-id>/BooksPage.jsp</to-view-id>
    </navigation-case>

    <navigation-case>
      <from-outcome>Courses</from-outcome>
      <to-view-id>/CoursesPage.jsp</to-view-id>
    </navigation-case>

    <navigation-case>
      <from-outcome>Home</from-outcome>
      <to-view-id>/Page1.jsp</to-view-id>
    </navigation-case>
  </navigation-rule>
</faces-config>
```

4. Click the Save All icon on the toolbar and click the Navigation button to return to the Navigation editor. Figure 7–28 shows the Navigation view after you modify the **navigation.xml** source file.

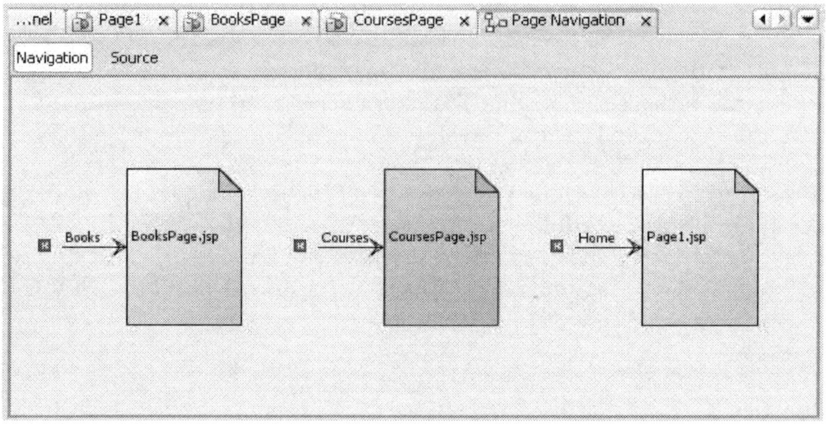

Figure 7–28 **Navigation editor with source code wildcard expressions**

Logout Event Handler

The last task is to add the logout event handler code, which will reset the session bean properties. The hyperlink `logout` is in the NavigationPanel page fragment.

1. Bring up **NavigationPanel.jspf** page fragment in the design editor.
2. Double-click hyperlink component `logout`. Creator generates the hyperlink's event handler, `logout_action()`. Note that Creator transforms the `action` property "Home" to the correct return String value in the event handler.
3. The `logout_action()` method will reset the values for the three session bean properties. Copy and paste file **FieldGuide2/Examples/WebPageDesign/snippets/logout_action.txt**. The added code is bold.

```
public String logout_action() {
   getSessionBean1().setFirstname("");
   getSessionBean1().setLastname("");
   getSessionBean1().setLoggedIn(new Boolean(false));
   return "Home";
}
```

Deploy and Run

Deploy and run project Cactus1. Figure 7–29 shows project Cactus1 running in the browser displaying CoursesPage. The image hyperlink's tooltip is visible.

Reuse with Project Templates

Once you have the look and feel of your application defined, Creator lets you save the project as a template. Project templates promote reuse and uniformity within an organization. When you create a new project, you can select a project template as a starting point. Let's create a template from project Cactus1.

1. In the Projects window, right-click the project node Cactus1 and select **Save Project As**. Creator pops up the Save Project As dialog.
2. For Project Name specify **CactusTemplate**. Click the Add Project to Template List checkbox, as shown in Figure 7–30. Click OK.

Now when you create a project, you can select My Templates and view a list of saved project templates for your new project. This is the approach we'll take with project Cactus2 (see "Using Tab Sets and Page Fragments" on page 327.)

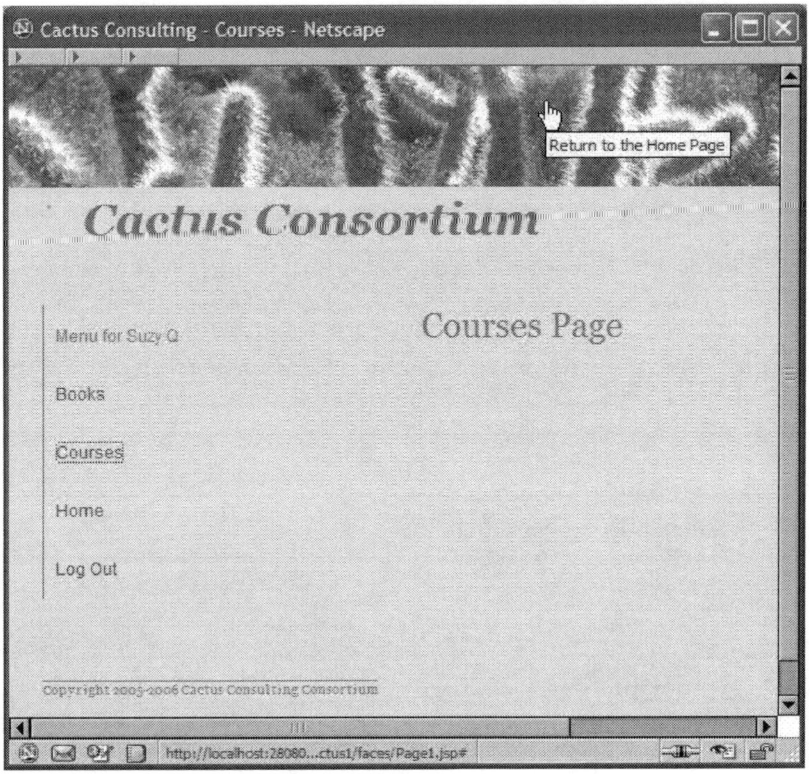

Figure 7–29 **Project Cactus1 running in a browser**

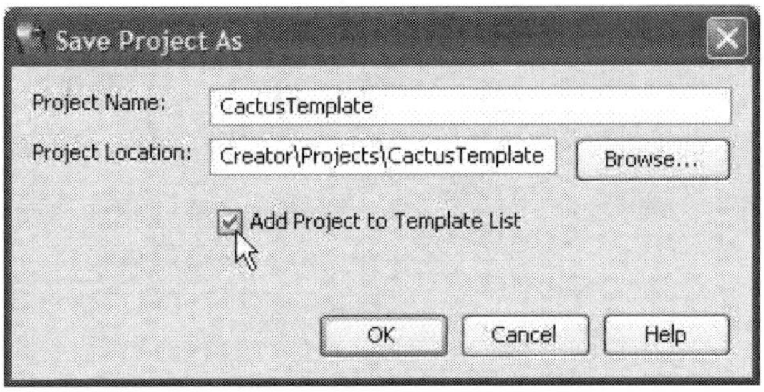

Figure 7–30 **Adding a project to the Template List**

7.7 Introducing Tab Sets

As we continue exploring Creator's components and configuration options for web applications, let's show you another useful layout component, the tab set. Many applications use tab set components for navigation and complex page management. With tab sets, you can display only those components that are relevant to the task at hand.

The tab set is a composite component. You place a tab set component on a page and then add tab components to the tab set. You have more than one way to manage an application with tab sets, however.

The simplest way places a separate tab set component on each page. If your application consists of three pages, for example, each page will hold its own distinct tab set and each tab set holds three tab components. Furthermore, each tab set has one tab that is always selected. The other two non-selected tabs act as hyperlink components and provide navigation to the other two pages where a different tab is always selected. This method is straightforward because you never have to manage the state of the tab sets. You place the components on each page with the visual design editor. Furthermore, you don't have to nest the page's components under the tab set.

A second approach is to put the tab set and tabs in a page fragment and include the page fragment on each page. Again, you place the components for each page directly on the page (you don't nest them under the tab set component). Because there is only one tab set component, you must maintain the state of its selected tab, however. Like the first approach, the tabs are used to navigate to the other pages. The advantage of using a page fragment for the tab set is that any customizing for the tab set must only be specified once.

A third approach uses a single page: the tab set and its tabs all go on one page. In this approach, you use the nested layout panel to hold the components corresponding to each tab. When the user selects a tab, the tab set renders only those components under the selected tab. Furthermore, the tab set automatically marks the selected tab, so you don't need to do anything to maintain its state. The disadvantage of this approach is that it is more difficult to design the page and the page is more complex.

We'll take you through building a project using the first approach. Then, you'll implement a version of the Cactus project (Cactus2), incorporating both a tab set and a navigation panel containing hyperlink components to perform navigation. The Cactus2 project uses the page fragment method for the tab set component. We illustrate the third approach in project TabSet3, which is included in the Creator2 download directory under **FieldGuide2/Examples/WebPageDesign/Projects/TabSet3**.

Using Separate Tab Sets

The first example uses a separate tab set on each page. For this project, you'll create three pages. Each page contains a tab set component with three tabs. The tabs enable users to navigate to the other pages.

Create a New Project

1. From Creator's Welcome Page, select button Create New Project. Creator displays the New Project dialog. Under Categories, select Web. Under Projects, select JSF Web Application. Click Next.
2. In the New Web Application dialog under Project Name, specify **TabSet1**. Click Finish.

   After initializing the project, Creator comes up in the design view of the editor pane. You can now set the title.

3. In the Properties window, select property `Title` and specify title **TabSet1 - Page1**. Finish by pressing **<Enter>**.

Add Components to Page1

Figure 7–31 shows the design view of Page1.

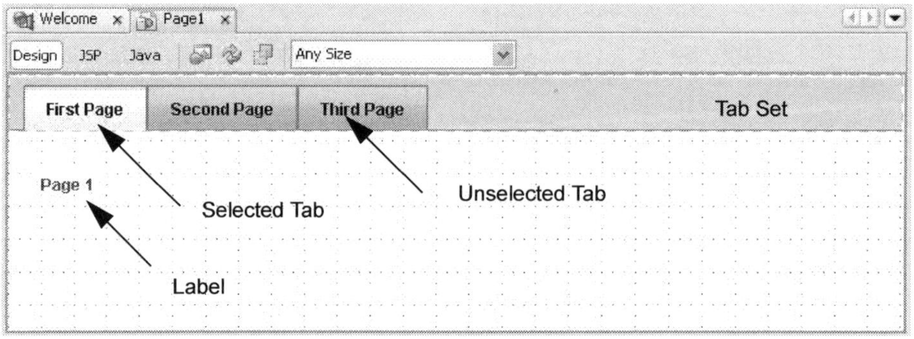

Figure 7–31 **Page1 design view for project TabSet1**

1. From the Layout Components palette, select Tab Set and drop it on the page. Position it in the top-left corner.
2. When you add the tab set component, Creator preconfigures a single tab nested in the tab set. Inside the tab component, Creator also preconfigures a layout panel. The tab should be selected. Change its `text` property to **First Page**, followed by **<Enter>**.

3. In the Page1 Outline view, select the nested layout panel, `layoutPanel1`. Right-click and select Delete from the context menu. Since you're placing a separate tab set on each page, you don't need the layout panel to hold the page's components.
4. In the Page1 Outline view, now select the tab set component. In the Properties window for the tab set component, add the property-value **; width: 100%** to the `style` property that is already configured. The background behind the tabs will expand.
5. From the Layout Components palette, expand node Tab Set and select the nested component Tab. Drop it on top of the tab set component that's on the page. Creator configures this as component `tab2`. In the Page1 Outline view, make sure that component `tab2` is at the same nesting level as `tab1`.
6. Component `tab2` should be selected. Change its `text` property to **Second Page**.
7. In the Page1 Outline view, delete the nested layout panel component (repeat the step you followed to delete the nested layout panel in the first tab).
8. From the Layout Components palette, select another Tab component and drop it on top of the tab set component. This is component `tab3`. Change its `text` property to **Third Page** and delete its nested layout panel component.
9. In the design view, click on component `tab1` (First Page) to make it selected.

Creator Tip

As you configure the tab set on each page, you specify the selected tab for that page. Each page has a different tab selected. Figure 7–31 shows `tab1` *selected (the Page1 configuration).*

Now you'll add a label component to the page to hold a page header.

1. From the Basic Components palette, select component Label and drop it on the page. (Drop it on the *page*, not on the tab set component.) In the Page1 Outline view, the label component should be nested under `form1`, at the same level as component `tabSet1`.
2. Set its `text` property to **Page 1**.

   You'll now create a second and third page and copy and paste these components to the new pages.

1. In the Projects view, right-click the Web Pages node and select **New > Page**. Creator pops up the New Page dialog.
2. Specify File Name **Page2** and click Finish. Creator brings up Page2 in the design view.
3. Set the `Title` property to **TabSet1 - Page 2**.

4. Repeat steps 1 through 3 to add a third page with file name **Page3** and `Title` **TabSet1 - Page 3**.

Since each page holds the same components (the tab set, three tabs, and a label) it's easier to copy and paste these components from Page1 and reconfigure them as needed for Page2 and Page3.

1. Select the Page1 tab above the editor pane to bring up Page1 in the design view.
2. In the Page1 Outline view, select component `tabSet1` and `label1` (use **<Shift+Click>** for multiple selection). The nested tabs will also be selected.
3. From the main menu bar, select **Edit > Copy**.
4. Now select the Page2 tab above the editor pane. In the Page2 Outline view, expand `page1 > html1 > body1` and select component `form1`.
5. Right-click on `form1` and select **Paste** from the context menu. This copies the Page1 components to Page2, maintaining the same position and other style attributes.
6. Repeat Steps 4 and 5 with Page3, pasting the components on this page.

Now you'll configure the tab set and label components for Page2 and Page3.

1. Select the Page2 tab above the editor pane to bring up Page2 in the design view.
2. In the design view, click on component `tab2` (Second Page) to make it selected. The tab will turn white and the other two tabs will be blue.
3. Select the label component and change its `text` property to **Page 2**.
4. Repeat Steps 1 through 3 for Page3. Make `tab3` (Third Page) selected and change the label's `text` property to **Page 3**.

Configure Navigation

The tab components behave like hyperlink components because you can define action event handlers or action labels for navigation. You'll define six navigation cases: each page will have two cases that originate from a tab component and terminate in one of the other two pages.

1. In the design view, right-click anywhere in the background and select Page Navigation from the context menu. Creator brings up the Navigation Editor.
2. You see the three pages that you defined for this project. Select **Page1.jsp**. When it enlarges, you'll see the three tab components.
3. Select `tab2`, click, and drag an arrow to **Page2.jsp**. Change the case label to **second**.
4. Select **Page1.jsp** again, click `tab3`, and drag an arrow to **Page3.jsp**. Change the case label to **third**.

5. Now repeat this sequence for **Page2.jsp**. Draw an arrow from component `tab1` to **Page1.jsp**. Use case label **first**. Draw a second arrow from component `tab3` to **Page3.jsp**. Use case label **third**.
6. Finally, configure the navigation cases for **Page3.jsp**. Draw an arrow from component `tab1` to **Page1.jsp**. Use case label **first**. Draw the second arrow from component `tab2` to **Page2.jsp**. Use case label **second**. Figure 7–32 shows the Navigation Editor with all of the cases configured and **Page2.jsp** enlarged.

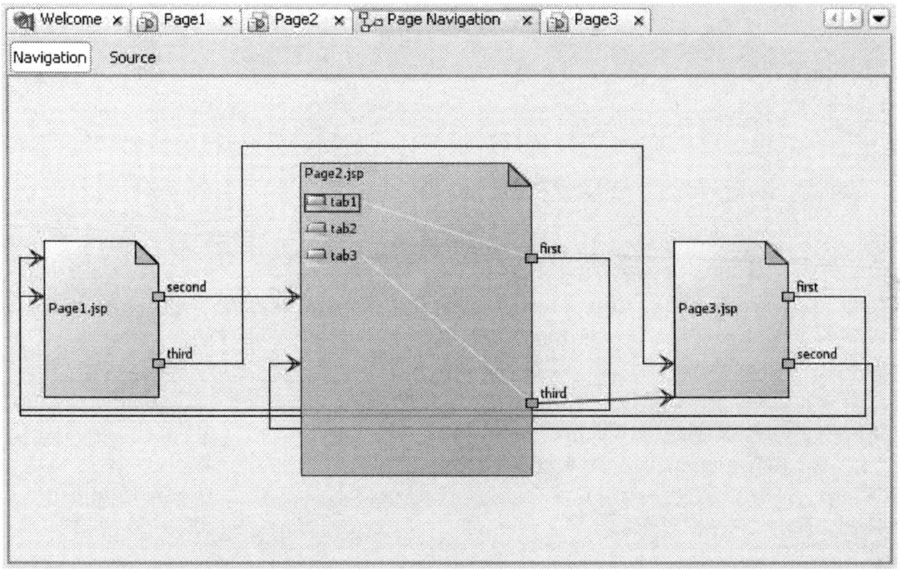

Figure 7–32 **Navigation Editor for project TabSet1**

Deploy and Run

Deploy and run project TabSet1. Figure 7–33 shows Page2 in the browser and the cursor is over the third tab.

Using Tab Sets and Page Fragments

You'll now add a tab set to the CactusBanner page fragment from project Cactus1. Instead of copying project Cactus1, you'll create a new project and use the project template you saved earlier.

1. From the Welcome page, click **Create New Project**.

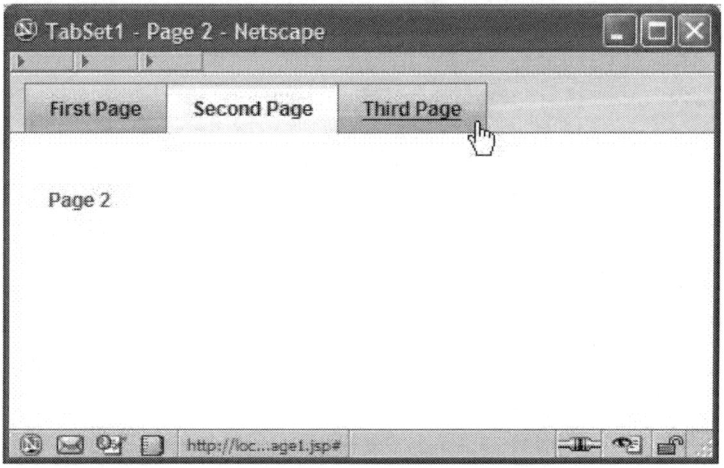

Figure 7–33 **Page2 of project TabSet1 running in a browser**

2. Creator pops up the New Project dialog. In the Categories window, select **My Templates.** Creator displays a list of available project templates.
3. Select **CactusTemplate** and click Next.
4. Creator displays the New JSF Web Application dialog. For Project Name specify **Cactus2** and click Finish.
5. Creator brings up Page1 of project Cactus2 in the design view. Click anywhere in the background of the design canvas of the Cactus2 project. In the Properties window, change the page's `Title` property to **Cactus Consulting 2.**

   Let's add another style rule to **stylesheet.css** to make the tab set blend with the pages better.

1. In the Projects window, expand the **Web Pages > resources** node and double-click **stylesheet.css** to bring it up in the Style Editor.
2. Add the following style rule for `TabGrp`.

```
.TabGrp {
  background-color: rgb(230,230,200);
}
```

Creator Tip

The standard Themes uses style rule `TabGrp` *to apply styles to tab sets. By customizing this rule, you can change the background color of the page behind the tabs. The default color is a gradient gray for the Gray Theme.*

Add Tab Set and Tabs to CactusBanner

First, let's add components to the CactusBanner page fragment. Figure 7–34 shows the design view for the CactusBanner page fragment with the tab set component added.

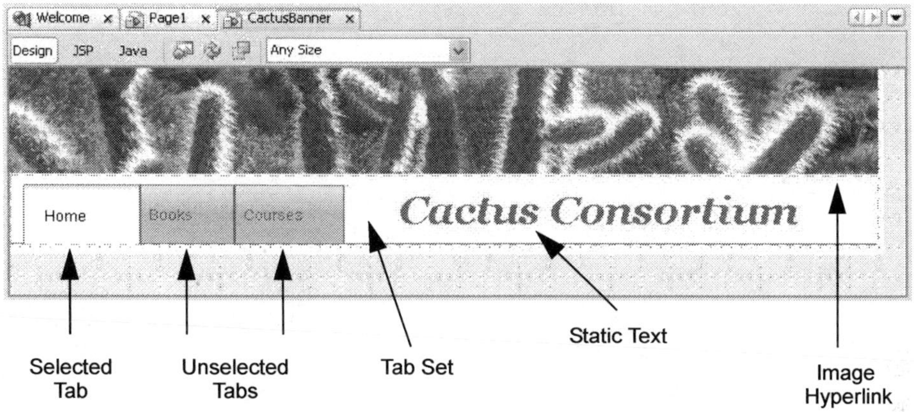

Figure 7–34 **Design view for CactusBanner.jspf**

1. In the Projects window, double-click **CactusBanner.jspf** to bring up the CactusBanner page fragment in the design view.
2. Click in the blue area to select the page fragment.
3. In the Properties view, change the page fragment's height to **150px**.
4. Select the Cactus Consortium static text component and move it over to the right to make room for the tab set component.
5. From the Layout Components palette, select Tab Set and drop it on the page fragment below the image hyperlink component.
6. The first tab is selected. Change its text to **Home**.
7. In the Outline view, select the nested layout panel, `layoutPanel1`, right-click and select **Delete** from the context menu.
8. In the Outline view, select the nested tab component, `tab1`. In the Properties window for the tab, change its `id` property to **homeTab**.

Creator Tip

The `selected` *property of the tab set component takes the* `id` *(passed as a String) of the tab that's selected. Renaming the component's id with meaningful names makes your code more readable.*

9. Now select component `tabSet1` in the Outline view. In the Properties window for the tab set, check the property `mini`. This changes the appearance of the tab set and makes the tabs smaller.

   Add two more tabs to the tab set.

1. From the Layout Components palette, expand the Tab Set component and select the nested Tab component. Drop it on top of the tab set you added. (Make sure that the new tab is at the same nesting level as component `homeTab`.)
2. Change the tab's `text` property to **Books**.
3. Change the tab's `id` property to **booksTab**.
4. Delete the nested layout panel under tab `booksTab`.
5. Repeat this and add another tab with `text` **Courses** and `id` **coursesTab**. Delete the nested layout panel under tab `coursesTab`.
6. Reposition the tab set component so that it is within the page fragment boundary (the white area) and that its left edge is flush with the fragment boundary (the `left` style attribute should be 0).
7. In the CactusBanner Outline view, select the Cactus Consortium static text component, drag it up to the `f:subview` component, and drop it on top of the subview.

The static text component is now listed *after* the tab set component in the CactusBanner Outline view. This makes the static text component render *on top of* the tab set component. When you moved the component in the Outline view, its `style` property was cleared. The component now appears in the design view in the upper-left corner (on top of the image).

8. In the design view, move the static text component back (next to) the tab set component, placing it to the right of the third tab.

   Add `style` and `styleClass` attributes to the tab set component.

1. Select the tab set component. In the Properties view for property `style`, add attribute **; width: 696px** to the end. This aligns the width of the tab set component with the image hyperlink component.
2. In the tab set Properties view for property `styleClass`, specify **TabGrp**.
3. In the tab set Properties view opposite property `selected`, click the check mark for the drop down list corresponding to the tabs. Choose the first, blank entry. Even though the property sheet will display Home (homeTab), property `selected` *should not appear in bold.*

Creator Tip

If the tab set's `selected` *property is bold, then Creator has generated a tag in the JSP file to set it. Because you'll set the tab set's* `selected` *property in each enclosing page's* `prerender()` *method, you must not generate the corresponding JSP tag. The JSP code executes after the* `prerender()` *method, rendering the method ineffective.*

4. Select the Save All icon on the toolbar to save these changes.

Setting the Currently Selected Tab

As you've seen from working with the tab set component in the first tab set example, the tab set displays tabs and renders them as either "selected" or "not selected." A selected tab (there can only be one selected tab) has a contrasting color and its link is inactive. It is the current tab. A non-selected tab has an active link. In this example, the action associated with clicking a non-selected tab causes page navigation. When the new page is rendered, the tab set must reflect the newly selected tab.

The most straightforward way to maintain the state of the currently selected tab is to set it in the enclosing page's `prerender()` method. Setting the selected tab in each page ensures that the correct tab is selected even when navigation to a new page happens through the hyperlink components in the Navigation-Panel page fragment or the image hyperlink.

As mentioned in the previous page's Creator Tip, the only caveat is you must ensure that Creator does not generate JSP code to set the tab set's `selected` property, since this will take precedence over the `prerender()` code.

1. In the Projects window under Web Pages, double-click **Page1.jsp** to bring it up in the design view.
2. Select the Java button in the editing toolbar to edit the Java source.
3. Add the following code to method `prerender()`. Copy and paste from **FieldGuide2/Examples/WebPageDesign/snippets/ cactus2_page1_tabset.txt**. The added code is bold.

```
public void prerender() {
   CactusBanner cactusBanner = (CactusBanner)getBean(
         "CactusBanner");
   cactusBanner.getTabSet1().setSelected("homeTab");
   // see if user is logged in
   . . .
}
```

You'll add the same code to the `prerender()` methods in **Courses.java** (with String `"coursesTab"`) and **Books.java** (with String `"booksTab"`).

1. Bring up **Courses.java** in the Java source editor. Add the same code to the `prerender()` method.
2. Change the tab set's `setSelected()` argument to `"coursesTab"`.
3. Bring up **Books.java** in the Java source editor. Add the same code to the `prerender()` method and change the tab set's `setSelected()` argument to `"booksTab"`.
4. Select the Save All icon on the toolbar to save these changes.

Configure Action Method for Tabs

The navigation rules have already been configured for this project. Because you used navigation wildcard notation in project Cactus1, these rules will apply to the tab set component as well. You do not need to make any adjustments to the navigation rules. However, you do need to specify the return string for each tab's action method. To do this, you'll generate action methods through the IDE and provide the code for the action event handler.

1. Bring up CactusBanner in the design view.
2. Double-click tab component `homeTab`. Creator generates the default `homeTab_action()` event handler and brings up **CactusBanner.java** in the Java source editor.
3. Replace the `return null` with `return "Home"` as shown.

```
public String homeTab_action() {
   // TODO: Replace with your code
   return "Home";
}
```

4. Return to the design view (click Design in the editor toolbar) and repeat steps 2 and 3 for tab component `booksTab`. Replace the `return null` with `return "Books"`.

```
public String booksTab_action() {
   // TODO: Replace with your code
   return "Books";
}
```

5. Return to the design view and repeat steps 2 and 3 for tab component `coursesTab`. Replace the `return null` with `return "Courses"`.

```
public String coursesTab_action() {
   // TODO: Replace with your code
   return "Courses";
}
```

6. Make sure that the tab set's `selected` property is not set in the Properties view. If it's bold, select the first (blank) entry in the drop down list for property `selected`. The property name should no longer be bold.
7. Click the Save All icon on the toolbar to save these changes.

Check Pages with Modified CactusBanner

Check and adjust the placement of the page fragments on each page. Once you've done this, deploy and run the application.

Creator Tip

Since the grid panel contains a vertical line on the left border, align this border with the first tab's left edge. This creates a pleasing visual connection between the grid panel component and the tab set component. The easiest way to adjust the page is to simultaneously select the NavigationPanel and CactusFooter page fragments. Then, while holding down the Shift key, move the fragments down and to the left to make the alignment with the tab set component. By moving both fragments together, you keep their relative position constant.

When you run the application, check to make sure the tab set component reflects the correct page navigation, whether you use the hyperlink components or the tab set component for navigation. Figure 7–35 shows project Cactus2 running in a browser with page BooksPage rendered.

7.8 Key Point Summary

This chapter explores some of Creator's tools and components that web designers use to compose web pages and visually organize their projects.

- Creator's visual editor helps you compose web pages by providing component dragging, dropping, and page positioning.

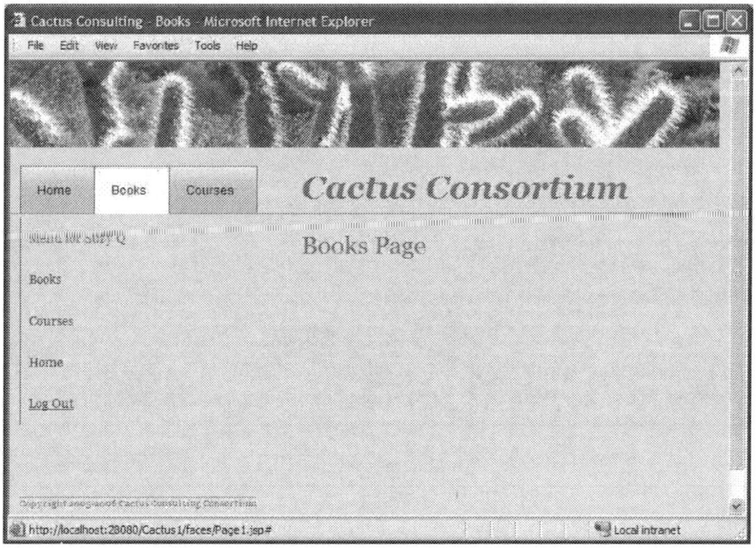

Figure 7–35 **Project Cactus2 running in a browser**

- By default the visual editor displays a grid that helps you align components. You can turn off the grid or change its size using the **Tools > Options > Visual Designer** menu. You can temporarily disable grid alignment by repositioning the component while holding down the Shift key.
- You can select multiple components by dragging a mouse around the target components, enclosing them in a box. You can also use **<Shift+Click>** to add components to those that are already selected.
- To align components with one another, select the target components, position the mouse over the reference component, right-click, and select **Align**. This brings up the Align context menu with choices for alignment.
- For horizontal alignment options, select Left, Center, or Right. For vertical alignment options, select Top, Middle, Bottom.
- Creator's Basic, Layout, and Composite components are rendered using *themes*. A theme is a bundled set of cascading style sheets, JavaScript files, and images that apply to the components and page. The available themes are listed in the Projects window under node Themes.
- To change the current theme, right-click a new theme selection in the Projects window and select **Set As Current Theme**. To make the new theme take effect for deployment, stop the application server and clean and rebuild the project.
- You can control the look of a component by modifying its `style` property. Property `style` accepts property-value pairs to control style attributes such as color, background color, font characteristics and page position.

- Creator provides a style editor to manipulate a component's `style` property. To use the style editor, click the editing box opposite property `style`.
- In addition to the `style` property, Creator also uses Cascading Style Sheets (CSS) to control the look of its components and pages. You can add style classes to a project's default style sheet, **stylesheet.css**. You can also provide your own style sheet.
- To edit the default style sheet, double-click file **stylesheet.css** in the Projects window under **Web Pages > resources**. Creator brings up the style sheet in the Style Sheet Editor.
- Apply one or more style classes to a component by specifying them in a comma separated list for the component's `styleClass` property.
- Using a style sheet with the `styleClass` property is easier than configuring a component's `style` property to achieve a uniform look.
- Creator provides several components that provide grouping and layout capabilities. The layout panel component provides the option of using a grid layout which lets you use the design view to easily position nested components.
- The grid panel component provides a cell for each nested component. Creator places each component in the next available cell. The default number of columns is one, but you can change this value in the grid panel's Properties window. The grid panel is especially useful when you want to include one or more components after a component with indeterminate sizing (such as a table that can have any number of rows).
- The anchor and hyperlink components control page scrolling. The hyperlink component jumps to a spot on the page marked by the anchor component. Jumping to an anchor does not perform a page request.
- Page Fragments are page building blocks for web applications. Typically, you use page fragments to hold parts of your web page that you'd like to standardize for a uniform look, such as page headers, standard menus, or footers.
- You can save a project as a template. When you create a new project, you can then select a saved template as a starting point.
- You can use wildcards in page navigation rules. Select the Source button in the Page Navigation editor and modify the **navigation.xml** source file directly. Wildcards simplify navigation rules by reducing the number of navigation cases you define.
- The tab set is a composite component that contains nested tabs. Under each nested tab is a layout panel component. Tabs are similar to hyperlinks in that you can specify action event handling code as well as navigation strings.
- You can use tab sets with page fragments or put a tab set and its nested tabs all on one page. You may also put a separate tab set on its own page.
- A tab set's `selected` property holds the component `id` (as a String) of the tab that is currently selected.

INTRODUCING DATA PROVIDERS

Topics in This Chapter

- Data Providers Class Hierarchy
- Property Binding with Data Providers
- Common Table Data Provider Methods
- Object Data Provider
- Object List Data Provider
- Cached RowSet Data Provider

Chapter 8

New to Creator 2 is the standardization of a data layer in between a web application's components and its persistence tier, such as a data base. This data layer allows the programmer to access data in a consistent way, even though the data may come from different sources. In this chapter, we'll introduce the Creator data providers and show you how they're used.

8.1 Data Provider Basics

Let's begin by examining the components in the Data Provider section of the Components Palette, as shown in Figure 8–1. All the data providers implement the basic DataProvider interface, which provides a consistent way to access data in an object using FieldKeys that correspond to property names. With the TableDataProvider interface, you can also use the concept of cursor-based access (using the "current" row) and random access (you specify both a FieldKey and a RowKey). We'll show you how to manipulate the data providers in this chapter.

More elaborate data providers provide transactional behavior (TransactionalDataProvider interface) and caching behavior (RefreshableDataProvider interface). The CachedRowSetDataProvider implements both of these interfaces.

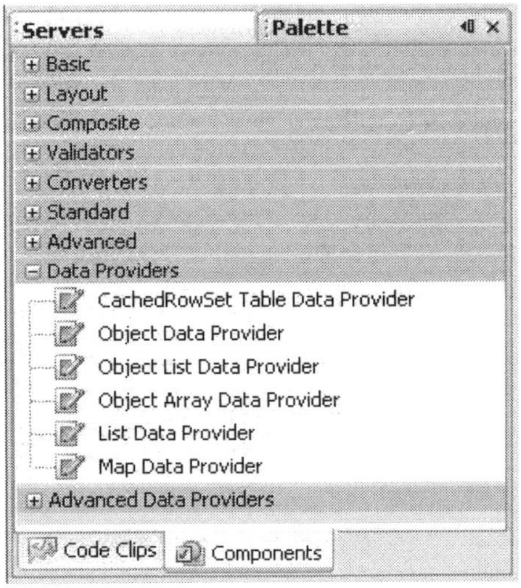

Figure 8–1 **Data Providers Palette**

The data provider you use depends on the source of the data and how you want to manipulate the data. For example, if your data originates from a data source, a cached row set table data provider, that is refreshable and transactional is suitable. On the other hand, if your data comes from another persistent source that is transactional but not a cached rowset, then you'll use an object list data provider that is transactional. Figure 8–2 depicts Creator's data provider class hierarchy, which shows the different data provider interfaces and their implementation classes.

Table 8.1 lists these data providers with descriptions of their use.

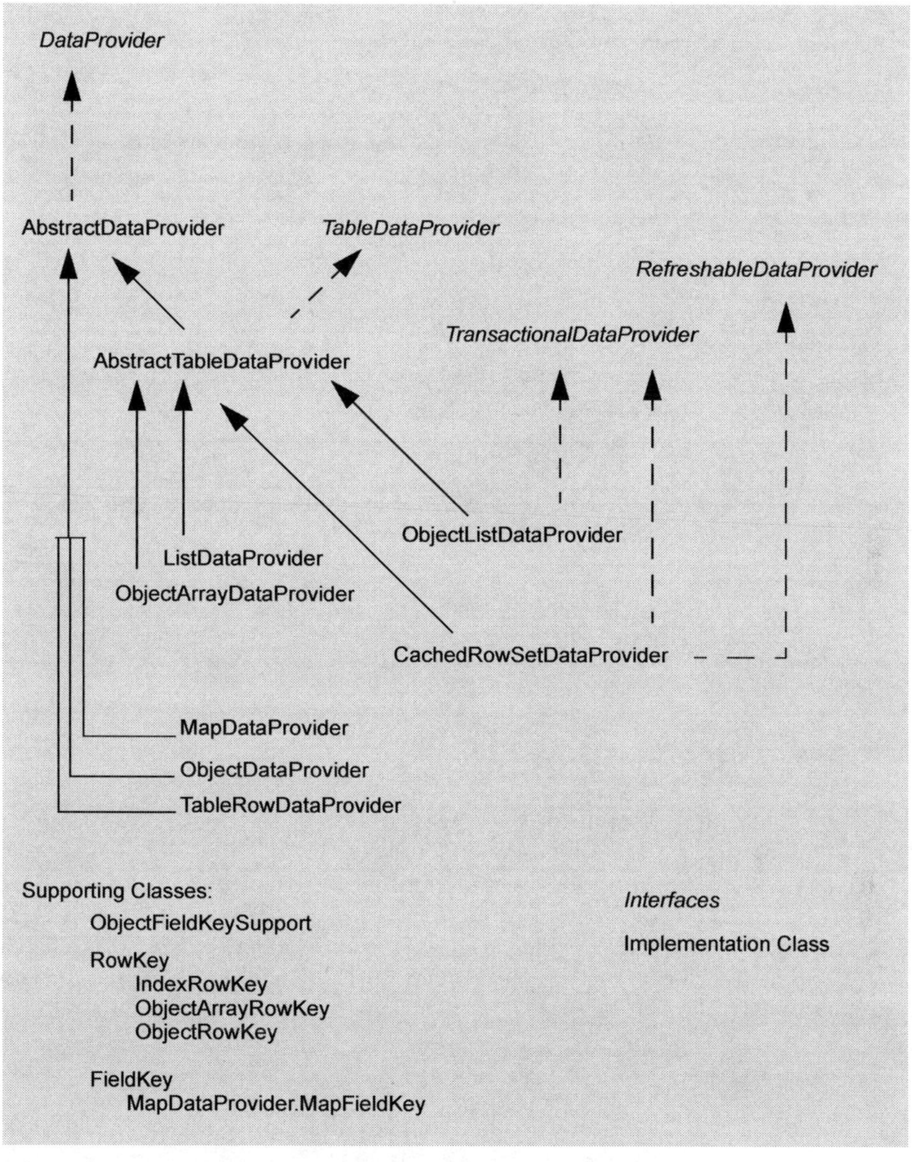

Figure 8–2 **Creator data provider class hierarchy**

Table 8.1 Creator Basic Data Providers

Data Provider	*Description*
Object Data Provider	Wraps the contents of a single object. Key fields have id values matching the properties of the object.
Object Array Data Provider	Wraps the contents of an array of objects. Key fields have id values matching the properties of the object type. Since an array's size is fixed, `canAppend()`, `canInsert()`, and `canRemove()` return false.
Object List Data Provider	Wraps the contents of a list of objects. Key fields have id values matching the properties of the object type. Objects can be added and removed to and from the list.
List Data Provider	Wraps the contents of a list. Key fields are ignored.
Map Data Provider	Wraps the contents of a map. Key fields have id values that match the keys of the wrapped map.
CachedRowSet Table Data Provider	Wraps a cached row set. This data provider is transactional and refreshable (cached).
Table Row Data Provider	Wraps a single row from a table data provider.

Table Data Providers

The Table Data Provider interface provides access to a set of data through row keys that identify a particular row and field keys that identify fields or columns in the table data provider. Let's examine some common tasks you'll perform with table data providers. For these examples, assume that `recordingsDP` is a CachedRowSetDataProvider that wraps a CachedRowSet. A CachedRowSetDataProvider is both transactional and refreshable. Unless otherwise noted, however, all of these examples apply to any Table Data Providers.

Row Data

You can get a single row from a table data provider. For example, if you have a Table component whose source variable is bound to a table data provider, here's how to obtain the current row of data using the `getBean()` helper function.

```
TableRowDataProvider rowdata = (TableRowDataProvider)
      getBean("currentRow");
```

Row Key

A row key is an index into a table row data provider. Many of the methods for manipulating the table row data provider use a row key parameter to identify the target row. Here's how you get the row key from a table row data provider (`rowdata`).

```
RowKey rowKey = rowdata.getTableRow();
```

The table data provider maintains a cursor marking the current row. Here's how to obtain the row key from the current row of a table data provider (`recordingsDP`).

```
RowKey rowKey = recordingsDP.getCursorRow();
```

You can manipulate the current row (the row key cursor) using a set of methods that change the cursor. The following methods, for example, set the current row to the first, next, previous, and last row, respectively. These methods return a boolean that give you the option of checking the validity of the cursor after calling the method.

```
boolean ok = recordingsDP.cursorFirst();
ok = recordingsDP.cursorNext();
ok = recordingsDP.cursorPrevious();
ok = recordingsDP.cursorLast();
```

You can also set the cursor by searching the data for a value of a particular field, as follows. The following example looks for the first occurrence of field RECORDINGTITLE that matches string "xyz".

```
recordingsDP.setCursorRow(recordingsDP.findFirst(
      "RECORDINGS.RECORDINGTITLE"), "xyz"));
```

Getting Data

You get data with the `getValue()` method and a field key. A row key fetches the data from the specified row. Otherwise, you get the data from the current row.

```
// use row key
String t = recordingsDP.getValue("RECORDINGS.RECORDINGTITLE",
      rowKey);
```

```
// use current row
String t = recordingsDP.getValue("RECORDINGS.RECORDINGTITLE");

// access through row data object
TableRowDataProvider rowdata = (TableRowDataProvider)
      getBean("currentRow");
String t = rowdata.getValue("RECORDINGS.RECORDINGTITLE");
```

Setting Data

You set data with the `setValue()` method and a field key. A row key sets the data in the specified row. Otherwise, you set the data in the current row.

```
// use row key
String t = new String("title");
recordingsDP.setValue("RECORDINGS.RECORDINGTITLE", rowKey, t);

// use current row
String t = new String("title");
recordingsDP.setValue("RECORDINGS.RECORDINGTITLE", t);

// use row data object
TableRowDataProvider rowdata = (TableRowDataProvider)
      getBean("currentRow");
String t = new String("title");
rowdata.setValue("RECORDINGS.RECORDINGTITLE", t);
```

Property Binding

You can bind a UI component's property to a field in a data provider. Here is a binding expression to bind the value of a particular field (RECORDINGTITLE) in the current row.

```
#{Page1.recordingsDP.value['RECORDINGS.RECORDINGTITLE']}
```

For a component that's part of the UI Table component, use variable `currentRow`, as follows.

```
#{currentRow.value['RECORDINGS.RECORDINGTITLE']}
```

Refreshable

A refreshable data provider is cached. To load (or reload) data into the table data provider from the underlying data source, use method `refresh()`. (You only use `refresh()` with data providers that implement the RefreshableData-Provider interface.)

```
recordingsDP.refresh();
```

Working With the Data Provider

Here's how to loop through a table data provider and perform an action on each row.

```
// only refresh if refreshable
if (recordingsDP instanceof RefreshableDataProvider)
  recordingsDP.refresh();
if (recordingsDP.cursorFirst()) {
  do {
    RowKey rowkey = recordingsDP.getCursorRow();
    try {
        info("Doing something to rowkey ", rowkey);
        recordingsDP.doSomething(rowkey);
    } catch(Exception e) {
        error("Failed for rowkey ", rowkey);
    }
  } while (recordingsDP.cursorNext());
} // end if
```

Removing a Row

Here's how to remove row `rowkey` from a table row data provider. Note that we check to see if the data provider can be resized before calling method `removeRow()`.

```
boolean ok = true;
if (recordingsDP.canRemoveRow(rowkey) {
  try {
      recordingsDP.removeRow(rowkey);
  } catch (Exception e) {
      error("Cannot remove row ", rowkey);
      ok = false;
  }
}
if (recordingsDP instanceof TransactionalDataProvider) {
  // commit or roll back changes depending on boolean ok
}
```

Appending a Row

Here's how to append row `rowkey` to a table row data provider. Note that we check to see if the data provider can be appended to before calling method `appendRow()`.

```
if (recordingsDP.canAppendRow()) {
  try {
    RowKey rowKey = recordingsDP.appendRow();
    // do this for each field
    recordingsDP.setValue("tablename.fieldname", rowKey,
          value);
    // after all fields are set, commit changes
    if (recordingsDP instanceof TransactionalDataProvider)
      recordingsDP.commitChanges();
  } catch (Exception e) {
      error(" . . . ");
  }
}
```

Working With Transactional Data Providers

Here's how to commit or rollback changes with a transactional data provider. Use these to commit appends, removes, and insert operations. Methods `commitChanges()` and `revertChanges()` are also used to commit (or not) data that the user edits from within a UI table component.

```
if (ok) {
  try {
      recordingsDP.commitChanges();
  } catch (Exception e) {
      error(" . . . ");
      try {
          recordingsDP.revertChanges();
      } catch (Exception e2) {
          error(" . . . ");
      }
  }
```

```
} else {
  try {
      recordingsDP.revertChanges();
  } catch (Exception e) {
      error(" . . . ");
  }
}
```

Working With RowSets

When a data provider wraps a row set, you may need to access the row set directly to set a query parameter. Here is an example of obtaining a query parameter from a SessionBean1 property and using it to execute the query. The `refresh()` method executes the underlying SQL query.

```
try {
     getSessionBean1().getRecordingsRowSet().setObject(1,
        getSessionBean1().getValue_of_query_parameter());
     recordingsDP.refresh();
} catch (Exception e) {
     error(" . . . ");
}
```

Chapter 9 (beginning on page 373) shows you projects that access a database for reading, updating, inserting new data, and deleting data.

8.2 Object Data Provider

The object data provider component wraps an individual JavaBeans component instance. This allows code in your web application to bind to the object data provider, isolating the instantiation of the underlying JavaBeans component. The client code (application code) accesses the properties of the JavaBeans component using a data provider. The object data provider wraps the JavaBeans component through its object property, which you can set in the Properties window. Data providers let you access the JavaBeans component both in the Java page bean code (such as event handlers) and in the property binding dialogs of the IDE.

Object Data Provider Methods

You access individual properties of the JavaBeans component using FieldKey objects. The data provider object provides the FieldKeys through method `get-`

`FieldKey(propertyName)` where *`propertyName`* is the JavaBeans component property.

Let's see how all of this works using the JavaBeans component you've already used in project Login2 (see "LoginBean" on page 229).

In project Login2, the JavaBeans component LoginBean is instantiated in session scope in SessionBean1 as property `loginBean`. In both the Page1 and LoginGood web pages, property bindings provide direct access to the object. For example,

```
#{SessionBean1.loginBean.username}
```

binds the `username` property of the LoginBean object to the `text` property of the `userName` text field. Similarly, in the Page1 `login_action()` event handler, you access the LoginBean object using

```
LoginBean login = getSessionBean1().getLoginBean();
if (login.isLoginGood() . . . )
```

Rather than access this SessionBean1 property directly, let's use an object data provider. All calls to the LoginBean component go through data provider calls. This lets you change the underlying mechanism for instantiating and maintaining this JavaBeans component without affecting your web application access code. For example, the object data provider `loginDP` provides access to the `username` property, as follows.

```
loginDP.setObject(
    (java.lang.Object)getValue("#{SessionBean1.loginBean}"));

// display the user name in a message component
info(loginDP.getValue(loginDP.getFieldKey("username")));
```

Method `getFieldKey()` returns the data provider's field key that correctly accesses the corresponding property value.

Here's how to bind the LoginBean `username` property to text field component `userName` using the following expression.

```
#{Page1.loginDP.value['username']}
```

Access to LoginBean boolean property `loginGood` is similar.

```
boolean loginOK = ((Boolean)loginDP.getValue(
    loginDP.getFieldKey("loginGood"))).booleanValue();
```

Copy the Project

Let's add the object data provider to project Login2. To avoid starting from scratch, make a copy of the Login2 project and save it as Login3. This step is optional. If you don't want to copy the project, simply skip this section and continue making modifications to the Login2 project.

1. Bring up project Login2 in Creator, if it's not already opened.
2. From the Projects window, right-click node Login2 and select Save Project As. Provide the new name **Login3**.
3. Close project Login2. Right-click Login3 and select Set Main Project. You'll make changes to the Login3 project.
4. Bring up Page1 in the design view.
5. Click anywhere in the background of the Page1 design canvas. In the Properties window, change the page's `Title` property to **Login 3**.

Add the Object Data Provider

Now you'll add and configure the object data provider.

1. Make sure that Page1 is active in the design window.
2. From the Components palette, scroll down and expand the Data Providers section.
3. Select component Object Data Provider and add it to the page (drop it on top of the page background). Creator adds the data provider component. Since the data provider is a non-visual component, it shows up in the Page1 Outline view.
4. Select the data provider component in the Page1 Outline view and in the Properties window, change its id to **loginDP**.
5. In the Properties window, select the editing box opposite property `object`. Creator pops up the **loginDP - object** dialog.
6. From the list, select **loginBean (SessionBean1)** and click OK, as shown in Figure 8–3. This is all you need to do to wrap the LoginBean JavaBeans component in the object data provider. Creator generates the following Java code in the Page1 private method `_init()`.

```
loginDP.setObject(
    (java.lang.Object)getValue("#{SessionBean1.loginBean}"));
```

Provide Binding to Components

The text field and password components on the page currently bind directly to the SessionBean1 LoginBean component. You'll now update the binding on these components.

Figure 8–3 **Set property object for data provider loginDP**

1. From the Page1 design canvas, select text field component `userName`.
2. Right-click and select Property Bindings. The Property Bindings dialog for component `userName` pops up.
3. Property **text *Object*** should already be selected under Select bindable property.
4. Under Select binding target, select **loginDP > key username *String***, as shown in Figure 8–4.
5. Click Apply then Close. Creator generates the following binding expression for the text field's `text` property.

```
#{Page1.loginDP.value['username']}
```

6. Repeat steps 1-5 for component `password`. For Select bindable property, choose **password *Object***. Under Select binding target, select **loginDP > key password *String***. The binding expression for this component is now

```
#{Page1.loginDP.value['password']}
```

Modify Event Handler Code

Now you'll modify the event handler code to use the object data provider.

1. From the Page1 design view, double-click the Login button. This brings up **Page1.java** and method `login_action()` in the Java source editor.

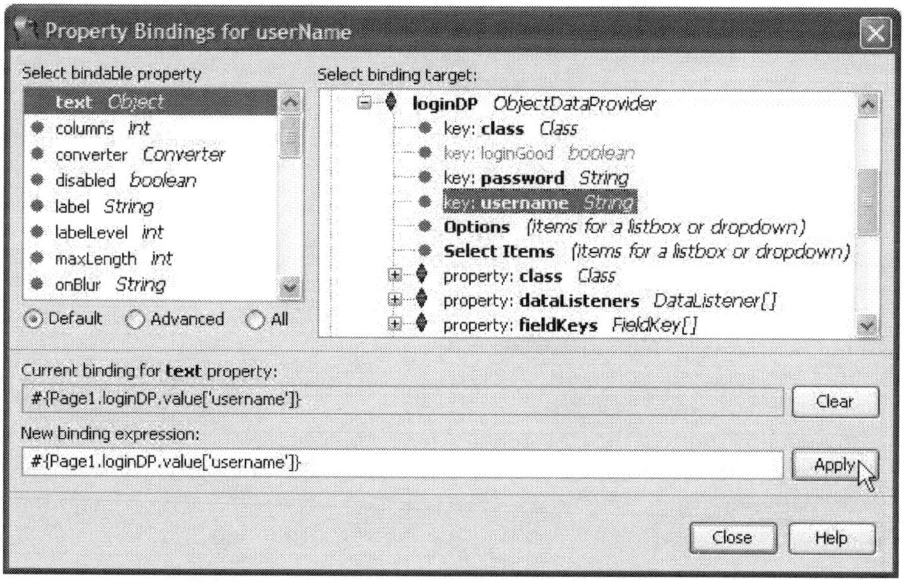

Figure 8–4 **Use loginDP object data provider for property binding**

This method currently queries property `loginGood` (a boolean) to see if the login process is successful. Rather than access the SessionBean1 property `loginBean`, you'll use the object data provider.

2. Provide the following code for method `login_action()`. Copy and paste from **FieldGuide2/Examples/DataProviders/snippets/ login3_login_action.txt**.

```
public String login_action() {
  boolean loginOK = ((Boolean)loginDP.getValue(
        loginDP.getFieldKey("loginGood"))).booleanValue();

  if (loginOK) {
    return "loginSuccess";
  } else
    return "loginFail";
}
```

Modify LoginGood Page

Note that page LoginGood displays the username after the user has successfully logged in. You can't use the same object data provider from Page1 since it has page (request) scope. Therefore, you'll use a second object data provider for this page and bind to the same underlying session bean property, the LoginBean object.

Creator Tip

You could optionally add the object data provider directly to SessionBean1 by dragging and dropping from the palette to SessionBean1 in the Outline view. Then you can use the same data provider in Page1 and LoginGood.

Here are the steps that configures an object data provider and binds it with the label component on the LoginGood page.

1. Double-click **LoginGood.jsp** under Web Pages in the Projects window to bring up this page in the design view.
2. From the Data Providers Components palette, select Object Data Provider and drop it on the page (anywhere on the background). Creator instantiates an object data provider, which you see in the Outline view under LoginGood.
3. Select the object data provider and in the Properties window, change its `id` property to **loginDP2**. (The name does not have to be different than the Page1 object data provider, but a different name helps reduce confusion.)
4. In the Properties window, select the small editing box opposite property `object`. In the dialog, select **loginBean (SessionBean1)** from the list. Click OK. This wraps SessionBean1 property `loginBean` with the data provider.
5. In the LoginGood design view, select the label component, right-click, and select Property Bindings.
6. Under Select binding target, select **loginDP2 > key username *String*** and click Apply.
7. In the New binding expression window, add the text **Welcome,** in front of the generated binding expression. Click Apply then Close. The binding expression for property `text` should now be set to

```
Welcome, #{LoginGood.loginDP2.value['username']}
```

Deploy and Run

Deploy and run project Login3. Although using the data provider here makes accessing the LoginBean component rather obtuse, you'll note that there are no dependencies on LoginBean's structure, as well as no dependencies on how it is acquired. The advantage of using data providers is that accessing data is similar regardless of the underlying structure. Later in this chapter we'll enhance the LoginBean component itself to access a database (through a data provider) to determine the success of the login process.

Other Singleton Object Data Providers

The Object Data Provider is meant to wrap a singleton data object. Creator also provides the Map Data Provider and the Table Row Data Provider (under Advanced Data Providers in the Palette window). The Map Data Provider wraps a data object that is a map construct. The Table Row Data Provider gives access to a structure that is a single row in a table.

8.3 Object List Data Provider

The Object List Data Provider is useful for wrapping an ArrayList (or other list-type) of objects. To illustrate this data provider, we're going to enhance the LoanBean component and add a property that provides an ArrayList of objects. This list is a payment schedule (an amortization table) of the fixed rate loan.

Because an array list is a dynamic array, the Object List Data Provider (*potentially*) allows you to insert and remove items. Potentially means that the ability to resize the list is dependent on several conditions.

- The underlying collection must be resizeable. An ArrayList is resizeable, an array of Objects is not.
- The object type (in our case PaymentVO) must have a zero-argument public constructor.
- The collection itself should be writable. In our case, property `monthlyAmortTable` is a read-only property.

The Table Data Provider interface provides methods that allow you to check the data provider to see if it can perform an insert, append, or remove operation (`canInsertRow()`, `canAppendRow()`, and `canRemoveRow()`). You should call these methods before attempting the resize operations. The Payment2 example does not perform any resizing.

Copy the Project

To avoid starting from scratch, make a copy of the Payment1 project and save it as Payment2. This step is optional. If you don't want to copy the project, simply skip this section and continue making modifications to the Payment1 project.

1. Bring up project Payment1 in Creator, if it's not already opened.

2. From the Projects window, right-click node Payment1 and select Save Project As. Provide the new name **Payment2.**
3. Close project Payment1. Right-click Payment2 and select Set Main Project. You'll make changes to the Payment2 project.
4. Bring up Page1 in the design view.
5. Click anywhere in the background of the Page1 design canvas. In the Properties window, change the page's `Title` property to **Payment Calculator 2.**

Replace LoanBean.java

In project Payment1, you added Source Packages **asg.bean_examples** and Java class **LoanBean.java**. In this project you'll replace the **LoanBean.java** source file with a version that includes additional properties. The new **LoanBean.java** will include property `startDate` (the beginning point for a payment schedule) and `monthlyAmortTable` (the loan's complete payment schedule).

1. In the Projects window, open the **Source Packages > asg.bean_examples** nodes.
2. Double-click file **LoanBean.java** to bring up the file in the Java source editor.
3. Replace the entire file using copy/paste with the source found in the Creator download at **FieldGuide2/Examples/DataProviders/snippets/LoanBean.java.** (There will be some syntax errors flagged. You can ignore these for now.)

Add PaymentVO.java

The enhanced LoanBean component uses a PaymentVO object to build the amortization schedule. Let's add this Java class to your project and then copy the contents of the file from the Creator download. Here are the steps.

1. In the Projects window, select node **Source Packages > asg.bean_examples**, right-click, and select **New > Java Class.**
2. Creator pops up the New Java Class dialog.
3. Provide Class Name **PaymentVO** (for Payment Value Object) and click Finish.
4. Replace the entire file using copy/paste with the source found in the Creator download at **FieldGuide2/Examples/DataProviders/snippets/PaymentVO.java.**
5. Build project Payment2, close it, and reopen it in the IDE. This ensures that the new LoanBean properties are visible in the Property Bindings dialogs. All of the files should now be free of syntax errors.

Deploy and Run

Project Payment2 should run the same as Payment1 without any further modifications. Test to make sure the application runs by deploying and running Payment2 now.

LoanBean Bean Patterns

Look at component LoanBean's bean patterns. From the Projects window, expand node **Source Packages > asg.bean_examples > LoanBean.java > LoanBean > Bean Patterns**, as shown in Figure 8–5. You'll see the properties you created earlier (`amount`, `payment`, `rate`, and `years`), as well as two new properties (`monthlyAmortTable` and `startDate`). Property `monthlyAmortTable` is a read-only property that returns an array list of payment objects. Property `startDate` is a read-write Calendar object that stores the beginning date of the loan. When you select **LoanBean.java** you see the Members View simultaneously displayed in the Navigator window (also shown in Figure 8–5).

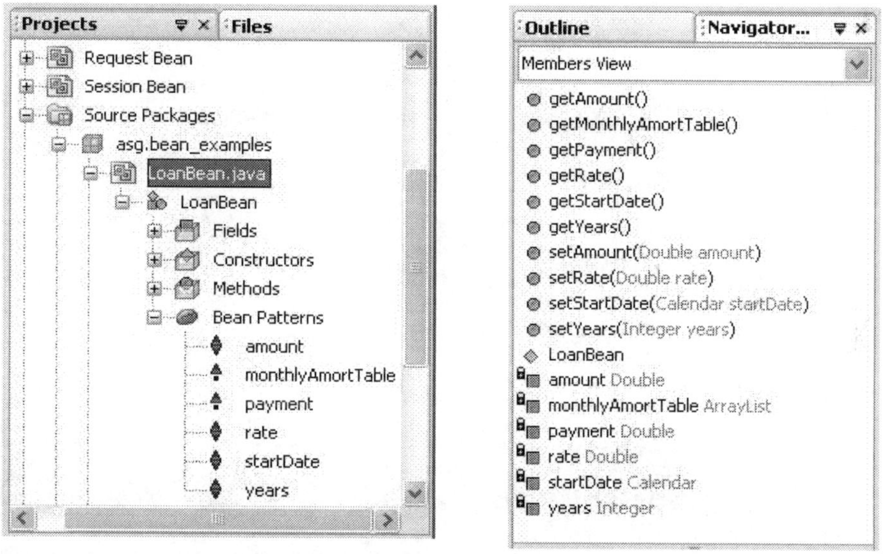

Figure 8–5 **Bean Patterns and Class Members for LoanBean**

PaymentVO Bean Patterns

Method `getMonthlyAmortTable()` is the getter for property `monthlyAmortTable`. Let's look at the data that this method returns. The data consists of the values that apply to each monthly payment for a fixed-rate loan: the payment number, date, interest amount, principal amount, accumulated interest and principal, and loan balance. This information is encapsulated in the PaymentVO component.

In the Projects window, scroll down a bit and select the **PaymentVO.java** node. Expand the **PaymentVO > Bean Patterns** nodes. The Projects window shows the bean patterns and the Navigator window shows the fields and property getters and setters, as shown in Figure 8–6. When you add a table component to the page, you'll access these properties through the table row data provider.

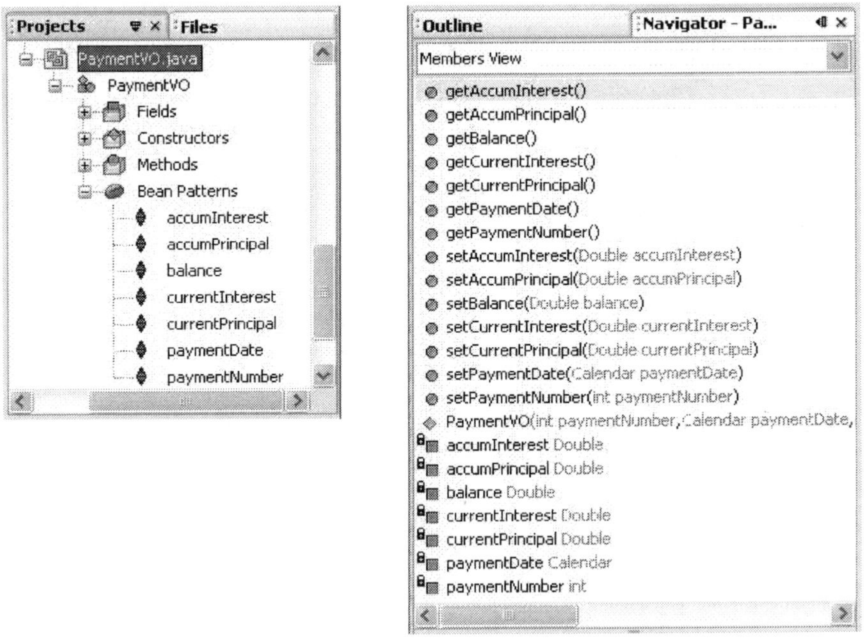

Figure 8–6 **Bean Patterns and Class Members for PaymentVO**

Add Components to Page1

You need a calendar component to obtain a starting date from the user and a button to display the payment schedule. Virtual forms will separate the Calculate use case from the Payment Schedule use case. The payment schedule will be displayed on a separate page using a table component. Recall that the LoanBean component is a property of SessionBean1, so it is accessible from any page throughout the session. Figure 8–7 shows the Page1 design view with the new components added.

1. Make Page1 active in the design view.

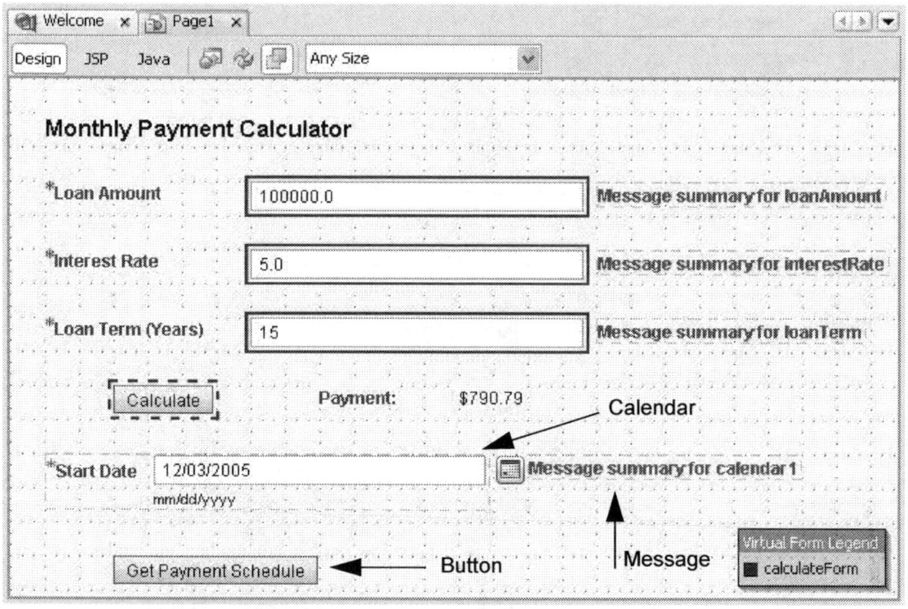

Figure 8–7 **Design view for Page1 of project Payment2**

2. From the Basics Components palette, select component Calendar and drop it on the page below the Calculate button.
3. From the Basic Component palette, select Button and drop it on the canvas below the calendar component.
4. While it is still selected, type in the text **Get Payment Schedule** to set the label text.
5. Change the button's `id` property to **schedule**.

Since the calendar component input is required and it performs validation, you'll need a message component.

1. From the Basic Components palette, select Message and add it to the canvas to the right of the calendar component.
2. Hold the **<Shift+Ctrl>** keys, left-click the mouse, drag the cursor over to the calendar component, and release the mouse. This sets the message component's `for` property.

Configure the Calendar Component

You'll bind the calendar component's `selectedDate` property to the LoanBean's `startDate` (`time`) property as well as configure some of its other properties.

1. Select the calendar component. In the Properties window, set the label property to **Start Date**.
2. In the Properties window, check the `required` property.
3. Select the calendar component, right-click, and select Property Bindings. Creator displays the now familiar Property Bindings dialog.
4. Under Select bindable property, select **selectedDate** ***Date***.
5. Under Select binding target, select **SessionBean1 > loanBean > startDate > time**, as shown in Figure 8–8. Click Apply then Close. Note that Creator displays today's date in the calendar component.

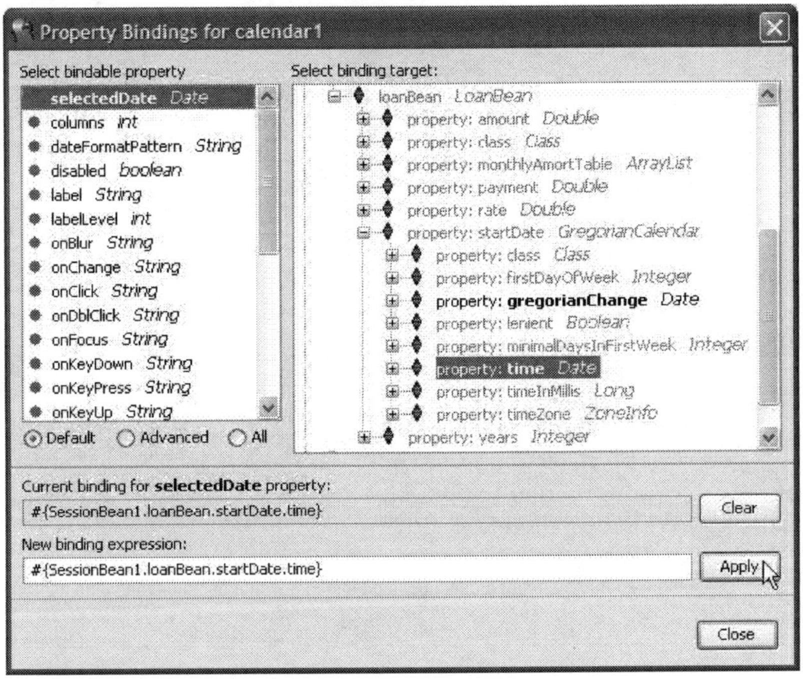

Figure 8–8 **Binding the** `selectedDate` **property to the LoanBean** `startDate.time` **property**

The Calendar component contains a built-in range validator for its `selectedDate` property. If you don't specify the range, the default minimum is today's date and the default maximum is four years from today's date. For Payment2, there's no reason to restrict the date to preclude specifying a date in the past or limiting a date further into the future. We'll use January 1, 1975 for the minimum start date and December 31, 2020 for the maximum start date. You can't specify a literal date through the Properties window, but you can add code in the page bean's `init()` method to set properties `minDate` and `maxDate`.

1. Click the Java button on the editing toolbar to bring up **Page1.java** in the source editor.
2. Find method `init()` and add the following code to the end. Copy and paste from **FieldGuide2/Examples/DataProviders/snippets/payment2_calendar_init.txt**. The added code is bold.

```
public void init() {
. . .
   // set minimum date to January 1, 1975
   calendar1.setMinDate(
        new GregorianCalendar(1975, 0, 1).getTime());
   // set maximum date to December 31, 2020
   calendar1.setMaxDate(
        new GregorianCalendar(2020, 11, 31).getTime());
}
```

3. Right-click inside the page and select Fix Imports to include an import statement for GregorianCalendar.

The calendar component method `setMinDate()` takes a `java.util.Date` object, which you can construct using the GregorianCalendar class. To read the corresponding Javadoc for this class, select it in the editor and press **<Ctrl+space>**. Creator pops up a detailed description of the class with examples on its use. The `getTime()` method returns the needed Date object.

Configure Virtual Forms

You can improve the user interaction with project Payment2 by using virtual forms. If you put all of the input components for the LoanBean calculation in one virtual form (excluding the calendar component) and make the Calculate button the submitter, then the user is not required to provide valid calendar input when requesting the payment calculation. However, because all fields are submitted for the payment schedule (including the loan parameter fields used for the payment calculation), the Get Payment Schedule button does not require a separate virtual form. By default, user input for all components will be converted and validated, which is the behavior we want.

1. Toggle the Show Virtual Forms icon on the editing toolbar.
2. From the Page1 design view, select text field components `loanAmount`, `interestRate`, and `loanTerm` (use **<Shift+Click>** to select all three components).
3. Right-click and select Configure Virtual Forms from the context menu. Creator pops up the Configure Virtual Forms dialog.

4. Click button New. Creator makes a new virtual form with color code blue. Edit the virtual form's Name to **calculateForm** (double-click the field name and it becomes editable) and change the Participate field to **Yes** using the drop down selection.
5. Click Apply then OK. The three text field components are outlined in a solid blue line indicating that they participate in the calculateForm virtual form.
6. Now select the Calculate button, right-click, and select Configure Virtual Forms.
7. Creator displays the calculateForm virtual form in the dialog. Change the Submit field to **Yes** using the drop down selection. Click Apply and OK. The design view now shows the Calculate button with a blue-dotted border, indicating that it is the submit component for the blue virtual form.

Add a New Page

The application displays the payment schedule on a separate page.

1. In the Projects window, right-click Web Pages and select New > Page. Creator displays the New Page dialog.
2. Supply Name **Schedule** and click Finish. Creator generates page **Schedule.jsp** and brings it up in the design view.
3. Click anywhere in the background and set the `Title` property to **Payment Schedule**.

Add Components to Schedule Page

The Schedule page contains a label and a static text component for the heading, a hyperlink to return to the loan parameters page, and a table component to display the payment schedule.

1. From the Basic Components palette, select Label and place it near the top of the page. Type in the text **Monthly Payment Schedule for payment:** followed by **<Enter>**.
2. Make sure the label is still selected. In the Properties window, change the labelLevel to **Strong(1)**.
3. From the Basic Components palette, select Static Text and place it on the page just to the right of the label.
4. Right-click the static text component and select Property Bindings.
5. In the Property Bindings dialog, under Select bindable property, select **text *Object***. Under Select binding target, select **SessionBean1 > loanBean > payment**. Click Apply, then Close.

Since the LoanBean's `payment` property is a Double, you'll need a converter. Use a number converter so that you can format the amount.

1. From the Converters Components palette, select Number Converter and drop it on the static text component. Creator pops up the Number Format dialog so that you can configure the converter.
2. Select the Pattern radio button and provide pattern **#,###.00**, as shown in Figure 8–9. This pattern supplies a comma separator if the value is greater than 999 and supplies two digits to the right of the decimal point. (You can test the pattern by providing a sample number in the Example field and click Test. The resulting conversion appears in the Results window.) Click Apply, then OK to close the dialog.

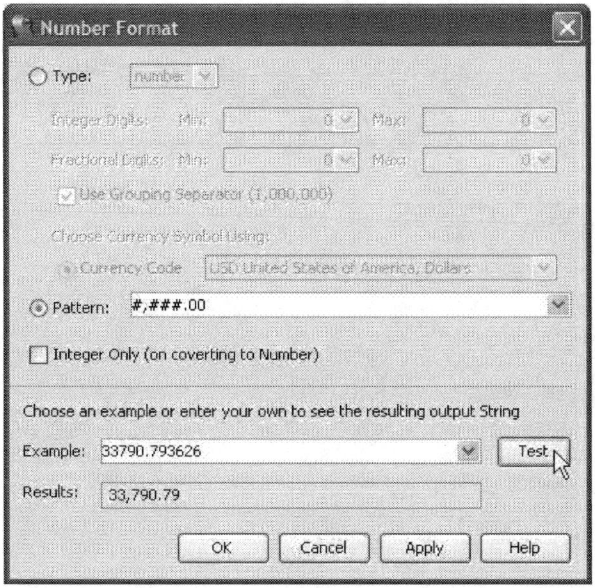

Figure 8–9 **Number Format dialog for number converter**

3. The number in the static text display should now read 790.70. (If the static text displays 0, close **Schedule.jsp** and reopen it in the design view. If it is not formatted correctly, in the Properties window opposite property `converter`, select `numberConverter1` from the drop down list opposite property `converter`.)
4. From the Basic Components palette, select Hyperlink and place it on the page below the label you added previously.
5. Type in the text **Return to Loan Parameters Page** followed by **<Enter>**. This is the hyperlink's text. You'll set the navigation links later.
6. From the Basic Components palette, select Table and drop it on the page under the hyperlink component. Creator configures a standard table with a default table data provider.

7. The table's title is selected for you. Type in the text **Amortization Table** followed by **<Enter>** to set the title.

Configure the Table

You'll provide a different data provider for the table and wrap the `monthlyAmortTable` property of the LoanBean component.

1. Open the Data Providers section of the Components palette. Select Object List Data Provider and drop it on the Table component. Make sure the entire table is outlined in blue before you release the mouse.
2. In the Outline view, select the object list data provider. In the Properties window, select the drop down opposite property `list` and choose **SessionBean1 > loanBean > monthlyAmortTable**. This wraps the ArrayList property of the LoanBean component. Creator adds the following `setList()` call to the `Schedule()` constructor.

```
objectListDataProvider1.setList((java.util.List)getValue(
    "#{SessionBean1.loanBean.monthlyAmortTable}"));
```

Now you'll configure the table layout.

1. In the design view, select the table component, right-click, and select Table Layout. Creator brings up the Table Layout dialog.
2. In the dialog, select the Options tab.
3. In the Options settings, enable pagination and set the number of rows to 12. Click Apply.
4. Now select the Columns tab. The PaymentVO component has seven fields (columns), which you've seen already in the PaymentVO Bean Patterns display. Creator binds these fields to the table columns for you automatically. Click the double arrow button (>>) to move all the PaymentVO fields from the Available window to the Selected window. Click Apply. Creator displays the columns in the table component in the design view.
5. Rearrange the columns to the following order by selecting the Up and Down buttons as needed. Change the Header Text to the text opposite each column name as shown here. Click Apply.

```
paymentDate           Payment Date
paymentNumber         Payment Number
currentPrincipal      Current Principal
currentInterest       Current Interest
balance               Balance
accumPrincipal        Accumulated Principal
accumInterest         Accumulated Interest
```

6. In order to apply a date time converter to the `paymentDate` column, you must first access its `time` property. Select the `paymentDate` column. Change its value expression from the default to the following (add the `.time` qualifier to the end of the expression). Click Apply then OK.

```
#{currentRow.value['paymentDate'].time}
```

7. Apply the number converter (the one you already configured for the payment display) to the current principal, current interest, balance, accumulated principal, and accumulated interest columns. For each of these columns, select `numberConvert1` from the Outline view (the same component you used for the static text component) and drag it over to the table to the target column. When the entire column is outlined in blue, release the mouse. The column will be reformatted with the number converter's pattern.
8. From the Converters palette, select Date Time Converter and drop it on the table's Payment Date column. Select the date time converter in the Outline view, and specify **MMM yyyy** followed by **<Enter>** for its pattern. The table will now display the date as a month and year only.

Figure 8–10 shows what the page looks like (running in a browser) after you've configured the table component and applied the number and date time converters to the appropriate columns.

Configure Page Navigation

You'll use simple navigation for this project. The Get Payment Schedule button on Page1 takes you to the Schedule page and the hyperlink on the Schedule page returns you to Page1.

1. Right-click in the background of the Schedule design view and select Page Navigation. Creator brings up the Navigation editor.
2. Click inside **Page1.jsp** and draw a navigation arrow from the schedule button and release the mouse inside Schedule.jsp.
3. Supply the navigation case label **schedulePage** on the navigation arrow and hit **<Enter>**.
4. Now click inside **Schedule.jsp**, select the hyperlink component, drag the cursor and release the mouse inside **Page1.jsp**.
5. Supply the navigation case label **loanPage** on the navigation arrow and hit **<Enter>**.

Deploy and Run

Deploy and run project Payment2. Test the application by providing different values for the loan parameters, as well as different start dates. Figure 8–10 shows the schedule page for the default values of the LoanBean component. Note that the user is about to display the next page of the table data. The relevant tooltip is configured for you.

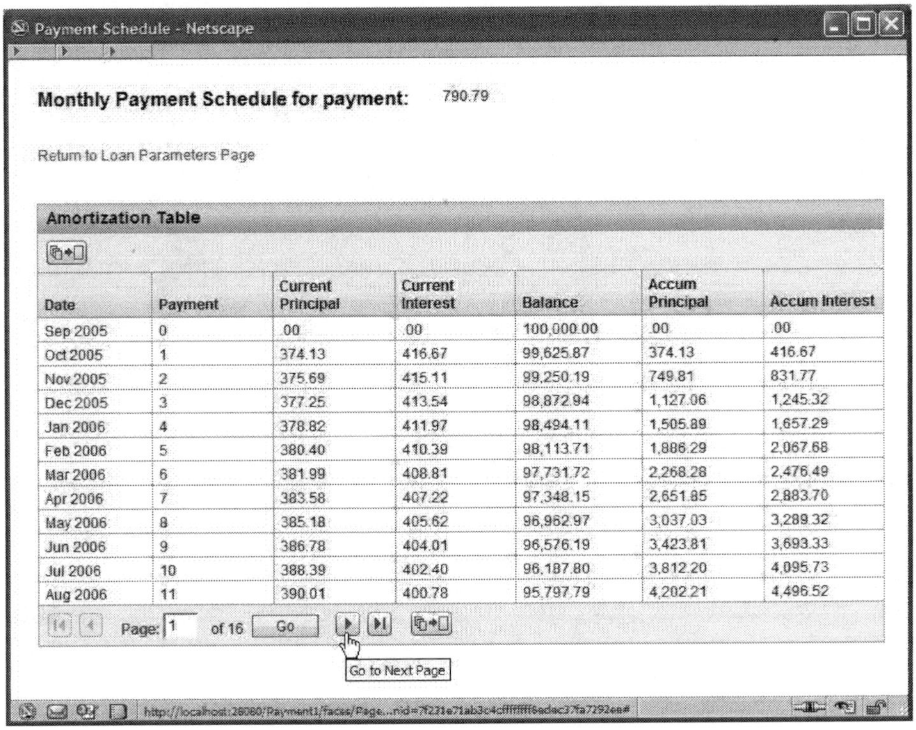

Figure 8–10 **Project Payment2 running in the browser**

8.4 Cached RowSet Data Provider

When you drop a database table on your project, Creator generates a Cached Rowset component, as well as a Cached Rowset Data Provider. This data provider wraps the CachedRowSet object. You manipulate the data in the same way using row keys and field keys, although the CachedRowSetDataProvider provides additional methods, such as `refresh()`, that are specific to the wrapped CachedRowSet.

Creator Tip

When you add a JDBC table to a page, by default Creator adds CachedRowSetDataProvider to the page and the wrapped CachedRowSet to SessionBean1. This enables you to reuse the CachedRowSet object in another data provider (as long as the SQL query is the same). To override the default behavior and place the CachedRowSet object in request scope, uncheck option Create RowSets in Session *from Tools > Options > Advanced > Data Source Drag and Drop.*

In this example, you'll modify the LoginBean component to access the database to determine whether or not the login parameters the user submits are valid. This is a simple database access and it will get your feet wet for the more involved database operations presented in the next chapter. First, you'll create the data base table and populate it with data by running a stand-alone utility program (provided with the book's download) from the IDE.

Configuring the Database

For the Login example, you'll use the bundled database. Here are the steps to configure the Login Data Source.

1. Make sure that the bundled database is running. If it's running, the Bundled Database Server node in the Servers window includes a green up-arrow badge. To start the server, select the Bundled Database Server node, right-click, and choose **Start Bundled Database**.
2. Open project UserBuild. Project UserBuild is included in the Creator book's download at **FieldGuide2/Examples/DataProviders/Projects/UserBuild**. When the project comes up in the IDE, Creator displays a Reference Problems dialog. You need to add the appropriate JAR file to the project. Click Close to remove the dialog.
3. In the Projects window expand the UserBuild node and right-click Libraries. Select Add JAR/Folder from the context menu. Creator pops up the Add JAR/Folder dialog.
4. Browse to the **<Creator-installation-directory>/rave2.0/core/** and select file **derbyclient.jar**. Click Open. Creator adds the JAR file to your project.
5. The UserBuild project is a stand-alone program that generates the sample Users database. You can inspect the code by expanding the **UserBuild > Source Packages > asg.databuild** nodes. Double-click **DerbyLoginDB.java**.

6. Run the project. Select the green arrow icon or select Run > Run Main Project from the main menu. Make sure that you see the following diagnostic in the Output window after running the application.

```
Login database was created.
```

7. When you're finished, close the Project. Right-click on the project name and choose Close Project.

Creator Tip

You can run project UserBuild multiple times to re-generate the Login database.

Add Data Source

Once you've generated the sample data, you'll add the Login schema as a data source. You'll add it as a schema using the same URL (`sample`) as the pre-installed database tables.

1. In the Servers window, right-click Data Sources, and select Add Data Source.
2. Creator displays the Add Data Source dialog. Supply the values shown in Table 8.2. Click Select and set the Validation Table to VALIDATIONONLY.

Table 8.2 Add Data Source Dialog

Prompt	***Value***
Data Source Name	**`Login`**
Server Type	`Derby`
Driver Class	`org.apache.derby.jdbc.ClientDriver`
Database Name	sample
Host Name	localhost
User ID	`login`
Password	`login`
Database URL	`jdbc:derby://localhost:`**`21527/sample`**
Validation Table	LOGIN.VALIDATIONONLY

Creator Tip

Make sure that the port number is ***21527*** *(there should be a 2 in front of the default port number).*

3. When you're finished filling in the dialog, click Test Connection to verify that all the values are correct. Click Add to finish.

Figure 8–11 shows the Add Data Source dialog filled in. Now when you open the Login and Tables node, you'll see two tables in the Login database: USERS and VALIDATIONONLY (used for testing the connection).

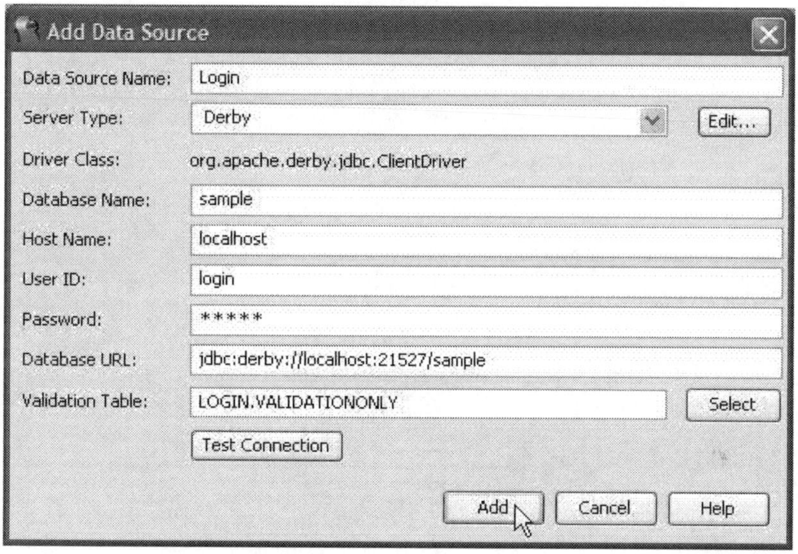

Figure 8–11 **Add Data Source dialog**

Inspect the Data Source

As you saw from Chapter 2, you can view the actual data from a database table interactively from the IDE. This allows a web developer to inspect the data and experiment with queries before building an application. Let's do that now.

1. From the Servers window, select Data Sources > Login > Tables > USERS. Open the USERS node (click on '+') and Creator displays the field names.

2. Double-click the USERS node. Creator displays the table's data in the editor pane. We show this view in Figure 8–12.

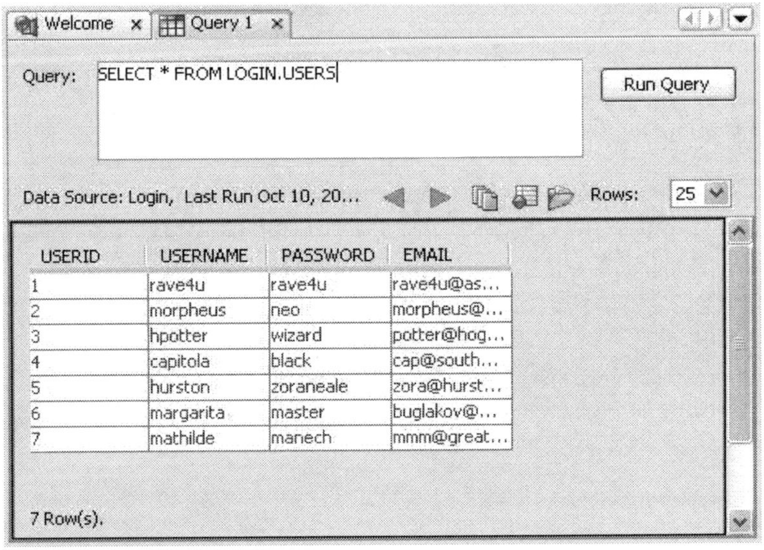

Figure 8–12 **USERS Query View**

The display not only shows the data, but it also provides an interactive query window at the top so that you can edit and run the query.

Copy the Project

Next, you'll modify the LoginBean component from projects Login2 and Login3. In this new project (Login4), the LoanBean `isLoginGood()` method will access the USERS data base table to determine valid login submissions. First, let's copy the project and save it as Login4. This step is optional. If you don't want to copy the project, simply skip this section and continue making modifications to your Login3 project.

1. Bring up project Login3 in Creator, if it's not already opened.
2. From the Projects window, right-click node Login3 and select Save Project As. Provide the new name **Login4**.
3. Close project Login3. Right-click Login4 and select Set Main Project. You'll make changes to the Login4 project.
4. Bring up Page1 in the design view.
5. Click anywhere in the background of the Page1 design canvas. In the Properties window, change the page's `Title` property to **Login 4**.

Add the Data Source

Now add the Login data source (the USERS data table) to SessionBean1 of the project. Creator will generate all the row set and data provider configuration code for you.

1. In the Outline window, expand SessionBean1. You'll see `loginBean` listed as a SessionBean1 property.
2. In the Servers window, expand Data Source > Login > Tables.
3. Select table USERS and drop it under the SessionBean1 section of the Outline window. (Move the mouse over to the left edge of the Outline window and make sure that a rectangular, dotted icon is visible before you release the cursor.) You'll see two new SessionBean1 properties: `usersDataProvider` and `usersRowSet`. The LoginBean component will access these to look up the user's username and password.

Replace LoginBean.java

The majority of the changes you'll make to the LoginBean object are the modifications to method `isLoginGood()`, which accesses the USERS table through the data provider you added to SessionBean1. However, because LoginBean accesses the database, it is convenient to access some Creator/JSF structures (SessionBean1) and services (methods `error()` and `log()`). This is easy if we make LoginBean extend AbstractSessionBean. Here are the steps to replace **LoginBean.java**.

1. In the Projects window, expand the **Source Packages > asg.bean_examples** node.
2. Double-click file **LoginBean.java**. Creator brings up the file in the Java source editor.
3. Replace file **LoginBean.java** with the file in your Creator's download directoy. Copy and paste file **FieldGuide2/Examples/DataProviders/snippets/LoginBean.java**.

Here's the code for the updated `isLoginGood()` method. Note that we obtain references the to data provider (`usersDataProvider`) and the row set (`usersRowSet`) components you added to SessionBean1.

Listing 8.1 Method isLoginGood()

```
public boolean isLoginGood() {
   boolean ok = true;
   CachedRowSetDataProvider usersDataProvider =
         getSessionBean1().getUsersDataProvider();
```

Listing 8.1 Method isLoginGood() *(continued)*

```
  CachedRowSetXImpl usersRowSet =
      getSessionBean1().getUsersRowSet();
  try {
    if (usersDataProvider instanceof
        RefreshableDataProvider)
            usersDataProvider.refresh();
    usersDataProvider.setCursorRow(
        usersDataProvider.findFirst(
            "USERS.USERNAME", username));

    correctName =
      (String)usersDataProvider.getValue("USERS.USERNAME");
    correctPassword =
      (String)usersDataProvider.getValue("USERS.PASSWORD");

    usersRowSet.release();
    usersRowSet.close();

  } catch (Exception e) {
    error("Cannot read USERS database: " + e.getMessage());
    log("Cannot read USERS database: ", e);
    usersRowSet.close();
    ok = false;
  }
  return (ok && username.equals(correctName) &&
                password.equals(correctPassword));
}
```

The code in this method still compares the submitted values stored in the LoginBean object to those in LoginBean's `correctName` and `correctPassword` fields. However, the method now sets these fields by searching through the data provider for a matching USERNAME field using method `findFirst()`, setting the row cursor with method `setCursorRow()`. The `refresh()` call executes the underlying SQL query and the `getValue()` calls read the data. The `release()` and `close()` calls to the underlying rowset free up any data source resources.

Method `error()` writes its error message to the FacesContext, which is displayed when the page is rendered. Therefore, you'll add a message group component to page LoginBad next.

Add a Message Group

Examine the code in **LoginBean.java**'s `isLoginGood()` method. You'll see that database access is inside a try block. If an exception is thrown (for whatever reason), then method `error()` writes its arguments to the FacesContext. A message group component on page LoginBad is necessary to display the error message on the page.

1. In the Projects view, expand node Web Pages and double-click **LoginBad.jsp** to display this page in the design view.
2. From the Basic Components palette, select Message Group and place it on the page.

Now any error messages generated due to a thrown exception inside `isLoginGood()` will be displayed on the LoginBad page.

Deploy and Run

Deploy and run project Login4. Test various valid and invalid username and password combinations (you can determine valid login data by displaying the USERS data table in the main editor pane.) Figure 8–13 shows a valid login scenario for username "margarita" and password "master."

Figure 8–13 **Successful login scenario**

8.5 Key Point Summary

Data providers supply a powerful link between UI components and a persistence layer. With data providers, you isolate code that is dependent on the source of data and implement a consistent interface where access to this data is required.

- All data providers implement the basic DataProvider interface. This provides a consistent way to access data in an object using field keys that correspond to property names.
- The TableDataProvider interface defines row keys that give you cursor-based access as well as random access.
- Data providers that wrap an underlying database provide transactional behavior and caching behavior.
- Each data provider depends on the source of the data and how you want to manipulate the data.
- A row key is an index into a table data provider. You can manipulate the current row with methods that change the cursor (the current row key).
- A table data provider has methods to remove a row, append a row, and insert a row. Not all table data providers are resizeable, however. Use methods `canRemoveRow()`, `canAppendRow()`, and `canInsertRow()` to test resizeability before invoking the table size modifying methods.
- Transactional data providers allow you to commit or revert changes made to the data with methods `commitChanges()` and `revertChanges()`, respectively. You can check whether a data provider is transactional with

```
if (myDataProvider instanceof TransactionalDataProvider) . . .
```

- Use an object data provider to wrap an individual JavaBeans object instance.
- Use an object list data provider to wrap an ArrayList of objects.
- Use an object array data provider to wrap an array of JavaBeans objects. (We show you how to use this data provider in the chapter on accessing web services. See "Add a Data Provider" on page 456.)
- Use a cached rowset data provider to wrap a CachedRowSet object. When you drag and drop a JDBC database table onto a page, Creator configures a cached row set data provider for you, as well as the wrapped CachedRowSet object.

ACCESSING DATABASES

Topics in This Chapter

- Database Basics
- JDBC Cached RowSet Technology
- Using Data Providers
- Master-Detail Relationship
- SQL Query Editor
- Database Operations: Update, Create, Delete
- Cascading Deletes

Chapter 9

One of Creator's key goals is to simplify web application development with databases. To that end, Creator lets you add data sources to your projects and select them from the Servers window. Once you configure a data source, you can view individual tables, field names and data types, and actual data.

Creator also gives you components that are data aware. Using the design canvas, you can select a number of different components and visually position them on your web page. You can select data source tables and add them to your application as cached rowsets, binding the components to the data using intermediary data providers. You can visually select or deselect columns to display, add tables to create database queries with "join" commands, and modify queries to include query parameters.

Creator relies on multiple technologies to make this all happen. Besides using the UI components and event models that we've already shown you, Creator makes use of JDBC and JDBC CachedRowSet technology to simplify accessing the database. Furthermore, Creator adds a "data provider" layer between the JDBC CachedRowSets and the data aware components. The data provider layer gives you flexibility in configuring your application and lets you isolate your client code from the persistence strategy that you choose. By using the data provider in the web application, you can change the persistence layer (say, use EJBs) without changing the client code (your web application).

In this chapter, we use a Music Collection Database for the project examples. Before we start, we review database and JDBC fundamentals and show you the organization of our Music database.

9.1 Database Fundamentals

We begin with an overview of databases and JDBC, discussing database tables and how to access data with JDBC. If you're already familiar with these subjects, you can skip to the next section.

A relational database consists of one or more tables, where each row in a table represents a database record and each column represents a field. Within each table, a record must have a unique key. This key, called a *primary key,* enables a database to distinguish one record from another. If a single field in a database table does not uniquely identify a record, a *composite primary key* can be used. A composite primary key combines more than one field to uniquely identify records in a database table. Each field of a composite primary key should be defined as a primary key.

A field within a table is either a primary key, a *foreign key* (used by the database to reference another table), or just plain data. To set up a database table, you must define fields so that the database software can maintain the integrity of the database. If a field is not "just data," then constraints are attached to the field. The description of the table's fields, data types, and constraints make up the metadata associated with the table. Creator uses metadata to help you configure your web application to access the database efficiently.

A very simple database consists of only a single table. However, many database schemata require multiple tables to efficiently represent related data. For example, our Music Collection database centralizes the information about each recording artist in one table. This table also cross-references a RecordingArtistID field in another table that stores data about a specific recording. Thus, if a recording artist has more than one recording, you don't have to duplicate the recording artist information.

To achieve cross-referencing and to avoid data duplication, you can mark a field in a database table as a foreign key. A foreign key in one table always matches either a primary or foreign key in another table. This is what helps you "relate" two or more tables.

Music Collection Database

The Music Collection database consists of four related tables. The database stores information about music recordings, a generic term we apply to music CDs and older LPs (long-playing records). Figure 9–1 shows the four tables, the fields in each table, and how they relate to each other through the foreign keys.

The Recordings table contains the bulk of the information about a recording. Its primary key (denoted PK) is the field RecordingID. It has two foreign key

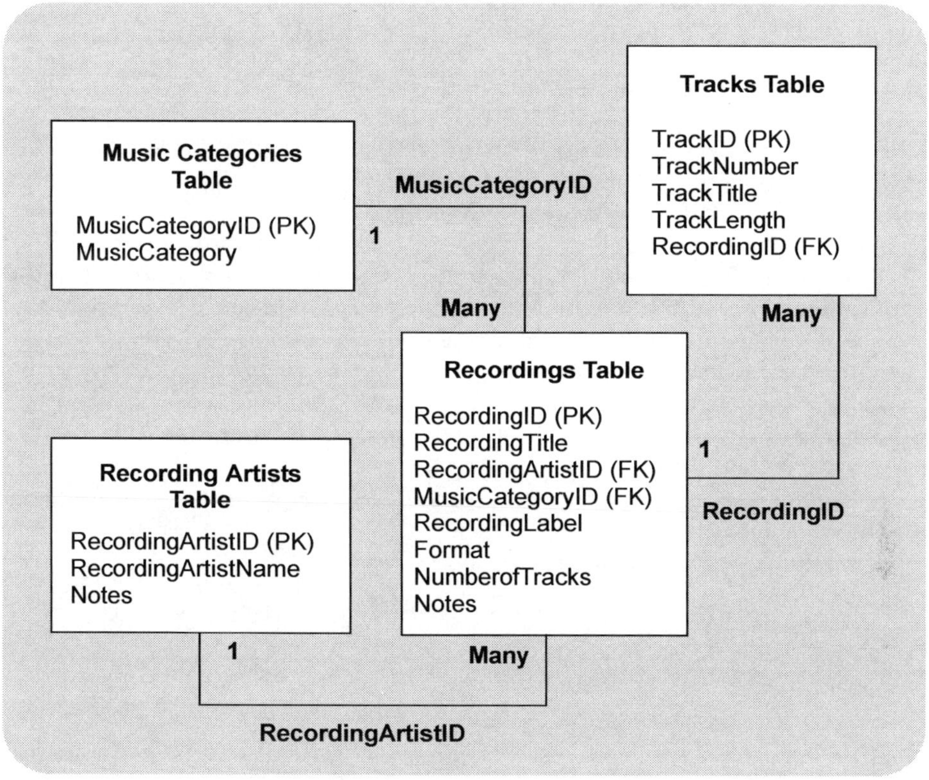

Figure 9–1 **Music Collection Database Schema**

fields (denoted FK): RecordingArtistID and MusicCategoryID. These foreign key fields refer to records in the Recording Artists table and the Music Categories table, respectively. For each row in the Music Categories table, there may be multiple rows in the Recordings table. (We indicate this relationship by placing the word **Many** next to the Recordings table and the numeral **1** next to the Music Categories table.) Similarly, for each row in the Recording Artists table, there may be multiple rows in the Recordings table. In the diagram, we show foreign key field names on the lines that relate two tables.

The Tracks table contains information about each track belonging to a recording. To determine which recording a track belongs to, we include the RecordingID as a foreign key in the Tracks table. Thus, for each row in the Recordings table, there are multiple rows in the Tracks table.

JDBC CachedRowSets

Java DataBase Connectivity (or JDBC) evolved as a standard way for Java programs to perform relational database operations. The JDBC API is database independent and relies on a JDBC driver that translates standard JDBC calls into specific calls required by the database it supports. Different drivers provide access to different database products.

Creator accesses the configured data sources using a `CachedRowSet` object, a JavaBeans component that is scrollable, updatable, and serializable. It is generally disconnected from the database, caching its rows into memory. The web application can modify the data in the cached rowset object. It then propagates back to the data source through a subsequent connection. By default, Creator instantiates a cached rowset object in session scope.

When you select a data source from Creator's Servers window, Creator generates code in session scope to access the data source through CachedRowSet objects. As you build the projects in this section, we'll look at the code Creator generates to access the data source, as well as connecting the data providers to the cached rowset.

Now let's build the sample data base and configure the data source.

9.2 Data Sources

The first step in our application is to create a Music database and make it available to Creator. Creator is bundled with a database server and JDBC driver for database access through Creator's IDE. Creator requires JDBC 3.0-compliant drivers. As of this writing, the Creator IDE includes drivers for DB2, Derby, Oracle, SQLServer, and Sybase. If you are using any of these database products, you should be able to configure Creator with the provided drivers to access your database. You can also add database servers to the IDE.

Configuring the Bundled Database

For our Music database example, we assume you're using the bundled database. Here are the steps to configure the Data Source in Creator.

1. Make sure that the bundled database is running. The Bundled Database Server node in the Servers window includes a green up-arrow badge when it's running. To start the server, select the Bundled Database Server node, right-click, and choose **Start Bundled Database**.
2. Open project MusicBuild. Project MusicBuild is included in the Creator book's download at **FieldGuide2/Examples/Database/Projects/MusicBuild**. When the project comes up in the IDE, Creator displays a Reference Prob-

lems dialog. The MusicBuild program references the JDBC driver needed to access the bundled database server. You need to add the appropriate JAR file to the project. Click Close to remove the dialog.

3. In the Projects window expand the MusicBuild node and right-click Libraries. Select Add JAR/Folder from the context menu. Creator pops up the Add JAR/Folder dialog.
4. Browse to the **<Creator2-installation-directory>/rave2.0/core/** and select file **derbyclient.jar**. Click Open. Creator adds the JAR file to your project.
5. The MusicBuild project is a stand-alone program that generates the sample Music database. You can inspect the code by expanding the **MusicBuild > Source Packages > asg.databuild** nodes. Double-click **DerbyMusicDB.java**.
6. Run the project. Select the green arrow icon or select Run > Run Main Project from the main menu. Make sure that you see the following diagnostic in the Output window after running the application.

```
Music database was created.
```

7. When you're finished, close the Project. Right-click on the project name and choose Close Project.

Creator Tip

You can run project MusicBuild multiple times to re-create the Music database. This is handy during testing of the projects that alter data in the database.

Add Data Source

Once you've generated the sample data, you must add the Music tables as a data source. You'll add it as a schema using the same URL (`sample`) as the preinstalled database tables.

1. In the Servers window, right-click Data Sources, and select Add Data Source.
2. Creator displays the Add Data Source dialog. Supply the values shown in Table 9.1. Click Select and set the Validation Table to MUSIC.VALIDATIONONLY.

Table 9.1 Add Data Source Dialog

Prompt	*Value*
Data Source Name	**`Music`**
Server Type	`Derby`
Driver Class	`org.apache.derby.jdbc.ClientDriver`
Database Name	sample
Host Name	localhost
User ID	`music`
Password	`music`
Database URL	`jdbc:derby://localhost`**`:21527/sample`**
Validation Table	MUSIC.VALIDATIONONLY

Creator Tip

Make sure that the port number is **21527** *(there should be a 2 in front of the default port number).*

3. When you're finished filling in the dialog, click Test Connection to verify that all the values are correct. Click OK, then Add to finish.

Figure 9–2 shows the Add Data Source dialog filled in. Now when you open the Music and Tables node, you'll see five tables in the Music database: MUSICCATEGORIES, RECORDINGARTISTS, RECORDINGS, TRACKS, and VALIDATIONONLY (used for testing the connection).

Inspect the Data Source

As you saw from Chapter 2, you can view the actual data from a database table interactively from the IDE. This allows a web developer to inspect the data and experiment with queries before building an application. Let's do that now.

1. From the Servers window, select Data Sources > Music > Tables > RECORDINGS. Open the RECORDINGS node (click on '+') and Creator displays the field names.
2. Double-click the RECORDINGS node. Creator displays the table's data in the editor pane. We show this view in Figure 9–3.

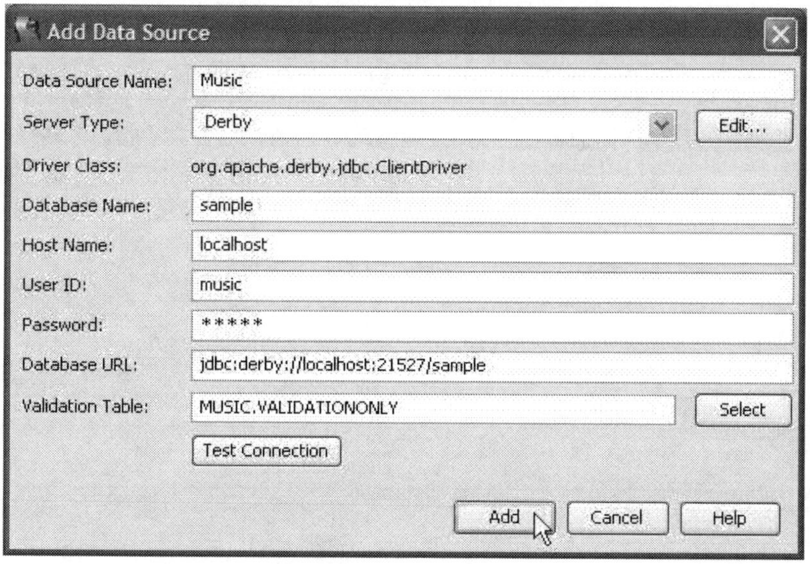

Figure 9–2 **Add Data Source dialog**

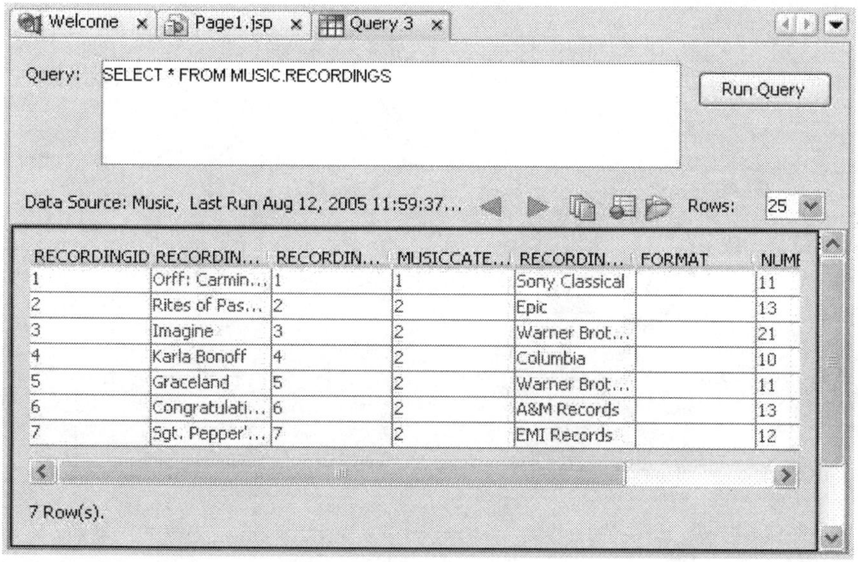

Figure 9–3 **RECORDINGS Query View**

The display not only shows the data, but provides an interactive query window so that you can edit and run the query. The data display provides controls for perusing lengthy result sets. Let's look at a second table from the Music schema.

1. From the Servers window, select Data Sources > Music > Table > TRACKS.
2. Double-click the TRACKS node. Creator displays the tracks table and the query used to read the data. It truncates the number of rows to 25. Note that all the tracks are returned in the result set from all the recordings.
3. Add the following WHERE clause to the query (the query is case insensitive).

```
where music.tracks.recordingid = 4
```

4. Click the Run Query button. Now you only see the tracks with RecordingID equal to 4. Creator displays the new results in the data window as shown in Figure 9–4.

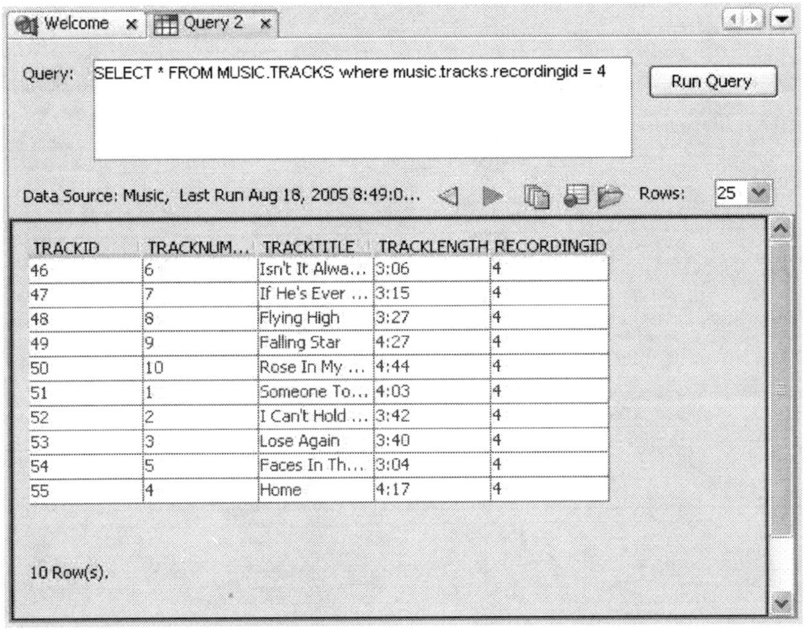

Figure 9–4 **TRACKS Query View**

5. Close the query windows by clicking the small 'x' on each Query tab above the editor pane.

Creator Tip

A word about case sensitivity: database field names (RecordingID) and table names (RECORDINGS) are NOT generally case sensitive. Java code, however, is. Thus, component id's, property names, method names, variable names, and data types are ALL case sensitive.

Loading Other Data Sources

If you configure Creator to use a Data Source other than bundled database server, see the **sql_readme.txt** file in your Creator book's examples (**FieldGuide2/Examples/Database/utils**). We also provide an SQL script (**createMusicDB.sql**) that you can adapt to any SQL-compliant database. This script loads sample music data into a Music database. After the database tables and data have been built, you tell Creator how to access the database.

Here are the steps to configure a new Data Source in Creator.

1. In the Server Navigator window, right-click Data Sources and select Add Data Source from the menu.
2. Under Server Type, select the database product from the dropdown list.
3. Creator supplies default values for the Host Name (localhost), Database URL, and Driver Class. You'll need to supply values for the Data Source Name, Database Name, User ID (if applicable), and Password (if applicable). Figure 9–5 shows an example screen shot of the Add Data Source window.
4. Use Test Connection to verify that Creator has all the information it needs to establish a connection to the database.
5. If the Test Connection succeeds, click Add. You should see the newly added Data Source under the Data Sources node in the Servers window.

9.3 Accessing the Music Database

Now that you have a configured database, let's use Creator's data-aware components to access it. You'll build several small projects that will help you learn about the Creator cached row set data provider, the data base row sets, and the data-aware components.

Create a New Project

In this section, you'll create a very simple project that reads the Music Collection database and displays the records in a table component. You'll see that

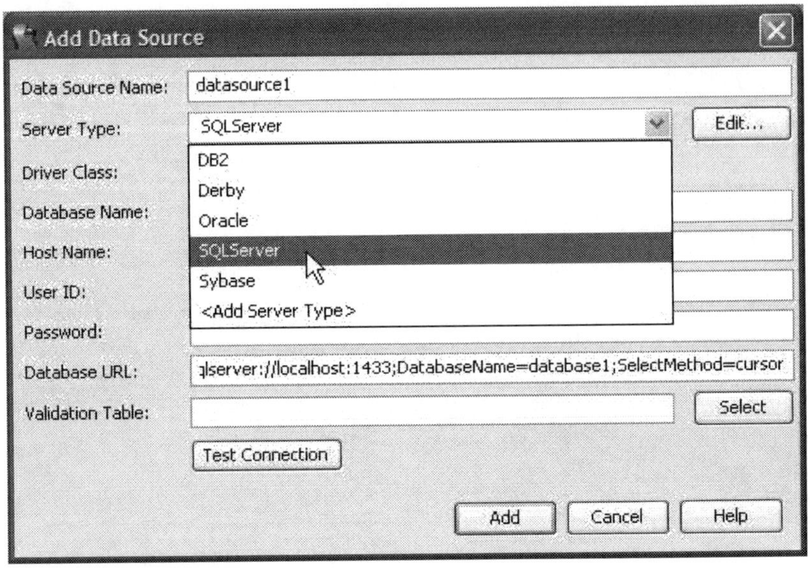

Figure 9–5 **Add Data Source window**

with minimum configuration of the table layout and the underlying SQL query, you can get a nicely formatted display.

1. From Creator's Welcome Page, select button Create New Project. From the New Project dialog, under Categories select **Web** and under Projects select **JSF Web Application**. Click Next.
2. In the New Web Application dialog, specify **MusicRead1** for Project Name and click Finish.

   After creating the project, Creator comes up in the design view of the editor pane. You can now set the title.

3. Select `Title` in the Properties window and type in the text **Music Read 1**. Finish by pressing **<Enter>**.

Add Components

Add a label component to place a title on the page and a table component to hold the data.

1. From the Basic Components palette, select Label and drop it on the page near the top.

2. Make sure that it is still selected and type in the text **Music Collection Database - Read** followed by **<Enter>**.
3. In the Properties window opposite property `labelLevel` select option **Strong(1)** from the drop down menu.
4. From the Basic Components palette, select component Table and drop it on the page under the label component you just added. Creator builds a table with default column and rows. Creator also adds a non-visual component, a default table data provider, which you can see in the Page1 Outline view.
5. The table title is selected for you. Change the title to **Recordings**. Figure 9–6 shows the design view after adding the table component with its default row and column configuration.

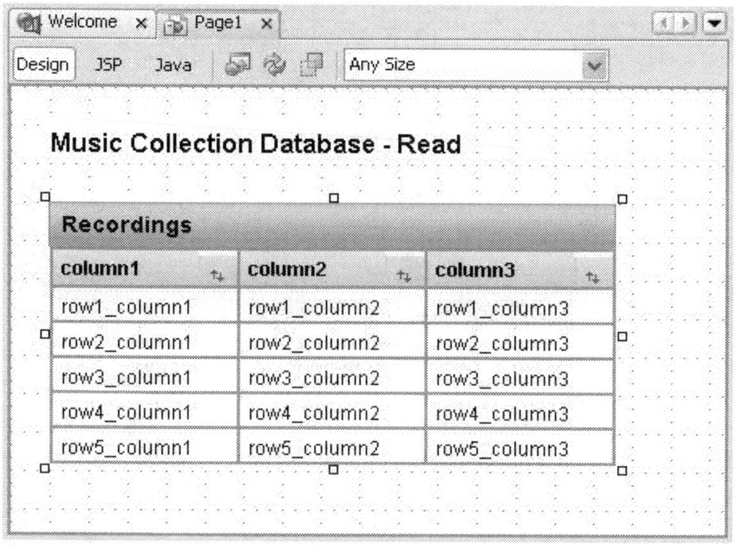

Figure 9–6 **Default table component**

Add a Database Table

Since you configured the Music Database source, you can now add it to your project by dragging and dropping a table onto the page.

1. From Servers window, expand Data Sources > Music > Tables nodes.
2. Select table RECORDINGS and drop it on top of the table component.

Creator Tip

Make sure that the entire table component is selected (it should be outlined in blue) before releasing the mouse. Otherwise Creator will display a Choose Target dialog. If you see this, select radio button table1 (Render a table) and click OK.

When you drop the database table onto the table component, Creator configures the table component to accommodate the RECORDINGS data and generates supporting components and code for you as well.

- The table component now contains a column for each field in the RECORDINGS table and each column heading contains the name of the field.
- The table row group component specifies the data provider for the table. To see this, click on the `tableRowGroup1` component under `table1` in the Outline view. In the Properties window under Data, examine properties `sourceData` (the data provider for this table) and `sourceVar` (how you access the data).
- Creator generates static text components to display data for each column. Select a static text component under one of the table column components in the Page1 Outline view. In the Properties view, hold the cursor over the `text` property. You see the following binding expression.

```
#{currentRow.value['RECORDINGS.fieldname']}
```

Token *`fieldname`* is the matching field name in the RECORDINGS table and `currentRow` specifies the current row of the data provider.

- Creator generates a cached row set data provider to wrap the row set object that communicates directly to the database source. You can see the cached row set data provider in the Outline view for Page1 (component `recordingsDataProvider`).
- Creator generates a `CachedRowSet` object in session scope to communicate directly with the database. In the Outline view under SessionBean1 you can see component `recordingsRowSet`.

Creator Tip

If the cached row set already exists in session scope (from a previous Data Source selection added to your project), Creator will ask you how to configure the new cached row set object. For example, if you add the RECORDINGS table to the page again, Creator pops up the Add New Data Provider with RowSet for Table RECORDINGS dialog as shown in Figure 9–7. The default selection uses the same RowSet object already configured in session scope. The other choice is to create a new RowSet object in the Page1, RequestBean1, SessionBean1, or ApplicationBean1 bean. You can use the same RowSet object if the SQL query is the same and the scoping requirements are the same. Otherwise, select the scope that matches the requirements of your application and edit the SQL query as needed.

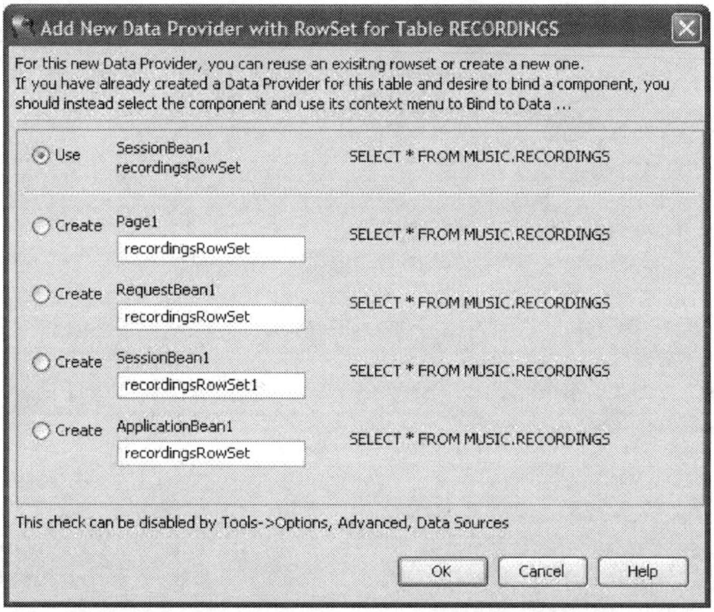

Figure 9–7 **Add New Data Provider with RowSet dialog**

Before proceeding, let's look at the Java code Creator generates for you.

1. Select the Java button in the editing toolbar. Creator brings up **Page1.java** in the editor pane.
2. In the Navigator window, double-click the private method `_init()`, which takes you to the method in the editor pane. Here is the code that connects

the data provider, `recordingsDataProvider`, to the cached row set in session scope (`recordingsRowSet`).

```
private void _init() throws Exception {
   recordingsDataProvider.setCachedRowSet(
         (javax.sql.rowset.CachedRowSet)getValue(
         "#{SessionBean1.recordingsRowSet}"));
}
```

3. Now examine the Java code for SessionBean1. In the Projects view, expand the **MusicRead1** node.
4. Double-click the Session Bean node. Creator brings up **SessionBean1.java** in the editor pane.
5. In the Navigator window, double-click the private method `_init()`, which takes you to the method in the editor pane. Here is the code that initializes the cached row set. Method `setCommand()` configures the SQL query.

```
private void _init() throws Exception {
   recordingsRowSet.setDataSourceName(
        "java:comp/env/jdbc/Music");
   recordingsRowSet.setCommand(
        "SELECT * FROM MUSIC.RECORDINGS");
   recordingsRowSet.setTableName("RECORDINGS");
}
```

Add a Message Group Component

It's a good idea to add a message group component to your web application to display possible error messages.

1. Return to the **Page1.jsp** design view. Click the **Page1** tab above the editor pane and then click the Design button in the editing toolbar.
2. From the Basic Components palette, select Message Group and place it on the page to the right of the page's title label. You may need to move the table component down to make room.

Deploy and Run

Deploy and run project MusicRead1. You'll see the entire RECORDINGS table displayed on the web page, including the primary key field and both foreign key fields. You've done no configuration of the data displayed, and some of the fields are more confusing than helpful. Let's modify the query, alter the table layout, and see if we can improve this display.

Query and Table Configuration

Note that two columns display foreign keys: RecordingArtistID and MusicCategoryID. Let's show the actual recording artist name and the music category label instead of numbers that represent foreign keys. To accomplish this, you add two tables to the query, creating an inner join clause.

1. From the Outline view, expand SessionBean1 and double-click the cached row set component, `recordingsRowSet`. This brings up Creator's Query Editor in the editor pane, as shown in Figure 9–8. (Close the Output window to make more room for the query editor.)

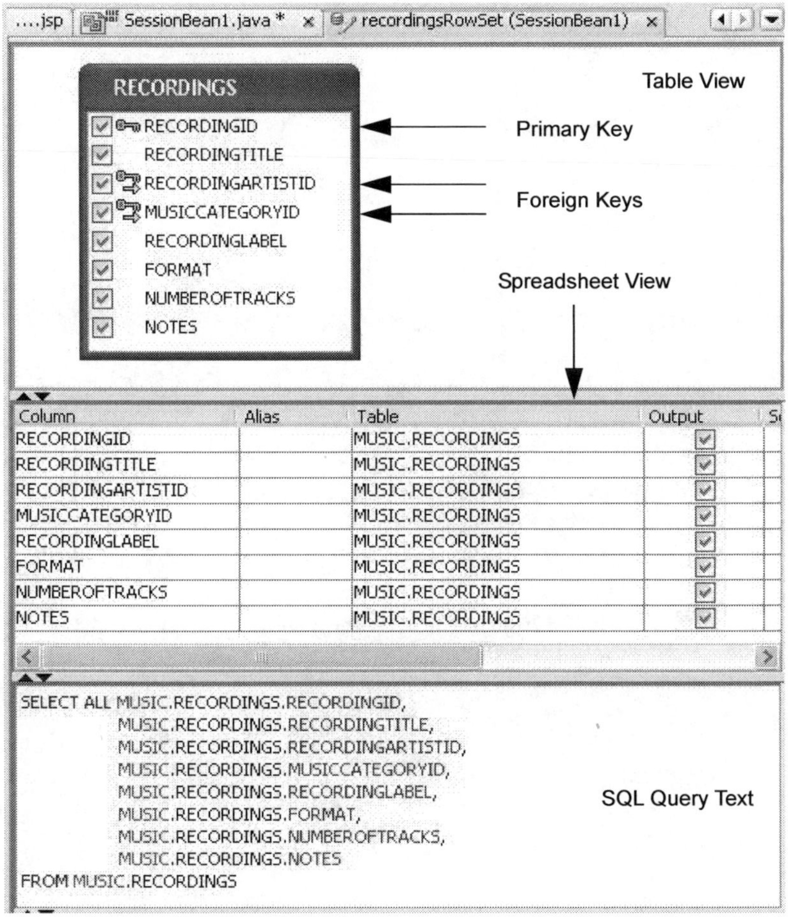

Figure 9–8 **Query Editor**

The Query editor consists of a table view, a spreadsheet view, and the SQL query text. Creator updates these views as you make modifications. Here, you'll add both the RECORDINGARTISTS table and the MUSICCATEGORIES table to the query so that the page displays names and category labels instead of foreign keys.

2. Right-click inside the table view and select Add Table from the context menu.
3. Creator pops up the Select Table(s) to Add dialog, as shown in Figure 9–9. Select both tables MUSICCATEGORIES and RECORDINGSARTISTS. (Use **<Ctrl+Click>** to select both tables.) Click OK. Creator adds an Inner Join clause to the query text. You now see two more tables in the Table view.

Figure 9–9 **Select Tables to Add dialog**

4. In the Table view, uncheck RECORDINGARTISTID and MUSICCATEGORYID from the RECORDINGS table. Uncheck MUSICCATEGORYID from the MUSICCATEGORIES table and uncheck RECORDINGARTISTID from the RECORDINGARTISTS table.
5. Select File > Save All to save these changes.
6. Return to the Design view by selecting the **Page1** tab at the top of the editor pane. Select the Design button in the editing toolbar if the Design view is not active.

You'll note that the table component has not changed even though you modified the underlying query. You'll now configure the table layout to display exactly the columns that you want.

1. Select the table component on the design view, right-click, and select Table Layout. Creator brings up the Table Layout dialog.
2. Because you unchecked some of the fields in the query editor, there are unused columns in the Selected window. Remove these by selecting each one and clicking the left-arrow button (<).

3. Remove RECORDINGS.RecordingID, RECORDINGS.Notes, RECORDINGS.NumberOfTracks, RECORDINGS.Format, and RECORDINGARTISTS.Notes from the Selected window by clicking the left-arrow button. (There should be two columns remaining in the Selected window.)
4. Move RECORDINGARTISTS.RecordingArtistName and MUSICCATEGORIES.MusicCategory to the Selected window using the right-arrow button.
5. Move the RecordingArtistName field up in the Selected window so that it is second.
6. Click Apply then OK.
7. The table component now has four columns. Expand the table component and widen the RecordingTitle column. Select the table component and use the handles to adjust the overall width. Then adjust the columns.

Deploy and Run

Deploy and run project MusicRead1 again. The RECORDINGS table now looks better; you see actual artist names and music categories displayed instead of foreign keys. Figure 9–10 shows MusicRead1 running in a browser.

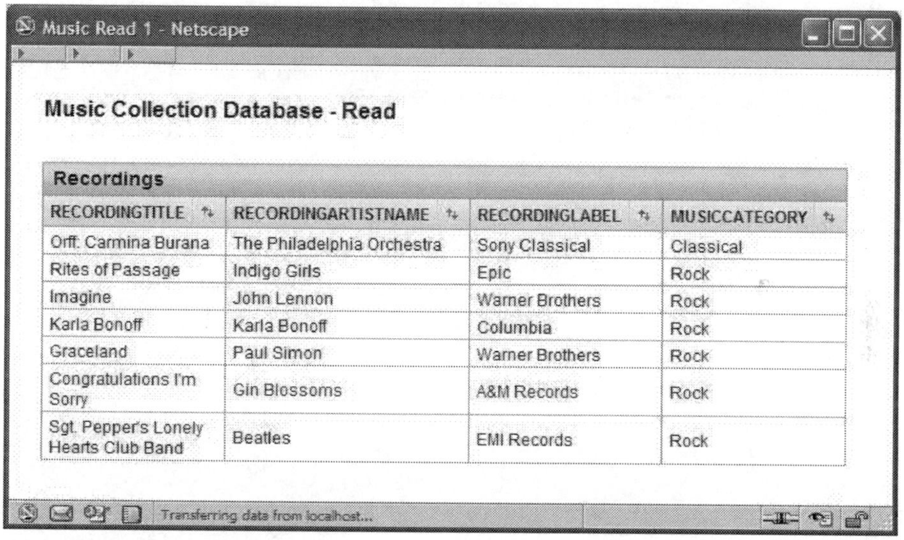

Recordings

RECORDINGTITLE	RECORDINGARTISTNAME	RECORDINGLABEL	MUSICCATEGORY
Orff: Carmina Burana	The Philadelphia Orchestra	Sony Classical	Classical
Rites of Passage	Indigo Girls	Epic	Rock
Imagine	John Lennon	Warner Brothers	Rock
Karla Bonoff	Karla Bonoff	Columbia	Rock
Graceland	Paul Simon	Warner Brothers	Rock
Congratulations I'm Sorry	Gin Blossoms	A&M Records	Rock
Sgt. Pepper's Lonely Hearts Club Band	Beatles	EMI Records	Rock

Figure 9–10 **MusicRead1 running in a browser**

9.4 Master Detail Application - Two Page

Web application MusicRead1 doesn't do much. While it displays data from the Recordings table in a pleasing format, a useful enhancement is to display the tracks when the user selects the recording. There are several ways to do this.

1. Replace the static text components in the first column with either a button component or a hyperlink component. These are both "command" components, allowing you to write event handler code to display the track information. You can place the tracks table on the same page, but it creates a rather busy, messy page. Navigating to a second page is preferable in this case.
2. Use a drop down component (instead of a table) to hold the recording data, displaying only the recording title. When the user selects a recording from the drop down component, the tracks belonging to that recording are displayed in a table. Because the drop down component takes up much less real estate than a table component, the tracks table fits nicely on the same page.

The the first method displays more information about the recording (you get the artist name, the label, the music category, etc.) However, you navigate to a second page and then return to choose another recording. The drop down component allows the web application to fit easily on a single page, but the artist name and other information are no longer displayed. Of course, one of the advantages of using Creator is that you can easily experiment with the layout on a single page and pick the configuration you'd like. We're going to go through both methods (using a command component in a table with a second page and using the drop down component on a single page) because each strategy shows you different features of Creator.

Copy the Project

Let's begin with the two-page approach. To avoid starting from scratch, copy the MusicRead1 project to a new project called MusicRead2. This step is optional. If you don't want to copy the project, simply skip this section and continue making modifications to the MusicRead1 project.

1. Bring up project MusicRead1 in Creator, if it's not already opened.
2. From the Projects window, right-click node MusicRead1 and select Save Project As. Provide the new name **MusicRead2**.
3. Close project MusicRead1. Right-click MusicRead2 and select Set Main Project. You'll make changes to the MusicRead2 project.

4. Expand MusicRead2 > Web Pages and open **Page1.jsp** in the design view.
5. Click anywhere in the background of the design canvas of the MusicRead2 project. In the Properties window, change the page's `Title` property to **Music Read 2**.

Add a RecordingID Request Bean Property

When the user clicks the hyperlink component associated with a specific title, you need a way to communicate the selected RecordingID to the second page. You can use either a Session Bean property or a Request Bean property.

Recall that the Request Bean property exists in the current HTTP request, making it available to the next page. Since the requesting page does not need to remember which track list is displayed, there's no need to put this information in session scope.

1. In the Projects view, expand the MusicRead2 node, select Request Bean, right-click, and select **Add > Property**.
2. Creator pops up the New Property Pattern dialog. For name, specify **recordingID**, for type specify **Integer**, and for Mode keep the default **Read/Write**.
3. Click OK. Creator adds property `recordingID` to **RequestBean1.java**.

Add a RecordingTitle Request Bean Property

It's a nice touch to also include the recording title on the second page. There are several approaches for accessing the recording title. You can add the RECORDINGS table to the Tracks row set, creating an inner join. A second approach is to add a second property to request scope to include the recording title. Let's use the request bean property approach.

1. In the Projects view, select MusicBean2 > Request Bean, right-click, and select Add > Property.
2. Creator pops up the New Property Pattern dialog. For name, specify **recordingTitle**, for type specify **String**, and for Mode keep the default **Read/Write**.
3. Click OK. Creator adds property `recordingTitle` to **RequestBean1.java**.
4. In the Outline view expand the RequestBean1 node. You'll see the two request bean properties you just added.

Command Components in a Table Column

Now you'll modify the Table Layout to use a hyperlink component instead of the default static text component.

1. Bring up **Page1.jsp** in the design view. Select the table component, right-click, and select Table Layout.

2. In the Selected window, select RECORDINGS.RECORDINGTITLE.
3. Under Column Details for Component Type, select **Hyperlink** from the drop down list, as shown in Figure 9–11. (You could also use Button here. The function is the same; the look is a bit different.)

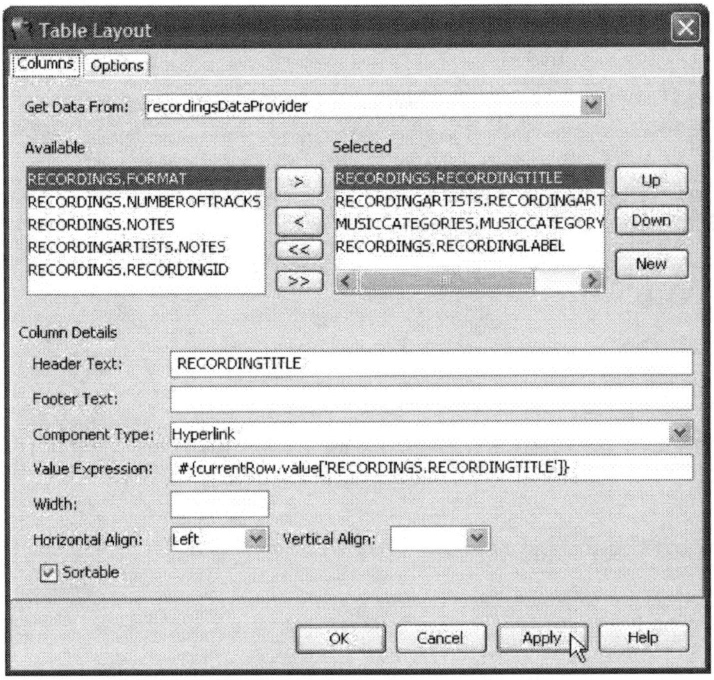

Figure 9–11 **Table Layout dialog**

4. Click Apply then OK. The component in the first column is now a hyperlink component.
5. In the Outline view, select the hyperlink component under the first column of the table.
6. Change the `id` property of the hyperlink component to **hyperlinkTitle**.
7. In the Outline view, right-click the hyperlink component and select Edit action Event Handler. Creator generates an action event handler and brings up the Java source editor.
8. Copy and paste the event handler code from the Creator book download **FieldGuide2/Examples/Database/snippets/ musicRead2_hyperlinkTitle_action.txt**. The added code is bold. Note that you replace the `return null` statement with `return "tracks"`.

Listing 9.1 Method `hyperlinkTitle_action()`

```
public String hyperlinkTitle_action() {
  // TODO: Replace with your code
  TableRowDataProvider rowData = (TableRowDataProvider)
        getBean("currentRow");

  getRequestBean1().setRecordingID(
        (Integer)rowData.getValue("RECORDINGS.RECORDINGID"));

  getRequestBean1().setRecordingTitle(
        (String)rowData.getValue(
        "RECORDINGS.RECORDINGTITLE"));
  return "tracks";
}
```

When the user selects a hyperlink from a particular row, the `currentRow` property holds data for the selected row. The RecordingID and RecordingTitle values of the selected row (object `rowData`) are then saved in request scope to make them available to the **tracksDetail.jsp** page, which you'll add to the project in the next section.

1. Right-click and select Fix Imports to fix the syntax errors.
2. Save these modifications by selecting the Save All icon on the toolbar.

Add a New Page

Now let's create a new page to display the track data. First, you'll place a label, a message group, and a table component on the new page. You'll then add the Music TRACKS table.

1. In the Projects view, right-click on node Web Pages and select **New > Page** from the context menu.
2. Creator pops up the New Page dialog. Specify **tracksDetail** for the file name and click Finish. Creator brings up page **tracksDetail.jsp** in the design view.
3. Click anywhere inside the page in the design view. In the Properties window opposite property `Title`, type in the following text followed by **<Enter>**.

```
Tracks Detail - #{RequestBean1.recordingTitle}
```

This displays the recording title in the browser's title bar.

4. From the Basic Components palette, select component Label and place it on the page, near the top left side.
5. Make sure it's selected and type in the text **Tracks Detail** and finish with **<Enter>**.
6. In the Properties window, specify **Strong(1)** for property `labelLevel`.
7. From the Basic Components palette, select component Message Group and drop it onto the page near the top to the right of the label you just added. When you post error messages to the faces context for this page, the message group component will display them.
8. From the Basic Components palette, select component Table and drop it onto the page. Creator builds a table with default rows and columns using a default table data provider.
9. From the Servers view, select the Data Sources > Music > Tables > TRACKS table and drop it on top of the table component you just added. Make sure that you select the *entire* table component when you release the mouse (it will be outlined in blue). Creator modifies the table to match the database fields from the TRACKS table and instantiates the `tracksRowSet` component in session scope.

Modify SQL Query

As it is currently configured, the `tracksRowSet` returns all of the track records from the Music database. You need to limit the query so that only the tracks that match the RecordingID selected in the Page1 table are returned. To do this, specify a query criteria so that each record in the Tracks row set matches the RecordingID saved in request scope. You'll use the query editor to modify the SQL query for the Tracks row set.

1. Open the SessionBean1 node in the Outline view and double-click the `tracksRowSet` component. Creator brings up the query editor. Close the Output window if it's open (to make more room).
2. In the spreadsheet view of the query editor, right-click opposite field RECORDINGID and select Add Query Criteria.
3. In the Add Query Criteria dialog, use the default (`= Equals`) for Comparison and select radio button Parameter, as shown in Figure 9–12. Click OK. Creator modifies the query text to include a WHERE clause.
4. In the spreadsheet view of the query editor, click inside cell Sort Type opposite column TRACKNUMBER and select Ascending from the drop down selection. This returns the records sorted by track number (in ascending

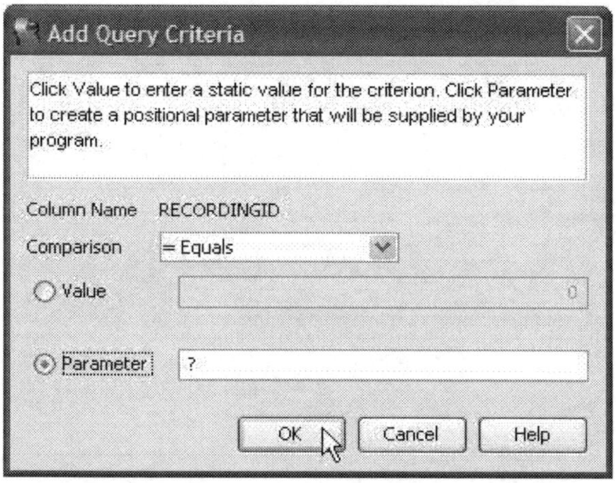

Figure 9–12 **Add Query Criteria dialog**

order). Here is the modified SQL query text with the WHERE and ORDER BY clauses you just added (shown in bold).

```
SELECT ALL MUSIC.TRACKS.TRACKID,
                    MUSIC.TRACKS.TRACKNUMBER,
                    MUSIC.TRACKS.TRACKTITLE,
                    MUSIC.TRACKS.TRACKLENGTH,
                    MUSIC.TRACKS.RECORDINGID,

FROM MUSIC.TRACKS
WHERE MUSIC.TRACKS.RECORDINGID = ?
ORDER BY MUSIC.TRACKS.TRACKNUMBER ASC
```

5. Save these modifications by selecting File > Save All from the main menu.

Add Page Navigation

Recall that the event handler code for the hyperlink components returns the string "tracks". This is the string JSF will send to the navigation handler. You'll now add the appropriate page navigation rule.

1. In the Projects view, double-click the Page Navigation node. Creator brings up the page navigation editor. You'll see the two pages, **Page1.jsp** and **tracksDetail.jsp**.
2. Select **Page1.jsp** and drag the cursor from the hyperlink component to page **tracksDetail.jsp**, releasing the mouse inside the page. Creator displays a navigation arrow.

3. Change the default name to **tracks**, as shown in Figure 9–13.

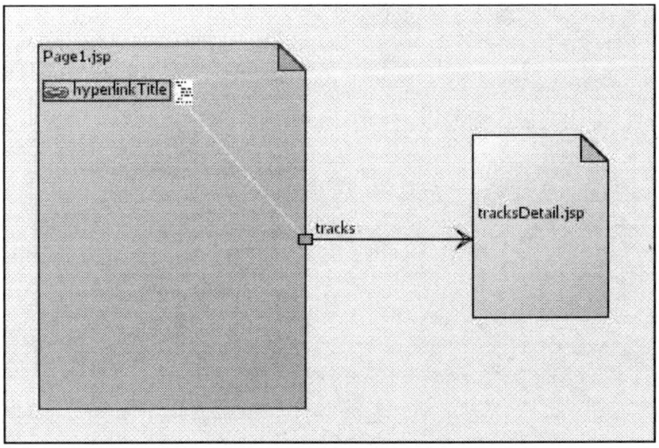

Figure 9–13 **Adding page navigation**

Add Prerender Code

It's time to add the code that will specify the query parameter for the `tracks-RowSet` component and update the `tracksDataProvider`.

1. Select the **tracksDetail** tab from the top of the editor pane. This displays the page in the design view.
2. Select the button labeled Java in the editing toolbar. Creator brings up **tracksDetail.java** in the Java editor.
3. Locate method `prerender()` and add the following code. Copy and paste from the book download file **FieldGuide2/Examples/Database/snippets/musicRead2_tracksDetail_prerender.txt**. The added code is bold.

```
public void prerender() {
  try {
    getSessionBean1().getTracksRowSet().setObject(1,
        getRequestBean1().getRecordingID());
    tracksDataProvider.refresh();

  } catch (Exception e) {
    error("Cannot read tracks for " +
        getRequestBean1().getRecordingTitle() +
        ": " + e.getMessage());
```

```
        log("Cannot read tracks for " +
          getRequestBean1().getRecordingTitle() + ": ", e);
    }
}
```

This code obtains the RecordingID from request scope and uses it to set the `tracksRowSet` query parameter. It forces an update of the tracks data provider with the `refresh()` call. Any errors are recorded in the Server Log (using method `log()`) and displayed in the message group component (using method `error()`).

Configure Table Component

The final step is to configure the table component.

1. Return to the design view by selecting the Design button in the editing toolbar.
2. Select the table component, right-click, and select Table Layout. Creator displays the Table Layout dialog.
3. Remove TRACKS.TRACKID and TRACKS.RECORDINGID from the Selected window using the left arrow (<).
4. Click Apply then OK.
5. In the design view, select the table component. In the Properties window, click the small editing box opposite property `title`.
6. Creator pops up a property editing dialog. Select radio button **Use binding** and tab **Bind to an Object.**
7. In the Select binding target window, choose **RequestBean1 > recordingTitle** ***String*** as shown in Figure 9–14 and click OK. This binds the table's title to the selected recording title from request scope.
8. In the design editor, resize the table so that the TracksTitle column is wider. First expand the table component and then adjust the columns.

Deploy and Run

It's time to deploy and run this project. Click the green arrow on the icon toolbar. Test out the application by selecting different titles. Use the browser's back arrow button to return to Page1. Figure 9–15 shows the tracks detail page for recording Graceland. Note that the recording title appears in the table title, as well as the browser's title bar. The track numbers appear in ascending order and the track title column is expanded to hold the longer titles.

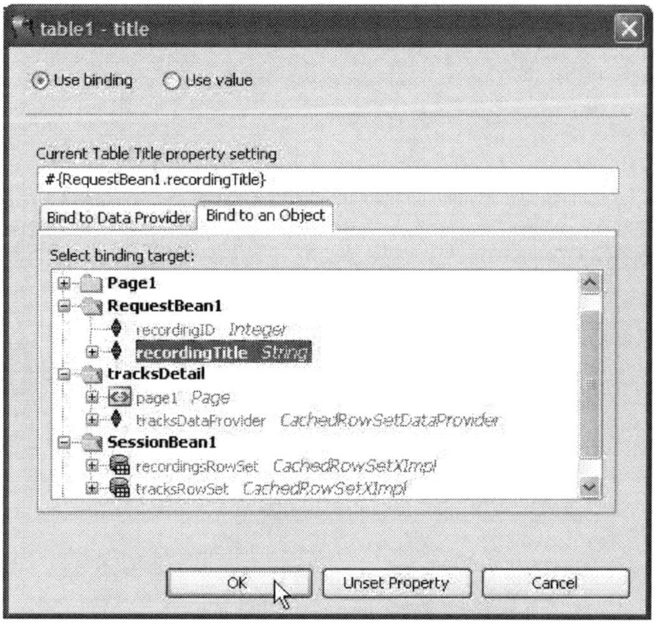

Figure 9–14 **Use binding dialog for property title**

9.5 Master Detail Application - Single Page

Project MusicRead2 provides a master-detail example using two pages. Now we'll build a master-detail project in a single page. A drop down list component will hold the "master" information from which the user selects a recording. You use the selected RecordingID to display the track information in a table component.

Create a New Project

Even though this project is very similar to the one you just built, it is easier to start with a new project. Close project MusicRead2 if it's open.

1. From Creator's Welcome Page, select button Create New Project. From the New Project dialog, under Categories select **Web** and under Projects select **JSF Web Application**. Click Next.

Figure 9–15 **Tracks detail for Graceland**

2. In the New Web Application dialog, specify **MusicRead3** for Project Name and click Finish.

   After creating the project, Creator comes up in the design view of the editor pane. You can now set the title.

3. Select `Title` in the Properties window and type in the text **Music Read 3**. Finish by pressing **<Enter>**.

Add Components

In this project, you'll add a label component to place a title on the page, a drop down list to display the recordings, and a message group component.

1. From the Basic Components palette, select Label and drop on the page near the top.
2. Make sure that it is still selected and type in the text **Music Collection Database - Master Detail** followed by **<Enter>**.
3. In the Properties window opposite property `labelLevel` select option **Strong(1)** from the drop down menu.

4. From the Basic Components palette, select component Message Group and place it on the page to the right of the label you just added.
5. From the Basic Components palette, select component Drop Down List and drop it on the page under the label component you just added. Creator configures the drop down list with a default options selections component. You can specify the options selections by editing the Properties window, or you can bind this component to a data provider and obtain the selection choices from a database (which is what you'll do for this project).

Creator Tip

Instead of a Drop Down List Component, you can also use a Listbox component here. The functionality is the same, but the Listbox is rendered as a box with all of its choices displayed at once. If the selection list is too long, the component includes a vertical scrollbar. If you'd like to use a Listbox component, skip this section and follow the steps under "Add a Listbox Component" .

6. Make sure that the drop down list component is selected. In the Properties window, change its `id` property to **recordingsDropdown**.

Skip over the next section "Add a Listbox Component" unless you've chosen to use a listbox in place of the drop down list component.

Add a Listbox Component

Instead of using a drop down list component to hold the data from the RECORDINGS table, let's use a listbox component. You can substitute the steps in this section for those outlined for the dropdown list component above. When you've finished the steps for adding a listbox component, continue to the next section ("Add a Data Source").

A listbox component creates a fixed list of choices that are all displayed. If the list is longer than the space allocated to the component, a vertical scrollbar provides access to the other choices. Just like the dropdown list component, you can specify the listbox choices directly by editing the Properties window, or you can bind this component to a data provider.

1. From the Basic Components palette, select Listbox and drag it to the design canvas. Center it under the previously placed label component.
2. Resize it so that it is wider and longer. (You can experiment with its size by right-clicking in the design canvas and selecting Preview in Browser.)
3. In the Properties window, change the `id` of the listbox component to **recordingsListbox**.

The rest of the build steps assume you selected the drop down list component, although the steps are the same for the listbox component.

Add a Data Source

You'll now add the Recordings data base table to your web page.

1. From the Servers window, expand the Data Sources, Music, and Tables nodes.
2. Select the RECORDINGS table and drag it to the design view. Drop it on top of the drop down list component. Make sure that the drop down component is outlined in blue before you release the mouse.
3. Creator automatically applies a converter (because the primary key is type Integer).

Let's see how Creator has configured the drop down list component.

1. Right-click the drop down list component. From the context menu, choose Bind to Data.
2. Make sure that the tab Bind to Data Provider is selected. You have already completed the binding in the previous steps, but this step shows you the database table's metadata (its fields and table names). Creator displays a dialog with the configured data provider, a Value field, and a Display field, as shown in Figure 9–16.

   The drop down list component's `selected` property (the Value field) is assigned field `RECORDINGS.RECORDINGID`, which is the primary key. Thus, when you invoke method

```
recordingsDropdown.getSelected();
```

   you'll get the value of the primary key for that selection.

   The text that's displayed in the dropdown list is the field selected in the Display field, which is set to `RECORDINGS.RECORDINGTITLE`.

3. Click OK to return to the design canvas.

Deploy and Run

Although we have only a page heading and a drop down list, it's a good idea to deploy and run the application at this point. Go ahead and click the green arrow on the toolbar.

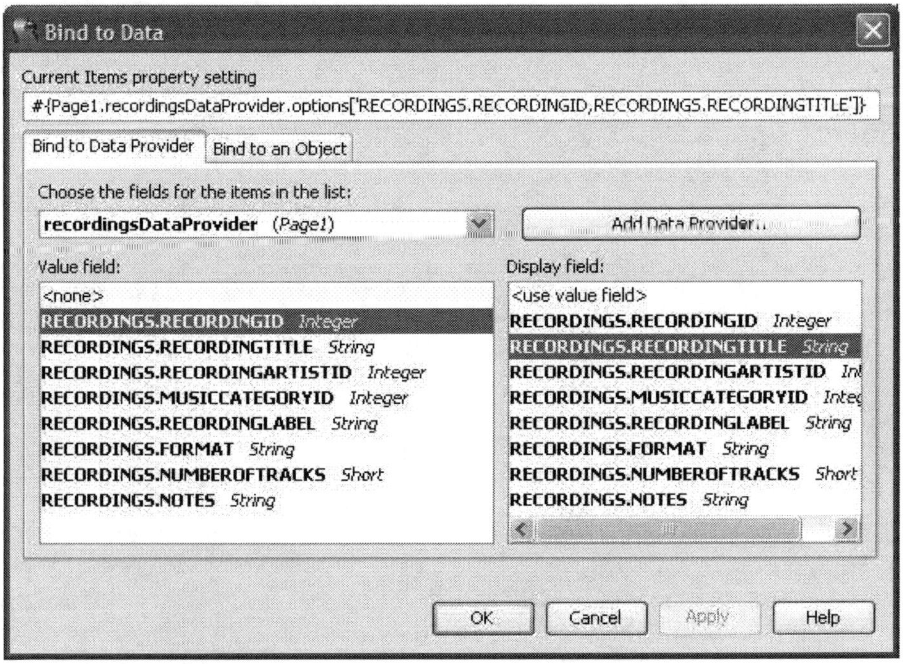

Figure 9–16 **Bind to Data dialog**

When you run the application, you'll see seven recording titles in the drop down list (or listbox component). Right now, selecting one doesn't do anything other than display a different title.

Part of the power of data binding is that you can associate the component's value with a primary key. To *display* a field other than the primary key typically has more meaning, however. The component in this example displays the recording's title. When a user selects a specific title, the corresponding primary key is returned with method `getSelected()`. The primary key allows you to build additional queries to the database and obtain more details about the recording associated with that primary key.

Add a Table Component

Now you're ready to do something when the user selects a recording title in the drop down list. In this section, you will display the recording's track information: the track number, its title, and its length. The track information is stored in the TRACKS table and is associated with the recording information through its foreign key, the RECORDINGID. In the Servers window, expand the TRACKS table under the Data Sources > Music > Tables node (click on '+') to see the field names. TRACKID is the primary key for the TRACKS table, and RECORD-

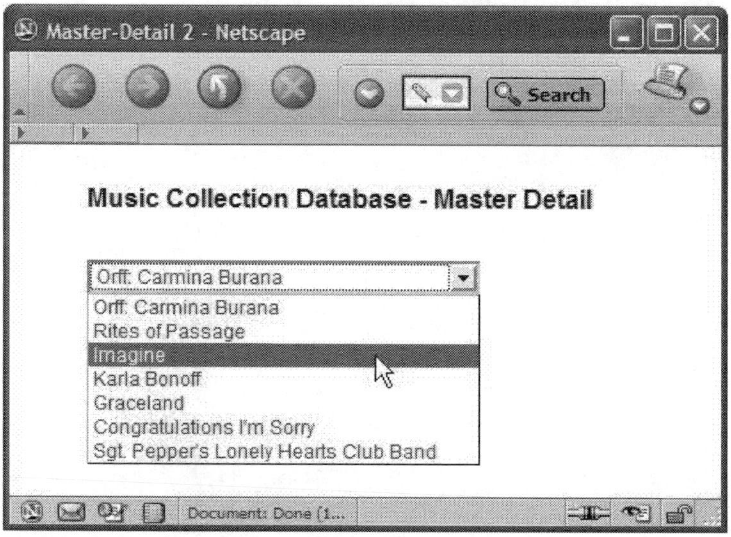

Figure 9–17 **Drop Down List component**

INGID is the foreign key (you may also want to refer to the diagram in Figure 9–1 on page 375 again).

1. Bring up the design canvas (**Page1.jsp**).
2. Select the Table component from the Basic Components palette and drop it onto the design canvas under the drop down list component that's already there.
3. Go to the Data Sources node in the Servers window, choose the TRACKS table, and drop it onto the data table. Make sure that the table is outlined in blue (indicating that the entire table is selected) before you release the mouse.

   The next step is to modify what the table component displays.

1. Select the table component. Now right-click and choose Table Layout.

   The Table Layout dialog appears. The Columns tab should be selected. There are two lists: Available columns and Selected columns.

2. In the Selected window, remove columns TRACKS.TRACKID and TRACKS.RECORDINGID by selecting these columns and clicking the left-arrow (<) button. There are now three columns in the Selected list, as shown in Figure 9–18.

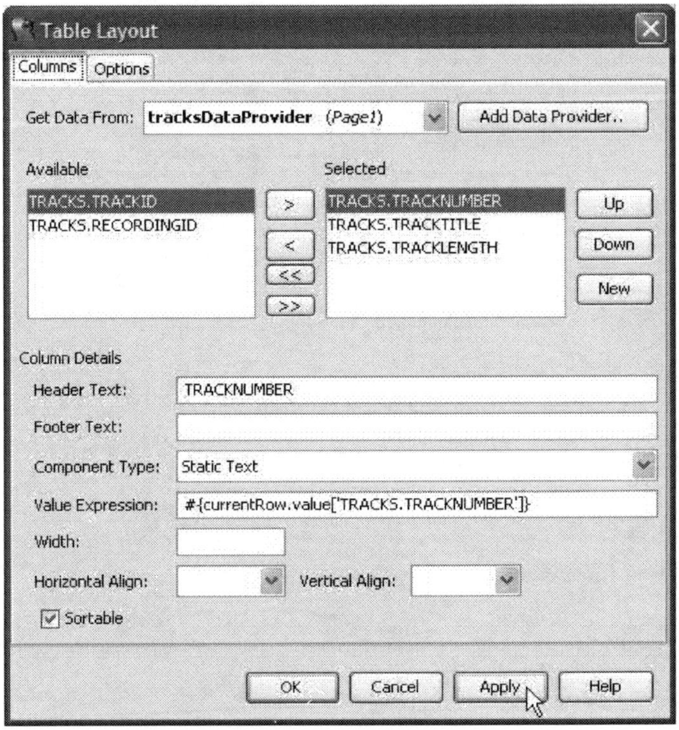

Figure 9–18 **Table Layout dialog**

3. Select Apply, then OK. The data table component should now have only three columns.

Creator generates code to populate the data table component and builds headers in the table with the column names. Figure 9–19 shows the design canvas with the data table component configured for the TRACKS table.

4. In the Outline view, select the nested static text component, `table1Title`. In the Properties window, click the small editing box opposite property `text`.
5. Creator pops up a property editing dialog. Select radio button **Use binding** and tab **Bind to Data Provider**.
6. In the drop down window, choose **recordingsDataProvider (*Page1*)**.
7. In the Data Field window, choose RECORDINGS.RECORDINGTITLE and click OK, as shown in Figure 9–20. (Hold the mouse cursor over the `text`

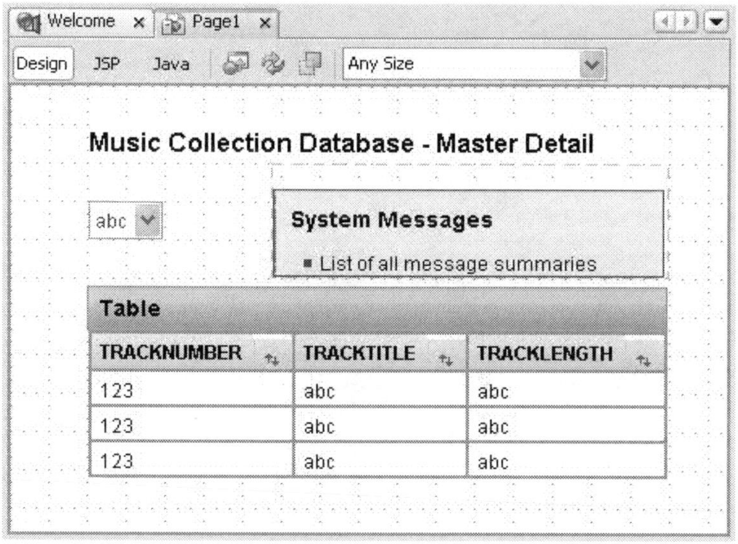

Figure 9–19 **Data-aware table component bound to TRACKS table**

property in the Properties window to see the binding expression.) This binds the `title` property to

```
#{Page1.recordingsDataProvider.value
    ['RECORDINGS.RECORDINGTITLE']}
```

Modify the SQL Query

You'll now use the Query Editor to modify the default query for the `tracks-RowSet` object.

1. In the Outline view, expand the SessionBean1 node, if necessary.
2. Double-click the `tracksRowSet` object. This opens the Query Editor for the `tracksRowSet` object, as shown in Figure 9–21. (Close the Output window to give more space to the Query Editor.)

When a user selects a recording title from the drop down list component, you want to display only those tracks that belong to the selected recording. You identify these tracks by matching the track's RECORDINGID foreign key with the drop down list component's `selected` property, the primary key of the RECORDINGS database table. Let's do this now.

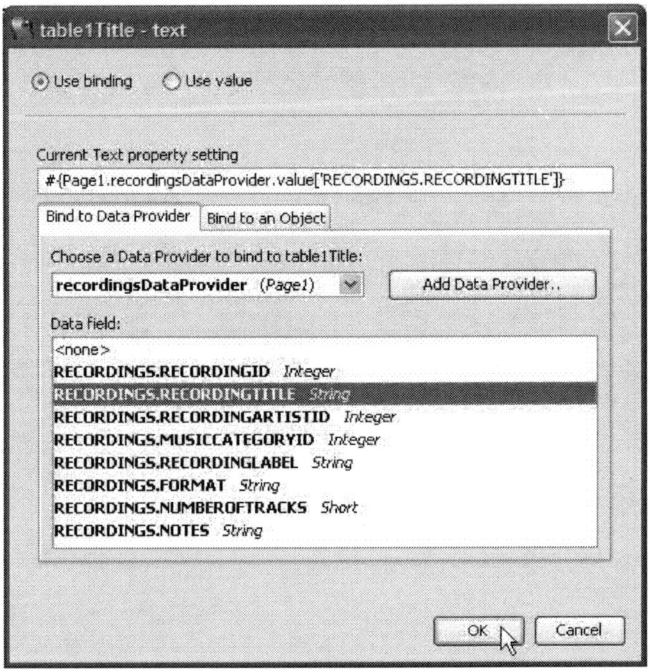

Figure 9–20 **Binding table's title property to recordingsDataProvider**

1. In the spreadsheet view, right-click the RECORDINGID field and choose Add Query Criteria from the context menu.
2. The Add Query Criteria dialog appears. Select radio button Parameter. Leave the Comparison at the default (`= Equals`), and click OK. These steps add a WHERE clause to the query.
3. Locate the TRACKNUMBER field in the spreadsheet view of the Query Editor. Opposite this field, select the Sort Type cell. Select Ascending from the drop down menu. This step adds an ORDER BY clause to the query.
4. In the table view of the Query Editor, uncheck the RECORDINGID and TRACKID fields. (Although the RECORDINGID field participates in the selection criteria of the query, we don't include this field in the data that are returned in the RowSet object.)

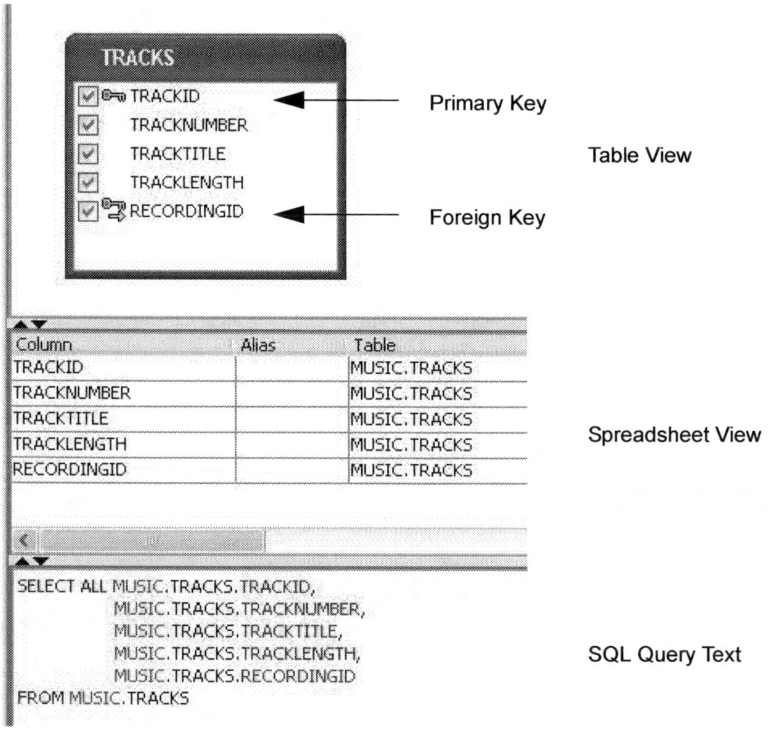

Figure 9–21 **Query Editor for TRACKS table**

Here is your modified query, shown at the bottom of the Query Editor.

```
SELECT ALL MUSIC.TRACKS.TRACKNUMBER,
                  MUSIC.TRACKS.TRACKTITLE,
                  MUSIC.TRACKS.TRACKLENGTH
FROM MUSIC.TRACKS
WHERE MUSIC.TRACKS.RECORDINGID = ?
ORDER BY MUSIC.TRACKS.TRACKNUMBER ASC
```

The WHERE clause expects a parameter to match with the RECORDINGID field, and the results will be ordered (in ascending order) by the TRACKNUMBER field.

Connect Dropdown List to Query

All that's left is to detect the change in the drop down list component's selection and use it to set the parameter for the query with the `tracksRowSet` object.

1. Return to the Page1 design canvas and double-click the drop down list component. Creator generates the default event handler, method `recordingsDropdown_processValueChange()`, and brings up **Page1.java** in the Java source editor with the cursor at the first line of the method.
2. Add code to the `recordingsDropdown_processValueChange()` method. Copy and paste from your Creator book's file **FieldGuide2/Examples/Database/snippets/musicRead3_Dropdown.txt**. (The added code is bold).

Listing 9.2 Method `recordingsDropdown_processValueChange()`

```
public void recordingsDropdown_processValueChange(
      ValueChangeEvent vce) {
   // TODO: Replace with your code
   try {
      recordingsDataProvider.setCursorRow(
            recordingsDataProvider.findFirst(
            "RECORDINGS.RECORDINGID",
            recordingsDropdown.getSelected()));

      getSessionBean1().getTracksRowSet().setObject(1,
            recordingsDropdown.getSelected());
      tracksDataProvider.refresh();

   } catch(Exception e) {
      error("Cannot read recording for " +
            recordingsDataProvider.getValue(
            "RECORDINGS.RECORDINGTITLE") + ": " + e.getMessage());
      log("Cannot read recording for " +
            recordingsDataProvider.getValue(
            "RECORDINGS.RECORDINGTITLE") + ": ", e);
   }
}
```

Note that the first statement in the try block sets the recordings data provider's cursor to the selected entity of the drop down component. This enables you to access *any field* in the current row of the recordings data provider. By keeping the recordings data provider in sync with the drop down's selection, you can access the data provider (for example, to bind the table title to the recording title).

The code in the drop down list's event handler sets the parameter of the `tracksRowSet` query to the `selected` property of the `recordingsDropdown` component (the primary key of the specific record in the RECORDINGS table). The `refresh()` method forces the data provider to be in sync with the underlying rowset object, which in turn executes the query.

3. Locate method `prerender()` and add initialization code. If the drop down component has not been selected yet, the code initializes the recordings data provider to the first row. It then sets the `tracksRowSet` object's query parameter to the RecordingID of the first selection. The `refresh()` call to the data provider for the tracks table executes the `tracksRowSet` query and populates the table component with the corresponding track information. Copy and paste from your Creator book's file **FieldGuide2/Examples/Database/snippets/musicRread3_prerender.txt**. (The added code is bold.)

Listing 9.3 Method `prerender()`

```
public void prerender() {
  if (recordingsDropdown.getSelected() == null) {
    try {
      recordingsDataProvider.cursorFirst();

      getSessionBean1().getTracksRowSet().setObject(1,
          recordingsDataProvider.getValue(
          "RECORDINGS.RECORDINGID"));
      tracksDataProvider.refresh();

    } catch (Exception e) {
      error("Cannot read tracks for " +
          recordingsDataProvider.getValue(
          "RECORDINGS.RECORDINGTITLE") + ": " +
          e.getMessage());
      log("Cannot read tracks for " +
          recordingsDataProvider.getValue(
          "RECORDINGS.RECORDINGTITLE") + ": ", e);
    }
}
```

4. Return to the design canvas (select Design button in the editing toolbar).
5. Right-click the drop down list component and enable Auto-Submit on Change. This adds the JavaScript element

```
common_timeoutSubmitForm(this.form, 'recordingsDropdown');
```

to the drop down list component's JavaScript `onChange` property in the Properties window. Now when a user selects a new title from the menu, the system submits and updates the page with the new track list.

6. Save these modifications by selecting the Save All icon on the toolbar.

Deploy and Run

It's time to deploy and run this web application. Figure 9–22 shows what the page looks like as the user is selecting a title in the drop down list. Note that as the user selects different recording titles, the data table is updated with the corresponding track information. The selected recording name appears in the table title and the number of rows as well as the width of the columns changes with the new data. You also see that the track numbers appear in ascending order. (Some of the recordings do not have track lengths.)

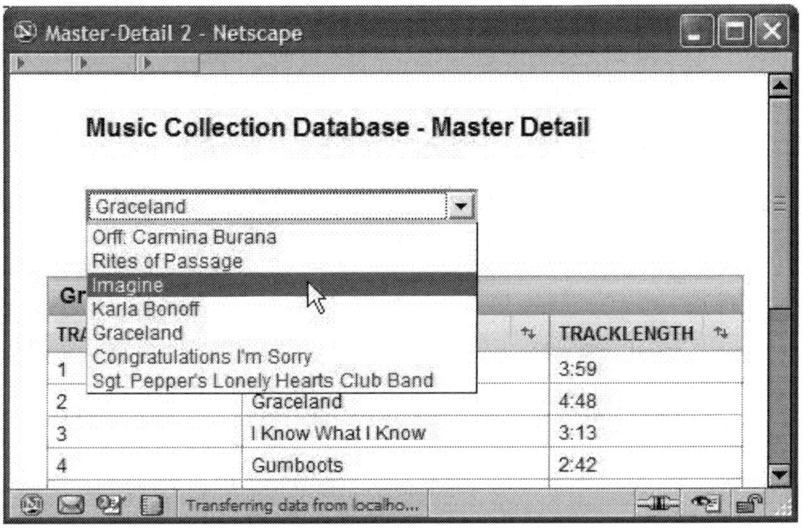

Figure 9–22 **The Music Collection Database application: selecting title Imagine**

9.6 Database Updates

The previous examples accessed the Music Collection database in a read-only mode. Furthermore, the embedded components of the data table component are static text components, which are read-only components.

In this section you'll create a project that allows a user to modify data fields in the MUSICCATEGORIES table of the Music database. You'll see that by using the data providers, the code to update a database is quite simple. Let's begin by creating a new project. Close Project MusicRead3 if it's open.

Create a New Project

1. From Creator's Welcome Page, select button Create New Project. From the New Project dialog, under Categories select **Web** and under Projects select **JSF Web Application**. Click Next.
2. In the New Web Application dialog, specify **MusicUpdate** for Project Name and click Finish.

   After creating the project, Creator comes up in the design view of the editor pane. You can now set the title.

3. Select `Title` in the Properties window and type in the text **Music Category: Update**. Finish by pressing **<Enter>**.

Add Components

In this project, you'll add a label component to place a title on the page, a message group component for system messages, button controls, and a table component to hold the data. Figure 9–23 shows the design canvas with the components added for this project and the table layout modified.

1. From the Basic Components palette, select Label and drop on the page near the top.
2. Make sure that it is still selected and type in the text **Update Music Category** followed by **<Enter>**.
3. In the Properties window opposite property `labelLevel` select option **Strong(1)** from the drop down menu.
4. From the Basic Components palette, select component Message Group and place it on the page to the right of the label component. You'll use the message group component to display information and error status to the user.

Add Buttons and a Table

You'll now add two button components: one to submit editing changes to the database and a second to cancel the edited table data.

1. From the Basic Components palette, select component Button and place it on the page below the label component.
2. It should be selected. Type in the text **Update Categories** followed by **<Enter>**.

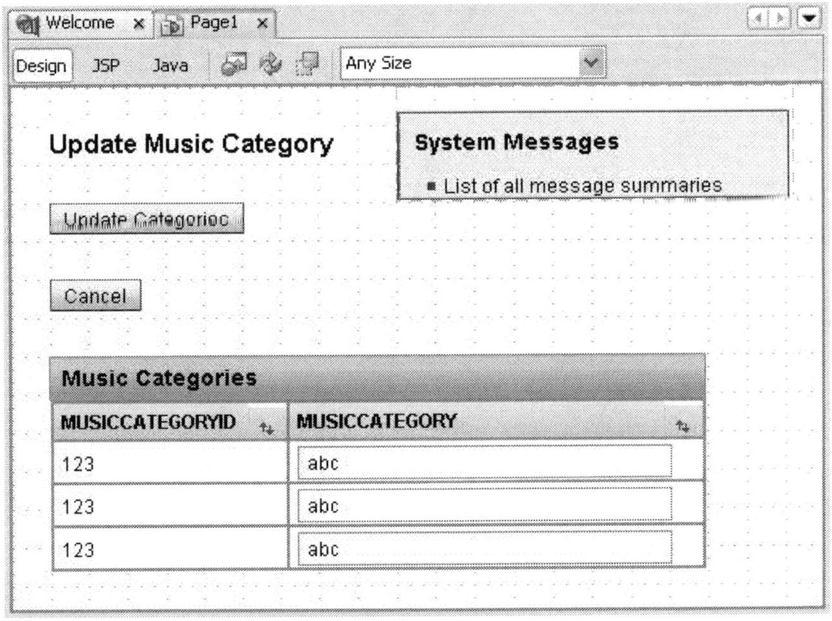

Figure 9–23 **Design canvas after adding components and modifying the table layout**

3. In the Properties window, change its `id` property to **update**.
4. Add a second button. Set its text to **Cancel**.
5. In the Properties window, change its `id` property to **cancel**.
6. From the Basic Components palette, select component Table and drop it on the page under the Cancel button you just added. Creator builds a table with default column and rows. Creator also adds a non-visual component, a default table data provider (visible in the Page1 Outline view).
7. The table title is selected for you. Change the title to **Music Categories**.
8. From the Servers view, select the Data Sources > Music > Tables > MUSICCATEGORIES table and drop it on top of the table component you just added. Make sure that you select the *entire* table component when you release the mouse (it will be outlined in blue). Creator modifies the table to match the database fields from the MUSICCATEGORIES table and instantiates the `musiccategoriesRowSet` component in session scope. Creator also replaces the default table data provider with `musiccategoriesDataProvider`, a cached row set data provider.

Modify the Table Layout

Now let's modify the data table's layout.

1. Select the data table component, right-click, and choose Table Layout.

   The Table Layout dialog appears. The Columns tab should be selected. Both columns appear in the Selected columns window.

2. Under the Selected window, select column MUSICCATEGORIES.MUSIC-CATEGORY (the second column). From the drop down menu, change the default component type to Text Field.
3. Click Apply, then OK. Figure 9–24 shows the Table Layout dialog for this step.

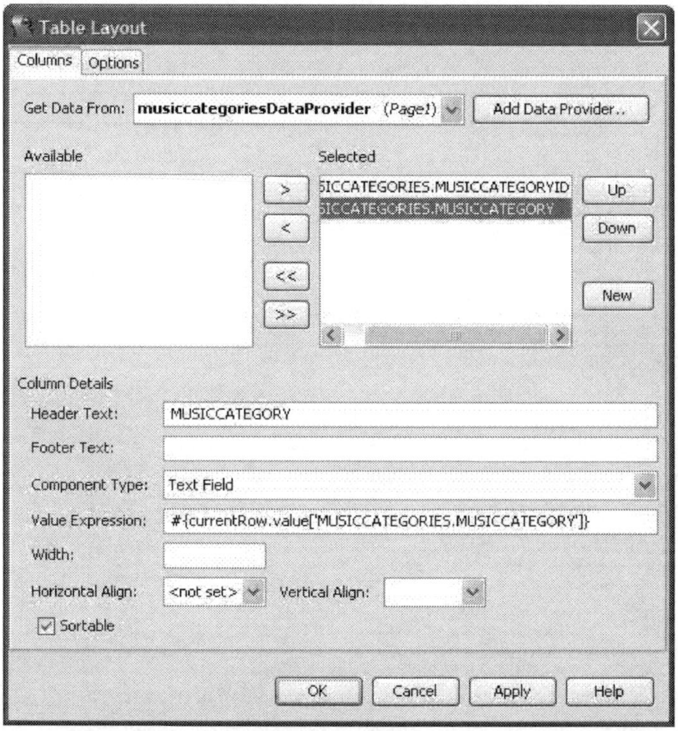

Figure 9–24 **Table Layout dialog: changing the component type**

The data table component displays two columns. The first column (MusicCategoryID) holds the primary key and retains the default display component, static text. The second column (MusicCategory) uses a text field component to enable editing.

Add the Button Event Handlers

The event handler for the Update Categories button will commit the changes to the database and the handler for the Cancel button will revert the fields in the data providers to the original data.

1. From the design canvas, double-click the Update Categories button component you added earlier. Creator brings up **Page1.java** in the Java source editor with the cursor at the `update_action()` method.
2. Add code to the event handler. Copy and paste from your Creator book's file **FieldGuide2/Examples/Database/snippets/musicUpdate_update.txt**. (The added code is bold.)

Listing 9.4 Method `update_action()`

```
public String update_action() {
   // TODO: Process the button click action.
   // Return value is a navigation
   // case name where null will return to the same page.

   try {
     musiccategoriesDataProvider.commitChanges();
     log("update: changes committed");
     info("Update committed");

   } catch(Exception e) {
     log("update: cannot commit changes ", e);
     error("Cannot commit changes: " + e.getMessage());

   }
   return null;
}
```

This event handler updates the editing changes to the database by calling Data Provider method `commitChanges()`, which causes any cached changes to values of the data elements to be written to the supported data store. Method `log()` records the update in the Server Log and method `info()` writes its text argument to the FacesContext, which is displayed by the message group component you added to the page.

3. Return to the Design view by selecting the button labeled Design in the editing toolbar.
4. Double-click the Cancel button. Creator brings up **Page.java** in the Java editor with the cursor at the `cancel_action()` method.

5. Add code to the event handler. Copy and paste from your Creator book's file **FieldGuide2/Examples/Database/snippets/musicUpdate_cancel.txt**. (The added code is bold.)

Listing 9.5 Method `cancel_action()`

```
public String cancel_action() {
   // TODO: Process the button click action.
   // Return value is a navigation
   // case name where null will return to the same page.

   try {
      musiccategoriesDataProvider.revertChanges();
      log("cancel: revert changes");
      info("Update cancelled");

   } catch(Exception e) {
      log("cancel: cannot revert changes ", e);
      error("Cannot revert changes: " + e.getMessage());

   }
   return null;
}
```

This event handler cancels the editing changes by calling Data Provider method `revertChanges()`. Any cached changes to values of the data elements are discarded, restoring the initial values.

Creator Tip

After clicking the Update Categories button, cancel has no effect on the updated data since they are already written to the database. Cancel restores the initial values from the database before Update Categories is clicked.

Deploy and Run

Deploy and run the application. Figure 9–25 shows you what the page looks like after the user changes the Rock category to Rock & Roll and clicks the Update Categories button. Note that you can make changes to more than one row before updating the database. You can't edit the primary key field, however. To confirm the music category data changes, select Data Sources from the Server Navigator window. Expand Music > Tables and double-click table MUSICCATEGORIES. Creator displays the table's data (including the changed fields) in the editor pane.

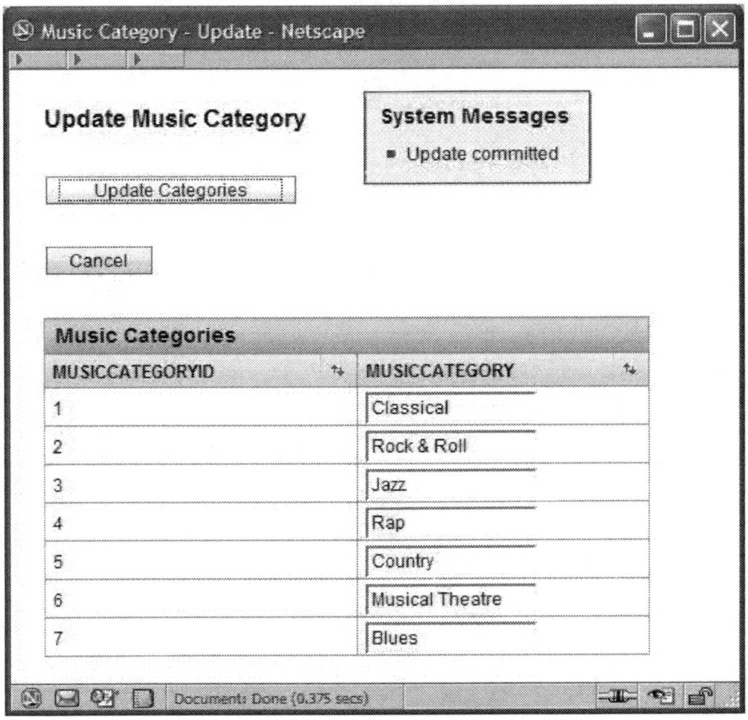

Figure 9–25 **The Music Collection Database: updating the Music Categories table**

9.7 Database Row Inserts

Let's modify the Music Update project to allow the user to insert new rows into the data base table, as well as make editing changes. This application is straightforward and demonstrates how to manipulate a Data Provider to insert a row.

While the Data Provider layer provides a consistent API, not all Data Providers are the same. For example, a Data Provider that wraps an object array cannot grow, and hence, you cannot insert "rows." The approach here is to provide a text field component that allows the user to supply a new category name and a way to obtain a new primary key. Then after you add the new values to the data provider, the application should display a revised music category list in the table. Of course, the user can then edit the new category as well.

Virtual Forms

You'll use virtual forms in this application to separate the new music category input from the Cancel and Update MusicCategories actions. You want to make new music category input required, but only if the user is adding a new row. Therefore, the text field component and its associated button to add the data should fall under the same virtual form. To prevent the Cancel and Update MusicCategories buttons from triggering validation for the new input, you'll place these in separate virtual forms. We'll provide the step-by-step approach to do this during the project construction.

Copy the Project

This step is optional. If you don't want to copy the project, simply skip this section and continue making modifications to the UpdateMusic project.

1. Bring up project MusicUpdate in Creator, if it's not already opened.
2. From the Projects window, right-click node MusicUpdate and select Save Project As. Provide the new name **MusicAdd**.
3. Close project MusicUpdate. Right-click MusicAdd and select Set Main Project. You'll make changes to the MusicAdd project.
4. Expand MusicAdd > Web Pages and open **Page1.jsp** in the design view.
5. Click anywhere in the background of the design canvas of the MusicAdd project. In the Properties window, change the page's `Title` property to **Music Category - Update/Add**.
6. Select label component `label1` and change its `text` property to **Music Category - Update and Add**.

Add Components

First, you'll add components to effect the new category portion of the web application. This includes a text field component, label, validator, message component, and button. Figure 9–26 shows the design view with the new components added. It also shows the configured virtual forms. You might want to refer to this figure as you add components to the project.

1. From the Basic Components palette, select Text Field. Place it on the page to the right of the Update Categories button. In the Properties window change its `id` property to **newCategory**.
2. In the Properties window, check property `required`.
3. From the Basic Components palette select Label and place it above the text field component you just added.
4. It should be selected. Type in the label text **New Music Category:** and finish with **<Enter>**.

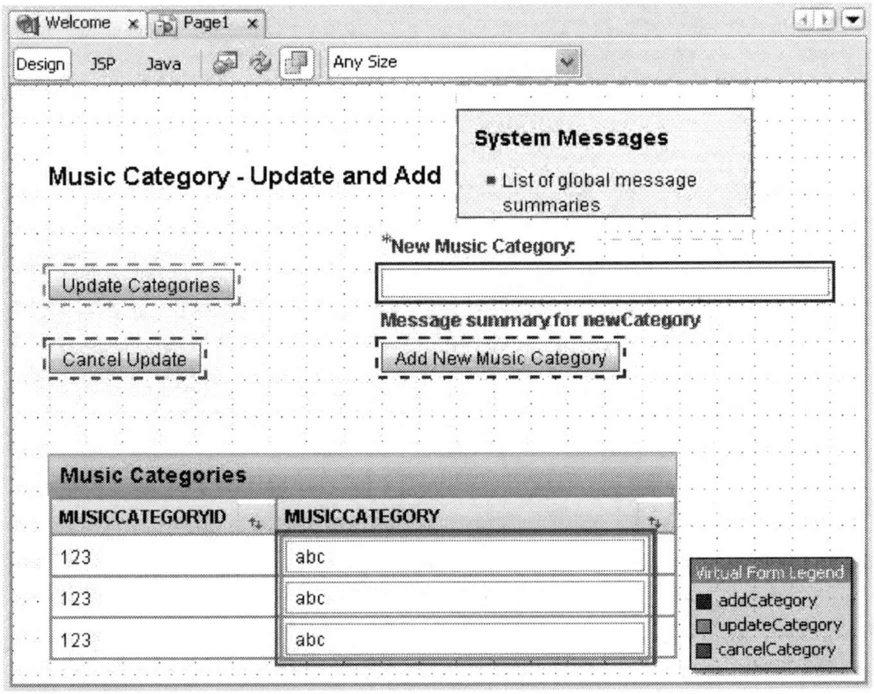

Figure 9–26 **Music Category Add project's design view**

5. Connect the label to the text field. Click inside the label component, type **<Ctrl+Shift>** and drag the cursor to the text field component. When you release the mouse, the label should have an asterisk indicating that its associated component is a required field.

Creator Tip

You're using a separate label component here instead of the text field's built-in label property because the label component's placement is more flexible. By default Creator places the built-in label on the left.

The database field MUSICCATEGORY is a VARCHAR with maximum length 20. You'll need a validator to make sure that its length doesn't exceed this maximum.

Creator Tip

You can check the type and other properties of a database table column through the Data Source portion of the Servers window. For example, to check the maximum size of the MUSICCATEGORY field, select Data Source > Music > Tables > MUSICCATEGORIES in the Servers window and right-click field MUSICCATEGORY. Select Properties from the context menu. Creator pops up a Properties window as shown in Figure 9–27. You see that the column size is 20 and its SQL Type is VARCHAR.

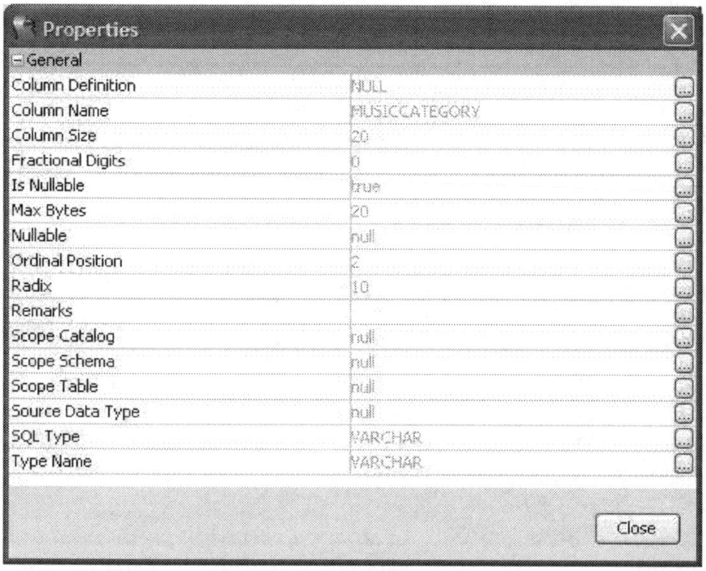

Figure 9–27 **Examine the Properties of a database column**

1. In the Palette window, expand the component Validators section and select Length Validator. Drag the component to the page and release the mouse over the text field component. Creator instantiates `lengthvalidator1` on your page.
2. In the Page1 Outline view, select `lengthValidator1`. In the Properties window, specify property `maximum` as **20** and property `minimum` as **3**.
3. Select the text field component and make sure its `validator` property is set to `lengthvalidator1` in the Properties window. (If it's not set, choose `lengthvalidator1` from the drop down menu opposite property `validator`.)

You'll need a message component since the text field has validation and its `required` property is enabled.

1. From the Basics Components palette, select component Message and place it on the design canvas directly under the text field component.
2. Type **<Ctrl+Shift>** and drag the cursor to the text field component, releasing the mouse when the cursor is over the component. This sets the message component's `for` property to the text field. The message component will display "Message summary for newCategory," as shown in the Design View in Figure 9–26.

As it is currently configured, the message group component you added in the previous section will display validation messages associated with the text field component `newCategory`. This means that a validation message will appear in *both* the message component you just added as well as the message group component that's already on the page. You'll now limit the message group component so that it displays global (page-level) messages only.

1. Select the message group component.
2. In the Properties window under Behavior, check the property `showGlobalOnly`. Creator now displays "List of global message summaries" in the component's box in the design view.

Now let's add the Add New Music Category button component.

1. From the Basics Components palette, select component Button and place it on the page under the message component.
2. Type in the text **Add New Music Category** for its label.
3. In the Properties window, change its `id` property to **addNewCategory**. (As with the other buttons on this page, you're changing the `id` property to reflect the button's function.)
4. Select the Cancel button. In the Properties view, change its `text` property to **Cancel Update**.

This completes the new component additions to the page. You might want to compare the page in your project with Figure 9–26 on page 418.

Configure Virtual Forms

Like many pages that have more than one "function," this page needs virtual forms to keep the various components correctly grouped. While any given form can have more than one component that participates in a virtual form, only one component can submit the form. Table 9.2 shows the command components on the page and which virtual form they submit.

Table 9.2 Virtual Form Description

Activity	*Submitting Component*	*Virtual Form Name*
Add a new category	`addNewCategory` button	addCategory (blue)
Update edits to database	`update` button	updateCategory (green)
Cancel edits	`cancel` button	cancelCategory (red)

With virtual forms, you decide which component submits the form and which component(s) participate in the form. For example, the `newCategory` text field participates in the addCategory virtual form. Therefore, if you click the `addNewCategory` button and neglect to specify a category in the text field, validation kicks in and provides feedback to the user. However, if you click the `cancel` or `update` buttons, you do not want the `newCategory` text field to be validated. Therefore, it should *not* participate in the updateCategory or cancel-Category virtual forms. Table 9.3 lists the two input components and assigns them to the appropriate virtual forms. Note that `textField1` belongs to the table component and must participate in the update and cancel operations for these components to correctly display the modified data.

Table 9.3 Virtual Form Participation

Component	*Activity*	*Virtual Form Participation*
`newCategory` (text field)	user supplies new category name	addCategory (blue)
`textField1` (text field)	user edits column2 in data table	updateCategory (green) cancelCategory (red)

Let's configure the virtual forms for this page now.

1. In the design view, select button Add New Music Category, right-click, and select Configure Virtual Forms. Creator brings up the Configure Virtual Forms dialog. Component `addNewCategory`, the button's `id` property, is displayed near the top of the dialog.
2. In the dialog, click button New. Creator builds a new virtual form with code color blue.
3. Double-click inside cell `virtualForm1` under Name and change the name to **addCategory**.
4. Under column Submit, select **Yes** from the drop down menu. Don't change the Participate column. Click Apply, then OK.

5. Enable the Virtual Form Legend in your design view by toggling the Show Virtual Forms icon in the editing toolbar (use the tooltips to identify the icon). The Virtual Form Legend appears in the lower-right portion of the design editor. The Add New Music Category button is now outlined in a dotted blue line, indicating that it is the submitting component for the blue virtual form.

Creator Tip

To change the default color legend Creator uses, select an alternate color from the drop down menu in the Color column for each virtual form.

Now let's add two more virtual forms to the page (one for updating edited category text and one for canceling edited category text).

1. In the design view, select button Update Categories, right-click, and select Configure Virtual Forms. Creator brings up the Configure Virtual Forms dialog and component `update` is displayed near the top of the dialog.
2. In the dialog, click button New. Creator builds a new virtual form with code color green.
3. Double-click inside cell `virtualForm1` under Name and change the name to **updateCategory**.
4. Under column Submit for the updateCategory virtual form (green), select **Yes** from the drop down menu. Don't change the Participate column. Click Apply, then OK.
5. The Update Categories button is now outlined in a dotted green line, indicating that it is the submitting button for the green virtual form.
6. Follow the same steps (Steps 1 through 5 above) to add virtual Form **cancelCategory** for button Cancel Update. Change the Submit column for virtual form cancelCategory to **Yes** for the Cancel button. When you're finished the Cancel button will be outlined in a red dotted line, indicating that it is the submitting button for the red virtual form.

Now you'll specify which input components (not buttons) participate in the virtual forms you've created. There are two text fields on the page: the text field in which users supply a new music category name (id `newCategory`) and the text field that is generated for each row in the table (id `textField1`).

1. Select text field `newCategory`, right-click, and select Configure Virtual Forms.
2. You'll see all three virtual forms in the Configure Virtual Forms dialog.
3. Select **Yes** from the drop down menu under heading Participate for virtual form `addCategory` (blue). Click Apply then OK. The component is now out-

lined in a solid blue line, indicating that it participates in the blue virtual form.

4. Now select `textField1` from the table (or select it from the Outline view), right-click, and select Configure Virtual Forms.
5. Select **Yes** from the drop down menu under heading Participate for *both* virtual forms `updateCategory` (green) and `cancelCategory` (red). Click Apply then OK. The second column (the text field) is now outlined in *both* solid green and solid red lines, indicating that it participates in both the green and red virtual forms.

Add ApplicationBean1 Property

When you insert data into a database, you have to have a way to generate unique primary keys. You also have to allow other users to add data at the same time.

Recall that application scope endures for the lifetime of the application and all data stored in application scope is shared among all sessions and users. Therefore, we'll put the primary key generation code in application scope, assuring that only one instance of this code exists at a time. You'll create a property, `nextCategoryId`, whose getter will return the next primary key for the MusicCategories database table. First you'll create the property, then configure a row set and data provider that will enable you to generate the next primary key. The new primary key will be the next integer value above the maximum primary key returned from an SQL query for the MusicCategories table.

Primary Keys

There are several ways to tackle the problem of generating unique primary keys. One approach is to generate a unique string using the current time, the IP address of the host machine concatenated with a hash code of the address of the current object, and a secure random number as a three-part hexadecimal string. A scheme which gets the next primary key from a database is simple and works with our example. However, getting the next primary key from a database could create a bottleneck with a high-usage system.

Let's add an Integer property to ApplicationBean1 that is read-only and does not have an associated instance variable (since its value is generated each time).

1. Expand the MusicAdd node in the Projects window and right-click Application Bean. Select Add > Property from the context menu.

2. Creator pops up the New Property Pattern dialog. For Name, specify **next-CategoryId**, for Type select **Integer**, and for Mode select **Read Only**. *Uncheck* the Generate Field option, as shown in Figure 9–28. (Check that your capitalizations exactly match those in the figure.) Click OK.

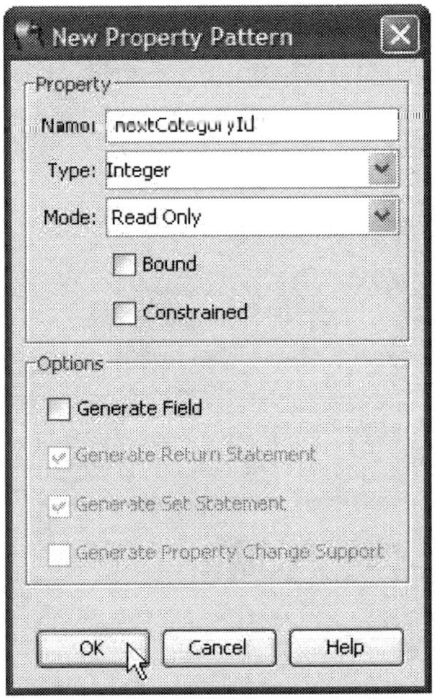

Figure 9–28 **Add property nextCategoryId to application scope**

Before adding the code for the property's getter, let's add the MusicCategories table to ApplicationBean1.

1. Double-click Application Bean in the Projects window. Creator brings up **ApplicationBean1.java** in the source editor. By default, Creator displays the Navigate window when the Java source editor is active.
2. Select the Outline tab and scroll down until you see the ApplicationBean1 node.
3. From the Servers window, select Data Sources > Music > Tables > MusicCategories and drop it on top of the ApplicationBean1 node. This creates a `musiccategoriesRowSet` object and `musiccategoriesDataProvider` in application scope.

You'll now edit the query and configure property `nextCategoryId`.

1. Open the ApplicationBean1 node and double-click the `musiccategories-RowSet`. This brings up the SQL Query editor in the editing pane. (Close the Output window to give more space to the editor.)
2. In the MUSICCATEGORIES Table, uncheck field MUSICCATEGORY.
3. In the Query Text view, edit the query as shown below.

```
SELECT ALL MAX(MUSIC.MUSICCATEGORIES.MUSICCATEGORYID)
   AS MAXCATEGORYID
FROM MUSIC.MUSICCATEGORIES
```

4. Save the changes (select the Save All icon in the toolbar) and close the SQL Query editor.
5. Return to **ApplicationBean1.java** in the Java editor and expand the Creator-managed Component Initialization code in the `ApplicationBean1()` constructor. You'll see the modified `musiccategoriesRowSet` command.
6. Scroll to the end of the file and add the following code to the `nextCatego-ryId` getter, `getNextCategoryId()`. (Ignore any red-underlined errors for now.) Copy and paste from your Creator book's file **FieldGuide2/Examples/Database/snippets/musicAdd_GetNextCategory.txt**. (The added code is bold.)

Listing 9.6 Method `getNextCategoryId()`

```
public Integer getNextCategoryId() {
   // force execution of command from underlying rowset
   musiccategoriesDataProvider.refresh();
   musiccategoriesDataProvider.cursorFirst();

   // get the max value returned (see rowset's sql query)
   Integer maxCategoryId =
        (Integer)musiccategoriesDataProvider.getValue(
        "MAXCATEGORYID");

   // close the rowset
   try {
     musiccategoriesRowSet.release();
     musiccategoriesRowSet.close();
   } catch (Exception e) {
     log("[getNextCategoryId]: Cannot close/release rowset");
   }

   Integer nextCategoryId = new Integer(
          maxCategoryId.intValue() + 1);
   return nextCategoryId;
}
```

Each time the method is called, the row set connects to the database and executes the command (the data provider `refresh()` method causes all of this). Field name "`MAXCATEGORYID`" returns the maximum primary key. This value is then increased by one and returned to the caller. Note that the row set is released and closed, making access available for the next caller.

Add Button Event Handler Code

You'll now add the event handler code that adds the new music category to the MusicCategories table.

1. Return to the Page1 design view and double-click button Add New Music Category. Creator generates a default button event handler for you and brings up **Page1.java** in the Java editor with the cursor set to the `addNewCategory_action()` method.
2. Copy and paste from your Creator book's file **FieldGuide2/Examples/Database/snippets/musicAdd_addNewCategory_action.txt**. (The added code is bold.)

Listing 9.7 Method `addNewCategory()`

```
public String addNewCategory_action() {
   // TODO: Process the button click action.
   // Return value is a navigation
   // case name where null will return to the same page.

   // Add a new music category to the data base
   if (musiccategoriesDataProvider.canAppendRow()) {
      try {
         RowKey rowKey =
            musiccategoriesDataProvider.appendRow();

         // put the new data in the data provider
         musiccategoriesDataProvider.setValue(
            "MUSICCATEGORIES.MUSICCATEGORYID", rowKey,
            getApplicationBean1().getNextCategoryId());
         musiccategoriesDataProvider.setValue(
            "MUSICCATEGORIES.MUSICCATEGORY", rowKey,
            newCategory.getText());

         musiccategoriesDataProvider.commitChanges();
         info("New Category " + newCategory.getText() +
               " added to MUSICCATEGORIES table");
         newCategory.setText(null);
```

Listing 9.7 Method `addNewCategory()` *(continued)*

```
        } catch (Exception e) {
            log("Cannot add new music category ", e);
            error("Cannot add new music category: " +
                    e.getMessage());
        }

    } else {
        log("Cannot append new music category");
        error("Cannot append new music category");
    }
    return null;
}
```

3. From within the Java source editor, right-click and select Fix Imports. This adds the import statement for class RowKey.

Deploy and Run

Deploy and run the application. Figure 9–29 shows project MusicAdd running in a browser after category Hip Hop is added.

After running the MusicAdd web application, you can check the status of the database by inspecting the tables using the Servers window. Select Data Sources > Music > Tables > MUSICCATEGORIES. Double-click the MUSICCATEGORIES table. Creator displays the data in the editor pane.

9.8 Database Deletions

Four database operations are represented by the acronym CRUD: Create (insert), Read, Update, and Delete. The previous sections have shown you all these operations except delete.

Delete operations are typically more involved than the others in a relational database schema, since you (or the underlying database software) must take into account what to do if you attempt to delete a record to which other records refer. You have two choices: you can disallow the delete of records that have links (foreign keys), or you can perform a cascading delete.

When you target a row for deletion that is referenced with a foreign key in another (related) table, you will have to delete the related records first. For example, to delete a record in the MUSICCATEGORIES table that is referenced in the RECORDINGS table, you must first delete the related row in the

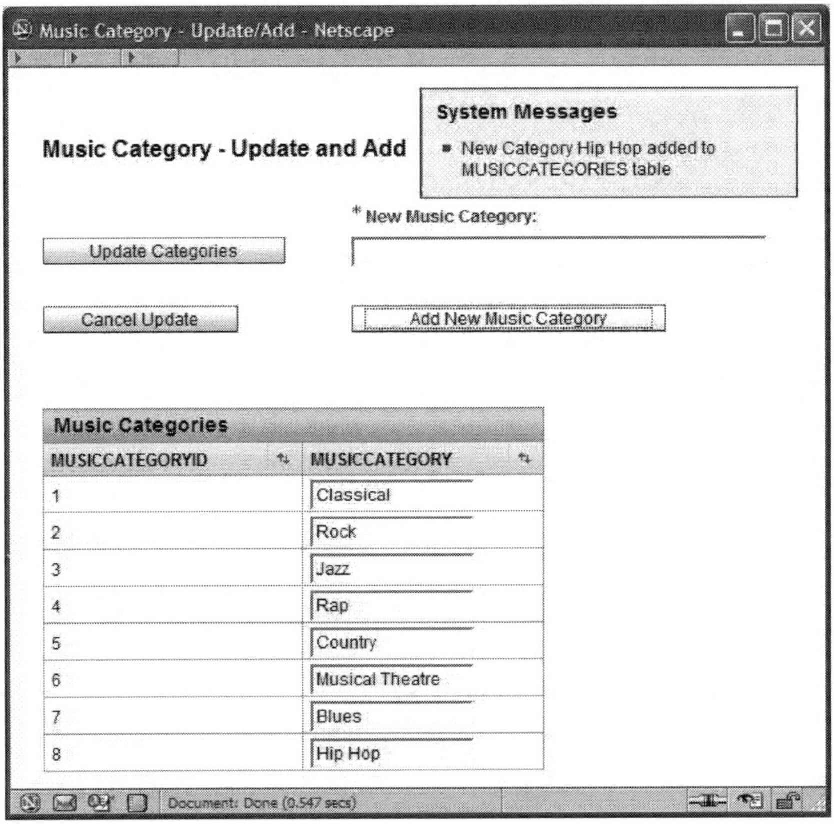

Figure 9–29 **After the insert row operation to the MusicCategories table**

RECORDINGS table. You can locate the row by matching its foreign key value for MusicCategoryID.

Furthermore, to delete the row in the RECORDINGS table, you'll also have to delete the related rows in the TRACKS table. These you find by locating all tracks with a foreign key that matches the RecordingID. This "cascading" effect that trickles through the database is called *cascading deletes*.

The database enforces data integrity by preventing deletes on rows referenced by other tables. In our example, deleting a row in the MUSICCATEGORIES table means we have to find and delete the related records in the RECORDINGS table and TRACKS table.

Alternatively, you can decide to only allow delete operations on records that don't have foreign key references to them. In the initial version of the MusicDelete project, this is the approach you'll take. How do you prevent delete operations on these records? Fortunately, the underlying database software prevents deletions by throwing an exception during the data provider's `commit-Changes()` call. By putting this method call in a try block, you can invoke the data provider's `revertChanges()` method in the corresponding catch handler. This puts the database back in a consistent state. In the second version of the MusicDelete project, you'll add code to perform cascading deletes.

Copy the Project

This step is optional. If you don't want to copy the project, simply skip this section and continue making modifications to the MusicAdd project.

1. Bring up project MusicAdd in Creator, if it's not already opened.
2. From the Projects window, right-click node MusicAdd and select Save Project As. Provide the new name **MusicDelete**.
3. Close project MusicAdd. Right-click MusicDelete and select Set Main Project. You'll make changes to the MusicDelete project.
4. Expand MusicDelete > Web Pages and open **Page1.jsp** in the design view.
5. Click anywhere in the background of the design canvas of the MusicDelete project. In the Properties window, change the page's `Title` property to **Music Category - Update/Add/Delete**.
6. In the design view, select component `label1` (it holds the title that's displayed on the page). Change its text to **Music Category - Update/Add/Delete**.
7. In the Properties window for `label1`, change property `labelLevel` to **Medium (2)**. This provides more space on the page for the other components.

Add Components

First, you'll add components to implement the delete function of the web application: a "Delete" checkbox column in the table so that users can delete more than one row at once, a button to perform the delete operation, and a corresponding virtual form. Figure 9–30 shows the design view with the new components added. It also shows the newly configured virtual form (yellow). You might want to refer to this figure as you add the components to the project.

1. Make sure that Page1 is active in the design view.
2. Select the table component, right-click, and select Table Layout from the context menu. You're going to add a new column at the beginning (left-side) of the table.
3. Click button New to add a new column. Click button Up to move it up in the Selected window until it is at the top.
4. Under Header Text, type in **Delete**.
5. Under Component Type, select Checkbox from the drop down menu. Select Apply then OK. Figure 9–31 shows the Table Layout for the new column.

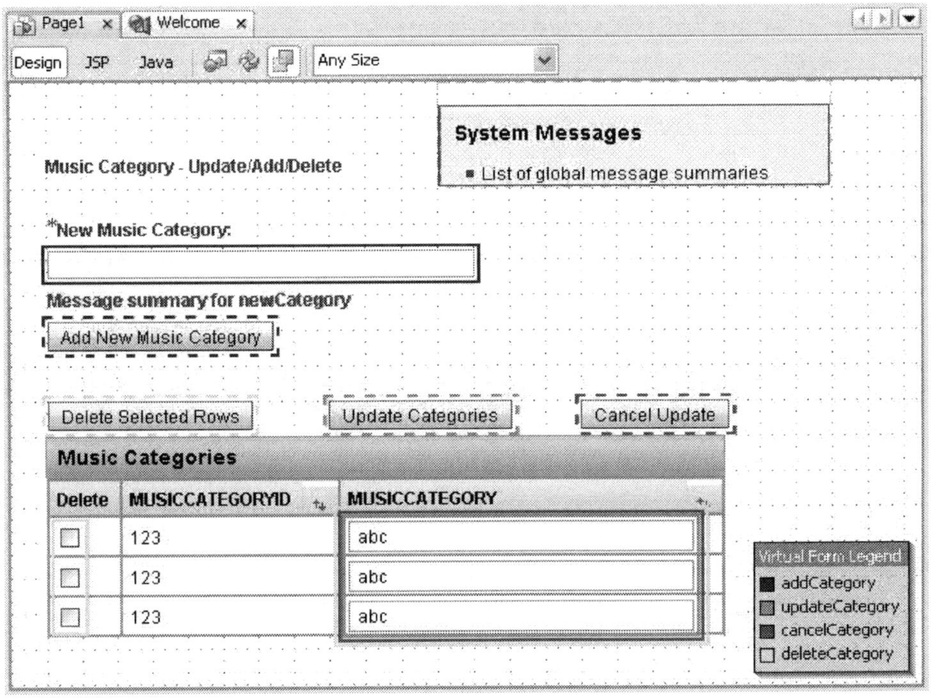

Figure 9–30 **Music Category Delete project's design view**

6. From the Basic Components palette, select Button and drop it on the page in the design view. Place it directly above the table, aligned on the left.
7. Change its `text` property to **Delete Selected Rows**; change its `id` property to **delete**.
8. Using Figure 9–30 as a guide, arrange the Delete Selected Rows, Update Categories, and Cancel Update buttons in a row above the table component.
9. Select the label, text field, message, and button components associated with adding a new music category and move these components over to the left side of the page.

Configure Checkbox Components

There are several steps involved in building the code to maintain the set of checked rows in the table. First, you create a Page1 boolean property (`selected`) and bind this to the checkbox component. Second, you create a HashSet object to hold the selected RowKeys from the table's data provider. This keeps track of the selected rows. Then you provide the setter and getter methods for the `selected` property that either adds a row key to the selected set or removes it from the selected set. You don't ever need to call the `setSe-`

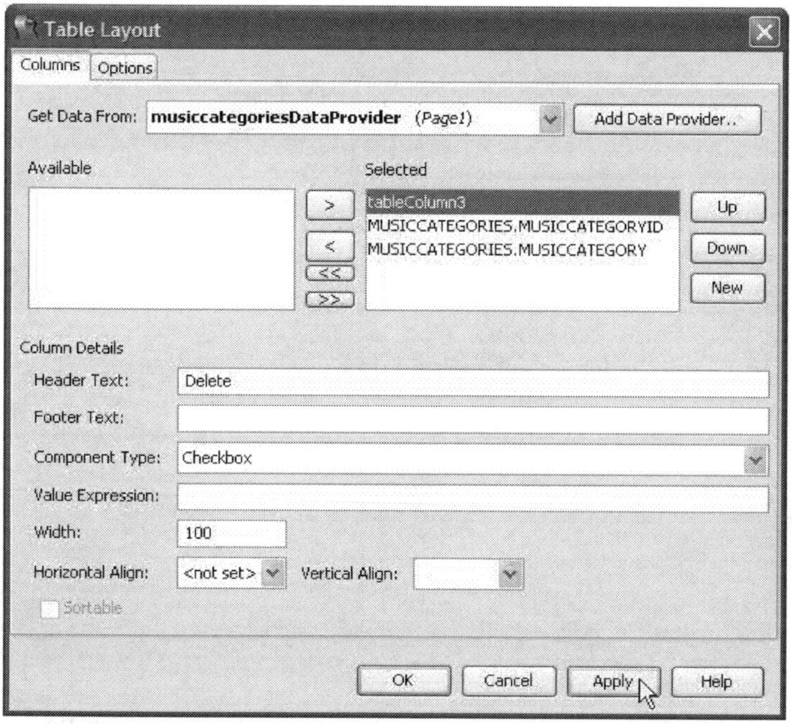

Figure 9–31 **Table Layout for checkbox column**

`lected()` and `isSelected()` methods yourself; Creator takes care of that when you bind the checkbox's `selected` property to the Page1 `selected` property.

1. From the Projects window, expand the Source Packages and default package name node.
2. Right-click **Page1.java** and select Add > Property from the context menu. Creator pops up the New Property Pattern dialog.
3. For Name specify **selected**, for Type specify **boolean**, and for Mode use the default **Read/Write**. Uncheck the Generate Field checkbox. Click OK. Creator adds property `selected` to Page1.
4. From the design view, select the checkbox component (its id is `checkbox1` unless you changed it). In the Properties window, select the small editing box opposite property `selected`. Creator pops up a property editing dialog.
5. Select radio button Use Binding. From the list of properties, select **Page1 > selected *Boolean*** and click OK. This binds the checkbox `selected` property to `#{Page1.selected}`.

You'll now provide the code for methods `isSelected()` and `setSelected()`.

1. Click the Java button in the editing toolbar to bring up **Page1.java** in the Java source editor.
2. Locate method `isSelected()`, which was generated by Creator when you added property `selected` to Page1. (Use the Navigator window to locate `isSelected()` in the methods list and double-click.)

   Note that when you added property `selected`, you specified that Creator should not generate the field. Therefore, **Page1.java** has compilation errors because the default getter and setter assume that field `selected` exists. These errors will disappear when you add the code for these methods.

3. Add private variable `selectedRows` above method `isSelected()`, as follows.

```
// HashSet of RowKeys to keep track of selected rows
private Set selectedRows = new HashSet();
```

   Right-click inside the editor and select Fix Imports.

4. Supply the following code for method `isSelected()`. Fix imports, if necessary. Copy and paste from your Creator book download **FieldGuide2/Examples/Database/snippets/musicDelete_isSelected.txt**.

Listing 9.8 Method `isSelected()`

```
public boolean isSelected() {
  // called for every row
  // returns true if rowkey exists in HashSet
  TableRowDataProvider trdp = (TableRowDataProvider)getBean(
        "currentRow");

  if (trdp == null) {
    return false;
  }
  RowKey rowKey = trdp.getTableRow();
  boolean exists = false ;
```

Listing 9.8 Method `isSelected()` *(continued)*

```
    for(Iterator i = selectedRows.iterator(); i.hasNext();) {
      RowKey rk = (RowKey)i.next() ;
      if ( rk.equals(rowKey)) {
        exists = true ;
        break ;
      }
    }
    return exists;
}
```

This method is invoked for every row in the table. (When you bind the checkbox `selected` property to the Page1 `selected` property, this method is called for every checkbox.) The method iterates through `selectedRows` hash set to find a match with the current row's row key.

5. Supply the following code for method `setSelected()`. Copy and paste from your Creator book's download **FieldGuide2/Examples/Database/snippets/musicDelete_setSelected.txt**.

Listing 9.9 Method `setSelected()`

```
public void setSelected(boolean selected) {
    // called for every row
    TableRowDataProvider trdp = (TableRowDataProvider)
        getBean("currentRow");

    RowKey rowKey = trdp.getTableRow();
    if (checkbox1.isChecked()) {
      selectedRows.add(rowKey);

    } else {
      selectedRows.remove(rowKey);
    }
}
```

Method `setSelected()` is also invoked for every row in the table. If the current row's checkbox component is checked, the corresponding row key is added to the `selectedRows` hash set. Otherwise, the row key is removed from the hash set.

Add the Delete Button Event Handler

You'll now add the code to the Delete button's event handler.

1. Return to the Page1 design view. Double-click button Delete Selected Rows. Creator generates the default action event method and brings up **Page1.java** in the Java source editor with the cursor set to the `delete_action()` method.
2. Provide the following code for method `delete_action()`. Type **<Alt+Shift+F>** to fix imports. This method does not perform cascading deletes, but calls method `revertChanges()` when the database disallows a row delete. Copy and paste from the Creator book download **FieldGuide2/Examples/Database/snippets/musicDelete_delete_action.txt.**

Listing 9.10 Method `delete_action()`

```
public String delete_action() {
   // TODO: Process the button click action.
   // Return value is a navigation
   // case name where null will return to the same page.

   // Make sure all the selected rows can actually be removed
   boolean ok = true;
   Iterator rowKeys = selectedRows.iterator();
   while (rowKeys.hasNext()) {
      RowKey rowKey = (RowKey) rowKeys.next();

      if (!musiccategoriesDataProvider.canRemoveRow(rowKey)){
         error("Cannot delete row " + rowKey);
         log("Cannot delete row " + rowKey);
         ok = false;
      }

   }
   if (!ok) {
      return null;
   }

   // Delete the currently selected rows
   rowKeys = selectedRows.iterator();
   while (rowKeys.hasNext()) {
      RowKey rowKey = (RowKey) rowKeys.next();
      try {
         musiccategoriesDataProvider.removeRow(rowKey);

      } catch(Exception e) {
         log("Cannot delete row " + rowKey + ": ", e);
         error("Cannot delete row " + rowKey + ": " + e);
         ok = false;
      }
   }
```

Listing 9.10 Method `delete_action()` *(continued)*

```
  // Commit or rollback the database transaction
  if (musiccategoriesDataProvider instanceof
          TransactionalDataProvider) {
    if (ok) {
      try {
        musiccategoriesDataProvider.commitChanges();
      } catch (Exception e) {
        log("Cannot commit deletes ", e);
        error("Cannot commit deletes: " + e);
        try {
          musiccategoriesDataProvider.revertChanges();
          musiccategoriesDataProvider.refresh();
        } catch (Exception e2) {
          log("Cannot roll back deletes ", e2);
          error("Cannot roll back deletes: " + e2);
        }
      }

    } else {
      log("Rolling back deletes");
      info("Rolling back deletes");
      try {
        musiccategoriesDataProvider.revertChanges();
        musiccategoriesDataProvider.refresh();
      } catch (Exception e) {
        log("Cannot roll back deletes ", e);
        error("Cannot roll back deletes: " + e);
      }
    }
  }

  // Clear the checkboxes
  selectedRows = new HashSet();
  info("Cleared selectedRows");
  return null;
}
```

This `delete_action()` performs the following tasks.

1. It calls the data provider method `canRemoveRow()` for each row key in the `selectedRows` hash set. The data provider associated with this table may not be a CachedRowSetDataProvider and it may not allow row removals.
2. If all rows are removable, data provider method `removeRow()` is invoked for each row key in the `selectedRows` hash set.

3. Once the rows are removed, data provider method `commitChanges()` is invoked if the data provider is transactional (such as the CachedRowSet-DataProvider). This is the call that will fail if the target row has referrals from other tables.
4. If an exception is thrown, method `revertChanges()` restores the underlying row set to a consistent state. Data provider method `refresh()` makes sure the data provider and the underlying row set are in sync with each other.
5. Finally, if `ok` is false, this means that the `removeRow()` call failed and methods `revertChanges()` and `refresh()` must be called to put the underlying row set in a consistent state with the data provider.

Configure Virtual Forms

Return now to the design view to configure virtual forms.

1. In the design view, right-click button Delete Selected Rows and select Configure Virtual Forms from the context menu. Creator brings up the Configure Virtual Forms dialog. Component `delete`, the button's `id` property, is displayed near the top of the dialog.
2. In the dialog, click button New. Creator builds a new virtual form with code color yellow.
3. Double-click inside cell `virtualForm1` under Name and change the name to **deleteCategory**.
4. Under column Submit, select **Yes** from the drop down menu. Click Apply, then OK. The Delete Selected Rows button is now outlined in a dotted yellow line, indicating that it is the submitting component for the yellow virtual form.
5. Select both the checkbox and text field components in the table (use **<Shift+Click>** to select more than one component). Right-click and select Configure Virtual Forms. Creator displays the Configure Virtual Forms dialog with both components listed above (`checkbox1` and `textField1`) and all four virtual forms.
6. Select **Yes** from the drop down menu under heading Participate for virtual form deleteCategory (yellow). Select Apply then OK. In the design view, both the checkboxes in the first column and the text field components in the third column are outline in solid yellow lines.

Deploy and Run

It's now time to test the application with all functions: Update, Add, and Delete. You'll probably want to open project MusicBuild in Creator and periodically run this project to re-initialize the data base so that's it is in a known, consistent state. Here's how to run MusicBuild.

1. From the Welcome Page, select button Open Existing Project and select MusicBuild. (If a Library Reference error appears, ignore it.)
2. From the Projects menu, select MusicBuild, right-click and select Set Main Project.
3. Again select MusicBuild, right-click and select Run Project. You should see the diagnostic Music database was created in the Output window.
4. Now select project MusicDelete, right-click and select Set Main Project.
5. Deploy and run project MusicDelete. Figure 9–32 shows this project running in a browser.

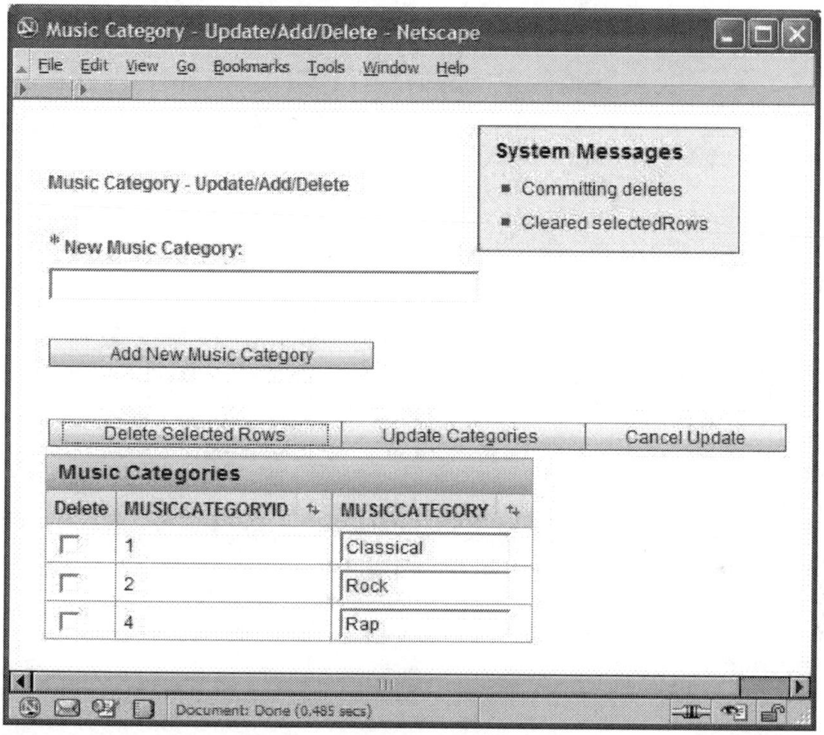

Figure 9–32 **Project MusicDelete running in a browser**

6. Delete a music category and verify that it was deleted. You can check the status of the database by inspecting the tables using the Servers window. Select Data Sources > Music > Tables > MUSICCATEGORIES. Double-click the MUSICCATEGORIES table. Creator displays the data in the editor pane.

9.9 Handle Cascading Deletes

As you test the MusicDelete project, you'll note that if you attempt to delete Music Category Classical or Rock, the `commitChanges()` call throws an exception. This is because the RECORDINGS table contains foreign keys that reference these rows. You'll now implement a version of this project that checks the RECORDINGS table to see if its foreign key for MUSICCATEGORYID matches the target row in method `delete_action()`. If the recording matches, then it will be removed from the RECORDINGS table. Likewise, you must remove all tracks in the TRACKS table that have a foreign key RECORDINGID that matches the target recording.

In order for the RECORDINGS data provider's `commitChanges()` call to succeed, the referring tracks must be removed first. Likewise, in order for the MUSICCATEGORIES data provider's `commitChanges()` call to succeed, the referring recordings must be removed. The algorithm you will use is as follows.

1. Identify the music category row that you want to delete and get its primary key (MUSICCATEGORYID).
2. Set the `recordingsRowSet` query parameter to this MUSICCATEGORYID and refresh the data provider. This will build a data provider row set with recordings whose MUSICCATEGORYID foreign key matches the target MUSICCATEGORIES row.
3. For each recording, get its primary key and set the `tracksRowSet` query parameter to this RECORDINGID. This will build a data provider row set with tracks whose RECORDINGID foreign key matches the target RECORDINGS row.
4. For each track, remove the row from the data provider.
5. When you're finished, commit the changes. This will update the TRACKS table in the data base.
6. Now remove the target recording and get the next recording, building a new data provider row set with tracks. Remove these tracks and commit the changes. Repeat until all the matching recordings and their tracks have been removed.
7. When you've finished removing all the target recordings, commit the changes. This will update the RECORDINGS table in the data base.
8. Remove the target music category row.
9. Repeat with the next music category row that's been selected on the web page. When all the music category rows have been deleted, you can now commit the changes. The `commitChanges()` call will succeed, since there are no more RECORDINGS with a matching MUSICCATEGORYID. If you select a music category that has no matching recordings, the `recordings-`

`DataProvider.refresh()` call builds an empty data provider object and `recordingsDataProvider.cursorFirst()` returns false.

Copy the Project

This step is optional. If you don't want to copy the project, simply skip this section and continue making modifications to the MusicDelete project.

1. Bring up project MusicDelete in Creator, if it's not already opened.
2. From the Projects window, right-click node MusicDelete and select Save Project As. Provide the new name **MusicCascadeDelete**.
3. Close project MusicDelete. Right-click MusicCascadeDelete and select Set Main Project. You'll make changes to the MusicCascadeDelete project.
4. Expand MusicCascadeDelete > Web Pages and open **Page1.jsp** in the design view.
5. Click anywhere in the background of the design canvas of the MusicCascadeDelete project. In the Properties window, change the page's `Title` property to **Music Category - Cascade Deletes**.
6. In the design view, select component `label1` (it holds the title that's displayed on the page). Change its text to **Music Category - Cascade Deletes**.

Include Additional Data Source Tables

Because the cascade delete operation has to access some of the other tables from the Music database, you'll need to add these to the page. When you add them, Creator also adds the corresponding row set objects to SessionBean1. Note that except for these data source tables, you don't add any new components to this project.

1. From the Data Sources > Music > Tables node in the Servers window, select the RECORDINGS table and drop it directly on top of the design canvas. (Don't drop it on any components.)

   Creator adds the `recordingsDataProvider` component to Page1 (it's visible in the Outline view) and `recordingsRowSet` component to SessionBean1 (also visible in the Outline view).

2. Again from the Data Sources > Music > Tables node in the Servers window, select the TRACKS table and drop it directly on top of the design canvas.

   The `tracksDataProvider` component appears in the Outline view under Page1 and the `tracksRowSet` component appears under SessionBean1.

Modify the SQL Queries

When you access these tables from the application, you'll perform a query to select only those rows that have matching foreign keys for the target row deletion in the MUSICCATEGORIES table (for the `recordingsRowSet` object) or the target row deletion in the RECORDINGS table (for the `tracksRowSet` object). Therefore, you'll need to modify the default query for both of these objects to add query criteria. This is the same type of master-detail relationship you built in the MusicRead2 and MusicRead3 projects. Let's modify the `recordingsRowSet's` query first.

1. In the Outline view under SessionBean1, double-click the `recordingsRowSet` object. This brings up the Query Editor.
2. In the spreadsheet view, right-click the MUSICCATEGORYID field and choose Add Query Criteria from the context menu.
3. The Add Query Criteria dialog appears. Select radio button Parameter and leave the Comparison at the default (`= Equals`). Click OK.

   This adds a WHERE clause to the query. Here is the modified query as shown at the bottom of the Query Editor.

```
SELECT ALL MUSIC.RECORDINGS.RECORDINGID,
                    MUSIC.RECORDINGS.RECORDINGTITLE,
                    MUSIC.RECORDINGS.RECORDINGARTISTID,
                    MUSIC.RECORDINGS.MUSICCATEGORYID,
                    MUSIC.RECORDINGS.RECORDINGLABEL,
                    MUSIC.RECORDINGS.FORMAT,
                    MUSIC.RECORDINGS.NUMBEROFTRACKS,
                    MUSIC.RECORDINGS.NOTES
FROM MUSIC.RECORDINGS
WHERE MUSIC.RECORDINGS.MUSICCATEGORYID = ?
```

4. Close the query editor for the `recordingsRowSet` object.
5. In the Outline view under SessionBean1, double-click the `tracksRowSet` object.
6. In the spreadsheet view, right-click the RECORDINGID field and choose Add Query Criteria.
7. In the Add Query Criteria dialog, select radio button Parameter and click OK. Here is the modified query for the `tracksRowSet`.

```
SELECT ALL MUSIC.TRACKS.TRACKID,
                    MUSIC.TRACKS.TRACKNUMBER,
                    MUSIC.TRACKS.TRACKTITLE,
```

```
 MUSIC.TRACKS.TRACKLENGTH,
                    MUSIC.TRACKS.RECORDINGID
FROM MUSIC.TRACKS
WHERE MUSIC.TRACKS.RECORDINGID = ?
```

8. Close the Query Editor for the `tracksRowSet` object and save the changes (select the Save All icon on the toolbar).

Modify Button Event Handler Code

You'll now modify method `delete_action()` to perform the cascading delete operation.

1. From the **Page1.jsp** design canvas, double-click the Delete Selected Rows button. This brings up **Page1.java** in the Java source editor and places the cursor at the `delete_action()` event handler.
2. Find the `while` loop in the `delete_action()` method that begins with the comment "Delete the currently selected rows." Replace the code with the following statements. The added lines are in bold (all the rest of the code is unchanged). Copy and paste from your Creator book's file **FieldGuide2/Examples/Database/snippets/musicDelete_deleteMods.txt.**

```
// Delete the currently selected rows
rowKeys = selectedRows.iterator();
while (rowKeys.hasNext()) {
  RowKey rowKey = (RowKey) rowKeys.next();
  Integer pK = (Integer)
      musiccategoriesDataProvider.getValue(
      "MUSICCATEGORIES.MUSICCATEGORYID",  rowKey);
  log("Removing music category PK = " + pK);
  try {
    cascadeDelete(pK);
    musiccategoriesDataProvider.removeRow(rowKey);
  } catch (Exception e) {
    log("Cannot delete row " + rowKey + ": ",  e);
    error("Cannot delete row " + rowKey + ": " + e);
    ok = false;
  }
}
```

After you add the code for method `cascadeDelete()`, the red underlines will disappear.

Add Method Cascade Delete

Let's discuss the `cascadeDelete()` method before you add it to your project. Its argument is a key, specifically, the MUSICCATEGORYID corresponding to the selected row in the MUSICCATEGORIES table. This method finds the related records in both the RECORDINGS and TRACKS tables.

Creator Tip

Method `cascadeDelete()` *may not be necessary for some database configurations. Check with your database software.*

Method `cascadeDelete()` has a `throws` clause. This allows you to call RowSet object methods without creating a new `try` block. Since the button event handler calls `cascadeDelete()` within its own `try` block, it will catch any thrown exceptions from `cascadeDelete()`. Inside the method, nested `while` loops iterate through the data. The outer `while` loop steps through the recordings data provider and finds the related records in the TRACKS table. The inner `while` loop steps through the tracks data provider.

Here is the code for the `cascadeDelete()` method, which you can place in front of or after the button handler. (Type **<Alt+Shift+F>** to fix imports.) Copy and paste your Creator book's file **FieldGuide2/Examples/Database/snippets/musicDelete_cascade.txt**.

Listing 9.11 Method `cascadeDelete()`

```
private void cascadeDelete(Integer foreignKey)
        throws SQLException
{
  getSessionBean1().getRecordingsRowSet().setObject(
        1, foreignKey);
  recordingsDataProvider.refresh();
  if (!recordingsDataProvider.cursorFirst()) return;
  boolean ok = true;
  do {
    getSessionBean1().getTracksRowSet().setObject(1,
         (Integer)recordingsDataProvider.getValue(
         "RECORDINGS.RECORDINGID"));
    tracksDataProvider.refresh();
```

Listing 9.11 Method `cascadeDelete()` *(continued)*

```
if (tracksDataProvider.cursorFirst()) {
  // delete all tracks with matching RECORDINGID FK
  do  {
    RowKey rowKey = tracksDataProvider.getCursorRow();
    try {
      log("Removing track PK=" +
        tracksDataProvider.getValue(
        "TRACKS.TRACKID",  rowKey));
      tracksDataProvider.removeRow(rowKey);

    } catch (Exception e) {
      log("Cannot delete tracks row " + rowKey
            + ": ", e);
      error("Cannot delete tracks row " + rowKey
            + ": " + e);
      ok = false;
    }
  } while (tracksDataProvider.cursorNext());

  if (ok) {
    try {
      tracksDataProvider.commitChanges();
    } catch (Exception e) {
      log("Cannot commit changes for tracks: ", e);
      error("Cannot commit changes for tracks: " + e);
    }

  } else {
    log("rolling back deletes for tracks");
    info("rolling back deletes for tracks");
    try {
      tracksDataProvider.revertChanges();
    } catch (Exception e) {
      log("Cannot revert changes for tracks: ", e);
      error("Cannot revert changes for tracks: " + e);
    }
  }      // end else
}
```

Listing 9.11 Method `cascadeDelete()` *(continued)*

```
      // delete matching recording
      RowKey rk = recordingsDataProvider.getCursorRow();
      try {
        log("Removing recording PK=" +
            recordingsDataProvider.getValue(
            "RECORDINGS.RECORDINGID",  rk));
        recordingsDataProvider.removeRow(rk);
      } catch (Exception e) {
        log("Cannot delete tracks row " + rk + ": ", e);
        error("Cannot delete tracks row " + rk + ": " + e);
        ok = false;
      }
    } while (recordingsDataProvider.cursorNext());

    if (ok) {
      try {
        recordingsDataProvider.commitChanges();
      } catch (Exception e) {
        log("Cannot commit changes for recordings: ", e);
        error("Cannot commit changes for recordings: " + e);
      }

    } else {
      log("rolling back deletes for recordings");
      info("rolling back deletes for recordings");
      try {
        recordingsDataProvider.revertChanges();
      } catch (Exception e) {
        log("Cannot revert changes for recordings: ", e);
        error("Cannot revert changes for recordings: " + e);
      }
    } // end else
}
```

Deploy and Run

Deploy and run project MusicCascadeDelete. Figure 9–33 shows the application after the user has selected and deleted categories Classical (primary key 1), Country (primary key 5), and Musical Theatre (primary key 6). Because the cascading delete function is implemented, the application also removes the recording whose category is set to Classical (Orff: Carmina Burana). As you test the application, use project MusicBuild to return the Music database to its original state.

Figure 9–33 **MusicCascadeDelete after deleting categories Classical, Country, and Musical Theatre**

9.10 Key Point Summary

- The Java Database Connectivity (JDBC) and JDBC RowSets technology provide a portable way to access a relational database using SQL.
- Creator provides components that allow you to easily connect component behavior with underlying data from a JDBC-compliant database.
- Creator generates code in session scope (by default) to access the data source using JDBC CachedRowSets.
- A JDBC CachedRowSet object is a disconnected rowset that extends a ResultSet object.

- Creator adds a data provider layer between the JDBC CachedRowSets and the data aware components, enabling you to isolate client code from the persistence strategy.
- When you select a data source (a table) from Creator's Servers window, Creator generates code in the Java page bean to manipulate this data through a data provider. It configures the data-aware component, applies converters when necessary, and provides configuration dialogs that allow you to customize the component.
- The Music Collection Database consists of four related tables, as diagrammed in Figure 9–1 on page 375. Relational databases use foreign keys to relate records from one table to records of another table.
- A dropdown list creates a selection menu from a fixed list of choices. You can drop a database table onto the component to obtain the selection choices from a database. Creator builds and configures the data provider and cached row set for you.
- A listbox component creates a fixed list of choices that are all displayed. You can also bind this component to a data provider.
- Selection components (such as dropdown and listbox) let you specify a database field for display and a different database field for its value. This allows meaningful text to be displayed to the user and at the same time the selection is automatically tied to a row's primary key.
- You can add a Creator table component and bind it to a data provider. You can modify which columns are displayed and the embedded component to use with the table (static text is the default). Creator's table component provides a paging mechanism, sort controls, and options for selecting and deselecting rows.
- You can control the data that is returned by invoking the Query Editor.
- You can use the Query Editor to sort the rowset, add a criterion based on a parameter or a fixed value, or create a JOIN by adding additional database tables.
- You use data provider methods to manipulate the underlying data, such as `appendRow()`, `deleteRow()`, `commitChanges()`, `revertChanges()`, and set/get values.
- You can edit and update data in your underlying database when you bind a data table component to a rowset and edit the fields in the component.
- You can insert or delete rows in a database by manipulating the data's RowSet object.
- Database applications that perform delete operations must handle cascading delete situations when the database contains related tables.

ACCESSING WEB SERVICES

Topics in This Chapter

- Google Web Services
- Adding and Testing a Web Service
- Nested Components
- Exceptions and Error Handling
- Message and Message Group Components
- Hyperlink Component
- String Validation
- Table Component and Data Providers
- Saving and Restoring Page Data

Chapter 10

Web services are software APIs that are accessible over a network in a heterogeneous environment. This network accessibility is achieved with a set of XML-based open standards such as the Web Services Description Language (WSDL), the Simple Object Access Protocol (SOAP), and Universal Description, Discovery, and Integration (UDDI). Both web service providers and clients use these standards to define, publish, and access web services.

Creator's default application server provides support for web services. Pre-installed with Creator is a Google Web Service client, which appears in the Servers window under node **Web Services > Samples > GoogleSearch**. The Google Web Service APIs provide a SOAP interface to search Google's index, accessing information and web pages from its cache. With SOAP and WSDL, Google enables clients to access these services in a variety of programming environments (including, of course, Java).

This chapter shows you how to create an application that uses the Google Web Service API. Then, you'll enhance it. After creating a project that uses web services, you'll (hopefully) exclaim, "Is that all?" because the steps are fairly simple. And that's the way technology should be when industry-wide standards are adopted. You'll see that once we drag and drop the web service onto the design canvas in Creator, we spend most of our time showing you elaborate ways to manipulate and display the data that Google returns.

10.1 Google Web Services

We've divided this example into several projects that incrementally build on features of the previous project. With each increment, you'll start with the project you previously built. Alternatively, you can pull up any of the projects from the Creator download and make changes to these projects.

Note

You must register with Google before using their web service. You'll also want to download the Google Web APIs developer's kit since it has additional documentation. Registration is free and painless. Once you register, Google will email you a key, which is required for access to their service. The Google Web Service URL is at `http://www.google.com/apis/`.

Let's look at a summary of the projects you'll be building. In this first version, you'll submit a search query to Google's search service and display just the first result that's returned. This is equivalent to the "I'm Feeling Lucky" submit button on the Google web site. In subsequent versions, you'll add validation for the query text field and display (up to) all ten results returned. Finally, you'll add pagination so that you can obtain and display subsequent groups of results.

Figure 10–1 shows Creator's design canvas with the components you'll add for project **Google1**. The image component holds Google's recognizable logo, a button component initiates the search, and a text field holds the search string. For the results display, static text component `timeCount` displays the search time and results count, the hyperlink component and an embedded static text component display the target URL, and static text component `snippet` displays the URL's "snippet" description. You'll bind these components to the various properties of the result object and you'll nest them inside a grid panel container to more easily manipulate them as a group.

Create a New Project

1. From Creator's Welcome Page, select button Create New Project. From the New Project dialog, under Categories select **Web** and under Projects select **JSF Web Application**. Click Next.
2. In the New Web Application dialog, specify **Google1** for Project Name and click Finish.

After creating the project, Creator comes up in the design view of the editor pane. You can now set the title.

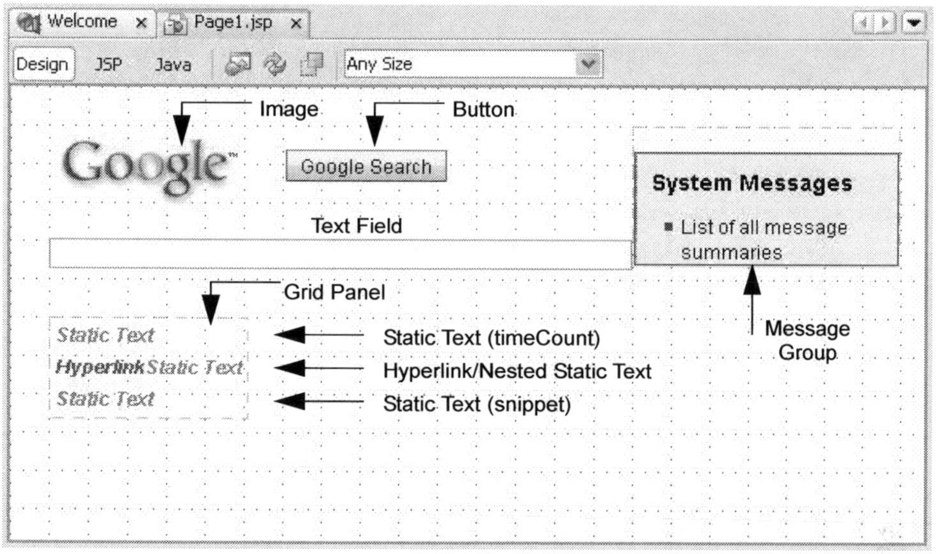

Figure 10–1 **Creator's design canvas view showing project Google1's components**

3. Select `Title` in the Properties window and type in the text **Google Search 1**. Finish by pressing **<Enter>**.

Add the Google Logo

It's a nice touch to include the Google logo when building a web application with Google's search service. To add an image on the page you simply drop the image's file directly on the design canvas.

- Using a file utility program (such as Windows Explorer), drag file **FieldGuide2/Examples/WebServices/images/Logo_40wht.gif** to the Design view and drop it on the canvas (consult Figure 10–1 for positioning).

  This places the Google logo on the page (using the image component) and copies the file into your project's resources directory. You can see this in the Projects window (select **Google1 > Web Pages > resources**).

Add a Text Field Component

You'll need a text field component to obtain the user's search query.

1. In the Basic Components palette, select component Text Field and drag it onto the design canvas. Place it below the Google logo.

2. Make sure it is selected and stretch it so that it's approximately 15 grid units wide.
3. In the Properties window, change its `id` property to **searchString**.
4. To provide a tooltip for this text field, type the text **Type in a search string** followed by **<Enter>** for the `toolTip` property (under Behavior).

Add a Button Component

In this application, a button component initiates a search using Google's Web Service API.

1. In the Basic Components palette, select Button and drag it onto the design canvas. Place it to the right of the Google logo.
2. Make sure the button is still selected. Type in the text **Google Search** followed by **<Enter>**. Creator resizes the button to accommodate the longer text string, which now appears inside the button on the design canvas. This sets the button's `text` property.
3. In the Properties window, change the button's `id` attribute to **search**.
4. To provide a tooltip for the button, edit its `toolTip` property in the Properties window (under Behavior). Type in the text **Search Google for the Search String** followed by **<Enter>**.
5. Align the Google logo with the button. Select the button component in the design canvas. While pressing **<Shift>**, move the mouse to the Google logo and left-click, which simultaneously selects the logo.
6. With both components selected, make sure the mouse is over the logo and right-click. Select option **Align > Middle** from the context menu. The button will move so that it is centered vertically in relation to the logo.

Creator Tip

Creator provides several ways to help you place components on the canvas. By default, components "snap to the grid lines." To adjust components without regard to the grid lines, hold the Shift key as you move the component on the canvas. You can select multiple components using the Shift key while you left-click with the mouse. Then it is possible to move the selected components as a group. Finally, make adjustments between components by selecting them and right-clicking the mouse inside the "anchor" component, as described above. The Align menu selection has several options that you can use to manipulate the selected components.

Add the Google Web Services

Since the Google Web Service client is preinstalled for you, you can simply drag and drop this component to add it to your project.

1. In the Servers window, expand the **Web Services > Samples > Google-Search** nodes.
2. Drag the **doGoogleSearch** node and drop it anywhere on the editor pane. Nothing appears in the design canvas; however, you will see **googleSearchClient1** and **googleSearchDoGoogleSearch1** in the Outline view for Page1, as shown in Figure 10–5 on page 460.

Adding a Web Service to the IDE

The Creator installation process configures the Google web service as well as other web services listed under the **Web Services > Samples** node in the Servers window. Creator also provides a way to *add* a web service to the Services view. For example, here are the steps to load the Google web service client into Creator manually.

Creator Tip

Since the GoogleSearch web service client is included with Creator, you do not need to follow these steps to access it from a Creator project. We include this procedure in case you'd like to add a web service that has not been pre-configured with Creator.

Before you can add a web service, you must provide the location (URL) of its Web Services Description Language (WSDL) page. This is the information that describes the particular web service's API.

We're going to step through the process to add the Google Search to Creator as an example. Once you've determined the Web Service URL, you can use these steps to add any web service.

1. Go to the Servers view.
2. Right-click on Web Services.
3. Select Add Web Service. Creator pops up the Add Web Service dialog.
4. In the URL field at the top, supply the URL of the WSDL file of the target web service. Here is the URL for Google's WSDL file.

```
http://api.google.com/GoogleSearch.wsdl
```

This is the location of the WSDL (Web Services Description Language) file for the Google Search Service.

5. Click Get Web Service Information. The Google web service API appears in the Web Service Information window, as shown in Figure 10–2.

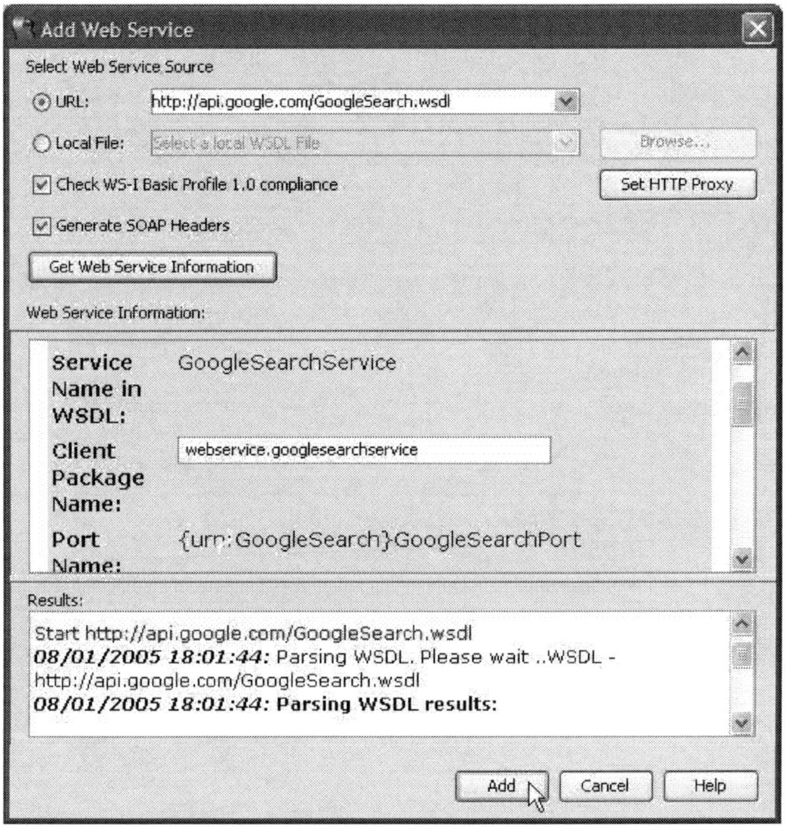

Figure 10–2 **Add Web Service dialog**

6. Scroll through the information in the Web Service Information window. Creator displays detailed information about the web service, including its name, the package name, port name, port display name, port address, and the methods. Information on the methods include the method names, the parameters and their types, and the return type. We'll examine the search method `doGoogleSearch()` in more detail later in this chapter.
7. Click Add. The name GoogleSearch appears under the Web Services node in the Servers window.

Once a web service is listed in the Servers view, you can select it and add it to your Creator project (as you did with GoogleSearch).

Add Search Result Properties to Page1

The trick to easily manipulating the results of the Google search web service is make the return object accessible through the IDE. The search web service returns an object (GoogleSearchResult) that contains information that you'll access. Object GoogleSearchResult also includes an object array (`result-Elements`) that contains specific information on the search result sites. You'll make both of these objects properties, then add an object array data provider to bind to the components on the page.

1. In the Projects window, expand the **Sources Packages > google1** nodes.
2. Right-click on **Page1.java** and select **Add > Property.** Creator pops up the New Property Pattern dialog, as shown in Figure 10–3.

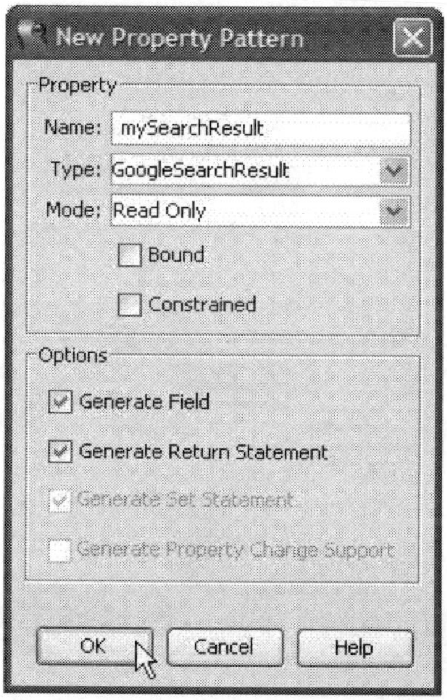

Figure 10–3 **Adding property mySearchResult to Page1.java**

3. For Name, specify **mySearchResult**, for Type, use **GoogleSearchResult**, and for Mode select **Read Only**. Name and Type are case sensitive, so be sure to match the capitalizations. Click OK.

4. Add a second property to Page1. For Name, specify **resultArray**, for Type specify **ResultElement[]**, and for Mode select **Read Only**.

> **Creator Tip**
>
> *Make sure that property* `resultArray` *is* ***NOT*** *an indexed property, but that Type includes the array notation* `[]`.

5. Select the Java label in the editing toolbar to bring up **Page1.java** in the Java source editor.
6. Scroll to the end of the file where you'll see the generated code that added properties `mySearchResult` and `resultArray`. You'll see syntax errors. Fix these using the shortcut **<Alt+Shift+F>** (fix imports), or **<Alt+Shift+I>** (import shortcut). (You must put the cursor anywhere inside **GoogleSearchResult** and **ResultElement[]** before using the **<Alt+Shift+I>** import shortcut.)
7. Add the following initialization statement to the end of method `init()` in **Page1.java**, as shown (the added code is bold). This allows you to control the visibility of the grid panel container component by binding its `rendered` property to whether or not property `mySearchResult` is null.

```
public void init() {
. . .
   super.init();
. . .
   // Creator-managed Component Initialization
. . .
   mySearchResult = null;
}
```

8. Save the project files by clicking the Save All icon on the toolbar.

Add a Data Provider

Using an object array data provider will make the types contained in ResultElement visible through the IDE. This, in turn, will make component binding easy.

1. Select Design in the editing toolbar to return to the design view.
2. Expand the Data Providers node in the Components palette.
3. From the Data Providers Components palette, select Object Array Data Provider and drop it on the design view.You'll see component `objectArrayDataProvider1` in the Page1 Outline view.
4. In the Properties window, change the object array data provider's `id` property to **myResultObject**.

5. Still in the Properties window, select the drop down opposite property `array` and select **resultArray**. This connects the data provider to the array returned in the GoogleSearchObject.

Layout and Grouping with Grid Panel

You'll now add the components that will display the results of the Google Search. Because you want to control these components as a group, you'll use a Grid Panel component as a container for the display components.

1. From the Components palette, expand the Layout node, if necessary.
2. From the Layout Components palette, select Grid Panel and place it on the page below the text field component.
3. In the Properties window under Advanced, *uncheck* property `rendered`. This sets the `rendered` property to `false` and causes the grid panel to disappear from the design view.
4. Select the JSP label in the editing toolbar to bring up **Page1.jsp** in the editor pane.
5. Scroll down to the grid panel tag and locate the `rendered` property. Change its setting from `false` to the following.

```
rendered="#{not empty Page1.mySearchResult}"
```

This means that the grid panel (and all of its sub-components) will be rendered (displayed) if `Page1.mySearchResult` is not empty (`null`).

Creator Tip

By nesting the display components (static text and hyperlink components) inside a grid panel, we can control the rendering of all of these components by specifying the rendered property of the container component (the grid panel).

6. Return to the design view by selecting the Design label in the editing toolbar. The grid panel should reappear on the design canvas.
7. Check the setting for property `rendered`. In the Properties window, locate property `rendered` and hold the mouse pointer over the cell. Creator displays a tooltip with the current setting for this property, as shown in Figure 10–4.

Add a Static Text Component

Next, let's add a static text component to display some of the search results from Google. You'll add this component to the grid panel container.

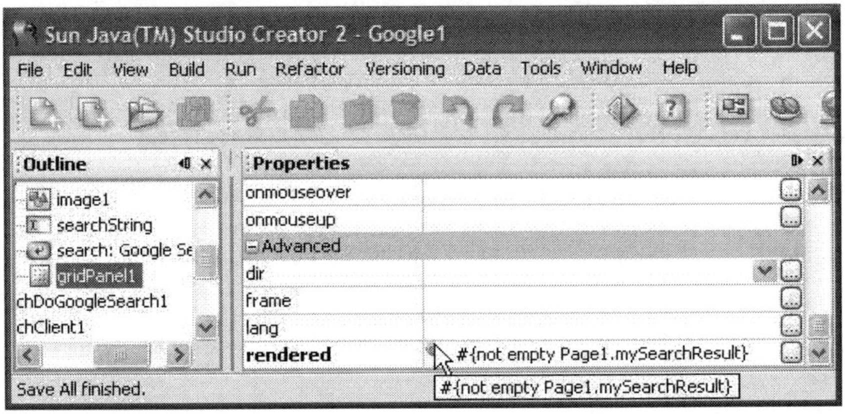

Figure 10–4 **Showing the grid panel's rendered property binding expression**

1. From the Basic Components palette, select Static Text. Place it on top of the grid panel. You can make it a sub-component of grid panel by dropping it on top of the grid panel component in the Outline view, or dropping it on the grid panel in the design view.
2. In the Properties window, change its `id` property to **timeCount**.

The static text component `timeCount` will display the amount of time in seconds that the search request took on Google's server, as well as the estimated number of search results found. Although Google's search returns at most ten results, this number is the estimated total (anywhere from zero to thousands).

Using Hyperlink with a Nested Static Text

The hyperlink component allows application writers to submit a form, navigate to an external URL, or navigate to an anchor within the same page. You'll use it to hold the URL returned in the Google search results. Normally, the `text` property of the hyperlink component is sufficient to display descriptive text for its URL. However, in this situation, the text will contain embedded HTML code supplied by the Google search web service. To correctly render this, use a *nested* static text component and *uncheck* its `escape` property.

1. In the Basic Components palette, select Hyperlink and drop it onto the grid panel in the Page1 Outline view. It should appear nested under the grid panel at the same level as the `timeCount` static text component you already added. The `id` property of this component is `hyperlink1`.
2. In the Basic Components palette, select Static Text and drop it directly on top of the hyperlink component you just added. (You can drop it on top of the

component on the design canvas, or you can drop it on top of the hyperlink displayed in the Page1 Outline view.)

Creator Tip

When you drop it on top of the hyperlink component in the design view, make sure that the hyperlink component is outlined in blue. This is an indication that you have selected it for placement and that the static text component will be nested. If you drop it onto the hyperlink component in the Outline view, the hyperlink component should be selected (white text in a blue background), making the static text component nested.

3. Make sure that the nested static text component is selected. In the Properties window, change its `id` property to **nestedText**.
4. Under Data in the Properties window, *uncheck* the `escape` property. This allows correct rendering of HTML tags embedded within the text.
5. Add another static text component and drop it on top of the grid panel in the Outline view. This second static text component will display the "snippet" returned by the Google search.
6. In the Properties window, change the `id` property to **snippet**.
7. The snippet that Google returns will also contain embedded HTML tags. To display the HTML formatting correctly, *uncheck* the `escape` property in the static text's Properties window.

Add a Message Group to Display Errors

When you access an external web service, there is always a possibility that the access could fail. The server that provides the web service could be inaccessible, the machine that runs the web application could fail, or the access key may be incorrect. In any case, you want to know that the web services call has failed and why.

We'll show you the code that guards against any type of failure later in this section. For now, you'll use a Message Group component to display messages for this web application.

- From the Basic Components palette, select Message Group component and drop it onto the design canvas. Place it to the right of the text field.

  The Message Group component renders messages that are tied to any component, as well as messages generated by the message routines, `info()`, `warn()`, `error()`, and `fatal()`. You can use these routines to report information back to the user from any bean (Java class) that extends class FacesBean.

You've finished adding the components to the page. Compare the components you have placed on the page with those shown in Figure 10–5, the Outline view for Page1.

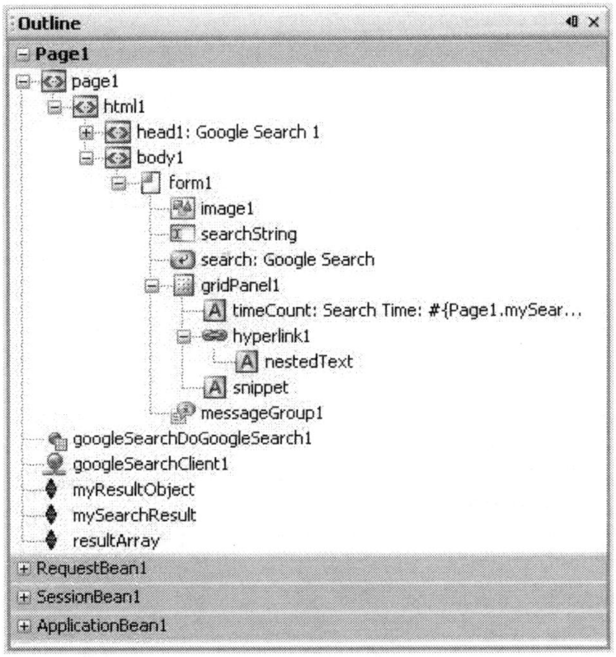

Figure 10–5 **Page1 Outline view of project Google1**

Deploy and Run

Creator Tip

Although you haven't added the calls to the Google Web Service yet, let's build and run the web application anyway. When the application runs, the page is redisplayed when you click the Search Google button (admittedly, not much).

To run the project, click the green arrow in the toolbar or select **Run > Run Main Project** from the main menu. The page should display the Google logo in the upper-left corner, as well as the text field and button. The grid panel and all of its nested components will not be visible since property `mySearchResult` is empty (null). You can type in a test search string, but clicking the button does not (yet) access the Google web service. It does, however, redisplay the page.

Now it's time to look at the methods in the Google web service API.

Inspect the Web Service

The Google web service is already included in your application, so let's use Creator to learn more about it.

When you added the Google web service to your page, Creator modified the Java page bean file (**Page1.java**) to import the Google web service package, as shown here.

```
import webservice.googlesearchservice.googlesearch.
       GoogleSearchClient;
import webservice.googlesearchservice.googlesearch.
       GoogleSearchDoGoogleSearch;
```

In the Navigator window Creator displays the Page1 methods (orange circle icon), the constructor (yellow diamond icon), and private variables (blue rectangle icon). Find the blue rectangle next to variable `googleSearchClient1` and double-click. In the Creator-managed code, you'll see private variable `googleSearchDoGoogleSearch1` defined as follows.

```
private GoogleSearchDoGoogleSearch googleSearchDoGoogleSearch1
         = new GoogleSearchDoGoogleSearch();
```

This is the object that you use to make calls to Google's web service API, as follows.

```
mySearchResult = (GoogleSearchResult)
       googleSearchDoGoogleSearch1.getResultObject();
```

Creator Tip

At this point, you will undoubtedly find Google's documentation to be helpful. A detailed description of the methods and their parameters can be found on the Google Web Site: `http://www.google.com/apis/reference.html`

Table 10.1 contains a list of the parameters for initiating a search with the `googleSearchDoGoogleSearch` object. The search returns a `GoogleSearchResult` object.

Table 10.1 `doGoogleSearch()` **parameters**

Name	*Type*	*Description*
`key`	`String`	Key provided to you by Google. A key is required for access to the Google service.
`q`	`String`	Search query.
`start`	`int`	Zero-based index of the first desired result.
`maxResults`	`int`	Number of results desired per query. This is at most 10.
`filter`	`boolean`	Specifies whether or not you want filtering, which helps eliminate very similar results.
`restricts`	`String`	Limits the search to a subset of the Google Web index.
`safeSearch`	`boolean`	Enables filtering of adult content.
`lr`	`String`	Language Restrict–limits the search to documents with the specified languages.
`ie`	`String`	Input Encoding–deprecated.
`oe`	`String`	Output Encoding–deprecated.

Table 10.2 contains some of the methods for return object `GoogleSearch-Result`. Note that these methods are the getter form of JavaBeans object properties. Therefore you can call the getter method, or access the property using a JSF EL expression, such as the following.

```
#{Page1.mySearchResult.startIndex}
```

which evaluates to the starting index of the returned results.

Table 10.2 `GoogleSearchResult` **public methods**

Name	*Return Type*	*Description*
`getDirectoryCategories`	`Array`	Array of the Directory Category items corresponding to the ODP[a] directory matches for this search.
`getEndIndex`	`int`	Index (1-based) of the last search result in the `ResultElements` array.
`getEstimatedTotalResultsCount`	`int`	Estimates of the total number of results for the query.
`getResultElements`	`ResultElement[]`	Array containing the results.
`getSearchComments`	`String`	Search comments.
`getSearchQuery`	`String`	Search query you provided.
`getSearchTime`	`double`	Time it took the Google server to compute the results.
`getSearchTips`	`String`	Tips for searching.
`getStartIndex`	`int`	Index (1-based) of the first search result in the `ResultElements` array.
`isDocmentFiltering`	`boolean`	True if document filtering is enabled.
`isEstimateIsExact`	`boolean`	True if the total results estimate is exact.

a. "The **Open Directory Project** is the largest, most comprehensive human-edited directory of the Web. It is constructed and maintained by a vast, global community of volunteer editors." (See About the Open Directory Project, `http://dmoz.org`.)

Finally, each response includes an array of `ResultElement` objects. Some of the methods you use to access a `ResultElement` object are listed in Table 10.3.

Table 10.3 ResultElement public methods

Name	*Return Type*	*Description*
`getCachedSize`	`String`	Size of the cached document.
`getDirectoryCategory`	`DirectoryCategory`	Name of the ODP category in which the result occurs.
`getDirectoryTitle`	`String`	Name of the result as it appears in the Open Directory.
`getHostName`	`String`	Hostname of the result.
`getSnippet`	`String`	Short description of the result page.
`getSummary`	`String`	Description of the result as it appears in the Open Directory.
`getTitle`	`String`	Page title of the result.
`getURL`	`String`	URL of the result page.
`isRelatedInformationPresent`	`boolean`	True if there are related documents to this result.

Testing the Google Web Service

Creator provides a web services testing mechanism. This is a quick way to study the method, provide parameters, and look at the results. Here's how.

1. In the Servers window under **Web Services > Samples > GoogleSearch**, right-click method `doGoogleSearch()` and select **Test Method**. Creator pops up the Test Web Service Method dialog.
2. Fill in the dialog as shown in Figure 10–6. For `key`, provide your key (sent to you by Google after you register at their web site), for `q`, provide a query string (we used "I M Pei Louvre"), and for `maxResults`, use **1**. You can use default values for all of the other parameters.
3. Click Submit. A successful test displays the results in the Results window. Expand **GoogleSearchResult > ResultElement[] > ResultElement** to see the results.
4. Click Close to finish.

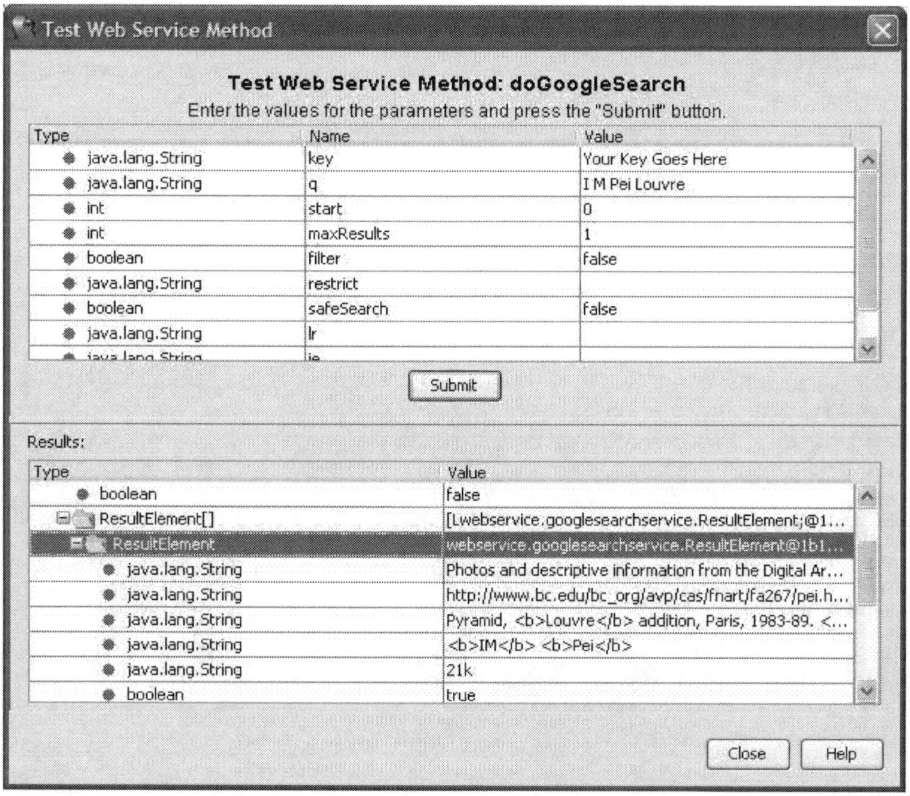

Figure 10–6 **Testing Web Service Method doGoogleSearch**

Configure Web Service Call

Instead of supplying method parameters in the event handling code, you can configure the web service through the Properties window, as follows.

1. Select **googleSearchDoGoogleSearch1** in the Page1 Outline view.
2. In the Properties window, the method's arguments are all listed under the General heading. For property `key`, provide your key (the one Google sent to you) and for `maxResults`, use **10**. These are the only properties that you need to set.

Creator Tip

Make sure you include your Google Web API's License Key for property `key`. *Otherwise, your application will return an exception. You'll configure the search query (property* `q`*) later.*

Add Event Handling Code for Button

You'll now add the Java code to access Google's search method. You'll put the code in the action method associated with the Google Search button on the page.

1. Make sure the Page1 design view is active in the editor pane.
2. Double-click the Google Search button. Creator generates default code for the button's action method, `search_action()` and brings up **Page1.java** in the Java source editor.
3. Add the following code to the `search_action()` method. From your Creator book download, copy and paste the file **FieldGuide2/Examples/WebServices/snippets/google1_search.txt** into the `search_action()` event handler. The added code is bold.

Listing 10.1 Method `search_action()`

```
public String search_action() {
  try {

    mySearchResult = (GoogleSearchResult)
      googleSearchDoGoogleSearch1.getResultObject();
    resultArray = mySearchResult.getResultElements();
    myResultObject.setArray(
      (java.lang.Object[])getValue("#{Page1.resultArray}"));

  } catch (Exception e) {
    log("Remote Connect Failure: ", e);
    mySearchResult = null;
    error("Remote Site Failure: " + e.getMessage());
  }
  return null;
}
```

Handling Exceptions and Error Messages

Let's examine the search button's action event code.

Because method `doGoogleSearch()` (which you invoke through the client `googleSearchDoGoogleSearch1`) throws `RemoteException`, you should include its call inside a `try` block. In this case, the accompanying catch handler will catch *any* exception, including `RemoteException`. The catch handler performs several tasks. First, it logs the error with the application server's log. You can view the log by selecting **Deployment Server** in the Servers window. Right-click and select **View Server Log**. Creator displays the log in the Output window (by default this is below the editor pane) under the tab for the application server host machine and port (ours is **localhost:24848**).

The next line sets the Page1 property `mySearchResult` to null. Recall that you bound the `rendered` property of the grid panel to whether or not this property is empty. Since there is nothing to display when an exception occurs, it makes sense to make sure the screen is not cluttered with a previous call's results.

The last line of the catch handler is a call to method `error()`. Method `error()` posts a message to the FacesContext. This message is not associated with a particular component, but is a generic user message. Generic messages will be displayed by a message group component if there is one on the page. (This is why you placed a message group component on the page.) Along with method `error()`, Creator provides methods `info()`, `warn()`, and `fatal()` for reporting messages back to the user. These message reporting methods render differently on the page, depending on their severity level.

If the call to `googleSearchDoGoogleSearch1` succeeds, you store the results in variable `mySearchResult` (a property), making the results accessible to the rest of the web application. You also set property `resultArray` and the data provider's `array` property. In the next section, you'll bind the components using these Page1 components.

Specify Binding for the Display Components

The static text and hyperlink components that you nested inside the grid panel display portions of the result returned from the call to Google's search method. Instead of setting these components' properties inside the event handler, you can specify the bindings through the Properties window. Let's provide the bindings now. (You may want to refer to Table 10.3 on page 464, which lists the properties for the returned result object.)

Design Note

Because taking small steps is always better than attempting a giant leap, let's display only the first result on your web page. In a later section, we'll have you display all of the returned results (a maximum of ten).

---

1. Click the Design label in the editing toolbar to return to the design view.
2. Select the static text component `timeCount`. In the Properties window for property `text`, type in the following binding expression. (Note that this expression combines literal text with expressions.) Type in the complete text on a single line and finish with **<Enter>**. The text will appear on the design canvas.

```
Search Time: #{Page1.mySearchResult.searchTime}; Approx.
Results: #{Page1.mySearchResult.estimatedTotalResultsCount}
```

This will display the search time and the estimated total number of results returned from the search.

Creator Tip

If you hold the mouse over the text property in the Properties window, the value is displayed in a tooltip. Use this to check that you entered the expressions and literal text correctly.

Now you'll bind the display components to the object array data provider, `myResultObject`.

1. Select the hyperlink component (use the Outline view). In the Properties window, select the editing box opposite property `text`. Creator pops up a property customizer. Click button Unset Property to remove the default text, Hyperlink.
2. The hyperlink component holds the URL property of the result returned from the Google search. In the Properties window, select the editing box opposite property `url`. Creator displays the `url` property customizer.
3. Select radio button **Use binding** and tab **Bind to Data Provider**. Make sure that data provider **myResultObject** is selected, as shown in Figure 10–7. Select property **URL** in the Data field window. Click OK.

   Creator generates the following binding expression for the hyperlink's `url` property.

```
#{Page1.myResultObject.value['URL']}
```

4. Select the nested static text component `nestedText`. This component will display the title of the returned search result. In the Properties window for property `text`, click the editing box to bring up the `text` property customer.

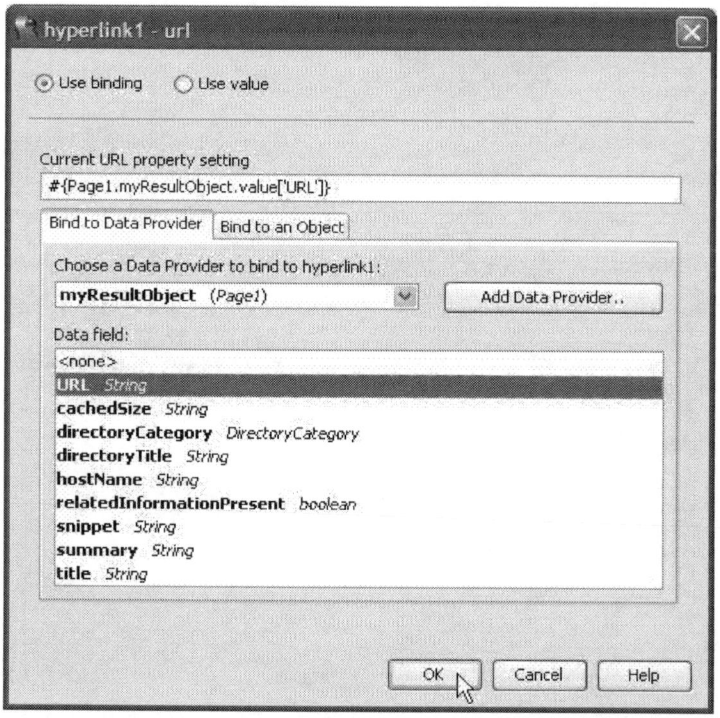

Figure 10–7 **Bind url property to the object array data provider myResultObject**

5. Select radio button **Use binding**, tab **Bind to Data Provider**, Data Provider **myResultObject**, and Data field **title**. Select OK. Creator generates the following expression.

```
#{Page1.myResultObject.value['title']}
```

6. Make sure that the `escape` property for this static text component is *unchecked* (set to false). This allows the embedded HTML elements that Google supplies to be rendered correctly on the page.
7. Select the static text component `snippet`. This components displays a short description of the returned URL. In the Properties window, bring up the customizer for property `text`.
8. Select radio button **Use binding**, tab **Bind to Data Provider**, Data Provider **myResultObject**, and Data field **snippet**. Select OK. Creator generates the following expression.

```
#{Page1.myResultObject.value['snippet']}
```

9. Make sure that the `escape` property for this static text component is also *unchecked* (set to false).

Finally, you'll bind the text field `searchString` to the query parameter q in the `googleSearchDoGoogleSearch1` object.

1. In the Design view, select text field component `searchString`. In the Properties window, bring up the customizer for property `text`.
2. Select radio button **Use binding** and tab **Bind to an Object**.
3. In the **Select binding target** window, expand **googleSearchDoGoogleSearch1** node and select property **q**, as shown in Figure 10–8. Click OK.

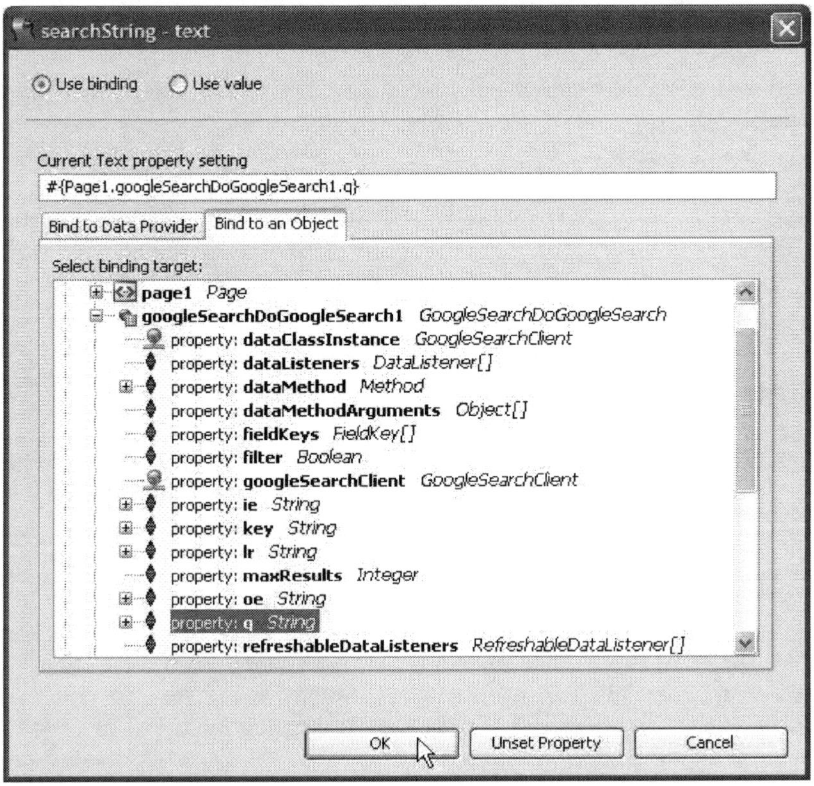

Figure 10–8 **Bind searchString text property to property q (query)**

Deploy and Run

You're ready to test this initial version of the Google search web application.

- From the main menu bar, select **Run > Run Main Project** or select the green arrow on the icon bar. You can test the Google Search API by typing in various search queries. Click on the URL (displayed as the title) and go to that web page. Figure 10–9 shows a screen shot of the application.

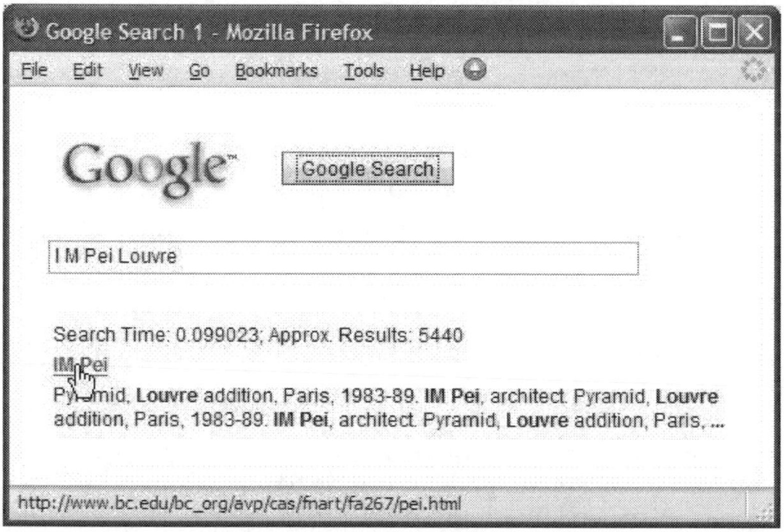

Figure 10–9 **First version of the Google Web Search application**

10.2 Validation - Project Google2

You have created a simple web application that uses a published web service. Now you're going to build on this example and enhance it in the following ways.

- Provide validation for the text field component and require that the user provide something. That is, you want to prevent a zero-length string and require a minimum length for the search string (three characters).
- Place a message component on the page to report validation errors associated with the text field component.
- Configure the message group component so that it displays global messages only.

Copy the Project

To avoid starting from scratch, make a copy of the Google1 project. This step is optional. If you don't want to copy the project, simply skip this section and continue making modifications to Google1.

1. Bring up project Google1 in Creator, if it's not already opened.
2. From the Projects window, right-click node Google1 and select Save Project As. Provide the new name **Google2**.
3. Close project Google1. Right-click Google2 and select Set Main Project. You'll make changes to the Google2 project.
4. Expand **Google2 > Web Pages** and open **Page1.jsp** in the design view.
5. Click anywhere in the background of the design canvas of the Google2 project. In the Properties window, change the page's `Title` property to **Google Search 2**.

Add a Validator

It's always a good idea to validate user input. Included in the components palette are a set of validators to help with this task. With text strings, two validators are of interest. First, a length validator can control a String's length. You can specify a maximum and a minimum for the number of characters input. Interestingly enough, if you want to prevent a zero-length string, you cannot use the length validator (and set the minimum to 1). Instead, you must use the component's *required* property. The `required` property is set in the Properties window for each text field component. If you check it (set it to true) and the component's value is a String, then its length must be greater than zero.

Validation in this application is important for two reasons. First, the web application developer has better control over user input and can give feedback to increase program usability. Secondly, by requiring valid input at the application's server site, you prevent access to Google's web site with an invalid search request.

For this example, let's prevent a zero-length string and set a length minimum of three characters and a maximum of 2,048 characters (this is the maximum search query allowed by Google).

Creator Tip

For testing, you'll set the length minimum to 3 and its maximum to 25. Coupled with the required validator, you should get the following behavior. If the user leaves the text field empty, you'll get a message from the required validator saying that a value is required. If you type in a 1- or 2-character text value, you'll get feedback from the length validator saying that it was less than the minimum of 3. Likewise, if you type in more than 25 characters, the length validator will complain that the string was more than the maximum. Note that a zero-length string does not trigger the length validator even if the minimum is set to 1. You must use the required property of the component!

Let's add validation to the application now.

1. Make sure Page1 is active in the design canvas.
2. Select the text field component, `searchString`.
3. In the Properties window, click the checkbox for the `required` attribute. This means the text field component cannot be empty.
4. From the Components palette, expand the Validators node, select Length Validator, and drop it on top of the `searchString` text field component. Creator sets the `validator` attribute for `searchString` to `lengthValidator1`. Component `lengthValidator1` appears in the Page1 Outline view.

   You've instantiated a length validator for the text field component. Now you have to give it length boundaries: the minimum and maximum allowable.

5. Select `lengthValidator1` in the Outline view. In its corresponding Properties window, change attribute `maximum` to **25** and `minimum` to **3**.

These values are probably not the limits you'd want to use in your production application, but they're good values for testing. Once you're convinced that the application is working the way you want, set the maximum to 2048, which is the maximum imposed by Google. The advantage of using the validator instead of letting Google complain is that you save a trip to the Google server.

Note also that the private `_init()` method in the Java page bean has been modified to include the minimum and maximum settings you defined in the Properties window, as follows. (Unfold the Creator-managed Component Definition block to see the `_init()` method.)

```
lengthValidator1.setMaximum(25);
lengthValidator1.setMinimum(3);
```

Add a Message Component

You've already placed a message group component on the page. And, if you run the web application now, the message group component will display error messages detected during validation. However, the look of the message group component is not really what you want, since validation messages aren't really "System Messages." For validation error reporting, use the message component. Like the message group component, the message component retrieves messages from the JSF context. The difference is that the message component is associated with a single component. That way, the web application designer can control exactly where on the page the error message for a specific input component appears. This is particularly useful for pages that contain many input components (such as a form that submits a whole page of personal information). Thus, when the validator sends an error message to the JSF context, it identifies the component whose input is marked invalid. A message component tied to this input component will pick up the error message and display it on the page.

1. Return to the Design view.
2. From the Basic Components palette, select Message component and drop it onto the design canvas. Place it in between the text field and the grid panel.
3. When you place the message component on the canvas, you can associate it with the text field using the mouse. Press and hold **<Ctrl+Shift>**, left-click the mouse, and drag the cursor to the `searchString` text field. This sets the message component's `for` property. In the design view, the message component now displays the text **Message summary for searchString**.

Message and Message Group Components

Go ahead and run the web application (select **Run > Run Main Project** from the main menu). Either leave the input field blank or type in less than three characters and press the Google Search button. You'll see that the application displays the error message twice: both the message component (which is tied to the text field) and the message group component (which displays all messages) display the validation error.

By default, a message group component displays all messages associated with a page, both messages tied to a specific component (such as the validation error message you just saw) and system messages (such as a problem with your Google authorization key). But when you also use message components specific to an input component, it's better to restrict a message group component to display global messages only. Global messages are those that are not tied to a specific component.

1. Make sure that Page1 is active in the design view.

2. Select the message group component.
3. In the Properties window, check property `showGlobalOnly` (set it to true). The message group component now displays the text "List of global message summaries."
4. Rerun the application and check its behavior for reporting validation errors as well as system errors. To simulate a system error, temporarily disconnect your test machine from the internet or use an incorrect access key. The Google web services call will fail. Figure 10–10 shows the application running with a validation error message (from the length validator).

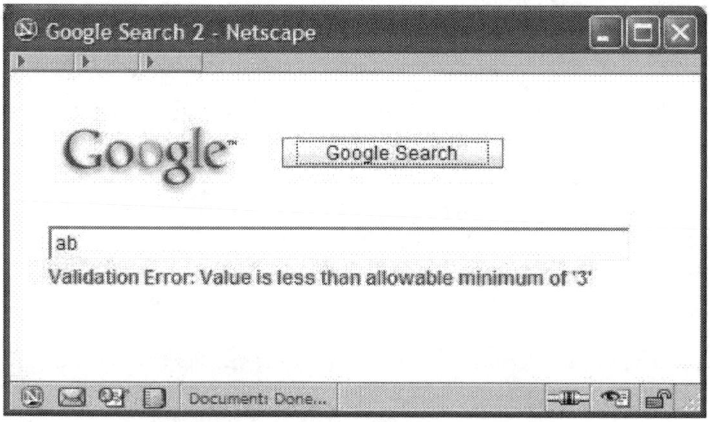

Figure 10–10 **Google Web Search with input validation**

Creator Tip

During testing, note that when you complete a successful search and follow this with invalid input, the previous results are cleared from the page. You get this behavior because you reset property `mySearchResult` *to null during the Page1 method* `init()`. *JSF calls method* `init()` *with each page access, assuring that the page will only render results from a new, valid call to* `doGoogleSearch()` *method.*

10.3 Displaying Multiple Result Elements

The previous version of the application displays only the first result element returned from a Google search. Most of the time, the Google search returns an array of ten results. You get the first ten results of the query if parameter `start` is set to zero and `maxResults` is set to 10. To get the next set of ten results, set `start` to 10 (instead of 0). For the third set of ten results, set `start` to 20, and so on.

Google returns the total result count with method `getEstimatedTotalResultsCount()`; you can easily determine the number of results returned by getting the `length` attribute of the ResultElement array. This will be at most ten. Furthermore, Google imposes a 1,000 count limit, so even if the query returns 30,000 hits, Google will give you at most 1,000 (in ten-count page increments).

In this version of our Google search application, you're going to display all (up to ten) elements of the ResultElement array (that is, the first *page*). You'll use Creator's Table component and the object array data provider you already configured.

Our approach is not so different from the project you just built: you use a hyperlink component to hold the ResultElement's URL, a nested static text holds the result's title, and a second static text component holds the result's snippet. To make sure that the snippet information starts on its own line in the table, you'll use a static text component to hold the HTML `<br/>` tag, which forces a line break in the table cell.

Here are the enhancements that you're going to make to this project.

- Use a Table component to format and display the results from a Google search web service call.
- Use an Object Array Data Provider (component `myResultObject`) to map the `ResultElements[]` array into the table component.
- Specify binding expressions for the table title, column title, as well as each component that you'll add to the table column.

Copy the Project

To avoid starting from scratch, make a copy of the Google2 project. This step is optional. If you don't want to copy the project, simply skip this section and continue making modifications to Google2.

1. Bring up project Google2 in Creator, if it's not already opened.
2. From the Projects window, right-click node Google2 and select Save Project As. Provide the new name **Google3**.
3. Close project Google2. Right-click Google3 and select Set Main Project. You'll make changes to the Google3 project.
4. Expand **Google3 > Web Pages** and open **Page1.jsp** in the design view.
5. Click anywhere in the background of the design canvas of the Google3 project. In the Properties window, change the page's `Title` property to **Google Search 3**.

Add a Table Component

The table component is a convenient way to present tabular data, such as an array of objects. You'll be using a single column (to mimic the display you see from Google's web site). In each cell, you'll display the result web site's title followed by the snippet. The title is the text for the hyperlink to the result's site.

1. Make sure that Page1 is active in the design view. Close the Output window to give yourself more room to work in the design editor.
2. From the Basic Components palette, select Table and drag it to the canvas. Place it below the grid panel component that's already on the page. (You'll delete the grid panel component later. For now, leave it on the page.) You'll see a default table rendered on the design canvas and the default table data provider, `defaultTableDataProvider1`, appears in the Outline view.
3. When you place the table component on the canvas, the table's title is selected so that you can provide your own title.
4. Type in the following text to set the title.

```
Search Results (#{Page1.mySearchResult.startIndex} to
  #{Page1.mySearchResult.endIndex})
```

   Type the text all on a single line and finish with **<Enter>**. The title text will appear in the table's title area.

Configure the Table

When you place the table component on the page, creator configures it with a default data provider. You'll use the object array data provider you configured earlier instead.

1. Select the table component, right-click, and choose Table Layout from the context menu.
2. In the drop down menu for Get Data From, choose **myResultObject**. Creator displays the data fields in the Selected window.
3. Use the < (left arrow) to remove all fields except URL, snippet, and title. Click Apply.
4. Select column URL and change the component type to Hyperlink. Click Apply and OK to close the dialog.

Creator binds each of these columns to the URL, snippet, and title fields of the data provider for you. You'll need a bit more customizing to get a look that's similar to the page the Google web site builds. Look at the Page1 Outline view. You'll see the table component (`table1`), a nested table row group, and three table column components with headings URL, snippet, and title. You'll now rearrange these components a bit.

1. From the Page1 Outline view, select the static text component under the column entitled **title** and drop it on top of the hyperlink component under the **URL** column. (This should nest component `staticText3` under component `hyperlink2`.)
2. In the Properties window for `staticText3`, change its `id` property to **nestedText** and *uncheck* its `escape` property.
3. In the Properties window, hold the cursor over the `text` property and verify that its binding is set to the following.

```
#{currentRow.value['title']}
```

4. Now select the hyperlink component (`hyperlink2`). In the Properties window, set property `url` to the following. (By default, Creator binds the `text` property instead.)

```
#{currentRow.value['url']}
```

5. In the Properties window for the hyperlink component, select the editing box opposite property `text` to bring up the property customizer and select **Unset Property**.
6. From the Basic Components palette, select Static Text and drop it on component `tableColumn1` in the Page1 Outline view. The static text should appear at the same level as the hyperlink component.
7. In the Properties window, *uncheck* its escape property and set its `text` property to **
**. (This will provide a line break in the table cell and improve the formatting.)
8. From the Page1 Outline view, select the static text component under the column entitled **snippet** and drop it on top of component `tableColumn1`.
9. In the Properties window, change its `id` property to **snippet** and *uncheck* its `escape` property. Now hold the cursor over the `text` property and verify that its binding is set to the following.

```
#{currentRow.value['snippet']}
```

You'll now make final configuration changes to the table component.

1. In the Page1 Outline view, remove components `tableColumn2` and `tableColumn3` (there shouldn't be any nested components in these unused columns).
2. Select the table component. In the Properties view, set property `width` to **500**.

3. In the Page1 Outline view, select static text component `timeCount` and bring up the property customizer for property `text`. Copy it using **<Ctrl+C>** and click OK.
4. Now select component `tableColumn1` and bring up the property customizer for property `headerText`. Paste (use **<Ctrl+V>**) the value from `timeCount`'s `text` property. Click OK. The column's header shows the new value.
5. Select the table component. In the Properties view, *uncheck* property rendered. The table disappears from the design view.
6. Click button JSP to bring the the JSP source editor.
7. Change the table's `rendered` property to the following. (You might want to copy and paste from the grid panel's `rendered` property.)

```
#{not empty Page1.mySearchResult}
```

8. Return to the design view. Delete the grid panel component (and all of its nested components).
9. Move the table component up so that it is directly underneath the message component, as shown in Figure 10–11.

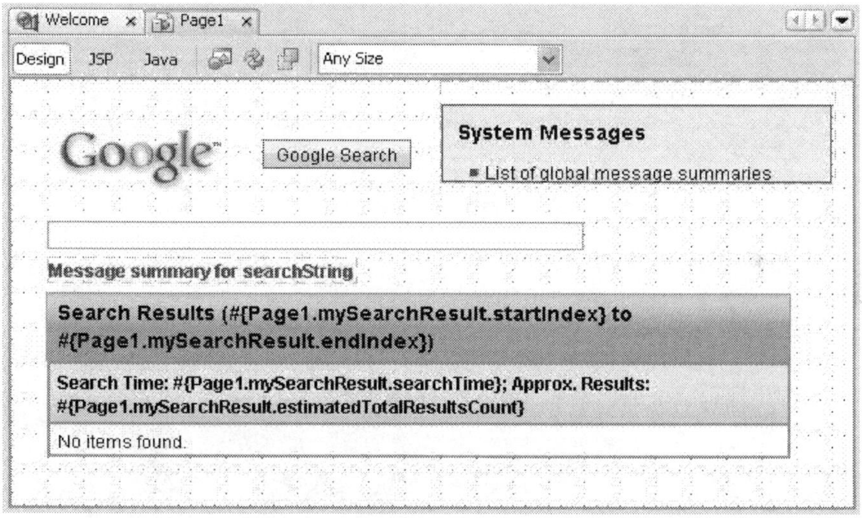

Figure 10–11 **Google Search application using Data Provider and Table components**

Deploy and Run

- Deploy and run the **Google** application. Depending on the input you provide for the search query, you should see up to ten results displayed on the page. Figure 10–12 shows an example screen shot.

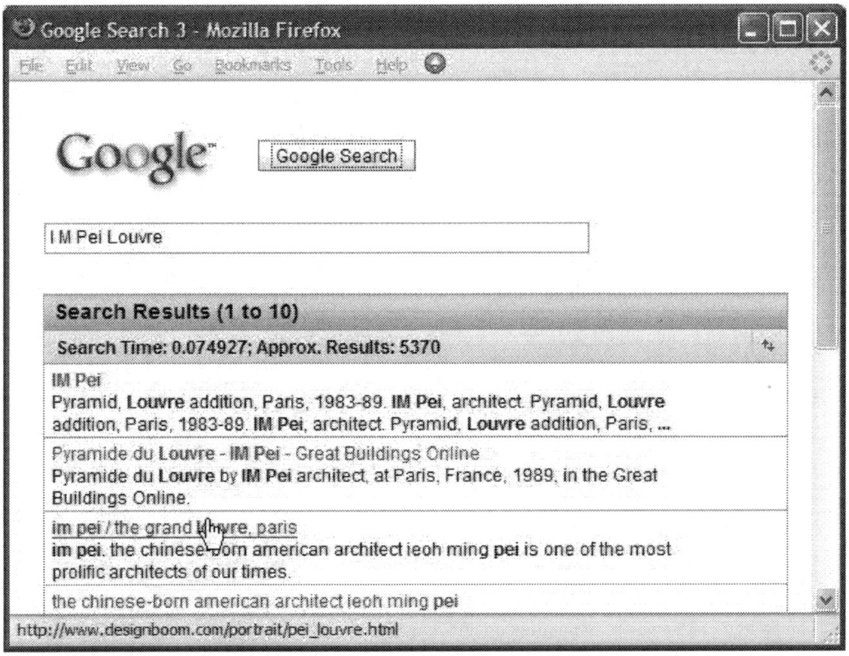

Figure 10–12 **Google Web Search application using HTML to build a results table**

10.4 Displaying Multiple Pages

Each Google request displays up to ten results. It's time to add controls that move forward to retrieve additional results or move backward to display earlier results. You've seen how to use a button component to initiate an action. Now you'll use two image hyperlink components. The images will be forward and backward pointing arrows. Since a hyperlink component is a command component, you can configure an action method that will be invoked when the hyperlink (that is, the arrow image) is clicked.

The image files you'll use are in your Creator book's **FieldGuide2** download bundle (**FieldGuide2/Examples/WebServices/images**), but if you'd like to use arrow graphics of your own, simply substitute the appropriate **.gif** or **.jpg** file.

The modifications for this project include adding two new image hyperlink components and image files for their display. You'll also install action event methods for the hyperlink components to page forward or backward through the Google search results. These additions are straightforward. What's a bit tricky is that you have to keep track of some of the parameters across page requests when you call Google. That means you can't use local variables with request scope inside **Page1.java**, since the Page1 bean is instantiated with each page request. Therefore, you'll need to save and restore these control variables in session scope using the Page1 methods `destroy()` and `init()`. (Ironically, `destroy()` refers to the *destruction* of Page1 but is used to *save session state* before said destruction. To review the different types of scope for web application objects, see "Scope of Web Applications" on page 224.)

Although Creator's table component has sophisticated paging controls, these are used to page through a large data set. In this application, the maximum array size is ten. In order to access the subsequent results, you must submit a new call to the Google web service search method with a different starting index and obtain a new result array.

Copy the Project

To avoid starting from scratch, make a copy of the Google3 project. This step is optional. If you don't want to copy the project, simply skip this section and continue making modifications to Google3.

1. Bring up project Google3 in Creator, if it's not already opened.
2. From the Projects window, right-click node Google3 and select Save Project As. Provide the new name **Google4**.
3. Close project Google3. Right-click Google4 and select Set Main Project. You'll make changes to the Google4 project.
4. Expand **Google4 > Web Pages** and open **Page1.jsp** in the design view.
5. Click anywhere in the background of the design canvas of the Google4 project. In the Properties window, change the page's `Title` property to **Google Search 4**.

Add an Image Hyperlink Component

Before you add components to project **Google4**, look at Figure 10–13, the design canvas for this project. You can see the placement of the image hyperlink components (the two arrows).

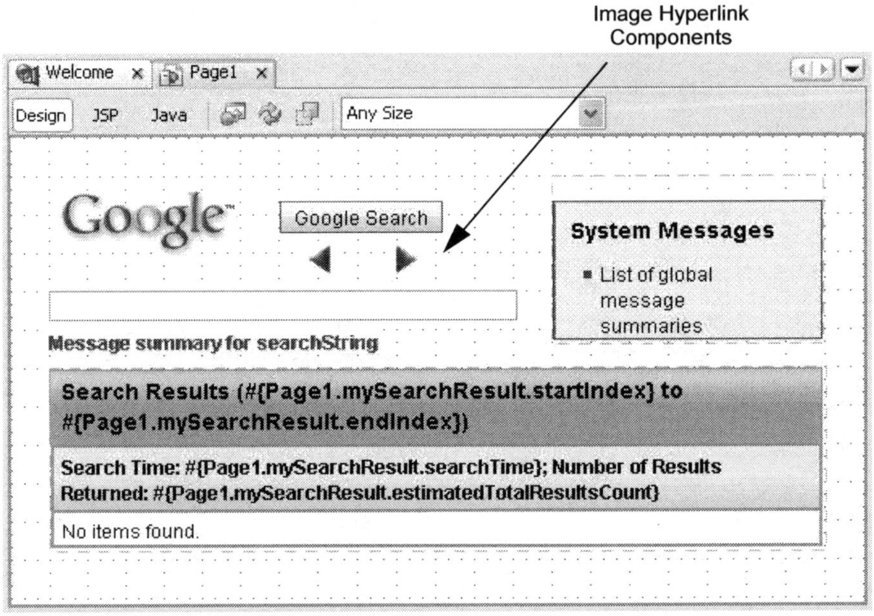

Figure 10–13 **Design canvas showing component layout for project Google4**

1. From the Basic Components palette, select Image Hyperlink and drop it onto the design canvas under the Google Search button.
2. In the Properties window, change its `id` property to **previous**.

Creator Tip

You're changing the standard `id` *that Creator uses because it's easier to keep track of the components in the Java page bean file. By using meaningful* `id` *names (such as* `previous` *and* `next`*), the associated action methods that Creator generates will have meaningful names, too.*

3. In the Properties window under Behavior, set property `toolTip` to **View the previous set of results.**
4. Make sure that the image hyperlink component is selected, right-click, and select Set Image from the context menu. Creator pops up an Image Customizer dialog that allows you to specify the URL, File, or Theme Icon for the image.
5. In the dialog, select radio button Choose File, browse to the Creator book download, and specify directory **FieldGuide2/Examples/WebServices/images** for the field labeled "Look in:", as shown in Figure 10–14.

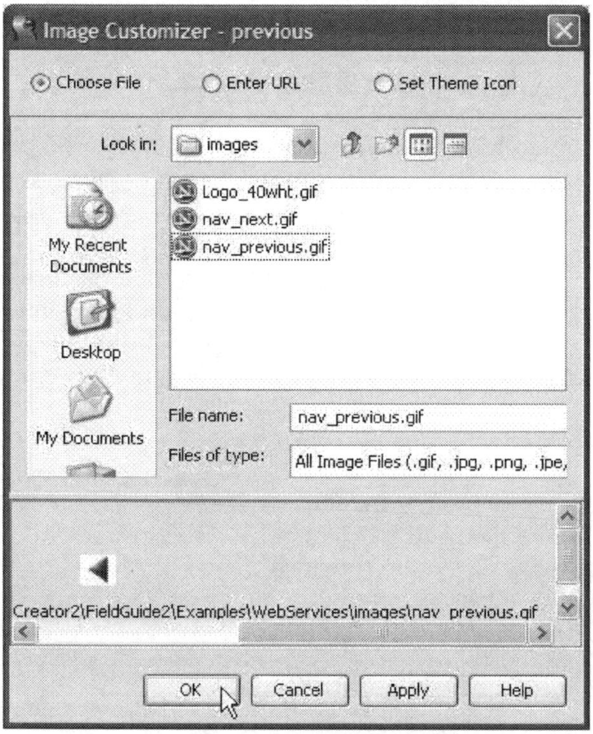

Figure 10–14 **Image Customizer dialog for image component**

6. Select file **nav_previous.gif**. Click Apply. Creator displays the arrow in the dialog's Preview window and the image appears on the design canvas.
7. Click OK. Creator copies the image file to the project's **Web Pages > resources** directory.
8. In the Properties window for the image hyperlink, click the editing box opposite property `text` and select **Unset Property** in the customizer dialog.

A Second Image Hyperlink Component

Follow the same procedure to add a second image hyperlink component and a second image to the page.

1. From the Basic Components palette, select Image Hyperlink and drop it onto the design canvas under the Google Search button.
2. In the Properties window, change its `id` property to **next**.
3. In the Properties window under Behavior, set property `toolTip` to **View the next set of results**.

4. Make sure that the image hyperlink component is selected, right-click, and select Set Image from the context menu.
5. In the dialog, select radio button Choose File, browse to the Creator book download, and specify directory **FieldGuide2/Examples/WebServices/images** for the field labeled "Look in:". Select file **nav_next.gif**. Click OK. Creator copies the image file to the resources folder and the right-arrow image should now appear on the design canvas.
6. In the Properties window for the image hyperlink, click the editing box opposite property `text` and select **Unset Property** in the customizer dialog.
7. Adjust the image hyperlink components so that they're aligned vertically to each other. Select the hyperlink component `next`, press and hold the Shift key, and then select the hyperlink component `previous`. With both components selected, right-click and select **Align > Middle** from the context menu.

Deploy and Run

You might want to experiment with the placement of these newly added graphic components. Right-click and select Preview in Browser. Check the placement of the components and adjust them if necessary. Now deploy and run project **Google4**. (The arrow buttons won't do anything useful, but you should be able to display the ten results as before.)

Creator Tip

The arrow buttons erase the table (why?). To see the search results again, click the Google Search button. The table is cleared because clicking an arrow button generates an action event, which initiates the JSF page life cycle process. You haven't specified any action, but the system proceeds through the different life cycle phases anyway. When JSF instantiates the Page1 page bean, it invokes `Page.init()`*, which sets* `mySearchResult` *to* `null` *and the table component is not rendered.*

Add SessionBean1 Properties

You will soon add control variables to the **Page1.java** file. These values keep track of the current index and other controls you need for displaying more than the first page of results. To maintain these values across page requests, you add them to the SessionBean1 managed bean as *properties*. This automatically puts them in session scope. The following properties are all type Integer and mode Read/Write:

- `startIndex` - index of the first result (parameter `start`)
- `currentCount` - length of the `ResultElements[]` array

- `totalCount` - estimated total number of results for the query; used to test end conditions

  Here are the steps to add properties to SessionBean1.

1. From the Projects window, select **Session Bean**, right-click and select **Add > Property**.
2. Creator pops up the New Property Pattern dialog.
3. For Name, specify **startIndex**, for Type, specify **Integer**, and for Mode, select the default **Read/Write**. Click OK.
4. Repeat these steps for **currentCount** and **totalCount**. Specify Type **Integer** and Mode **Read/Write** for both.
5. In the Projects window, double-click node **Session Bean**. This brings up file **SessionBean1.java** in the Java source editor.
6. Add the following code to the end of method `init()` to initialize the three properties. Copy and paste from file **FieldGuide2/Examples/WebServices/snippets/google4_session_init.txt**. The added code is bold.

```
public void init() {
. . .
   startIndex = new Integer(0);
   currentCount = new Integer(0);
   totalCount = new Integer(0);
}
```

Specify the Action Code

When a user clicks the right-arrow hyperlink, the web application should display the next ten results from the Google search. Conversely, clicking the left-arrow hyperlink displays the previous ten results. Because you'll make similar calls to the Google search API, you should place this code in its own method. Once you determine the correct start index, you can call this method from the action event handlers for the search button and from both hyperlinks.

1. To return to the design view for Page1, select the tab labeled **Page1.jsp** at the top of the editor pane.
2. In the design canvas, select the right-arrow hyperlink `next` and double-click.
3. Creator brings up the Java page bean file, **Page1.java**, and displays the generated event handler, `next_action()`.
4. To keep track of the index variables and the result count information that Google returns, you'll need integer control variables. Place these declara-

tions above method `next_action()`. Copy and paste file **FieldGuide2/Examples/WebServices/snippets/google4_variables.txt.**

```
private int startIndex = 0;
private int prevIndex = 0;
private int currentCount = 0;
private int totalCount = 0;
```

The `startIndex`, `currentCount`, and `totalCount` integer variables are saved and restored in session scope for the action handlers. To do this, you'll use the Page1 methods `destroy()` and `init()` to save and restore the SessionBean1 properties. Recall that method `init()` is invoked after the page is constructed and method `destroy()` is invoked after the page is rendered. (Table 6.6 on page 266 describes these life cycle methods.)

1. Add the following code to method `destroy()`. Copy and paste from **FieldGuide2/Examples/WebServices/snippets/google4_destroy.txt**. This code calls setters to store `startIndex`, `currentCount`, and `totalCount` as equivalently named properties in the SessionBean1 object. The added code is bold.

Listing 10.2 Method `destroy()`

```
private void destroy() {
   getSessionBean1().setStartIndex(new Integer(startIndex));
   getSessionBean1().setCurrentCount(
         new Integer(currentCount));
   getSessionBean1().setTotalCount(new Integer(totalCount));
}
```

2. Next, add the following code to the end of method `init()`. Copy and paste from **FieldGuide2/Examples/WebServices/snippets/google4_init.txt**. The added code is bold.

Listing 10.3 Method `init()`

```
private void init() {
. . .
   mySearchResult = null;
   startIndex = getSessionBean1().getStartIndex().intValue();
   currentCount =
       getSessionBean1().getCurrentCount().intValue();
   totalCount = getSessionBean1().getTotalCount().intValue();
}
```

Most of the code that resides in the `search_action()` event handler can be pulled out and placed in a method that all three action event handlers will call. Let's call this new method `doSearch()`. The difference is that the start index, which was previously hard-coded to zero, has been parameterized (`int start`). The second difference is that we're saving the total search count (`totalCount`) and the length of the `ResultElements[]` array (`currentCount`).

3. To create the `doSearch()` method, use **FieldGuide2/Examples/WebServices/snippets/google4_doSearch.txt** and place it directly before the `search_action()` method (near the end of the Java page bean file). Note that this method sets the starting index value by calling method `setStart()`. It also sets `totalCount` and `currentCount` from the `mySearchResult` object.

Listing 10.4 Method `doSearch()`

```
public void doSearch(int start) {
   try {
        googleSearchDoGoogleSearch1.setStart(start);
        mySearchResult = (GoogleSearchResult)
          googleSearchDoGoogleSearch1.getResultObject();

        resultArray = mySearchResult.getResultElements();
        myResultObject.setArray(
          (java.lang.Object[])getValue
          ("#{Page1.resultArray}"));

        totalCount =
          mySearchResult.getEstimatedTotalResultsCount();
        currentCount =
          mySearchResult.getResultElements().length;

   } catch (Exception e) {
        log("Remote Connect Failure: ", e);
        mySearchResult = null;
        error("Remote Site Failure: " + e.getMessage());
   }
}
```

4. The `search_action()` method is now simpler, since all that's required is to reset the index control variables and call `doSearch()`. Copy and paste from

file **FieldGuide2/Examples/WebServices/snippets/google4_search_action.txt** to modify this method. Here's the new code.

Listing 10.5 Method `search_action()`

```
public String search_action() {
   startIndex = 0;
   prevIndex = 0;
   doSearch(startIndex);
   return null;
}
```

Clicking the right-arrow hyperlink returns the next set of results from Google. To effect this return, update the `start` parameter (see Table 10.1 on page 462) of the `doGoogleSearch()` method. Also note that the code in the action handler `next_action()` is similar to the code in the above `search_action()`. You just need to check for upper limits in the index control variables.

5. Add code to the `next_action()` event handler. Copy and paste from file **FieldGuide2/Examples/WebServices/snippets/google4_next_action.txt**. Note that the index variables from the session object are automatically restored and saved through methods `init()` and `destroy()`. (The added code is bold.)

Listing 10.6 Method `next_action()`

```
public String next_action() {
   prevIndex = startIndex;
   startIndex = startIndex + currentCount;

   if (startIndex >= totalCount||startIndex>= 1000) {
      startIndex = prevIndex;
      prevIndex -= currentCount;
   }

   doSearch(startIndex);
   return null;
}
```

Now let's add a `previous_action()` method to handle action events associated with the left-arrow hyperlink.

6. Return to the design canvas by selecting **Design** from the editing toolbar.

7. Select the left arrow hyperlink `previous` and double-click. This creates the event handler method in the Java page bean for you and places the cursor at the beginning of the method.
8. Add the following code to the default `previous_action()` method. Copy and paste from file **FieldGuide2/Examples/WebServices/snippets/google4_previous_action.txt**. The added code is bold.

Listing 10.7 Method `previous_action()`

```
public String prev1_action() {
   prevIndex = startIndex - currentCount;
   startIndex = prevIndex;

   if (startIndex <= 0) {
      startIndex = 0;
      prevIndex = 0;
   }

   doSearch(startIndex);
   return null;
}
```

You'll note that the structure of `previous_action()` is similar to the `next_action()` method.

Deploy and Run

Deploy and run the project. You should be able to page through multiple result sets by using the arrow graphics "right" and "left." Figure 10–15 shows the fourth page of a result set.

10.5 Key Point Summary

Creator provides an easy drag and drop feature for accessing a web service through your project. You can add a web service so that it is accessible through the Servers window, test a web service method, and view the returned results.

- Web services provide a standard way to access services over a network in a heterogeneous environment.
- You can add a web service client to Creator by supplying the URL of its Web Service Description Language (WSDL) page.

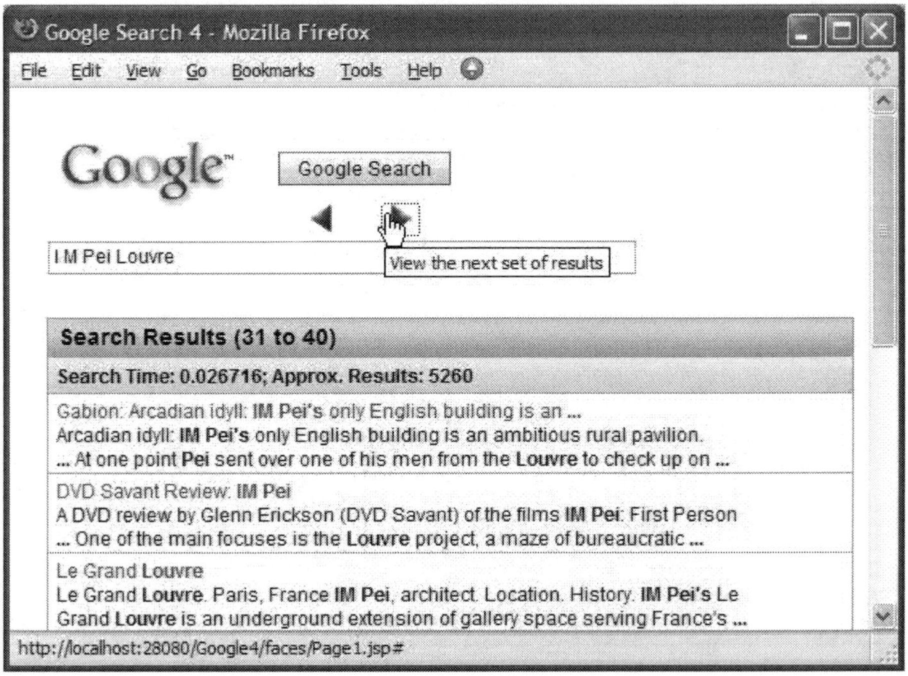

Figure 10–15 **The Google Web Search application displaying the third page of results**

- You can test a web service by selecting one of its methods, right-clicking on the method, and selecting Test Method. Creator displays a Test Web Service Method dialog in which you supply parameter values, submit the call, and examine the results.
- You can access methods of a web service by dragging its node onto the design canvas. Web services appear in the Outline view for the page.
- The Google web service API provides a SOAP interface to search Google's index of pages.
- Initiate a search of the Google engine by dragging the `doGoogleSearch` web service onto your page.
- Web service methods should be invoked within a try block.
- Use image components to add graphics to your web pages.
- Use a static text component to display read-only text. Setting its `escape` attribute to false allows correct rendering of HTML tags. JSF dynamically sizes the output text component for you.
- Use a hyperlink component to submit a form, navigate to an external URL, or navigate to an anchor within the same page.
- Use an image hyperlink component to render an action component using an image.

- You can nest a static component within a hyperlink component and use it to display the text for the hyperlink. This allows you to render HTML tags correctly by *unchecking* the escape property.
- You can control whether or not a component is displayed through its `rendered` property.
- You can nest components inside a grid panel or other layout component. This allows you to easily control the rendering on these components as a group through the parent component's `rendered` property.
- The length validator makes sure that input is within a certain range for length. It does not check for empty fields.
- The `required` attribute makes sure the field is not empty.
- Validators write error messages to the JSF context. Use a message component to display error messages generated by a specific component.
- Use the message group component to display generic user messages. Set its `showGlobalOnly` property to `true` to suppress error messages that are already displayed through component-specific message components.
- You can generate user messages using one of `info()`, `warn()`, `error()`, and `fatal()` from within any FacesBean object.
- Page1 lives in *request scope*. You can maintain information you need to access across page requests as properties in SessionBean1, which is defined in *session scope*.
- Use page bean method `destroy()` to save session state in SessionBean1. Use page bean method `init()` to restore session state from SessionBean1.

USING EJB COMPONENTS

Topics in This Chapter

- Consuming EJBs
- Adding EJB Clients to Projects
- Adding EJB Method Data Providers to Projects
- Invoking EJB Methods
- Initializing EJB Method Data Providers
- Using EJBs that Supply Data
- Adding a Set of Session EJBs to Creator

Chapter 11

Enterprise JaveBeans (EJBs) are server-side components that encapsulate an applications's business logic. While they are similar to JavaBeans components that you've already used and incorporated into your projects, the underlying architecture of EJBs are different. First of all, EJBs are distributed objects. They execute within a J2EE application server. A web application can access them remotely. Furthermore, EJBs provide a level of abstraction between the web application and a backend data store, such as a database. By using EJBs to access a database, the details of the structure and location of the database access are not exposed to the web application. EJBs also provide a highly scalable model. Since a web application can access EJBs remotely, more of an application's processing can be distributed among separate machines if needed.

Furthermore, when you drop an EJB method on your page, Creator generates a data provider for you (if the EJB method has a non-void return), allowing you to bind components (such as drop down lists and tables) exactly like database sources. In fact, with some of the examples, you'll access a data base indirectly through the EJB.

11.1 Consuming EJBs

Creator comes bundled with several sets of session EJBs. These EJBs are all stateless session beans. This means that user state is not saved and that users may share an instance of the bean in the application container. It also means the application server can create multiple copies of the bean to improve performance. Before we start building examples, let's take a moment to examine some of the EJBs that are pre-configured with Creator's IDE and pre-deployed in the bundled application server.

1. Open the Servers view (select View > Servers) if it's not already open.
2. Expand node Enterprise JavaBeans and open Currency Converter > ConverterEJB, HelloWorld Application > GreeterEJB, and Travel Center > TravelEJB. Figure 11–1 shows the Servers view with these nodes expanded.

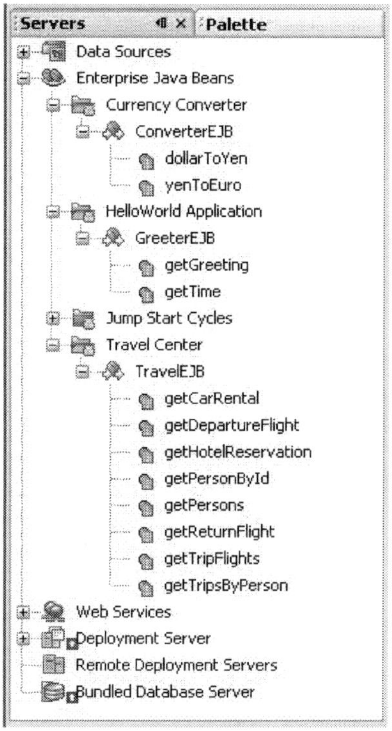

Figure 11–1 **Servers view showing Enterprise JavaBeans display**

With the Servers view, you can determine the EJBs available and the methods exposed through the EJB. In the Servers window, if the method is associated with a data provider, then the icon includes a data provider badge (a table-like grid image). Creator provides two ways to consume EJBs:

- Invoke the EJB method through the Creator-generated client (using Java statements in a page bean or other managed bean).

- Instantiate a data provider that invokes the EJB method for you. Currently, all "EJB" data providers are for retrieving data only—you cannot use the EJB data providers to update data. (Invoke the EJB method through the Creator-generated client to update data.)

The method you choose depends on several factors, so let's briefly describe these two approaches. We'll use both approaches in the examples that you'll build. Along the way, we'll show you the advantages of each method.

Invoke the EJB Method

In order to invoke an EJB method in your page bean, you select the EJB and drop it on the page. For example, to invoke method `getGreeting()` in the GreeterEJB, select GreeterEJB under the HelloWorld Application and drop it on your page. Creator generates an EJB Client (`greeterClient1`). You can then invoke method `getGreeting()`, as follows. Here, `greeting` is the `id` property associated with a static text component.

```
try {
   greeting.setText(greeterClient1.getGreeting());
} catch (Exception ex) {
   log("Error Description", ex);
   error("GreetingEJB: " + ex);
}
```

How do you determine what arguments to supply to the method (if any), and the expected return value? (Since all EJB methods throw at least RemoteException, you always need to put the method call inside a try/catch block or specify a throws clause.)

When you select an EJB method name in the Servers view, Creator displays the information you need in the Properties window. Here is the Properties window for method **getGreeting** under HelloWorld Application > GreeterEJB in the Servers window.

From its signature, you see the method returns a String, takes no arguments, and throws RemoteException.

Let's look at another EJB method. In the Servers window under Currency Converter > ConverterEJB, select **dollarToYen**. Figure 11–3 shows the Properties window for this method. Here, the method expects a BigDecimal argument (the amount in dollars) and returns a BigDecimal. To invoke this method through the Creator-generated client, use the following steps.

1. From the Servers window under Currency Converter, select ConverterEJB and drop it on the page. Creator generates the EJB client (`converterClient1`) you'll need to call the EJB method.

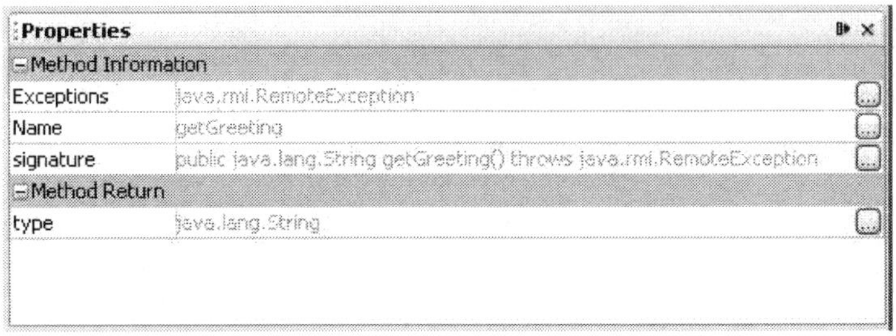

Figure 11–2 **Properties view for GreeterEJB's method getGreeting**

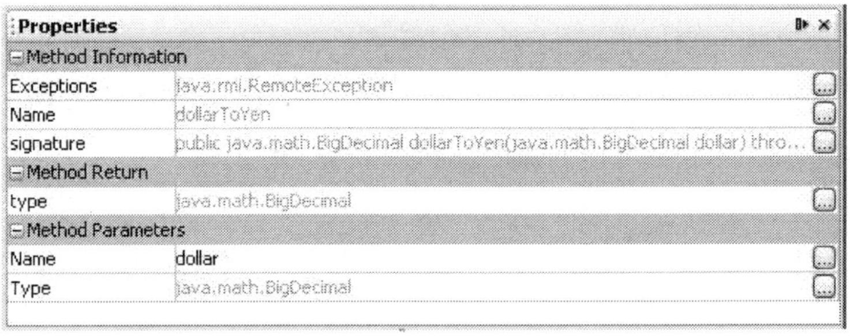

Figure 11–3 **Properties view for ConverterEJB's method dollarToYen**

2. Provide the following code to invoke the method.

```
BigDecimal amount = new BigDecimal(10.0);
try {
   dollars.setText(converterClient1.dollarToYen(amount));
} catch (Exception ex) {
   log("Error Description", ex);
   error("ConverterEJB: " + ex);
}
```

Here, `dollars` is the `id` property of a static text component. Since method `dollarToYen()` returns a BigDecimal, you would apply a number converter to format the display.

There are several advantages for calling an EJB method through the client. One, you can call it exactly where you need to in your code. You may need to gather input for a method's argument (for example, the dollar amount required by `dollarToYen()`), so placing the call in the appropriate event handler after processing user input is straightforward. Second, the method call is trivial. You simply invoke it using the Creator-generated client. Third, as stated earlier, you must invoke a method through the client to update or create data through an EJB method.

Instantiate a Data Provider

The second approach lets you select a method name from the Servers window and drop it on the page. In this case, Creator generates the client (as in the first approach) and also generates a data provider that wraps the return object (or objects) from the call. Creator configures the data provider to hold a reference to the client. When you bind the data provider to a component (such as a drop down list, a static text component, or even a table), the property resolver mechanism invokes the method through the client for you. This approach is also straightforward, but you must initialize any required arguments beforehand (usually in the page bean's `init()` method). This method is especially appropriate when the EJB is connected to a data store and the method returns one or more data transfer objects.

Note that only EJB methods that return non-void types have data providers. If a method does not return anything, then there is no data provider generated for the method and the method is not droppable. Note that if the method is associated with a data provider, then the method's icon in the Servers window includes a data provider badge (a table-like grid image).

Let's look at an example that shows how simple this approach is.

Creator Tip

If you want to deploy this small example, go ahead and create a new project. Call the project EJBTest. When the page comes up in the design view, set the page title to EJB Test.

1. Make sure that the bundled database server is running. In the Servers menu the Bundled Database Server should have a green up-arrow badge next to the database icon. If not, right-click the server name and select Start Bundled Database from the context menu.
2. From the Basic Components palette, select Drop Down List and place it on the page.
3. From the Servers window under Travel Center > TravelEJB, select method **getPersons** and drop it on top of the drop down list. (Hold the mouse over the drop down list component until it is outlined in blue. Be patient.) When you release the mouse, you'll see that Creator generated the EJB client (`travelClient1`), the data provider (`travelGetPersons1`), and an Integer converter (`dropDown1Converter`).
4. Select the drop down list component, right-click, and select Bind to Data. Creator pops up the Bind To Data dialog.

5. The dialog has a Value window and a Display window (corresponding to the value and display properties of the drop down list). Make sure **personId** is selected for Value and **name** is selected for Display, as shown in Figure 11–4. Click Apply then OK to close.
6. Deploy and run the application. You'll see the drop down list populated with names supplied by the EJB.

Let's see how all this magic works.

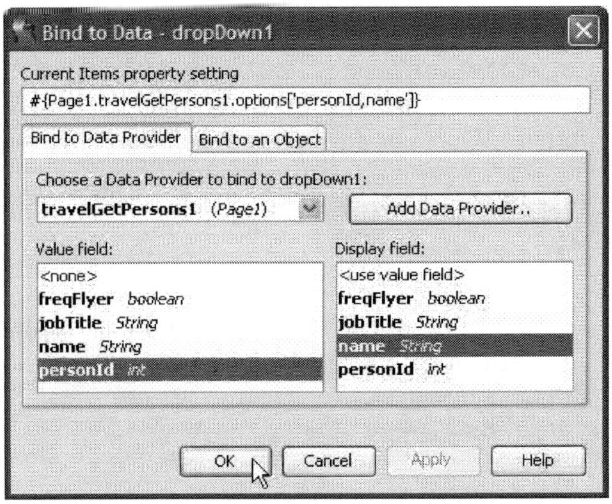

Figure 11–4 **Bind to Data dialog**

1. First, select method **getPersons** in the Servers window under Travel Center > TravelEJB and examine the Properties view, as shown in Figure 11–5.

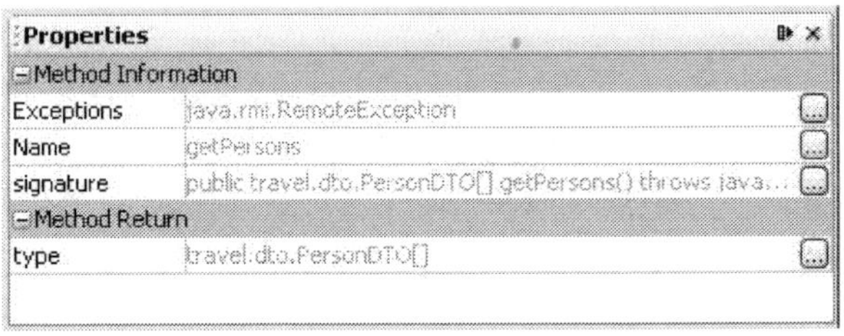

Figure 11–5 **Properties view for TravelEJB's getPersons method**

Method `getPersons()` takes no arguments and returns a PersonDTO (Person Data Transfer Object) array. A PersonDTO contains fields (these are displayed in the Bind to Data dialog in Figure 11–4). Here, you are binding the drop down component to the key fields of the data provider.

2. Now click Java in the editing toolbar to bring up **Page1.java** in the Java editor.
3. Double-click private method `_init()` in the Navigator view to display this method in the Java editor. Method `_init()` holds the Creator-generated code that configures the data provider.

```
private void _init() throws Exception {
   travelGetPersons1.setTravelClient(
        (travel.ejb.session.travel.TravelClient)
            getValue("#{Page1.travelClient1}"));
}
```

Method `_init()` invokes `setTravelClient()` to connect data provider `travelGetPersons1` with the TravelEJB client. Once this is configured, JSF's property resolvers invoke EJB method `getPersons()` to populate the data provider and honor the data binding between the drop down list component and the data provider.

Since method `getPersons()` does not require any arguments, no initialization is necessary. Furthermore, `_init()` has a throws clause in its signature; hence, the call to `setTravelClient()` does not have to be inside a try block.

When an EJB method requires no arguments, there's no need to provide initialization code. However, if an EJB method requires an argument (for example TravelEJB method `getTripsByPerson()`), you must provide this argument during initialization (typically in method `init()`). We'll show you how to do this shortly when you build a more involved example project.

Data providers are extremely convenient when binding components to data. You access and manipulate a data provider interfaced with an EJB method in exactly the same way as a data provider interfaced with a database (as we did in Chapter 9). This transparency allows an application the flexibility to change how it acquires data without restructuring or refactoring the code.

Creator Tip

The data providers for EJBs (as well as web services) are read-only. That is, you cannot update the data source using the data provider. For update operations, you invoke the EJB method directly.

11.2 EJBs as Business Objects

You can implement business objects with JavaBeans components. You can also implement them with Enterprise JavaBeans components, providing scalability within a distributed environment. In our first example, let's show you the ConverterEJB sample bundled with the Creator software.

This example is more suited to calling the EJB method directly. After completing the project, however, you'll go back and implement this application with the data provider method. This approach, although not as straightforward (in this example), is very instructive for familiarizing yourself with the requirements for using data providers with EJB components.

Create a Project

1. From Creator's Welcome Page, select Create New Project. Creator displays the New Project dialog. Under Categories, select Web. Under Projects, select JSF Web Application. Click Next.
2. In the New Web Application dialog under Project Name, specify **EJBConverter**. Click Finish.

   After initializing the project, Creator comes up in the design view of the editor pane. You can now set the title.

3. In the Properties window, select property `Title` and specify title **Currency Converter**. Finish by pressing **<Enter>**.
4. In the Properties window, select the customizer box opposite property `Background`. Creator displays a property customizer dialog. Select the yellow swatch from the top row of the color chooser and click OK to close. This sets the background color to **RGB(255, 255, 204)**.

Add an EJB Client

Like the Web Services node and the Data Sources node, the Enterprise JavaBeans node in Creator's Servers window provides information about the available services you can add to your project. Once you select one of the EJB session sets, you can inspect the methods and determine how to call them in your project. For now, let's look at Currency Converter node under Enterprise JavaBeans.

1. In the Servers view, expand Enterprise JavaBeans > Currency Converter.
2. Select ConverterEJB and drop it on the page in the design view. Creator adds component `converterClient1` to the Page1 Outline view. That's all you need to access the methods provided by the ConverterEJB.
3. Now expand node ConverterEJB and you'll see two methods: `dollarToYen()` and `yenToEuro()`.
4. Right-click on the first method, `dollarToYen()`, and select Properties. Creator displays a method Properties window, as shown in Figure 11–6. This window shows you the complete method signature, including the type of

each parameter, the return type, and the Exceptions thrown. You'll need this information when you write event handling code that invokes these methods.

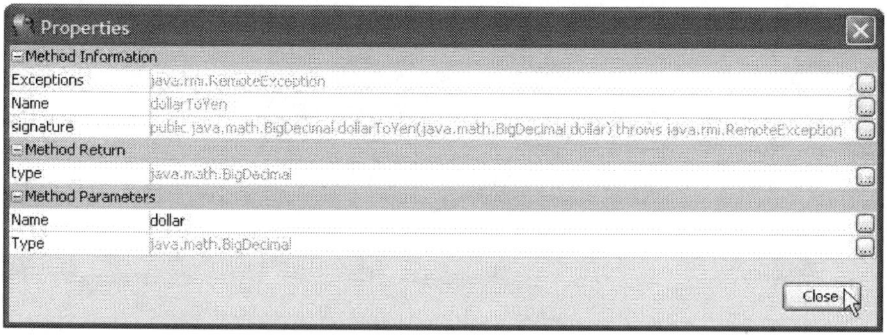

Figure 11–6 **Visual design editor in the editor pane**

Add Session Bean Properties

This converter application stores monetary data and conversion results in session scope. Session scope is preferable to request scope because the project can then easily be implemented as a portlet (see "Portlet Life Cycle" on page 541 for a discussion on differences between portlet and non-portlet applications).

You'll add three properties to session scope, all of type BigDecimal: `myDollar`, `myYen`, and `myEuro`.

1. From the Projects view, select Session Bean, right-click, and select Add > Property. Creator pops up the New Property Pattern dialog.
2. For Name specify **myDollar**, for Type specify **BigDecimal**, and for Mode, select the default **Read/Write**. Click OK to add the property.
3. Repeat Steps 1 and 2 and add properties **myYen** and **myEuro**. The Type and Mode of all three properties are the same.
4. Double-click node Session Bean to bring up **SessionBean1.java** in the source editor.
5. Right-click anywhere inside the editor pane and select Fix Imports. This adds the import statement for type BigDecimal.

6. Add the following code to the end of method `init()`. Copy and paste from **FieldGuide2/Examples/EJB/snippets/converter_session_init.txt**. The added code is bold.

```
public void init() {
   . . .
   // TODO - add your own initialization code here
   myDollar = new BigDecimal(10);
   myYen = new BigDecimal(0);
   myEuro = new BigDecimal(0);
}
```

Note that property `myDollar` is set to 10. The other two properties are set to zero.

Add Components to the Page

Figure 11–7 shows the project in the design view with the components added. To help with the layout, a grid panel with two columns holds the components, using static text components as place holders. The three static text components that display dollars, yen, and euros are nested in a second grid panel with three columns.

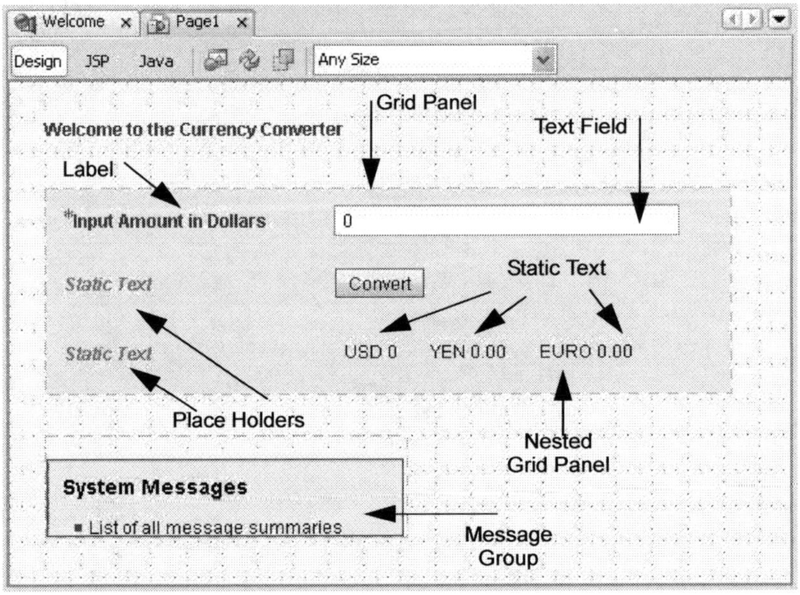

Figure 11–7 **Visual design editor in the editor pane**

First, you'll add a label component for the page title and a grid panel to help with the layout.

1. From the Basic Components palette, select component Label and drop it on the page. Specify **Welcome to the Currency Converter** for its `text` property.
2. From the Layout Components palette, select Grid Panel and place it under the Label you just added.
3. In the Properties window, set property `bgcolor` to **#eeeeee**, `cellpadding` to **10**, and `columns` to **2**. The grid panel's background color changes to a light grey-blue.

Next, you'll add components to the grid panel. Recall that the order you add components determines their placement. If you need to rearrange the components, you can drag and re-drop them on top of the grid panel (it's easier if you use the Outline view).

1. From the Basic Components palette, select component Label and drop it on the grid panel component in the Page1 Outline view. Set its text to **Input Amount in Dollars**.
2. From the Basic Components palette, select Text Field and drop it on the grid panel (using the Outline view).
3. In the Properties window, *check* property `required`.
4. Select the Label component and in the Properties view, set property `for` to **textField1** using the drop down list. A red asterisk appears in front of the label's text.
5. From the Validators Components palette, select Double Range Validator and drop it on top of the text field component in the design view. This sets property `validator` to **doubleRangeValidator1**.
6. From the Converters Components palette, select Big Decimal Converter and drop it on top of the text field component in the design view. This sets property `converter` to **bigDecimalConverter1**, converting the text field's string input to BigDecimal.
7. In the design view, select the text field component, right-click, and choose Property Bindings from the context menu.
8. In the Property Bindings dialog, for Select bindable property, choose **text *Object***. For Select binding target, choose **SessionBean1 > myDollar *BigDecimal***. Click Apply then Close for the setting to take effect.
9. In the Page1 Outline view, select component `doubleRangeValidator1`. In the Properties view, set `maximum` to five million (**5000000**) and `minimum` to one (**1**).

You've configured the first row of the grid panel. Now you'll add a place holder (static text) and a button for the second row.

1. From the Basic Components palette, select Static Text and drop it on the grid panel component in the Page1 Outline view. Set its `id` property to **placeholder1**. This component will occupy the first cell in the second row of the grid panel (below the label).
2. From the Basic Components palette, select Button and drop it on the grid panel component in the Page1 Outline view. Set its `id` property to **convert** and its `text` property to **Convert**. You'll configure its action event handler later.

The third row of the grid panel contains another place holder component and a second grid panel. Nested inside the grid panel, you'll add three static text components to display the dollar, yen, and euro amounts.

1. From the Basic Components palette, select Static Text and drop it on the grid panel component in the Page1 Outline view. Set its `id` property to **placeholder2**. This component occupies the first cell in the third row of the grid panel.
2. From the Layout Components palette, select Grid Panel and drop it on the first grid panel (`gridPanel1`) component in the Outline view.
3. In the Properties window, set property `id` to **nestedPanel**, `cellpadding` to **5**, and `columns` to **3**.

Each column in the nested grid panel holds a static text component. The first one displays the amount in dollars, which requires configuring a number converter.

1. From the Basic Components palette, select Static Text and drop it on the nested grid panel in the Outline view.
2. In the Properties window, set property `id` to **dollar**.
3. Select the static text component, right-click and select Property Bindings from the context menu. Creator pops up the Property Bindings dialog.
4. In the Property Bindings dialog, for Select bindable property, choose **text** ***Object***. For Select binding target, choose **SessionBean1 > myDollar** ***BigDecimal***. Click Apply then Close.
5. In the Converters Components palette, select Number Converter and drop it on top of the static text component dollar in the design view. This sets property `converter` to **numberConverter1**. Creator pops up the Number Format dialog, as shown in Figure 11–8.
6. Select radio button Pattern and provide pattern **USD #,###.00**, which uses the accepted abbreviation for U.S. Dollars (USD) followed by the pattern. Click Apply then the Test button to test the pattern. Click OK to close the dialog. **USD 0** should now display in the static text component.

You'll now repeat these steps for the second static text component, which displays the amount in yen.

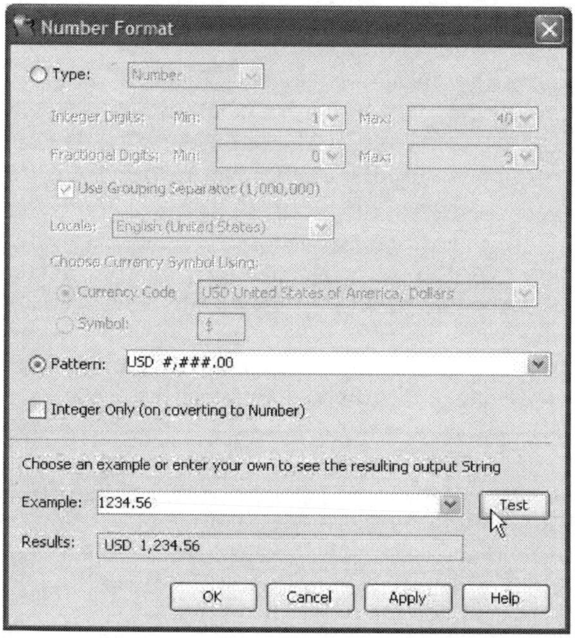

Figure 11–8 **Number Format dialog**

1. From the Basic Components palette, select Static Text and drop it on the nested grid panel in the Outline view.
2. In the Properties window, set property `id` to **yen**.
3. Select the static text component, right-click and select Property Bindings from the context menu. Creator pops up the Property Bindings dialog.
4. In the Property Bindings dialog, for Select bindable property, choose **text *Object***. For Select binding target, choose **SessionBean1 > myYen *BigDecimal***. Click Apply then Close.
5. In the Converters Components palette, select Number Converter and drop it on top of the static text component dollar in the design view. This sets property `converter` to **numberConverter2**. Creator pops up the Number Format dialog.
6. Select radio button Pattern and provide pattern **YEN #,###.00**. Click Apply then OK to close the dialog. **YEN 0** should now display in the static text component.

Finally, repeat these steps for the third static text component, which displays the amount in euros.

1. From the Basic Components palette, select Static Text and drop it on the nested grid panel in the Outline view.
2. In the Properties window, set property `id` to **euro**.
3. Select the static text component, right-click and select Property Bindings from the context menu. Creator pops up the Property Bindings dialog.
4. In the Property Bindings dialog, for Select bindable property, choose **text** ***Object***. For Select binding target, choose **SessionBean1 > myEuro** *BigDecimal*. Click Apply then Close.
5. In the Converters Components palette, select Number Converter and drop it on top of the static text component dollar in the design view. This sets property `converter` to **numberConverter3**. Creator pops up the Number Format dialog.
6. Select radio button Pattern and provide pattern **EURO #,###.00**. Click Apply then OK to close the dialog. **EURO 0** should now display in the static text component.

The last component to add is a message group. Since the text field requires both conversion and validation, you'll need some type of message component. Furthermore, to access the EJB component, you'll put the method call inside a try block. The catch handler will produce a system error message.

Creator Tip

A single message group component allows you to use one component for all error messages (system, validation, and conversion). This is a typical practice if the page contains only one input component and the source of any conversion or validation errors is clear to the user.

- From the Basic Components palette, select Message Group and drop it on the page below the grid panels.

Figure 11–9 shows the Outline view with all of the components added, including the Session Bean properties and the EJB client component (`converterClient1`).

Add Event Handling Code

When the user clicks the Convert button, the action event handler invokes the methods from the ConverterEJB to convert the dollars to yen and yen to euros. The methods' parameters are set from session bean properties and likewise the results are stored in the session bean properties.

1. In the Page1 design view, double-click the Convert button.

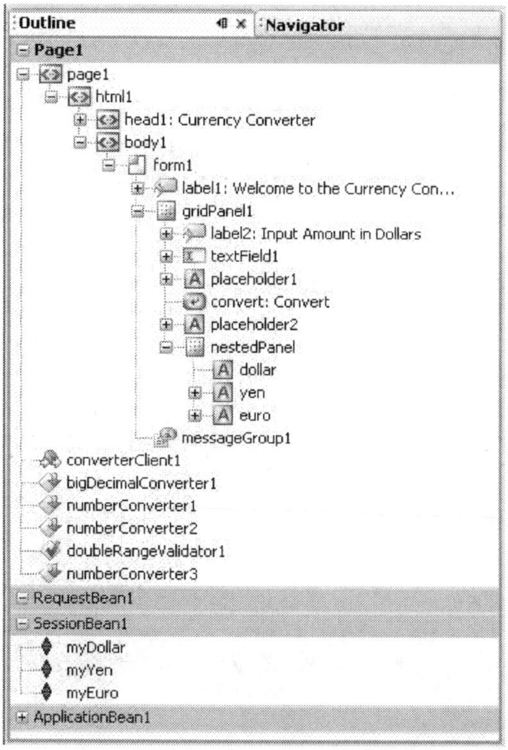

Figure 11–9 **Outline view for project EJBConverter**

2. Creator generates default code for method `convert_action()` and brings up **Page1.java** in the source editor with the cursor at the first line of this method.
3. Add the following code to the event handler. Copy and paste from **FieldGuide2/Examples/EJB/snippets/converter_convert_action.txt**. The added code is bold.

Listing 11.1 Method `convert_action()`

```
public String convert_action() {
   try {
      getSessionBean1().setMyYen(converterClient1.dollarToYen(
            getSessionBean1().getMyDollar()));
      getSessionBean1().setMyEuro(converterClient1.yenToEuro(
            getSessionBean1().getMyYen()));
```

Listing 11.1 Method `convert_action()`

```
    } catch (Exception ex) {
      log("Error Description", ex);
      error("ConverterEJB: " + ex);
    }
    return null;
}
```

Since both methods potentially throw RemoteException, you must either encase the call in a try block (as shown here), or include a throws clause with method `convert_action()`. To control the application when an exception is thrown here, we use a catch handler to record the error message in the server log (with `log()`) and write an appropriate message to the faces context (with `error()`). JSF displays the error using the message component you added to the page.

Deploy and Run

Deploy and run the application by clicking the Run icon on the main toolbar. Figure 11–10 shows application EJBConverter running in a browser. Try out several numbers to convert, including input that fails either validation or conversion to test these scenarios.

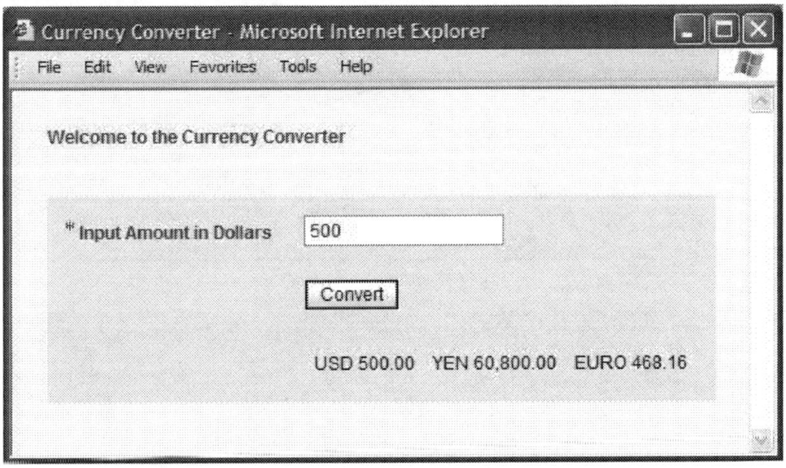

Figure 11–10 **Currency Converter application running in a browser**

The event handling code in this example invokes the EJB methods through the Creator-generated client. Now let's show you how to implement this same application with a data provider.

Copy the Project

To avoid starting from scratch, copy the EJBConverter project to a new project called EJBConverter2. This step is optional. If you don't want to copy the project, simply skip this section and continue making modifications to the EJB-Converter project.

1. Bring up project EJBConverter in Creator, if it's not already opened.
2. From the Projects window, right-click node EJBConverter and select Save Project As. Provide the new name **EJBConverter2**.
3. Close project EJBConverter. Right-click EJBConverter2 and select Set Main Project. You'll make changes to the EJBConverter2 project.
4. Expand EJBConverter2 > Web Pages and open **Page1.jsp** in the design view.
5. Click anywhere in the background of the design canvas of the EJBConverter2 project. In the Properties window, change the page's `Title` property to **Currency Converter 2**.

Add EJB Method Data Providers

Instead of adding the EJB to your page, you'll add the EJB method.

1. From the Servers window under Enterprise JavaBeans > Currency Converter > ConverterEJB, select **dollarToYen** and drop it on the page. Creator uses `converterClient1` and generates `converterDollarToYen1` data provider.
2. Repeat this and add method **yenToEuro** to the page. Creator uses `converterClient1` and generates `converterYenToEuro1` data provider.

Bind Components to Data Object

Currently, the static text components `yen` and `euro` are bound to their respective session bean properties. Instead, you'll bind these components to the data object returned within the data provider.

1. From the Page1 design view, select static text component `yen`. In the Properties view, click the property customizer box opposite property `text`. Creator pops up the text customizer dialog.
2. Tab Bind to an Object should be set. Retain this setting.
3. Under Select binding target, choose **Page1 > converterDollarToYen1 > resultObject** ***BigDecimal***, as shown in Figure 11–11. Click OK. Binding target `resultObject` holds the EJB method's returned object. The text component now displays YEN 123.
4. Repeat Steps 1 through 3 for static component `euro`, binding its `text` property to **Page1 > converterYenToEuro1 > resultObject** ***BigDecimal***.

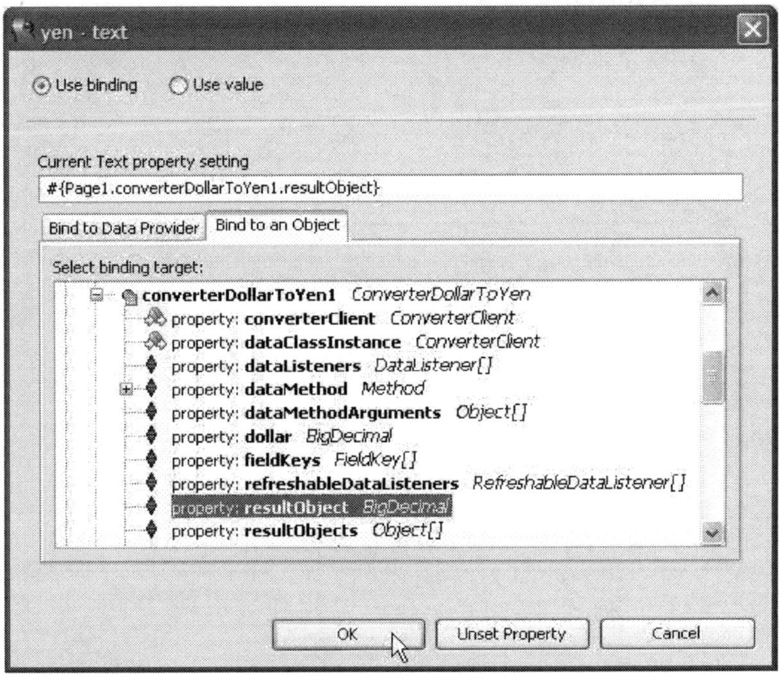

Figure 11–11 **Bind to an Object dialog for component yen**

Modify Event Handler Code

Instead of invoking the EJB methods directly, you'll manipulate the Creator-generated data providers.

1. From the Page1 design view, double-click button Convert. Creator brings up **Page1.java** in the editor and places the cursor at the button's event handler, method `convert_action()`.
2. Replace the event handler code with the following. Copy and paste from **FieldGuide2/Examples/EJB/snippets/converter2_convert_action.txt**. The replaced code is bold.

Listing 11.2 Method `convert_action()`

```
public String convert_action() {
   // get dollar amount from session to set method parameter
   converterDollarToYen1.setDollar(
        getSessionBean1().getMyDollar());
```

Listing 11.2 Method `convert_action()` *(continued)*

```
    // refresh() calls method dollarToYen()
    converterDollarToYen1.refresh();
    // store resultObject in session property
    getSessionBean1().setMyYen(
          (BigDecimal)converterDollarToYen1.getResultObject());

    // get yen amount from session to set method parameter
    converterYenToEuro1.setYen(getSessionBean1().getMyYen());
    // refresh() calls method yenToEuro()
    converterYenToEuro1.refresh();

    // store resultObject in session property
    getSessionBean1().setMyEuro(
          (BigDecimal)converterYenToEuro1.getResultObject());
    return null;
}
```

Compare the code in this listing with Listing 11.1 on page 507. To modify the event handler to use the EJB-connected data provider requires three steps in place of the single EJB method call: you provide the method parameter, invoke `refresh()` (which calls the actual EJB method), and obtain the result (with `getResultObject()`). As verbose as this approach seems to be, it is the preferred tactic when the EJB method returns an array (or collection) of data transfer objects. The returned objects are mapped to a data provider and then to one of Creator's data-aware components, such as the drop down list, listbox, or table component.

Method `setDollar()` allows you to provide the method's argument. Recall that method `dollarToYen()` takes a BigDecimal method parameter that is the amount in dollars. Once you've provided a new dollar amount, you then update the data provider with `refresh()`. This invokes the EJB method. Method `getResultObject()` returns the BigDecimal return value.

Specify Data Provider Initialization

If you deployed and ran the project now, you'd get a run time exception. That's because the data provider's return value is bound to the static text component. During the JSF life cycle, the property resolving mechanism attempts to obtain the result object. However, you haven't yet set the method parameter. This you need to do during initialization, in the Page1 method `init()`.

1. **Page1.java** should still be active in the Java editor. Scroll up and find method `init()`.

2. Add the following code to the end of the method. Copy and paste from **FieldGuide2/Examples/EJB/snippets/converter2_init.txt**. The added code is bold.

```
public void init() {
   . . .
   // TODO - add your own initialization code here
   converterDollarToYen1.setDollar(
        getSessionBean1().getMyDollar());
   getSessionBean1().setMyYen(
        (BigDecimal)converterDollarToYen1.getResultObject());
   converterYenToEuro1.setYen(getSessionBean1().getMyYen());
   getSessionBean1().setMyEuro(
        (BigDecimal)converterYenToEuro1.getResultObject());
}
```

This code is similar to the event handling code. Here, it is not necessary to call `refresh()`, since this is the initial call to `getResultObject()`.

Deploy and Run

Deploy and run application EJBConverter2. There is a slight difference in the run time behavior between EJBConverter and EJBConverter2. Since EJBConverter2 provides initialization code, the static text components `yen` and `euro` are initialized when the page is rendered in the browser the first time. These amounts were set to zero in project EJBConverter, where the first EJB call occurred in the event handling code.

11.3 Greeting Two Ways

Let's now build an application that uses the data provider method, since is the most straightforward approach here. After, we'll make a modification that uses the method call approach.

The GreeterEJB (under HelloWorld Application in the Servers view) has two methods: `getGreeting()` and `getTime()`. Neither method requires parameters and both methods return Strings. When you use the data provider approach, you can bind a static text component to `resultObject` to display a return value. Here, you'll use a button component to submit the page and update the display. (Method `getTime()` returns a new, updated time with each call.)

Create a Project

1. From Creator's Welcome Page, select Create New Project. Creator displays the New Project dialog. Under Categories, select Web. Under Projects, select JSF Web Application. Click Next.
2. In the New Web Application dialog under Project Name, specify **EJBGreeting**. Click Finish.

   After initializing the project, Creator comes up in the design view of the editor pane. You can now set the title.

3. In the Properties window, select property `Title` and specify title **EJB - Simple Greeting**. Finish by pressing **<Enter>**.

Add Components to the Page

Figure 11–12 shows the project in the design view with the components added. The page includes an Update button and two static text components.

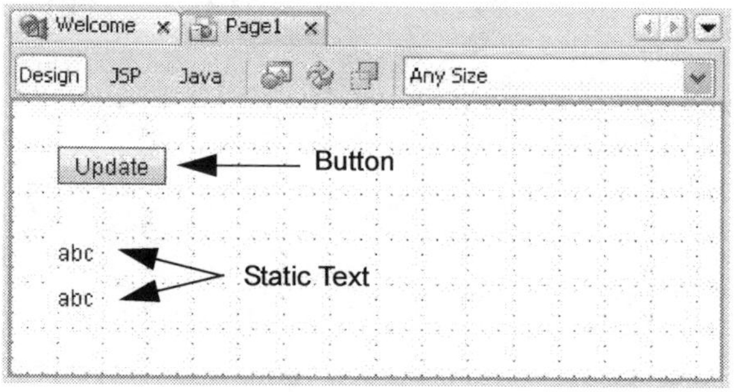

Figure 11–12 **Page1 design view for EJBGreeting**

1. From the Basic Components palette, select component Button and drop it on the page. Specify **Update** for its `text` property.
2. From the Basic Components palette, select Static Text and place it under the button you just added.
3. In the Properties window, set property `id` to **greeting**.
4. Repeat Steps 2 and 3 and add a second static text component. Set its `id` property to **time**.

Add EJB Method Data Providers

You'll now add both EJB methods to the page.

1. From the Servers window under Enterprise JavaBeans > HelloWorld Application > GreeterEJB, select **getGreeting** and drop it on the page. Creator generates EJB client `greeterClient1` and `greeterGetGreeting1` data provider.
2. Repeat this step and add method **getTime** to the page. Creator reuses `greeterClient1` and generates `greeterGetTime1` data provider.

Bind Components to Data Object

You'll bind the two static text components to the data object returned within the data provider.

1. From the Page1 design view, select static text component `greeting`, right-click, and select Bind to Data. Creator pops up the Bind to Data dialog.
2. Select tab Bind to an Object.
3. Under Select binding target, choose **Page1 > greetingGetGreeting1 > resultObject *String***. Click Apply then OK, as shown in Figure 11–13. The text component now displays **abc**.

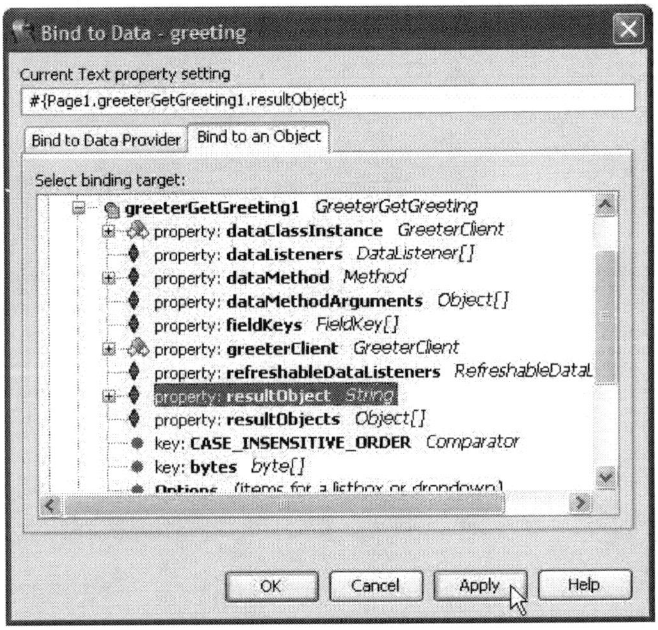

Figure 11–13 **Page1 design view for EJBGreeting**

4. Repeat Steps 1 through 3 for static component `time`, binding its `text` property to **Page1 > greetingGetTime1 > resultObject *String***.

Deploy and Run

Deploy and run application EJBGreeting. Note that as you successively click Update, the time is refreshes. If you run the application at different times of the day, the text of the greeting changes as well. Figure 11–14 shows the EJBGreeting project running in a browser.

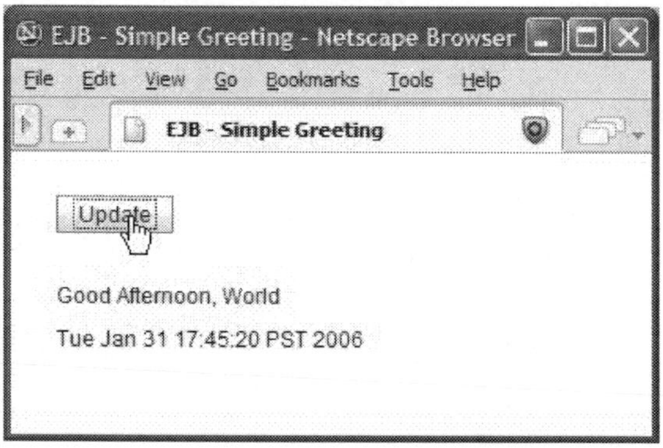

Figure 11–14 **Application EJBGreeting running in a browser**

Let's now personalize this application by having the user select a name from the sample Travel database. You'll use the TravelEJB to access the list of names. Instead of binding the static text components to the GreetingEJB data providers, you'll call the EJB methods directly in the event handler code.

Copy the Project

To avoid starting from scratch, copy the EJBGreeting project to a new project called EJBGreeting2. This step is optional. If you don't want to copy the project, simply skip this section and continue making modifications to the EJBGreeting project.

1. Bring up project EJBGreeting in Creator, if it's not already opened.
2. From the Projects window, right-click node EJBGreeting and select Save Project As. Provide the new name **EJBGreeting2**.
3. Close project EJBGreeting. Right-click EJBGreeting2 and select Set Main Project. You'll make changes to the EJBGreeting2 project.
4. Expand EJBGreeting2 > Web Pages and open **Page1.jsp** in the design view.
5. Click anywhere in the background of the design canvas of the EJBGreeting2 project. In the Properties window, change the page's `Title` property to **EJB - Simple Greeting 2**.

Delete Unneeded Components

Since you're accessing the GreetingEJB methods directly, you no longer need the Creator-generated data providers. You also don't need the button.

1. Bring up Page1 in the design view.
2. In the Page1 Outline view, select component `greeterGetGreeting1`, right-click, and select Delete. Creator removes the component from the page and the `greeting` static text component displays the default *Static Text*.
3. In the Page1 Outline view, select component `greeterGetTime1`, right-click, and select Delete. The `time` static text component also displays the default *Static Text*.
4. In the design view, select the Update button, right-click, and select Delete. This leaves the two static text components on the page.

Add Components to the Page

Next, you'll add a listbox component to display the selection of names from the Travel database, a message group component to report errors, and a label component. Figure 11–15 shows the page with the new components.

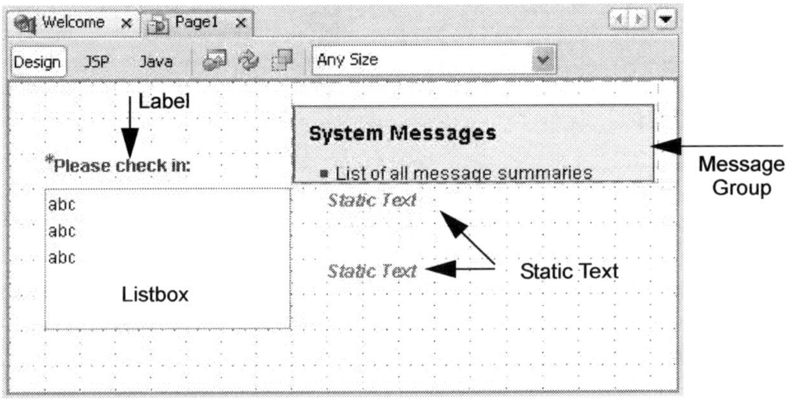

Figure 11–15 **Project EJBGreeting2 Page1 design view**

1. Make sure that the bundled database server is running. In the Servers menu the Bundled Database Server should have a green up-arrow badge next to the database icon. If not, right-click the server name and select Start Bundled Database from the context menu.
2. Use Figure 11–15 as a guide for component placement. Before adding the additional components, move the two static components as shown.

3. Select static text component `time`. In the Properties view, *uncheck* property `escape`. This allows HTML characters to be interpreted by the browser.
4. From the Basic Components palette, select Label and drop it on the page. Set its text to **Please check in:**.
5. From the Basic Components palette, select Listbox and drop it on the page under the label you just added.
6. In the Properties view, *check* property `required`.
7. Resize the listbox so that it is approximately 5 by 5 grids.
8. In the design view, select the label component. In the Properties view, select component `listbox1` from the drop down list opposite property `for`. This connects the label to the list box. A red asterisk appears in front of the label's text since the listbox has its `required` property set to true.
9. From the Basic Components palette, select Message Group and place it on the page. This component will display any system error messages, as well as validation error messages generated from listbox input.

Add EJB Method Data Provider

The GreetingEJB client is already included with the Page1's components. You'll now add one of the TravelEJB methods to the page.

1. From the Servers window under Enterprise JavaBeans > Travel Center > TravelEJB, select **getPersons** and drop it on the listbox component. Don't release the mouse until the listbox component is outlined in blue. (Be patient.) Creator generates EJB client `travelClient1` and `travelGetPersons1` data provider. Creator binds the data provider to the listbox component. The listbox component displays **abc** in the selection area.
2. Select the listbox component, right-click, and select Bind to Data. Creator pops up the Bind to Data dialog, as shown in Figure 11–16.
3. Make sure that **travelGetPersons1 (*Page1*)** is selected in the Data Provider selection window.
4. Select **name *String*** for both the Value and Display fields. The listbox component (like the drop down list component) uses a Value field and a Display field. The Value field is returned with method `getSelected()` and the Display field is what is displayed in the component. In this application, you use the Person field **name** for both the Value and the Display fields. Click Apply then OK to close the dialog.

Add Event Handling Code

When the user selects a name from the listbox, the process value change event handler invokes the methods from the GreetingEJB to display a greeting and the time.

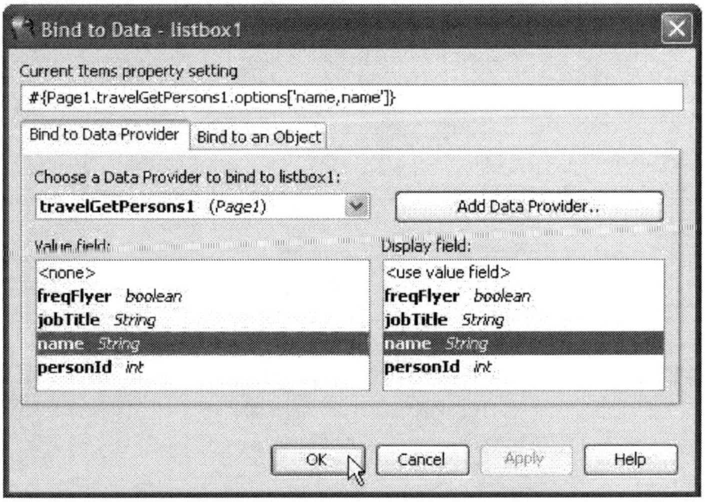

Figure 11–16 **Bind to Data dialog**

1. In the Page1 design view, right-click the listbox component and select Auto-Submit on Change. This submits the page when the user changes the selection.
2. Now double-click the listbox.
3. Creator generates default code for method `listbox1_processValueChange()` and brings up **Page1.java** in the source editor with the cursor at the first line of this method.
4. Add the following code to the event handler. Copy and paste from **FieldGuide2/Examples/EJB/snippets/greeting2_listbox1.txt**. The added code is bold.

Listing 11.3 Method `listbox1_processValueChange()`

```
public void listbox1_processValueChange(
        ValueChangeEvent event) {
   String name = listbox1.getSelected().toString();
   String greetingStr = "";
   String timeStr = "";
```

Listing 11.3 Method `listbox1_processValueChange()`

```
    try {
      greetingStr = greeterClient1.getGreeting();
      timeStr = greeterClient1.getTime();
    } catch (Exception ex) {
      log("Error Description", ex);
      error("GreetingEJB: " + ex);
    }

    int stop1 = greetingStr.indexOf(',');
    int stop2 = name.indexOf(',');
    greeting.setText(greetingStr.substring(0, stop1+2)
        + name.substring(stop2+2) + "!");
    time.setText("<b>Today is:  </b>" + timeStr);
}
```

The event handler uses String methods `indexOf()` and `substring()` to manipulate the Strings returned from EJB method `getGreeting()` and listbox method `getSelected()`.

Deploy and Run

Deploy and run application EJBGreeting2. As you change the listbox selection, the greeting changes as well as the time. Figure 11–17 shows the EJBGreeting2 project running in a browser.

Note that this application does not require initialization code for the EJB-connected data provider, since EJB method `getPersons()` does not take a parameter.

11.4 Implementing a Master-Detail Page with EJBs

In a previous chapter (see "Master Detail Application - Single Page" on page 398) you built an application that accessed a database. From the Servers window, you selected specific tables and dropped them on the page. You then built the appropriate query by adding criteria. You supplied the necessary search parameters by selecting the search criteria data from a drop down list component. To display data in the table, you attached various data fields to the table component's columns.

This method of accessing the database through the IDE requires that the application developer know the structure of the data. If, on the other hand, you

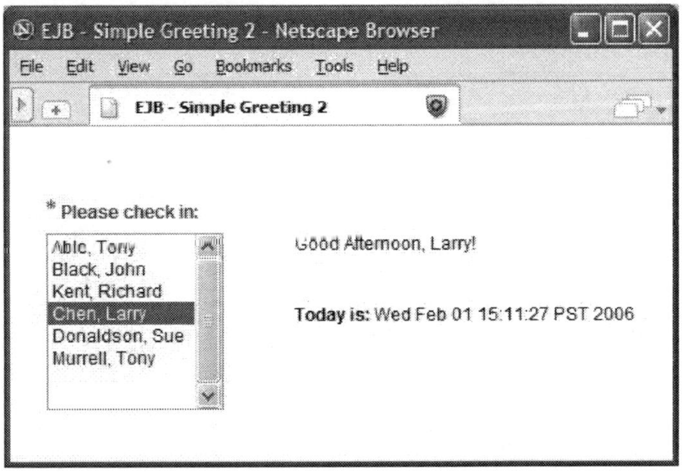

Figure 11–17 **Application EJBGreeting2 running in a browser**

access the data through EJB components, knowledge of the database structure is not necessary. The EJB component developer decides how to expose the data by providing methods that you call through the EJB client. This level of indirection means that the data store details can change as long as the EJB component's outside view remains constant.

In this section, you'll build a master-detail application based on TravelEJB, the sample Travel Center EJB included in Creator. From the Servers window, expand Enterprise JavaBeans > Travel Center > TravelEJB. Table 11.1 lists the available methods in TravelEJB.

Table 11.1 TravelEJB Methods

Method Name	*Parameter*	*Return Type*
getCarRental	tripId (Integer)	CarRentalDTO
getDepartureFlight	tripId (Integer)	FlightDTO
getHotelReservation	tripId (Integer)	HotelReservationDTO
getPersonById	id (Integer)	PersonDTO
getPersons	none	PersonDTO []
getReturnFlight	tripId (Integer)	FlightDTO

Table 11.1 TravelEJB Methods *(continued)*

getTripFlights	tripId (Integer)	FlightDTO []
getTripsByPerson	personId (Integer)	FlightDTO []

For example, method `getPersons()` returns a PersonDTO array and takes no parameters. Method `getPersonById()` requires parameter `id` (an Integer) and returns a single PersonDTO. Method `getTripsByPerson()` requires parameter `personId` (an Integer) and returns a FlightDTO array. Let's use these three methods to build our master-detail example.

Creator Tip

The Enterprise JavaBeans components bundled with Creator that access the database perform database reads only. This is a limitation only when using the data provider wrapper. Other database operations with remote session EJBs are possible, as long as the EJB method is invoked directly. EJBs must be remote session beans (consuming entity beans is not supported).

Create a Project

1. From Creator's Welcome Page, select Create New Project. Creator displays the New Project dialog. Under Categories, select Web. Under Projects, select JSF Web Application. Click Next.
2. In the New Web Application dialog under Project Name, specify **EJBTravel**. Click Finish.

   After initializing the project, Creator comes up in the design view of the editor pane. You can now set the title.

3. In the Properties window, select property `Title` and specify title **EJB Travel**. Finish by pressing **<Enter>**.

Add Components to the Page

Figure 11–18 shows the project in the design view with the components added. The page includes a grid panel for layout, a drop down list for selection, and two tables to display the selected data. You'll start by adding components to the page. Then, you'll select the EJB methods and bind them to the appropriate components.

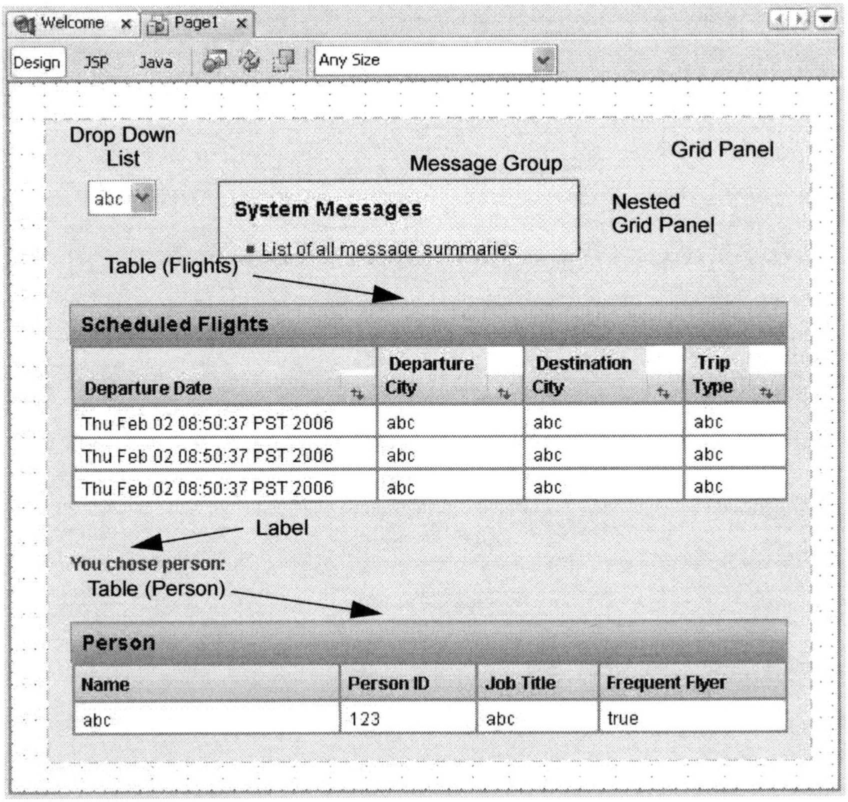

Figure 11–18 **Page1 design view for EJBTravel**

1. From the Layout Components palette, select Grid Panel and drop it on the page.
2. In the Properties view, set property `bgcolor` to **#eeeeee**, `cellpadding` to **15**, `columns` to **1**, and `width` to **90%**. The grid panel's background color changes to a light blue-gray.
3. From the Layout Components palette, select a second Grid Panel and drop it on top of the grid panel you just added.
4. In the Properties view, change its `id` property to **nestedPanel**, `cellpadding` to **10**, and `columns` to **2**. This nested grid panel will hold a drop down list and a message group component.
5. From the Basic Components palette, select Drop Down List and drop it on top of the nested grid panel (either use the Page1 Outline view or check that the desired target component is outlined in blue in the design view).

6. From the Basic Components palette, select Message Group and drop it on top of the nested grid panel. The message group will appear next to the drop down list component.

   You'll now add two tables and a label component to the page.

1. From the Basic Components palette, select Table and drop it on top of the top-level grid panel component (`gridPanel1`). Use the Outline view.
2. Change the table's title to **Scheduled Flights**.
3. From the Basic Components palette, select Label and drop it on top of the top-level grid panel component. Set its text to **You chose person:**.
4. From the Basic Components palette, select a second Table and drop it on top of the top-level grid panel in the Outline view.
5. Change the table's title to **Person**.

Add EJB Method Data Providers

Now let's add the EJB methods to the page. Table 11.1 on page 520 lists the available methods with TravelEJB. Only one method, `getPersons()`, does not require a parameter. This is the method you'll use to perform the initial data display.

1. From the Servers window under Enterprise JavaBeans > Travel Center > TravelEJB, select **getPersons** and drop it on top of the drop down list. (Release the mouse after the drop down list is outlined in blue.) Creator generates EJB client `travelClient1` and `travelGetPersons1` data provider.
2. In the design view, select the drop down list component, right-click, and select Bind to Data.
3. Creator pops up the Bind to Data dialog. The Bind to Data Provider tab should be selected.
4. In the Value field window, select **personId** ***int***. In the Display field window, select **name** ***String***. Click Apply and OK to close. Creator will generate a converter for the `personId` integer field.

   You'll now add two more EJB methods: `getTripsByPerson()` and `getPersonById()`.

1. From the Servers window under Enterprise JavaBeans > Travel Center > TravelEJB, select **getTripsByPerson** and drop it on top of the first table (`table1`). (Release the mouse after the table is outlined in blue.) Creator generates data provider `travelGetTripsByPerson1`. Creator configures the table component to reflect the fields in the `travelGetTripsByPerson1` data provider.
2. Repeat this step and add **getPersonById**. Drop it on top of the second table component (`table2`). Again, wait until the table is outlined in blue. Creator

configures the table component to reflect the fields in the `travelGetPersonById1` data provider.

Configure the Table Components

You'll now configure the first table component.

1. Select component `table1`, right-click, and select Table Layout. Creator pops up the Table Layout dialog.
2. Move columns **personId** and **tripId** from the Selected window to the Available window using the left-arrow (<).
3. Using the Up and Down buttons, rearrange the order of the Selected fields to **depDate**, **depCity**, **destCity** and **tripType**.
4. Select column **depDate** and change its Header Text to **Departure Date**.
5. Select column **depCity** and change its Header Text to **Departure City**.
6. Select column **destCity** and change its Header Text to **Destination City**.
7. Select column **tripType** and change its Header Text to **Trip Type**.
8. Select Apply then OK to close the dialog. The design view reflects the reconfigured table.

Make similar configuration changes to the second table.

1. Select component `table2`, right-click, and select Table Layout. Creator pops up the Table Layout dialog.
2. Using the Up and Down buttons, rearrange the order of the Selected fields to **name**, **personId**, **jobTitle**, **freqFlyer**.
3. Select column **name** and change its Header Text to **Name**.
4. Select column **personId** and change its Header Text to **Person ID**.
5. Select column **jobTitle** and change its Header Text to **Job Title**.
6. Select column **freqFlyer** and change its Header Text to **Frequent Flyer**.
7. Select Apply then OK to close the dialog. The design view reflects the reconfigured table.

Add a Session Bean Property

This application requires a session bean property to keep track of the currently selected value from the drop down list component. This requirement is subtle and is only necessary if a user selects one of the sorting options on the table. When a sorting selection is made, the page is rendered and the Page1 method `init()` is invoked. Method `init()` must make sure it uses the currently selected value stored in session scope. (This will be clearer when you add the initialization code to the Page1 method `init()`.)

1. In the Projects view, right-click Session Bean and select Add > Property. Creator pops up the New Property Pattern dialog.
2. For Name specify **myPersonId**, for Type specify **Integer**, and for Mode keep the default **Read/Write**. Click OK to close the dialog.
3. Double-click node Session Bean. Creator brings up **SessionBean1.java** in the Java source editor.
4. Add the following code to the end of method `init()`. The added code is bold.

```
public void init() {
   . . .
   // TODO - add your own initialization code here
   myPersonId = null;
}
```

Add Event Handling Code

When a user selects a name from the drop down list, the process value change event handler provides parameters to refresh the data providers and supply the requested data to the tables.

1. In the Page1 design view, right-click the drop down list component and select Auto-Submit on Change. This submits the page when the user changes the selection.
2. Now double-click the drop down list component.
3. Creator generates default code for method `dropDown1_processValueChange()` and brings up **Page1.java** in the source editor with the cursor at the first line of this method.
4. Add the following code to the event handler. Copy and paste from **FieldGuide2/Examples/EJB/snippets/travelEJB_dropDown1.txt**. The added code is bold.

Listing 11.4 Method `dropDown1_processValueChange()`

```
public void dropDown1_processValueChange(
        ValueChangeEvent event) {
   Integer personId = (Integer)dropDown1.getSelected();
   travelGetTripsByPerson1.setPersonId(personId);
   travelGetTripsByPerson1.refresh();
   travelGetPersonById1.setId(personId);
   travelGetPersonById1.refresh();
   getSessionBean1().setMyPersonId(personId);
}
```

The event handler obtains personId from the drop down list and calls method `setPersonId()` for the `travelGetTripsByPerson1` data provider. The `refresh()` call invokes the EJB method for that data provider. The event handler also uses personId from the drop down list to call method `setId()` for the `travelGetPersonById1` data provider. Method `refresh()` updates the second data provider as well. The last statement saves the newly selected personId in session scope.

Specify Initialization

The design approach for this application requires an initial value for the personId. Otherwise, an attempt to invoke the data providers' methods without valid arguments causes a run time exception.

1. **Page1.java** should still be active in the Java editor. Scroll up and find method `init()`.
2. Add the following code to the end of the method. Copy and paste from **FieldGuide2/Examples/EJB/snippets/travelEJB_init.txt**. The added code is bold.

```
public void init() {
  . . .
  // TODO - add your own initialization code here
  Integer personId = getSessionBean1().getMyPersonId();

  if (personId == null) {
    personId = (Integer)travelGetPersons1.getValue(
          travelGetPersons1.getFieldKey("personId"));
    getSessionBean1().setMyPersonId(personId);
  }

  dropDown1.setSelected(personId);
  travelGetTripsByPerson1.setPersonId(personId);
  travelGetPersonById1.setId(personId);
}
```

Here `init()` checks to see if a non-null value for session bean property `myPersonId` exists. If not, the data provider method `getValue()` obtains an initial personId using FieldKey. The rest of `init()` uses this value to initialize property `myPersonId`, the drop down component, and the method parameters.

Deploy and Run

Deploy and run application EJBTravel. Figure 11–19 shows one result for a selection from the drop down list.

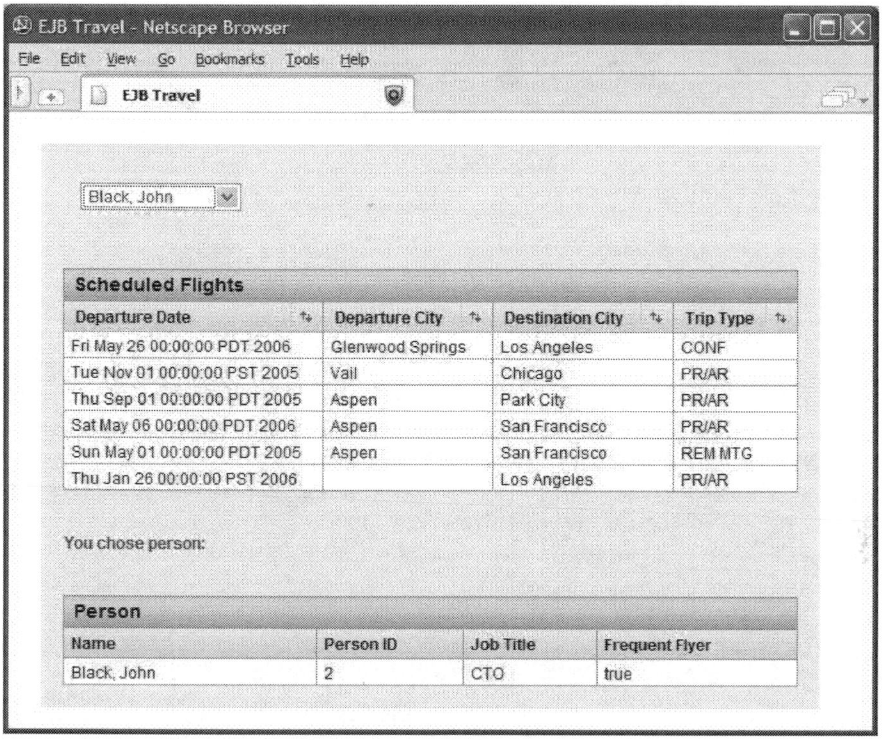

Figure 11–19 **Application EJBTravel running in a browser**

11.5 Adding EJBs to Creator

When you use EJBs in Creator applications, you'll need to add application target EJBs to the IDE. These EJBs must be deployed, but they don't have to be deployed on your local server. Adding EJBs to the Servers window involves inspecting deployed JAR files and extracting the information Creator needs to invoke EJB method calls. This is not a difficult task, but there are a few guidelines to follow.

- Creator supports the consumption of remote session beans only. In reality, this restriction shouldn't be prohibitive, since a common way of accessing entity beans is through a session facade EJB.
- You must deploy the EJB before you can add it to Creator's Servers window.

- Currently, Creator supports adding EJBs from application servers listed in Table 11.2.

Table 11.2 Supported Application Servers for EJB Adds

Sun Java System Application Server 8.2
Sun Java System Application Server 8.1
Sun Java System Application Server 8
Sun Application Server 7
BEA WebLogic 8.1
IBM WebSphere 5.1

- You must provide a Server Host and RMI-IIOP port for the application server. (With the bundled application server, use `localhost` for the Server Host and `24700` for the default RMI-IIOP port.)
- You supply an EJB Set Name and the name and location of the client JAR file.

  (The client JAR file contains all the necessary classes for a client (that is, your web application) to call the EJBs. If the web application is running in a J2EE environment, the client JAR file needs to include the home interfaces, remote interfaces, and the classes those interfaces depend on. Creator also requires the EJB deployment descriptors in order to display the EJBs in the Servers window.)

- As you step through adding the EJB set to the IDE, you'll have a chance to specify the element class for collection return values (if applicable), as well as the names of any method parameters. The default method parameter name is `arg0` (the historical influence of the C Programming Language lives on).

Creator Tip

If an EJB returns an Array of objects, Creator figures out the element class for the return values. A Collection (such as ArrayList) return value requires that you specify the element class when you add the EJB to the Servers window.

Add LoanEJB

Let's add an example EJB to the Servers window in Creator. Before you can manipulate the Enterprise JavaBeans node, you must deploy the EJB. Let's do that now.[1]

1. Make sure the Deployment Server is running. From the Servers window, the Deployment Server node should display a green up-arrow badge indicating that it is running.
2. If the application server is not running, right-click the Deployment Server node and select Start / Stop Server. Creator displays the Server Status dialog.
3. Click Start Server.

You'll now deploy the EJB (jar file) provided with the book's examples. This requires that you login into the server's Admin Console. Here are the steps.

1. From Creator's Servers window (the Deployment Server should be running), right-click Deployment Server and select View Admin Console.
2. Creator pops up a Log In window.
3. For User Name specify **admin** and for Password use **adminadmin.**
4. Under Common Tasks, select Application Server > Applications > EJB Modules. The Admin Console displays all deployed EJB Modules (if any).
5. Select button Deploy. The Admin Console displays Deploy EJB Module.
6. Under Location, select **Specify a package file to upload to the Application Server** and select Browse.
7. In the File Upload dialog, browse to your Field Guide download directory, select file **FieldGuide2/Examples/EJB/ejb-jar-loanBean.jar**, and click Open.
8. Select Next and then OK. Figure 11–20 shows the console after you finish deployment.
9. Select the LOGOUT button at the top of the window to end your session.

Now that the LoanEJB is deployed, let's add it to the IDE so you can access it in your projects. Note that you can access EJBs deployed on other machines as well (not just the local machine), as long as the application server is listed in Table 11.2 on page 528.

1. The Deployment Server should be running and LoanEJB should be deployed.
2. From the Servers window, right-click Enterprise JavaBeans and select Add Set of Session EJBs. Creator displays the Add Set of Session EJBs dialog.

---

1. This EJB example is taken from "The Loan Enterprise Bean," Anderson and Anderson, *Enterprise JavaBeans Component Architecture,* Sun MicroSystems Press, Prentice Hall, 2002.

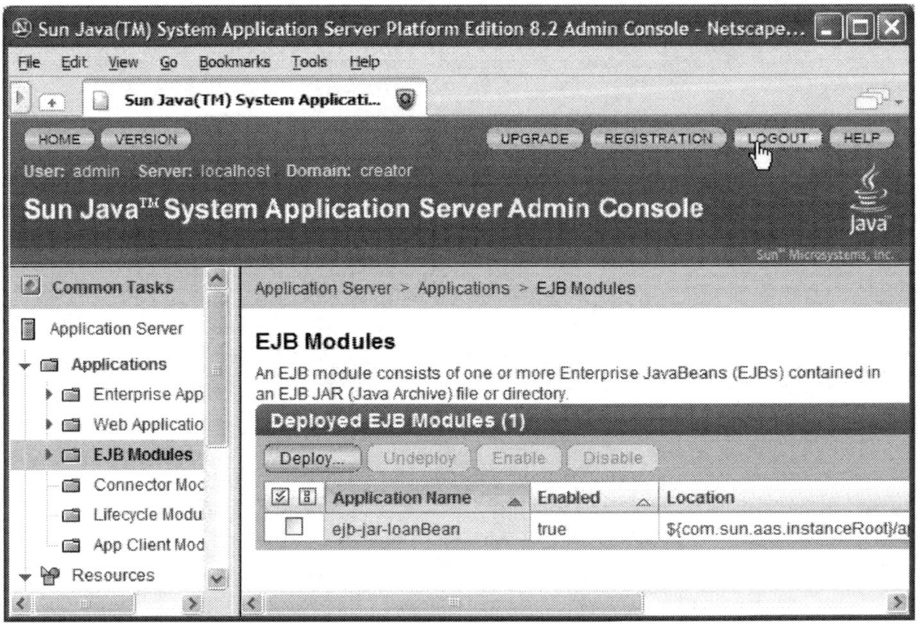

Figure 11–20 **System Application Server Admin Console**

3. For EJB Set Name specify **LoanEJB**, for Application Server use the default **Sun Java System Application Server 8.2**, and for RMI-IIOP port specify **24700**.

Creator Tip

The correct value for the bundled application server RMI-IIOP port is 24700.

4. Click Add to add the client jar.
5. Browse to **<Creator-install-directory>/SunAppServer8/domains/creator/applications/j2ee-modules/ejb-jar-loanBean/ejb-jar-loanBeanClient.jar** and click Open. (The client jar file is embedded in the deployed EJB jar file.) Click Next.
6. You'll now configure the EJB methods `annualAmortTable`, `monthlyAmort-Table`, and `monthlyPayment`. The first two methods require an Element Class for the ArrayList return object. Use `asg.LoanEJB.PaymentVO` for both methods. You should also change the method parameter name from `arg0` to **loanVO** (use lower-case for the initial letter) for all three methods. Class LoanVO stands for Loan Value Object. Table 11.3 shows the settings.

Table 11.3 EJB Method Configuration for LoanEJB

Method Name	*Element Class*	*Parameter Name*
annualAmortTable	asg.LoanEJB.PaymentVO	loanVO
monthlyAmortTable	asg.LoanEJB.PaymentVO	loanVO
monthlyPayment	not applicable	loanVO

When you're finished configuring the methods, each of them should have an orange circle next to the method name. Figure 11–21 shows the setting for method `monthlyAmortTable`.

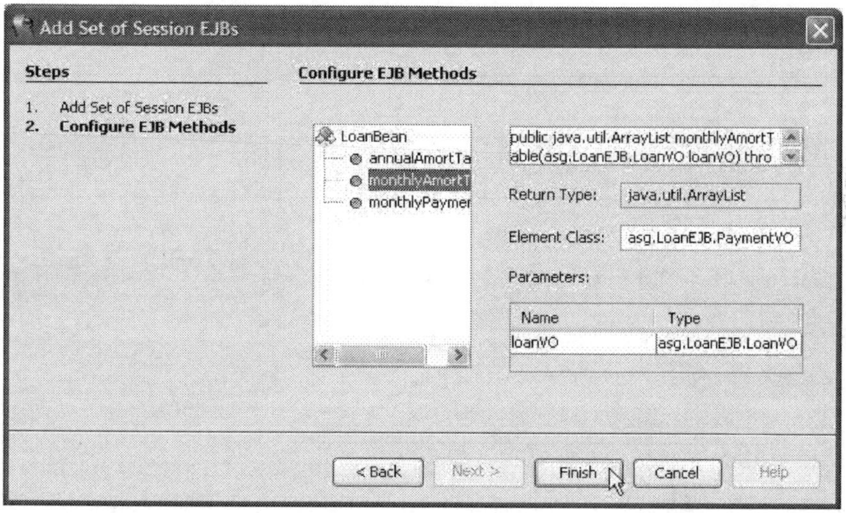

Figure 11–21 **Configure EJB Methods during Add**

7. Click Finish. The Servers window should now include LoanEJB under node Enterprise JavaBeans, as shown in Figure 11–22. Note that each method includes a data provider badge with the icon. This means the method is droppable and its return value(s) can be wrapped by a data provider.

Consuming the LoanEJB

In this section, you're going to modify project Payment1 (see "LoanBean" on page 242 from Chapter 6) to use an EJB component instead of the project's LoanBean JavaBeans component. The design approach is similar to Payment1, where you'll define a session bean property to hold loan information. The dif-

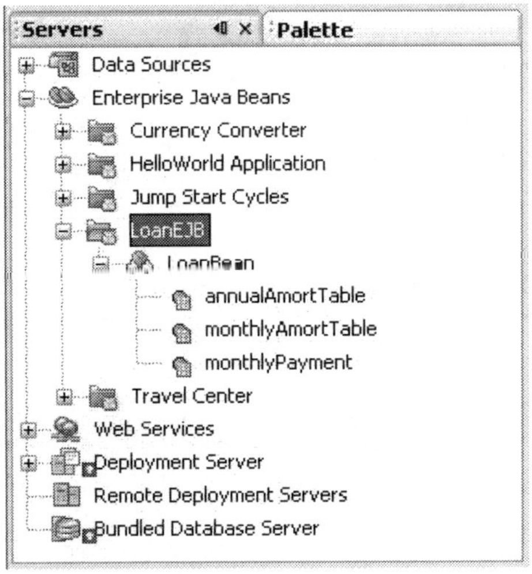

Figure 11–22 **Servers view showing LoanEJB added to Enterprise JavaBeans node**

ference is you'll invoke EJB method `monthlyPayment()` to calculate the mortgage's payment.

Copy the Project

To avoid starting from scratch, copy project Payment1 to a new project called EJBPayment1. This step is optional. If you don't want to copy the project, simply skip this section and continue making modifications to project Payment1.

1. Bring up project Payment1 in Creator, if it's not already opened. (If you didn't build project Payment1, use the pre-built project found in **FieldGuide2/Examples/JavaBeans/Projects/Payment1**.)
2. From the Projects window, right-click node Payment1 and select Save Project As. Provide the new name **EJBPayment1**.
3. Close project Payment1. Right-click EJBPayment1 and select Set Main Project. You'll make changes to the EJBPayment1 project.
4. Expand EJBPayment1 > Web Pages and open **Page1.jsp** in the design view.
5. Click anywhere in the background of the design canvas of the EJBPayment1 project. In the Properties window, change the page's `Title` property to **EJB - Payment Calculator**.

Add an EJB Method

Use the Servers window to add the LoanBean method data provider to your project.

1. In the Servers view, expand Enterprise JavaBeans > LoanEJB > LoanBean.
2. Select **monthlyPayment** and drop it on the page in the design view. Creator adds EJB client `loanClient1` and data provider `loanMonthlyPayment1` to the Page1 Outline view.

Delete Local LoanBean Component

You'll replace the **asg.bean_examples/LoanBean** component you added to the project to build Payment1. In this step, you'll first delete the source for this component and then delete the corresponding session bean property.

1. In the Projects view, expand EJBPayment1 > Source Packages. You'll see a node for **payment1** as well as **asg.bean_examples**.
2. Right-click **asg.bean_examples** and select Delete to remove this node (and all source code under it) from the project. Select Yes in the confirmation dialog.
3. In the Outline view, expand the SessionBean1 node, right-click `loanBean`, and select Delete. This deletes session bean property `loanBean` from your project.
4. In the Projects view, double-click node Session Bean to bring up **SessionBean1.java** in the source editor.
5. Find method `init()` and delete the initialization statement of `loanBean` from the method.
6. Delete the remaining comments from the deleted `loanBean` property (at the end of the file).

Add a Session Bean Property

You'll now add a session bean property to replace the `loanBean` property you just deleted.

1. In the Projects view, right-click node Session Bean and select Add > Property.
2. For name specify **loanBean**, for type specify **LoanVO**, and for Mode specify **Read/Write**. Click OK. Recall that LoanVO stands for Loan Value Object, which is the method parameter type required by the EJB `monthlyPayment()` method.
3. Double-click node Session Bean to bring up **SessionBean1.java** in the Java source editor.

4. Place the cursor in the background, right-click, and select Fix Imports to add the import statement for class LoanVO. This also removes the import statement for the removed **asg.bean_examples.LoanBean** class.
5. Add an initialization statement to the end of method `init()`, as follows. The added statement is bold.

```
public void init() {
    . . .
    loanBean = new LoanVO(100000.0, 5.0, 15);
}
```

Provide Property Bindings

The three text field components hold the amount, interest rate, and term. You'll bind the `text` property of each of these components to the related property of the LoanVO session property.

1. In the Page1 design view, select text field component `loanAmount`, right-click, and select Property Bindings. Creator pops up the Property Bindings dialog.
2. Under Select bindable property choose **text *Object***. For Select binding target, choose **SessionBean1 > loanBean > amount *double***. Select Apply and Close.
3. Repeat Steps 1 and 2 for text field component `interestRate`. Choose binding target **SessionBean1 > loanBean > rate *double***.
4. Repeat Steps 1 and 2 for text field component `loanTerm`. Choose binding target **SessionBean1 > loanBean > years *int***.

You'll now bind the static text component `cost` with the `resultObject` (return object) of the `loanMonthlyPayment1` data provider.

1. In the Page1 design view, select static text component `cost`. Right-click and select Bind to Data.
2. Select tab Bind to an Object. In the Select binding target window, choose **Page1 > loanMonthlyPayment1 > resultObject *Double***. Click Apply and Close as shown in Figure 11–23. The `cost` component now renders as $123.45 in the design view.

Since method `monthlyPayment()` requires a parameter, you need to invoke method `setLoanVO()` to initialize it.

1. Click the Java label in the editing toolbar to bring up **Page1.java** in the Java source editor.

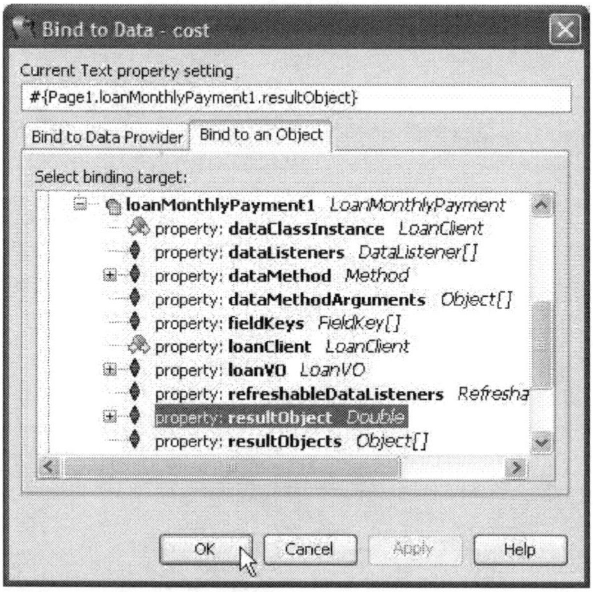

Figure 11–23 **Bind to Data dialog**

2. Add the following initialization statement to the end of method `init()`, as follows. The added code is bold.

```
public void init() {
   . . .
   // TODO - add your own initialization code here
   loanMonthlyPayment1.setLoanVO(
            getSessionBean1().getLoanBean());
}
```

Deploy and Run

Deploy and run application EJBPayment1. Figure 11–24 shows the project running in a browser with the tooltip for the Loan Amount field displayed.

Project Payment2 Alternative

You can also adapt project Payment2 (see "Object List Data Provider" on page 351) to use LoanEJB method `monthlyAmortTable`. Follow the same modifications for implementing EJBPayment1 from project Payment1. Drop `monthlyAmortTable` directly on the table component in **Schedule.jsp**. You can then

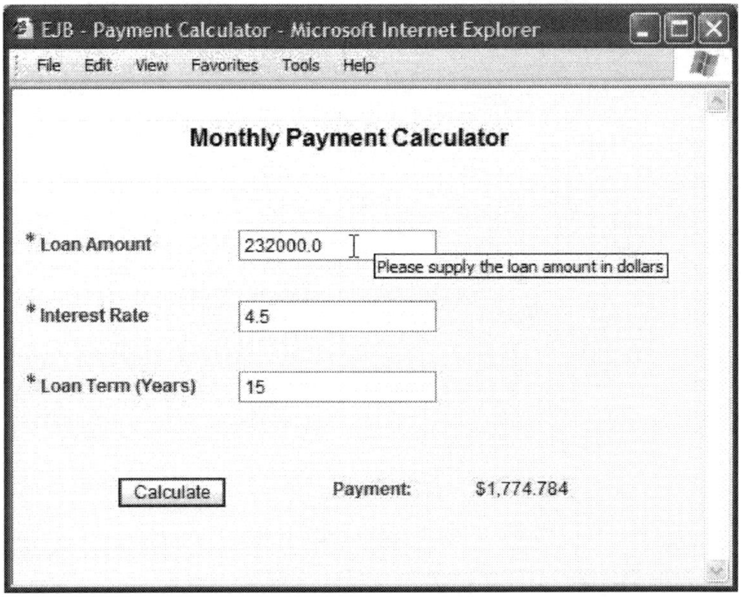

Figure 11–24 **Application EJBPayment1 running in a browser**

configure the table with the desired fields from the EJB data provider. We show this implementation in **FieldGuide2/Examples/EJB/Projects/EJBPayment2.**

11.6 Key Point Summary

Enterprise JavaBeans (EJBs) provide an important architectural option for adding scalable functionality to a web application. Creator allows you to consume session beans by generating clients that access the EJB methods. It also builds a data provider interface so that you can bind method return objects to Creator's data-aware components.

- EJBs are server-side components that encapsulate an application's business logic. They provide a distributed alternative to JavaBeans components.
- Creator comes bundled with several sample sets of session EJBs that you can add to your projects.
- If you add an EJB component to your design page, Creator generates a client that invokes the desired EJB method. When used in this way, you place the method call in a try block.

- If you add an EJB *method* to your design page, Creator generates both a client and a data provider that invokes the method and generates return values. You can access these return values through the data provider.
- If you bind a component to an EJB method data provider, you must provide initialization data if the method takes a parameter.
- You can bind Creator's data-aware components to the EJB method data providers. This is a convenient way to fill components such as list box, drop down list, and table.
- When an EJB method is selected, the Properties window displays important usage information about the method, such as its signature, name, return type, and method parameter.
- You can add sets of session EJBs to the Creator Servers window. The EJBs must be deployed on one of the supported application servers listed in Table 11.2 on page 528. The EJBs can be deployed on an application server on the local machine or a remote server.
- When you add an EJB set that's deployed on the bundled application server, use RMI-IIOP port 24700.
- You can configure an EJB method during the process that adds the EJB set to Creator's Servers window. You specify the element class for any method that returns a collection. You also rename the method parameter (from the default name `arg0`).
- If the EJB method returns an Array then Creator can determine the element class for the return value, making Arrays the preferred return type (instead of Collections).

PORTLETS

Topics in This Chapter

- JSF Portlets and JSR-168
- Design Time Experience with Portlets
- Portlet View Mode, Edit Mode, Help Mode
- Page Navigation with Portlets
- Page Layout with Portlets
- Portlet Life Cycle

Chapter 12

Portlets provide a customized view within a fragment of a web page. The job of the portal is to aggregate portlets into a complete page. With Creator, you can create a JSF portlet application that conforms to the Java Specification Request (JSR) 168 Portlet specification, ensuring that your portlet application works with any JSR-168 compliant portlet server.

In this chapter we look at portlet application development using Creator. We show you how portlet development differs from non-portlet Creator web applications and show you how to leverage Creator's IDE to build portlet applications. You'll see that many of the web application features apply to portlets, such as JavaBeans objects, page navigation, and database, web service, and EJB access.

12.1 What Are Portlets?

A portlet is an application that runs on a web site managed by a server called a *portal*. A portal server manages multiple portlet applications, displaying them on the web page together. Each portlet consumes a fragment of the page and manages its own information and user interaction. Portlet application developers will typically target portlets to run under portals provided by various portal vendors. JSR-168 establishes a standard for creating portlets, which allows any portlet that conforms to JSR-168 to run in any JSR- 168 compliant portal.

Creator includes a bundled portal driver called Pluto, developed at the Apache Software Foundation. Pluto is a reference implementation of the JSR-168 specification for portal servers. When you deploy a portlet project, Creator deploys the portlet container for you and brings up your portlet project in Pluto in your target web browser.

You can also deploy the portlet application to other JSR-168 compliant portal servers. Creator provides a dialog that allows you to export the portlet Web Archive (WAR) and configure it for deployment on the target portal server. Final deployment takes place on the target system where you can also specify deployment options (which may also include portal-specific configuration).

Creator builds JSF portlets. This means your design-time experience in building portlet web application using the visual, drag-and-drop features of Creator will be familiar. Most of the interaction with the IDE is exactly the same as it is for non-portlet JSF projects.

Portlet Modes

Portlets have three standard modes: View, Edit, and Help. The portal server manages the modes for an application and provides page decorations that allow you to switch modes.

View mode is the default and normal mode for user interaction with a portlet. When you develop a portlet with Creator, the initial page, **PortletPage1.jsp**, is the initial View mode page. Edit mode allows users to customize the portlet and Help mode provides information about the portlet to the user. You can create Edit and Help mode pages (and additional View mode pages) for your portlet through the IDE.

Portlet Navigation

JSF-based portlets use the standard JSF navigation engine. Thus, you can use Creator's navigation editor to provide navigation for your portlet. Each portlet mode has its own navigation rules. As a portlet designer, you should treat each mode separately for navigation. Therefore, if your View mode contains three pages, you'll define the navigation among these three pages in isolation of any Edit or Help mode interaction. Similarly, you would define Edit mode navigation in isolation of View or Help modes.

Creator Tip

Creator's IDE lets you define navigation links to any page, regardless of its mode. However, mixing modes through JSF navigation presents a confusing model for the user, since the portal server manages navigation among a portlet's modes. To keep the user experience consistent, don't define navigation links across portlet modes.

Portlet Real Estate

Because a portlet is a page fragment (managed by the portal server), you'll have a smaller area to work with when building the portlet application. Like the page fragment box component that Creator provides, the IDE design view for portlets is a subset of a full page. Creator marks the usable design area with a white background. This reduced real estate means that your mind set must shift a bit when designing portlet applications. Typically, you'll "down size" your target page layout. You'll start thinking in terms of "small is good" or "how can I display this information in a small area?"

Some of Creator components have alternate, "lite" or "mini" versions that are more suitable for portlets. For example, the button component has a `mini` property which renders a smaller version of a button. The table and tab set component also offer smaller (lite) versions.

Portlet Life Cycle

You've seen the life cycle of a JSF application in a previous chapter (see "The Creator-JSF Life Cycle" on page 260). Here, we'll briefly describe the JSF *portlet* life cycle. A portlet application shares the browser page with other portlets. The user interacts with only *one portlet* at a time. Thus, only *one portlet* processes user input and possibly invokes event handlers. All portlets on the page, however, must go through the render phase. For this reason, the normal JSF life cycle for portlets is split into *two cycles*—one for the form submit processing and one for rendering.

How does this difference affect the portlet application model? It means you cannot use request scope objects to transfer data from the form submission phase to the rendering phase. Request scope objects include objects within **RequestBean1.java** and any request scope managed beans (the page beans). You can, however, use session scope objects to cache data. You can pull data out of session scope objects in method `prerender()` for the rendering phase, or use property bindings with session scope objects. For example, during a form submission (without navigating to a new page), the JSF life cycle phases and framework calls are as follows.

```
Restore View Phase
  PortletPage1.init()
  PortletPage1.preprocess()
Apply Request Values Phase
Process Validations Phase
Update Model Values Phase
Invoke Applications Phase
  PortletPage1.destroy()

  PortletPage1.init()
  PortletPage1.prerender()
RenderResponse Phase
  PortletPage1.destroy()
```

Thus, data acquired in the page bean during the first cycle (Restore View Phase through the first page bean `destroy()` call) will not be retained when the page bean is instantiated during the rendering process.

If you navigate to a new page, the framework calls the second `init()` through `destroy()` on the new page (here, PortletPage2) during the rendering process, as follows.

```
Restore View Phase
  PortletPage1.init()
  PortletPage1.preprocess()
Apply Request Values Phase
Process Validations Phase
Update Model Values Phase
Invoke Applications Phase
  PortletPage1.destroy()

  PortletPage2.init()
  PortletPage2.prerender()
RenderResponse Phase
  PortletPage2.destroy()
```

The JSF component tree (containing the actual UI component objects) *is* maintained throughout the JSF life cycle. Therefore, you *can* store data in the components themselves. However, using session scope objects to pass data to the render phase is the method we'll use in our example projects.

Note that currently you can deploy only one portlet at a time using the bundled portal server in Creator.

12.2 Creating a Portlet Project

Let's begin with a simple portlet application. Our example is a portlet that echoes text provided by the user. You'll see how the development steps generally mirror non-portlet applications. Along the way, we'll point out differences between portlet applications and non-portlet applications built with Creator.

Create a Portlet Project

1. From Creator's Welcome Page, select button Create New Project. From the New Project dialog, under Categories select **Web** and under Projects select **JSR-168 JSF Portlet Project**. Click Next.
2. In the New Portlet dialog, specify **PortletEcho** for Project Name and click Next.
3. Creator displays the New Project dialog which includes the Portlet Deployment Descriptor for the portlet project, as shown in Figure 12–1. Accept the defaults and click Finish.

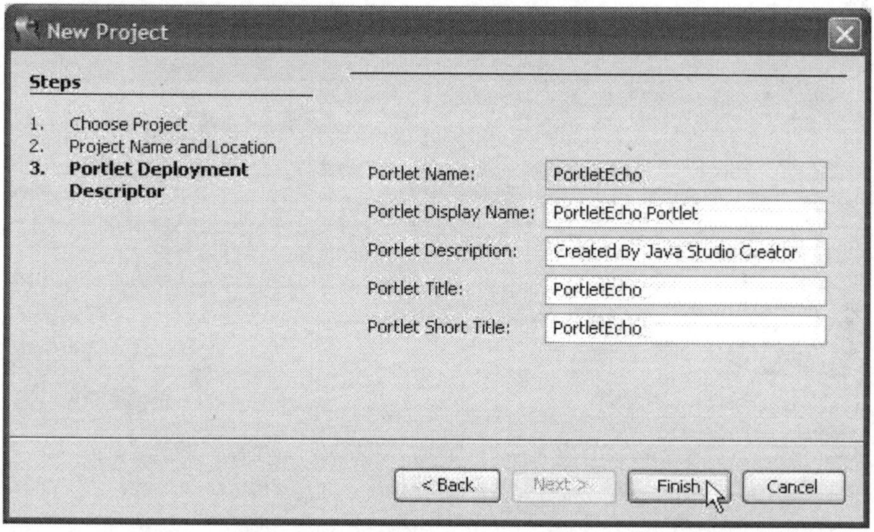

Figure 12–1 **New Project dialog for JSF portlet projects**

Creator Tip

You can change default information about the portlet, including its display name, description, and titles (regular and short). You can also edit this deployment descriptor later. In the Projects window, right-click the portlet project name and select Edit Deployment Descriptor.

After initializing the project, Creator comes up in the design view of the editor pane. It creates an initial page with default name PortletPage1 and uses the `div` element (similar to the Page Fragment Box) to contain the page's `form` element. The portlet page fragment default size is 400 by 400 pixels.

Add Components to PortletPage1

The portlet page is configured in a white background by default and the design editor displays a contrasting background for the area outside the fragment boundary. Figure 12–2 shows the design view with several components added. You'll use normal drag-and-drop component selection to add components to the page.

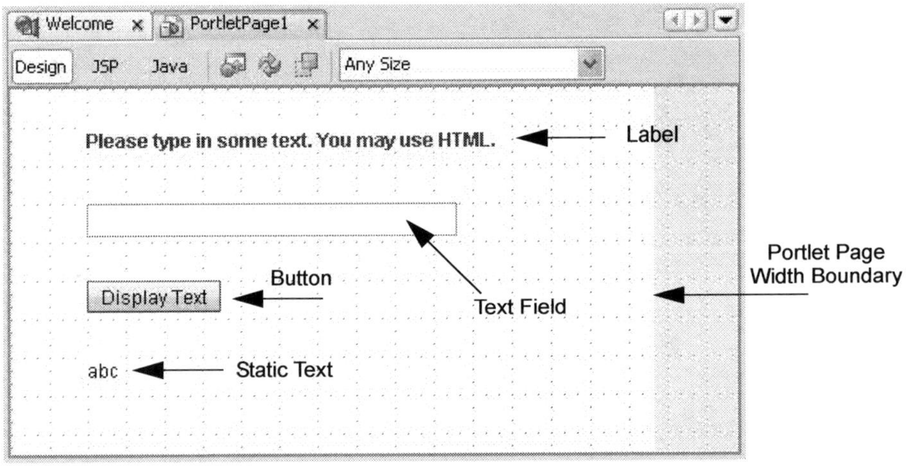

Figure 12–2 **PortletPage1 design view for project PortletEcho**

1. From the Basic Components palette, select Label and drop it on the page near the top, left-hand portion of the design area.
2. The label will be selected. Type in the text **Please type in some text. You may use HTML.** followed by **<Enter>**.
3. From the Basic Components palette, select Text Field and drop it on the page under the label component.

4. From the Basic Components palette, select Button and place it below the text field component. Supply the text **Display Text** followed by **<Enter>** to set the button's label.
5. Make sure the button is still selected. In the Properties view, change property `id` to **display**.
6. From the Basic Components palette, select Static Text and place it below the button component.
7. Make sure the component is still selected. In the Properties view, *uncheck* the `escape` attribute. This allows HTML tags to be interpreted by the browser.

Figure 12–3 shows the PortletPage1 Outline view after the components are added to the page.

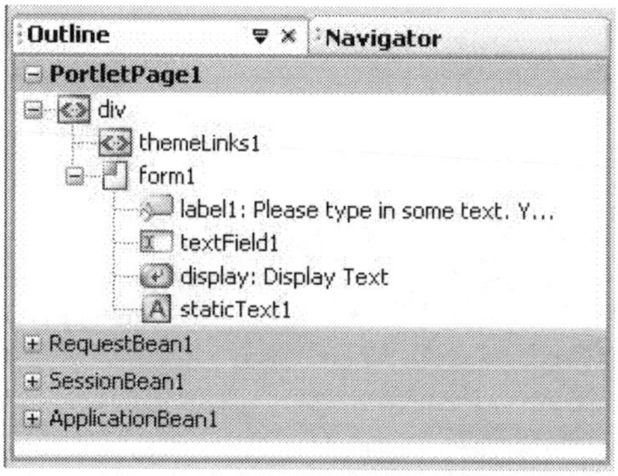

Figure 12–3 **PortletPage1 Outline view**

Add a Save Text Session Bean Property

We now encounter one of the biggest differences between portlet JSF projects and non-portlet JSF projects. With portlet projects, you cannot use request scope objects to cache data within a HTTP request. With regular JSF projects, data in request scope survives the HTTP request, allowing the rendering page to access data that comes from processing the request. Therefore, instead of binding component `textField1` to the static text component `staticText1`, we use a session scope property for data caching. To do this, we'll add a property to SessionBean1 called `saveText` (a String).

1. In the Projects window, right-click Session Bean and select **Add > Property**. Creator displays the New Property Pattern dialog.
2. For Name, specify **saveText**, for Type use **String**, and for Mode, select the default **Read/Write**.
3. Click OK to add the property.

Specify Property Bindings

You can use the JSF property binding mechanism to display the text that the user provides. When you bind both the text field and the static text components to the `saveText` property, user-provided text is stored in property `saveText` during the Update Model Values phase. Similarly, the data in property `saveText` is transferred to both the text field and the static text component during the Render Response phase. If the user provides formatting tags, such as `<b> </b>` pairs, these will affect the text in the static text component since its `escape` property is unchecked.

1. In the PortletPage1 design view, select text field component `textField1`, right-click, and select Property Bindings. Creator displays the Property Bindings dialog.
2. In the Select bindable property window, select **text *Object***. In the Select binding target window, select **SessionBean1 > saveText *String***. Click Apply, as shown in Figure 12–4.

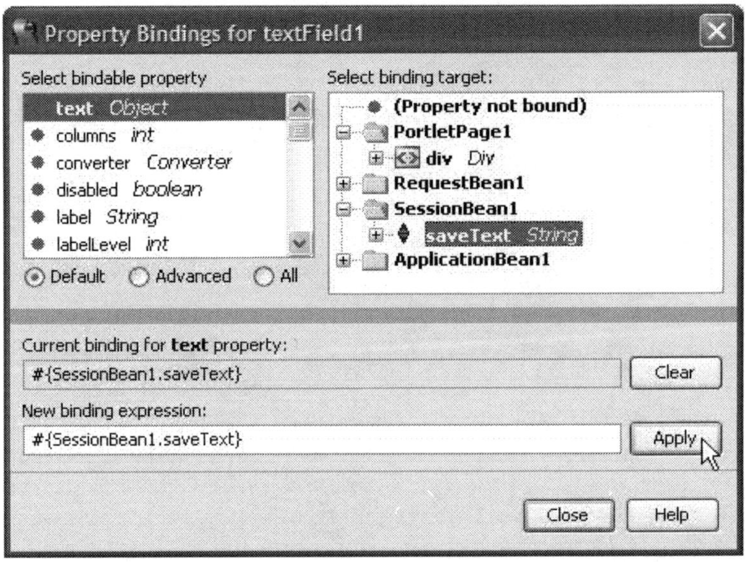

Figure 12–4 **Property Bindings for textField1**

3. Click Close. Creator sets the text field's `text` property to

```
#{SessionBean1.saveText}
```

4. Repeat the property binding for component `staticText1`. Select the component, right-click, and select Property Bindings.

5. Select **text *Object*** for the bindable property and **SessionBean1 > saveText *String*** for the binding target. Click Apply and Close.

Deploy and Run

Click the Run icon on the toolbar to build, deploy, and run the portlet application. The Output window displays several status lines pertaining to the portlet container (which is deployed within the application server). When your portlet comes up in the browser, it is running within the Pluto portlet container, as shown in Figure 12–5. Note that the project's name and title is displayed on the page.

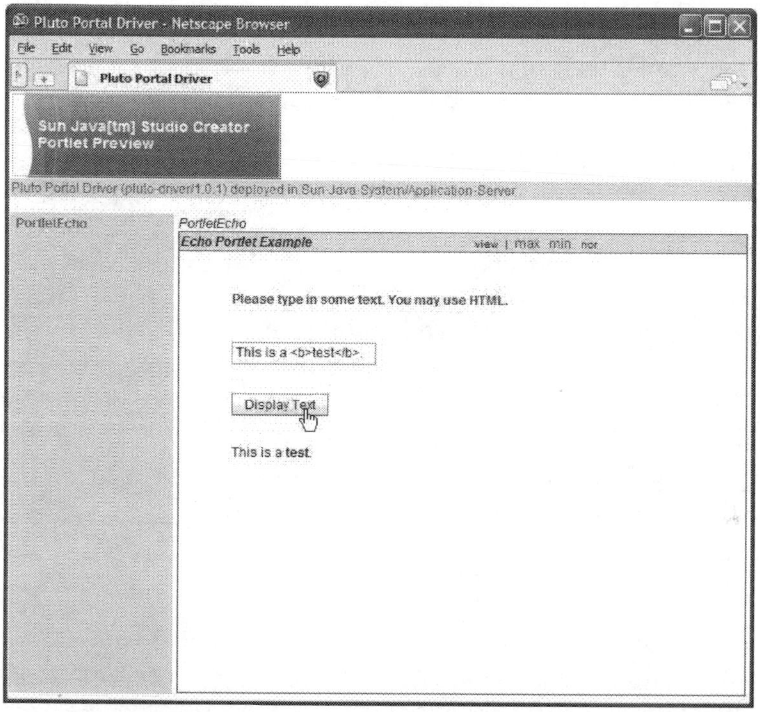

Figure 12–5 **Portlet project PortletEcho running in the portlet container**

12.3 Database Access with Portlets

Creating a portlet that accesses a database is the same as creating a non-portlet JSF project using Creator. The differences are smaller browser real estate and portlet life cycle treatment of request-scope data.

Let's adapt project MusicRead2 (see "Master Detail Application - Two Page" on page 390) and implement it as a portlet. The approach is the same—a table component lists recordings on the first page with a hyperlink component to take users to the second page. This second page displays track details for the selected recording. Because the target application is a portlet, however, you'll make several changes. First, the table component will display only two columns. Second, you'll store the selected RecordingID and RecordingTitle values in session scope rather than request scope. On the tracksDetail page, the table component will implement pagination, limiting the number of rows to seven.

Create a Portlet Project

1. From Creator's Welcome Page, select button Create New Project. From the New Project dialog, under Categories select **Web** and under Projects select **JSR-168 JSF Portlet Project**. Click Next.
2. In the New Portlet dialog, specify **PortletMusic** for Project Name and click Next.
3. Creator displays the New Project dialog which includes the Portlet Deployment Descriptor for the portlet project. Accept the defaults and click Finish.

After initializing the project, Creator comes up in the design view of the editor pane. The initial page has the default name PortletPage1.

Add Session Bean Properties

When the user selects a recording, you'll need to save the RecordingID and the RecordingTitle so that components on the tracksDetail page can access the data. Recall that project MusicRead2 used request scope to store the data, since request scope data is available to the next page in a standard JSF application. With portlets, you must use session scope.

1. In the Projects view, expand the PortletMusic node, select Session Bean, right-click, and select **Add > Property**.
2. Creator pops up the New Property Pattern dialog. For name, specify **recordingID**, for type specify **Integer**, and for Mode keep the default **Read/Write**.
3. Click OK. Creator adds property `recordingID` to **SessionBean1.java**.

Now add a second property, `recordingTitle`, to session scope.

1. In the Projects view, select PortletMusic > Session Bean, right-click, and select **Add > Property**.
2. Creator pops up the New Property Pattern dialog. For name, specify **recordingTitle**, for type specify **String**, and for Mode keep the default **Read/Write**.
3. Click OK. Creator adds property `recordingTitle` to **SessionBean1.java**.
4. In the Outline view expand the SessionBean1 node. You'll see the two session bean properties you just added.

Add Components to the Page

The design view marks the default portlet area, so you'll position the components inside this white background. You'll need a label for the title, a message group component for error messages, and a table component to display the data, as shown in Figure 12–6. The first column uses a hyperlink component and the second columns uses a static text component (the default).

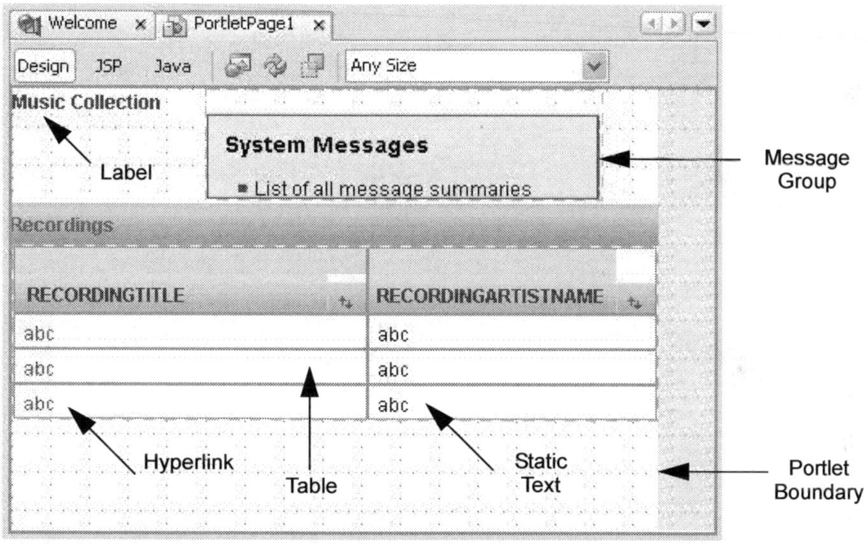

Figure 12–6 **PortletPage1 design view for project PortletMusic**

1. Make sure that PortletPage1 is active in the design view.
2. From the Basic Components palette, select Label and drop it on the page in the top left corner.
3. Supply the text **Music Collection** followed by **<Enter>** to specify the label's text.
4. From the Basic Components palette, select Message Group and drop it on the page to the right of the label.

5. From the Basic Components palette, select Table and drop it on the page. Place it flush to the left and as high as possible without overlapping the message group component. Creator configures the table with a default data provider and default columns and rows.
6. The table title is selected. Change the title to **Recordings**. You'll configure the rest of the table after you add the database table.

Add a Database Table

You can now add the database table to the page. (If you haven't configured the Music database, do this now. See "Configuring the Bundled Database" on page 376 in Chapter 9.)

1. From the Servers window, expand Data Sources > Music Tables nodes.
2. Select table RECORDINGS and drop it on top of the table component (make sure the table component is outlined in blue before releasing the mouse).

Creator configures the table component to accommodate the RECORDINGS data and generates a cached rowset data provider to wrap the cached rowset in session scope.

Query and Table Configuration

You'll first modify the default SQL query and then configure the table component. The portlet will display the recording title and the recording artist name. The recording artist name requires an inner join.

1. From the Outline view, expand SessionBean1 and double-click the cached row set component, `recordingsRowSet`. This brings up the Query Editor in the editor pane. (Close the Output window to make more room for the query editor.)
2. Right-click inside the table view (the top area that shows the RECORDINGS table) and select Add Table from the context menu. Creator pops up the Select Table(s) to Add dialog. Select table RECORDINGARTISTS and click OK. Creator adds an Inner Join clause to the query text. You now see a second table in the Table view.
3. In the Table view, uncheck all fields in the RECORDINGS table except RECORDINGID and RECORDINGTITLE. Uncheck all fields in the RECORDINGARTISTS table except RECORDINGARTISTNAME. (Only three fields total are now checked.)
4. Select File > Save All to save these changes.
5. Return to the design view by selecting the **PortletPage1** tab at the top of the editor pane.

You'll now configure the table layout to display the columns that you want.

1. Select the table component in the design view, right-click, and select Table Layout. Creator brings up the Table Layout dialog.
2. Move the fields between the Available window and the Selected window so that RECORDINGS.RECORDINGTITLE and RECORDING-ARTISTS.RECORDINGARTISTNAME are both in the Selected window. (Make sure that field RecordingTitle is listed first.) Field RECORD-INGS.RECORDINGID should be in the Available window.

Creator Tip

Although you won't display field RECORDINGID, you still need it to identify the relevant tracks in the TRACKS table. That's why this field remains checked in the query editor.

3. In the Selected window, select RECORDINGS.RECORDINGTITLE.
4. Under Column Details for Component Type, select **Hyperlink** from the drop down list. Click Apply then OK. The table component has two columns and the component in the first column is now a hyperlink component.
5. In the Properties window for the table component, set property `width` to **400** (the default width of the portlet area).
6. Still in the Properties window, check property `lite` (this provides a more streamlined looking table component appropriate for portlets).

Now let's provide event handling code for the table's hyperlink component.

1. In the Outline view, select hyperlink component under the first column of the table.
2. Change the `id` property of the hyperlink component to **hyperlinkTitle**.
3. In the Outline view, right-click the hyperlink component and select Edit action Event Handler. Creator generates a default action event handler and brings up the Java source editor.
4. Copy and paste the event handler code from the Creator book download **FieldGuide2/Examples/Portlets/snippets/portletMusic-**

_hyperlinkTitle_action.txt. The added code is bold. (Be sure to replace the `return null` statement with `return "tracks"`.)

Listing 12.1 Method `hyperlinkTitle_action()`

```
public String hyperlinkTitle_action() {
  TableRowDataProvider rowData = (TableRowDataProvider)
      getBean("currentRow");
  getSessionBean1().setRecordingID(
      (Integer)rowData.getValue("RECORDINGS.RECORDINGID"));
  getSessionBean1().setRecordingTitle(
      (String)rowData.getValue("RECORDINGS.RECORDINGTITLE"));
  return "tracks";
}
```

The RECORDINGID and RECORDINGTITLE values of the selected row (object `rowData`) are saved in session scope properties so that they are available to the **tracksDetail.jsp** page, which you'll add to the project in the next section.

1. Right-click and select Fix Imports to fix the syntax errors.
2. Save these modifications by clicking the Save All icon on the toolbar.

Add a New Page

Now let's create a new page to display track data. First, you'll place a label, message group, hyperlink and table component on the tracksDetail page. You'll then add the Music TRACKS table. Figure 12–7 shows the tracksDetail page in the design view.

1. In the Projects view, right-click on node Web Pages and select **New > Portlet Page** from the context menu.
2. Creator pops up the New Portlet Page dialog. Specify **tracksDetail** for the file name and click Finish. Creator brings up page **tracksDetail.jsp** in the design view.
3. From the Basic Components palette, select component Label and place it on the page, near the top left side.
4. Make sure it's selected and type in the text **Tracks Detail** and finish with **<Enter>**.
5. From the Basic Components palette, select component Message Group and drop it onto the page near the top to the right of the label you just added. When you post error messages to the faces context for this page, the message group component will display them.
6. From the Basic Components palette, select component Hyperlink and place it on the page underneath the label component.

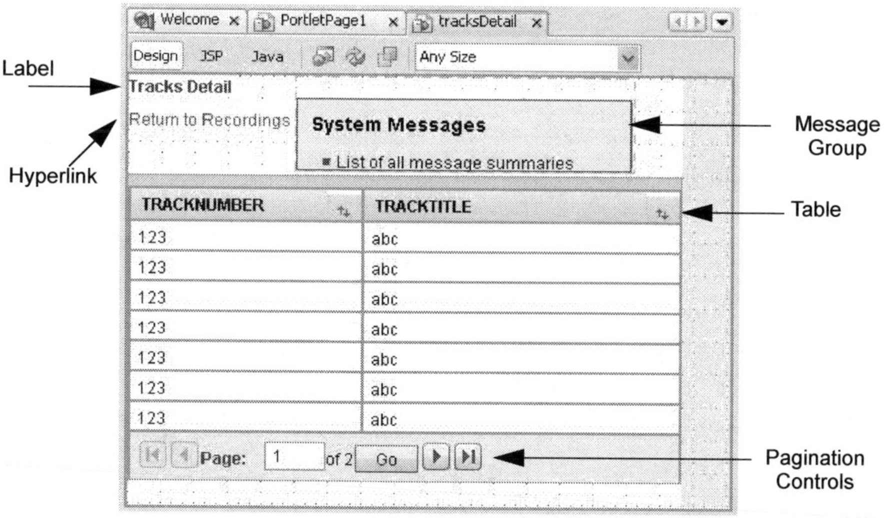

Figure 12–7 **tracksDetail design view for project PortletMusic**

7. Specify **Return to Recordings** for its text. You'll use this component to navigate back to PortletPage1.
8. From the Basic Components palette, select component Table and drop it onto the page. Creator builds a table with default generated rows and columns and a default table data provider.
9. From the Servers view, select the Data Sources > Music > Tables > TRACKS table and drop it on top of the table component you just added. Make sure that you select the *entire* table component when you release the mouse (it will be outlined in blue). Creator modifies the table to match the database fields from the TRACKS table and instantiates the `tracksRowSet` component in session scope.

Modify SQL Query

As it is currently configured, the `tracksRowSet` returns all track records from the Music database. You need to limit the result set so that only the tracks that match the RecordingID selected in the PortletPage1 table are returned. To do this, specify a query criteria so that each record in the Tracks row set matches the RecordingID saved in session scope. You'll use the query editor to modify the SQL query for the Tracks row set.

1. Open the SessionBean1 node in the Outline view and double-click the `tracksRowSet` component. Creator brings up the query editor. Close the Output window if it's open (to make more room).

2. In the spreadsheet view of the query editor, right-click opposite field RECORDINGID and select Add Query Criteria.
3. In the Add Query Criteria dialog, use the default (`= Equals`) for Comparison and select radio button Parameter, as shown in Figure 12–8. Click OK. Creator modifies the query text to include a WHERE clause.

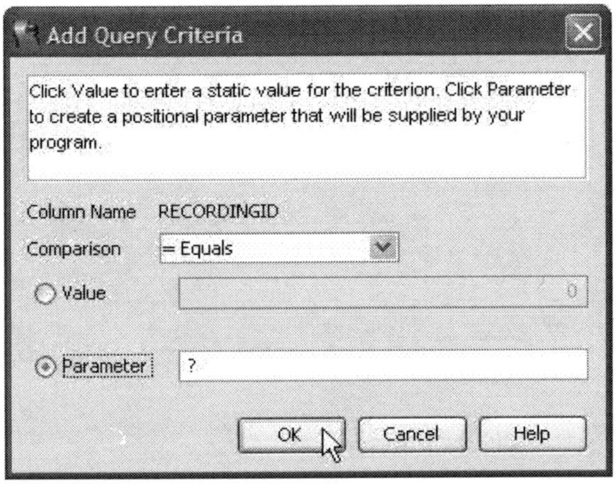

Figure 12–8 **Add Query Criteria dialog**

4. In the Table view, uncheck all fields except TRACKNUMBER and TRACKTITLE in the TRACKS table.
5. In the spreadsheet view of the query editor, click inside cell Sort Type opposite column TRACKNUMBER and select Ascending from the drop down selection. This returns the records sorted by track number (in ascending order). Here is the modified SQL query text with the WHERE and ORDER BY clauses you just added (shown in bold).

```
SELECT ALL MUSIC.TRACKS.TRACKNUMBER, MUSIC.TRACKS.TRACKTITLE
FROM MUSIC.TRACKS
WHERE MUSIC.TRACKS.RECORDINGID = ?
ORDER BY MUSIC.TRACKS.TRACKNUMBER ASC
```

6. Save these modifications by selecting File > Save All from the main menu.

Add Page Navigation

Recall that the event handler code for the first page table's hyperlink component returns the string "tracks". This is the string JSF will send to the navigation handler. You'll now add the appropriate page navigation rule. You'll also add the navigation rule to return to PortletPage1 from the tracksDetail page.

1. In the Projects view, double-click the Page Navigation node. Creator brings up the page navigation editor. You'll see the two pages, **PortletPage1.jsp** and **tracksDetail.jsp**.
2. Select **PortletPage1.jsp** and drag the cursor from the hyperlink component to page **tracksDetail.jsp**, releasing the mouse inside the page. Creator displays a navigation arrow.
3. Change the default name to **tracks**, as shown in Figure 12–9.

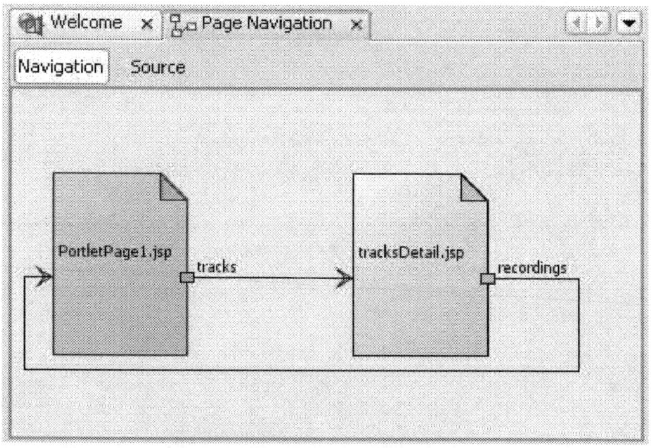

Figure 12–9 **Adding page navigation**

4. Now select page **tracksDetail.jsp** and drag the cursor from the hyperlink component to page **PortletPage1.jsp**. Release the mouse inside the page.
5. Change the default name to **recordings**.

Add Prerender Code

It's time to add the code that will specify the query parameter for the `tracksRowSet` component and update the `tracksDataProvider`. This code belongs in method `prerender()`, since the page bean object during this portion of the life cycle is the one used for rendering the page.

1. Select the **tracksDetail** tab from the top of the editor pane. This displays the page in the design view.
2. Select the button labeled Java in the editing toolbar. Creator brings up **tracksDetail.java** in the Java editor.

3. Locate method `prerender()` and add the following code. Copy and paste from the book download file **FieldGuide2/Examples/Portlets/snippets/portletMusic_tracksDetail_prerender.txt**. The added code is bold.

```
public void prerender() {
  try {
    getSessionBean1().getTracksRowSet().setObject(1,
        getSessionBean1().getRecordingID());
    tracksDataProvider.refresh();

  } catch (Exception e) {
      error("Cannot read tracks for " +
        getSessionBean1().getRecordingTitle() +
        ": " + e.getMessage());

      log("Cannot read tracks for " +
        getSessionBean1().getRecordingTitle() + ": ",  e);
  }
}
```

This code obtains the RecordingID from session scope and uses it to set the `tracksRowSet` query parameter. The call to `refresh()` forces an update of the tracks data provider. Any errors are recorded in the Server Log (using method `log()`) and displayed in the message group component (using method `error()`).

Configure Table Component

The final step is to configure the table component on the tracksDetail page.

1. Return to the tracksDetail design view by selecting the Design button in the editing toolbar.
2. Select the table component, right-click, and select Table Layout. Creator displays the Table Layout dialog.
3. Make sure that both TRACKNUMBER and TRACKTITLE appear in the Selected window. Click Apply.
4. Select the Options tab and check option Enable Pagination. Specify 7 for the number of rows. Click Apply and OK.
5. In the design view, select the table component. In the Properties window, click the small editing box opposite property `title`.
6. Creator pops up a property editing dialog. Select radio button **Use binding** and tab **Bind to an Object**.
7. In the Select binding target window, choose **SessionBean1 > recordingTitle *String*** as shown in Figure 12–10 and click OK. This binds the table's title to the selected recording title from session scope.

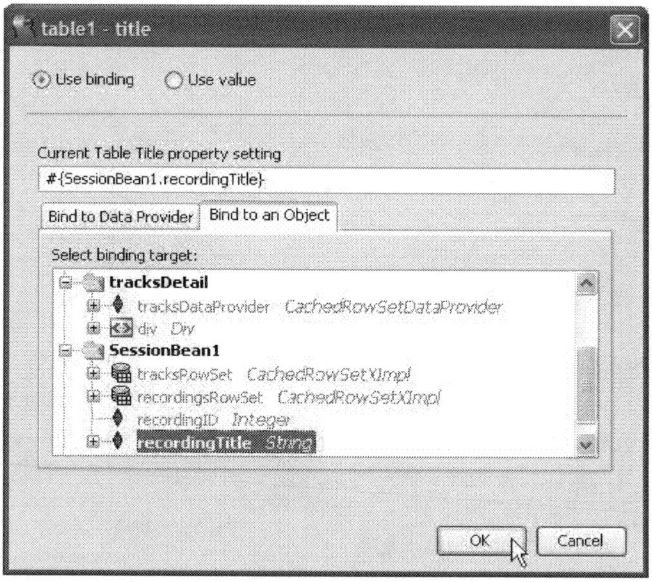

Figure 12–10 **Use binding dialog for property title**

8. Make sure the table component is still selected. In the Properties window, uncheck the box opposite property `paginateButton`. (This removes the paginate toggle from the table.)
9. Still in the Properties window, set the table's `width` property to **400** (to match the width of the portlet).

Deploy and Run

Figure 12–11 shows project PortletMusic running in a browser displaying the initial portlet page. Figure 12–12 shows the tracksDetail page after selecting the hyperlink for *Congratulations I'm Sorry.*

12.4 Web Services and Portlets

In this section you'll create a portlet that accesses the Google Search web service. It's a repeat of the project you built in the web services chapter (the final version is discussed in "Displaying Multiple Pages" on page 480), but you'll make changes specifically to adjust to the smaller foot print of a portlet. You'll also make adjustments to the application to accommodate the life cycle differences with portlet applications. You can read about the Google Search web ser-

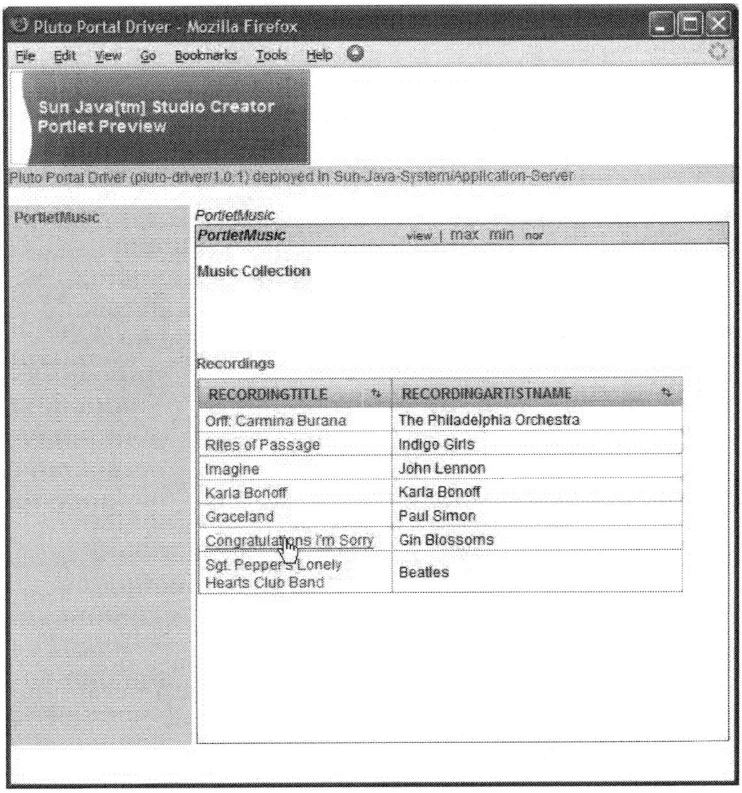

Figure 12–11 **Project PortletMusic running in a browser**

vice in "Inspect the Web Service" on page 461. In the following discussions, we assume you're familiar with the Google Search web service and the general organization of project Google4 built previously.

Create a Portlet Project

1. From Creator's Welcome Page, select button Create New Project. From the New Project dialog, under Categories select **Web** and under Projects select **JSR-168 JSF Portlet Project**. Click Next.
2. In the New Portlet dialog, specify **PortletGoogle** for Project Name and click Next.
3. Creator displays the New Project dialog which includes the Portlet Deployment Descriptor for the portlet project. Accept the defaults and click Finish.

After initializing the project, Creator comes up in the design view of the editor pane. The initial page has the default name PortletPage1. Project Portlet-

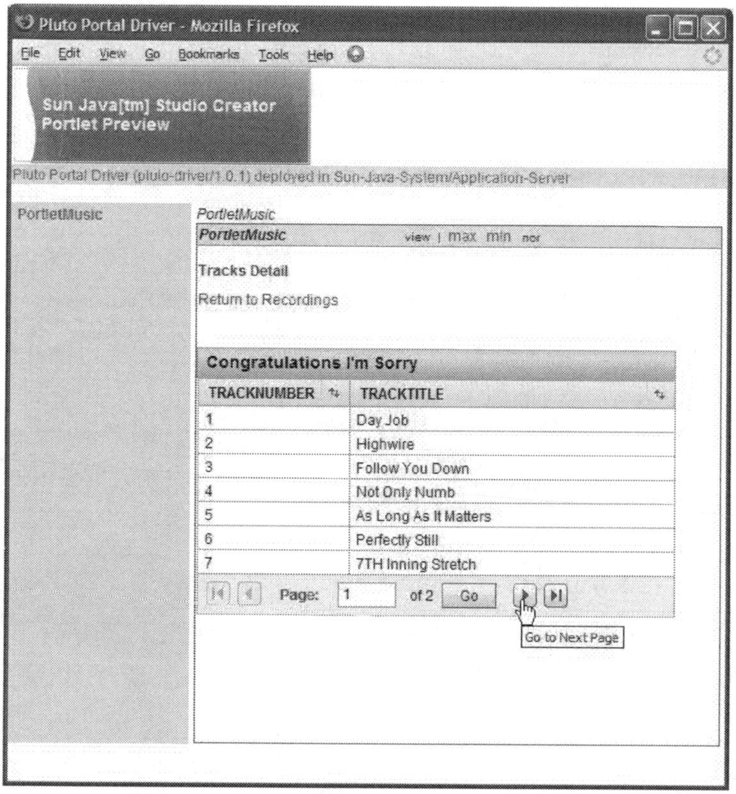

Figure 12–12 **Portlet page tracksDetail in browser**

Google will use a different background color and default page fragment size, since Google search results default to a wider format.

1. In the Properties window, select the custom editor box opposite property Background. Creator pops up the Background property editor.
2. Select tab RGB and specify values **234** for Red, **234** for Green, and **255** for Blue. Click OK. The new background is a light blue.
3. In the Properties window opposite property `Width`, specify **500** to change the width to 500 pixels.

Add Session Bean Properties

Recall that to display multiple pages from the Google search result, you must keep track of the start index, the current count, and the total results count in session scope variables. You'll also place the query search string in session scope and bind it to the input text field component, which you'll add in the next section. Furthermore, the object array data provider and the google search result variables will be in session scope. This is necessary to maintain the portlet's rendering state. Let's add the bookkeeping counters `startIndex`, `currentCount`, and `totalCount` first.

1. In the Projects view, expand the PortletGoogle node, select Session Bean, right-click, and select **Add > Property**.
2. Creator pops up the New Property Pattern dialog. For name, specify **startIndex**, for Type specify **Integer**, and for Mode keep the default **Read/Write**.
3. Click OK. Creator adds property `startIndex` to **SessionBean1.java**.
4. Repeat these steps to add properties **currentCount** and **totalCount**, both Type **Integer** and Mode **Read/Write**.

Now add String property `query` to hold the search query.

1. In the Projects view, select PortletGoogle > Session Bean, right-click, and select **Add > Property**.
2. Creator pops up the New Property Pattern dialog. For name, specify **query**, for type specify **String**, and for Mode keep the default **Read/Write**.
3. Click OK. Creator adds property `query` to **SessionBean1.java**.

Now let's add two properties to keep track of the Google search results, `mysearchResult` and `resultArray`.

1. In the Projects view, select PortletGoogle > Session Bean, right-click, and select **Add > Property**.
2. Creator pops up the New Property Pattern dialog. For name, specify **mySearchResult**, for type specify **GoogleSearchResult**, and for Mode keep the default **Read/Write**.
3. Click OK. Creator adds property `mySearchResult` to **SessionBean1.java**.
4. Repeat these steps to add property **resultArray**. For Type, specify **ResultElement[]** and Mode **Read/Write**.

Creator Tip

Make sure you specify type **`ResultElement[]`** *(use the array notation). Also, do* **NOT** *use the Indexed Property menu option.*

Finally, you'll need a data provider component in SessionBean1. You can use Creator's drag and drop facility to add the data provider component to SessionBean1 in the Outline view.

1. From the Components palette, expand the Data Providers section.

2. Select data provider Object Array Data Provider and drag the mouse to SessionBean1 in the Outline View. Release the mouse while the cursor is over SessionBean1. Creator adds component `objectArrayDataProvider1` to SessionBean1.
3. Make sure the object array data provider is selected. In the Properties window, change its `id` property to **myResultObject**.
4. In the Properties window, select the drop down list opposite property `array` and select **resultArray**.
5. In the Outline view expand the SessionBean1 node. You'll see the session bean properties (and object array data provider component) you just added, as shown in Figure 12–13.

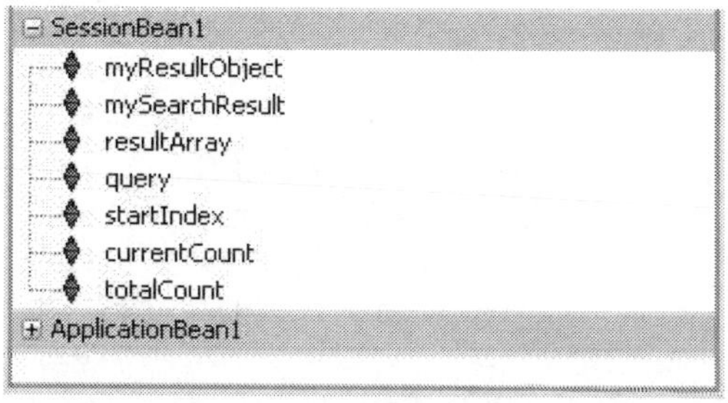

Figure 12–13 **SessionBean1 properties and components for project PortletGoogle**

You'll now fix the imports in the **SessionBean1.java** file, as well as add initialization code for the properties you just added.

1. In the Projects window, double-click **Session Bean** to bring up **SessionBean1.java** in the Java source editor.
2. Right-click and select Fix Imports to include import statements for types `ResultElement` and `GoogleSearchResult`.
3. Add the following code to the end of method `init()` to initialize the properties you added. Copy and paste from file **FieldGuide2/Examples/Portlets/snippets/portletGoogle_session_init.txt.** The added code is bold.

```
public void init() {
   . . .
   mySearchResult = null;
   query = new String("");

   startIndex = new Integer(0);
   currentCount = new Integer(0);
   totalCount = new Integer(0);
}
```

4. Click the Save All icon on the toolbar to save these changes.

Creator Tip

Note that we initialize `mySearchResult` *to null. Recall from building this project earlier (see "Creator Tip" on page 475) that property* `mySearchResult` *is used to compute the rendering of the table component. Because of portlet life cycle differences,* `mySearchResult` *must be set to null in the page's* `preprocess()` *method as well. This keeps the display clear of old results and leaves more room for validation error messages. (See "Portlet Life Cycle Issues" on page 574 where you'll add the initialization code.)*

Add Components to the Page

The design view marks the default portlet area in a lighter color, so you'll position the components inside this background. You'll use a text field component for the query, an image component for the Google logo, image hyperlink components for the left and right arrows, a button component to submit the query, and a table component to display the results (see Figure 12–14). Hidden behind the table are the message and message group components to report validation errors and system errors, respectively. As in the previous (non-portlet) versions of this project, the table component consists of a single column containing hyperlink and static text components.

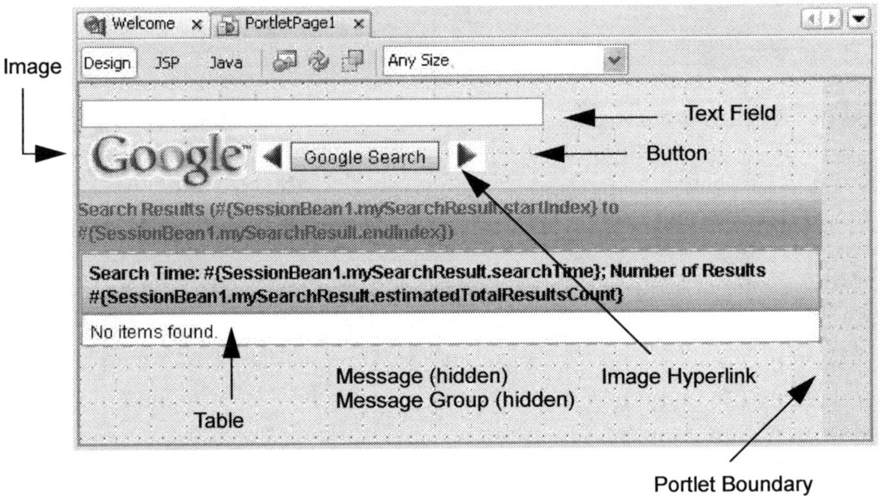

Figure 12–14 **PortletPage1 design view for project PortletGoogle**

1. Make sure that PortletPage1 is active in the design view.
2. From the Basic Components palette, select Text Field and drop it on the page in the top left corner. Expand it so that it is approximately 14 grids wide.
3. In the Properties window, change its `id` to **searchString**.
4. In the Properties window, *check* property `required`.
5. In the Properties window, click the editor box opposite property `text`. Creator pops up a custom property editor.
6. Select radio button **Use binding**, then tab **Bind to Object**. Expand node **SesionBean1** and select property **query *String***, as shown in Figure 12–15. Click OK to close. This sets property `text` to

```
#{SessionBean1.query}
```

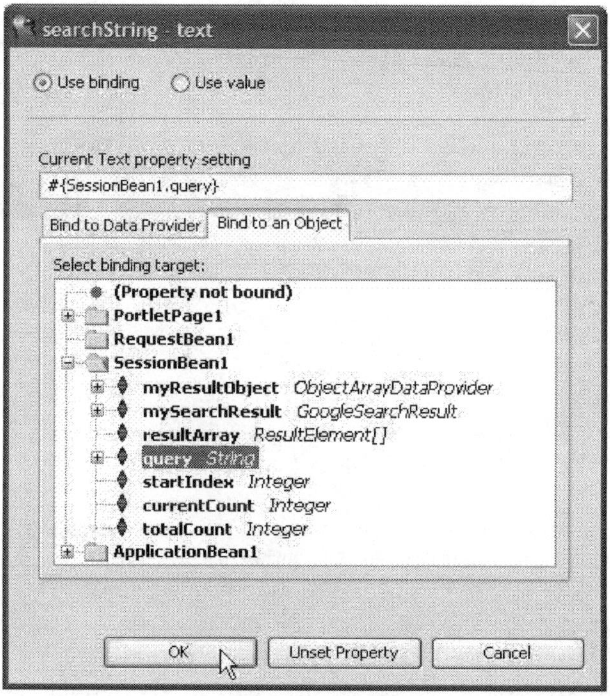

Figure 12–15 **Property binding to session bean property query**

You'll need a length validator and a message component to validate the query string.

1. From the Components palette, expand the Validators node, select Length Validator, and drop it on top of the `searchString` text field component. Creator sets the `validator` attribute for `searchString` to `lengthValidator1`. Component `lengthValidator1` appears in the PortletPage1 Outline view.
2. Select `lengthValidator1` in the Outline view. In its corresponding Properties window, change attribute `maximum` to **2,048** (the limit imposed by the Google web services) and `minimum` to **3**.
3. From the Basic Components palette, select Message component and drop it onto the design canvas. Place it below the text field component, leaving room for the Google logo and search buttons that you'll add next.
4. Press and hold **<Ctrl+Shift>**, left-click the mouse, and drag the cursor to the `searchString` text field. The sets the message component's `for` property. In the design view, the message component now displays the text **Message summary for searchString.**

An image component displays the Google logo and a button component submits the search. You can place an image component on the page by dropping an image file directly on the page.

1. Using a file utility program (such as Windows Explorer), drag file **FieldGuide2/Examples/Portlets/images/Logo_40wht.gif** to the Design view and drop it on the canvas below the text field (consult Figure 12–14 for positioning).

   This places the Google logo on the page and copies the file into your project's resources directory. You can see this in the Projects window (select **PortletGoogle > Web Pages > resources**).

2. In the Basic Components palette, select Button and drag it onto the design canvas. Place it to the right of the Google logo (leave room for the left-arrow image hyperlink).
3. Make sure the button is still selected. Type in the text **Google Search** followed by **<Enter>**. Creator resizes the button to accommodate the longer text string, which now appears inside the button on the design canvas. This sets the button's `text` property.
4. In the Properties window, change the button's `id` attribute to **search**.
5. To provide a tooltip for the button, edit its `toolTip` property in the Properties window (under Behavior). Type in the text **Search Google for the Search String** followed by **<Enter>**.

   Two image hyperlink components provide paging of the search results.

1. From the Basic Components palette, select Image Hyperlink and drop it onto the design canvas to the left of the Google Search button.

2. In the Properties window, change its `id` property to **previous**.
3. In the Properties window under Behavior, set property `toolTip` to **View the previous set of results**.
4. In the Properties window, click the editing box opposite property `imageURL`. Creator pops up the imageURL customizer.
5. Click Add File, browse to **FieldGuide2/Examples/Portlets/images**, and select file **nav_previous.gif**. Click Add File again. Creator copies the file into the project's resources directory, as shown in Figure 12–16.

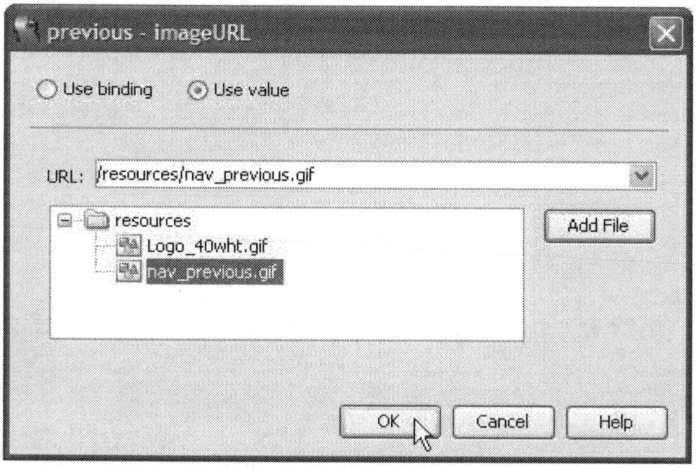

Figure 12–16 **Property imageURL customizer dialog**

6. Click OK. Creator displays the arrow on the design canvas.
7. In the Properties window for the image hyperlink, click the editing box opposite property `text` and select **Unset Property** in the customizer dialog.

Follow the same steps to add a second image hyperlink component, placing it to the right of the Google Search button.

1. Specify **next** for property `id`, set property `toolTip` to **View the next set of results**, and set property `imageURL` to **nav_next.gif** (add the file from **FieldGuide2/Examples/Portlets/images**).
2. In the Properties window for the image hyperlink, click the editing box opposite property `text` and select **Unset Property** in the customizer dialog.

Now align the Google image, image hyperlink, and button components together.

1. Use **<Shift+Click>** to multiply-select the four components: the Google image, the two image hyperlink components, and the button.

2. Hold the mouse over the Google image and right-click. Select **Align > Middle** from the context menu. This aligns all four components vertically on the canvas.
3. In the Design view, select the button component and right-click. Select **Bring to Front** from the context menu. This ensures that neither image hyperlink component will block the edges of the button component.

Add the Google Web Service Client

Creator comes with the Google Web Service client preinstalled. Here are the steps to add the Google web service client and the message group component that displays system errors.

1. In the Servers window, expand the **Web Services > Samples > Google-Search** nodes.
2. Drag the **doGoogleSearch** node and drop it anywhere on the editor pane. Nothing appears in the design canvas; however, you will see **googleSearchClient1** and **googleSearchDoGoogleSearch1** in the Outline view for PortletPage1.
3. From the Basic Components palette, select Message Group and drop it onto the design canvas. Place it directly below the message component you added earlier.
4. In the Properties window, *check* property `showGlobalOnly` (set it to true). The message group component now displays the text "List of global message summaries." (Recall that since the project contains *both* a message component and a message group component on the same page, setting this property to true prevents the message group component from displaying validation error messages.)

Configure Web Service Call

You can configure some of the web service parameters through the Properties window, as follows.

1. Select **googleSearchDoGoogleSearch1** in the PortletPage1 Outline view.
2. In the Properties window, the method's arguments are listed under the General heading. For property `key`, provide your key (the one Google sent to you) and for `maxResults`, use **5**. Note that 5 (instead of the maximum possible, 10) is more suitable for the smaller portlet foot print. These are the only properties that you need to set.

Creator Tip

Make sure you include your Google Web API's License Key for property `key`. *Otherwise, your application will return an exception. You'll set the search query parameter (property* `q`*) in the event handler code.*

Add a Table Component

Next, you'll need a table component to work with the object array data provider you added previously. The table displays the results from the Google search web service call.

1. From the Basic Components palette, select Table and drag it to the canvas. Place it on top of the message and message group components. You'll see a default table rendered on the design canvas and the default table data provider, `defaultTableDataProvider1`, appears in the Outline view.
2. When you place the table component on the canvas, the table's title is selected so that you can provide your own title.
3. Type in the following text to set the title.

```
Search Results (#{SessionBean1.mySearchResult.startIndex} to
  #{SessionBean1.mySearchResult.endIndex})
```

Type the text all on a single line and finish with **<Enter>**. The title text will appear in the table's title area.

Configure the Table

Only a single column is required to mimic the display you see from Google's web site. In each cell, you'll display the result web site's title followed by the snippet. The title is the text for the hyperlink to the result's site.

1. Select the table component, right-click, and choose Table Layout from the context menu.
2. In the drop down menu for Get Data From, choose **myResultObject *(SessionBean1)***. Creator displays the data fields in the Selected window.
3. Use the < (left arrow) to remove all fields except URL, snippet, and title. Click Apply.
4. Select column URL and change the component type to Hyperlink. Click Apply and OK to close the dialog.

Creator binds each of these columns to the URL, snippet, and title fields of the data provider for you. You'll need a bit more customizing to get a look that's similar to the page the Google web site builds. Look at the PortletPage1 Outline view. You'll see the table component (`table1`), a nested table row group, and three table column components with headings URL, snippet, and title. You'll now rearrange these components a bit.

1. From the PortletPage1 Outline view, select the static text component under the column entitled **title** and drop it on top of the hyperlink component under the **URL** column. (This should nest component `staticText2` under component `hyperlink1`.)
2. In the Properties window for `staticText2`, change its `id` property to **nestedText** and *uncheck* its `escape` property.
3. In the Properties window, hold the cursor over the `text` property and verify that its binding is set to the following.

```
#{currentRow.value['title']}
```

4. Select the hyperlink component (`hyperlink1`). In the Properties window, set property `url` to the following. (By default, Creator binds the `text` property instead.)

```
#{currentRow.value['URL']}
```

5. In the Properties window for the hyperlink component, select the editing box opposite property `text` to bring up the property customizer and select **Unset Property**.
6. From the Basic Components palette, select Static Text and drop it on component `tableColumn1` in the PortletPage1 Outline view. The static text should appear at the same level as the hyperlink component.
7. In the Properties window, *uncheck* its escape property and set its `text` property to **
**. (This will provide a line break in the table cell and improve the formatting.)
8. From the PortletPage1 Outline view, select the static text component under the column entitled **snippet** and drop it on top of component `tableColumn1`.
9. In the Properties window, change its `id` property to **snippet** and *uncheck* its `escape` property. Now hold the cursor over the `text` property and verify that its binding is set to the following.

```
#{currentRow.value['snippet']}
```

Let's make a few more configuration changes to the table component.

1. In the PortletPage1 Outline view, remove components `tableColumn2` and `tableColumn3` (there shouldn't be any nested components in these unused columns). Right-click and select Delete from the context menu.
2. Select the table component. In the Properties view, set property `width` to **500**.
3. In the PortletPage1 Outline view, select component `tableColumn1` and bring up the property customizer for property `headerText`. Select radio button **Use value** and provide the following text (type it on a single line). Click OK to close the dialog. The column's header shows the new value.

```
Search Time:
     #{SessionBean1.mySearchResult.searchTime};
Number of Results:
     #{SessionBean1.mySearchResult.estimatedTotalResultsCount}
```

4. Select the table component. In the Properties view, *uncheck* property rendered. The table disappears from the design view.
5. Still in the Properties window, *check* property lite (rendering a lighter version of a table).
6. Click button JSP to bring the the JSP source editor.
7. Change the table's `rendered` property to the following.

```
#{not empty SessionBean1.mySearchResult}
```

8. Click the Save All icon to save these changes. Figure 12–17 shows the PortletPage1 Outline view with the components configured.

Add Event Handling Code

You've configured all of the components. Now it's time to add the event handling code. The code is the same you used in project Google4, except that the properties storing the query and the results data are now in session scope.

1. Make sure that PortletPage1 is active in the design view. Double-click the Google Search button. Creator generates the default action event handler (`search_action()`) and brings up **PortletPage1.java** in the Java source editor.
2. To keep track of the index variables and the result count information that Google returns, you'll need integer control variables. Place these declara-

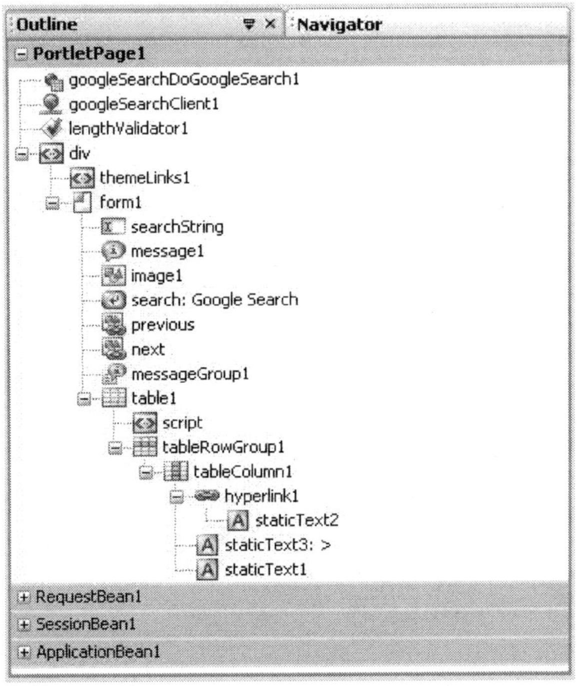

Figure 12–17 **PortletPage1 Outline view for project PortletGoogle**

tions above method `search_action()`. Copy and paste file **FieldGuide2/Examples/Portlets/snippets/portletGoogle_variables.txt**.

```
private int startIndex = 0;
private int prevIndex = 0;
private int currentCount = 0;
private int totalCount = 0;
```

The `startIndex`, `currentCount`, and `totalCount` integer variables are saved and restored in session scope for the action handlers. To do this, use PortletPage1 methods `destroy()` and `init()` to save and restore the corresponding SessionBean1 properties. Recall that methods `init()` and `destroy()` are invoked during the portlet request and rending phases.

1. Add the following code to method `destroy()`. Copy and paste from **FieldGuide2/Examples/Portlets/snippets/portletGoogle_destroy.txt**. This code calls setters to store `startIndex`, `currentCount`, and `totalCount` as

equivalently named properties in the SessionBean1 object. The added code is bold.

Listing 12.2 Method `destroy()`

```
private void destroy() {
   getSessionBean1().setStartIndex(new Integer(startIndex));
   getSessionBean1().setCurrentCount(
         new Integer(currentCount));
   getSessionBean1().setTotalCount(new Integer(totalCount));
}
```

2. Next, add the following code to the end of method `init()`. Copy and paste from **FieldGuide2/Examples/Portlets/snippets/portletGoogle_init.txt**. The added code is bold.

Listing 12.3 Method `init()`

```
private void init() {
. . .
   // TODO - add your own initialization code here
   startIndex = getSessionBean1().getStartIndex().intValue();
   currentCount =
       getSessionBean1().getCurrentCount().intValue();
   totalCount = getSessionBean1().getTotalCount().intValue();
}
```

Method `doSearch()` is the common method that is invoked when the user clicks either the Google Search button or the left or right arrow image hyperlink components.

3. To create the `doSearch()` method, use **FieldGuide2/Examples/Portlets/snippets/portletGoogle_doSearch.txt** and place it directly before the `search_action()` method (near the end of the Java page bean file). Note that this method sets the starting index parameter by calling method `set-`

Start() and the query by calling method setQ(). It also sets totalCount and currentCount from the mySearchResult object.

Listing 12.4 Method doSearch()

```
public void doSearch(int start) {
  try {
    googleSearchDoGoogleSearch1.setStart(start);
    googleSearchDoGoogleSearch1.setQ(
        getSessionBean1().getQuery());
    getSessionBean1().setMySearchResult((GoogleSearchResult)
        googleSearchDoGoogleSearch1.getResultObject());

    getSessionBean1().setResultArray(getSessionBean1().
        getMySearchResult().getResultElements());
    getSessionBean1().getMyResultObject().setArray(
        (java.lang.Object[])getValue(
        "#{SessionBean1.resultArray}"));

    totalCount = getSessionBean1().getMySearchResult().
        getEstimatedTotalResultsCount();
    currentCount = getSessionBean1().getMySearchResult().
        getResultElements().length;

  } catch (Exception e) {
      log("Remote Connect Failure: ", e);
      getSessionBean1().setMySearchResult(null);
      error("Remote Site Failure: " + e.getMessage());
  }
}
```

4. The search_action() method is exactly the same code you used in the Google4 project. Copy and paste from file **FieldGuide2/Examples/Portlets/snippets/portletGoogle_search_action.txt** to add the code. The added code is bold.

Listing 12.5 Method search_action()

```
public String search_action() {
  startIndex = 0;
  prevIndex = 0;
  doSearch(startIndex);
  return null;
}
```

Clicking the right-arrow returns the next set of results from Google.

1. Return to the design canvas by selecting **Design** from the editing toolbar.
2. Select the right arrow image hyperlink `next` and double-click. This creates the event handler method in the Java page bean for you and places the cursor at the beginning of the method.
3. Add code to the `next_action()` event handler. Copy and paste from file **FieldGuide2/Examples/Portlets/snippets/portletGoogle_next_action.txt**. The added code is bold.

Listing 12.6 Method `next_action()`

```
public String next_action() {
   prevIndex = startIndex;
   startIndex = startIndex + currentCount;

   if (startIndex >= totalCount || startIndex >= 1000) {
      startIndex = prevIndex;
      prevIndex -= currentCount;
   }

   doSearch(startIndex);
   return null;
}
```

Now add the `previous_action()` method to handle action events associated with the left-arrow image hyperlink.

1. Return to the design canvas by selecting **Design** from the editing toolbar.
2. Select the left arrow image hyperlink `previous` and double-click. This creates the event handler method in the Java page bean for you and places the cursor at the beginning of the method.
3. Add the following code to the `previous_action()` method. Copy and paste from file **FieldGuide2/Examples/Portlets/snippets/portlet-Google_previous_action.txt**. The added code is bold.

Listing 12.7 Method `previous_action()`

```
public String previous_action() {
   prevIndex = startIndex - currentCount;
   startIndex = prevIndex;

   if (startIndex <= 0) {
      startIndex = 0;
      prevIndex = 0;
   }
```

Listing 12.7 Method `previous_action()` *(continued)*

```
    doSearch(startIndex);
    return null;
}
```

Portlet Life Cycle Issues

If you run the PortletGoogle project as it is, any validation error messages will appear on top of the previously displayed results table. Solving this problem requires an understanding of the portlet life cycle.

Recall that the `rendered` property of the table depends on the session scope property `mySearchResult`, as follows.

```
rendered="#{not empty SessionBean1.mySearchResult}"
```

The non-portlet version of this project included the initialization

```
mySearchResult = null;
```

in the page bean's `init()` routine. However, with portlets, a page's `init()` routine is invoked twice, and the second time would wipe out the results you stored in session scope in the `doSearch()` event handler. You can't put this code in method `destroy()` for the same reason. Putting the initialization code in the event handler won't work either, since the event handler is not invoked when a validation error occurs. Where should this initialization code go?

The answer is in method `preprocess()`, which is invoked during the page submission cycle but not during page rendering. By setting the session bean property `mySearchResult` to null in `preprocess()`, you are assured that if a validation error occurs, the table component will not be rendered. Furthermore, once valid data from the Google search call is stored in session scope, it remains there until the next request cycle.

1. You should still have **PortletPage1.java** active in the Java source editor.
2. Find method `preprocess()` and add the following call to `setMySearchResult()`, as follows. The added code is bold.

```
public void preprocess() {
    getSessionBean1().setMySearchResult(null);
}
```

3. Click the Save All icon to save these changes.

Deploy and Run

It's time to deploy and run the project. Page through multiple results sets. Then, leave the search query empty to test component validation. Figure 12–18 shows the Google Search application running as a portlet, displaying the second page of results.

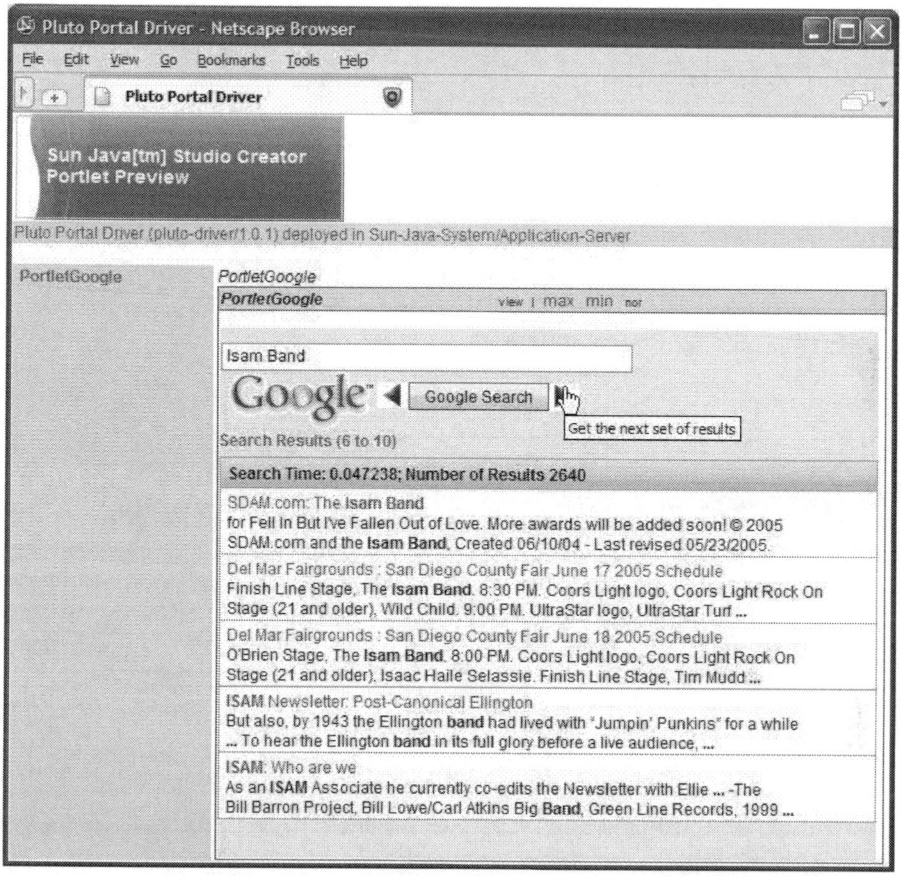

Figure 12–18 **The Google Web Search application running as a portlet**

12.5 Portlet Edit Mode

Portlet applications have three modes: View, Edit, and Help. View is the default mode, and the mode you have been working with in the previous examples. In this section, you'll add an Edit mode to the PortletGoogle application that allows a user to adjust the Google search parameters. In the next section, you'll add a Help mode so that users can learn about configuring the Google search parameters.

Copy the Project

To avoid starting from scratch, make a copy of the PortletGoogle project. This step is optional. If you don't want to copy the project, simply skip this section and continue making modifications to PortletGoogle.

1. Bring up project PortletGoogle in Creator, if it's not already opened.
2. From the Projects window, right-click node PortletGoogle and select Save Project As. Provide the new name **PortletGoogleEdit**.
3. Close project PortletGoogle. Right-click PortletGoogleEdit and select Set Main Project. You'll make changes to the PortletGoogleEdit project.

Add a New Edit Mode Page

You add an edit mode page by first creating a new portlet page. Then you designate the page as the initial edit mode page. Here are the steps.

1. In the Projects view, right-click on node Web Pages and select **New > Portlet Page** from the context menu.
2. Creator pops up the New Portlet Page dialog. Specify **EditParams** for the file name and click Finish. Creator brings up page **EditParams.jsp** in the design view.
3. In the Projects view under Web Pages, right-click node **EditParams.jsp** and select **Set as Initial > Edit Mode Page**. Creator changes the page's icon and sets EditParams as the initial edit mode page. When the user selects Edit on the portlet page, the portal server will display this page.

Creator Tip

Note that if you don't define an Edit mode page, the Edit selector does not appear on the portlet page. Similarly, the Help selector only appears if you define a Help mode page.

4. Click anywhere inside the page. In the Properties window, select the custom editor box opposite property `Background`. Creator pops up the Background property editor.
5. Select tab **RGB** and specify values **234** for Red, **234** for Green, and **255** for Blue. Click OK. This light blue color matches the background color for the View page.

Add SessionBean1 Properties

Before you add components to the page, you'll add the session bean properties that store submitted values for the Google search parameters. You'll have three properties: property `safeSearch` (Boolean), property `filter` (Boolean), and property `languageRestrict` (String).

1. From the Projects window, select **Session Bean**, right-click and select **Add > Property**.
2. Creator pops up the New Property Pattern dialog.
3. For Name, specify **languageRestrict**, for Type, specify **String**, and for Mode, select the default **Read/Write**. Click OK.
4. Repeat these steps for **filter** and **safeSearch**. Specify Type **Boolean** and Mode **Read/Write** for both.
5. In the Projects window, double-click node **Session Bean**. This brings up file **SessionBean1.java** in the Java source editor.
6. Add the following code to the end of method `init()` to initialize the three properties. Copy and paste from file **FieldGuide2/Examples/Portlets/snippets/portletGoogleEdit_session_init.txt**. The added code is bold.

```
public void init() {
. . .
   safeSearch = new Boolean(false);
   filter = new Boolean(false);
   languageRestrict = new String("");
}
```

Add ApplicationBean1 Data

In order to initialize the choices for the drop down list component (that you'll add in the next step), add a read-only property to ApplicationBean1 to hold the drop down list's selections.

Creator Tip

You'll put this property in Application scope since it is read-only and can be shared by all users of the application.

1. In the Projects window, right-click Application Bean and select New > Property. Creator pops up the New Property Pattern dialog.
2. For Name specify **languages**, for Type specify `com.sun.rave.web.ui.model.Option[]`, and for Mode specify **Read Only**, as shown in Figure 12–19.
3. Click OK to add the property to ApplicationBean1.

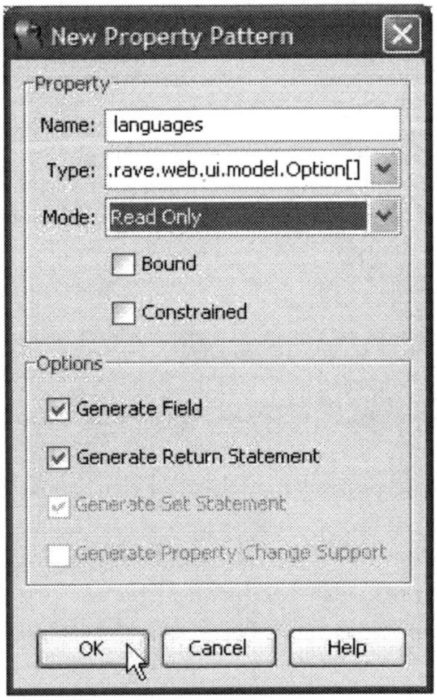

Figure 12–19 **Adding application scope property** `languages`

The `languages` array contains objects of type `Option`, used by components like the drop down list or listbox to display options on the page. Each option has both a Value (that is returned with the drop down list's method `getSelected()`) and a Display Name (that is visible in the drop down list component). The Display Name is always a String. The Value can be any kind of Object. In this example, Value is also a String.

You'll now initialize the `languages` array with data.

1. In the Projects window, double-click Application Bean to bring it up in the Java source editor.
2. Add the following code to the ApplicationBean1 method `init()`. Copy and paste from file **FieldGuide2/Examples/Portlets/snippets/languages_init.txt**. The added code is bold. (The first object in an Option element is the Value; the second object is the Display Name.)

```
public void init() {
   . . .
   // TODO - add your own initialization code here
   languages = new Option[] {
     new Option("", "No language restrictions"),
     new Option("lang_ar", "Arabic"),
```

```
        new Option("lang_zh-CN", "Chinese (S)"),
        new Option("lang_zh_TW", "Chinese (T)"),
        new Option("lang_cs", "Czech"),
        new Option("lang_da", "Danish"),
        new Option("lang_nl", "Dutch"),
        new Option("lang_en", "English"),

        new Option("lang_et", "Estonian"),
        new Option("lang_fi", "Finnish"),
        new Option("lang_fr", "French"),
        new Option("lang_de", "German"),
        new Option("lang_el", "Greek"),
        new Option("lang_iw", "Hebrew"),

        new Option("lang_hu", "Hungarian"),
        new Option("lang_is", "Icelandic"),
        new Option("lang_it", "Italian"),
        new Option("lang_ja", "Japanese"),
        new Option("lang_ko", "Korean"),
        new Option("lang_lv", "Latvian"),

        new Option("lang_lt", "Lithuanian"),
        new Option("lang_no", "Norwegian"),
        new Option("lang_pt", "Portuguese"),
        new Option("lang_pl", "Polish"),
        new Option("lang_ro", "Arabic"),
        new Option("lang_ar", "Romanian"),

        new Option("lang_ru", "Russian"),
        new Option("lang_es", "Spanish"),
        new Option("lang_sv", "Swedish"),
        new Option("lang_tr", "Turkish")};
}
```

3. Right-click in the editor and select Fix Imports. Make sure that the imported class for `Option` is **`com.sun.rave.web.ui.model.Option`**.
4. Select the Save All icon on the toolbar to save these changes.

Add Components to the Page

Figure 12–20 shows the components added to the Edit mode page that allow you to specify the filter, safe search, and language restrictions search parameters. Table 10.1 on page 462 lists the parameters. You'll provide check box components to edit boolean parameter `safeSearch` and `filter` and a drop down list component to specify parameter `lr` (language restrict).

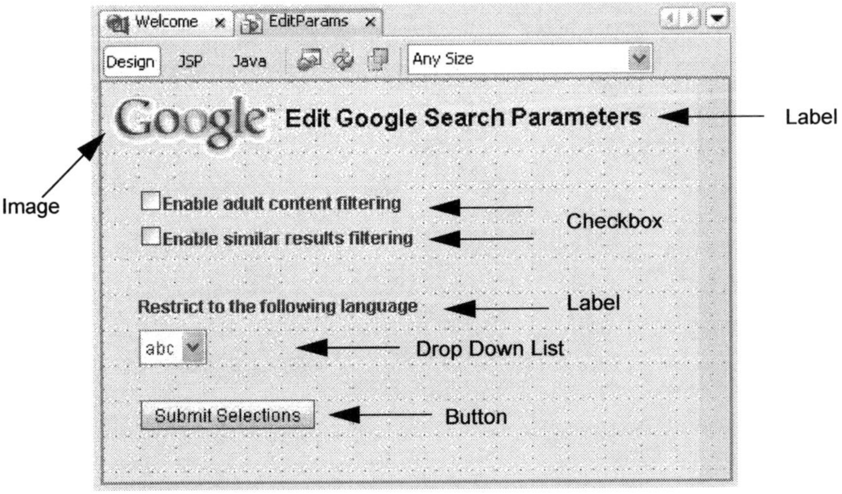

Figure 12–20 **Design view for EditParams edit mode page**

1. Select the EditParams tab to make page EditParams active in the design view.
2. From the Projects view, expand **PortletGoogleEdit > Web Pages > resources**. Select file **Logo_40wht.gif** and drag it to the page. Drop it in the upper-left corner. This puts the Google logo on the page.
3. From the Basic Components palette, select Label and drop it on the page to the right of the logo. Specify **Edit Google Search Parameters** for its text.
4. In the Properties window, change property labelLevel to **Strong(1).**

Now you'll add the input components for the Google search parameters.

1. From the Basic Components palette, select Checkbox and place it on the page under the logo.
2. Change its label to **Enable adult content filtering.** Change property `labelLevel` to **Medium(2)**.
3. In the Properties window, change its `id` to **safeCheckbox**.
4. From the Basic Components palette, select Checkbox and place it under the checkbox component you just added.
5. Change its label to **Enable similar results filtering.** Change property `labelLevel` to **Medium(2)**.
6. In the Properties window, change its `id` to **noDuplicateCheckbox**.
7. From the Basic Components palette, select Label and place it below the two checkbox components. Change its text to **Restrict to the following language**.

8. From the Basic Components palette, select Drop Down List and place it below the label you just added.

Creator Tip

You can also use a text field component here. However, the drop down list component restricts its selections to a specific set of options, ensuring that the parameter submitted with the Google search is valid.

Now supply the selections for the drop down list by binding property `items` to the ApplicationBean1 property `languages` that you configured in the previous section.

1. In the Properties window, select the editing box opposite property `items` for component `dropDown1`.
2. Make sure tab **Bind to an Object** is selected.
3. Scroll down and select **ApplicationBean1 > languages *Option[]***, as shown in Figure 12–21.

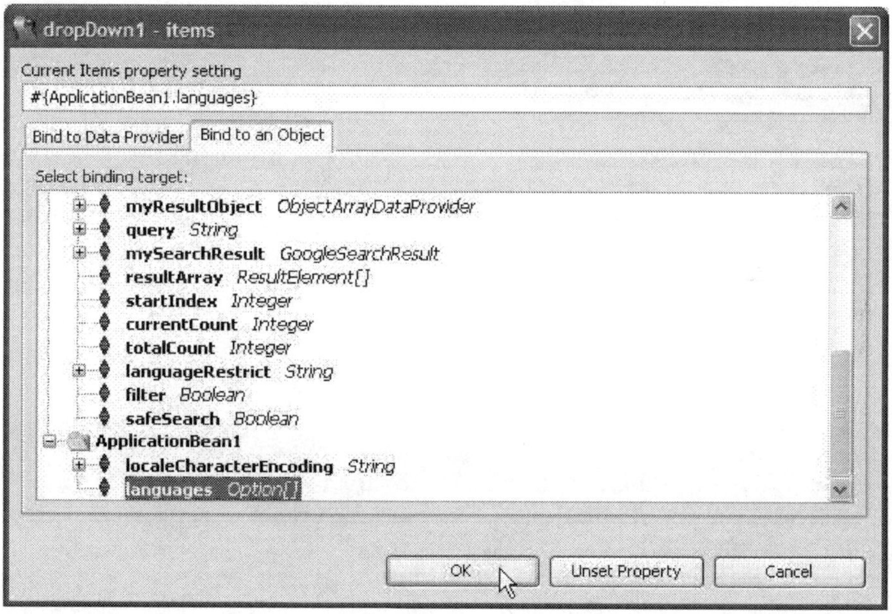

Figure 12–21 **Bind** `items` **property to ApplicationBean1 property** `languages`

4. Click OK. The drop down component displays **abc**, indicating its display is bound to an alphabetic string.

Creator Tip

The first selection, No language restrictions, has value empty (null), matching the default value for the parameter.

Add the button component to the page.

1. From the Basic Components palette, select Button and place it below the drop down list.
2. Change the button's `text` to **Submit Selections**.

Creator Tip

The button component will submit the page, but you do not need to supply an action event handler. Page submission will update the session bean properties that hold the Google search parameter values.

Specify Property Bindings

You'll now specify property bindings between the EditParams components and the Session Bean properties and connect these Session Bean properties to the Google Search web services call.

1. In the EditParams design view, select checkbox component `safeCheckBox`, right-click, and select Property Bindings. Creator pops up the Property Bindings dialog.
2. For Select bindable property, choose **Selected *Object***. For Select binding target, choose **SessionBean1 > safeSearch *Boolean***. Click Apply then Close. In the Properties window opposite property `selected`, you'll see the following binding expression.

```
#{SessionBean1.safeSearch}
```

3. Repeat this step using property `selected` for component `noDuplicate-Checkbox`. Specify the binding with SessionBean1 property `filter`. Creator generates the following binding expression.

```
#{SessionBean1.filter}
```

4. Finally, specify the binding using property `selected` for component `dropdown1` with SessionBean1 property `languageRestrict`. Creator generates the following binding expression.

```
#{SessionBean1.languageRestrict}
```

5. Click the Save All icon on the toolbar to save these changes.
6. Bring up PortletPage1 in the design view. Click the Java button to bring up **PortletPage1.java** in the Java editor.
7. Add the following code to method **`doSearch()`** at the beginning of the try block. Copy and paste from the Creator download file **FieldGuide2/Examples/Portlets/snippets/portletGoogleEdit_doSearch.txt**. The added code is bold.

```
public void doSearch(int start) {
  try {
    googleSearchDoGoogleSearch1.setLr(
        getSessionBean1().getLanguageRestrict());
    googleSearchDoGoogleSearch1.setSafeSearch(
        getSessionBean1().getSafeSearch().booleanValue());
    googleSearchDoGoogleSearch1.setFilter(
        getSessionBean1().getFilter().booleanValue());
  . . .
```

Deploy and Run

Deploy and run the portlet. When the initial View page comes up in the browser, the page will now include an Edit option. Click Edit and the application displays the initial Edit mode page, **EditParams.jsp**, as shown in Figure 12–22. After customizing the Google search options, return to the View page by selecting View and run the Google search.

12.6 Portlet Help Mode

The final step is to add a Help mode page to your Google portlet. The Help page will describe the Google Search parameters that a user can configure.

Copy the Project

To avoid starting from scratch, make a copy of the PortletGoogleEdit project. This step is optional. If you don't want to copy the project, simply skip this section and continue making modifications to PortletGoogleEdit.

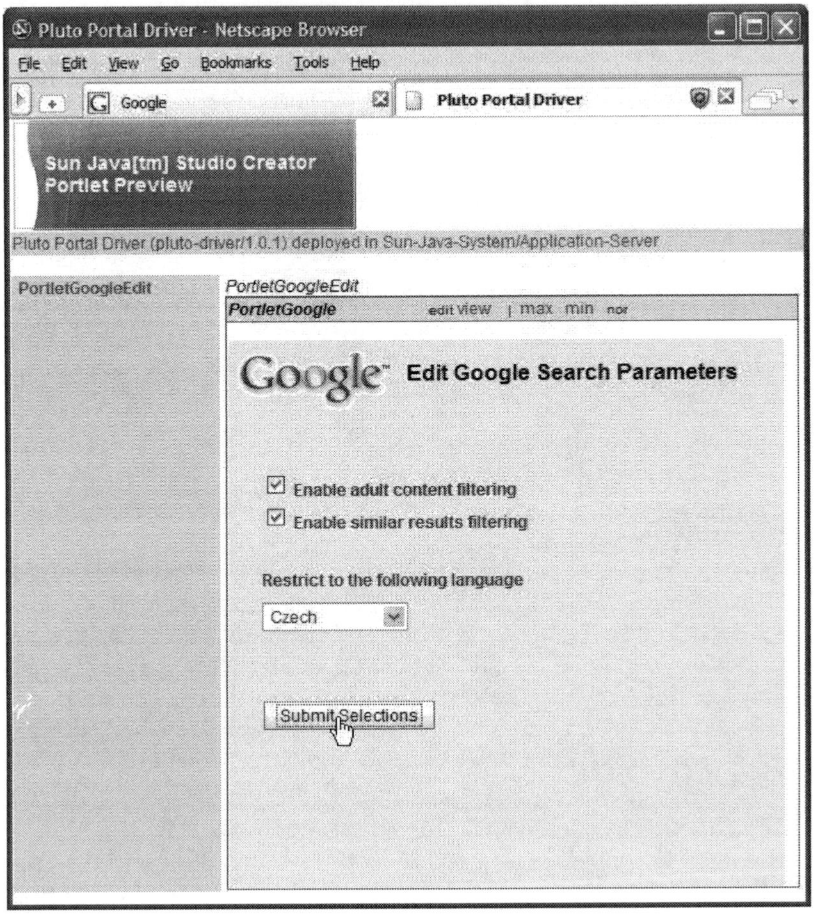

Figure 12–22 **Portlet Edit mode page running in a browser**

1. Bring up project PortletGoogleEdit in Creator, if it's not already opened.
2. From the Projects window, right-click node PortletGoogleEdit and select Save Project As. Provide the new name **PortletGoogleHelp**.
3. Close project PortletGoogleEdit. Right-click PortletGoogleHelp and select Set Main Project. You'll make changes to the PortletGoogleHelp project.

Add a New Help Mode Page

You add a help mode page to your portlet by first creating a new portlet page. Then you designate the page as the initial help mode page. Here are the steps.

1. In the Projects view, right-click on node Web Pages and select **New > Portlet Page** from the context menu.
2. Creator pops up the New Portlet Page dialog. Specify **GoogleHelp** for the file name and click Finish. Creator brings up page **GoogleHelp.jsp** in the design view.
3. In the Projects view under Web Pages, right-click node **GoogleHelp.jsp** and select **Set as Initial > Help Mode Page**. Creator changes the page's icon and sets GoogleHelp as the initial help mode page. When the user selects Help on the portlet page, the portal server will display this page.
4. Click anywhere inside the page. In the Properties window, select the custom editor box opposite property `Background`. Creator pops up the Background property editor.
5. Select tab **RGB** and specify values **234** for Red, **234** for Green, and **255** for Blue. Click OK. This light blue color matches the background color for the View and Edit pages.

Add ApplicationBean1 Property

You'll add a read-only application scope property to hold the help contents that the Help page displays. Recall that application scope objects are shared among all users of the application.

1. From the Projects window, select **Application Bean**, right-click and select **Add > Property**.
2. Creator pops up the New Property Pattern dialog.
3. For Name, specify **helpContents**, for Type, specify **String**, and for Mode, select **Read Only**. Click OK.
4. From the Projects view, double-click node **Application Bean** to bring up **ApplicationBean1.java** in the Java source editor.

5. Add the following code to the end of method `init()` to initialize property `helpContents`. Copy and paste from file **FieldGuide2/Examples/Portlets/snippets/portletGoogleHelp_application_init.txt**. The added code is bold.

```
public void init() {
   . . .
   // TODO - add your own initialization code here
   String hc  = new String(
        "<b>Google Search Parameters</b><p/>");
   hc = hc + "<b>Enable adult content filtering</b><br/>- ";
   hc = hc +
     "When checked, filters out adult-content results<p/>";
   hc = hc + "<b>Enable similar results filtering</b><br/>- ";
   hc = hc +
     "When checked, helps eliminate very similar results<p/>";
   hc = hc + "<b>Language restrict</b><br/>- ";
   hc = hc +
     "Limits search to documents with the chosen language<p/>";
   helpContents = new String(hc);
}
```

Add Static Text Component to the Page

Figure 12–23 shows the single static text component added to the Help mode page.

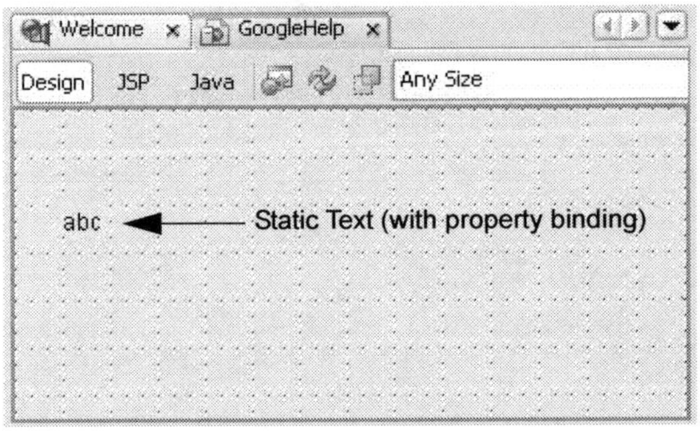

Figure 12–23 **Design view for page GoogleHelp (help mode page)**

1. From the Basic Component palette, select Static Text and drop it on the page as shown in Figure 12–23.
2. In the Properties window, *uncheck* property `escape`. This allows HTML tags to be interpreted by the browser.

Specify Property Binding

You'll now specify property binding between the GoogleHelp static text component and the Application Bean property `helpContents`.

1. In the GoogleHelp design view, select the static text component, right-click, and select Property Bindings. Creator pops up the Property Bindings dialog.
2. For Select bindable property, choose **text** ***Object***. For Select binding target, choose **ApplicationBean1 > helpContents** ***String***. Click Apply then Close. In the Properties window opposite property `text`, you'll see the following binding expression.

```
#{ApplicationBean1.helpContents}
```

3. Click the Save All icon on the toolbar to save these changes.

Deploy and Run

Deploy and run the portlet. When the initial View page comes up in the browser, you'll see a Help option as well as the Edit option. Click Help and the application displays the initial Help mode page, **GoogleHelp.jsp**, as shown in Figure 12–24.

12.7 Key Point Summary

Creator allows you to build a JSF portlet application that conforms to the JSR-168 Portlet specification.

- A portlet is an application that runs on a web site managed by a server called a portal.
- A portal server manages multiple portlet applications, displaying them on the web page together. Each portlet consumes a fragment of the page and manages its own information and user interaction.
- When you deploy a portlet project, Creator deploys the portlet container for you and brings up your portlet project in Pluto in the target web browser.
- Portlets have three standard modes which Creator supports: View, Edit, and Help. The portal server manages the modes for the application.
- JSF-based portlets use the standard JSF navigation engine. Although it is possible, it is not a good idea to define navigation rules across portlet modes. You should treat each mode separately for navigation.

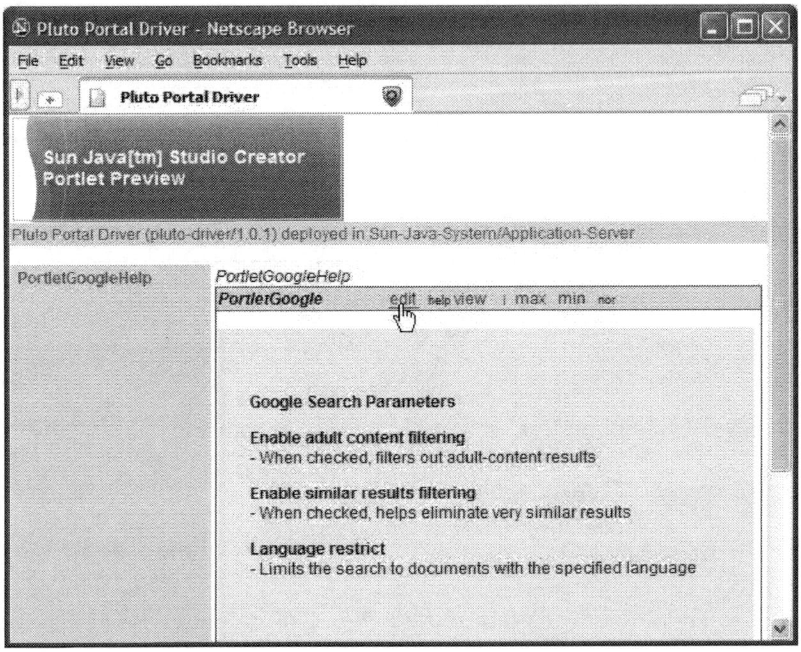

Figure 12–24 **Portlet Help mode page running in a browser**

- The design time experience for building portlet applications (component placement, specifying property values and property binding, and adding event handling code) is the same as with non-portlet applications.
- Portlets must share a web page with possibly other concurrently running portlets.
- The reduced real estate for portlets means you should design applications that stay within the defined page fragment size of the portlet page.
- Creator offers some components (such as the table component or the button component) that have smaller or "lighter" versions more appropriate for the portlet environment.
- The portlet page life cycle differs from a non-portlet page life cycle. A portlet application shares the browser page with other portlets. The user interacts with only one portlet at a time. Hence, only one portlet processes user input and possibly invokes event handlers. All of the portlets on the page, however, must go through the render phase.
- The normal JSF life cycle for portlets is split into two cycles—one for the form submit processing and one for rendering.

- Don't use request scope objects to transfer data from the form submission phase to the rendering phase. Instead, use session scope objects to cache data.
- Currently you can deploy only one portlet at a time using the bundled portal server in Creator.
- The default portlet page size is 400 by 400 pixels.
- You can build portlets that access a database, call a web service, or use EJBs.
- You designate a portlet page as an initial view mode, edit mode, or help mode page using the Projects window.

CUSTOMIZING APPLICATIONS WITH CREATOR

Topics in This Chapter

- Localizing and Internationalizing Applications
- Setting Up Properties Files
- Locales and Languages
- Configuring Your Browser
- Setting a Locale from Your Application
- Custom Validation
- Working with AJAX-Enabled Components

Chapter 13

An IDE like Creator is only as good as its supporting technology. Fortunately, Creator is built on the solid foundation of JSF, and under that, live a host of other Java technologies that we've touched upon. One area that you'll explore in this chapter is the duo of localization and internationalization.

Another important facet of web application design is providing custom validation. We show you how to write a custom validator method for your Creator project. You'll validate a component's input, control error message display with a message component, and use localized error messages.

As JSF and Creator both mature, more third-party component libraries become available. One such offering is an AJAX-enabled component library available from Sun. We'll show you how to use the auto complete text field in several project examples.

13.1 Localizing an Application

Localization means you customize an application to a given locale. The Java programming language has the concept of a locale that affects many objects. For example, the String class has a version of `toLowerCase()` that takes a Locale object as its argument. When you supply this argument, `toLowerCase()` uses the Locale's idea of translating a String to lowercase letters. More commonly, you use Locale to control the format of a Date object or a monetary amount using the local currency symbol.

Consider the following Java code fragment.

```
import java.util.*;
import java.text.*;
. . .
Locale currentLocale = new Locale("en", "US");
Date myDate = new Date();

DateFormat df = DateFormat.getDateInstance(
     DateFormat.LONG, currentLocale);
System.out.println(df.format(myDate));
```

The `DateFormat` class uses the locale argument (if provided) to determine how to format the date. Here we provide a locale language ("en" for English) and region ("US" for the United States). The `println` statement produces

```
April 2, 2006
```

But if we change the region locale to "GB" for Great Britain, the output becomes

```
02 April 2006
```

to reflect the customary British date format. Furthermore, if we use Spanish and Spain ("es" and "ES" for español and España, respectively), we get

```
2 de abril de 2006
```

However, it's not good enough to simply customize an application for a specific locale. You also need to make your application language independent. To accomplish this task, you gather all the text messages, error messages, and labels from your web page and put them in a "properties" file. Each properties file isolates messages for a specific Locale. To run a program, you "bundle" those messages that are specific to the user's Locale. This creates a ResourceBundle containing locale-specific objects.

The project example in this section shows you how to

- create a property file that holds localized messages;
- configure your application to accept localized messages;
- create and load the resource bundle that makes localized messages available to the pages in your application; and

- allow users to dynamically change the locale.

A Word About Locales

Locales designate both a language and a country (or region). Many readers are aware of the differences between British English and American English, for example, so specifying just a language isn't always good enough. The Spanish spoken in Mexico is different from that spoken in Spain. Similarly, the French spoken in Montreal is distinct from the French spoken in Paris.

On the other hand, specifying a generic language (without a country) may be just fine. A locale may represent just a language or a language and a region.

You can learn more about internationalization[1] from the following tutorial.

```
http://java.sun.com/docs/books/tutorial/i18n/index.html
```

To learn about internationalization support in Java, visit

```
http://java.sun.com/j2se/corejava/intl/index.jsp
```

Localize Application Labels and Text

All too often we neglect to plan ahead for localization and are therefore forced to localize an application after it's already written. In our first example, let's localize project **Login2** from Chapter 6. Then we'll internationalize it and provide a way for the user to select the application's language. We'll also discuss some layout tricks for accommodating variable-sized labels and text.

Localizing an application means that the messages and labels on the page are determined by the locale. When there are no explicit instructions to use a particular locale, a properly localized application simply uses the default locale. Let's start with opening up project **Login2** from Chapter 6.

Copy the Project

To avoid starting from scratch, copy project **Login2** to a new project called **Login2I18N**. This step is optional. If you don't want to copy the project, simply skip this section and continue making modifications to the **Login2** project.

1. Bring up project **Login2** in Creator.
2. From the Projects window, right-click node Login2 and select **Save Project As**. Provide the new name **Login2I18N**.

---

1. The term "i18n" refers to the word internationalization: the 18 letters sandwiched between the initial *i* and final *n*.

3. Close project Login2. Right-click **Login2I18N** and select **Set Main Project**. You'll make changes to the **Login2I18N** project.
4. Expand Login2I18N > Web Pages and open Page1 in the design view.
5. Click anywhere in the background of the design canvas of the Login2I18N project. In the Properties window, change the page's `Title` property to **Login2-I18N**.

Isolate Labels and Text Messages

Go ahead and deploy project **Login2I18N** unchanged. Recall that the project consists of three pages: the initial page (**Page1.jsp**), the page you get when you successfully login (**LoginGood.jsp**), and the login failure page (**LoginBad.jsp**). Provide input for a successful login as well as errors. (For a successful login, type "rave4u" for both the username and password fields.) Note that you get validation errors when you fail to provide any input. (Fortunately, the JSF validators are already localized components. You'll notice that when you provide support for different locales, these components automatically provide locale-specific text.)

To isolate the text in a web page, you must extract each label or message and place it in a property file. (You don't need to extract validation error messages.) Let's look at the localized property file in English for this application.

Listing 13.1 asg.messages.login.properties

```
welcomeGreeting = Welcome
loginPageTitle = Members Login Page
usernameLabel = Username
passwordLabel = Password
usernameTip = Please type in your username

passwordTip = Please type in your password
loginButtonLabel = Login
resetButtonLabel = Reset
badLogin = Invalid username or password. To try again click
hereHyperlink = HERE
```

Fortunately, there are not many messages and component labels to extract, but the format here is important. The format includes a *key* (for example, `welcomeGreeting` listed above), an equal sign (=), followed by the message or label *text*. Spaces around the equal sign are optional. You place these key/value pairs in a text file and give it a name with a **.properties** extension. If the file represents the default locale, the name doesn't need a locale identifier. Otherwise, append **_LOCALE** to the base filename.

With English as the default locale, the name of this file is **login.properties** (with no locale designation) in package **asg.messages**. Later, you'll implement translations to German and Spanish. These files will have the names **login_de.properties** (for German) and **login_es.properties** (for Spanish).

With country codes as well as language codes, use **login_es_ES.properties** (for Spanish in Spain) and **login_de_DE.properties** for German in Germany. (By the way, American English is **login_en_US.properties** and British English is **login_en_GB.properties**.) Adding country-specific translations involves creating additional translations with the country-specific filename. You can easily add these to your application later.

Add the asg.jar Jar File

The **login.properties** file is in JAR file **asg.jar** found in the Creator2 download. Once you add the JAR file to your project, you can access the login properties file.

1. In the Projects window right-click Libraries. Select Add JAR/Folder from the context menu. Creator pops up the Add JAR/Folder dialog.
2. Browse to the **FieldGuide2/Examples** and select file **asg.jar**. Click Open. Creator adds the JAR file to your project.

Creator lets you view the properties file as a key-value database in the editor pane, showing all of the locales. Here's how you can view it.

1. In the Projects window under Libraries, expand the **asg.jar > asg.messages** nodes.
2. Select **login.properties** file and double-click. Creator displays the key-value data in the editor as shown in Figure 13–1.

Localize the JSF Source

Once you've created a properties file for at least one locale, you must tell your program where to access these messages. JSF has a `loadBundle` tag that accomplishes this. Let's put a `<f:loadBundle/>` tag in each of your page's JSP source files, as follows.

1. Bring up **Page1** in the design editor.
2. Click the JSP label in the editing toolbar to bring up the file in the JSP editor.
3. Directly after the `<f:view/>` tag, open a new line and add the following `loadBundle` tag. (Put the tag all on one line.)

```
<f:loadBundle basename="asg.messages.login" var="messages"/>
```

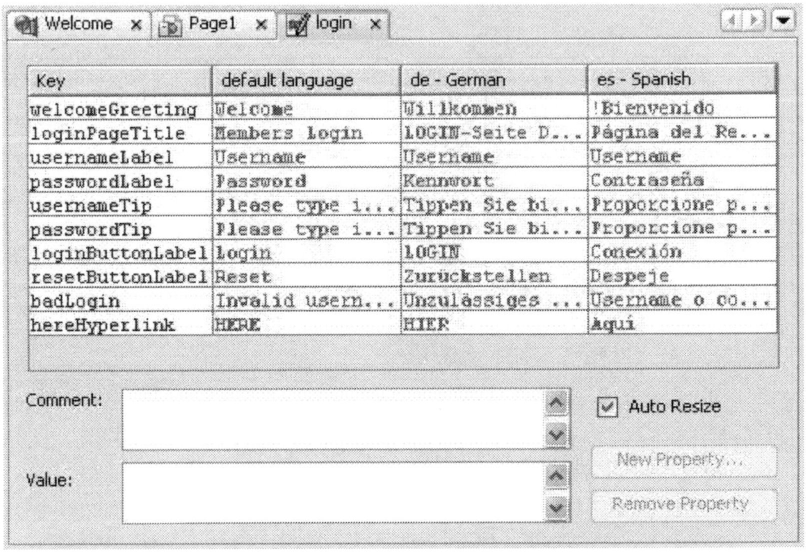

Figure 13–1 **Viewing the properties file in Creator's editor pane**

The `loadBundle` tag now appears in the Page1 Outline view.

With the `loadBundle` tag, JSF loads the resource bundle from the properties file with basename **login** in package **asg.messages**. This selects the properties file that corresponds to the current locale. If no locale is specified, JSF loads resource property file **login.properties**.

The `var` property specifies how you'll refer to the message text in the rest of the JSF source. Here, you've set `var` to "messages," so the value binding expression that grabs the text corresponding to the key `welcomeGreeting` is

```
#{messages.welcomeGreeting}
```

Note that `messages` is the value of the `var` property and `welcomeGreeting` is the key in the properties file that corresponds to the text you want.

Creator Tip

There is a big advantage to having a distinct `var` *property specify a "handle" to the properties file. If the properties file name changes, you only have to modify the* `basename` *attribute of the* `loadBundle` *tag. All of the value binding expressions for your application's components remain unaffected, since they reference the* `var` *property.*

Now add the `loadBundle` tag to pages **LoginGood.jsp** and **LoginBad.jsp**.

1. In the Projects view, expand Web Pages and double-click the filename.
2. Click the JSP label to bring the file up in the JSP editor.
3. Copy and paste the `loadBundle` tag into each JSP source file at the same spot.

Using Grid Panel to Improve Page Layout

When you build an application with just one language, you can determine the placement of the components on the page. You just use the design view editor to align components in the grid. However, when labels and other text are locale-specific, you cannot gauge component placement. Either components are placed too far apart to accommodate translated text that is longer than the original, or text overwrites adjacent components.

Fortunately, the grid panel component helps immensely. Figure 13–2 shows the Page1 design view with grid panel components holding the text field and password components (as well as their labels and message components). You'll also put the two button components inside their own grid panel. Page LoginBad contains two adjacent components that nest inside a grid panel as well. (*We modified the components to display the* **key** *from the properties file. You'll provide a more complete value binding expression, which we'll show you during component configuration.*)

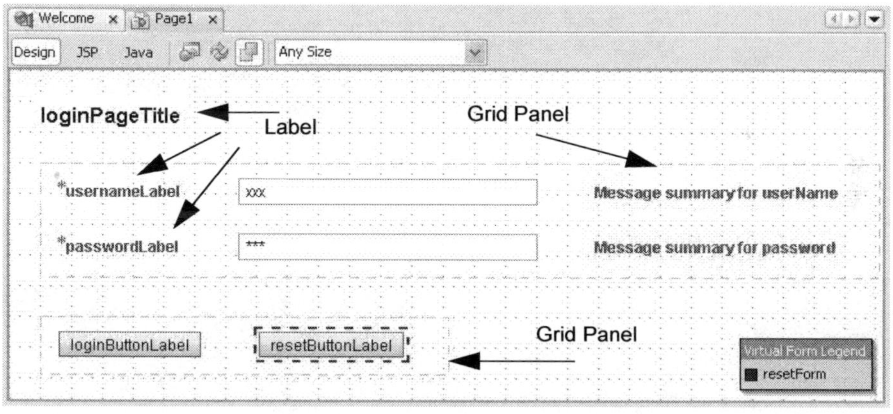

Figure 13–2 **Page1 with components nested in grid panels**

Before you modify the components to use the properties file, let's update the layout with grid panel components. You'll also use the label component instead of the built-in label property with the text field and password components.

1. Bring up Page1 in the design view.
2. From the Layout Components palette, select Grid Panel and drag it to the page. Place it under the label component that holds the title. (Don't worry about its exact placement; you can easily move it later.)
3. Make sure the grid panel is still selected. In the Properties window, change property `id` to **gridPanelInput**.
4. In the Properties window under Appearance, specify **10** for `cellpadding` and **3** for `columns`.
5. From the Basic Components palette, select Label and drop it on top of the grid panel component (make sure the grid panel is outlined in blue before you release the mouse).
6. Leave the label's `text` property set to Label for now. Make sure the label is selected. In its Properties window, set property `id` to **usernameLabel** and property `for` to **userName** (the text field component) from the drop down list. The label component will now include a red asterisk.
7. Select the text field component and unset property `label` (it should be empty).
8. In the Page1 Outline view, select component `userName` and drag it, dropping it on top of the grid panel component you just added.
9. Repeat this step for the message component associated with the `userName` component. Since the grid panel contains three columns, the label, text field, and message components will appear adjacent to each other in the grid panel's first row.

   You'll organize the password components in the same way.

1. From the Basic Components palette, select Label and drop it on top of the grid panel component (make sure the grid panel is outlined in blue before you release the mouse).
2. Leave the label's `text` property set to Label. Make sure the label is selected. In its Properties window, set property `id` to **passwordLabel** and property `for` to **password** from the drop down list. The label component will now include a red asterisk.
3. Select the password component and unset property `label` (it should be empty).
4. In the Page1 Outline view, select component `password` and drag it, dropping it on top of the grid panel component.
5. Repeat this step for the message component associated with the password component.

   You'll put the two button components in a separate grid panel.

1. From the Layout Components palette, select Grid Panel and drag it to the page. Place it under the first grid panel component.

2. Make sure the grid panel is still selected. In the Properties window, change property `id` to **gridPanelButtons**.
3. In the Properties window under Appearance, specify **10** for `cellpadding` and **2** for `columns`.
4. In the Page1 Outline view, drag the Login button and drop it on top of component `gridPanelButtons`.
5. Repeat this step with the Reset button. Both buttons should appear side by side in the second grid panel.
6. Adjust the grid panel components on the page so that the layout is the way you want it.
7. Click the Save All icon from the toolbar to save these changes.

Page LoginBad also needs a grid panel component to accommodate the various lengths of the text in both components.

1. Bring LoginBad up in the design view.
2. From the Layout Components palette, select Grid Panel and drag it to the page. (Don't worry about its exact placement.)
3. Make sure the grid panel is still selected. In the Properties window under Appearance, specify **10** for `cellpadding` and **2** for `columns`.
4. In the LoginBad Outline view, drag the static text component and drop it on top of the grid panel.
5. Repeat this step with the hyperlink component. Both components should appear side by side in the grid panel.
6. Click the Save All icon from the toolbar to save these changes.

Modify the Components for Localized Text

It's time to return to the task of configuring the components to use the text in the properties file.

1. Bring up Page1 in the design view.
2. Select the label component that displays the page's title. Property `text` is set to **Members Login**. In the Properties window, replace property `text` with the following expression followed by **<Enter>**.

```
#{messages.loginPageTitle}
```

3. Select label component `usernameLabel`. In the Properties window, replace property `text` with the following expression.

```
#{messages.usernameLabel}
```

4. Repeat this process for the password component's label (its `text` property), the Login button's `text` property, and the Reset button's `text` property. Use the following value binding expressions.

```
#{messages.passwordLabel}
#{messages.loginButtonLabel}
#{messages.resetButtonLabel}
```

5. The text field component and password component both have tooltips. Change the `toolTip` property for components `userName` and `password` to the following.

```
#{messages.usernameTip}
#{messages.passwordTip}
```

   Each of the other two pages contains components as well.

6. Bring up **LoginGood** in the design view. Select the static text component (there's only one) and change its `text` property to the following (type it on a single line).

```
#{messages.welcomeGreeting},
#{SessionBean1.loginBean.username}!
```

   This expression concatenates the welcome greeting text with the user's login name. Figure 13–3 shows page LoginGood in the design view.

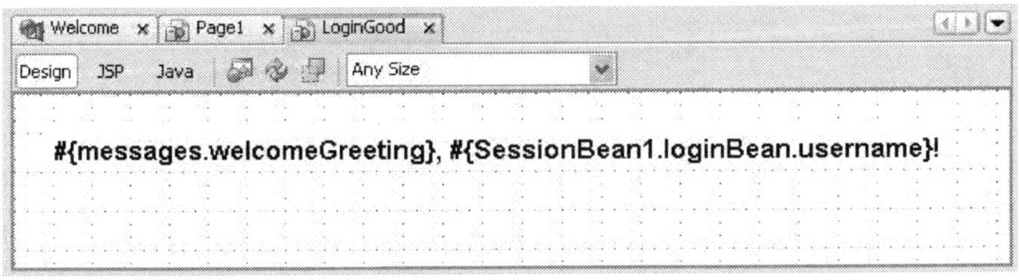

Figure 13–3 **Using localized messages and property binding**

7. Select tab **LoginBad** to make it active in the design view. There are two components: a static text component and a hyperlink component.
8. Change the `text` property of the static text component to

```
#{messages.badLogin}
```

9. Change the `text` property of the hyperlink component to

```
#{messages.hereHyperlink}
```

Deploy and Run

Ok, you've completed the steps for localization, so now it's time to deploy and run the application. If you've done everything right, you should not see any changes from the **Login2** application (except for the slight layout changes due to nesting components inside the gird panels). The messages are still in English and the login procedure is unchanged. Underneath, however, there is a big difference. No hard-wired English labels or messages appear on the page. Everything is read from the properties file you reference for the default locale. The next step is internationalization.

Creator Tip

If you're having trouble with your application working correctly, here are some things to check. First, if deploying throws an exception, open the **Page1** *in the JSP editor and make sure you have the* **asg.messages.login** *properties file spelled correctly in the* `<f:loadBundle>` *tag. Check the other pages, too. If the application deploys but doesn't work properly, use the Properties window or the JSP source to check the value binding expressions.*

13.2 Internationalizing an Application

A localized application is much easier to internationalize than one that is not localized. Since you've already extracted the messages and labels, it won't be difficult to configure your application to access translated versions of the text.

Provide Translations

Fortunately, you can provide translations at any time once you've isolated the text that requires translation. (This is when you hire a bank of native speakers who can translate your English language text into the target languages.) Here is our translation for Spanish, in file **login_es.properties**.

Listing 13.2 asg.messages.login_es.properties

```
welcomeGreeting = !Bienvenido
loginPageTitle = Página del Registro Para Los Miembros
usernameLabel = Username
passwordLabel = Contraseña
usernameTip = Proporcione por favor su Username
passwordTip = Proporcione por favor su Contraseña

loginButtonLabel = Conexión
resetButtonLabel = Despeje
badLogin = Username o contraseña inválido. Para tratar otra
vez escoge
hereHyperlink = Aquí
```

Here is the translation for German, in file **login_de.properties**.

Listing 13.3 asg.messages.login_de.properties

```
welcomeGreeting = Willkommen
loginPageTitle = LOGIN-Seite Des Mitgliedes
usernameLabel = Username
passwordLabel = Kennwort
usernameTip = Tippen Sie bitte Ihr Username ein
passwordTip = Tippen Sie bitte Ihr Kennwort ein

loginButtonLabel = LOGIN
resetButtonLabel = Zurückstellen
badLogin = Unzulässiges Username oder Kennwort. Um es erneut
zu versuchen klicken Sie
hereHyperlink = HIER
```

Note that the text *keys* are unchanged from the original version. In any properties file, the keys remain constant across all translations. In the Projects window, expand **Libraries > asg.jar > asg.messages > login.properties** to see all three properties files listed (see Figure 13–4). With Spanish and German text isolated into properties files, the only step left is to tell JSF which locales the application supports.

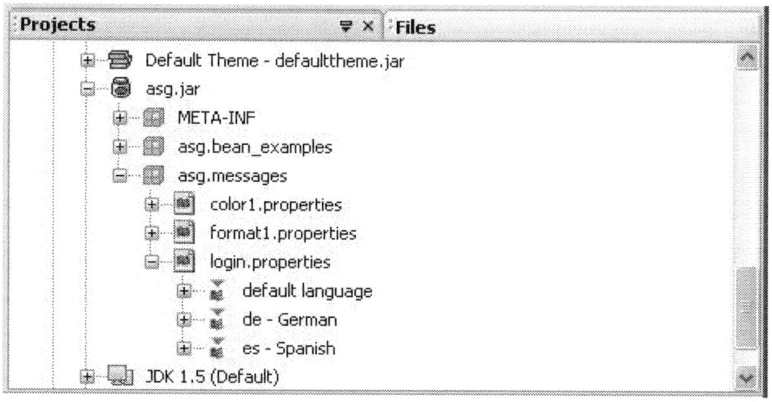

Figure 13–4 **Properties files for English (default), German, and Spanish locales**

Specify Supported Locales

You specify supported locales in the XML configuration file **faces-config.xml**. Creator includes it in your project; you just have to remove the comments around the XML tags.

1. Select the Files tab to activate the Files view (or select **View > Files** from the main menu if the Files tab is not visible).
2. Expand nodes **Login2I18N > web > WEB-INF** and you'll see several XML files Creator generates for each project.
3. Double-click file **faces-config.xml** to bring it up in the XML editor. You'll see the template of the file you'll need. Delete the comment lines (<!-- and -->) surrounding the `<application> </application>` tags.
4. Delete locale **`fr`** (or provide the necessary French properties file for this project). Here is the modified file **faces-config.xml**.

Listing 13.4 faces-config.xml

```
<faces-config>
   <application>
      <locale-config>
       <default-locale>en</default-locale>
        <supported-locale>es</supported-locale>
        <supported-locale>de</supported-locale>
      </locale-config>
   </application>
</faces-config>
```

The default locale is English (`en`); Spanish (`es`) and German (`de`) are supported locales.

Configure Your Browser

If you normally use English, you'll have to configure your browser to see the German and Spanish versions of project Login2I18N. Here are the steps you need with Internet Explorer.

1. Select **Tools > Internet Options > Languages**. Click the Add button and select the following lines in the supported languages box.

```
Spanish [es]
English [en]
German [de]
```

2. Click OK.
3. To change your locale, select the target language and move it to the top with the Move Up button.

If you use Netscape Navigator (version 8) as your browser, follow these steps.

1. Select **Tools > Options**.
2. Select category **General** from the options on the left.
3. Select **Languages**.
4. From the drop down component in the middle of the dialog, select the language you'd like to add. Then click Add to add it to the list.
5. Select the target locale and move it to the top with the Move Up button, as shown in Figure 13–5. Click OK when you're finished.

Deploy and Run

With the preceding changes, the application runs in either English, Spanish, or German by configuring your browser for these different locales. Note that if you don't supply a username or password, the application displays error messages in the selected language. This is because the JSF validator is already configured to get its text from locale-specific messages.

Figure 13–6 shows the login page in the Spanish version (with Netscape 8) and Figure 13–7 displays the German version (with Internet Explorer).

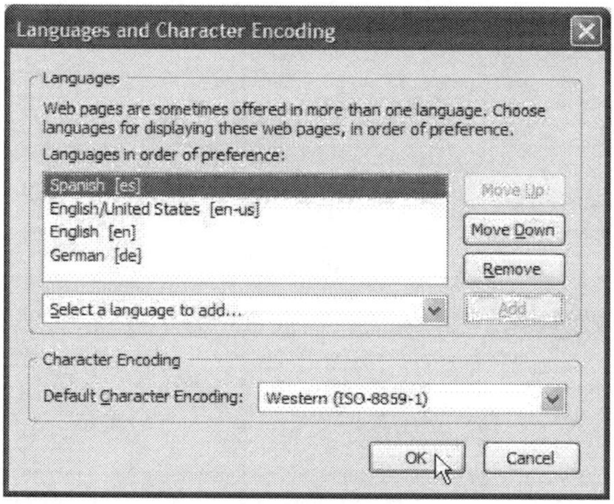

Figure 13–5 **Configuring Netscape for other languages**

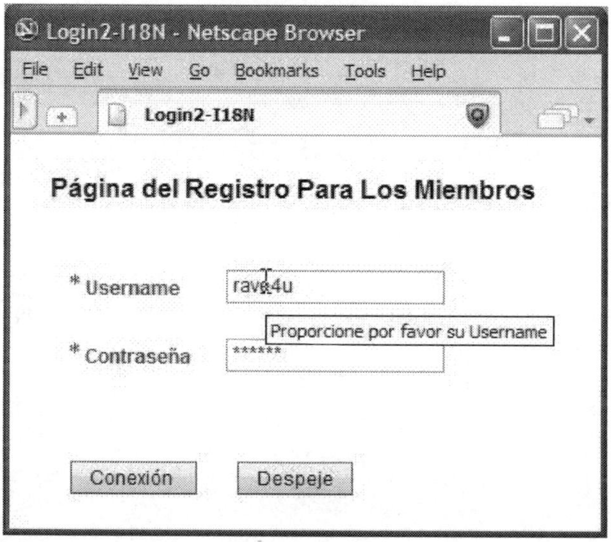

Figure 13–6 **Logging in with the Spanish version**

Figure 13–7 **Logging in with the German version**

13.3 Controlling the Locale from the Application

You may want users of your web application to select a language directly without having to modify browser configurations or change default locale settings. In this example, you'll add a drop down list component to the initial page that offers language selection for the application. Since the web application has already been internationalized (for three languages, at least), these modifications are minor.

Here's the approach. You'll use a drop down list to hold the locale choices. When the user changes the locale, you save the choice as a property in session scope by binding the selected value of the drop down component to the session bean property. Then, when the user returns to the application's initial page, the correct language is still selected in the drop down component. Your first step, then, is to copy the project and add a property to session scope.

Copy the Project

To avoid starting from scratch, copy project **Login2I18N** to a new project called **Login2I18N-Alt**. This step is optional. If you don't want to copy the project, simply skip this section and continue making modifications to the **Login2I18N** project.

1. Bring up project **Login2I18N** in Creator.
2. From the Projects window, right-click node **Login2I18N** and select **Save Project As**. Provide the new name **Login2I18N-Alt**.
3. Close project **Login2I18N**. Right-click **Login2I18N-Alt** and select **Set Main Project**. You'll make changes to the **Login2I18N-Alt** project.
4. Expand **Login2I18N-Alt > Web Pages** and open Page1 in the design view.
5. Click anywhere in the background of the Page1 design canvas. In the Properties window, change the page's `Title` property to **Login2-I18N-Alt**.

Add a SessionBean1 Property

In this project, you will save the drop down list's current selection in session scope. Call the property `myLocale`; it will be type String. Here are the steps to add property `myLocale` to SessionBean1.

1. In the Projects window, right-click **Session Bean** and select **Add > Property**. Creator displays the New Property Pattern dialog.
2. Fill in the fields as follows. For Name specify **myLocale**, for Type select **String**, and for Mode select **Read/Write**. Click OK.

Now you you'll provide code to initialize property `myLocale` to English in SessionBean1 method `init()`.

1. From the Projects window, double-click node **Session Bean** to bring up **SessionBean1.java** in the Java source editor.
2. Add the following initialization code to the end of method `init()`. The added code is bold.

```
public void init() {
   . . .
   // Default to English locale
   myLocale = new String("en");
}
```

Add Components to Page1

You'll place the drop down list component at a prominent place at the top of the page. To account for the variable size of the page title's text, place both the title and the drop down list component inside a grid panel. Figure 13–8 shows the design view with the components placed inside grid panels and the drop down component added. Note that the drop down component submits its own virtual form (green localeForm).

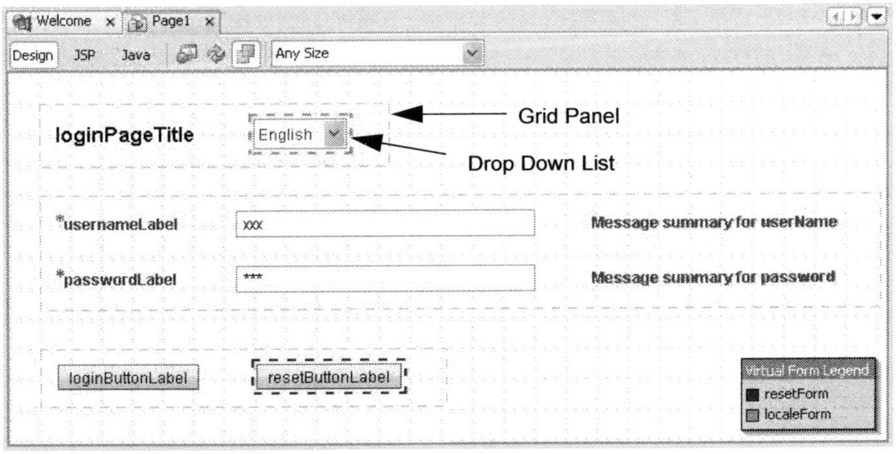

Figure 13–8 **Design view showing component layout for Login2I18N-Alt**

1. Bring up Page1 in the design view.
2. From the Layout Components palette, select Grid Panel and drag it to the page. (Don't worry about its exact placement.)
3. Make sure the grid panel is still selected. In the Properties window, change its `id` property to **gridPanelTitle**.
4. In the Properties window under Appearance, specify **10** for `cellpadding` and **2** for `columns`.
5. In the Page1 Outline view, drag the label component (that holds the page title) and drop it on top of the grid panel.
6. From the Basic Components palette, select Drop Down List and drop it on top of the grid panel you just added. The label component and the drop down list will appear adjacent to each other inside the grid panel. In the Page1 Outline view, these components will be nested under the grid panel.

   Now you'll define the options for the drop down list.

1. In the Page1 Outline view, select component `dropdown1DefaultOptions` (it's near the bottom of the Outline view).
2. In the Properties window, select the small editing box opposite property `options`. A dialog pops up.
3. Replace the default items with **English**, **Deutsch**, and **Español** under Display and **en**, **de**, and **es** under Value, as shown in Figure 13–9.
4. Click OK to close the dialog.

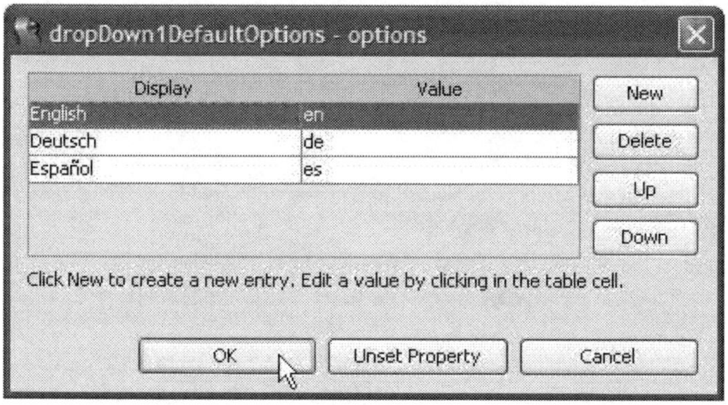

Figure 13–9 **Specifying language selections for the drop down component**

The drop down list requires its own virtual form (so that the text field and password components are not validated during language selection).

1. Toggle the Virtual Forms icon in the editing toolbar to enable the virtual forms display. There should be one virtual form defined (blue resetForm).
2. Select the drop down component, right-click, and select Configure Virtual Forms. Creator pops up the Configure Virtual Forms dialog.
3. Click New to create a new form (green). Change its name to localeForm and select Yes under heading Submit.
4. Click Apply and OK. A dotted, green outline now encloses the drop down list component.

Method `processValueChange()` is invoked when the user changes the selection in the drop down component.

1. Select the drop down list component. Right-click and select Edit Event Handler > processValueChange from the context menu. Creator generates method `dropDown1_processValueChange()` and brings up **Page1.java** in the Java source editor.
2. Add the following code to method `dropDown1_processValueChange()`. Copy and paste from file **FieldGuide2/Examples/Custom/snippets/login2I18N_dropdown.txt**. The added code is bold.

```
public void dropDown1_processValueChange(
        ValueChangeEvent event)
{
    FacesContext context = FacesContext.getCurrentInstance();
    UIViewRoot viewRoot = context.getViewRoot();
```

```
      String loc = dropDown1.getSelected().toString();
      viewRoot.setLocale(new Locale(loc));
   }
```

This method retrieves the faces context and the root view (the top level for all the components on the page). It then obtains the selected value from the drop down list (either *en*, *de*, or *es* for English, German, and Spanish, respectively) and uses it to set a new locale.

Fix the syntax errors by defining the necessary import statements.

3. Right-click anywhere inside the file and select Fix Imports from the context menu. This should take care of any syntax errors.
4. Click the Save All icon on the toolbar to save these changes.

Final Configurations

There's a few more settings to configure for the drop down list component.

1. Return to the Page1 design view by selecting Design in the editing toolbar.
2. Select the drop down list component, right-click, and check selection **Auto-Submit on Change** from the context menu. This submits the page for processing when the user changes the drop down selection.

Creator Tip

Auto-Submit on Change also sets property immediate to true.

3. Right-click the drop down list again and select Property Bindings from the context menu. Creator pops up the Property Bindings dialog.
4. For Select bindable property, choose **selected *Object***. For Select binding target, choose **SessionBean1 > myLocale**, as shown in Figure 13–10. Click Apply then Close. Property binding between the drop down component's selected value and property `myLocale` saves the chosen locale in session scope.

Finally, you'll remove the locale configurations from file **faces-config.xml**. This is to prevent the locale settings performed by the event handler from interfering with the settings indicated by your browser. Without the configuration information in **faces-config.xml**, the drop down component's event handler will determine the current locale.

1. Select the Files tab to activate the Files view.

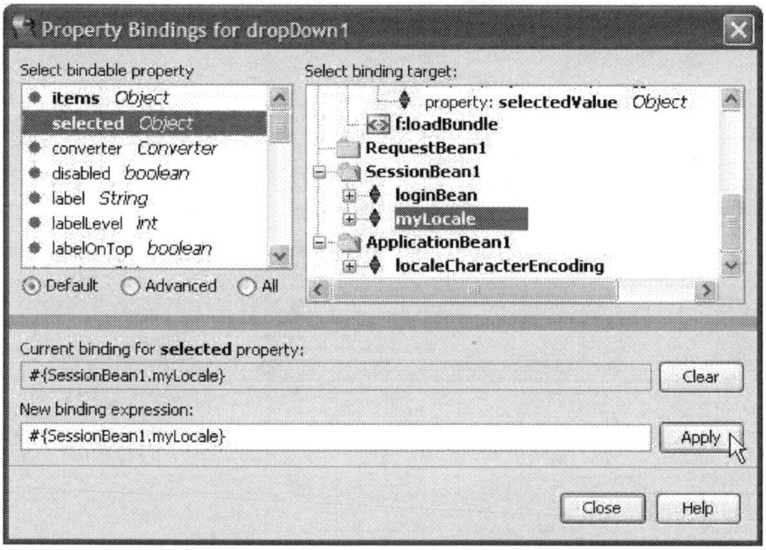

Figure 13–10 **Specifying property bindings for the drop down component**

2. Expand nodes **Login2I18N-Alt** > **web** > **WEB-INF**. Under **WEB-INF**, double-click file **faces-config.xml**. This brings it up in the XML editor.
3. Add comments `<!--` and `-->` around the `<application>` and `</application>` tags to comment-out the locale configuration (or remove the XML tags from the file).
4. Click the Save All icon and close file **faces-config.xml**.
5. Click Projects to return to the Projects view.

Deploy and Run

Deploy and run the application. You can now select the target language without configuring your browser. Figure 13–11 shows the initial page (in German) as the user is about to select Spanish.

13.4 Custom Validation Method

Sometimes you need to provide your own validation for input. There are two approaches to take here. One is to write a custom validator that you can use with other projects. Writing your own validator is a lot more work, but it gives you a reusable component. The other approach is to write a validation method and add it to your page bean. This is appropriate when you don't expect to use

Figure 13–11 **Setting the locale from the application**

the validation with other pages or other applications. It's the easier of the two approaches and a good first step if you're thinking about creating a validator.

You learned about localization and internationalization in the previous sections. Now we'll show you how to make your validation method access the current locale for error messages and post messages to the faces context. Using the current locale, you can provide international support for your validator error messages. Also, by posting error messages to the faces context, you can use Creator's message components to report validation errors generated by your custom validation method.

You'll accomplish all this with a simple application that uses a JavaBeans component called ColorBean to store red-green-blue (RGB) color values. Each color property of ColorBean stores its value as a two-digit hexadecimal string. A `getColor()` method returns a String that sets HTML colors. The String's format is `#rrggbb`, where `rr` is a two-digit hex value for red, `gg` is a two-digit hex value for green, and `bb` is a two-digit hex value for blue.

A user can modify the two-digit value of each color, but a custom validator makes sure that user input is only two digits in length and that the digits are valid. The validator also allows upper- and lowercase letters for the hex digits `a` through `f`.

This application comes up with all color properties set to the String `"ff"` (white). See Figure 13–12 for the page layout. When the user modifies an RGB color value, the background color of the enclosing grid panel changes to the new color.

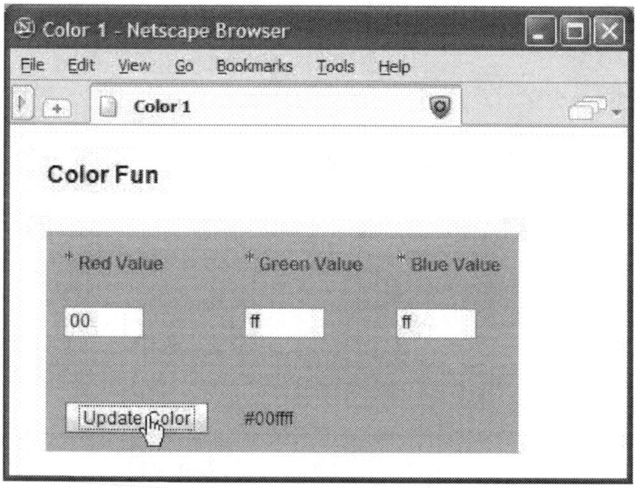

Figure 13–12 **Using custom validation**

Create a Project

Let's start by creating a project called **Color1**. When the design canvas comes up, change the Page1 title to **Color 1**.

Add a JAR File to Your Project

Before you add components, configure properties files, and create a **faces-config.xml** file, you'll add a JAR file to your project. You'll use the same JAR file from the previous project. This file contains **ColorBean.java** (the source for your JavaBeans component), **ColorBean.class** (the compiled class file), and the **.properties** files that internationalize the application.

1. In the Projects view, right-click the Libraries node and select Add JAR/Folder from the context menu. Creator opens up the Add JAR/Folder dialog.
2. Browse to your Creator2 download to **FieldGuide2/Examples**.
3. Select file **asg.jar** and click Open.
4. Expand the Libraries node and you'll see file **asg.jar** listed.

Add a ColorBean Property to SessionBean1

Now that you've added the JAR file containing the ColorBean class file, you'll need to make it accessible within your project. Since the ColorBean should have session scope, let's add it to the managed bean SessionBean1 as a property. This enables JSF to automatically instantiate the bean when it instantiates SessionBean1. The bean will also become available to the UI components as a SessionBean1 property.

Creator Tip

You could just as easily put the ColorBean object in RequestBean1, which uses request scope (unless you plan on implementing the project as a portlet).

1. In the Projects view, right-click the node Session Bean and select **Add > Property**. Creator pops up the New Property Pattern dialog, as shown in Figure 13–13.

Figure 13–13 **New Property Pattern dialog**

2. Fill in the dialog as follows. Under Name specify **colorBean**, under Type specify **ColorBean**, and under Mode, select **Read/Write**.

Creator Tip

Since Name and Type are case sensitive, make sure you copy the capitalizations exactly.

3. Keep the default for options Generate Field, Generate Return Statement, and Generate Set Statement as shown. Click OK to close the dialog.

4. Still in the Projects window, double-click node Session Bean. This brings up **SessionBean1.java** in the Java source editor.
5. You'll see that the code is marked with syntax errors because type Color-Bean is unknown in the current compilation scope. Right-click anywhere inside the file and select Fix Imports from the context menu. This adds the following import statement for the ColorBean class near the top of source file **SessionBean1.java**.

```
import asg.bean_examples.ColorBean;
```

Now you'll add the Java code that instantiates (with operator `new`) the Color-Bean object.

1. Still editing file **SessionBean1.java**, place the cursor after the comment line at the end of method `init()`.
2. Add instantiation with operator `new` for property `colorBean`, as follows.

```
public void init() {
   . . .
   // TODO - add your own initialization code here
   colorBean = new ColorBean();
}
```

The code you added to **SessionBean1.java** makes the `colorBean` object a property of SessionBean1. To access the `redColor` property of `colorBean` (for example), use the following JSF EL expression.

```
#{SessionBean1.colorBean.redColor}
```

This is how you'll bind the UI components on your web page to the Color-Bean's properties. Before you specify binding for the components, however, let's look at the source code for **ColorBean.java**.

ColorBean.java Code

The source for **ColorBean.java** is included in the **asg.jar** JAR file. Since the JAR file is installed in your project as a library, you can easily view the file in Creator's Java source editor.

1. In the Projects window under Libraries, expand nodes **asg.jar > asg.bean_examples**.

2. Double-click file **ColorBean.java**. Creator brings it up in the Java source editor as a read-only file. Listing 13.5 shows the source for **ColorBean.java**.

Listing 13.5 `ColorBean.java`

```
// ColorBean.java

package asg.bean_examples;

public class ColorBean {
    private String redColor;
    private String greenColor;
    private String blueColor;

  /** Creates a new instance of ColorBean */
    public ColorBean() {
        redColor = "ff";
        greenColor = "ff";
        blueColor = "ff";
    }

  // Setters
    public void setRedColor(String c) { redColor = c; }
    public void setGreenColor(String c) { greenColor = c; }
    public void setBlueColor(String c) { blueColor = c; }

  // Getters
    public String getRedColor() { return redColor; }
    public String getGreenColor() { return greenColor; }
    public String getBlueColor() { return blueColor; }
    public String getColor() {
        return "#" + redColor + greenColor + blueColor;
    }
}
```

ColorBean has four properties: three are read/write and the fourth is a read-only property (`color`). All properties have String values. You will bind three text field components to the properties `redColor`, `greenColor`, and `blueColor`. You'll also bind the background color of a grid panel to the `color` property.

Isolate Localized Text

This time you'll plan ahead for localization. Your application will have a page title, labels for three text field components, a button label, and two different error messages that result from validation. The properties file contains the labels and error messages in (American) English. The name of this file is

color1.properties and it lives in the **asg.jar** library under package **asg.messages**. The file's text is shown in Listing 13.6.

Listing 13.6 asg.messages.color1.properties

```
pageTitleLabel = Color Fun
redValueLabel = Red Value
greenValueLabel = Green Value
blueValueLabel = Blue Value
updateButtonLabel = Update Color
lengthError = Hex numbers must be two digits exactly.
digitError = Hex characters must be [0-9][A-F][a-f] only.
```

Creator Tip

You can also view the properties file with Creator. In the Projects window under Libraries, expand the **asg.jar > asg.messages** *folders. Double-click* **color1.properties**. *Creator displays each key-value pair for both the default locale and Spanish locale in the editor pane.*

You'll now add a JSF loadBundle tag to your **Page1.jsp** source page. This tells JSF to use the resource bundle from the current locale. Here are the steps.

1. Bring up Page1 in the design view.
2. Click the JSP label in the editing toolbar.
3. Add the <f:loadBundle> tag after the <f:view> tag in the JSP source. Here's the JSF tag. (Put the tag all on one line.)

```
<f:loadBundle basename="asg.messages.color1" var="messages"/>
```

With the loadBundle tag you'll be able to bind the components that you place on the page to the text messages in the **.properties** files.

Add a Validation Method

To "hook" into JSF's component validation process, all custom validation methods must conform to the correct format. Specifically, they must accept arguments that include the faces context, the input component that's being validated, and the input string that's being validated.

Furthermore, to keep with the stipulation that all messages are localized, you'll have to access the resource bundle from the current context to build the error message. Once the error message is formed, you add the message to the faces context and mark the component "not valid."

Custom method `validateHexString()` calls `toLowerCase()` to convert possible uppercase letters to lower case. Note that we supply the optional Locale argument to the call.

1. Click the Java label in the editing toolbar to open **Page1.java** in the Java source editor.
2. Place the `validateHexString()` method at the end of the file, as shown in Listing 13.7. Copy and paste from file **FieldGuide2/Examples/Custom/snippets/color1_validateHexString.txt**.

Listing 13.7 Method `validateHexString()`

```
public void validateHexString(FacesContext context,
            UIComponent toValidate, Object value) {
  String hexString = value.toString().toLowerCase(
        context.getViewRoot().getLocale());
  boolean valid = true;
  String message = "";

  if (hexString.length() != 2) {
    valid = false;
    message = hexString + ": " +
        lookup_message(context, "lengthError");
  }

  else {
    for (int i = 0; i < 2; i++) {
      char hd = hexString.charAt(i);
      int v = Character.digit(hd, 16);

      if (v < 0 || v > 15) {
        valid = false;
        message = hexString + ": " +
            lookup_message(context, "digitError");
        break;
      }
    }
  }

  if (!valid) {
    ((UIInput)toValidate).setValid(false);
    context.addMessage(toValidate.getClientId(context),
          new FacesMessage(message));
  }
}
```

You'll see some syntax errors due to missing import statements. You'll fix these errors after you add the code for the `lookup_message()` method.

Method `lookup_message()` is a private helper function that looks up the resource bundle associated with this context and locale. This method finds the message text with the key from the resource bundle.

3. Add method `lookup_message()` to **Page1.java**, as shown in Listing 13.8 Copy and paste from file **FieldGuide2/Examples/Custom/snippets/color1_-lookup_message.txt**.

Listing 13.8 Method `lookup_message()`

```
private String lookup_message(
      FacesContext context, String key) {
  String text = null;

  try {
    ResourceBundle bundle =
        ResourceBundle.getBundle("asg.messages.color1",
          context.getViewRoot().getLocale());
    text = bundle.getString(key);

  } catch (Exception e) {
    text = "???" + key + "???";
  }
  return text;
}
```

4. To fix the syntax errors, right-click anywhere in the background and select Fix Imports from the context menu. Here are the import statements.

```
import java.util.ResourceBundle;
import javax.faces.application.FacesMessage;
import javax.faces.component.*;
import javax.faces.context.FacesContext;
import javax.faces.validator.*;
```

Adding Components to the Page

With all the setup work complete, it's time to add components to the page. Figure 13–14 shows the design canvas with the components you need. (*We modified the components to display the* **`key`** *from the properties file. You'll provide a more complete value binding expression during component configuration.*)

You'll add all the components to the page first. Then you'll configure them to access the properties file.

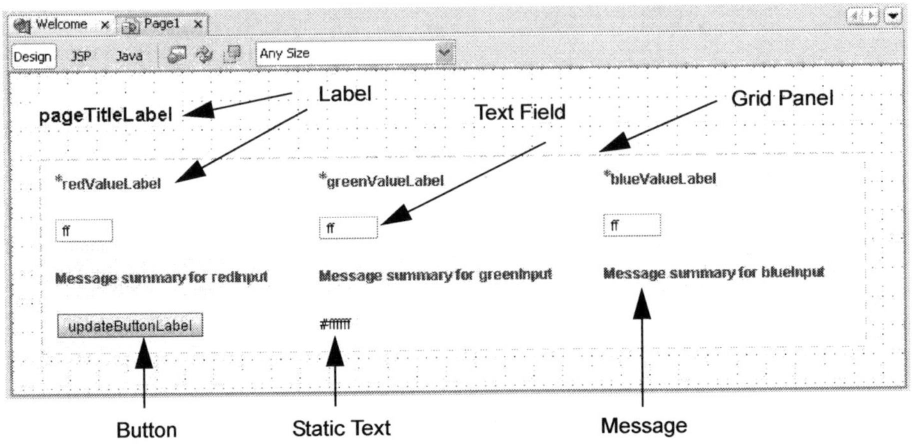

Figure 13–14 **Design canvas with components added to Page1 for project Color1**

1. Bring up Page1 in the design view.
2. From the Basic Components palette, select Label and drag it to the canvas.
3. From the Layout Components palette, select Grid Panel and add it to the page. This component lets you nest components within a grid. It's useful when components are not a constant size (for example, when using localized text for labels).
4. In the Properties window, change `cellpadding` to **10** and `columns` to **3**.
5. Bind the grid panel's `bgcolor` property to the ColorBean `color` property. Select the grid panel component, right-click, and choose Property Bindings. Creator pops up the Property Bindings dialog.
6. For Select bindable property, choose **bgcolor *String***. For Select binding target, choose **SessionBean1 > color *String***. (See Figure 13–15 for the Property Bindings dialog.) Click Apply then Close. Creator sets the binding expression to the following.

```
#{SessionBean1.colorBean.color}
```

Add Components for Input

For each of the three color values (red, green, and blue) you'll need a label, a text field component to gather input, and a message component for validation error messages. Each color will occupy a column in the grid panel.

There are a lot of components to add here, so it's best to place all three labels on the page first, followed by all three text field components, and finally all

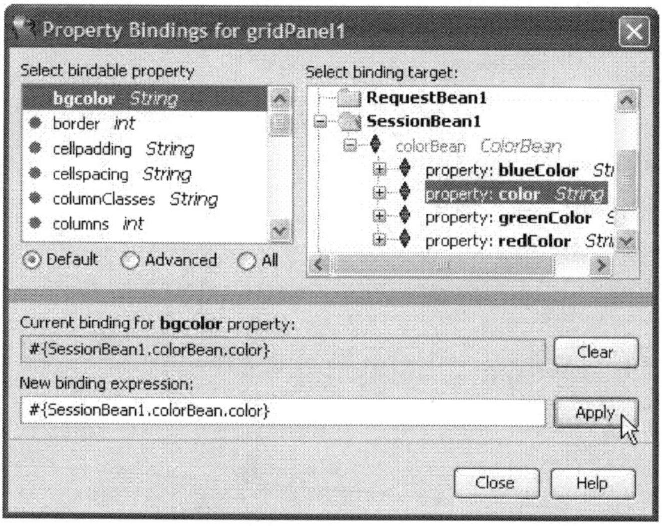

Figure 13–15 **Property Bindings dialog**

three message components. As you add the components, check the Outline view to make sure you're nesting components properly.

Creator Tip

You might find it easier to drop each of the components onto the grid panel in the Outline view. Creator places them in the grid according to the order that you add them. Each cell in the grid panel is used in order until the first row is full. Creator uses the columns property to determine how many columns it should create. You can always re-arrange the components by dropping them on top of the grid panel again. This moves the component to the "end" of the grid. Figure 13–16 shows the Outline view after all the components have been added.

1. From the Basic Components palette, select Label and drop it on top of the grid panel in the Outline view. You'll set its `text` property later.
2. In the Properties view, change its `id` property to **labelRed**.
3. Repeat this and add two more label components, dropping each one on top of the grid panel in the Outline view. Change the second label's `id` property to **labelGreen** and the third one's to **labelBlue**. There should now be three label components side by side in the first row of the grid panel.
4. From the Basic Components palette, select Text Field and drop it on top of the grid panel in the Outline view.

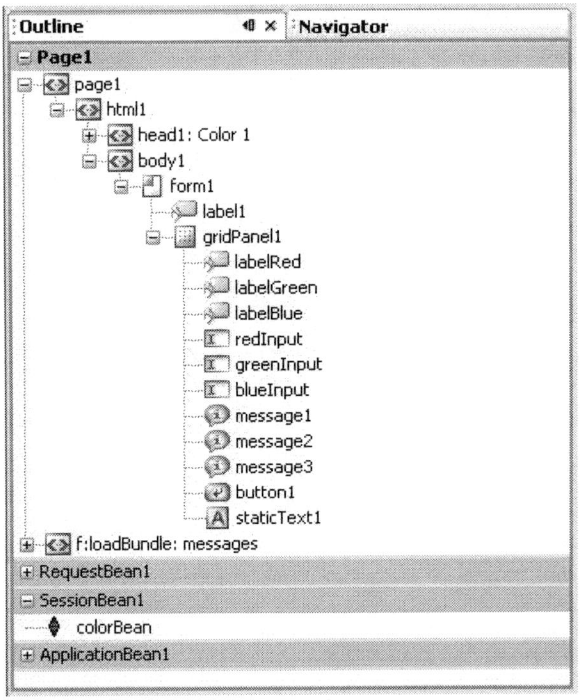

Figure 13–16 **Outline view for project Color1**

5. Configure the text field component as follows. Set its `id` property to **redInput**, *check* the `required` property (set it to true), and bind its `text` property to the `redColor` property of the ColorBean object, as follows. (Figure 13–17 shows the Property Bindings dialog.)

```
#{SessionBean1.colorBean.redColor}
```

6. From the Basic Components palette, select Text Field and drop it on top of the grid panel in the Outline view. This is the second text field component used for green color input.
7. Configure the text field component as follows. Set its `id` property to **greenInput**, *check* the `required` property (set it to true), and bind its `text` property to the `greenColor` property of the ColorBean object, as follows.

```
#{SessionBean1.colorBean.greenColor}
```

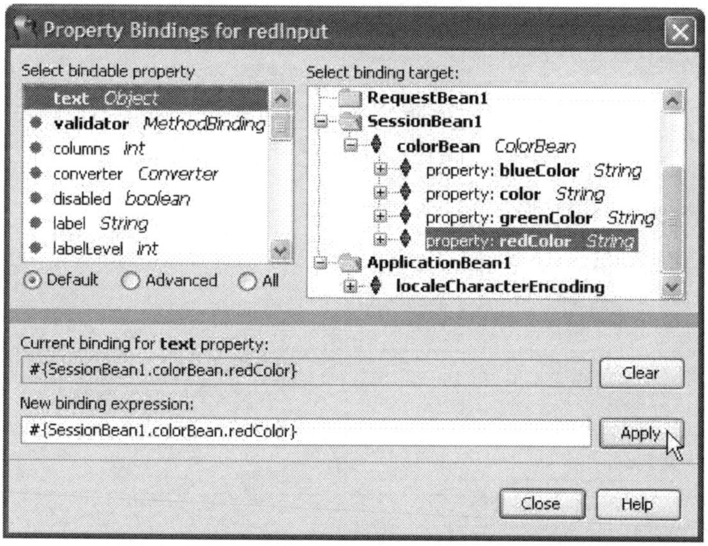

Figure 13–17 **Property Bindings dialog to specify binding for text field redInput**

8. From the Basic Components palette, select Text Field and drop it on top of the grid panel in the Outline view. This is the third text field component used for blue color input.
9. Configure the text field component as follows. Set its `id` property to **blueInput**, *check* the `required` property (set it to true), and bind its `text` property to the `blueColor` property of the ColorBean object, as follows.

```
#{SessionBean1.colorBean.blueColor}
```

There are now three text field components, all in the second row of the grid panel component. You'll now add the three message components and tie them to their respective text field components.

1. From the Basic Components palette, select Message and drop it on top of the grid panel in the Outline view.
2. Type and hold **<Ctrl+Shift>** and drag the mouse to the first text field component. The message component should display "Message summary for redInput."
3. Repeat steps 1 and 2 and add two more message components to the grid panel. Use **<Ctrl+Shift>** to associate each message component with the correct text field component.
4. Now select the first label component. In the Properties view, set its `for` property using the drop down list. Choose **redInput** for the first label.

5. Repeat this step and set the second label's `for` property to **greenInput**. Set the third label's `for` property to **blueInput**. The labels should all have red asterisks indicating required input.

Add a Button and a Static Text Component

You'll now add the button and static text components.

1. From the Basic Components palette, select Button and drop it on top of the grid panel in the Outline view. The button should appear in the fourth row of the grid panel. You'll set its `text` property later.
2. From the Basic Components palette, select Static Text and drop it on top of the grid panel in the Outline view.
3. Select the static text component, right-click, and select Property Bindings. Bind the `text` property of the static text component to property `color` of the ColorBean, as follows.

```
#{SessionBean1.colorBean.color}
```

The grid panel is now set. It has three component labels, three text fields, and three inline messages. In the last row (the fourth row), it has the button and the static text component.

Note that this example does not require an action method for the button component. That's because we just want the page to be submitted when the user clicks the button. All the work is done by input validation and component binding.

Configure for the Validator Method

You must set the `validator` property for each text field component. Normally, you select a validator from the drop down list in the Properties window or simply drag a validator onto the text field component. With a custom validator method, however, you set the `validate` property (under Events in the Properties window).

1. Select the text field component `redInput`.
2. In the Properties window under Events, set property `validate` to **validateHexString**. After you save these changes, the JSP tag contains the following element.

```
validator="#{Page1.validateHexString}"
```

3. Repeat Steps 1 and 2 and set the `validate` property to the same method name for the other two text fields.

Configure the Components for Localized Text

It's time to configure the components to use the text in the properties file. The page title label, the three labels in the grid panel, and the button component will all reference keys in the properties file.

Use Table 13.1 for the correct binding expression for each component.

Table 13.1 Binding to the Properties File

Component Id	*Property*	*Setting*
label1 (Label)	`text`	`#{messages.pageTitleLabel}`
labelRed (Label)	`text`	`#{messages.redValueLabel}`
labelGreen (Label)	`text`	`#{messages.greenValueLabel}`
labelBlue (Label)	`text`	`#{messages.blueValueLabel}`
button1 (Button)	`text`	`#{messages.updateButtonLabel}`

Deploy and Run

Deploy and run the application by clicking the Run icon on the toolbar. Figure 13–18 shows the page after the user changes the color to yellow (`#ffff00`) and then supplies invalid input for the red color value.

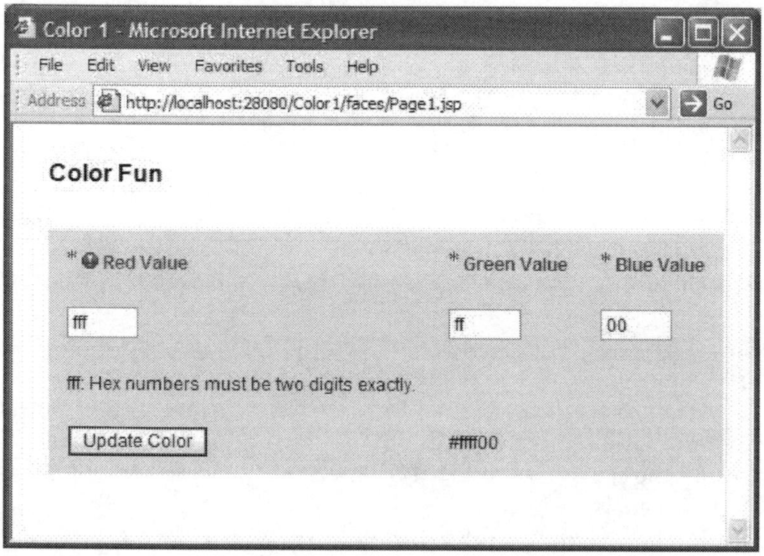

Figure 13–18 **Custom validation with localized error messages in English**

Creator Tip

If you're having trouble with your application working correctly, here are some things to check. First, if deploying throws an exception, open the **Page1.jsp** *file in source mode and make sure you have the* **asg.messages.color1** *properties file spelled correctly in the* `<f:loadBundle>` *tag. If the application deploys but doesn't work properly, use the Properties window in Creator to check that all the property bindings are correct.*

Internationalize for Spanish

In keeping with our two-step process for internationalization (localization being the first step), let's look at the Spanish text for the keys we already created in the default **color1.properties** file. We'll call this file **color1_es_ES.properties** (for Spanish as it's spoken in Spain). The file is already in the **asg.jar** file installed in your project. You can view all locales by double-clicking file **color1.properties** under **Libraries > asg.jar > asg.messages** in the Projects view. Here is the properties file.

Listing 13.9 asg.messages.color1_es_ES.properties

```
pageTitleLabel = Diversión con color
redValueLabel = Valor Rojo
greenValueLabel = Valor Verde
blueValueLabel = Valor Azul
updateButtonLabel = Fije el Color
lengthError = Los números hexadecimales deben ser dos dígitos
  exactamente.
digitError = Los caracteres hexadecimales deben ser
  [0-9][A-F][a-f] solamente.
```

Specify Supported Locales

Specify supported locales in the **faces-config.xml** file. Here are the steps.

1. Select the Files tab to activate the Files view (or select **View > Files** from the main menu if the Files tab is not visible).
2. Expand nodes **Color1 > web > WEB-INF**. You'll see several XML files Creator generates for each project.
3. Double-click file **faces-config.xml** to bring it up in the XML editor. This is the template of the file you'll need. Delete the comment lines (`<!--` and `-->`) surrounding the `<application> </application>` tags.

4. Delete locale **fr** and **de** (French and German). Add a region notation to English (en_US) and Spanish (es_ES). Here is the modified file **faces-config.xml**.

Listing 13.10 faces-config.xml

```
<faces-config>
  <application>
    <locale-config>
      <default-locale>en_US</default-locale>
        <supported-locale>es_ES</supported-locale>
    </locale-config>
  </application>
</faces-config>
```

Configure Your Browser

Here are the steps you need to configure your browser to use other locales with Internet Explorer.

1. Select **Tools > Internet Options > Languages**. Click the Add button and select the following lines in the supported languages box.

```
Spanish [es-ES]
English [en-US]
```

2. Click OK.
3. To change your locale, select the target language and move it to the top with the Move Up button.

If you use Netscape Navigator (version 8) as your browser, follow these steps.

1. Select **Tools > Options**.
2. Select category **General** from the options on the left.
3. Select **Languages**.
4. From the drop down component in the middle of the dialog, select the language you'd like to add. Then click Add to add it to the list.
5. Select the target locale and move it to the top with the Move Up button. Click OK when you're finished.

Deploy and Run

Deploy and run the application by clicking the Run icon on the toolbar. Figure 13–19 shows the page after the user changes the color to `#88eedd` and then supplies invalid input for the red color value. Note that when you configure your browser for Spanish, the system automatically displays the messages you supplied for the Spanish locale.

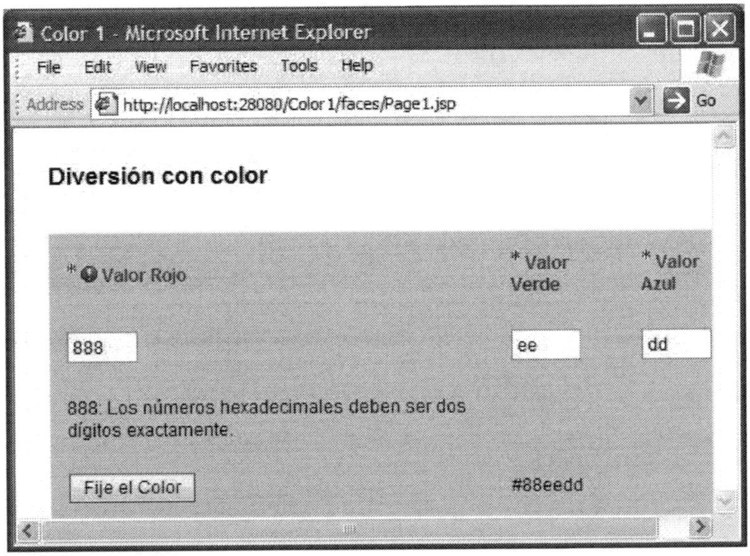

Figure 13–19 **Custom validation with localized error messages in Spanish**

13.5 Using AJAX-Enabled Components

Asynchronous JavaScript Technology and XML (AJAX) is a web development technique for building interactive web applications. Its main purpose is to allow asynchronous updates on a web page without refreshing the whole page and without performing a submit and postback. Even though calls are made to the server, the overall experience for the user is an extremely responsive web application, since only a small portion of the page's display is affected.

The AJAX approach relies on a group of (mostly) standardized technologies working together; it is not itself a new technology. AJAX incorporates

- page markup and presentation using XHTML and CSS (Creator's generated JSP pages use XHTML code and CSS style sheets);
- an application programming interface to access and modify the content, structure and style of a document using Document Object Model (DOM) (DOM is a description of an HTML or XML document in an object-oriented representation);
- asynchronous data retrieval using an XMLHttpRequest object;
- JavaScript to perform the client-side processing.

Readily accessible web applications that use AJAX include Google Suggest, Google Maps, and Flickr (a photo sharing web site). For example, with Google Suggest you can begin typing in a search query and, with the first key stroke, the application gives you a set of suggested search strings that match what you've typed in so far. As you continue typing, the list of suggestions dynamically (and instantly) changes. Even though each key stroke causes a call to the server, the amount of data returned is very small and the page update is minimal. User *perceived* bandwidth is excellent.

The good news for JSF (and Creator) developers is that it is possible to build JSF components with built-in AJAX support. This means that the necessary JavaScript and the required artifacts to communicate asynchronously with the server are built into the component. The end result is sweeter still when the JSF component is enhanced to run within the Creator IDE. We assume that you've already imported a component library containing (at least) the AJAX-enabled auto complete JSF component. (We step you through the process in Chapter 3. See "Importing a Component Library" on page 129.)

State Codes Auto Complete Example

The project that you'll build requests a two-letter state postal code, and based on what the user types in, will provide up to ten two-letter strings that the user can select. After making a selection, the user clicks the Submit button. As a later enhancement, the application will display the state name associated with the provided code in a static text component.

1. From Creator's Welcome Page, select button Create New Project. From the New Project dialog, under Categories select **Web** and under Projects select **JSF Web Application**. Click Next.
2. In the New Web Application dialog, specify **StateCodes** for Project Name and click Finish.

After creating the project, Creator comes up in the design view of the editor pane. You can now set the title.

3. Select `Title` in the Properties window and type in the text **AJAX Example 1**. Finish by pressing **<Enter>**.

Add myStateCode Session Property

To keep track of the state code that the user selects, you'll use a String property called `myStateCode` and add it to session scope.

1. In the Projects view under **StateCodes**, select Session Bean, right-click, and select **Add > Property**.
2. Creator pops up the New Property Pattern dialog. For name, specify **myStateCode**, for type specify **String**, and for Mode keep the default **Read/Write**.
3. Click OK. Creator adds property `myStateCode` to **SessionBean1.java**.
4. In the Projects window, double-click Session Bean to bring up **SessionBean1.java** in the Java editor.
5. Add the following initialization code to the end of method `init()` in **SessionBean1.java**, as follows (the added code is bold).

```
public void init() {
  . . .
  // TODO - add your own initialization code here
  myStateCode = new String();
}
```

6. Scroll to the end of the file and you'll see the generated code for property `myStateCode`.
7. Add the call to method `toUpperCase()` in the setter for property `myState-Code`, as follows (the modified statement is bold).

```
public void setMyStateCode(String myStateCode) {
   this.myStateCode = myStateCode.toUpperCase();
}
```

Add stateCodes Application Property

The AJAX auto complete text field uses a sorted array of Strings to find potential matches. It matches the prefix that the user has typed in so far and grabs the ten strings that potentially match the prefix. Since the array of Strings is sorted, it only needs to find a potential match for the first item.

The array of Strings goes in application scope since it is read-only and it can be shared by all users of the application. First you'll add the property, then you'll insert the code to initialize the array with the state code data.

1. In the Projects view under **StateCodes**, select Application Bean, right-click, and select **Add > Property**.
2. Creator pops up the New Property Pattern dialog. For name, specify **stateCodes**, for type specify **String[]**, and for Mode select **Read Only**.
3. Click OK. Creator adds property `stateCodes` to **ApplicationBean1.java**.

Creator Tip

Make sure you specify Type `String[]` *using array notation.*

4. In the Projects window, double-click Application Bean to bring up **ApplicationBean1.java** in the Java editor.
5. Add the following code to the end of the `init()` method in **ApplicationBean1.java**. Copy and paste from **FieldGuide2/Examples/Custom/snippets/ajax_stateCodes_init.txt**. The added code is bold.

```
public void init() {
   . . .
   // TODO - add your own initialization code here
   stateCodes = new String[] {
      "AK", "AL", "AR", "AZ", "CA", "CO", "CT", "DC", "DE",
      "FL", "FM", "GA", "GU", "HI", "IA", "ID", "IL",
      "IN", "KS", "KY", "LA", "MA", "MD", "ME", "MH",
      "MI", "MN", "MO", "MP", "MS", "MT", "NC", "ND",
      "NE", "NH", "NJ", "NM", "NV", "NY", "OH", "OK",
      "OR", "PA", "PR", "PW", "RI", "SC", "SD", "TN",
      "TX", "UT", "VA", "VI", "VT", "WA", "WI", "WV", "WY"
   };
}
```

6. Click the Save All icon on the toolbar to save these changes.

(The state postal codes are available on the U.S. Postal Service's web site.) Note that the state codes are in alphabetical order here and that this order is different than the alphabetical order of the state names. Also, note that there are several codes that refer to non-state territories and countries, such as MP (Northern Mariana Islands) and PR (Puerto Rico).

Add Components to the Page

Figure 13–20 shows this simple one-page application in the design view. Use the figure as a guide when you add these components to your project.

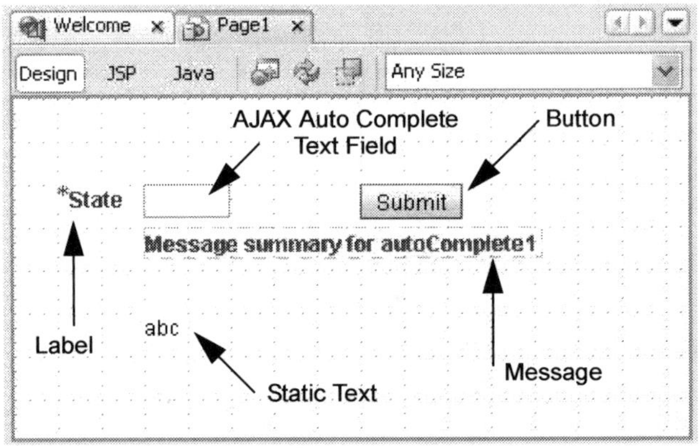

Figure 13–20 **AJAX Auto Complete Text Field component added to Page1**

1. Select the Page1 tab to bring up Page1 in the design view.
2. From the Basic Components palette, select component Label and place it on the page, near the top left side.
3. Make sure it's selected and type in the text **State** and finish with **<Enter>**.
4. From the end of the Components palette, expand section BluePrints AJAX Components and select component Auto Complete Text Field. Drag it to the design canvas and drop it on the page to the right of the label you just added.
5. Make sure it's selected. Adjust its size so that it's smaller (it only needs to hold 2 letters.)
6. In the Properties window under Data, check property `required`. (If property `required` does not appear in the Properties view, add `required="true"` to the `<bp:autoComplete>` tag in the JSP file.)
7. In the Properties window under Data, set property `maxlength` to **2**. (Property `maxlength` limits the number of characters that can be input.)
8. In the design view, select the label component. In the Properties window under Appearance, select **autoComplete1** from the drop down list opposite property `for`. This ties the label component to the auto complete text field component.

   You'll now add a button, a message, and a static text component.

1. From the Basic Components palette, select component Button and drop it onto the page to the right of the auto complete text field component.
2. Type in the text **Submit** followed by **<Enter>** to set the button's label.

3. From the Basic Components palette, select component Message and drop it onto the page under the auto complete text field component. The message component will display input validation errors associated with the text field.
4. Select the message component, type and hold **<Ctrl+Shift>**, and drag the mouse, releasing it when it is over the auto complete text field. This sets the message component's `for` property to `autoComplete1`.
5. From the Basic Components palette, select component Static Text and drop it onto the page below the message component.
6. In the Properties view, change its id to **stateResult**.
7. In the design view, select the static text component, right-click, and select Property Bindings. In the Property Bindings dialog, under Select bindable property, choose **text *Object***. Under Select binding target, choose **SessionBean1 > myStateCode**. Click Apply, as shown in Figure 13–21, then Close.

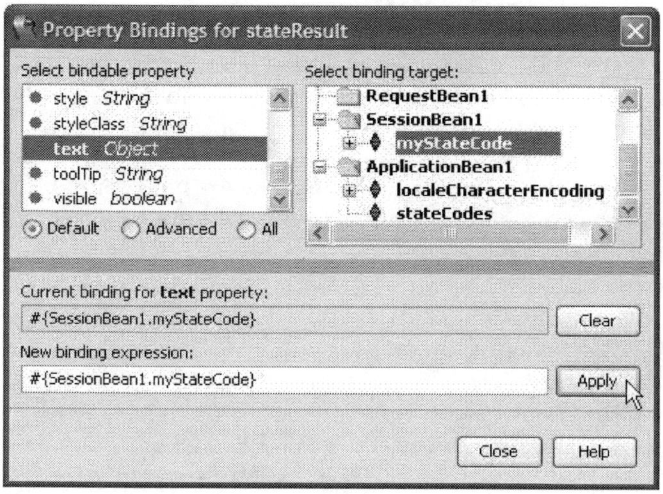

Figure 13–21 **Property Bindings dialog**

8. Repeat this step and bind the auto complete text field `value` property to the same session bean property, `myStateCode`.

Now you'll add a length validator for the auto complete text field component.

1. From the Validators section of the Components palette, select Length Validator and drop it onto the page.
2. Now select the auto complete text field (`autoComplete1`). In the Properties window under Data, select **lengthValidator1** from the drop down list oppo-

site property `validator`. This applies the length validator to the auto complete text field component.
3. In the Page1 Outline view, select `lengthValidator1`. In the Properties window, specify **2** for both the `minimum` and `maximum` properties.
4. Click the Save All icon on the toolbar to save your project.

Creator Tip

Although the length validator makes sure that the length is exactly two and the required property makes sure that the user doesn't leave the field empty, property `maxlength` *(set earlier) prohibits input beyond two characters. This avoids server-side validation for three or more characters since the user can't type in more than two characters to begin with.*

Configure the AJAX Component

The auto complete text field's ability to supply the asynchronous feedback to the user is its `completionMethod` property, which you can bind to a method that provides data to display on the page. Let's do this now.

1. In the design view, double-click the auto complete text field component. Creator generates the complete method event handler and brings up **Page1.java** in the Java source editor.
2. Add the call to `addMatchingItems()` to the `autoComplete1_complete()` event handler. Here's the method with the call to `addMatchingItems()` added (in bold).

```
public void autoComplete1_complete(FacesContext context,
      String prefix, CompletionResult result) {
   // TODO: Return your own list of items here
   // based on the prefix
   //result.addItem("Hello");
   //result.addItem(prefix.toUpperCase());
   AutoCompleteUtilities.addMatchingItems(
        getApplicationBean1().getStateCodes(), prefix, result);
}
```

3. Right-click inside the editor and select Fix Imports to generates the import statement for class `AutoCompleteUtilities`.

Method `autoComplete1_complete()` has three arguments. Argument `prefix` is the text that the user has typed in so far. Argument `result` is an array of Strings that the embedded JavaScript will access to display the current "choice list." You can add items to the `result` array manually inside the complete event handler (as shown by the statements that are commented-out).

Our example uses a utility method included with the AJAX component library to build the `result` array. This method, `addMatchingItems()`, builds the `result` array using the `prefix` String (match target) and a sorted array of Strings as its match source. In our example, the match source is the application scope property `stateCodes`, whose getter returns a (sorted) array of Strings.

As the user types in letters in the auto complete text field, each key stroke causes a call to `addMatchingItems()` to build a new result array. Since the call is made outside of the normal HTTP Request cycle, only the small pop-up containing the selection choices needs rendering.

Deploy and Run

Build, deploy and run the application by selecting the Run icon on the toolbar. When you initially click inside the auto complete text field, a list pops up that consists of the first 10 entries in the state code String array, as shown in Figure 13–22. If the user then types the letter 'm', a new list pops up, starting with the first entry that begins with the letter m. The second window shows this scenario.

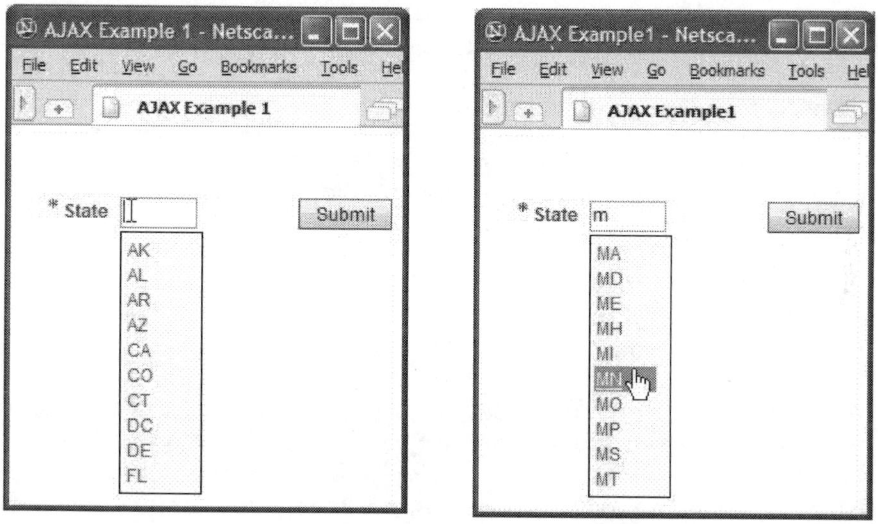

Figure 13–22 **AJAX Auto Complete Text Field component responding to user input**

After the user selects an entry (such as MN, as shown in Figure 13–22) and clicks the Submit button, the state code is displayed in the static text field. If the user leaves the field empty or clicks the button after entering only one letter, the validator kicks in and a validation message is displayed.

If the user selects one of the choices from the pop-up, the selection will be in all upper case. However, if the user types in a code manually, then the setter for property `myStateCode` converts it to all upper case. In this case, it will be displayed in upper case both in the text field and in the static text component only after the user clicks the Submit button.

We'll now enhance the application to display the state name (instead of its code) in the static text component. This requires adding an application property to access a mapping of the codes to the state names and creating a session property to store the user's state selection (to bind to the static text component). By converting the state code to uppercase, we don't have to worry about case sensitivity when using the state code as a lookup key for the map.

Add statesMap Application Property

You'll continue making modifications to the StateCodes project.

1. In the Projects view under **StateCodes**, select Application Bean, right-click, and select **Add > Property**.
2. Creator pops up the New Property Pattern dialog. For name, specify **statesMap**, for type specify **LinkedHashMap**, and for Mode select **Read Only**.
3. Click OK. Creator adds property `statesMap` to **ApplicationBean1.java**.

Creator Tip

LinkedHashMap implements the java.util.Map interface and is useful for retrieving the state name that corresponds to the state code (the key).

4. In the Projects window, double-click Application Bean to bring up **ApplicationBean1.java** in the Java editor.
5. Inside the editor pane right-click and specify Fix Imports to generate the import statement for class `LinkedHashMap`.
6. Add the following code to the end of the `init()` method (after the initialization you already provided for property `stateCodes`) in **ApplicationBean1.java**. Copy and paste from **FieldGuide2/Examples/Custom/snippets/ajax_statesMap_init.txt**. The added code is bold. (To save space, we omit many of the calls to `put()`. There will be a `put()` call for each state code.)

```
public void init() {
   . . .
   statesMap = new LinkedHashMap(stateCodes.length);
   statesMap.put("AK", "Alaska");
```

```
    statesMap.put("AL", "Alabama");
    statesMap.put("AR", "Arkansas");
    statesMap.put("AS", "American Samoa");
      . . .
    statesMap.put("WA", "Washington");
    statesMap.put("WI", "Wisconsin");
    statesMap.put("WV", "West Virginia");
    statesMap.put("WY", "Wyoming");
}
```

7. Click the Save All icon on the toolbar to save these changes.

Add myStateName Session Property

To keep track of the state name, you'll use a read-only String property called `myStateName` and add it to session scope.

1. In the Projects view under **StateCodes**, select Session Bean, right-click, and select **Add > Property**.
2. Creator pops up the New Property Pattern dialog. For name, specify **myStateName**, for type specify **String**, and for Mode select **Read Only**.
3. Click OK. Creator adds property `myStateName` to **SessionBean1.java**.
4. In the Projects window, double-click Session Bean to bring up **SessionBean1.java** in the Java editor.
5. Scroll to the end of the file and you'll see the generated code for property `myStateName`.
6. Replace the code for getter `getMyStateName()` with the following code. Copy and paste from **FieldGuide2/Examples/Custom/snippets/ajax_getMyStateName.txt**. The modified code is bold.

```
public String getMyStateName() {
   myStateName = (String)
      getApplicationBean1().getStatesMap().get(
      getMyStateCode());
   if (myStateName == null) {
      myStateName = new String("State Code Not Set");
   }
   return myStateName;
}
```

Method `getMyStateName()` uses the `LinkedHashMap get()` method with `myStateCode` property for the key. If the `LinkedHashMap` can't find the key, it returns null.

7. Click the Save All icon on the toolbar to save these changes.

Configure Static Text Component

You'll now re-configure the static text component `stateResult` and bind it to the `myStateName` session bean property.

1. Click tab Page1 at the top of the editor pane to return to the design view.
2. Select the static text component `stateResult`, right-click, and select Property Bindings from the context menu. Creator pops up the Property Binding dialog.
3. The Select bindable property should already be set to **text** ***Object***. Under Select binding target, choose **SessionBean1 > myStateName** and click Apply. This changes the binding expression to

```
#{SessionBean1.myStateName}
```

4. Click Close to exit the dialog.

Deploy and Run

Deploy and run project StateCodes. Figure 13–23 shows the page when it initially comes up in a browser. The second screen shot shows the page after the user has selected "FM" for Federates States of Micronesia and is about to select "IL" for Illinois. The AJAX auto complete displays the matching codes beginning with "FM." Note that the state name display is not updated until *after* the user clicks the Submit button.

13.6 Using AJAX-Enabled Components with Web Services

In the previous example, the AJAX `complete()` method invoked the supplied AJAX utility `addMatchingItems()` to build the completion array. You are not limited to using the component this way; you can build the `result` array by accessing a database, an EJB method, or a web service method (for example). In this section, we'll show you how to use the supplied Dictionary Web Service to perform the text completion function of the AJAX component.

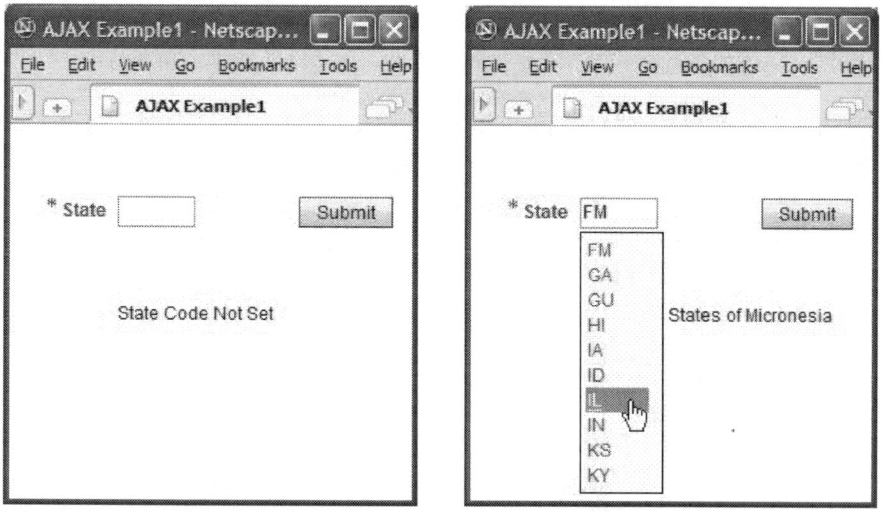

Figure 13–23 **AJAX Auto Complete Text Field component responding to user input**

Adding the Dictionary Web Service

The Dictionary Web Service included with the Creator product was built to work with the AJAX auto complete text field. In order to use it, you must add it to the Web Services section in the Servers window. It should be deployed by the bundled application server. To check, do the following.

1. If the server isn't running, start it. From the Servers window, right-click node Deployment Server and select Start / Stop Server. Creator pops up the Server Status dialog.
2. Click Start Server to start the deployment server.
3. When the server is running, Creator displays a green-arrow badge on the Deployment Server node.
4. In the Servers window under the Deployment Server node, expand the Deployed Components node. You should see the Dictionary Service web service listed.

Now you'll add the Dictionary Service to the Web Services section.

Creator Tip

If DictionaryService appears under the Web Services node in Creator's Servers window, then the web service has already been added and you should skip this section.

1. In the Server window, right-click the Web Services node and select Add Web Service. Creator pops up the Add Web Service dialog.
2. You access the Google Web Service Web Service Description Language (WSDL) file (for example) remotely. Here, however, you'll access the Dictionary Web Service WSDL *locally*. Under Select Web Service Source, click radio button Local File and then Browse, as shown in Figure 13–24.

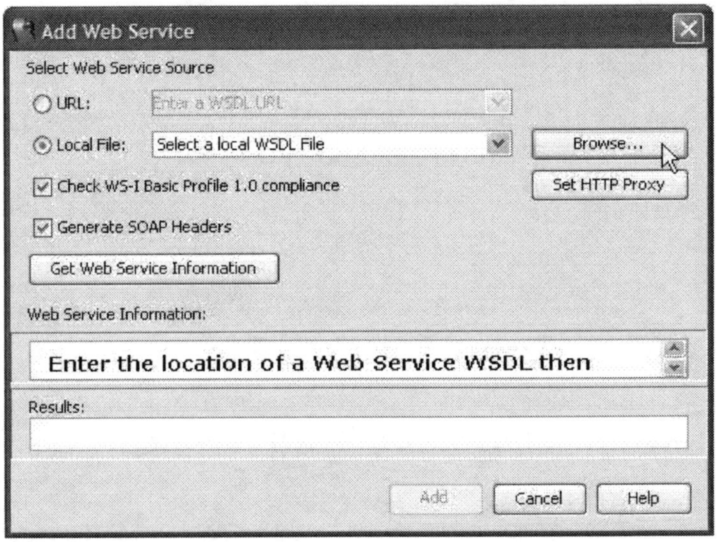

Figure 13–24 **Add Web Service dialog**

3. Creator pops up a file selection dialog. It will default to the **websvc** directory under your user configuration directory for Creator. Select file **DictionaryService.wsdl** and click Open.
4. Creator parses the WSDL file and displays information about the methods as shown in Figure 13–25. Click Add to add the Dictionary Web Service to the Web Services node.

The Dictionary Web Service consists of two methods, as follows.

```
java.lang.String[] matchPrefix(java.lang.String prefix)
java.lang.String define(java.lang.String word)
```

Method `matchPrefix()` performs the same function as the AJAX utility `addMatchingItems()` you used in the previous section. Here, `matchPrefix()` returns an array of Strings from its 180,00 word dictionary that matches the user-typed prefix. You then use `addItems()` to build the `result` array used by the auto complete text field. Method `define()` returns the definition of the

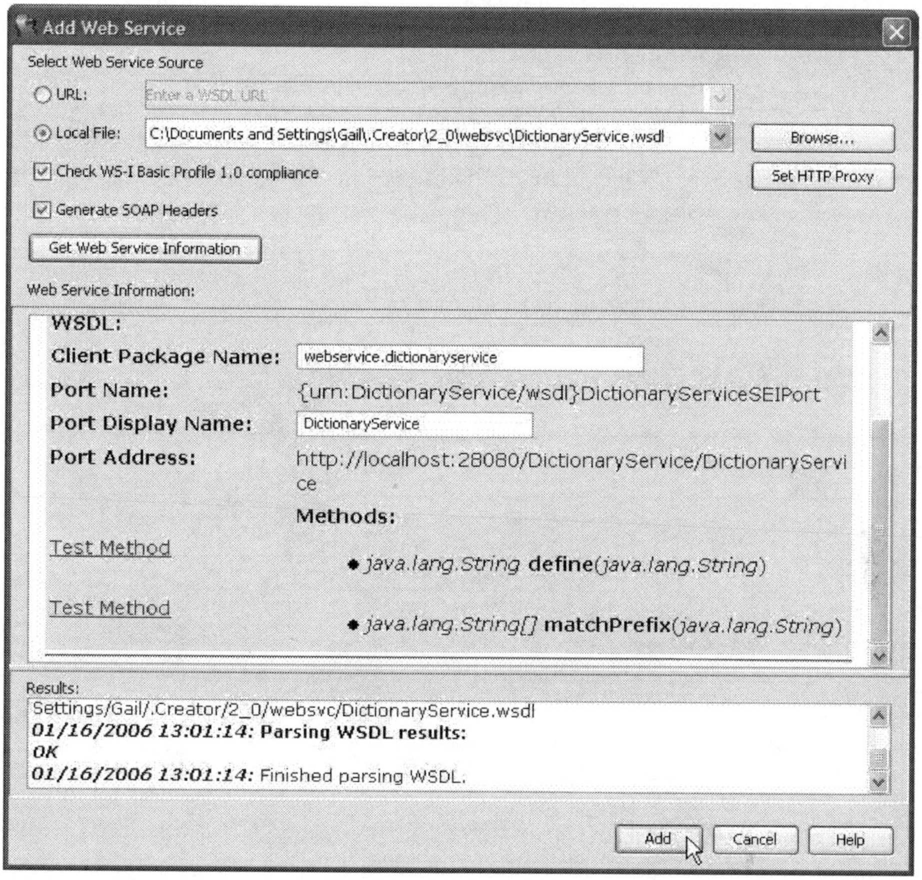

Figure 13–25 **Add Web Service dialog displaying the Dictionary Web Service**

word supplied as its argument. You'll use both these methods to provide a dictionary lookup application that performs auto-completion on the input text field.

Create a New Project

Let's build the dictionary lookup application.[2]

2. This application is based on the Creator/AJAX Demo presented by Sun Microsystems' Tor Norbye at JavaOne.

1. From Creator's Welcome Page, select button Create New Project. From the New Project dialog, under Categories select **Web** and under Projects select **JSF Web Application.** Click Next.
2. In the New Web Application dialog, specify **AjaxLookup** for Project Name and click Finish.

   After creating the project, Creator comes up in the design view of the editor pane. You can now set the title.

3. Select `Title` in the Properties window and type in the text **AJAX Lookup**. Finish by pressing **<Enter>**.

Add Components to the Page

Figure 13–26 shows the dictionary lookup project in the design view. Use the figure as a guide when you add the components to your project.

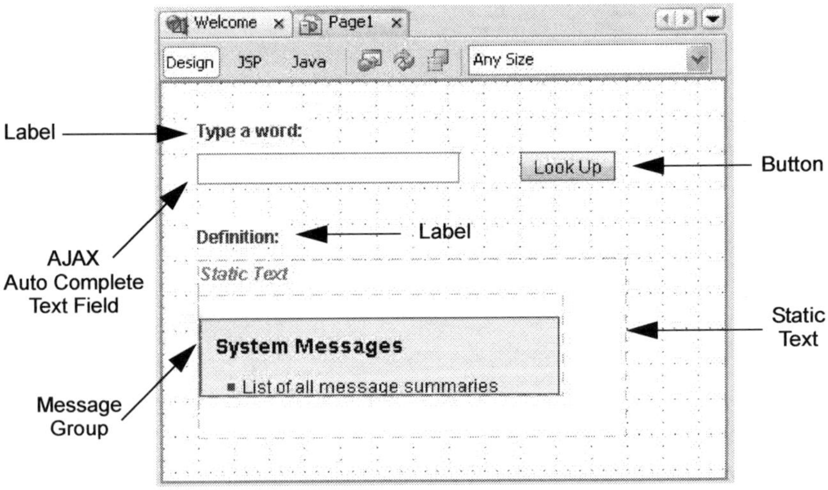

Figure 13–26 **Design View for project AJAXLookup**

1. From the Basic Components palette, select component Label and place it on the page, near the top left side.
2. Make sure it's selected and type in the text **Type a word:** and finish with **<Enter>**.
3. From the BluePrints AJAX Components palette, select component Auto Complete Text Field. Drag it to the design canvas and drop it on the page below the label you just added.

4. Make sure the AJAX component is selected. In the Properties window under Appearance, opposite property `title`, specify **Type in a word for dictionary lookup** followed by **<Enter>**. This sets its tooltip.

You'll now add a button, a second label, a static text component, and a message group component.

1. From the Basic Components palette, select component Button and drop it onto the page to the right of the auto complete text field component.
2. Type in the text **Look Up** followed by **<Enter>** to set the button's label.
3. In the Properties view, change its id to **lookup**.
4. From the Basic Components palette, select component Label and drop it onto the page under the auto complete text field component.
5. Type in the text **Definition:** and finish with **<Enter>** to set its label.
6. From the Basic Components palette, select component Static Text and drop it onto the page below the label component.
7. In the Properties view, change property `id` to **meaning** and *uncheck* property `escape`.
8. In the design view, resize the static text component so that it is approximately 12 grids wide and 5 grids high.
9. From the Basic Components palette, select Message Group component and drop it onto the design canvas. Place it on top of the static text component as shown in Figure 13–26.

Add the Dictionary Web Service to the Page

Before you can make any calls to the Dictionary Web Service, you must add it to your project.

- In the Servers window, select **Web Services > DictionaryService** and drag it to the Page1 design view. Nothing appears in the design canvas; however, you will see **dictionaryServiceClient1** in the Page1 Outline view.

Configure the Event Handlers

You'll now provide the code for the AJAX component's auto-completion event handler. You'll also add the event handling code for the button component to perform the dictionary lookup.

1. In the design view, double-click the auto complete text field component. Creator generates the complete method event handler and brings up **Page1.java** in the Java source editor.

2. Add the following code to the `autoComplete1_complete()` event handler. Copy and paste from **FieldGuide2/Examples/Custom/snippets/ajax_lookup_match.txt**. The added code is bold.

```
public void autoComplete1_complete(FacesContext context,
            String prefix, CompletionResult result) {
  try {
    String[] items =
        dictionaryServiceClient1.matchPrefix(prefix);
    result.addItems(items);
  } catch (Exception ex) {
    log("Error Description", ex);
    error("Could not access dictionary service matchPrefix: "
          + ex);
  }
}
```

Recall that `prefix` contains the text that the user has typed in so far. Method `matchPrefix()` returns an array of Strings (up to ten words) that match the provided prefix. These you add to the complete method's `result` array for display in the completion popup window.

The catch handler includes a call to `error()` which will display any system errors in the message group component you added to the page.

1. Return to the design view by clicking the Design label on the editing toolbar.
2. Double-click the Look Up button component. Creator generates the action event handler for the button and brings up **Page1.java** in the Java source editor.
3. Add the following code to the `lookup_action()` method. Copy and paste from **FieldGuide/Examples/Custom/snippets/ajax_lookup_action.txt**. The added code is bold.

```
public String lookup_action() {
  try {
    String definition =
        dictionaryServiceClient1.define(
            autoComplete1.getText());
    meaning.setText(definition);
```

```
    } catch (Exception ex) {
        log("Error Description", ex);
        error("Could not access dictionary service define: "
            + ex);
    }
    return null;
}
```

When the user clicks the Look Up button, the event handler calls the Dictionary Service method `define()` with the text in the AJAX auto complete text component. The `define()` method returns the word's definition, which method `lookup_action()` stores in the static text component's `text` property.

Deploy and Run

Build, deploy and run the application by selecting the Run icon on the toolbar. Figure 13–27 shows the application after the user types an initial 'x'. If the user then types the letter 'i', a new list pops up, matching the prefix 'xi'.

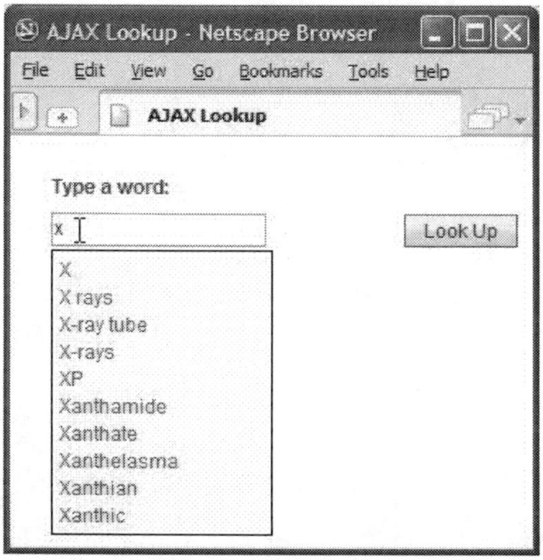

Figure 13–27 **AJAX Auto Complete Text Field component responding to user input**

Figure 13–28 shows the application after the user selects entry 'Xiphioid.'

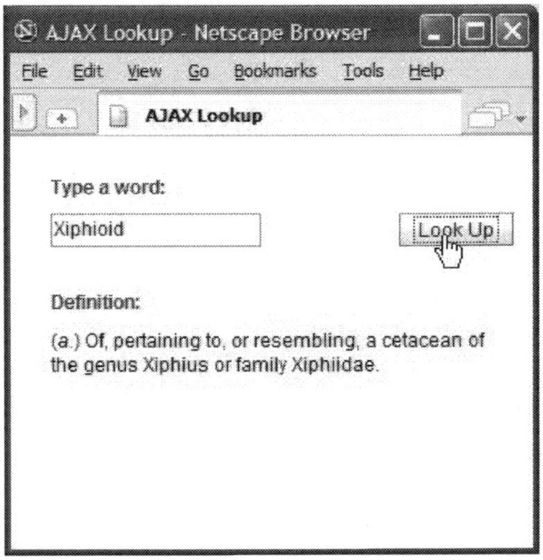

Figure 13–28 **AJAX Lookup application displays the definition for 'Xiphioid'**

13.7 Key Point Summary

- Localization and internationalization enable your applications to run in a global environment.
- Java uses a Locale to customize an application for a target language and region.
- To localize an application, first isolate all textual labels and messages and organize them into key-value pairs.
- Java uses a properties file to hold key-value pairs of text to identify text data.
- Use the `loadBundle` JSF tag to identify the resource bundle of the current locale.
- To internationalize an application, translate the messages and labels in the properties file to the target languages you intend to support.
- Each supported locale has its own properties file.
- Components access message keys in the properties file instead of using literal text. JSF uses value binding for this.
- When you want to support more than one locale by configuring your browser, specify the supported locales in file **faces-config.xml**. Creator supplies a template for this file, which you can access in the Files view. Expand the project name node, then **web > WEB-INF**.

- You can also control the locale programmatically by invoking the `setLocale()` method of `UIViewRoot`.
- You can provide custom validation by writing a validation method in your Java page bean.
- You must modify a component's `validator` property to use a custom validator method.
- The custom validator method should access the current locale to obtain localized error messages.
- The custom validator should add error messages to the faces context so that you can use message components to display them.
- Creator lets you import third-party component libraries and add them to the Components palette.
- Asynchronous JavaScript Technology and XML (AJAX) is a web development technique that provides (asynchronous) updates on a web page. Calls are made to the server to obtain new data, but only a portion of the page's display is affected. User perceived bandwidth and application responsiveness is excellent.
- An AJAX-enabled JSF auto complete text component is available on Sun's web site for importing.
- The AJAX auto complete text field includes the necessary JavaScript and other artifacts to communicate asynchronously with the server.
- Creator generates the complete method event handler when you double-click the AJAX auto complete text field component in the design view.
- The complete method is invoked with each user keystroke in the auto complete text field.
- Inside the complete method, you build a `result` object (an array of Strings) that is then displayed in a popup menu on the page.
- The AJAX component library includes utility `addMatchingItems()`, which you invoke inside the complete method to build the `result` object.
- You can alternatively build the `result` object by accessing a web service, a database, or EJBs.

DEBUGGING WITH CREATOR

Topics in This Chapter

- Planning for Debugging
- Debugging Commands
- Breakpoints
- Stepping Through Your Code
- Tracking Variables
- Setting Watches
- Using the Call Stack
- Detecting Exceptions
- Debug Methods
- Using the HTTP Monitor

Chapter 14

Let's face it, everyone makes mistakes. Designing and coding a web application is certainly no exception. Even simple web applications can be complex to work with, and there are lots of things to keep track of. As a programmer you have to be conversant with Java programming as well as XML. If all goes well, there's no problem. But when things don't work right, you can use all the help you can get.

Fortunately, Creator has a built-in debugger that can assist you in troubleshooting your web applications. The debugger is smart, includes lots of features, and has a user-friendly interface. You can use the debugger to monitor program flow, find out why variables aren't set to proper values, and help decipher why you're getting a Java exception. All this is not difficult if you know what to do. This chapter shows you how. And if you haven't used a debugger before, don't worry, we take it one step at a time.

This chapter shows you the different features of the Creator debugger as we look at an application that you've already seen. We'll examine breakpoints, watches, call stacks, variable tracking and show you how to apply the debugging features of Creator while your web application is running. You'll also learn about the HTTP monitor, a very useful tool that tracks the data flow between your application and the web server it's communicating with. To make it easier to follow, we include lots of screen shots so you can see what's going on. You are also welcome to perform each step as you read along, too.

Before we begin, however, let's talk about debugging in general.

14.1 Planning for Debugging

Unless you are very bold and confident, it's best to plan ahead for debugging. This mode of operation is often called *defensive programming*. Although a broad topic that covers many things, the main philosophy here is to simply plan ahead. Don't be too fancy with your code and follow some simple rules. Here are some of our rules.

- Keep methods short in size. Call other methods as needed (this practice is often called *stepwise refinement*).
- Use local variables to store important data so that it's easier to track the data with a debugger.
- Use assertions in your program to perform consistency checks on assumptions you've made (such as "This value will never be null.").
- Use log files to record data, monitor program flow, or document the capture of a critical exception.
- Provide catch handlers to capture uncaught or unexpected exceptions early in your designs.

Although we won't show you all these suggestions in this chapter, here are several to look at.

Local Variables

In the following method, the calculation of a monthly interest payment is performed in the return statement. This approach makes it difficult to access the payment amount in a debugger.

```
public double getPayment() {
     double monthly_interest = this.rate / 1200;
     int months = this.years * 12;
     return this.amount * (monthly_interest /
        (1-Math.pow(1+monthly_interest,-1*months)));
}
```

A better approach for debugging is to store the payment in a local variable before returning its value, as follows.

```
public double getPayment() { {
     double monthly_interest = this.rate / 1200;
     int months = this.years * 12;
     double pmt = this.amount * (monthly_interest /
        (1-Math.pow(1+monthly_interest,-1*months)));
     return pmt;
}
```

Now you can track the `pmt` variable in memory as you test out the algorithm with different input values. A class field, rather than a local variable, can also be used here.

Assertions

Another programming technique for debugging is a Java assertion.[1] There are two formats.

```
assert expression1;
assert expression1 : expression2;
```

An assertion is a boolean expression that is expected to be true at run time. In the first format, an `AssertionError` is thrown if *`expression1`* evaluates to false. The second format customizes the message for `AssertionError` from *`expression2`*, which is typically a String.

There are many ways to use assertions in Java. Here's an example with a private class method that tests a precondition.

```
private void myMethod(int arg) {
     assert arg >=0 && arg <= 100 : "Bad argument: " + arg;
     // rest of code here...
}
```

Displaying Debug Information

The last example of defensive programming is a simple output statement, strategically placed where it might be important to see in a log file or in a message component. Here's an example with Creator's `log()` method, which writes to the application server's log file.

```
log("button was clicked");
```

---

1. Java assertions were introduced in JDK 1.4.

You can also use Creator's `info()` method to write to a message group component on a web page.

```
info("database updated");
```

We discuss these methods in more detail in "Debug Methods" on page 672.

14.2 Debugger Overview

The Creator Debugger has a lot of helpful features. Before you run your project with the debugger, let's show you the debugging commands in Creator and what they mean. We'll also discuss the contents of the Debugger Window, which gives you a visual look at your running program.

Debugger Features

What kinds of things can you do with the Creator debugger? Here's a list of some of the major features.

- Step through application code or JDK source code a line at a time.
- Execute part of your code using breakpoints as delimiters.
- Suspend execution at a breakpoint, which can be at a specific line number in your code, a condition that is met, or when an exception is thrown.
- Track the value of a variable or an expression.
- Use a fixed watch to track an object referenced by a variable in your program.
- Use the Apply Code Changes command to fix code on the fly within the current debugging session.
- Monitor and control the execution of threads in your program.
- View the call stack to see what methods were called and when.
- Run multiple debugger sessions at the same time.
- Use the HTTP monitor to track data flow between your application and the web server.

Debugger Windows

To work effectively with the Creator debugger, you'll need to use Debugger windows. On the Creator toolbar, the **View > Debugging** menu offers you various options for displaying debug information in a debugger window. Figure 14–1 shows you the debugger views that are available and the hot keys you can use to enable them.

We'll examine these windows later as we show you how to use the debugger.

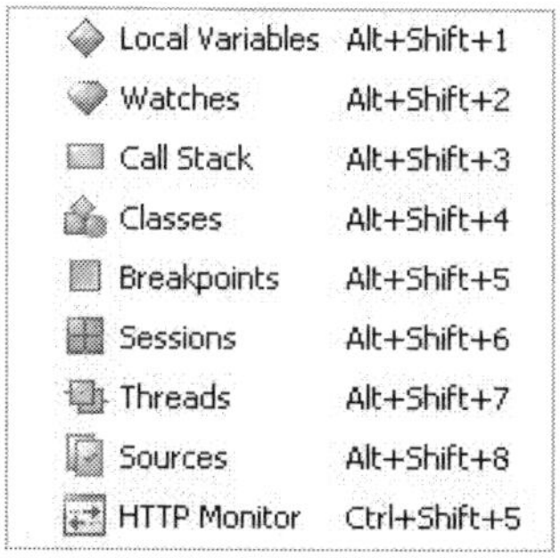

Figure 14–1 **The Debugger views**

Debugging Commands

The **Run** menu on the Creator menu bar lists the debugging commands as shown in Table 14.1. Most of these commands also have hotkeys listed in the menu.

Table 14.1 Run Menu Debugging Commands

Command	***Short Cut Keys***
Run Main Project	**<Ctrl+F5>**
Debug Main Project	**<F5>**
Test Project	**<Alt+F6>**
Run File	
Finish Debugger Session	**<Shift+F5>**
Pause	
Continue	**<Alt+F5>**
Step Over	**<F10>**
Step Into	**<F11>**
Step Out	**<Shift+F11>**
Run to Cursor	**<Ctrl+F10>**

Table 14.1 Run Menu Debugging Commands *(continued)*

Apply Code Changes	
Stack	
Toggle Breakpoint	**<F9>**
New Breakpoint	**<Ctrl+B>**
New Watch	**<Ctrl+Shift+W>**

Debug Main Project runs Creator in debugging mode, and **Finish Debugger Session** stops the debugging session. You can use the **Test Project** and **Run File** commands to test your code or run a selected file with your project, respectively. The **Apply Code Changes** command lets you fine tune your code in the middle of a debug session and the **Stack** command lets you view the call stack during the execution of your program.

Most of the other commands deal with *breakpoints,* a central concept in a debugger. A breakpoint is a spot in your program at which you can stop the execution of your program. Once you're at a breakpoint, you can examine the values of program variables or monitor program flow by means of a call stack of method calls. Breakpoints allow you to use other debugging commands to find out why your code is not working correctly. Here is a description of the debugging commands that affect breakpoints.

- **Pause** – Temporarily halt the execution of your program.
- **Continue** – Execute to the next breakpoint or if there are no more breakpoints, run until the program completes.
- **Step Over** – Execute only the next statement, then pause again. If the statement is a method call, execute the entire method code and pause after returning from it.
- **Step Into** – Execute only the next statement, but if it's a method, pause before executing the first statement in the method.
- **Step Out** – Execute the rest of the current method and pause in the method that called it.
- **Run to Cursor** – Execute up to the point where the cursor is positioned.

We'll show you how to set breakpoints and use these debugging commands later in this chapter.

14.3 Running the Debugger

Let's fire up the Creator Debugger now and show you some of its handy features.

Open Project and Files

We'll start our tour of the Creator Debugger with the Monthly Payment Calculator program from Chapter 6 (see "LoanBean" on page 242). Here's what you do.

1. From the Welcome Page, select project **Payment1** from the list of projects. Or, select the button entitled **Open Existing Project**, browse to project **Payment1**, and select **Open**.
2. Expand the **Payment1 > Web Pages** nodes in the Projects window and double-click **Page1.jsp**. You should see the **Page1.jsp** page appear in the design view.
3. In the Projects window, expand **Source Packages** and **asg.bean_examples** nodes. Double-click **LoanBean.java** to bring it up in the source editor.
4. You'll need to see line numbers in both Java files, so move the cursor to the darkened left margin area of the editor pane. Right-click and choose **Show Line Numbers**. (This will make line numbers visible in Creator's editors for all of your source files.)

Run and Deploy in Debug Mode

Now let's run the Payment program in debug mode with Creator.

- In the Creator toolbar, select **Run**, then **Debug Main Project** (or use the F5 shortcut).

Creator will compile and deploy the system. If the server is already running, Creator will stop the server and restart it in debug mode. After deployment, the Calculator page appears in the browser window. You can execute the program by typing in various input values for the loan amount, interest rate, and loan term (in years). Figure 14–2 shows the Design view and Debugger window.

Debugging Views

You'll note that in Figure 14–2 we currently have Watches, Local Variables, and Call Stack enabled in our Debugging Window. To see these views in your display, select **View > Debugging > Watches** (**<Alt+Shift+2>**) from the Creator

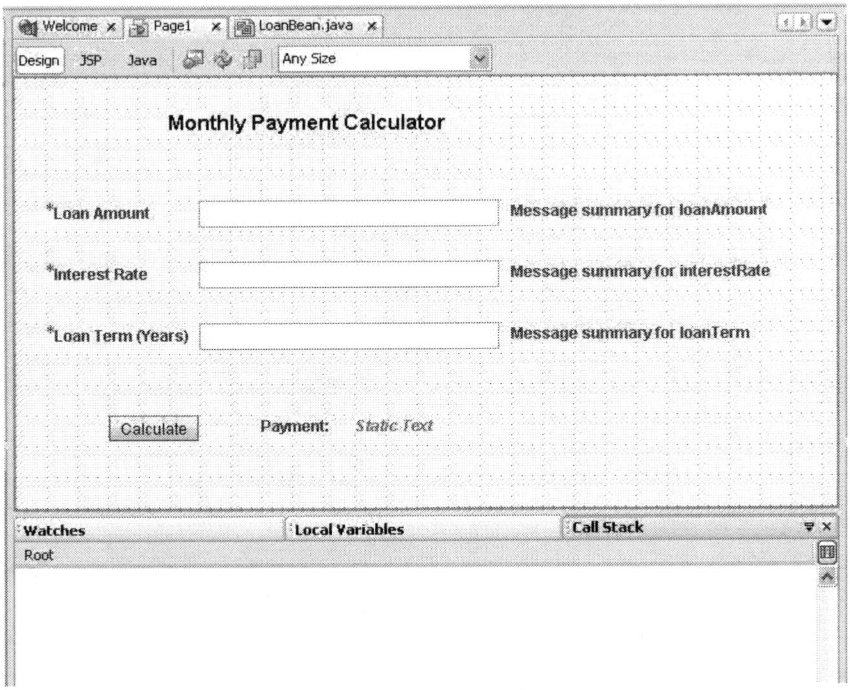

Figure 14–2 **The Debugger window**

toolbar. This brings up the Watches display. Select **View > Debugging > Local Variables** (**<Alt+Shift+1>**) to bring up the Local Variables display and **View > Debugging > Call Stack** (**<Alt+Shift+3>**) to bring up the Call Stack display.

It's also possible to change the display format of any view in the Debugger window. If you right-click the title bar of an individual display, you can maximize (**<Shift+Esc>**), minimize (**<Ctrl+Backspace>**), or close the window (**<Ctrl+F4>**).

Now you are ready to work with the Debugger window and learn its features. Let's start with breakpoints.

14.4 Setting Breakpoints

Go to the Calculator Page and exit the browser to end the current session. Switch back to Creator. The first thing you'll do now is set a *breakpoint*. Recall that a breakpoint is a place in your program at which the debugger stops the execution of your program. In Creator, you can set a breakpoint for any of the following.

Line	Suspend before executing line.
Method	Suspend when method is called.
Exception	Suspend when exception occurs.
Variable	Suspend when variable is accessed.
Thread	Suspend when thread is started or terminated.
Class	Suspend when class is referenced

For line breakpoints, Creator marks the line in red and you may specify additional conditions. Exception breakpoints let you stop execution when an exception is caught, uncaught, or both. For variables, you can suspend execution when a variable is read or modified. Thread breakpoints can be set for the start of a thread, the death of a thread, or both.

Let's set breakpoints for a line[2] and a method in our Java code. Here's what you do.

1. Click the **LoanBean.java** tab to open this file in the Java source editor.
2. Set a breakpoint in the constructor at the line where the `amount` field is initialized. Right-click Line 21 and select **Toggle Breakpoint**. (Or, move the cursor to the darkened left margin where the line numbers are displayed and left-click the mouse.) Creator will highlight Line 21 in red for you, showing that a breakpoint has been set, as shown in Figure 14–3.

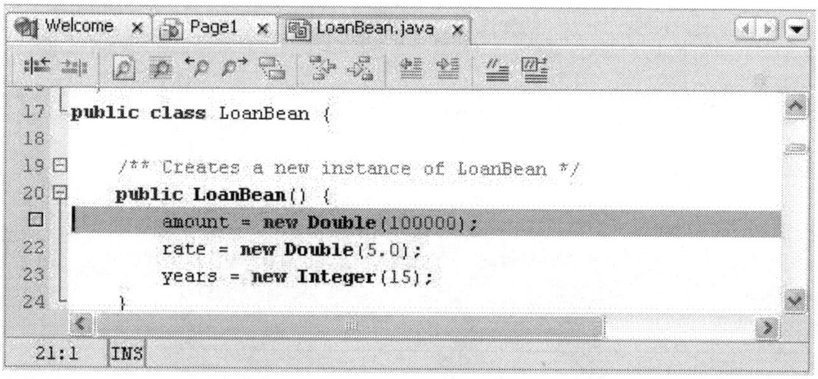

Figure 14–3 **Setting a breakpoint**

---

2. The format of your program may be slightly different than ours. If so, use your line numbers from the same spots in the program.

3. Move the cursor down to the `getPayment()` method at line 104. Put the cursor on the line and click the left button of the mouse. The selected line is highlighted in yellow.
4. Select **Run > New Breakpoint** from the Creator toolbar. Creator pops up the New Breakpoint dialog.
5. You will see a Breakpoint Type selection menu at the top of the New Breakpoint dialog. Select **Method** from this list. (See Figure 14–4.) This is how you set a breakpoint to a Java method. This means the Creator debugger will stop the execution of your program when the method is called.

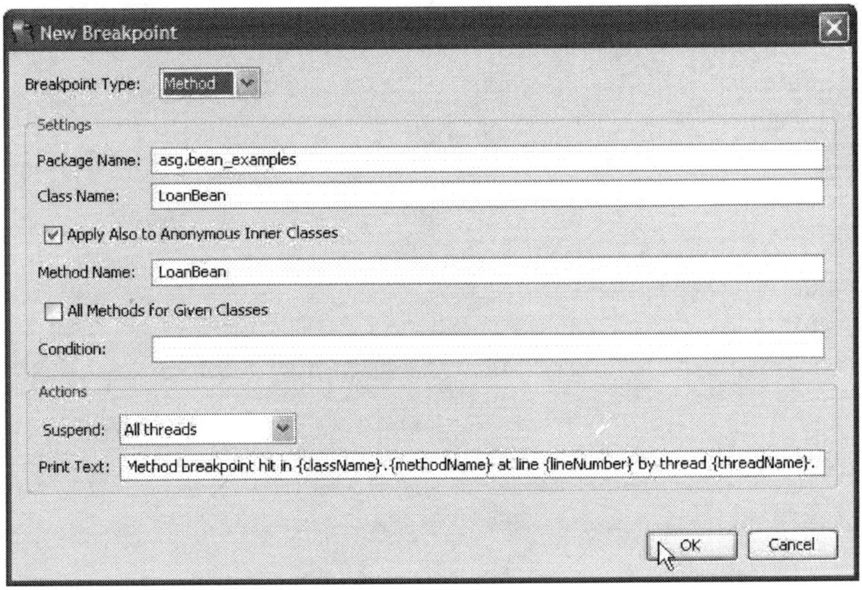

Figure 14–4 **New Breakpoint dialog**

6. Click OK to finish setting the breakpoint.

Enable the Breakpoints window by selecting **View > Debugging > Breakpoints**. Figure 14–5 shows you the Breakpoints Display, indicating the two breakpoints you just set.

Now you are ready to run and deploy the program again, so select **Run > Finish Debugger Session**. Select **Run > Debug Main Project** from the main menu. Several things will happen.

Line 21 changes color from red to green in the **LoanBean.java** window. This means that the first breakpoint was reached and the program has stopped. Since we are inside the LoanBean constructor at this point and Creator has not finished initializing the LoanBean object, Page1 cannot be rendered. Hence, your browser window is empty.

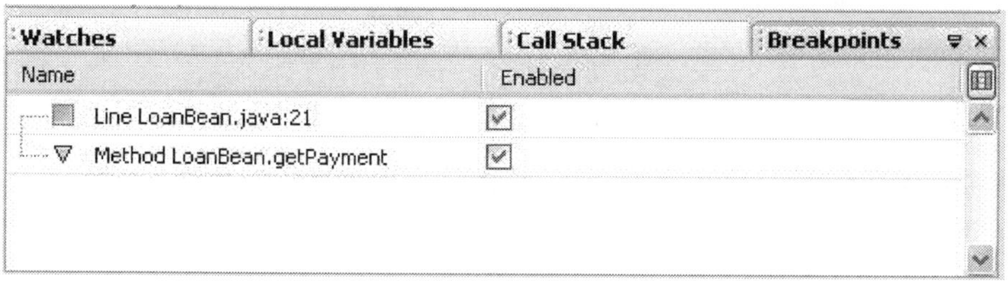

Figure 14–5 **Breakpoints display**

14.5 Managing Breakpoints

Before we step though the code, let's show you how to manage your breakpoints. If you right-click any breakpoint in the Breakpoints window, a context menu gives you several options to choose from. Figure 14–6 shows you what's available when you right-click the `getPayment()` method breakpoint.

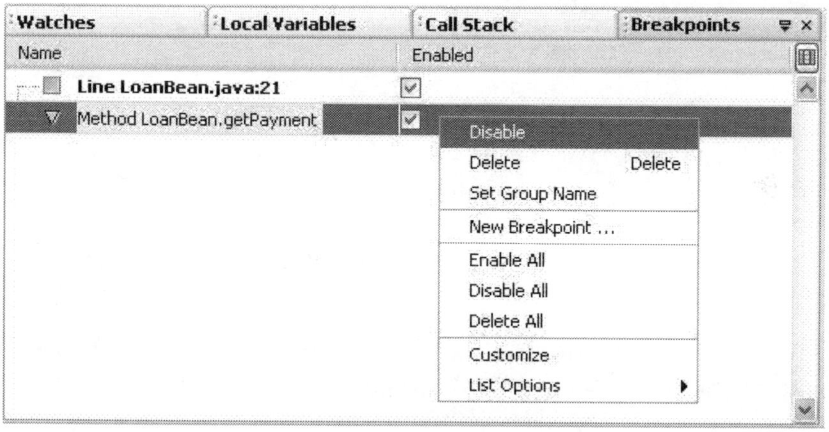

Figure 14–6 **Managing Breakpoints Options**

Note that you can Enable/Disable/Delete all breakpoints, or disable/delete an individual breakpoint. It's also possible to consolidate breakpoints under one node to make the Breakpoints window less cluttered. To do this, select the breakpoints you want to group, then choose **Set Group Name**. The breakpoints will be grouped under an expandable node with the name you choose.

The **Customize** command lets you manage other aspects of a breakpoint. Figure 14–7 shows you the Customize Breakpoint window when you select this command from the menu.

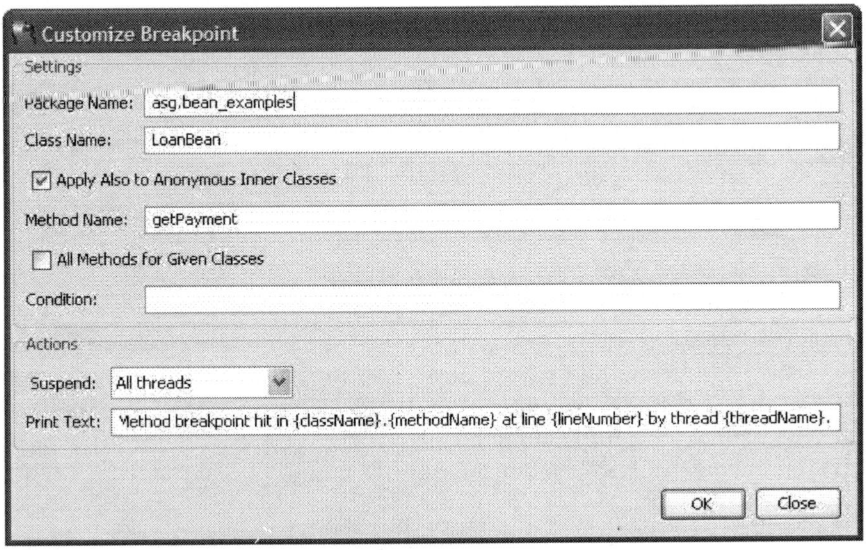

Figure 14–7 **Customizing Breakpoints**

The **Condition** box lets you set up a breakpoint to suspend execution only if a certain condition is met. You could type in expressions like `i==10` or `pVar!=null`, for example. It's also possible to log a breakpoint without suspending execution. Instead of stopping your program at the breakpoint, a message is written in the Debugger console window. To enable this option with a breakpoint, choose **No thread (continue)** in the **Suspend** combo box under **Actions**.

The **Customize** command also lets you create your own console messages when breakpoints are hit. The **Print Text** combo box contains a default message, but you can use the following substitution codes to customize messages.

`{className}`	Name of class where breakpoint was hit.
`{lineNumber}`	Line number where execution was suspended.
`{methodName}`	Method in which execution was suspended.
`{threadName}`	Thread in which the breakpoint was hit.
`{variableValue}`	Value of variable, with variable or exception breakpoints.
`{variableType}`	Type of variable, with variable or exception breakpoints.

Now let's show you how to step through code using breakpoints.

14.6 Stepping Through the Code

Debuggers typically allow you to execute your code one line at a time as it executes. This is called *stepping*. Let's step through the LoanBean constructor code now with the Creator debugger to initialize the LoanBean's fields. This is where we'll use the Debugger window, so make sure you have that window open. Here's what you do.

1. Modify your Debugger window so that the Local Variables display is visible. (Click the tab labeled Local Variables.) The Local Variables window displays all variables currently in scope for the execution context of your program.
2. Click the '+' for the `this` reference. Underneath this name, you will see the fields for the LoanBean constructor: `amount`, `rate`, `years`, and `payment`. If you right-click any field and select **Go to Source**, you can jump to the statement in the source code where it's defined.
3. From the toolbar, select **Run > Step Over** (you may also hit the F10 key). This makes the Creator debugger execute Line 21 and stop at Line 22, which will now be displayed in green.

   In the Local Variables display, the `amount` field should be set to 100000.0, as shown in Figure 14–8.

4. Now **Step Over** Line 22 to Line 23, and then **Step Over** again to Line 24.
5. In the Local Variables display, the `rate` field should now be 5.0 and the `years` field should be 15.

Figure 14–9 shows you what the screen looks like after the LoanBean constructor has finished executing.

TroubleShooting Tip

It's easy to change the value of a local variable in memory with Creator. Just click the rounded box to the right of the variable you want to change and use the custom editor to modify its value. If the variable is an object (Integer, Double, etc.) make sure you use new to create it with the value you want. This feature can be very handy for checking out boundary conditions and algorithm correctness during debugging.

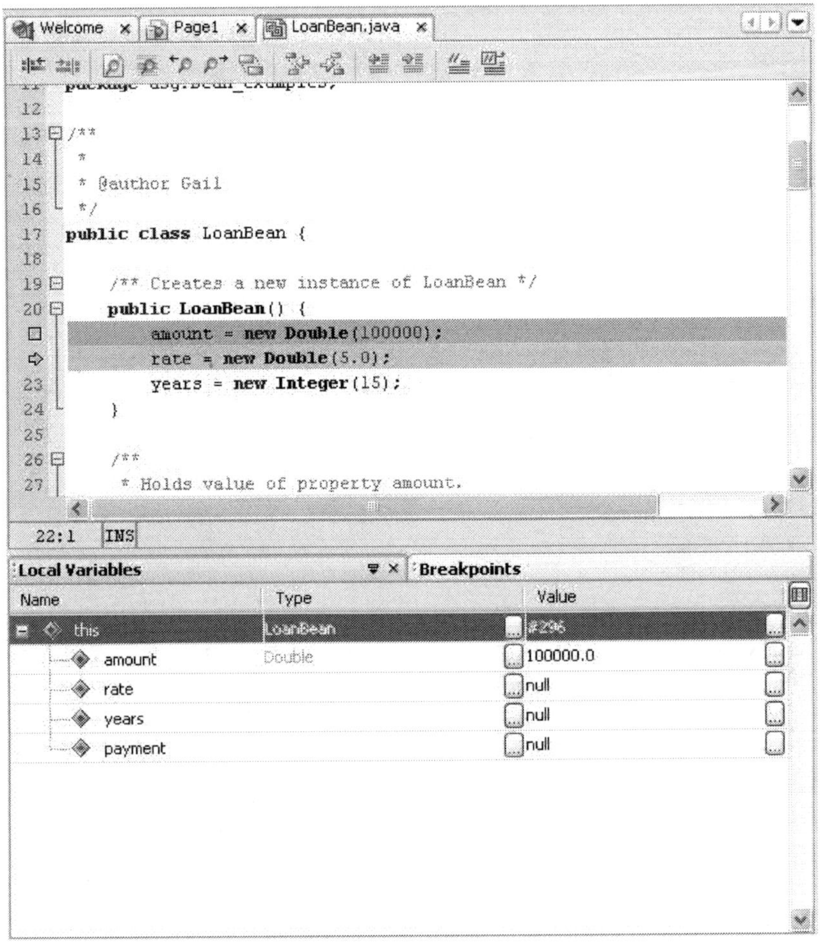

Figure 14–8 **After issuing a Step Over command**

Creator Tip

There are other ways to step through your code in Creator. You can, for instance, select ***Run > Step Into*** *a method or* ***Run > Step Out*** *of a method. You can also move the cursor to a line and select* ***Run > Run to Cursor****.*

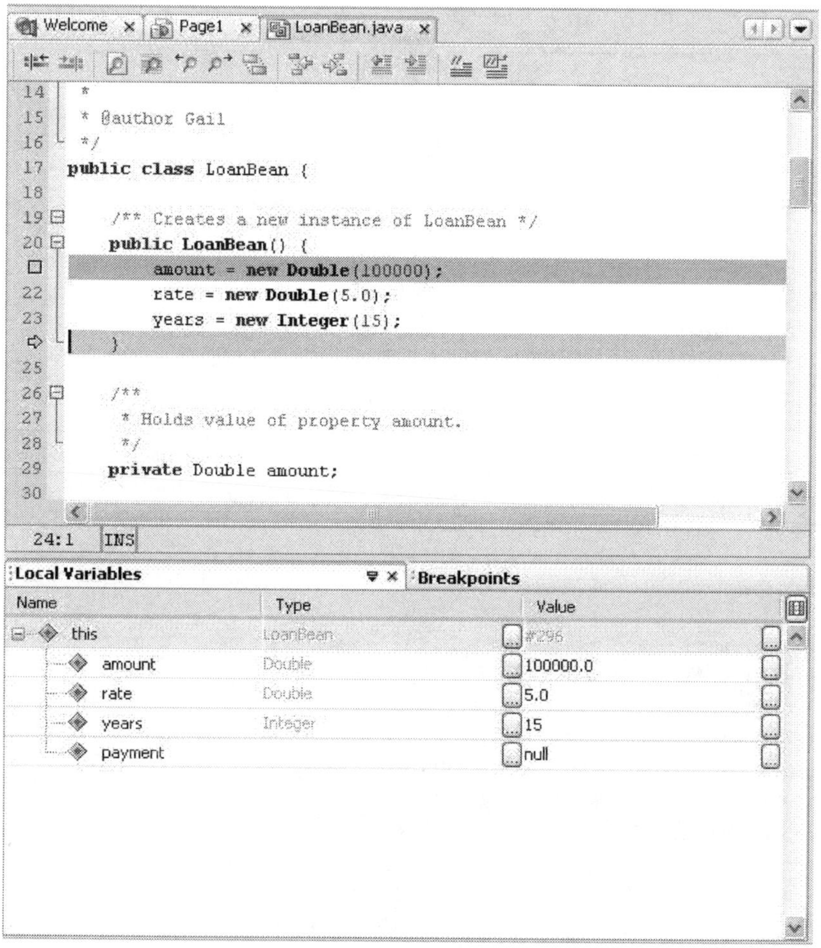

Figure 14–9 **Display after LoanBean constructor executes**

14.7 Tracking Variables

Now let's make Creator execute our program to the next breakpoint. To do this, click **Run > Continue** from the main menu. The Continue command makes the Creator debugger continue execution from the current breakpoint to the next one.

Inside the **LoanBean.java** window, you'll see that Creator has stopped execution at the second breakpoint. This is the first statement in the `getPayment()`

method (Line 105), and is highlighted in green. Note that this method calculates the loan payment, using local variables to store data. Let's see how to monitor these variables with a Creator debugger feature called *tracking*. Here are the steps.

1. In the Local Variables display, you should see the same values for the LoanBean fields as before.
2. Click **Run > Step Over** (or F10) from the main toolbar. This moves the focus to Line 106. In the Local Variables display, a new entry appears below the `this` reference. The local variable `monthly_interest` shows up with a value of 0.00416666.
3. Click **Run > Step Over** from the toolbar. This moves the focus to Line 107. The local variable `months` appears in the Local Variables display with a value of 180.
4. Click **Run > Step Over** one more time. The LoanBean `payment` field changes to a value of 790.79362. Figure 14–10 shows the result. Note that the browser page is still blank.
5. Click **Run > Continue** from the toolbar and switch to the Payment Calculator page in your browser. You will see a Loan Payment of $790.79 displayed on the page.

TroubleShooting Tip

You can repeat this whole exercise again by changing any of the input fields on the Calculator page. When you click the Calculate button and return to the Creator screen, you will see the program stop at the same breakpoint. By stepping through `getPayment()` *as before, you can see the changed values in the Local Variables display. When you click* ***Run > Continue*** *from the toolbar, the Payment Calculator page will show the new payment. This is a handy way to test an algorithm and see whether a method is working correctly for a wide range of input test values.*

14.8 Setting Watches

With the debugger, you can monitor the running values of fields and local variables in several different ways.

- Move the cursor to an identifier in the Source Editor. A tool tip displays the value of the identifier in the current debugging context.
- Use the Local Variables window to display the values of fields and local variables.
- Set a watch for an identifier and track its value in the Watches window.

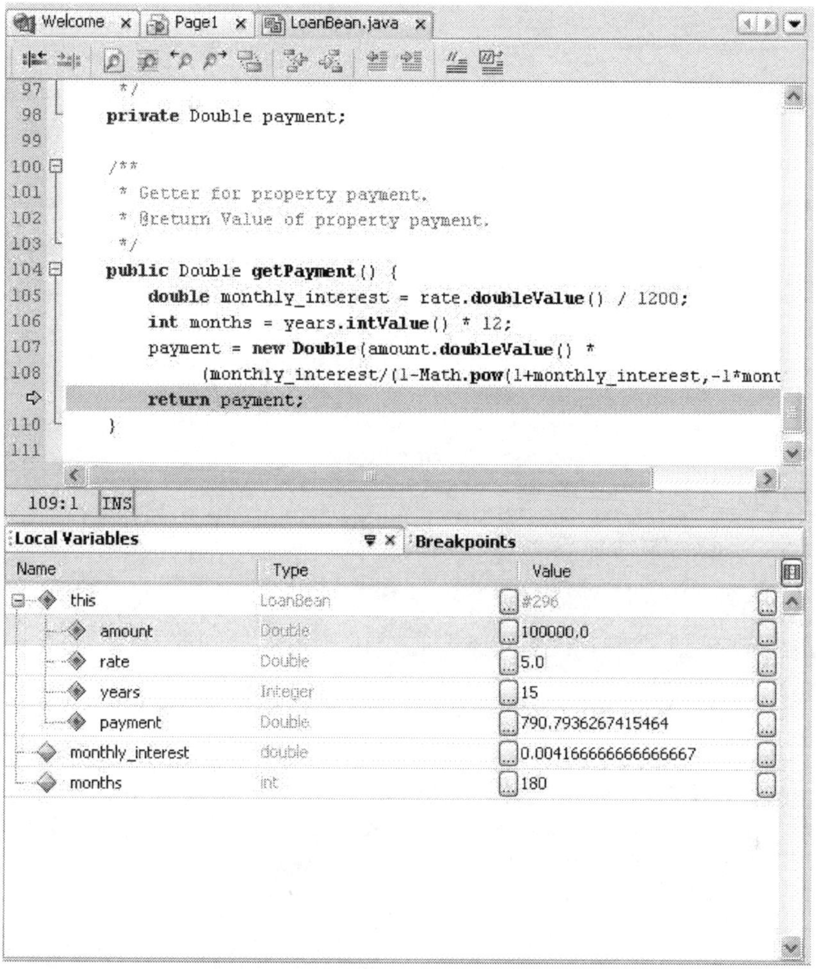

Figure 14–10 **Displaying `getPayment()` local variables**

There are several local variables inside the `getPayment()` method, but the LoanBean `payment` field is the most interesting. Since this field holds the payment amount that will be displayed on our web page, let's use another feature of the Creator debugger called a *watch*. With watches, you can monitor key variables as they change values during the execution of a program. Whereas the Local Variables window shows values for variables in the currently executing method, the Watch window monitors values of variables selected by you (including class fields). Watches also persist across debugging sessions. Here's how to set a watch.

1. Return to Creator. Click the small 'x' on the Local Variables tab to close the Local Variables display.
2. To enable the Watches display, select **View > Debugging > Watches** from the main menu.
3. Click the **Breakpoints** tab to show the current list of breakpoints.
4. In the Breakpoints display, disable all the breakpoints by clicking the check-boxes underneath the Enabled heading. (Alternatively, you can right-click in the Breakpoints display and select **Disable All**.)
5. Put a new breakpoint at line 109 in **LoanBean.java** at method `getPayment()`'s return statement. (Again, use the line numbers relevant to your file if the line numbers don't match exactly.) To do this, place the cursor on the line number, right-click, and select **Toggle Breakpoint**. Line 109 should now be highlighted in red and appear enabled in the Breakpoints display in the Debugger window.
6. Right-click line 109 on the `payment` variable and select **New Watch**. Creator pops up the New Watch dialog and displays the `payment` variable for the Watch Expression.
7. Click OK to make `payment` a watch variable. Click the **Watches** tab in the Debugger window. The `payment` variable appears in the Watches display. Note that its value is not defined at this point (no current context).
8. Return to your browser to interact with the Calculator page. Change the Loan Term field to 30 and click the Calculate button. Switch back to the Creator window.

Creator Tip

*If your current session has timed out, then the changes you submitted in the browser window are thrown away and the payment variable remains 790.79 in the Watches display. In this case, select **Run > Continue** and return to the browser. Resubmit the Loan Term input and click the Calculate button once more.*

Figure 14–11 shows the result for the Watches display. The value of the payment field is now set to the current payment (536.821 . . .). (If you didn't supply the same input fields on the Calculator page, your payment variable will have a different value.)

9. Select **Run > Continue** from the main menu. When you go back to the Calculator page, you will see the same loan payment amount displayed (rounded to 2 places after the decimal point).
10. Now type in various input values for the amount, interest rate, and loan term. Click the Calculate button again and switch back to the Creator screen.

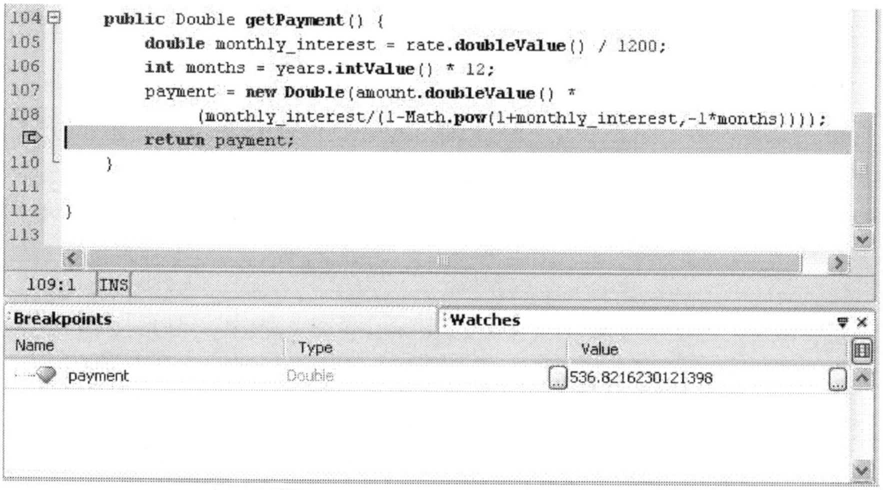

Figure 14–11 **Monitoring watches**

11.The breakpoint at line 109 is reached and is highlighted in green. Click **Run > Continue**. Each time you do this, the payment watch variable displays the new loan payment. This is the same value that is printed on the Calculator web page in your browser.

TroubleShooting Tip

*Watches are a handy way to monitor how a variable changes during the execution of a program. Use **Run > Continue** in Creator to step through the breakpoints as you do this.*

Creator Tip

*You can also create a **fixed** watch to monitor an object that is assigned to a variable, rather than the value of the variable. In the Local Variables window, right-click a field or local variable and select **Create Fixed Watch**. Fixed watches have a different icon in the Watches window and are removed when the debugging session terminates.*

14.9 Using the Call Stack

The Java Virtual Machine executes your Java code and maintains a call stack list. This list shows the order of method calls that have been invoked but have not yet returned (this type of list is often called a *call chain*). The current method is at the top of the list, and the invocations of each parent method appears below it as you work down the call list.

To see the Call Stack in action, perform the following steps

1. Click the Calculate button on the Calculator web page in your browser.
2. Now switch back to Creator and make sure line 109 (or the line number you used earlier) is highlighted in green.
3. Select **View > Debugging > Call Stack** to enable the Call Stack display.

Figure 14–12 shows the result. At the top of the Call Stack is the current method `LoanBean.getPayment()`, which was called from a series of methods in the underlying system. If you scroll through this display, you'll see various calls to binder methods, UI components, and servlets. At the very bottom of the Call Stack is `WorkerThread.run()`, which starts it all.

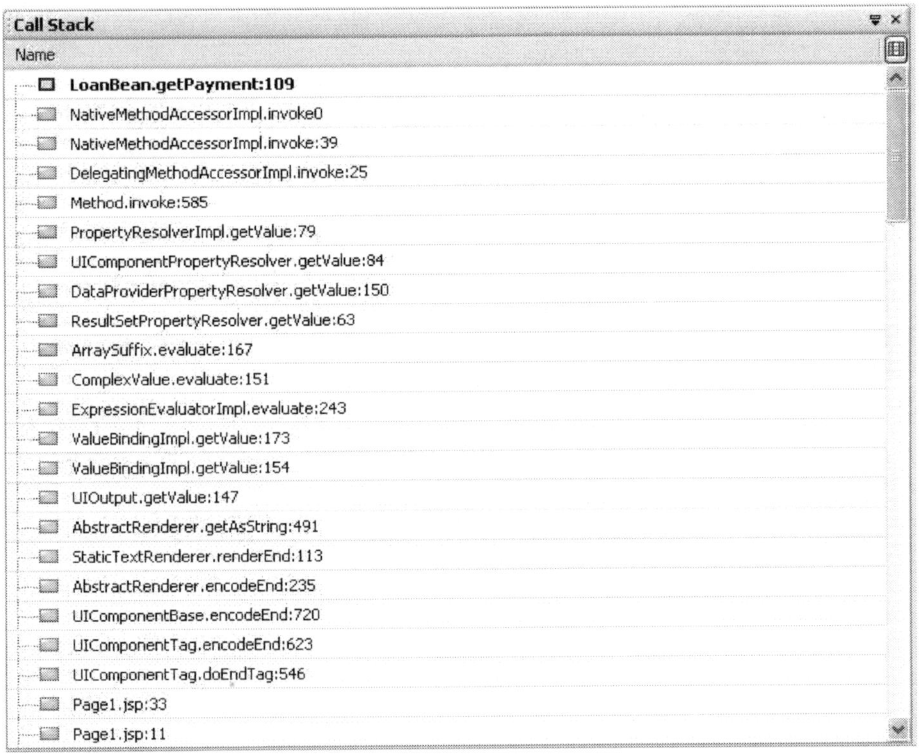

Figure 14–12 **Displaying the Call Stack**

Creator also lets you manipulate the Call Stack. When you click **Run > Stack** on the Creator menu bar, you'll see a list of choices in a dropdown list. With the Call Stack, you can select from any of the following.

Make Callee Current	**<Ctrl+Alt+Up>**
Make Caller Current	**<Ctrl+Alt+Down>**
Pop Topmost Call	

The first two commands let you change the current method of the call stack. The pop command removes the current method from the top of the stack.

TroubleShooting Tip

The Call Stack display is useful when your program calls a method and you aren't sure why. When you set a breakpoint at a method and run your program, the Call Stack tells you the call chain of methods up to and including the breakpoint. Call stacks are also handy when you need to determine which method threw an exception.

14.10 Detecting Exceptions

When using Creator's debugger, you can detect and track thrown exceptions. We'll show you how to do this now.

Our working Calculator program doesn't throw any exceptions directly, but it does generate an internal exception that is handled by JSF. This happens when you don't type anything in one of the input text fields and click the Calculate button. In this case, an error message appears on the Calculator page, because an exception was thrown and handled.

Here are the steps for detecting an exception with the debugger.

1. Remove all breakpoints. To do this, open the Debugger window and bring up the Breakpoint display. Right-click anywhere in the Breakpoint display, and select **Delete All**.
2. Select **Run > New Breakpoint** from the main toolbar. Creator pops up the New Breakpoint dialog
3. In the dropdown list for Breakpoint Type, select **Exception**.
4. In the dropdown list for Package Name, select `java.util`. (If the package name does not appear in the list, type it in.)
5. In the dropdown list for Exception Class Name, choose **MissingResource-Exception**. (Again, type in the name if it doesn't appear in the dropdown list.)

6. In the dropdown list for Stop On, choose **Caught**, as shown in Figure 14–13.

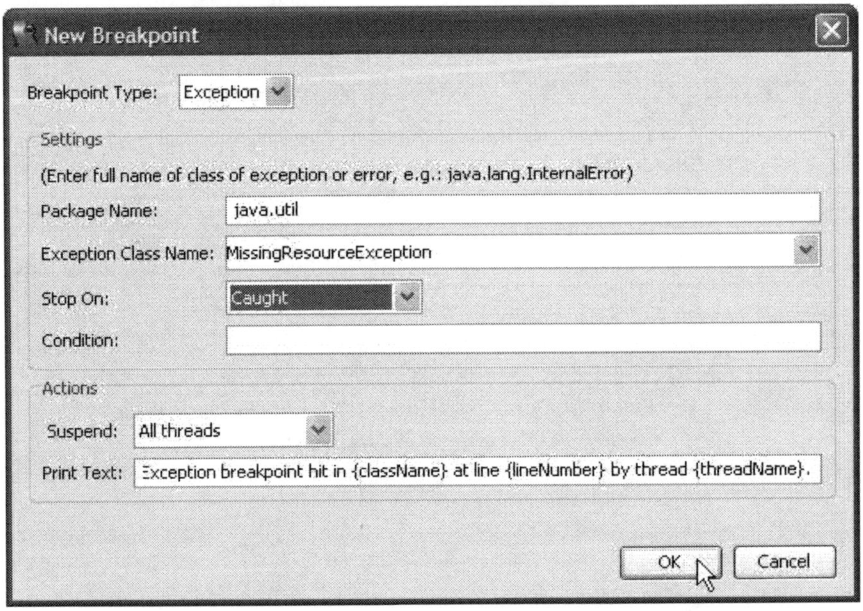

Figure 14–13 **Setting a breakpoint on a caught exception**

7. Click OK. In the Breakpoint display of the Debugger window, you should see the breakpoint on `Exception MissingResourceException` caught enabled.
8. Click **Run > Continue** from the main toolbar. Switch to the Calculator page and clear the input for the Interest Rate field.
9. Click the Calculate button and then switch back to Creator. Figure 14–14 shows you what the Call Stack in the Debugger window looks like. Because you did not type anything into the interest rate input field, a `MissingResourceException` was caught by the `ResourceBundle()` method. At the top of the Call Stack, you will see `ResourceBundle.getObject()` as the current method.
10. Now view the Output Display (select View > Output). Click the **Debugger Console** tab. Inside the window, you should see this message:

```
Exception breakpoint hit in java.util.ResourceBundle at line
326 by thread httpWorkerThread-28080-8. Thread httpWorker-
Thread-28080-8 stopped at ResourceBundle.java:326.
```

11. Disable the breakpoint. From the Breakpoints display, uncheck the breakpoint.

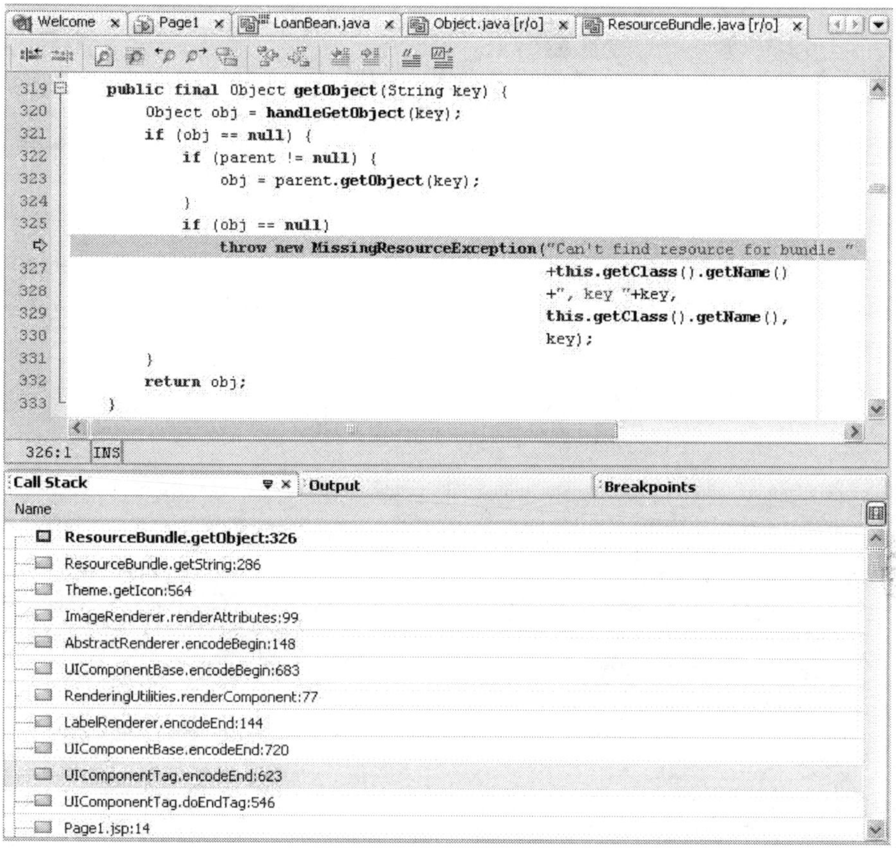

Figure 14–14 **Exception caught**

12.Select **Run > Continue** and switch to the browser window. You'll see that the application displays a validation error message for the missing interest rate text field input.

Creator Tip

*In Creator, click **Run > New Breakpoint** again from the main toolbar. In the dialog box for Breakpoint Type, choose **Exception** at the top and then peruse the choices in the checkbox for **Exception Class Name**. Note that there are lots of choices. If you select an exception class name from this list, you will see the corresponding package name that it belongs to. If you examine the checkbox for **Stop On**, you'll notice that you can monitor uncaught exceptions as well as caught exceptions, or both. All this gives you a variety of ways to track exceptions as you debug your applications with Creator.*

14.11 Finish Debugging

To finish your debugging session, click **Run > Finish Debugger Session** (or type **<Shift+F5>**) on the Creator tool bar.

TroubleShooting Tip

A good way to end a debugging session is to clear all breakpoints before you finish the session. In the Breakpoints display of the Debugger window, you can either disable your breakpoints or delete them.

14.12 Debug Methods

It's easy to record debugging information as your application runs. You can use method calls to write text to a message group component on a web page or write data to a log file. These techniques work for any managed bean class extended from FacesBean. Let's look at message group component methods first.

Method info()

The `info()` method, defined in FacesBean, can display debug information on a web page. You can use this to verify that some event has occurred or to provide some visual output to the user. The `info()` method has two formats.

```
void info(String);
void info(UIComponent, String);
```

The first format is handy for writing event information (such as "button clicked") to a message group component. The second format displays error messages for components with invalid entries. We'll use the first format for `info()` to display debug information in a message group component.

Recall that `info()` can only be called from Creator's preconfigured managed bean files, since it extends the FacesBean class. Calls to `info()`, therefore, are valid only in **Page1.java**, **RequestBean1.java**, **SessionBean1.java**, **ApplicationBean1.java**, or other page beans that you create in your project.

Let's show you how `info()` works for debugging. Here's what you do.

1. Bring up **Page1** in the design view.
2. Drag a Message Group component from the Component Palette and drop it underneath the Calculate button in the design view.
3. Double-click the Calculate button. This makes Creator write Java code for the button action method. Creator opens the **Page1.java** file and puts the cursor in the `calculate_action()` method.
4. Add the following call to `info()` in the button handler.

```
public String calculate_action() {
     info("button clicked");
     return null;
}
```

You don't really need a button handler in this program, but we include it to show you how to write text to the message group component. When the user clicks the Calculate button, JSF submits the page. If no validation errors occur, JSF invokes the button handler method. The text in the message group component tells us that the `calculate_action()` method was invoked.

Recompile and redeploy the program. Click the Calculate button with *valid entries* for the amount, interest rate, and loan term.[3] The loan payment should appear on the Calculator page. You should also see the text "button clicked" appear in the System Messages message group component (see Figure 14–15).

Method log()

The `log()` method, also defined in FacesBean, is useful for writing debugging information to the server log file. Like the `info()` method, you can only invoke method `log()` from Creator's preconfigured managed bean files or other page beans that you create in your project.

---

3. Remember that validation errors cause the life cycle process to skip some of life cycle stages and `calculate_action()` won't be called (see "The Creator-JSF Life Cycle" on page 260).

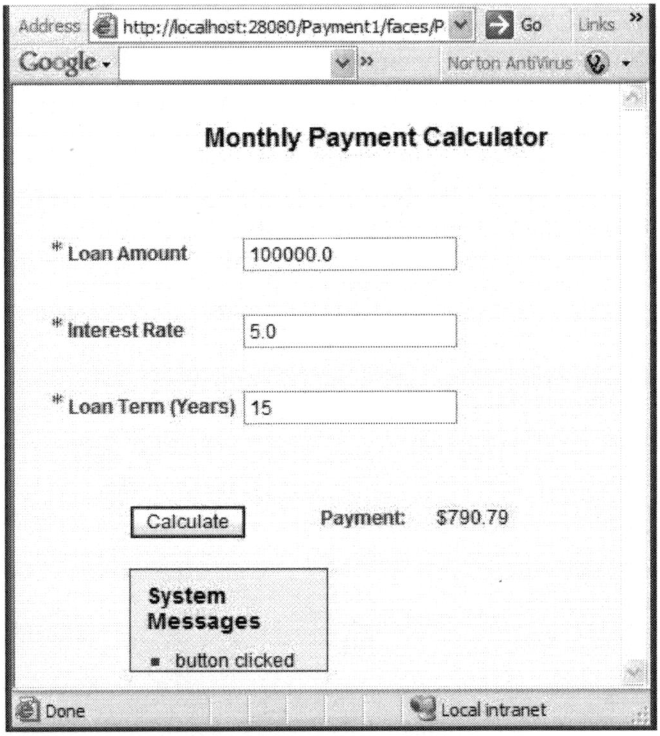

Figure 14–15 **Message Group Display**

The `log()` method has two formats.

```
void log(String);
void log(String, Throwable);
```

The first format is handy for printing event information (such as "button clicked"). The second format is useful in catch handlers with thrown exceptions.

```
catch (Exception e) {
     log("SQL ROWSET UPDATE ERROR", e);
     throw new FacesException(e);
}
```

Note that this form of the `log()` method uses the `Exception` object with the textual message you want to use.

The information from the `log()` method is available in Creator's output window. To see what this looks like, replace the `info()` statement in your button handler with a call to `log()`, as follows.

```
public String calculate_action() {
     log("button clicked");
     return null;
}
```

Now deploy and run the application. After you click the Calculate button and return to Creator, here's how to display the log file.

1. Click the **Servers** tab and right-click **Deployment Server** to select **View Server Log**. The server log is displayed in its own Output window at the bottom of your screen.
2. Move the scroll bars to the bottom and to the right to see the most recent information written to the log file. Near the end of the file you should see output similar to the following.

```
[#|2005-08-30T22:48:51.250-0700|INFO|
sun-appserver-pe8.1_02|
javax.enterprise.system.container.web|_ThreadID=39;
|WebModule[/payment1]button clicked|#]
```

(The output from the server log file on your system may be slightly different.) Note that the output from the `log()` method shows you more than the text you called it with. The output includes date and time information, the thread ID of your application, and the web module name (project name).

It's also possible to access the server log file directly in your file system, if you need to print it out or parse the information in the file. Here is the location on our system (yours may be slightly different).

```
D:\Sun\Creator2\SunAppServer8\domains\creator\logs\server.log
```

14.13 Using the HTTP Monitor

Another useful tool in the Creator debugger is the HTTP monitor. This tool lets you track the HTTP GET and POST commands that can occur in a deployed web application. Specifically, the HTTP monitor lets you monitor the data flow from JSP and servlet execution on the web server. When debugging applications, the HTTP monitor can let you see what's happening "under the hood" as you isolate problems between web application components.

Enabling the HTTP Monitor

Before you can use the HTTP Monitor, you need to make sure it's enabled within the Application Server in Creator. To do this, perform the following steps.

1. Bring up the Servers window if it's not already visible by clicking the Servers tab.
2. Right-click the Deployment Server's node and select Properties.
3. Find the Enable HTTP Monitor property and examine its value.
4. If it's set to false, the Monitor is not enabled. Use the checkbox to change the value to true, as shown in Figure 14–16. This enables the HTTP monitor.

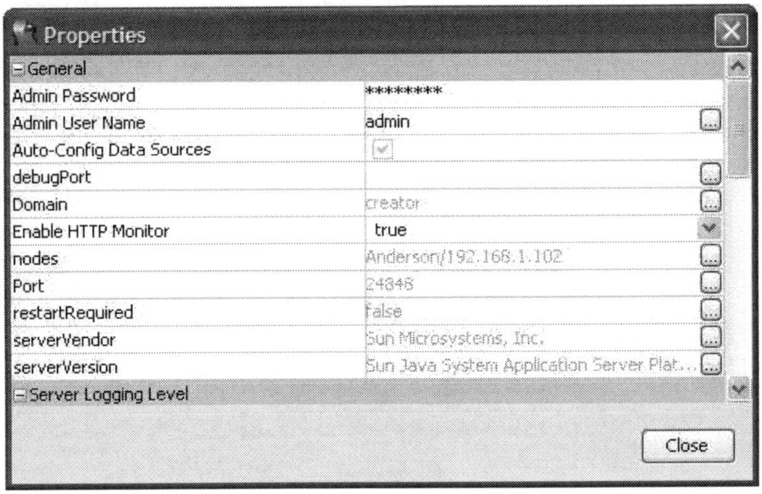

Figure 14–16 **Enabling the HTTP Monitor**

5. Click Close to close the Servers Properties window.

The Application Server can now record HTTP events for deployed applications.

The HTTP Monitor Window

Let's use the HTTP Monitor window with our Payment calculator web application. To bring up the HTTP Monitor window for viewing in the debugger, follow these steps.

- From the Creator toolbar, select **View > Debugging- > HTTP Monitor** (or use **<Ctrl+Shift+5>**). Figure 14–17 shows the HTTP monitor window.

Figure 14–17 **HTTP Monitor Window**

The HTTP Monitor window consists of two panels. The left panel is a tree view of HTTP request records for the client-side of your application. This includes current records that you are processing and saved records from previous sessions. Every HTTP request made to the web server is recorded by the HTTP Monitor as your web application executes. Current records persist across restarts of the server, but you can delete them during a session or have them cleared automatically when you exit Creator. The Saved Records, however, will persist until you explicitly delete them. There are also icons on the tool bar in the left panel to reload the records, sort them, and show/hide time stamp information for each record.

The right panel is additional information for any HTTP request that you select in the left panel. For each record, you can display request information, cookie name/value pairs, session data, and servlet context. You can also view HTTP header data and client-server information, such as client protocol and IP address, and the server platform and host name.

Viewing Record Data

1. Now click the green run icon (or select **Run > Run Main Project** from the Creator toolbar) to deploy the **Payment1** application.
2. After the payment page appears in your browser window, switch back to Creator. Expand the **Current Records** node in the left panel and select the GET Payment1 record. Figure 14–18 shows the request information that appears in the right panel for this record.
3. Select some of the other tabs in the right panel to view additional information about this GET record. You will see a wealth of information displayed to tell you everything you need to know about the data flow between your JSP page and the servlet execution on the web server. Figure 14–19 shows the client/server information for the GET record on our system.

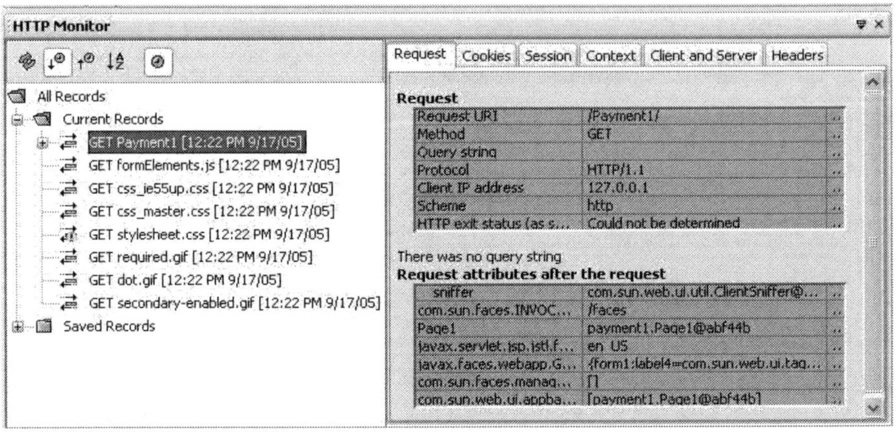

Figure 14–18 **HTTP GET Request**

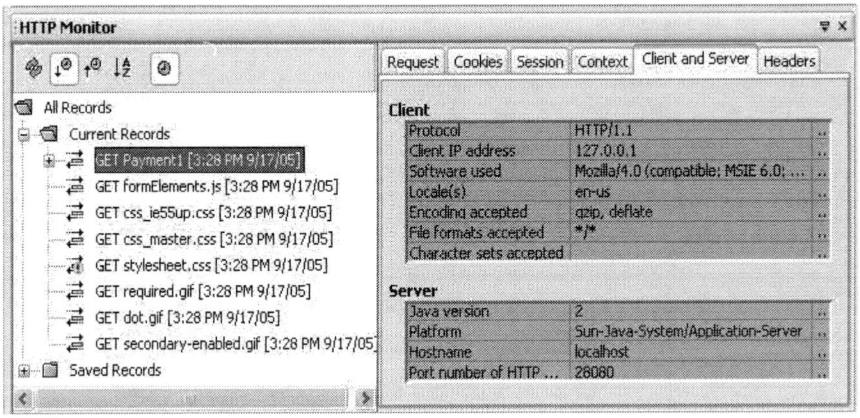

Figure 14–19 **HTTP Client/Server Data**

Editing HTTP Requests

The HTTP monitor lets you edit HTTP records and replay them during a debug session. Before we show you how to do this, let's generate a POST record in our HTTP monitor window. Here are the steps.

1. Click the **Request** tab in the right panel of the HTTP monitor window.
2. Switch to your browser and return to the Payment page. Type in **200,000** for the loan amount, **5.5** for the interest rate, and **30** for the loan term.

3. Click the Calculate button and switch back to Creator. You should see a POST record appear in the HTTP monitor window. Click the POST record to see the request information, as shown in Figure 14–20.

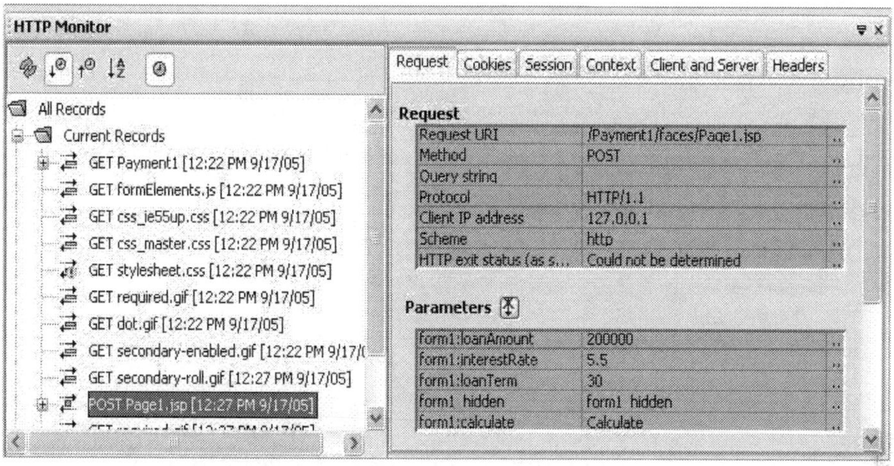

Figure 14–20 **HTTP POST Request**

Note that the input numbers that you typed on the calculator page in your browser now appear in the **Parameters** window as input forms for the POST request.

4. Right-click the POST **Page1.jsp** record in the left pane of the HTTP monitor window. Creator displays a context menu, as shown in Figure 14–21.
5. Select **Edit and Replay** from this list.
6. An **Edit and Replay** window will appear to let you edit fields in the POST request record. Let's change the loan term to 15 years. Select the **form1:loan-Term** field and click the rounded box at the far right. Edit the field and change its value from 30 to 15. Figure 14–22 shows you what the display should look like at this point.
7. Click the **Send HTTP Request** button and switch back to your browser. You should see the loan term set to the new value (15) and the loan payment will change, too. This all happens because we resent the modified POST request to the web server.

Saving HTTP Requests

As we said earlier, HTTP requests in the HTTP monitor do not survive a debugging session unless you explicitly save them. Let's save our POST request now. To do this, perform the following steps.

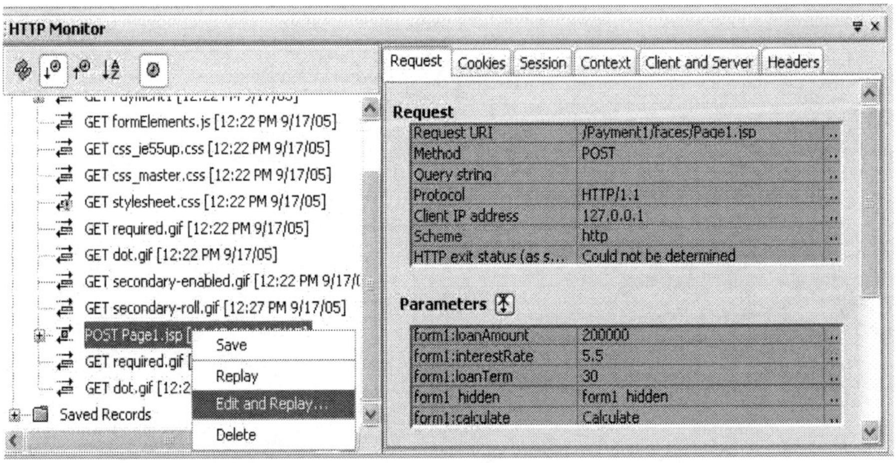

Figure 14–21 **HTTP POST Menu Selections**

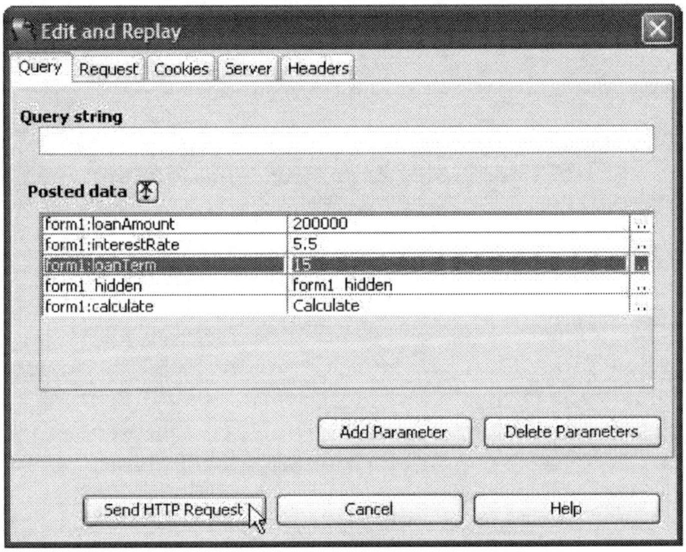

Figure 14–22 **Edit and Replay dialog**

1. If the POST request record is not already selected, select it now in the left pane of the HTTP monitor window.
2. Right-click the POST request record and choose **Save**. The POST request record will be saved under the **Saved Records** node in the left pane of the HTTP monitor window.

3. Expand the **Saved Records** node and select the POST record. Click the **Request** tab in the right pane of the HTTP monitor window. Figure 14–23 shows you what the display looks like.

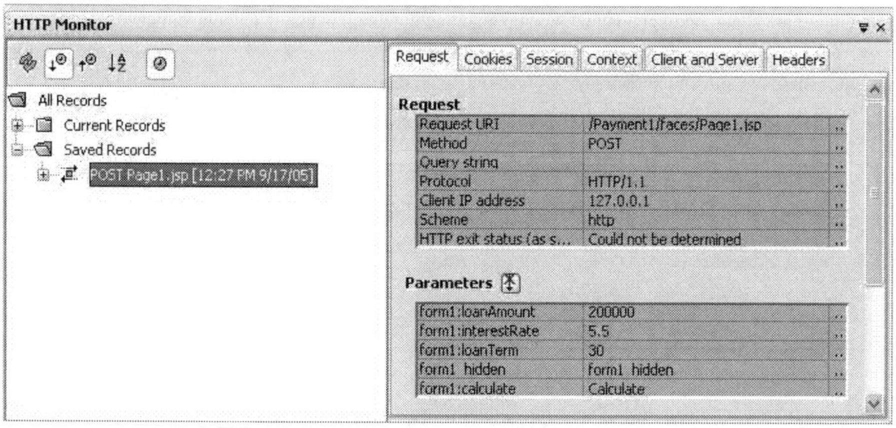

Figure 14–23 **HTTP Saved Records**

Now if you exit from Creator and start a new debugger session, you can replay the POST request record at any time.

Replaying HTTP Requests

With Saved Records, there are several options available to you. If you right-click the POST **Page1.jsp** record, a list of option appears (Figure 14–24).

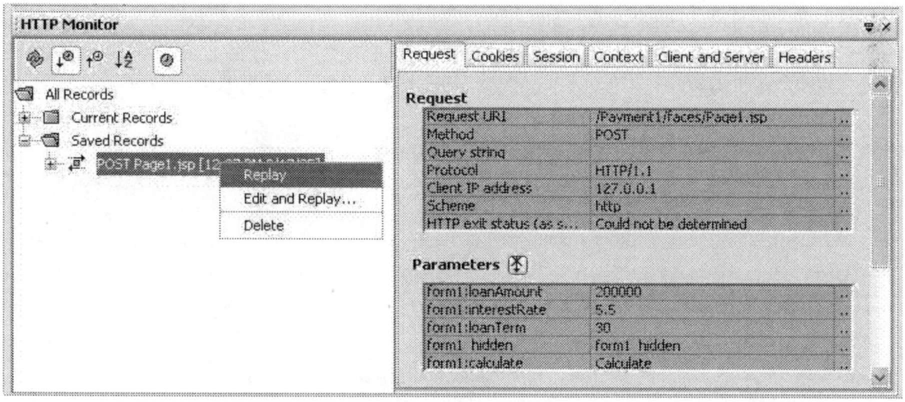

Figure 14–24 **HTTP Saved Record Selections**

The **Delete** option deletes Saved Records when you no longer need them. Note that you may **Replay Saved Records** at any time and **Edit and Replay** them as well.

Creator Tip

*All of these examples used the HTTP monitor window with a deployed application (**Run Main Project**). You can also use the HTTP monitor in debug mode (**Debug Main Project**). Together with breakpoints, local variables, and watches, the HTTP monitor can be a powerful tool to help you debug web applications across the enterprise.*

14.14 Key Point Summary

- Defensive programming means that you plan ahead for debugging.
- An assertion is a boolean expression that is expected to be true at run time. If an assertion fails, the Java Virtual Machine throws an `AssertionError`.
- You can run and deploy programs with Creator in debug mode.
- Creator has debugging features with which you can set breakpoints, step through code, track variables, and set watches.
- When using the Creator Debugger, you can examine sessions, threads, the call stack, local variables, watches, classes, breakpoints, and properties.
- A breakpoint is a spot in your program at which the debugger stops the execution of your program.
- The Creator debugger can step you through your code one line at a time. You can also step in or out of a method or run your program to a selected line.
- Tracking allows you to follow the creation and initialization of a local variable in a method. Tracking is a handy way to see if a method is working correctly for a range of test values.
- Watches let you monitor key variables as they change values during the execution of a program. Creator lets you display watches as your program runs.
- The Call Stack shows you the order of method calls as your program runs, with the most recent method at the top. Call stacks are useful for determining when a method was called and which method threw an exception.
- The Creator debugger lets you select exception breakpoints from a wide variety of different Java packages.
- In debugging mode, you can set a breakpoint when an exception is caught, uncaught, or both.

- Creator lets you view the server log to which you can write from your code. Log files are useful to monitor program flow, show intermediate data, and determine whether an event occurred.
- The `info()` and `log()` methods are handy for displaying debug information during debugging. These methods can only be called from Creator's preconfigured managed bean files. The `info()` method writes text to a message group component on a web page and `log()` writes text to the server log file.
- The HTTP monitor lets you monitor the data flow from JSP and servlet execution on the web server. The HTTP monitor can display request information, cookie name/value pairs, session data, and servlet context. You can also save HTTP request records between debug sessions and replay them to track down bugs.

Index

Symbols

A

D

J

K

L

P

Q

R

T

U

V

W

X

Z

Printed in Dunstable, United Kingdom

84160297R00409